T0254300

Java™ Security Solutions

Rich Helton and Johennie Helton

WILEY

Wiley Publishing, Inc.

Java™ Security Solutions

Published by
Wiley Publishing, Inc.
10475 Crosspoint Boulevard
Indianapolis, IN 46256
www.wiley.com

Published simultaneously in Canada

Library of Congress Control Number: 2002107908

ISBN: 0-7645-4928-6

10 9 8 7 6 5 4 3 2 1

1B/RV/QY/QS/IN

About the Authors

Rich and Johennie Helton are a husband and wife team whose collective experience in the computer industry spans over 30 years. Together their work history covers most of the facets of the software development life cycle. Their focus has been security as it applies to networks, applications, and enterprise solutions. The Heltons operate a consulting firm known as RichWare, LLC (www.richware.com).

Rich Helton's career in computers and security spans over 20 years. His early interest was in amateur radio. During the 80s he joined the Air Force, and he spent most of the decade in Frankfurt, Germany, working with computers and secured communications. After serving in the Air Force, Rich was offered a consulting position at OmniPoint Data Corp, where he helped the inventors of wireless PCS communications. He finished his MSCS in computer communications at the University of Colorado. He has enjoyed many consulting positions over the past 12 years, specializing in network security, protocols, and architecture for many companies. His experience includes building Secure NFS, secure Internet and Intranets, building monitoring software for enterprise communications and many distributed products. He has served as lead Java architect specializing in security in such industries as brokerage, financial, telecommunications, and logistics. He is a Sun Certified Java Programmer and Developer. He is also BEA WebLogic 6.0 Developer Certified. Rich is a co-author of BEA WebLogic Server Bible [Wiley Technology Publishing, 2002].

Johennie Helton is a systems architect specializing in J2EE technologies. Her professional life has included design, development, and software consulting in numerous n-tier distributed solutions for the automobile, financial, healthcare, retail, and coupon industries. During her career she has focused on leading-edge technologies. She has a strong background in object-oriented analysis, design and implementation, databases, application modeling, and hypermedia systems. She has helped companies move to Java and has experienced firsthand the needs and realities of providing a secure solution to the enterprise. She has a MSCS from the University of Colorado, and she is a contributing author to Java Data Access: JDBC, JNDI, and JAXP [Wiley Technology Publishing, 2002].

Credits

Executive Editor
Chris Webb

Senior Acquisitions Editor
Grace Buechlein

Project Editor
Sharon Nash

Technical Editors
Ashutosh Bhonsle
David Wall
Greg Wilcox

Copy Editor
Kim Cofer

Editorial Manager
Mary Beth Wakefield

Vice President & Executive Group Publisher
Richard Swadley

Vice President and Executive Publisher
Bob Ipsen

Vice President and Publisher
Joseph B. Wikert

Executive Editorial Director
Mary Bednarek

Project Coordinator
Maridee Ennis

Proofreading
Kim Cofer

Indexing
Johnna VanHoose Dinse

For Ashley and Courtney

Preface

Welcome to *Java Security Solutions*, a book that explains security in general and Java security in particular. This book includes cryptography, algorithms, and architecture. It provides practical solutions to security problems and not only describes the different security technologies, but explains why the different technologies exist and why you should use them. The source code is done in Java and illustrates how security in Java works. This book also shows how to extend Java to provide a more secure organization. In this book, we wanted to show more than just how to use Java components. We also wanted to show how to extend them, explain the reasons why algorithms like RSA are important, and inform readers about the basic protocols. In short, we wanted to answer the what, when, how, and why of the Java components used in security solutions.

Why This Book?

Some of the specifications that we address in this book include J2EE, WebServices, CORBA, JAAS, RMI, JSSE, SKIP, SASL, GSS-API, IPSec, X.509 certificates, cryptography, RSA, Elliptical Curve Cryptography, DSS, DSA, Kerberos, LDAP, TLS, WTLS, message digests, key agreements, key management, java access, ciphers, firewalls, network security, PKI, and much more. This book helps you:

♦ Think as a hacker so that you can avoid the security pitfalls that hackers exploit

♦ Understand the building blocks of security so that you can take full advantage of security features

♦ Learn how to apply Java security features effectively and efficiently

♦ Get hands-on experience with security algorithms and their implementation

♦ Understand procedures for ensuring secure communications within the enterprise

♦ Learn how to add security to enterprise applications

♦ Understand ciphers

♦ Ensure message authentication and data integrity

♦ Understand network security architecture

♦ View your solution from beginning to end and look for vulnerable points along the way

Why Java?

These days, Java is the language of choice for the development of Web applications and enterprise solutions. Typically, these are distributed systems requiring distributed communication among the components. This distributed communication is supported by

CORBA, RMI, or RMI over IIOP, and the combination of these technologies along with Java provide a tool set that allows the development of secure solutions. Security has been a major design goal for Java ever since the creation of the language. Java provides a language, runtime environment, APIs, and tools that are ideal for the development of secure systems. The Java Development Kit (JDK) 1.4 comes standard with many cryptography components in its distribution and technologies that allow the support and development of secure solutions. Some of these technologies include X.509 certificates, key agreement, a way to specify security policies, authentication, authorization, code signing, and cryptographic support.

The JDK 1.4 now integrates into its distribution the Java Cryptography Extension (JCE) as cryptography components and Java Authentication and Authorization Services (JAAS). Java also provides the Java Secure Socket Extension (JSSE). Although you can create solutions without these technologies, these solutions will probably be less portable and more expensive than if you use the JDK 1.4. It is definitely worth it to take your time and learn what Java has to offer. In order for you to understand how these technologies can be used successfully, however, you need to understand the why, when, how, and what behind the different Java components. That is where this book comes in.

What You Need to Know

This book is for anyone who wants to understand security issues and how to prevent security violations. If you want to understand how to address security concerns and how to implement many of the standards and protocols in Java, this book is for you. The typical reader of this book is the intermediate to advanced Java developer, Java architect, and systems architect. Basic Java programming knowledge is assumed, and therefore, concepts such as EJB deployment, Java language constructs, HTML, Web server and application server technologies are not covered in detail. We address these concepts from the security perspective and not at an introductory level.

How This Book Is Organized

This book provides a discussion on all aspects of security. We begin by introducing security and its requirements. Then we introduce the Java components that address these requirements, including the reasons why and how these components are to be used. Then we move on to resource, enterprise, and network security.

This book is divided into nine parts.

Part I: Introduction to Security

This part covers the basics of security, explains the need for security, and introduces you to the way hackers think, the tools that are available to hackers, and the most common attacks. In addition, this part categorizes security elements and the different Java components available for security. If you cannot wait to start with Java security, its components, and implementation, we suggest you skip to Chapter 3, "Java Security Components."

Part II: Identity and Authentication

This part provides an overview of key management algorithms, Elliptic Curve Cryptography (ECC), and Java implementation to keys and key management. It includes key pair examples, a discussion of the mathematics, Diffie-Hellman, key generation, man-in-the-middle attack, RSA key exchange, ECC, secure random, and DES examples.

Part III: Data Integrity

This part covers data integrity, hash functions, message digest algorithms, message authentication, and digital signatures. This discussion includes RSA, ECC, MAC, SHA-1, and others. It includes an MD5 implementation, a SHA-1 algorithm, a MAC algorithm, and DSA signature examples.

Part IV: Data Hiding

This part presents ciphers, and how to implement ciphers including how to use CipherSpi. Also, it presents a discussion on PBE, Blowfish, and Java Smart Cards. This part includes examples on RSA and an example implementation, Stream Ciphers, PBE, and Blowfish.

Part V: Resource Access Using Java

This part provides an overview of the common criteria for security. It also helps you understand the need for security in your applications and how to satisfy those requirements using Java. It presents JAAS, Kerberos, GSS-API, and the Security Manager. It includes examples on security context, policies, configurations, guarded objects, signed objects, and JAAS.

Part VI: Enterprise Data Security

This part covers the needs to secure your enterprise data. This is mainly a discussion of why and how you can secure your database, and the communication between your application and the data repository. It contains container-managed and application sign-on, and a discussion on the connector API.

Part VII: Network Access

This part focuses on network security and architecture. It discusses the OSI model, DMZs, firewalls, HTTP tunneling, Java Sockets, SSL, TLS, and JSSE. It includes socket examples (including the server, client, and channel), routing tables, and X509 examples.

Part VIII: Public Key Management

This part discusses Java digital certificates such as X500, and X.509. Also, this part describes PKI management with certificate chaining, X.500, LDAP, and the need for non-repudiation, including how to import certificates, CRL, CertPath, and LDAP examples.

Part IX: Enterprise Access

This part covers the need for security of enterprise solutions. It describes, including programming examples, the Java security model, Java permissions, Web-tier security, Web Services, JNDI, RMI, IIOP, and EJB security. Finally, it presents a discussion of how BEA's WebLogic, IBM's WebSphere, and Borland's Enterprise Server handle security.

Conventions Used in this Book

This book uses special fonts to highlight code listings and commands and other terms used in code. For example:

```
This is what a code listing looks like.
```

In regular text, `monospace font` is used to indicate items that would normally appear in code.

This book also uses the following icons to highlight important points:

> **NOTE:** Note icons, like this one, provide information about the subject being discussed. They generally contain relevant information or elaborate on a detailed technical point.

> **TIP:** Tip icons provide a more efficient way of doing something, and suggest or give pointers on the subject being discussed.

> **CAUTION:** Caution icons provide a warning of a potential missuse, misconception, or the requirement of a defensive approach.

> **CROSS-REFERENCE:** Cross-reference icons provide you with a guide to other chapters that discuss a particular subject in more detail.

Companion Web Site

This book provides a companion Web site. The Web site provides you with all the source code found in this book. The code listings are organized by chapters, or you can download all the examples at once. Simply go to www.wiley.com/extras.

There is a companion Web site (www.richware.com/JavaSecuritySolutions) that contains a list of links, which takes you to the relevant RFCs, documentation, and sites associated with different topics covered in the book.

What Resources You Need

The source code has been tested with the Java 2 Platform Standard Edition JDK 1.4, and the Java 2 Software Development Kit, Enterprise Edition, on Windows 2000.

The http://java.sun.com/java2/ provides links to the Java 2 technologies that are needed (http://java.sun.com/j2ee/download.html, http://java.sun.com/j2se/1.4/download.html).

The book's Web site provides all source code in the book along with test scripts (run.bat) for each chapter. Some sample code requires a Sun Certificate, which is also provided for you along with the source code. Links to other important resources are provided in the relevant chapter.

Contacting the Authors

We are interested in hearing from you, your impressions (either good or bad) of this book, the chapters, and contents. Please, do contact us if you find anything that you think needs a better explanation or that can be improved in any way.

You can contact the authors directly at jssbook@richware.com.

Acknowledgments

This book would not be possible without the inspiration, encouragement, and assistance of our friends and family, and especially the following people:

Big thanks to Grace Buechlein, a Sr. Acquisitions Editor at Wiley Publishing, Inc., who trusted in us at every step of the way and provided guidance and moral support so that we could do this book. She also kept us on track with the deadlines and guided us through the process.

Also, thanks to Sharon Nash, our Project Editor at Wiley Publishing, Inc., for helping us through this project and helping this book become a reality.

Thanks to Ashutosh Bhonsle, David Wall, and Greg Wilcox who provided technical feedback, and Kimberly Cofer, who helped us make this a more readable book. Your attention to detail drove us crazy at times, but without it this book would not be of the quality it is.

Thanks to our friend Glen Wilcox who provided invaluable insight early on in the adventure that became this book.

— *Rich and Johennie Helton*

Contents

Preface vii

Acknowledgments xii

Part I: Introduction to Security **1**

  Chapter 1: Security Basics **3**

    Introduction 3

    Protecting Your Information in Today's World 3

    The Four Pillars of Security.. 6

    Mapping Security Features to the Digital World... 10

    Summary... 11

  Chapter 2: Hackers and Their Tools **13**

    Introduction 13

    Looking for the Hack 14

    Different Types of Hacks and How They Work 15

    Understanding Network Attacks 19

    Protecting Against Hackers 35

    Summary... 36

  Chapter 3: Java Security Components **39**

    Introduction 39

    Categorizing Security Elements 40

    Categorizing Security Components in Java 46

    How Do the Components Fit Together? 56

    Summary... 58

Part II: Identity and Authentication **59**

  Chapter 4: Key Management Algorithms **61**

    Introduction 61

    Understanding the Purpose of Keys 62

    Understanding the Mathematics 65

    Symmetric versus Asymmetric Keys 70

    The Diffie-Hellman Key Exchange 70

    The Rivest, Shamir, and Adleman Key Exchange.. 92

    The Future of Key Exchanges 106

    Summary... 107

  Chapter 5: Elliptic Curve Cryptography... **109**

    Introduction 109

Understanding the Mathematics of ECC 111
The ECCDH Key Exchange 113
Summary 127

Chapter 6: Key Management Through the Internet Protocol...................................**129**

Introduction..129
The Internet Protocol Security Protocol 129
The Simple Authentication and Security Layer 136
Summary 138

Chapter 7: Implementing Keys with Java...**139**

Introduction..139
Understanding DSA: The Digital Signature Algorithm..140
Generating Key Pairs with Java 141
Generating the Secret Key with Java 157
Summary 161

Chapter 8: Java Implementation of Key Management **163**

Introduction..163
KeyStore..164
PKCS #12 KeyStore 168
Truststore 168
TrustManager...169
Policy File 179
Policytool 181
Summary 185

Part III: Data Integrity..**187**

Chapter 9: Ensuring Data Integrity..**189**

Introduction..189
Understanding the Hash Function...190
Understanding the Message Digest 190
Understanding the Different Message Digest Algorithms 194
Implementing the Different Message Digest Algorithms in Java.............................217
Summary 218

Chapter 10: Ensuring Message Authentication..**219**

Introduction..219
Understanding the MAC...219
Implementing the MAC..221
Summary 230

Chapter 11: Signature Integrity **231**

Introduction..231
Understanding the Digital Signature Algorithm (DSA)..233
Understanding the RSA Digital Signature Algorithm...237
Understanding the Elliptic Curve Digital Signature Algorithm 238

Implementing the Digital Signature Algorithm (DSA) 239
Summary 254

Part IV: Data Hiding **255**

Chapter 12: Understanding Ciphers **257**
Introduction 257
Understanding Symmetric Ciphers 258
Implementing RSA Public Key Encryption 266
Some Security Suggestions 286
Summary 287

Chapter 13: Extending New Ciphers with the JDK **289**
Introduction 289
Implementing a CipherSpi 289
Implementing the RC4 Stream Cipher 299
Summary 303

Chapter 14: Applying Ciphers **305**
Introduction 305
Understanding PBE 305
Understanding Blowfish 310
Some Implementations in Ciphers 316
Java Smart Card Basics 319
Summary 324

Part V: Resource Access Using Java **325**

Chapter 15: Securing Enterprise Resources **327**
Common Criteria for Security Systems 327
Understanding Your Security Needs 330
Fulfilling Your Security Requirements 332
Summary 336

Chapter 16: Java Authentication and Authorization Through Kerberos **337**
Introduction to Kerberos 337
Principal Names and Key Distribution Center 338
The Kerberos Authenticator 346
The Kerberos Principal Database 346
Java Kerberos 350
Summary 351

Chapter 17: Securing Messages with the Java GSS-API **353**
Introduction 353
Implementing the GSS with Initiators and Acceptors 374
Authenticating with JAAS 375
Summary 379

Chapter 18: Java Access: The Security Manager **381**
Introduction 381

The Class Loader 382
The Security Manager 383
The Access Controller 384
The Policy 392
The Permission Collection 397
Summary 398

Chapter 19: Java Authentication and Authorization Service............401
What Is JAAS?..401
Using Authentication 402
Understanding JAAS Authorization 418
Summary 428

Part VI: Enterprise Data Security 431
Chapter 20: Working with Database Security..433
Introduction..433
Connecting Your Database through JDBC..434
Connecting Your Database through the Connector Architecture 436
Securing Enterprise Data in the Database..439
Summary 440

Part VII: Network Access...441
Chapter 21: Network Security Architecture..443
Understanding Network Security...444
Network Concepts Overview 444
Firewalls...463
De-Militarized Zones (DMZs) 468
Understanding Proxying Firewalls...470
HTTP Tunneling...473
Java Sockets 474
Summary 484

Chapter 22: SSL and TLS 487
The Secure Socket Layer (SSL) 487
The SSL Layers 490
SSL Sessions and Connections 495
Security and Attacks...498
HTTPS: HTTP over SSL 499
WLS 500
Summary 502

Chapter 23: Java Secure Socket Extension 503
JSSE Architecture....:...503
Summary 533

Part VIII: Public Key Management **535**

    Chapter 24: Java Digital Certificates **537**

        Introduction to Digital Certificates 537

        A Quick Overview of X.500 538

        The X.509 Specification 540

        Certificate Revocation 556

        Summary 573

    Chapter 25: PKI Management **575**

        Introduction 575

        Certificate Chaining 576

        X.500 577

        LDAP 581

        Certificate Components 583

        Certificate Path Validation.. 584

        Non-repudiation 595

        Summary 596

Part IX: Enterprise Access **597**

    Chapter 26: Java Enterprise Security and Web Services Security **599**

        Introduction 599

        Java Security Models 600

        Java Permissions 603

        Enterprise Component Models 604

        Understanding Web Services.. 605

        Summary 616

    Chapter 27: Securing Client-Side Components **617**

        Introduction 617

        Exploring Java Directory Services 617

        Using Authentication 621

        Using Access Control 624

        Working with Client-Side Security 624

        Using Servlets 627

        Using Java Server Pages 628

        Client-Side Code Example 630

        Summary 643

    Chapter 28: Securing Server-Side Components **645**

        Introduction 645

        Securing Your Enterprise with CORBA 646

        RMI 651

        Enterprise Security with EJBs 655

        Server-side code example 660

        Summary 670

Chapter 29: Application Security with Java..**671**

BEA's WebLogic Basics...671

IBM's WebSphere Basics 673

Borland's Enterprise Server Basics...675

Summary 677

Index **679**

Part I

Introduction to Security

Chapter 1: Security Basics

Chapter 2: Hackers and Their Tools

Chapter 3: Java Security Components

Chapter 1
Security Basics

In This Chapter

- ♦ Determining security needs in the modern world
- ♦ Authenticating identity and authorizing access to system resources
- ♦ Ensuring confidentiality and integrity of data
- ♦ Relating the four pillars of security to the digital world

This chapter is intended to provide a basic introduction to security concepts that I call the pillars of security: authentication, authorization, confidentiality, and integrity. These concepts are used throughout the book. I do not intend to present a complete discussion on all the details of security in this chapter; instead, my intention is to establish the basic terminology to be built on and to be addressed in detail later. Security is a complicated topic and having a common understanding of the terminology and concepts is a good starting point. If you are already familiar with authentication, authorization, confidentiality, and integrity, you can skip this chapter entirely.

Introduction

Most people practice some form of security every day, such as locking their houses and putting their keys and wallets in their pockets or purses. Similarly, organizations need to use security techniques to protect their resources and information. No company gives away its assets unless it no longer wishes to stay in business, and information is one of the most important and strongest assets a company has. This chapter explores the basic security concepts of authentication, authorization, confidentiality, and integrity and discusses why these concepts are relevant to an enterprise solution. It also presents some basic examples of security techniques that will be expanded upon in later chapters.

Protecting Your Information in Today's World

The old adage "Information is power" is more true than ever for the corporate world. Even the release of very general information about a company (for example, an upcoming merger between company A and company B) can have a profound impact on a company. For example, in the case of a corporate merger, if confidential information about a proposed merger is leaked to the press or other companies, the merger could be in jeopardy. In today's corporate environment, these basic principles can have a dramatic impact on the security of the organization. Developers who implement security measures must be mindful of not only the complex security techniques that are discussed throughout this book, but also the basic, commonsense concepts that apply to any discussion of confidentiality and security.

Protecting resources from the hacker

In today's corporate world, what we are protecting and from whom we are protecting it is important. The corporate world no longer revolves around written information as the medium of documentation; it revolves around digital information. Spies no longer wear trench coats and exchange information in dark alleys. Nowadays, spies are more often than not sitting in front of a computer screen. This new type of spy is called a *hacker*. He is trained in technology and willing to use it for a price. The hacker personality takes many forms and spans a wide range. Today's hacker profiles include:

♦ A disgruntled employee who releases viruses into the system before he quits his job.

♦ A teenager who uses the high school's computer to hack into an organization that somebody told him about in church.

Hackers no longer belong to a club that meets in the basement of a home. They are people who belong to newsgroups. The hacker has evolved over time from the computer amateur to the computer professional. The hacker now practices social engineering.

> **NOTE:** Social engineering is the ability to gain access to systems by social interaction, which may be formal or informal. Social interaction is discussed in depth in Chapter 2.

To the hacker, the goal is an organization's Information Technology (IT) department. The IT department should be ready and expecting such attacks.

Hack attacks: different scenarios

Many company resources need protection from hack attacks, including e-mail messages, network addresses, lists of employees, and confidential documents describing technology. Any of these items may lead to other items that a hacker can use for intrusion. For example, a person's e-mail could contain a personal note along with the user's name. This personal information can be re-used to try to break a person's password. For instance, the password may be a pet's name, a favorite sports team, and the like. In another example, the user (or hacker that knows the username) may go to a site that gives the option 'send me my password' when the user has forgotten the password. If the attacker can impersonate an SMTP server and the user's e-mail address, the attacker can receive e-mails addressed to the user. E-mails receiving passwords are sometimes not password protected and can be sniffed.

> **NOTE:** If an attacker knows an e-commerce site that requires a username and password, he may monitor the site in order to detect the transmission of the data.

Another means of attack is when the hacker sends an e-mail posing as the IT department and requests that the person install a new software patch in his computer. Once the person installs the patch, the computer is no longer secure — the attacker owns it.

Like spies, the best hackers are those who are never caught and never heard of. They don't have a "hacker" license plate or an "I hack for a living" t-shirt. Appearance-wise, they blend in with their targets. The best hackers look like the people working in the IT department of an organization. They may even walk into the company carrying a fake badge and wearing a company shirt, and use a conference room just as if they worked there.

A common attack employed by hackers is the call-in approach: A hacker may impersonate an IT technician calling a salesperson, especially one offsite, and say that he needs to remotely install some software. If the salesperson believes the hacker, then the hacker can easily install any harmful software he wants. Another type of call-in is the hacker impersonating a salesperson to the IT technician, where the hacker tells the IT technician that his or her password is no longer working and the IT technician walks the hacker through logging on to the salesperson's machine.

Weapons against attack

The two most important weapons a company has against hackers, spies, and attacks are:

♦ Adequate security training for staff
♦ A secure infrastructure in place that allows the organization to adequately meet potential threats

The better IT professionals understand hackers, security measures, and potential attacks, the better the IT professionals are prepared to handle threats. Even a simple attack can do great damage if the IT professional is not prepared to handle it.

There have been many instances where organizations were hacked but were never aware of it until it was too late. An organization should work hard to ensure that its information and resources are protected because it is the resources and information that make the organization. A recurrent problem I have observed through the years across companies and organizations is confidential information received by one person (director, vice president, and so on) not being secured. In order for information to be secure, each individual within the organization needs to understand how and what needs protection.

To understand how information can be secured, you need to understand the security principles that form the foundation (or "pillars") of security. The next section describes the pillars of security.

The Four Pillars of Security

There are four basic principles that apply for most security systems: authentication, authorization, confidentiality, and integrity. Figure 1-1 gives an overview of these four principles. These pillars of security are discussed in the next few sections.

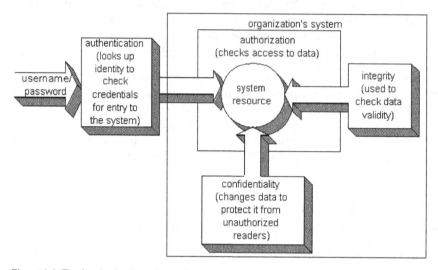

Figure 1-1: The four basic pillars of security

Authentication: proving identity with credentials

Authentication is the process of proving the identity of a user of a system by means of a set of credentials. *Credentials* are the required proof needed by the system to validate the identity of the user. The *user* can be the actual customer, a process, or even another system. A person is *validated through a credential*. The *identity* is who the person is. If a person has been validated through a credential, such as attaching a name to a face, the name becomes a *principal*.

In this case the principal is associated with the username. The principal represents the identity of the user for a given service. Since a user may access many different services that have different usernames, we need to introduce the concept of a subject. A *subject* represents a collection of principals.

> **CROSS-REFERENCE:** Chapter 19 gives more details on principals, subjects, and related concepts (such as credentials, permissions, and policies).

The credential set is highly dependent on the requirements of the organization's system for proving the identity, but is most likely a set of user attributes such as passwords, certificates, or smart cards. People in everyday life apply authentication at different levels. One level could be locking the front door to the house. Another could be verbally asking an employer to verify information that is circulating as a rumor.

Every day we meet people and introduce ourselves. This is a form of authentication. The person we meet may give a form of credential by describing his role or his work. Other forms of credentials are required when writing checks or using credit cards. If a cashier requires further validation from a person, he or she may ask for a driver's license. The driver's license also represents a form of credential to the cashier. The cashier is authenticating the person to allow a transaction, the purchase of an item, to take place in a store. E-commerce systems require a similar, digital form of authentication and credentials to access an online store.

Credentials allow one party to recognize another. Recognition can occur through various means. For example, people might use physical appearance or some other characteristic in order to identify someone. Using physical characteristics for authentication is known as biometrics. Biometric controls use the following characteristics to identify individuals:

- Fingerprints
- Voice
- Handwritten signature dynamics
- Retina and iris scans
- Palm scans and hand geometry

Biometric access control devices are considered physical access security control devices. In this book, I do not address physical security specifically. There are many ways you can physically secure your systems, such as using employee badges, multiple doors, and video surveillance.

Authorization: providing access to system resources

Once a user's identity has been validated, the user can be checked for access to a system resource. The process by which a user is given access to a system resource is known as *authorization*. For example, after a user logs in to a commerce system, which validates his or her identity, the user needs access to his or her account history; that is, the user needs authorization to retrieve the user's records. The user's records are the system resources needed by the user. The authorization process is the check by the organization's system to see whether the user should be granted access to the user's record. The user has logged in to the system, but he still may not have the permission necessary from the system to access the records.

You probably practice authorization every day by giving others access to your resources. Examples of authorization include inviting someone into your home, giving an administrator access to your computer, storing your money in a bank, or giving someone your credit card number so that the person can access your funds. In all these cases, it is important to be aware of the person's identity (by applying authentication) to make sure the person can be trusted with your resources.

> **NOTE:** When you give out your credit card number, you are authorizing the charge to your account, and your funds are the resource you are authorizing access to. Cognitively speaking, people may apply more authentication rules when giving a credit card number than a system can apply when giving access to a resource such as a database. An organization giving access to a system resource usually does a lookup, and based on the proven identity of a user match to the permission of the resource, it gives the user access to the resource. The authorization checks the permission and simply allows or denies access to the resource.

When deploying a system, access to system resources should also be mapped out. Security documents that detail the rights of individuals to specific resources must be developed. These documents must distinguish between the owners and the users of resources as well as read, write, delete, and execute privileges.

> **CROSS-REFERENCE:** Chapter 15 describes common criteria that can be used as a guide to define the security needs.

There might be property files that are used to configure servers. Sometimes these property files contain usernames and passwords so anyone who has read access to these files can potentially break into the server. Files such as these should be given a high level of security.

> **TIP:** A common approach when deploying a system is giving a level of 1 to 5 to each file, 5 being the highest, and mapping out the permissions allowed to access the files based on the level of security. Allow only system administrative people to access level 5 files. This notion of categorizing files is a first step toward implementing an access control model. An access control model allows the operating system and other applications (such as SiteMinder) to enforce a company's security policy. For example, the military uses a classification scheme that has unclassified, confidential, secret, and top secret.

Mapping the level of security allowed for each file in a deployment of the system is an example of establishing an authorization rules set. An organization needs to have a plan for the rules for authorization. Who is allowed to access what? When developing such a plan, a question set is important. The question set addresses issues such as how important the file is, whether it contains sensitive material, and how this resource should be accessed and by whom. Examples of sensitive material include passwords and files that have settings that change the system, such as configuration files.

Confidentiality: protecting information from unauthorized readers

To protect data from being accessed by unauthorized readers, the data is changed to keep it confidential. This process is known as *obfuscation* (which literally means to "darken" — that is, to make obscure or to confuse). *Confidentiality* is the means of keeping information secret, not by blocking the access, but by making the information unreadable by the public. Only people allowed to read the information can unlock the secret file for the original message (usually with a key). Such techniques have been dated to 1900 B.C. in Egypt. Throughout history, there has always been a process, or an organization, that is responsible for encrypting and decrypting messages. Before keys were used, anyone who understood the algorithm could decrypt the message. So the knowledge of how the algorithms worked was kept secret, and there was a person educated in the algorithm who needed to understand both the encryption and how to reverse the process (for decryption). Today, besides having the technique done in a digital form, the algorithms have also been modified to protect the algorithm itself by providing an extra variable called a key.

An organization should be concerned about confidentiality techniques whenever it wants to protect information that is being transmitted to another system. When the information is in its original form, it is called *plaintext*. When the information is in a protected form, it is called *ciphertext*. Ciphertext uses a *cipher*, which changes the plaintext into ciphertext. The cipher requires keys to change the information from one form to the other.

> **CROSS-REFERENCE:** For more detailed information on ciphers and how to implement them, refer to Chapters 12 through 14.

Two types of cryptographic systems are in use today for commercial applications. They are either symmetric or asymmetric systems. The symmetric systems use a shared secret key, whereas asymmetric systems use a key pair.

> **CROSS-REFERENCE:** Keys are discussed more fully in Chapters 3 through 8.

Many techniques for security have evolved over time, but are based on algorithms that are decades old. A modern variation of passing a public key and checking the key's integrity is the X.509 certificate. The X.509 is a called a public certificate. The X.509 is guaranteed to be unforgeable by having an issuing authority encrypt a digital signature and using a public key for validating the digital signature. The X.509 comprises several older algorithms that make up the X.509 certificate. The RSA algorithm created decades ago makes up the cipher algorithm for using the key pair. The X.509 uses a private key from an issuing authority (those agencies that create the certificate) and a public key accessed by the user to verify that public certificate has not been modified. X.509 is a more recent technique, but makes use of signatures in a digital form that has been around for a long time.

> **CROSS-REFERENCE:** Chapter 24 describes X.509 certificates in detail.

Integrity: validating your data

During the transmission or storage of data, information can be corrupted or changed, maliciously or otherwise, by a user. *Validation* is the process of ensuring data integrity. When data has *integrity,* it means that the data has not been modified or corrupted.

One technique for ensuring data integrity is called data hashing. Under this process, the computer system hashes information and stores the hash result at a later time. A *hash* is an algorithm that is applied to information and produces a unique result. If the hash is applied to different information, changed by even one character, it produces a different result.

> **CROSS-REFERENCE:** Chapter 9 provides more information on hashing and data integrity.

When the integrity of the information needs to be checked, the process will hash the information to be checked and compare it with the stored hash. If both hash results match, the data hasn't changed. The integrity process may also be used during the transmission of data to ensure that the data did not get corrupted from one system to the next, and that the original information is still valid.

> **NOTE:** As with other basic security principles, it is easy to find processes for ensuring data in the non-digital world. For example, when you balance your checkbook, you are checking data integrity. If the balance is incorrect, especially in favor of the bank, you may call the bank to correct the error. By calling the bank, you are correcting the data that failed the bank's validation process.

Mapping Security Features to the Digital World

The physical world and the digital world have many similarities when it comes to security processes. The need for authentication, authorization, confidentiality, and integrity do not change from the physical world to the digital one. They do, however, change in execution through digital means and medium. For instance, the authentication of a person cannot always be done through physical recognition since the person could be across the world sitting in front of a computer. In such a case, the authentication process must be through digital means. Instead of identification cards and drivers' licenses, certificates with the user's information must be used. The *certificate* is a form of credential, a digital form similar to a driver's license. Another form of credential is the password used when a person logs in to a Web site.

Once the identity has been matched with a credential and accepted by an organization's system, authentication is achieved. The authorization process requires a lookup of the permission set and digital identification to see if the user has access to a resource.

In order to achieve confidentiality, the system can use the user's key for encryption and decryption. A secret key is a single key that can be used for both encryption and decryption. A key acts as a digital token for allowing data to be read by users who only have access to the secret key. To check the integrity of the information, the system hashes the information into a new hashed information block. The *hashed information block* is a smaller block of information that uniquely represents the original information. When the information must be checked, the hash block is created again and the two blocks are compared. If the blocks match, the system concludes that the information has not been modified.

> **CAUTION:** When authorization is performed digitally, an organization is susceptible to digital attacks. Chapter 2 provides examples of common attacks to an organization, and Part V provides detailed information on authorization.

The digital processes are merely personal security techniques applied to the digital world. The physical world simply does not apply anymore, except in the case of isolation, which is the process of physically isolating the systems from digital access to protect the systems.

Security is ever-evolving and dynamic; therefore, an enterprise's security architecture must be flexible and agile enough to change as the times and security requirements change. There is one concept that is constant in computer science: It is ever-evolving. At one time in my life, I was writing x86 assembler, and now I write JSPs and EJBs. Some of the concepts have remained the same; however, technology has changed. An organization's architecture must be designed so that one year it can use Kerberos and the next X.509 certificates with minimal change.

> **CROSS-REFERENCE:** Chapter 16 describes Kerberos and Chapter 24 describes X.509.

The endpoints of the organization must be constantly monitored to support security. It doesn't do much good if the Web site has a lot of security on a server sitting on a Windows NT machine accessed across the Internet (and open to the world). The network engineers should always be aware of which machines are open and which machines are not and make sure that the only way to pass into secure information is through proper security mechanisms.

The organization that wants to establish security needs to define security requirements, such as identifying which resources are sensitive. For example, the needs of a government and a non-profit organization could be very different. Therefore, the requirements are based on the type of organization, and a security policy is established to define how to enforce these requirements. The security policy governs and dictates the standards, procedures, and practices for the organization. The practices will elicit security rule sets for any resource that should be secure. It is best to assign a security advisor to keep a running list of administrative usernames and passwords so that, if access is lost to the system, it can be recovered by logging in as the administrator. A plan needs to be devised that regulates, tests, maintains, and updates the security system at regular intervals. All these points will be developed in more detail as we progress through the book.

Summary

Security is the process of allowing or disallowing others access to information and resources. This chapter introduced the basic concepts of security: authentication, authorization, confidentiality, and integrity. These concepts have evolved through the years in the physical world and have now been applied to the digital world.

Enterprises and organizations that need secure systems need to be knowledgeable about how these concepts are used and applied correctly in a secure system. The best secure solution is to have a flexible enough architecture to move forward with the technology, yet follow strict security rules with a plan that regulates, tests, and maintains the security system.

Chapter 2
Hackers and Their Tools

In This Chapter

- ♦ Understanding the hacker
- ♦ Exploring some common hacker tools
- ♦ Learning about the different type of hack attacks
- ♦ Protecting your systems against hackers

Information assets are very important to today's business; and malicious attackers and hackers, including industry espionage, present a danger. This chapter is intended to provide information on security concerns and weaknesses that attackers have historically explored to gain access to your valuable resources. The presentation is informal and anecdotal (including my personal experience) because I believe that some knowledge, even if it is rudimentary, will help you understand where security issues may arise. It may help you realize where the technologies discussed later in the book aid in your organization's security; however, feel free to skip this chapter if you cannot wait to start with Java security, its components, and implementation.

Introduction

A hacker is a person who infiltrates an organization's system through unauthorized means, or someone who harms the organization's systems. To define a hacker is not necessarily to define a specific person, but rather a culture of individuals. A hacker could be a person with a malicious intent or simply a person trying to prove his or her technical prowess. Some attackers are disgruntled employees and others are people who do it for personal gain, seeking fame or money.

Many hackers have achieved fame, and some have become computer consultants for security systems. The hacker is simply someone who attacks systems, sometimes for illegal gain. The hacker personality differs, and attacks are made on systems for different reasons. The purpose of some attacks is to shut down a competitor's Web site. Attacks that are seen at government Web sites are often similar to graffiti on a wall, where hackers might write "This page has been hacked" across the screen. Just as there are many different personalities that make up the hacker, there are many types of hacks.

Looking for the Hack

Anytime information is cached in memory, transmitted through a network, or stored in a computer, that information is susceptible to being read, written, or redirected. The same hacking principles apply just as much to redirecting keyboard input as to data being transmitted through the Internet since a common hacker attack is to sniff communication lines for usernames and passwords.

Grabbing and transmitting keys

A program that I was asked to write a long time ago needed to capture the keys being typed on the keyboard locally. Once these were captured, it needed to transmit the keystrokes through a telephone connection to a remote server for video streaming. Being a young engineer, I wasn't sure how to approach this issue. I proceeded to capture keyboard entries through an interrupt table and sent the keystrokes through the serial communications. After further observation, I noticed a `getSystemKey( )` function in an operating system kernel library that was callable by the "C" language. I wrote a thread that just called the undocumented function and sent the keys that were typed. It turned out the undocumented function in the operating system saved a lot of time for capturing keys. After I found the undocumented function, it took me about an hour to write and test the program to send the keys across the phone line.

A hacker can use the preceding approach. If the attacker wants to capture the keystrokes from a computer, he simply needs to store the keystrokes in a log file and transmit them when the computer connects to the Internet. Any password or username, credit card number, or company information typed into the computer could have been saved to a log. The unnamed operating system that I used was one from ten years ago, but the concept applies today. A hacker could use the same technique to read keyboard entries and send the entries to a log file on a temporary machine. The hacker can use a temporary machine to avoid being traced and pick up the keystroke file when the access seems safe. The log can contain everything that a user entered on the keyboard, including passwords.

> **CAUTION:** A possible attack is to monitor your keystrokes. The attacker needs an access point to the target machine through the network.

Keyboard sniffers

A keyboard sniffer is a common hacking routine. Some commercial products even use similar routines to keep tabs on employees or children to check their activities. The keyboard sniffer could masquerade as a driver or library. All a hacker needs is a chance to install the program on the computer.

> **TIP:** See
> `http://directory.google.com/Top/Computers/Security/Products_and_Tools/Keyloggers_and_Spyware/` for a list of keyboard sniffers or loggers.

There are several things that a hacker has to do to read the keyboard entries from a computer. First, a program has to be installed on the local machine with privileges to read the keyboard; and second, the program must transmit the information to the hacker's location. If the key log is transmitted to the hacker's site, the log can be used by the hacker for a replay attack.

> **NOTE:** A *replay attack* is typing the keystrokes that the user typed in order to re-create what the user has done. An attacker saves the keystrokes in a repository (a key log) and makes sure that he (the attacker) is not tracked.

The privilege to read from the keyboard has changed over the years in most operating systems. To read a keyboard, the process or program needs the same access that a device driver would have, which is the system-level privilege. A system-level privilege is the access that a "root" administrator is granted when logging in to the computer. The program would have to be installed by an administrator user. So the attacker would also have to have administrator privileges to install such a program. The hacker would normally need a key logging utility to get the administrator password in the first place.

> **CAUTION:** A possible attack is a replay attack; for example, the hacker may accomplish it through network sniffing.

Different Types of Hacks and How They Work

Most hacks seek an entry point to the system. The entry point could be reading the network packets or social engineering the person who has a password. The entry point is important because of its potential to expose the security leak.

In this section I address social engineering, cracks in the system, and passive and active hacks. A *passive hack attack* is one in which nothing is changed or harmed on the system. Both of the previous examples, keystroke monitoring and replay attacks, are examples of passive attacks. The other type of hack is an *active hack attack*. During an active hack programs are changed and corrupted. An example of an active hack is changing the organization's Web pages.

Social engineering

Social engineering is the ability to gain access to systems by social interaction. The interaction may be formal or informal in nature. A renowned tactic is to call in as a senior officer's wife or secretary to the IT department and complain that a password isn't working. The next step is to convince the IT department to perform the reset password process. IT departments and customer service centers could be a weak link unless they strengthen their authentication process. Some centers have employed techniques like requesting a mother's maiden name and other weak passwords before they regenerate a password. Once this is done, they will only send the password by e-mail, which further weakens the process.

Some of the biggest cracks into computers stem from people acquiring information in a social environment. Understanding an organization's systems can best be gained by being good friends with the people who install or maintain them.

> **CAUTION:** Social engineering is a very real threat that should not be ignored.

A crack in the system

Monitoring a secure system might not do much good unless there is a crack in the security of the system. A *crack* is a way to break a system. Just like someone who wants to rob a house and not get caught, the hacker must establish a plan for entering the system, grabbing assets, and covering his or her tracks. The difference between robbing a house and grabbing resources from an organization is that a hacker can leave digital fingerprints that can be erased after the crime. There is still the risk of getting caught, so the hacker usually has a motivation worth getting into trouble for if he is ever caught. For example, if an organization advertises the distribution of new software that will make a lot of money, a hacker is likely to go after that resource. A hacker will case the place or, in other words, monitor the traffic going in and out of the organization for security vulnerabilities.

The hacker might even attach a program to act as a listener, or *sniffer*, to discover security vulnerabilities. The sniffer can save the information to a log and send the information to the hacker's secure system. After the place looks safe and the hacker has sufficient knowledge to accomplish the hack, the hacker will perform the hack. The hack may involve further penetration into the system such as creating a backdoor (a login that bypasses security mechanisms), or grabbing a new program, or placing an e-mail monitoring device on a CIO's computer system. When the break in occurs, like any other professional, the hacker is going to have tools (in this case software tools) that are used to thwart security defenses.

Some attacks are not planned. For example, a hacker may FTP into a company site and accidentally find the company's source code open to the world and take it. Granted, the company source should be protected, but if it is not someone is bound to take it.

Other hackers may be a little more physical, such as stealing a laptop from the organization so that they can scan the hard disk; there are tools that can be used to scan the physical hard disk without login. They could then use the information found on the laptop. These resources could be bank account numbers, credit card numbers, passwords, computer programs, or anything else of value.

> **CAUTION:** Cracks in the system are explored to gain access to resources.

The passive hack attack

As I mentioned earlier, hacks are broken down into two modes of operation: the *passive hack attack* and the *active hack attack*. These hacks do not have to be done together or in any order.

The passive hack is merely observing information without corrupting or changing the information. The passive hack includes:

◆ Sniffing the network

◆ Probing the programs that are running

◆ Scanning the memory of the computer

◆ Scanning the files of the system

Nothing may come of the information found in these scans. The hacker could be doing a scan to understand the organization's systems. Figure 2-1 shows how a passive hack may work.

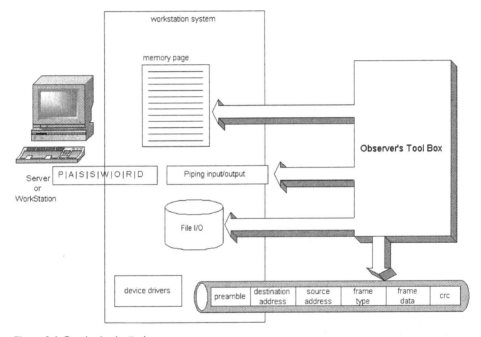

Figure 2-1: Passive hack attacks

CAUTION: Even though passive hack attacks do not modify your organization's information or infrastructure, they are a real threat and can affect your company's bottom line. Think of a passive attack as espionage.

The active hack attack

The purpose of the active hack attack is inherently different than the passive one; the active hack not only infiltrates but also corrupts the organization's systems for the hacker's use. The active hack may involve viruses, worms, backdoors, impersonators, and redirectors. An example of an active hack is a corrupted site or Web page. Another active attack is the *denial of service attack.*

The denial of service attack prevents users from accessing system resources. For example, some servers will not allow users to fail a login more than a specified number of times, so a hacker will try to log in until a user's account is disabled and the user no longer has access to the server.

Figure 2-2 demonstrates the active hack attack.

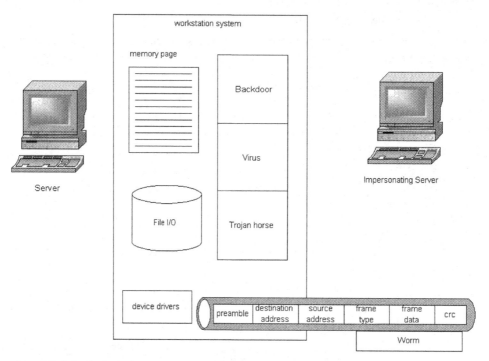

Figure 2-2: Active hack attacks

> **CAUTION:** Active hack attacks damage your organization's information and infrastructure.

The motivation behind active and passive attacks is different. The passive attack is similar to spying to retrieve information. The active attack is motivated by the need to destroy the organization's computer. A disgruntled employee or a competing company could motivate the active attack. The passive attack hides the attack by not showing signs that anyone has been on the system. The active attack hides the attack by destroying enough of the system so that no digital fingerprints are left on the system. The active and passive attack can be used in combination to both read information and cover the tracks of the hacker. The passive attack, while not destroying the systems, can also do harm to the overall organization. The hacker who gets information from the passive attack can use it for insider trading, to publish derogatory information about the organization, or to publish the organization's trade secrets.

NOTE: Attacks are not only described as active and passive, but can be organized by the system or subsystem that is attacked and the style in which it is attacked. The type of the attack could be a worm, virus, impersonator, redirector, or sniffer. The systems that can be attacked are networks, the computer system, or the enterprise system.

Understanding Network Attacks

Any computer that is on the Internet is susceptible to a computer attack. The attack may not be successful, but it is an attack nevertheless. Attackers may constantly test the system for vulnerabilities and keep track of possible weaknesses. It is up to the organization and individual to diligently keep track of the attacker to judge where these attacks have occurred and where they are headed.

If an organization does not monitor its networks and systems, it is susceptible to being attacked and not even knowing it. When a company is attacked and doesn't know it, the company may find that its private information has become public after it is too late. Any anomaly on a network should be investigated to ensure that security has not been breached. Many companies spend a lot of money to check the integrity of their networks. Some companies have rooms full of network engineers monitoring the packets of the networks.

Network monitoring terms

Network monitoring software is easy to get, and any network that is open to the Internet can easily be sniffed. *Sniffing the network* is when the protocol packets are being observed. Anyone who understands the socket *Application Programming Interface* (API) can write specialized sniffers and redirectors. By sniffing the packets, the hacker can understand the frame data. The frame may potentially include plaintext passwords. After the packets are understood on the network, they can be used for impersonation or redirection. Figure 2-3 demonstrates the sniffer technique.

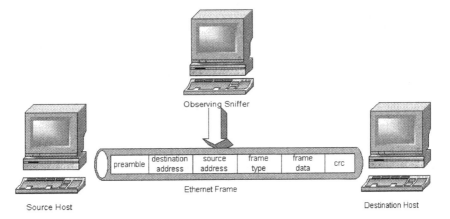

Figure 2-3: Network sniffing

> **NOTE:** The Socket API is supported on multiple systems and languages and is used to support network programming. However, it can also be misused for attacks.

Sniffing the network for a host

Many network programs and applications are described as sniffers. A simple query on a search engine can provide a list. One site is www.sniffer.com. The purpose of a sniffer application is to provide packet and statistics information for the protocol packets being transmitted on a network. Some sniffers may be programs that are run on a remote host, and others may involve hardware that is plugged into the network. An example of a sniffer that doesn't require a host computer is the Fluke LanMeter, which I helped develop. If the packet being sniffed is Ethernet, the packet will contain the destination address, source address, connection synchronization, data packet, protocol type, and cyclic redundancy check. If there is any plaintext information in the packet, such as a password, it can be observed. Firewalls use the source and destination of addresses as well as the connection synchronization to secure and filter the packets on the network. Once the hacker understands this information, the hacker can simulate the information to fake the firewall into believing that it came from a secure location.

Some operating systems support some of the protocol utilities that will be mentioned for sniffing the network. These protocol utilities can be pulled down by separate packages online for those operating systems that do not support them. The starting point for scanning services and ports can be found on your local machine. Common files that are searched for information are the etc/services, etc/hosts, etc/networks, and etc/protocols files. The etc/services file contains entries that have information about port numbers, the protocol type, and the protocol service. Listing 2-1 demonstrates the entries for *File Transfer Protocol* (FTP).

> **TIP:** Because hackers are familiar with and explore the weaknesses of the Request for Comments (RFCs), you should be at least familiar with the RFCs too. The site www.ietf.org provides network protocol information and specifications.

Listing 2-1: FTP entries

```
ftp-data            20/tcp                      #FTP, data
ftp                 21/tcp                      #FTP. control
```

Listing 2-1 shows the FTP entry for the data for the TCP protocol at port 20 and shows that the FTP control is at port 21. This is valuable information for a hacker because it details available port services.

> **CAUTION:** Some applications use host and service files to establish their connectivity, and overriding these files may redirect the service to different ports and allow hackers to impersonate services.

For Java sockets, the Java InetAddress class has the getByName() method which first looks in the etc/hosts file. If the host is not found in the etc/hosts file, it does a DNS lookup based on how the DNS is set up. Changing the `hosts` file affects an application using this method.

> **TIP:** Java sockets do not support the `getservbyname()` functionality for retrieving information from the services file.

The hacker's arsenal of utilities

Some of the hacker's arsenal includes the `whois` utility, the `ping` utility, and the `traceroute` utility. The `whois` utility lists the hosts of an organization that are publicly listed through the *Domain Name Service* (DNS). The `ping` utility is used to see if a computer is active on the network. The `ping` utility gives the time to the target host and back. The `traceroute` utility does one better and gives *hop* information, which is IP information on the devices in between the source and the target host. These utilities are common network protocols that can be picked up almost anywhere and that are used to find the target computer and the computers surrounding it. Finding a nearby host with less security helps hackers in launching their attacks. Hackers can launch their attacks from the nearby machine and check it occasionally when they think that it is safe.

> **CROSS-REFERENCE:** See Chapter 21 for more information on `ping` and network security.

The uninvited "guest"

Other utilities used by hackers include `telnet` and `FTP`. A typical example of what a hacker can do is log in to firewalls and routers using the `telnet` protocol with a "guest" account if one is enabled. The process of logging in often generates a screen output that is useful to the hacker. The screen output may contain essential information such as the type of device and the software version. The hacker can try a password cracker to guess the username and password.

`FTP` provides a means to copy files to and from the network devices. The `FTP` server utility and file system on the device must be compromised in order to be susceptible to an attack, but sometimes the hacker gets lucky and the system wasn't set up correctly. Firewalls and routers are complicated network devices to set up. Network administrators require years of training and experience to set them up correctly. The hacker's only advantage is that he could be more experienced with the device and the holes found in the devices. Holes for the network devices are published on hacker sites and in books. Many other network devices require routing tables and firewall access, so some of the tables allow read access to all the members in the organization. By reading the routing table, an understanding can be gained on how the networks are configured in the organization. Figure 2-4 demonstrates an attack on a target machine from a nearby machine.

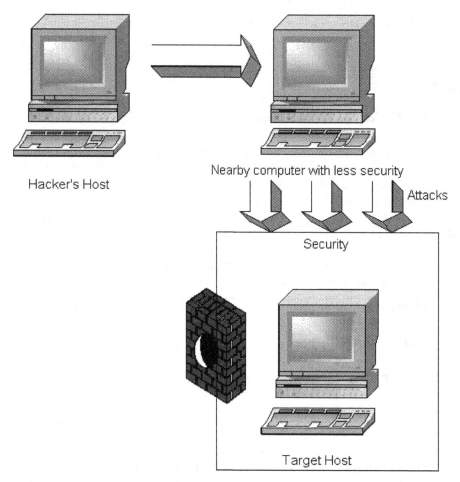

Figure 2-4: Attacks from a nearby local machine

> **NOTE:** The closer physical access that a hacker has to a machine, the more he can focus an attack to that particular machine. For instance, if the hacker has access to a machine in the same subnet as the target machine, it is easier for the hacker to try an attack because he bypasses the security measures established to protect the subnet.

Password crackers

If the password and other vital information are not displayed in packets from the network traffic, a hacker may use password crackers. Password crackers use dictionary attacks. *Dictionary attacks* use a dictionary for passwords and try every word in it.

Many systems that fear this attack will disable a user's account if many incorrect passwords are used to try to log in. If the user's account is disabled, the user can no longer log in. This is the nature of a *denial of service attack*. If the entire user set, including the administrator users, are denied login, the system can never be accessed again unless there is backdoor. The *backdoor* is a login that bypasses most of the enforced security mechanisms.

> **NOTE:** In a dictionary attack, the attacker performs guesses for the password, such as all possible combinations of six letters. Because passwords are small (by crytographic standards), they can be determined in a very short periods of time (days, hours, or even seconds) depending on the skill of the attacker, the system, and the password itself.

Another useful utility in the hacker's arsenal is the *port scanner*. The port scanner will scan all of the ports on a remote machine to see which are active. If port 20 and port 21 are active, the hacker can review the file in Listing 2-1 and know that the remote computer is supporting the FTP protocol. The `etc/services` file lists the ports that the services must use. Any service that uses port 20 and port 21 that is not an FTP service will have problems because FTP services will try to log in to those ports from the Internet. Once access is granted on a machine, even as a guest, files can be read, what processes are running can be determined, and users who are locally logged on can be observed. The *netstat utility* can be used to determine the current ports that are being used by services. The *ps utility* can be used to determine other processes running on the machine. Even a guest has access to many of these utilities.

Other information about access can be found at Web sites, such as e-mail addresses for contacts, information about the founders of the organization, and where the organization is located. Social engineering can be used in conjunction with some of this information. For example, if the IT department is listed on the Web site, the hacker can call and complain about not being able to log in to his account. If the hacker is believable, the IT department may be helpful.

IT impersonations

Another method is for the hacker to contact a salesperson and act as if he is from the IT department. This works best when the salesperson is telecommuting. The hacker tells the salesperson that there is an upgrade in software or new software that the salesperson must install and provides an FTP address for the salesperson to download the file. The file can be tainted for the hacker's use. Or, the hacker can say there is an issue with the salesperson's computer and say he (the hacker) needs to log in to fix it. Once a hacker accesses a system, he can access FTP or e-mail to transfer files to the hacker's machine. If the files are write accessible, the hacker can transfer them to the machine to overwrite key files.

Using sniffing tools provides packet information. Some of the first sniffers were hardware sniffers from companies such as Network General. Now sniffers can easily be run on remote machines. Listing 2-2 gives a fragment of a sniffer example of a telnet packet.

> **NOTE:** The following screen dump was made by the "analyzer" product, a public domain sniffer found at `http://analyzer.polito.it/`. Another public domain version is `http://www.ethereal.com/`. I recommend to anyone who wants more powerful port sniffers and protocol to visit `http://www.tigertools.net`.

Listing 2-2: Sniffer output example

```
----- General -----
Item number 1, position in logfile 1%
Timestamp: 14h:23m:00s:367000us
----- Description -----
Item type: Partial frame, 62 bytes available
Frame size is 62 (3E hex) bytes
----- MAC Header ----- [0-13]
Destination = Computer 004854-0133F7 (Universal; Vendor: ???) - [0-5]
Source = Computer 004854-013412 (Universal; Vendor: ???) - [6-11]
Ethertype = 0800h (DOD IP) - [12-13]
----- IP v4 Header ----- [14-33]
Version = 4 - {14-14}
Header length = 5 bytes - {14-14}
Type of service = 00h - [15-15]
 000. .... = priority 0 - {15-15}
 ...0 .... = normal delay - {15-15}
 .... 0... = normal throughput - {15-15}
 .... .0.. = normal reliability - {15-15}
Total length = 48 bytes - [16-17]
Identification = 8193 - [18-19]
Flags = 4h - {20-20}
 0... .... = must be 0 - {20-20}
 .1.. .... = do not fragment - {20-20}
 ..0. .... = last fragment - {20-20}
Fragment offset = 0 bytes - {20-20}
Time to live = 128 seconds/hops - [22-22]
Protocol = 6 (TCP [Transmission Control Protocol]) - [23-23]
Header checksum = C6C4h - [24-25]
Source address = [10.0.0.2] - [26-29]
Destination address = [10.0.0.1] - [30-33]
No IP options
----- TCP Header ----- - [34-61]
Source port = 1037 (???) - [34-35]
Destination port = 23 (telnet) - [36-37]
Sequence number = 742731 - [38-41]
Acknowledgement number = 0 - [42-45]
Header length = 28 bytes - {46-46}
Flags = 02h - [47-47]
 ..0. .... = No urgent pointer - {47-47}
 ...0 .... = No acknowledgement - {47-47}
 .... 0... = No push - {47-47}
 .... .0.. = No reset - {47-47}
 .... ..1. = SYN - {47-47}
 .... ...0 = No FIN - {47-47}
Window = 8192 - [48-49]
Checksum = F5A2h - [50-51]
Urgent pointer = 0 - [52-53]
```

```
Options = 8 bytes - [ 54-61]
 Code = 204 (MSS)
 Required MSS: 1029
 Other Options
Next Protocol: Unsupported (s:1037,d:23) - [ 34-37]
----- Telnet -----
[ 0 byte(s) of data]
===================================================================
==
* 00 48 54 01 | 33 F7 00 48 | 54 01 34 12 | 08 00 45 00
[ .HT.3..HT.4...E.]
* 00 30 20 01 | 40 00 80 06 | C6 C4 0A 00 | 00 02 0A 00 [ .0
.@...........]
* 00 01 04 0D | 00 17 00 0B | 55 4B 00 00 | 00 00 70 02
[ .........UK....p.]
* 20 00 F5 A2 | 00 00 02 04 | 05 B4 01 01 | 04 02      [ ............]
```

Listing 2-2 shows an extraction for a telnet packet. The output shows the computer MAC Header and the TCP Header. As you can see, the destination port is port 23 for telnet, and the packet information and data is also displayed. Knowing what is being transmitted into and out of the computer is useful for gaining access into the computer.

The information in the packet is a telnet session. If a secure shell or encryption is not used to shield the password, the plaintext password can be seen going across the session. A hacker could reuse the information and log in at a later time. The hacker could also use a port sniffer instead of a packet sniffer to see which protocols are being supported. If a telnet server is not available on the host machine, a hacker could impersonate a telnet session.

A hacker has to establish a reason for people logging in to the telnet session, such as broadcasting that there is a new machine to deliver source code. Just knowing that a telnet server is available will give reason to look for telnet packets being transported on the network. Some telnet servers may have the "guest" or "anonymous" user active, giving some access to start with to the telnet servers. Some telnet servers have known bugs and issues that can be used, such as backdoors, for hackers to gain access.

Once inside the computer, it is important to understand the operating system. Just as it is important to understand the network for reaching and impersonating a connection, it is important to understand the operating system to impersonate processes.

Sniffing the system computer

Understanding the security of the operating system is important for impersonating secure processes or embedding a process into the operating system. Also, it is important to understand the security that is used for accessing file systems and device drivers. The *file system* is a type of device driver for accessing files. To have access to everything on the computer, the current user must be set to the system or administrator user.

Device drivers and system daemons normally have to be installed and managed by the system administrator. Even though a user might have minimal access on a computer, some of the daemon services and device drivers that are running in the background are running as the system user at all times. The daemon services and device drivers have to run as a system user to access some of the operating system resources. For this reason, anyone who has administration privileges on a machine may take over the machine because he has write permission to all system files on that machine. Other users may have access to read the system and the files but are very limited on write access.

A gold mine for hackers

In the Microsoft Windows operating systems, one gold mine for the hackers is the registry entries. The *registry* describes the operation and setup to the devices and many of the processes. The registry database can be protected from read and write access. Sometimes administrators may not set this up correctly, or the hacker might have somehow cracked the registry. If the hacker accesses the registry, the computer can be mapped out for further hacks. If write access is granted to the hacker, the hacker can replace device drivers and system services with his own.

The difference in the UNIX operating system is that there are system environment configurations, and the UNIX operating system has a hierarchical file structure for where files should be placed, such as /dev for device drivers. The hacker can apply the same rules in that he can modify the startup shells for the user and redirect to his own processes and device drivers. The difference in the UNIX operating system is that the startup shells normally live under the user's home directory and they run with the user's privileges.

The file system is a common place for most hacks. The file system is a device driver such as NTFS, meaning the Window's NT File System, and is tightly integrated with the operating system. If the device driver is interrupted or overwritten, it is possible to read and write all files on a device; however, that hack is very complicated and requires complete administration access. A more passive hack is just to read any files that are accessible for information-gathering purposes.

Cracks to common encryption

Many users will now encrypt their files using Microsoft Word or other applications, but many cracks exist on hacker sites for some of these applications. When gathering information, users might have passwords for databases stored in files or even their e-mail files saved to hard disk. Many users do not have private read access on these files, and if others can read the files, hackers may copy these files and move them to a different location to be cracked at a later time. A waiting hacker might also pick up any log files that an application might leave around. Log files usually give detailed information on how the application is behaving and sometimes information on how it is connecting to other applications.

Some of the files that are susceptible in the J2EE applications are setup files that contain database identification and deployment descriptors that describe the security of the application components. If there is any file that has read access to a less secure user than an administrator, the hacker will probably target that user for file access. Once the hacker retrieves a database username and password and has access to a database, he can gain control of the database and implement backdoor passwords. Then the chase for the hacker will start to move from the system administrator to a database administrator.

JSP cookies

Other files from the J2EE that are used for information are the *Java Server Pages* (JSP) cookies. *Cookies* are files saved to a machine to retain session state information for a Web site. Some cookies are used to store usernames and passwords that can be sniffed from the cookie file. Other cookies retain personal information used when logging onto the Web site. Cookies keep information based on the Web site visited. If a hacker who understands cookies can gain access to the cookies in a system's machine, he can at a minimum gather the Web sites that a user has visited. By understanding the Web sites that a user has visited, the hacker can start with a hack at a Web site to try to impersonate the user.

A more active hack is to replace application setup files and deployment descriptors with the hacker's own version. The objective is to change the behavior of the application server. A hacker could only replace these files if he were granted write access to them. If the files were overwritten with the hacker's own files, he could create an identical server which would forward the credit card numbers to the hacker's private account. A hack like this would require a lot of skill and patience, but it can happen if requirements for the proper security on the files and file systems are not mapped out and enforced. Simply put, changing files on the system can change the behavior of the system.

> **CAUTION:** As you may already know, some of the most pervasive viruses live in the boot sectors of the file system, and these viruses are capable of infecting the files that the given file system manages.

Unsafe memory

The file system is not the only part of the operating system that is susceptible to hackers. Memory, either cached or shared, is also a possible target in the operating system.

> **NOTE:** The concept of *shared memory* refers to a read and write block of data directly to memory. Many operating systems support the concept of shared memory using the system's native language, such as C.

A hacker who has detailed knowledge of the memory system can peruse the memory allocation blocks and try to determine what is being loaded into memory. A person who has detailed knowledge of the operating system and its devices, such as NTFS, could use shared memory routines to try to rewrite a section of memory. Very few people can accomplish a hack like this one, and the operating system is prone to crash when something is written to its protected memory location.

Protected memory is used because the memory section is protected by the operating system, and if writes do occur without system access permissions, an operating system exception occurs. In Windows NT, the term for a system exception is a BSOD, or Blue Screen of Death. Other programs that use memory are not part of the operating system and are not loaded into protected memory. These programs could be changed, but a detailed knowledge of the operating system and assembly code is required.

> **NOTE:** Java doesn't use shared memory as an interprocess communication and so doesn't have some these security holes that can be programmatically used.

Debugging past and present

Because understanding the file system and operating system usually requires great skill, some hackers will try to change a system process by using the registry and debug commands that are part of the operating system or application. When MS-DOS was prevalent, many users would simply use the `DEBUG` command to change how a process operated. Many operating systems still support the `DEBUG` command for debugging an executable. By using available debug commands, the hacker can interrupt the normal operation of an executable. Java applications are not immune to the `DEBUG` command.

Java uses the `jdb` utility for its debugging. Debug commands can attach themselves to a process that is already running or to an address space of a running application. Some of the most pervasive hacks that I have witnessed in my career are accomplished when a person who is knowledgeable about machine or assembly language has gone in an application and changed the byte or assembly code. In older versions of operating systems, a person could use the `DEBUG` utility to change the behavior of running applications. These techniques require detailed knowledge of the operating system. A simpler method would be to impersonate a server to get information about a company.

Impersonating hosts

When I want to log in to a Web site, I put in a *Uniform Resource Locator* (URL) on a browser page, such as "www.somesite.com". The local machine will do a DNS lookup on the name servers specified from the local machine. *Domain name servers* (DNS) provide the logical mapping of names to IP addresses. The DNS servers use the `etc/hosts` file to map the information. The `etc/resolv.conf` file stores the name servers to do further lookups if the DNS could not resolve the host name. DNS spoofing is easier than IP spoofing in that the logical mapping is redirected to a different server.

> **TIP:** RFC 1033 and RFC 1034 describe the DNS system.

These domain name servers will search their `etc/hosts` file and may also do a name server lookup on the DNS servers that are specified. If the name is really obscure, it might do a lookup all the way to a master INTERNIC DNS server. The site host name will resolve to an IP address where an `etc/hosts` file will eventually have an entry with "www.somesite.com" if the host is valid.

The idea behind DNS spoofing is to resolve the host's name to the hacker's address for a set of users. When the user or set of users log in to the hacker's Web site or server, they are to believe that they are logging into a valid Web site. When the user logs into the hacker's Web site, the hacker is capturing the keystrokes for the username and password. The hacker now has access to one of the user's Web sites. The idea could apply to other network protocols such as FTP and telnet. In order to accomplish this task, the hacker will have to change either the DNS that the user will use or the hosts table that the DNS will use. Figure 2-5 demonstrates host impersonation.

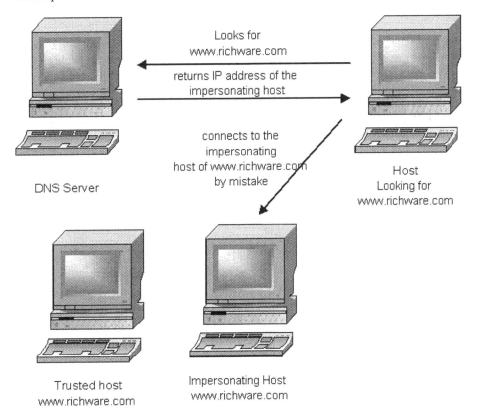

DNS Server

Looks for
www.richware.com

returns IP address of the
impersonating host

connects to the
impersonating
host of www.richware.com
by mistake

Host
Looking for
www.richware.com

Trusted host
www.richware.com

Impersonating Host
www.richware.com

Figure 2-5: Host impersonation

IP spoofing attacks

Many firewalls and other network security mechanisms give access to the host if the source of the connection comes from a trusted network or host. For example, the application server may only accept connections coming from the Web server at www.richware.com. The application server will look for the source address in the TCP/IP packet to verify that connection originated at the Web server. *IP spoofing* is the ability to fake the trusted network source.

In order to perform the operation of providing a fake IP source address, it cannot conflict with an active host on the network. The first step is to down or block the host that is being impersonated. The hacker will have to disconnect or interrupt the trusted Web server for a small period of time and access the application as if it came from the Web server. The Web server could even be down for a scheduled maintenance without the application server being aware of it, so the hacker, in this case, wouldn't have to ensure a disconnect from the valid Web server.

The concept of IP spoofing is to impersonate the trusted source of the connection for a trusted connection. After sniffing the packets across the network and knowing what the application server is expecting, the hacker duplicates the packets for the application server. Figure 2-6 demonstrates IP spoofing.

CROSS-REFERENCE: See Chapter 21 for more information on firewalls and network security.

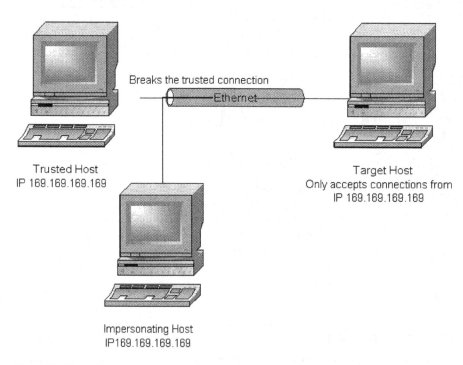

Breaks the trusted connection

Ethernet

Trusted Host
IP 169.169.169.169

Target Host
Only accepts connections from
IP 169.169.169.169

Impersonating Host
IP169.169.169.169

Figure 2-6: IP spoofing

Operating system active attacks

The passive attacks for operating systems have been discussed, but there are many more ways to corrupt an operating system. The attacks against operating systems to bring them down are active attacks against the operating system. These attacks may not be totally malicious, but rather a way for a hacker to get recognition by painting a message on your screen similar to "You have been hacked." These hacks may not even be geared toward any one organization. They might be geared toward any consumer that buys a specific software product. The attack could be directed to anyone, for instance someone who answers through a specific newsgroup or answers certain e-mail. I have seen hacks like these geared toward people who copy specific software packages onto other software packages in their systems. These hacks might not be done by someone just learning a system but by a competitor of a software package or done for some other business reason.

Backing up: the best defense

The first active hack that I was a victim of occurred when I pulled down a compiler off a *Bulletin Board System* (BBS) using a modem and a local number. The result was that my screen looked like it was raining and system files started deleting themselves. For those very reasons, I kept a backup of everything, but it was lot easier to reload a 128-megabyte hard drive. The amount of damage that active hacks can cause can be in the millions and can bring down an organization for days.

The jarsigner utility: a defense up to a point

One of the most significant additions to Java is the use of the `jarsigner` utility. The `jarsigner` allows the *Java Archive* (JAR) to be signed by principals who are located in the local `keystore` database of certificates. The `jarsigner` utility prohibits users from changing a JAR file. The JAR file can contain Java applications or Java components. The limitation of JARs and Java components is that many still use the operating system's native libraries, file system, and network system. The operating system, file system, and network system are still susceptible to hackers.

Even though Java provides a lot of security functionality as part of its basic foundation, the limitations of the operating system, file system, and network system still can affect Java applications. If the operating system could enforce Java security down to the device driver and operating system levels, I believe many of the hack attacks could be avoided by using the `jarsigner` utility. However, at this point there is no Java operating system. A Java operating system, with Java libraries and device drivers, could fully use the `jarsigner` utility and take advantage of the `jarsigner` utility security features right down to the device level. A possible way this could work is to have the entire operating system signed in a JAR file, which could not be overwritten unless one has the `keystore` to match the JAR. Therefore, the operating system would be as secure as how the `keystore` is protected.

> **TIP:** Because the operating system, at this point, does not support Java security, if you are a victim of an attack and suspect the operating system, you can easily verify your suspicion by moving the JAR to another operating system and verifying the attack.

Virus attacks

The most common active attack on an operating system is the virus. There are more than 69,000 known computer viruses. The purpose of a digital virus is to infect a host and replicate. Digital viruses, very much like the biological forms, will attack their hosts, disrupting the normal operation of the host. Just as a person slows down and becomes disrupted when they catch a virus, so does the host computer.

Biological and digital viruses: a frightening similarity

Biological viruses infect human cells by replicating thousands of the viruses and infecting the system. The digital virus replicates itself as well on the Internet or through the host computer systems. The virus may try to hide itself in the disk format or operating system of a specific system, surfacing occasionally to infect other systems. The biological virus takes on the same form by hiding itself in the human subsystem.

Like the biological virus, the computer virus can usually replicate itself to spread to other systems that it comes into contact with through a connection. The virus incubates in a particular system or set of systems and once it believes it can spread, it tries. When a virus lays waiting for a chance to spread, it is in its *dormant* phase. After the virus has the nutrients to spread, it will enter a replication phase where it reproduces. The digital virus will replicate itself in programs and disk sectors, as the biological form replicates through a bloodstream.

When a computer program contains a virus, it usually contains an exact clone of the virus. After the virus has significantly reproduced or realizes it is about to be caught, it may believe itself strong enough to attack the host system. An attack on the computer host system can take many forms, from changing the screen to deleting files. If the computer host contains the correct anti-virus software, like antibodies for biological virus, the virus can be fought and destroyed. If the computer host does not contain the correct anti-virus software, the computer host can be destroyed.

Types of viruses

The virus is meant to hide in the host's operating system through a variety of means. There are *boot sector viruses* that go live when the operating system boots up in hopes of being started before any anti-virus software. The objective here is to destroy the anti-virus software when it starts. There are *stealth viruses* that are built specifically to hide from anti-virus software. *Parasitic viruses* attach themselves to programs in the hopes that destroying them will also destroy the program. There are *macro viruses* that can only be executed by Microsoft Word or Microsoft Outlook that are started when these programs are started. There are also *polymorphic viruses* that change every time they reproduce to create a mutant virus, so that the anti-virus software doesn't recognize them. There are many more types of viruses. Studying them all, and their variations, is just as complex and overwhelming as studying biological viruses.

There are so many types of viruses now that knowing a programming language is not even required. Viral kits can be used from different hacking sites to create different types of viruses. The viral kit normally asks the creator a set of questions about how they would like their virus to behave. One of the questions might be "Should it delete system files?"

One thing that all digital viruses have in common is that they need a way to enter the system and they need a process to start them. The process could be an operating system call, a device driver call, or even the startup of a system service by the operating system. Just as easily as a network can be sniffed by hackers to find useful information, the user of the host computer can see what information is traveling to his system. The user of the host machine can monitor the operating system of the host machine just as easily as a hacker can. The best defense against a virus is to know your host machine and network. Something as simple as setting the security to its highest for Microsoft Outlook and not clicking on an attachment until the user knows what it is for can go a long way in the prevention of the macro virus alone. Equal steps must be taken for other viruses.

The cost of combatting a virus

One of the most difficult viruses that I had to track down happened almost ten years ago when I was installing a network operating system. The virus would infect the boot sector of the normal operating system, and it would occasionally spread itself to other operating systems. It turned out that the virus was on a floppy that a person copied the setup to from original disks for installation. The virus hid itself in the *File Allocation Table* (FAT) partition of the floppy. Copying new files to the floppy disk did not get rid of the virus. I eventually just bought a new box of floppies and went back to the original disks. Time and money was spent to destroy the virus.

The difficulty in finding this virus was that any virus protection software was always installed after the network operating system installation; and when the virus protection software was installed, the virus would prevent the virus protection software from looking for the virus. This scenario is an example of the complexities of finding viruses. The prevention was simply not to use copied disks. Constantly monitoring the processes and transmissions goes a long way in preventing viruses. There are many anti-virus programs that can help check for viruses whenever new software is brought into the machine.

Backdoors and logic bombs

Many programs have backdoors or even Easter eggs that never try to do anything malicious. With *Easter eggs*, when a certain combination of keys is pressed you get a surprise. For example, with the new Space Invaders games if certain keys are pressed, the old Space Invaders game can be played. Many games have Easter eggs and so do many programs. Most of the Easter eggs in some of my applications simply list the authors and contributors to the programs. Easter eggs are fun, but they can produce bugs just like any other program. If the

Easter egg is not part of the test plan, which it usually is not, it might not be fully tested and bugs can arise, which hackers take advantage of. For instance, if the authors of the program come up when pushing a key combination, using a similar combination can cause a security breach.

A developer or tester usually leaves a backdoor in order to bypass the main security to test or recover the system. Developers and testers use the backdoor to perform quick tests or debug the programs without having to go through the normal security in order to save time in their testing. The developer may also want to have a backdoor in case the normal security authentication breaks so there is an alternative way to enter the system to fix the issues. There have been incidents in some older operating systems, such as Multics, where backdoors were not planned at all but were a side effect of a bug. A *tiger team*, which is an offsite team that tests the system like a hacker would by using the same tools and techniques, later found the bug.

A *logic bomb* is a more malicious program. A logic bomb is code embedded in the application, and is set to "explode" when certain conditions are met. The bomb could be set up to go off on a certain date or when certain keys are pressed in sequence. Once it explodes, it damages the system by deleting data, forcing the machine to crash, or by some other damaging action. The software could also be set to go off if the system doesn't receive a certain combination of keys every week. Disgruntled employees or contractors may implement logic bombs that have to be updated with a key sequence into the organization's system at certain intervals. If they don't get paid or if they get laid off, they no longer enter the sequence. When the sequence is not entered, the bomb explodes and damages the system.

Trojan horses and worms

A *Trojan horse* is a seemingly useful program or utility that can be downloaded off a Web site, but when started on the machine it damages the system. The damage that it does may not be apparent at first, such as changing the access to files on the local machine. The program may even work and appear useful, but the idea is for the user to download it and install it so the hacker can get entry into the user's computer. Another example is downloading an FTP client that, when it is used, it keeps a running log of the keystrokes and passes them to the hacker. It is difficult to detect Trojan horses because they act as normal programs, and they usually give no warning that something malicious is taking place. The idea of the Trojan horse is to masquerade a hacker utility as a legitimate program and to attack when the user is executing the program. Backdoors would be considered a Trojan horse if the purpose of distributing the application is to apply a backdoor into the user's system.

Worms are viruses or Trojan horses that crawl from system to system. Unlike viruses, the worm depends on a network connection to spread. A worm will search for weaknesses in protocols in order to spread. Worms may be created to infect a particular protocol, such as e-mail, or a list of protocols, such as e-mail, FTP, TELNET, and RLOGIN. After a worm gets through a network protocol, it will replicate itself on the remote machine, and continue to spread in the same manner. The Internet worm attack of 1988 is the most famous example of a worm attack. Sending new code to the finger daemon created the spreading of the Internet worm. The Internet worm spread because there were logic errors in the finger daemon when retrieving data. The Internet worm of 1988 clogged the networks and brought down many machines that it encountered on the network. This worm brought a lot of organizations' systems down until they deleted the worm.

Protecting Against Hackers

Some reports state that someone on the inside, such as a disgruntled employee, performs 85% of all hacks suffered by organizations. Unlike a hacker who is entering through the outside system, the hacker for an internal attack knows the systems. The employee is familiar with the resources that are available and may have a set of passwords to start hacking. There may be internal systems that he is familiar with, and the employee could have applied logic bombs or backdoors to assist in any attacks.

Keeping tabs in the workplace

There are applications that can be purchased to keep tabs on what employees are doing on their workstation. Managers who are aware of what the software engineer or system administrator is doing on a daily basis can keep that person from becoming a hacker. An employee who knows he is being watched would likely be hesitant to do something he shouldn't do. It is the employee who works weekends and until midnight without the manager watching who has the time to establish a hack.

Always be aware of what is being loaded onto the system's machine. Keep a running inventory of the programs that were installed. Check the list with some of the security sites for potential security risks. Be a minimalist when it comes to installing new programs. Only install programs that are by trusted and well-known vendors. Sometimes, I need to install programs to use for a month and then not re-use them for several more months. The program can be un-installed and re-installed when I need it several months later. Also monitor and be aware of what is running on the system computer. If the CPU usage of a machine is maxed out and there should be nothing running on the machine, obviously something harmful could be running in the background of the machine.

Isolating your suspects

If a hacker is suspected, set up a machine and account just for the hacker. Isolate the hacker into a machine that can be monitored and controlled with almost no utilities and access on it. Have the keystrokes and commands captured to log files. Isolating, monitoring, and controlling the hacker in a remote site can lead to the search and capture of the hacker. In many cases, the hacker will not know that he has been isolated, but may think that he has accessed an organization's system. Think like the hacker. Give the hacker a Trojan horse to download and find him. Because the hacker uses viral kits, sniffers, and other toolboxes where very little programming and computer knowledge is involved, the hacker may not be aware of the total damage that he may cause to a system.

Many hackers are tracked by organizations to give the estimate of the damage done to the organization so they can fix the damage. It might be that the hacker cannot give detailed information but can only point to a hack kit that he got on the Internet. The organization should always be aware of the hacking products and security Web sites. Several hacking sites that I visited last year no longer exist, and I am sure that any information on their tools is hard to come by. Organizations should know their systems well enough that, if they are hacked, they can assess the damage themselves and not depend on any other information.

Understanding your security system

The biggest effort that can help in securing systems is to be security aware. Many companies are aware of the latest and greatest technologies, but when asked about security, their typical response is "We have a firewall." A firewall does help if properly configured, but I have seen people answering this question and then pulling down hundreds of software packages the next time they're attacked.

There were so many programs on this person's desktop that a hard drive was added and when asked about the origin of some of the files, the response was "Just things collected over the years. I don't know where most of it came from." Even if the person was very technology aware, security should also be a big consideration. Some of the programs could be malicious without the person knowing. The suggestion was to compress and backup all of the files to a CD-ROM and later retrieve the files only when necessary. When considering security, be a minimalist with downloading and using programs of unknown origin. There may or may not have been malicious programs on this person's desktop. Usually, the only time that a hack is found is when it affects a system and it starts to cost money.

Hiring an expert

The biggest advantage that an organization could have is having security requirements established by a security expert. Many organizations give the security requirements to a business analysis person who lacks the background to understand security issues. The security expert will always ensure that chances of a security risk are avoided. Security consciousness is, in many ways, just a frame of mind. Just as a person is motivated to learn new technology, so there is a frame of mind for someone who wants to learn new security techniques. In the security plan, have tiger teams test the organization's systems and plan to revisit the security needs of the organization at regular intervals. Have a designated security administrator visit the advisories of applications and operating systems found at `www.cert.org/advisories`.

> **CROSS-REFERENCE:** Chapter 21 discusses how to protect your system and unused ports against hackers.

Summary

Hackers are a diverse group that could have many reasons for hacking into a system. Their tools and techniques are as diverse as the hackers themselves. Even though they have diverse methods, the only way through a computer system is through a network. A hacked application can be pulled down by a user, e-mailed as a virus, or put on the computer by the hacker. The hacker can sniff the network to understand the packets that are being sent. The organization can sniff the network just as well to protect their networks.

The hacker, through a strong understanding of the operating system and applications, can control the computer once he gains access to it. The user, having access to the computer, can apply his knowledge of operating systems to contain the hacker. The hacker can be mapped to an isolated system to be contained and identified. The hacker is feared among the organizations of the world, but the hacker has more to lose, and there is always the chance that he is hacking into an organization that knows more about hacking than he does.

Chapter 3

Java Security Components

In This Chapter

♦ Learning the security elements for each security operation

♦ Introducing Java security components

♦ Understanding the role of each component

Introduction

The purpose of this chapter is to introduce some of the many Java components for security. The difference between the Java components lies in the purpose of the component, the supporting algorithm, and the supporting protocol. In Chapter 1, the operations for security are defined as authentication, authorization, data confidentiality, and data integrity. All Java security components do have similarities based on how they are constructed. To access the security interface to use in Java applications, the Sun JDK 1.4 provides the *Application Programming Interface* (API).

Java APIs are provided for the security operations defined in Chapter 1. The security operation, in turn, calls a *Service Provider Interface* (SPI) to allow other security mechanisms to be plugged in. By using an API and SPI methodology, security mechanisms can be updated or modified without modifying code. The SPI interface allows different security mechanisms to be plugged by adding entries to configuration files and adding Java engines for more algorithms. The SPI interface allows the Java security components to grow in supporting algorithms and security mechanisms. Figure 3-1 shows the association of the API and SPI. Implementations are discussed in more detail in subsequent chapters.

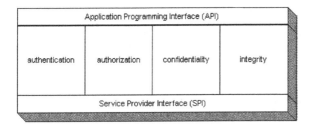

Figure 3-1: The association of the API and SPI

Categorizing Security Elements

Each security operation requires security elements. The security elements change depending on the security operation and algorithms that the security operation uses. Each security operation has a Java API and underlying security mechanism that implements the operation. The security elements define the security operation; for example, if the security operation uses keys, the security operation is confidentiality.

The principal, credential, key, and hash are all security elements that require management and storage. The management and storage are required for archival and retrieval of security elements. The security elements that are stored are considered trusted and will be used by the security operation. Most security operations will simply check incoming security elements with the trusted security element to ensure that they are valid. When a security element is created and used for a security operation, there must be a mechanism to support the security element creation, management, and storage.

TIP: The trusted security elements must be stored in a secure store to avoid tampering.

Defining authentication with principal and credential elements

At least one security element is needed for each security operation. Authentication requires a user principal with its associated credential information. Authorization is similar in that it requires at least one principal. The principal for authorization could be a principal or a principal that represents all principals.

NOTE: The difference between the authentication and authorization information is that the authentication validates the principal with a credential, and authorization checks the access permissions of the principal on a system resource.

Many principals, like groups and domains, may not have credentials associated with them. These principals cannot be authenticated without at least one credential. The user always has a credential and thus the term *user principal*. A system could also be a user principal as long as it has at least one credential associated with it. Once a principal is authenticated, most protocols will create a subject. The *subject* is the new set of principals and credentials retrieved by the authentication mechanism for further authentication and authorization throughout the organization's system. Further authentications and authorizations may be required to enter other organizations and their systems. A user logging in to a Web site could place an order that could interact with several other companies to see the order through. Figure 3-2 shows the user principal and credential association.

For example, I could log in to a Web site using a username and password. If the authentication is valid, the authentication process creates a subject that could contain a set of X.509 certificates for me to access the application server. The authentication mechanisms use both the username and password at the Web server, and use the X.509 certificate to authenticate at the application server. The principal in the X.509 could also be used for authorization to access the resources for the applications, such as the account information in the application server. The first authentication routine uses the username as my principal and the password as my credential. The authentication mechanism reads a store to retrieve my credential and then checks the trusted user principal and credential with the incoming principal and credential. If the principals and credentials pass the check, authentication passes; otherwise, the authentication fails.

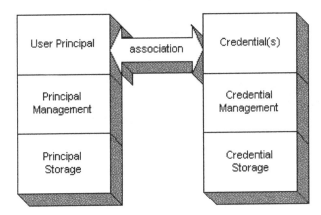

Figure 3-2: Authentication principal and credential mapping

The authentication and authorization process could consist of multiple layers of authentication and authorization mechanisms. The system could require an X.509 to enter the Web site and then a username and password to enter a second tier of security. Alternatively, the authorization could require a Kerberos token to enter a store and place an order, and then an X.509 certificate to read the profile and order history. Each principal mechanism must have an associated credential to validate the identity of the principal. For example, when I log in to a system with a username, how does the system know that the username actually belongs to me? I have to enter a password, which is a form of credential, to validate that the password belongs to me. A principal to a credential is a one-to-many relationship. A user principal requires at least one credential, but it can require more than one. I can easily write a login routine that requires two passwords.

Defining authorization with principal and permission elements

Authorization requires elements and mechanisms just like authentication. The difference is that the elements for authorization are principals and permissions. The principals for authorization can be group, domain, user, and more. No credential is required for this principal. For authorization, it is assumed that the principal has already been authenticated. The authentication confirms that the users entering the system are who they say they are.

> **NOTE**: The authentication could be implicit, meaning that some users accessing a resource in a system could be considered valid because it is assumed that they have been authenticated by the operating system. However, assumptions are dangerous.

The authorization mechanism, in most cases, will have a policy file or *Access Control List* (ACL) associated with the running Java application. The Java application will access a system resource and use the principal to check the entries of the policy file and ACL. The principal either will or will not have an entry. Some policy files will have the implicit entry of an empty principal, which means all principals can use the entry. Once the entry is found, the Java application will check the permission type and permission operation of the system resource and see if the principal has the access.

For example, the user could be `Rich`, the permission type could be `FilePermission`, the resource could be `secret.key`, and the permission operation could be `read`. When `Rich` reads the `secret.key` file, the authorization mechanism will find the entry and check that `Rich` has permission to read that file. The Java security manager provides this support as an authorization mechanism if the Java application has the security manager defined for being used at startup. See Figure 3-3 for the principal and permission association. If the principal does not have the correct principal for the system resource, then access to the resource is denied.

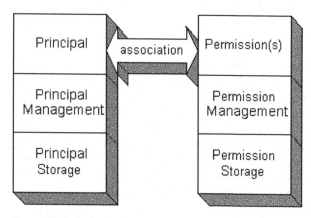

Figure 3-3: Authorization principal

Defining confidentiality with key elements

Confidentiality is the ability to change, or encrypt, data or messages into ciphertext and give only a selected group of users the ability to read, or decrypt, the original data and messages. The selected group can decrypt the message because they have been given keys to read it. Since messages are now constantly sent across the Internet in the form of e-mail, network packets, and more, no one can control who accesses these messages. However, a person can encrypt the message so that the people who sniff the message cannot understand it unless they have a key to unlock the message's meaning.

The selected groups of users who get the keys need to receive the keys in a secure distribution to ensure that only those who should receive the keys receive them and not the attackers of the system. If the keys are simply passed to the users on the Internet, anyone who is watching the data on the networks can pick up the keys and use them to decrypt the secure messages. In this case, the messages are no longer secure to those who were watching the data on the networks. The key distribution may be viewed as a form of key agreement. This is because it involves a method of different parties agreeing on which keys to use.

A simple form of key agreement is when two parties e-mail each other and agree to use key number 104 out of the 500 keys they have in separate files on their box. Key agreement is part of key management. The key management mechanisms can also interact with a key storage device in which the keys are stored. If the keys are stored, they need to be secure so that attackers cannot access them and decrypt the messages. Some types of key stores have the key encrypted.

There are two types of key elements. One uses a secret key for both encryption and decryption, and the other uses a separate private key and public key for encryption and decryption, respectively. This is called a key pair. See Figure 3-4 for the secret key and Figure 3-5 for the key pair.

The *key pair* requires both the private and public key to encrypt and decrypt the message or data. Only the public key from the associated private key can decrypt the message. No other public key can decrypt the same message. The most common key storage form for the public key is the X.509 certificate. The X.509 certificate can be stored in an unsecured key store because the certificate itself contains a public key. Following the path of the certificate can only decrypt the public key.

> **CROSS-REFERENCE**: X.509 certificates are described in Chapter 24 in more detail.

For the secret key agreement, there are algorithms that agree on which key to use. For example, two people have the same 12 keys, designated by the month, and each user uses the key based on the current month. Attackers watching the users know that the users might agree to the key of the month. But if the user's keys are not transmitted, the attackers will not know the agreed 12 keys.

The problem with this scenario is how the two users get the 12 keys originally. They could mail each other floppies, but there is always the chance that somebody might pick up the floppy from a mailbox and substitute keys that are known to an attacker. Therefore, the users not only need to agree on which key to use but also how to securely transmit the keys in the first place.

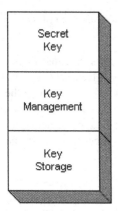

Figure 3-4: The secret key

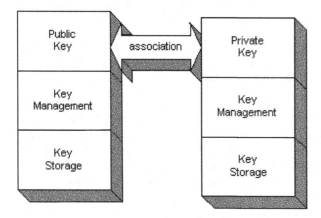

Figure 3-5: The key pair

Defining integrity with secure hash elements

Message integrity is checked to find out whether a message has been modified. When a message has been changed, it could have been changed to do harm. Software is pulled down from Web sites and online services all the time, and a message or program could be pulled down, have a virus added, and be put back on the Web site. *Integrity* is the ability to check that the data of the software has not been altered. A rudimentary way to check the data is to check the size of the file and the date that it was created. The problem with this method is that a file can have a virus introduced into it and be modified so that the size remains the same. The date of the machine can be altered for a few minutes so that when the file is uploaded it retains the original creation date, so the integrity check is easily broken in this scenario.

A more trusted method is to store an exact copy of the file in a trusted location and to periodically compare the entire stored file to the one that is used for downloading. The problem with this method, comparing entire questionable files and messages with an exact copy of trusted files and messages, is that a lot of storage is required. To avoid the storage problem, the file or message is hashed to a resultant block called a *hash* or *digest*. The hash is called a one-way hash because the original data cannot be reconstructed from the hash. Once the first hash is created, it is saved to a trusted store. When the message or file is questionable or needs a periodic check, it is hashed again into a new hash. The hash from the trusted store is retrieved and checked with the new hash. If the two hashes are identical, the original data has not been modified.

For a simple understanding of the hash and the hash function, I will start out with an *XOR* (exclusive-or) of a text message. The text message will be converted to ASCII. ASCII is a representation of text by digital numbers. As shown in Listing 3-1, the XOR function works by any two like digits resulting in a "0" and any two opposite digits resulting in positive "1."

Listing 3-1: Understanding an XOR

```
1 ^ 1 = 0
1 ^ 0 = 1
0 ^ 0 = 0
```

A very simple sample hash function is to take two text messages, convert them to ASCII, and XOR each ASCII digit. Listing 3-2 demonstrates two messages that are converted to ASCII. Then each ASCII digit is converted to binary. Finally each binary value is XOR'd with the next binary value.

Listing 3-2: Understanding a hash

```
"This is a hash ="
Changing the text in ASCII format will read the following:
84 104 105 115 32 105 115 32 97 32 104 97 115 104 32 61
The result is 114
---------------------------------------------------------------
"This hash is different ="
Changing the text in ASCII format will read the following:
84 104 105 115 32 104 97 115 104 32 105 115 32 100 105 102 102 101 114
101 110 116 32 61
The result is 118
```

The two results of XOR'ing the text messages execute two different results. Since the results are different, the messages are not the same. This is just a simple example to demonstrate how a hash function may work. The difference between this hash function and a real-world example is that a real-world hash function is a lot more complex to ensure that results of different messages can never equal. If the hashes do not match, the messages are different. If the hashes match, then the messages are the same. In order to compare the hash messages, a previous hash of the message is executed and saved into a trusted environment. When the message needs to be checked to see if it has been altered, the trusted hash is retrieved from the trusted store. The one-way hash can only generate an exact hash digest as a result. The data cannot be re-created from the hash result. See Figure 3-6 for the one-to-one hash association.

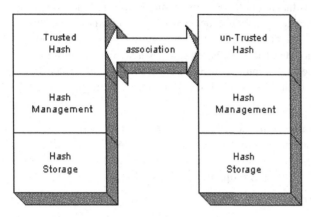

Figure 3-6: The hash

> **CROSS-REFERENCE**: Chapter 9 describes hash functions in more detail.

Categorizing Security Components in Java

Many Java components make up Java security. The components can be broken down into *element use* and *security operation*. The security operation is used to check the security elements and validate them to ensure that they match trusted security elements. An example of a trusted security element is a secure hash that is trusted to validate the message. The only security element that doesn't perform is the confidentiality operation. The key is not checked, but if it decrypts the message, then the key is considered valid from the user who encrypted the message.

Each of the security elements that have been discussed so far are created, managed, and stored. The Java security components can be broken down into those components that support the creation, management, and storage of the security elements and the security operations that are performed on those elements. For instance, the Java KeyStore is a very important security component for supporting the storage and management of keys.

Beyond key storage and management, the KeyStore is not used in any particular security operation. The KeyStore does provide authentication and authorization, but only for storing keys. The KeyStore uses multiple security operations to keep the keys secure. Since key storage and key management is needed to have a trusted set of keys to perform any confidentiality, the KeyStore makes up the necessary supporting utilities and APIs in order to ensure keys can be used for confidentiality. The use of the security elements for creation, management, and storage are supporting protocols, APIs, utilities, and mechanisms that are crucial for supporting the security operations.

Some of the most important mechanisms that are part of the Java API are *Java Authentication and Authorization Service* (JAAS), *Java Secure Socket Extensions* (JSSE), and *Java Generic Security Service Application Program Interface* (GSS-API). The JAAS handles authentication and authorization for securing system resources. The JAAS uses login modules that are defined in the configuration file and uses the Java 2 security manager to access privileged actions.

> **CROSS-REFERENCE:** See Chapter 19 for more on JAAS.

The JSSE provides a Java API for *Secure Socket Libraries* (SSL) and *Transport Layer Security* (TLS). The JSSE uses X.509 certificates for its key material. The X.509 certificate is a secure data structure format for managing public keys. JSSE provides key exchange, authentication, confidentiality, and message integrity.

> **CROSS-REFERENCE:** See Chapter 23 for more on JSSE.

The Java GSS-API provides authentication, confidentiality, and message integrity using different authentication mechanisms. By default the GSS-API uses Kerberos tickets as its key material and the Kerberos Server for authentication.

> **CROSS-REFERENCE:** See Chapter 17 for more on Java GSS-API and Chapter 16 for information on Kerberos.

Components that provide authentication

When logging on to a system, the principal in the form of a username and the credential in form of a password can be entered. To authenticate the username and password, the authentication mechanism must check the username and password with the ones retrieved by the authentication mechanism. The check compares the usernames and passwords and marks them as valid or invalid. JAAS, JSSE, and the Java GSS-API all provide some form of authentication. The JAAS supports the ability to change the authentication mechanisms in a configuration file. Java GSS-API supports the ability to change the authentication mechanism by passing in a different *Object Identifier* (OID) in the initialization of the security context.

Implementing principal and credential elements with Java components

The security elements for authentication are principals and credentials. A principal could be the name of a user or other system that is named. The authentication operation uses a user principal, meaning that it cannot accept the group principal or any other principal that does not have a credential associated with it.

Many types of principals are given in the Java API. The name of a principal is derived from the `java.security.Principal` interface. The `Principal` interface has many implementations that are distributed in the JDK 1.4. The different implementations are defined according the different protocols and operating systems that are being supported. The different principals that are defined for Microsoft WinNT operating system and subsequent uses in the Microsoft operating systems are as follows:

- `com.sun.security.auth.NTDomainPrincipal`
- `com.sun.security.auth.NTSidDomainPrincipal`
- `com.sun.security.auth.NTSidGroupPrincipal`
- `com.sun.security.auth.NTSidPrimaryGroupPrincipal`
- `com.sun.security.auth.NTSidUserPrincipal`
- `com.sun.security.auth.NTUserPrincipal`

The SID for Microsoft WinNT is the security identifier that uniquely identifies the group, user, or domain. From the Microsoft WinNT principal set, the Microsoft WinNT system can uniquely identify a domain, group, or user that contains properties specific for the Microsoft WinNT system. Like the Microsoft WinNT distinction of principals, UNIX also uniquely identifies the principals modeled after the UNIX operating system format. The different UNIX operating system principals are:

- `com.sun.security.auth.UnixUserPrincipal`
- `com.sun.security.auth.UnixNumericUserPrincipal`
- `com.sun.security.auth.UnixNumericGroupPrincipal`

The Numeric number is the UNIX *group identification number* (GID) for the group principal or the *user's UNIX identification number* (UID) for the user principal. The UNIX principals can uniquely identify a user or group by using the UNIX operating system's GID or UID. The UNIX principals allow the named principal to be used in a format for UNIX. Other principal formats are specific to the protocol being used for JSSE and Java GSS-API. JSSE uses the X.509 certificate format. The X.509 certificate format uses the X.500 protocol for the naming conventions. The JSSE can use the `javax.security.auth.x500.X500Principal` class for its API. The Java GSS-API uses Kerberos by default, so the Kerberos principal must be defined in Java.

The Kerberos principal is defined as the `javax.security.auth.kerberos.KerberosPrincipal` class. These principals make up all the different types of principals that are shipped with the JDK 1.4, however not all these principals are user principals. While all these principals can be used for authorization, not all of them can be used for authentication. Authentication requires credentials. User principals, such as `NTUserPrincipal`, can use credentials.

TIP: Group principals rarely, if ever, have credentials associated with them. Groups are used for giving a set of users access to the same system resources.

Credentials are the security element that identifies a principal. Most credentials take the form of a password. The password could be the same password that unlocks the keystore for that particular user to retrieve an X.509 certificate. There are normally many layers of authentication and authorization throughout an organization's system. Each layer throughout the system could provide a different path based on the authentication and different accesses of the resources based on the principal that was validated. It is important to map the authentication and resource paths that can be taken by different users, systems, and groups. An architect must ensure that a path or resource cannot be accessed unless it is defined by a set of requirements to be used.

> **TIP**: Documenting users and passwords through a central location such as a database or *Lightweight Directory Access Protocol* (LDAP) server is very valuable when revoking user access as the system evolves. For example, if a user set is used specifically for testing and development, the username might be `test` and the password might also be `test` for all testers to easily remember. This set might be given a lot of access to the system for full testing. Once the system is released, an attacker may find this forgotten password, and the attacker would then own a backdoor to the system with access to a lot of the system.

Validating principal and credential elements with Java components

All the authentication components support the notion of a credential. In JAAS, users are normally prompted for a series of passwords and their usernames. The series of passwords are given in a byte array and are dependent on the login module. The *login module* is the authentication mechanism that is defined for the JAAS client. The JAAS component can have multiple login modules. The login modules are defined in a configuration file for which ones are required and initialized. The username is normally given in the form of a string. After successful authentication, the JAAS creates a subject, which will contain principal entries and credential entries for further authentications and authorizations. Most of the authentication work is hidden in the login modules that provide the authentication mechanisms. The subject may provide a completely different set of principals and credentials for further use throughout the system.

If an NT login module is defined, there will be lookups in the Microsoft WinNT domain to also authenticate the user. In the `KeyStore` login module, there may be two sets of passwords, one for the administration rights to the keystore and one for the alias. The alias is the mapping of a logical name, usually the username, to an X.509 certificate. There are many login modules that can be changed to support different authentication mechanisms. The user can be prompted for the passwords and username so that the login modules can be changed without changing any code. The login module checks the username and password with the stored username and password that the login module manages. The only management of the user principal and password that is needed is if there is any automation to logging in from the JAAS client. Other than that, the login module manages the username and password for validation. For example, to validate the username and password for the `NTLoginModule`, the username and password must be defined and managed in the Microsoft Windows WinNT domain. See Figure 3-7 for the JAAS interface.

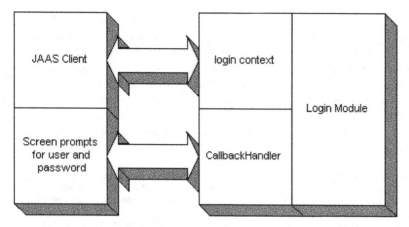

Figure 3-7: The JAAS interface

The credential for the JSSE API is normally the X.509 certificate. The X.509 certificate is normally stored in the `KeyStore`. The application surrounding the JSSE protocol normally has to retrieve the certificate from the `KeyStore`. In order to retrieve the certificate, the applications must use the alias, which consists of a name-associated certificate and the password to retrieve the certificate. The issuer's information and keys are defined in the X.509 certificate, and the origin of the certificate can be traced through a certificate path. The information in the X.509 is used for authentication. The JSSE protocol can also be set to use a username and password. The JSSE will use Java sockets as the transfer mechanism to exchange keys and perform authentication from the server to the client. When authentication is from the client to the server, it is called *one-way authentication*. The JSSE authentication may also require *mutual authentication*, where the authentication is also from the client to the server.

The Java GSS-API uses the `org.ietf.jgss.GSSName` and `org.ietf.jgss.GSSCredential` to define the principal name and credentials to be authenticated. A Kerberos server must be set up on the organization's domain to do the authentication. The Java GSS-API transport mechanisms are Java streams or byte arrays. Since Java streams are used, the streams can be written to Java sockets for network interaction. The implementation to Java sockets is not part of the GSS-API mechanism.

> **NOTE**: There are basically three choices that are out of the box for authentication: JAAS, JSSE, and Java GSS-API. The decision on which one to use is dependent on whether confidentiality and integrity also have to be used. The decision also depends on which choice of transportation is desired and the infrastructure of the organization systems.

Components that provide authorization

The only authorization that JSSE and Java GSS-API provides is the capability to keep anyone from reading the plaintext messages except for those individuals who possess the public or secret key. The confidentiality of JSSE and the GSS-API prevents other users from reading the original messages. JAAS and Java applications can enforce the access to system resources with the `SecurityManager`.

CROSS-REFERENCE: See Chapter 18 for more on the Security Manager.

Implementing principal and permission elements with Java components

The principal was discussed in the authentication section. The permission set is a number of permissions that are defined with a system resource. For example, the `FilePermission` may be defined in a policy file with read permissions on a `temp.txt` file. The `FilePermission` will always have a principal associated with it to define which principals can have the permission to the system resource. If one is not defined with the permission set in the policy file, it simply means that all principals have the permissions.

The resource permissions are implementations of the `java.security.Permission` interface. The permissions are collected in a collection data type in the `java.security.PermissionCollection` class.

Validating principal and permission elements with Java components

The `SecurityManager` uses the policy file that is defined in its system properties. The `SecurityManager` will look up the principal that is currently defined in its thread context in the policy file and get the permission set. When an operation is performed on a system resource, the operation will check with the `SecurityManager` to see if the operation is allowed on the resource. In the `FilePermission` example, if a `SecurityManager` is defined and the application is reading the `temp.txt` file, the read operation will check with the `SecurityManager` to see if it is allowed.

If no `SecurityManager` is defined, then all system resources can be accessed. The principals and permissions are managed in the form of policy files or ACLs used by databases or LDAP servers. The policy file that contains the principal and permission set must be trusted and secure to prevent attackers from modifying the policy file to give everyone access to the system resources. ACLs are normally stored in the database or LDAP to protect the access to the principals and permissions.

The JAAS component uses the `SecurityManager` in the manner just described, except the principals it will use are the principals returned in the subject. When a JAAS application successfully completes authentication, the login module returns a subject with the principals and credentials that are used for further authentication and authorization.

See Figure 3-8 for the `SecurityManager`.

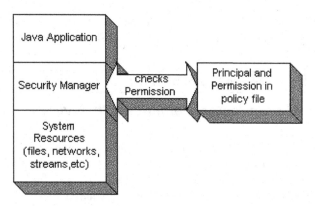

Figure 3-8: Security Manager

Components that provide confidentiality

Confidentiality is the act of encrypting data or a message with a key (which keeps attackers from understanding the message) and providing selected users with a key to unlock to understand the message. When selected users unlock the message to understand it, it is called *decrypting the message*. The JSSE and GSS-API components provide encryption. There are also Java APIs to encrypt a messages and data directly. In order to use a key, a key must be created, managed, and stored. The key to unlock the message must be given only to the selected users to decrypt the message. If others access the key, then they also can read the message.

Implementing key elements with Java components

The first step in using a key is to create it. A key can be created using the `keytool` utility that is shipped with the JDK, which will store the key in a keystore (database). Other Java APIs that support generating keys are the `java.security.KeyPairGenerator` for generating a key pair and the `javax.crypto.KeyGenerator` for generating a secret key.

> **TIP:** The `keytool` utility can create, store, and manage X.509 certificates in a keystore file.

After the key is created, it needs to be stored for later use. Keys can be stored in several ways. Some organizations may manage keys in their databases or LDAP server. One way to organize X.509 keys is to use the keystore. The keystore is a repository for X.509 certificates that is supported by the utility `keytool`, which is distributed with JDK. Java APIs also supports the keystore. The `javax.net.ssl.KeyManager` and `javax.net.ssl.TrustManager` are used to retrieve X.509 certificates from the keystore for use by JSSE. The `TrustManager` will retrieve X.509 certificates that are mark trusted from the keystore. When a certificate is mark trusted, it means that the organization knows to trust the certificate issuer.

> **CROSS-REFERENCE:** See Chapters 6, 7, and 8 for more on keys.

Using key elements with Java components

The purpose of the key elements is to encrypt and decrypt data or messages. When a message is encrypted, it is called *ciphertext*. When a message is decrypted, it is called *plaintext*. The cipher algorithms to encrypt and decrypt are created with the `javax.crypto.Cipher` class. Other Java components that are used to encrypt and decrypt messages, byte arrays, and streams are JSSE and the Java GSS-API. The JSSE will encrypt and decrypt messages going across Java sockets. Java GSS-API will encrypt and decrypt messages across Java streams and byte arrays.

When using a key pair combination, a private key is used to encrypt the message and only the associated public key can decrypt the message. Because only that particular public key can decrypt the message, some may say that establishes a form of authentication; however, this is not so. The authentication of the person refers to verification that he is who he says he is. The credential, in this case, is the public key.

> **NOTE**: *Public key authentication* is a type of authentication and can be accomplished by the use of a pubic key; however, it does not imply that the user principal is authenticated. The principal is part of a number of principals that have access to the public key and cannot be uniquely identifed.

When decrypting the message, the public key is being used. This does not imply that the user principal has been authenticated. Also, the public key may be distributed to many users instead of a specific user, so the validation of the user's identity really identifies the user as being a member of the group that receives the public key.

Even though the `keytool` is the utility for storing the key pairs, it is called a *keystore* because the resulting file is used to store keys. The keystore is used only in the key pair storage. Since the Java API does provide interfaces in the form of the `KeyStore` class, a Java application can be written to store secret keys. The `keytool` utility was never designed to store secret keys. Other key distribution mechanisms will have to be used in order to distribute and manage secret keys. In olden days, it was easy, but time consuming, to pass secret keys through the sneaker net. Sneaker net refers to when a developer has a floppy and walks to all the computers and installs the files. In this case, the file contained the secret keys to use. Secret keys and the keystore files can still be passed in this manner to keep hackers from reading the transfer of the key files.

Since secret keys do not normally use the keystore, secret keys require a different kind of access security than the key pair. Since the secret key cannot be managed in a keystore, other key agreement algorithms need to be supported. Java supports several key agreement algorithms to distribute a secret key through the `javax.crypto.KeyAgreement` class.

Key agreement

Key agreement is the ability for different parties to agree upon a key to use without transmitting the key over a network for fear of eavesdroppers getting a copy of the key. Most of the time, the parties simply calculate the same key. The keys are changed at periodic intervals to keep eavesdroppers guessing. Sometimes the periodic interval is every session of communication of messages. When the key changes every session, it is termed a *session key*. The most famous of the key agreement protocols is the *Diffie-Hellman* (DH) algorithm.

> **CROSS-REFERENCE:** See Chapter 4 for more information on key exchanges and key agreement.

The public key from the key pair is distributed in the form of an X.509 certificate. There are many associated protocols and third-party organizations that are used for the distribution of the X.509 certificate to update, distribute, revoke, and manage certificates. *Public Key Infrastructure* (PKI) is a means to provide the management and distribution of public keys.

> **CROSS-REFERENCE:** See Chapter 25 for more on PKI.

The JSSE and Java GSS-API can be set to automatically encrypt and decrypt messages during transportation and message passing.

Components that provide integrity

It has been mentioned that message and data integrity is accomplished through a hash or message digest. The term *message digest* is sometimes used because it is a digest, or unique block, representing the original message. When the message is ever so slightly different, so is the message digest. The JSSE and GSS-API support message integrity. Other Java APIs also directly support message integrity, however some work must be done to define what to do if the message does not check to be valid.

> **CROSS-REFERENCE:** See Chapter 9 for more on message digests.

The three forms of the message digest

There are three forms of the message digest, or one-way hash: *message digest*, *message authentication code* (MAC), and the *digital signature*. The differences between the message digests are their levels of security.

> **NOTE**: The different level of security for the message digest is established by their use of a key. The lowest security does not use a key, the middle level uses a secret key, and the highest uses a key pair.

The `java.security.MessageDigest` class in the JDK 1.4 supports the generic message digest. The `MessageDigest` creates a digest using a specific algorithm to create the hash. The algorithm to create the hash could be a MD5 or SHA-1. These algorithms are described in detail in a later chapter. The algorithms are actually implemented at the SPI layer of the Java API, like most other security algorithms, so that they may be updated or so that algorithms may be added without changing the Java API. The algorithms create a unique hash when a different message or data is passed in.

> **CROSS-REFERENCE**: Chapter 9 describes the message digest MD5 and SHA-1 in more detail.

Hash vs. message digest

Sometimes I may use the term hash instead of message digest because the hash can be produced from a file, data from a database, and from more types of data than a message. The `MessageDigest` supports data in the form of a byte array. The result of the hash is also a byte array. The `MessageDigest` class does not define the storage and management of the hashed byte array. Again, the storage and management in most organizations are in the forms of databases, LDAP, and files.

The LDAP server formats its database structure in the form of the X.500 protocol. The X.500 protocol defines groups and users and their information in the form of a tree structure. The tree structure of X.500 is how the X.509 certificates are named and stored. If the organization is using a database or file structure, the interface for X.500 support will have to be written and supported from the organization to extend any matching use of X.509. The file structure will need further security for authentication and authorization to protect the files from attackers. The database will have to be structured to support tree queries and X.500 support. LDAP provides a lot of functionality out of the box for security support by using the X.500 protocol.

> **TIP:** LDAP provides X.500 functionality and directory structures out of the box. The X.500 functionality can be used for management of X.509 certificates.

The first hash that the `MessageDigest` class will produce needs to be saved to a trusted store as the trusted hash. When the message is in question, the message is passed through a `MessageDigest` class again to produce a new hash. The trusted hash byte array and the new hash array are compared byte by byte. If the bytes are equal, then the message has not changed.

A *message authentication code* (MAC) is basically a keyed message digest. Like a message digest, a MAC takes an arbitrary amount of input data and creates a short digest value. Unlike a message digest, a MAC uses a secret key to encrypt the digest. Only those individuals who possess the secret key can check the message digest. The purpose of encrypting the message digest is to keep attackers from seeing the true message digest. If it happens that two unlike messages can produce the same message digest, an attacker can change the message data. The message digest will say that message is the same as long as the resulting digests are equal. The MAC is also used to encrypt the digest so that it may be stored in a secure form. The purpose of the MAC is simply to encrypt and decrypt the digest to secure it. The MAC is useful for protecting the integrity of data that is sent over an insecure network. The JDK 1.4 supports the MAC with the `javax.crypto.Mac` class.

To guarantee that the message can only come from a specific user, the user signs the message by using a private key. There is a one-to-one correspondence between the user and message because the private key can only originate from that specific user. This concept is referred to as a *digital signature*. The *digital signature* offers a higher level of security. When using a key pair, there is a private and public key that is created by a user. The user only distributes the public keys for selected users to decrypt the messages that they encrypt. The private key is used for encryption and cannot be duplicated. If the public key from that user decrypts the message, it can only have been encrypted with that specific private key. If only one user owns the private key, the people who decrypt the message know that the message derived from that particular user. The message could have been modified in transportation; but with the use of a message digest, it can be determined if the message has been altered. In addition, the private key encrypts the message digest and only the originator of the message has the private key. Therefore, the message is valid.

> **CROSS-REFERENCE**: Chapter 11 and Chapter 22 provide a discussion on digital signatures. For example, if I receive a message that has been digitally signed, which is a message digest encrypted in the message by the user's private key, I can say specifically that the particular user created the message. Since the digest the user encrypted can only be created by a very specific message, and if the message that he encrypted validates the message as coming from the user, there is both the message validation and the public key to prove that the message originated from that user.

Legal ramifications

In fact, some organizations will use the digital signature as a means to prove that a particular individual signs information. The digital signature has even been recognized by some law organizations as a means to verify that a specific individual, through a digital medium, has said something specific. If a contract has been negotiated through the Internet, the digital signature is a form of proof that it came from a specific individual because of his encrypting the digest that validates the message and his encryption with the private key. The digital signature is supported in Java from the `java.security.Signature` class.

> **CAUTION:** I am not a lawyer and cannot say that a digital signature will hold up in court. Please see a lawyer before holding somebody accountable through a digital signature.

Figure 3-9 demonstrates the different security levels of the hashed digest. The message digest is not encrypted, the MAC is secured through a secret key, and the digital signature is secured through a key pair.

Message Digest	Hash
MAC	Hash/Secret Key
Digital Signature	Hash/Key Pair

Figure 3-9: The message digest security level

How Do the Components Fit Together?

As previously mentioned, several Java components support the different security elements and security components. Several Java components require very little effort to write into a Java application, such as JAAS, JSSE, and Java GSS-API. Other Java components are handled individually and require more work and requirements to use in a Java application such as the

`MessageDigest` class. Several decisions have to be made when using the `MessageDigest` class. Some of the decisions include:

- The algorithm used to compare the digest with a trusted digest — for instance MD5 or SHA-1.
- The storage and the location of the trusted digest.
- The type of encryption algorithms — if any — to be used.

The organization should have a set of requirements specifically for handling decisions to ensure that the `MessageDigest` class is being used correctly and, if a message fails validation, that the organization has a method for not using the message. If a message fails validation, an attack could be in progress. If an attack is in progress, the organization should monitor the attack, usually in the form of an audit trail. The organization should have a plan of attack when an attack occurs and be prepared to dedicate tools, time, and resources to the attack to protect the organization.

There are many organizations that might not consider an attack important, but later find that their Web sites are down and that confidential information has been made public. An attack through an organization's systems should be seen as just that: an attack that could be an enemy trying to bring down the organization. The attacker <u>should</u> be seen as the enemy of the organization. There have been many instances where hackers have been prosecuted and the only evidence was an organization's audit files that logged the attack. If the organization fails to provide information such as this, then my question would be: How does the organization plan to stop an attacker?

Another security concept, besides auditing, that needs to be introduced is the concept of *isolation*. In several organizations that I have known, the only way to prevent hackers was to isolate their networks from the Internet or through firewalls. Java sockets and support in networks are still evolving.

Many applications exist in hardware and software packages and languages to support network security and firewalls. What Java does provide is authorization through the `java.net.SocketPermission` class to deny users rights to sockets through a Java application.

CROSS-REFERENCE: See Chapter 21 for more information on network security.

Figure 3-10 provides an overview of some of the Java components discussed in this chapter. This is merely a starting point in the discussion of Java components and many more will be discussed throughout the book. Organizations and individuals alike could greatly evolve and enhance the Java components because they are written to add protocols and algorithms in the SPI layer without changing the Java API.

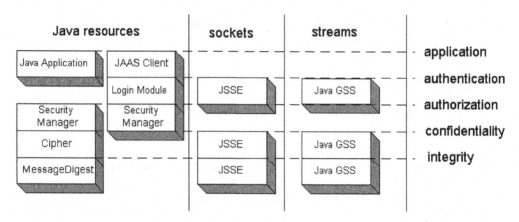

Figure 3-10: An overview of the Java components

Summary

This chapter introduced the purpose of several of the Java components. It cannot be overemphasized that this chapter is just a starting point. Organizations and individuals can add protocols and algorithms to the Java SPI layer without changing the Java API and evolve the security for their organization.

The security operations and elements discussed are given as a minimum to understand how to secure one's systems. If the creation, management, and trusted storage of the security elements are not considered, the security is compromised. For instance, you may have an application that depends on a trusted digest and you may be keeping the trusted digest in a non-secure location; thus, a hacker can change the digest used to check data. Equal amounts of consideration and requirements need to be applied to the security elements as are applied to the security operation.

There is never a point when an organization is considered too secure, unless the organization is never accessed by anyone. When an attacker attacks, the organization needs a plan to apply resources, time, and tools to isolate an attacker and protect its systems. Time, money, and materials can be applied ahead of time to try to prevent attacks. I will offer one quote that fully describes security: "If you think security is expensive, try the cost of recovering from an attack."

Part II

Identity and Authentication

Chapter 4: Key Management Algorithms

Chapter 5: Elliptic Curve Cryptography

Chapter 6: Key Management Through the Internet Protocol

Chapter 7: Implementing Keys with Java

Chapter 8: Java Implementation of Key Management

Chapter 4
Key Management Algorithms

In This Chapter

- ♦ Learning the need for key agreement
- ♦ Introducing mathematics for key exchanging
- ♦ Understanding the different key exchanges
- ♦ Understanding some of the issues involved with key exchanges

Introduction

In the previous chapter, a key scenario was mentioned. Two users have a copy of the same floppy. On the floppy is a file with secret keys that are assigned a number. For each session of secret communications, the two individuals agree on which key to use. So, there is an agreement of keys with information that someone sniffing the network cannot understand, unless I/O (input/output) sniffers have access to the file on the floppy.

However, there are many limitations with this method. If the file on the floppy were compromised, the individuals would need a new file to communicate. The two people could have a collection of floppies and hope that only one gets compromised so that they can continue to communicate. At some point, they might also run out of keys, in which case they would need a new set of files. Figure 4-1 demonstrates a basic key exchange for secret keys. Key exchanges are also needed for public keys so that messages can be decrypted. The purpose of the secret key and public key exchange is that users may decrypt messages that are encrypted by one of the owners of the secret key or the owner of a private key.

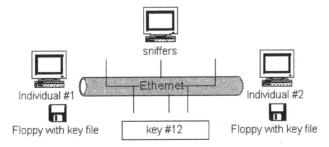

Figure 4-1: Secret key exchange by number

There are import control restrictions, and the JSDK has two versions, limited and unlimited, depending which restrictions apply to your application. Here is the description from SUN:

"Due to import control restrictions of some countries, the JCE jurisdiction policy files shipped with the Java 2 SDK, v 1.4 allow "strong" but limited cryptography to be used. An "unlimited strength" version of these files indicating no restrictions on cryptographic strengths is available for those living in eligible countries (which is most countries). You can download this version and replace the strong cryptography versions supplied with the Java 2 SDK, v 1.4 with the unlimited ones."

Understanding the Purpose of Keys

The purpose of a key is to ensure that an encrypted message cannot be decrypted except by a selected group of users who have access to the secret and public keys. If keys are not used, any user who has access to the algorithm can decrypt the message. Figure 4-2 shows that only the cipher algorithm is needed.

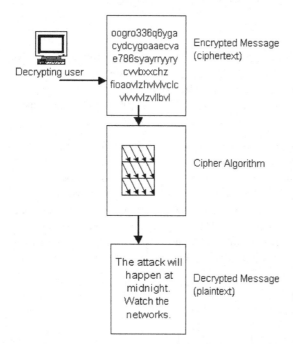

Figure 4-2: Cipher without the key

The key gives access to a specific user to decrypt the message. The key denies users who do not possess the key and the ability to decrypt the message. See Figure 4-3 for a demonstration.

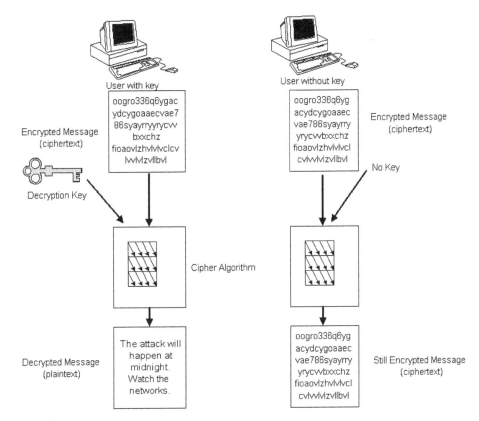

Figure 4-3: The key for decryption

Hackers have been known to break an encryption without a key, by trying a myriad of keys. The keys that are tried depend on the size of the key. For example, if the key is 129 bits long, the key can have 2 ^ 129 possibilities, which is a very large number. Even though there are 2 ^ 129 possibilities, not all have to be tried before finding the bit stream that matches the key. If the key is all zeros, and the cracker starts at zero, the key will be found during the first iteration. For this reason, a randomness is applied to the key to ensure that the key has an equal chance of appearing anywhere within the possibilities.

I have mentioned that the secret key is used for both encryption and decryption. The *key pair* consisting of a public key and private key uses the public key for decryption and the private key for encryption. When the key pair is generated, an association between the public key and private key is generated, so that only that specific public key will decrypt messages with that specific private key. The public key is distributed to users for decrypting the message. The private key is not for distribution but kept by the owner of the key to encrypt the messages. Figure 4-4 demonstrates the secret key, and Figure 4-5 demonstrates the key pair.

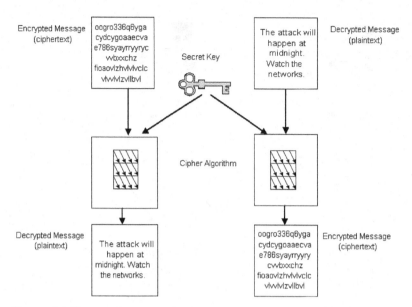

Figure 4-4: The secret key

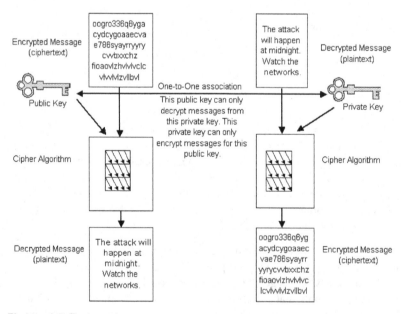

Figure 4-5: The key pair

The *key agreement* is how the key is exchanged or distributed to a user so that he or she may decrypt the message or data. The key used for encryption, in most cases, should not be distributed unless there are no other choices. Sometimes the keys may also be used for digital signatures, but that is discussed in a later chapter. The secret key produces only one key for the encryption and decryption; a generic, not Java code, method may look like Listing 4-1 to generate the ciphertext (the encrypted data) and the plaintext (the decrypted data).

CROSS-REFERENCE: Chapter 11 and Chapter 22 discuss digital signatures.

Listing 4-1: SecretKey cipher pseudocode

```
CipherText = Encrypt_secretKey(PlainText);
PlainText = Decrypt_secretKey(CipherText);
```

Listing 4-1 gives a pseudocode example of a secret key cipher. Pseudocode is a code-like example to describe functionality but is not specific to a programming language. The listing shows that the same secret key is used for both encrypting and decrypting the message. To understand the difference with the key pair, see Listing 4-2.

Listing 4-2: The key pair cipher pseudocode

```
CipherText = Encrypt_PrivateKey(PlainText);
PlainText = Decrypt_PublicKey(CipherText);
```

Listing 4-2 demonstrates the pseudocode for a key pair. The pseudocode demonstrates that the private key is used for encryption and the public key is used for decryption, but this is not always the case. Some algorithms, such as RSA (which is discussed later in this chapter), use the private key to decrypt and the public key to encrypt The difference between which key is required for the encryption and decryption is algorithmic specific. The definition of the *key pair* is that there is a matching pair of keys, one public and one private. Here the term "matching" means that there is an association between the private key and public key. The public key will only work for the matching private key and vice versa. The only way that the association can be made between the public and private key is a mathematical association. Most cryptographers who work with the keying mechanisms and ciphers are mathematicians.

TIP: Instead of the private key being released to the public, it is the result of the key — the ciphertext — that is released to the public.

Understanding the Mathematics

The key pair relationship in most algorithms is accomplished by the use of a *logarithm*.

NOTE: Recall that logarithms have the mathematical capability to have inverse functions, and also provide the result of the equation by using exponentials.

Logarithms

A *logarithm* function is simply a curve that has an inverse of an exponential function. Figure 4-6 demonstrates two logarithms $x = \log_2 y$ and $y = \log_2 x$, or the same functions in exponential form as $y = 2^x$ and $x = 2^y$, respectively.

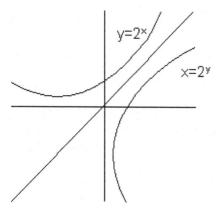

Figure 4-6: The logarithmic function

The formulas in Figure 4-6 cover all points along each curve. In most cases, when finding a key a positive integer is found. Ensuring that the logarithmic function results in an integer limits the logarithmic functions and numbers that can be used. The limitation to a specific result defines the logarithmic functions to be *discrete*.

> **TIP:** Keys are always integers, and in most cases positive. Some algorithms, such as Elliptic Curve, do use negative integers. With logarithmic algorithms, however, keys are positive integers.

Just using the formula and mapping all of the points, as in either formula in Figure 4-6, produces an infinite number of results. A discrete logarithm requires one point as the result. To help force the discrete logarithm into a non-negative integer result, modular exponentials are used. A modular exponential is used to compute the remainder of a value. Using a modulus that is positive from a positive number will usually produce these results. See Listing 4-3 for an example and the tip that follows for a simple explanation of modular math.

> **NOTE:** Recall that integers do not have a dot, such as 34454 rather than 34454.57567. There are many good mathematics books that address integers, natural numbers, logarithms, discrete logarithms, and modular exponentiation. A discussion of these concepts is beyond the scope of this book.

Listing 4-3: Modular exponential

```
An example:
5^9 mod 563 = 1953125 mod 563 = 78
1953125 / 563 roughly equals 3469, not an integer
```

```
563 X 3469 = 1953047, which is an integer
1953125 - 1953047 = 78, which is an integer
```

> **TIP:** Here are a few modular math concepts to refresh your memory:
>
> 1. Modular math uses division and only uses the whole number remainder (never fractions or negative numbers).
>
> 2. The modulus is the remainder.
>
> 3. Modular inverse pairs are two numbers that multiplied together equal one.
>
> 4. Use Fermat and Euler for exponentiation properties. Recall that:
>
>   Fermant showed $m^{(p-1)}$mod p = 1, when the modulus is prime.
>
>   Euler showed that $m^{(p-1)(q-1)}$mod n = 1, when m and n are relative prime numbers.

Most key algorithms start with at least two numbers that are used to calculate the key. The purpose of the key algorithms is to provide numbers without providing the key. Listing 4-3 shows a formula in which three numbers, 5, 9, and 563, can be used to calculate the key 78. If only two of the numbers are transmitted across the network, and the third number is agreed upon secretly, then anyone watching the network has no way to compute the key 78.

> **TIP:** Keys are usually prime numbers and some algorithms only work with prime numbers. Recall that a prime number is only divisible by one (1) and itself.

Listing 4-4 demonstrates performing the modular exponential calculation in Java using the `java.math.BigInteger` class and the `modPow` method. The sample code selects prime numbers at random. Many keying algorithms will use both prime numbers and random numbers. An output of the sample is shown in Listing 4-5.

Listing 4-4: The `TestRandomMod` class: A sample code for performing the modular exponential

```java
package com.richware.chap04;
import java.util.*;
import java.math.*;
import java.security.*;

/**
 * Class TestRandomMod
 * Description: This is an example of
 * a random modular exponent
 *
 * Copyright:    Copyright (c) 2002 Wiley Publishing, Inc.
 * @author Rich Helton <rhelton@richware.com>
 * @version 1.0
 * DISCLAIMER: Please refer to the disclaimer at the beginning of this
book.
 */
```

```
public class TestRandomMod
{
  /**
   * Method main
   * Description: Main Driver
   * @param args none
   *
   */
  public static void main(String[] args)
  {
    try
    {
      /*
       * bitLength - bitLength of the returned BigInteger.
       * certainty - a measure of the uncertainty
       * that the caller is willing to tolerate.
       * The probability that the new BigInteger
       * represents a prime number will exceed (1 - 1/2certainty).
       * The execution time of this constructor is proportional
       * to the value of this parameter.
       * rnd - source of random bits used to
       * select candidates to be tested for primality.
       */
      int           bitLength = 512;  // 512 bits
      SecureRandom rnd        = new SecureRandom();
      int           certainty = 90;   // 1 - 1/2(90) certainty
      System.out.println("BitLength : " + bitLength);
      System.out
        .println("Selecting Prime Numbers..............");
      BigInteger mod = new BigInteger(bitLength, certainty,
                                        rnd);

      /* probablePrime
       * Returns a positive BigInteger
       * that is probably prime, with the
       * specified bitLength.
       * The probability that a BigInteger
       * returned by this method
       * is composite does not exceed 2-100.
       * Parameters:
       * bitLength - bitLength of the returned BigInteger.
       * rnd - source of random bits
       * used to select candidates to be
       * tested for primality.
       */
      BigInteger exponent = BigInteger.probablePrime(bitLength,
                            rnd);
      BigInteger n        = BigInteger.probablePrime(bitLength,
                            rnd);
```

```
        /* modPow
         * Returns a BigInteger whose
         * value is (thisexponent mod m).
         *(Unlike pow, this method permits negative exponents.)
         */
        BigInteger result = n.modPow(exponent, mod);
        System.out
          .println("Number ^ Exponent MOD Modulus = Result");
        System.out.println("Number*****************");
        System.out.println(n);
        System.out.println("Exponent***************");
        System.out.println(exponent);
        System.out.println("Modulus****************");
        System.out.println(mod);
        System.out.println("Result*****************");
        System.out.println(result);
      }
    catch (Exception ex)
      {
        ex.printStackTrace();
      }
    }
  }
}
```

Listing 4-5: Output of Listing 4-4

```
>java com.richware.chap04.TestRandomMod
BitLength : 512
Selecting Prime Numbers.............
Number ^ Exponent MOD Modulus = Result
Number*****************
1243606098767677687463480608165050969754569073800525422867103841106424 64
64229619
8141006499400390197972035507090794157084901064559320878305629175822344 46
223
Exponent***************
1179652140134006069042118782173842502813356442131123786269582183530066 81
79928419
8977438309533988445321123675534659500562152479235949113810252652739818 21
493
Modulus****************
1154898777972164235453915030518332386926832045920380447801716209137147 73
58398072
6161961142325320832150561590390672855412212295082447823201385552513954 47
511
Result*****************
```

8467635180426724867734715736810727954009834828601448510768959033697807 11
74521773
3235442352217678748531194590056933473074847497290992116103616761710188 07
52

Listing 4-5 displays the results of choosing prime random numbers that are 512 bits long to perform the calculation.

Prime and random numbers

Many keys will use prime and random numbers for their agreements. A prime number is a natural number that has no integer factors except itself and 1. These numbers cannot be broken down into further multiplications. Listing 4-4 demonstrates getting prime numbers using the `java.math.BigInteger` class. The demonstration sets the certainty to 90, thus using $1/2^{90}$, or 8.0779356694631608874161005084957e-28 probability that the number might not be prime. The higher the certainty number, the longer the method takes to calculate the prime number. Prime numbers play a significant role because some of the algorithms to calculate the key will only work with a prime number.

Random numbers are used so that the same numbers or a pattern is not used to generate a key. For instance, if a user always used 9 and 10 as the primary numbers to generate the keys, the keys would most likely be same value. To avoid any type of pattern, a random number is used. The random number is required to be a certain bit size so that it is not too large or too small to be applied to the algorithm. Listing 4-4 displays the use of the `java.security.SecureRandom` class. This is discussed in more detail later in the book.

CROSS-REFERENCE: Chapter 7 describes random numbers and `SecureRandom`.

Symmetric versus Asymmetric Keys

There are two types of keys: asymmetric keys and symmetric keys. An *asymmetric* key is a key pair consisting of a public and private key. The public key is generated from the private key and, therefore, there is a one-to-one association between these keys. The generated public key only decrypts the ciphertext generated from the private key. A sy*mmetric* key is a secret key used for both encryption and decryption. In most cases it is a randomly generated prime number.

The Diffie-Hellman Key Exchange

The *Diffie-Hellman* (DH) key exchange was the first key exchange and the first to mention a public key. The key was first documented in 1979. The purpose of DH is key exchange; it does not define cipher suites.

Whitfield Diffie and Martin Hellman, from Stanford University, first published the public key algorithm in 1976. The DH algorithm enables two parties to compute a shared secret. The algorithm doesn't require encryption for low overhead. The fundamental concept underlying the DH algorithm is the mathematical difficulty of calculating discrete logarithms in a finite field.

Understanding the Diffie-Hellman key exchange

The key agreement for DH follows this procedure for User A and User B:

- First, an agreement between User A and User B is made on two large prime numbers, p and g.
- Next, User A generates a random number, Xa, and User B generates a random number, Xb; each must be less than $p - 2$.
- User A then calculates Ya and sends the results to User B.

  $Ya = g^{Xa} \bmod p$
- User B then calculates Yb and sends the results to User A.

  $Yb = g^{Xb} \bmod p$
- User A computes $K = Ya^{Xa} \bmod p = g^{XaXb} \bmod p$.
- User B computes $K = Yb^{Xb} \bmod p = g^{XaXb} \bmod p$.

The only calculations that are actually seen across the network are Ya and Yb. From Ya and Yb alone, the key cannot be determined. The user needs the p and g to perform the calculations. The p and g are normally agreed upon through a secure means, but without the user ever seeing Xa or Xb, the key cannot be derived. Listing 4-6 gives a small demonstration of these calculations.

Listing 4-6: Diffie-Hellman example

```
An example:
Step 1:
p = 47
g = 71

Step 2:
Xa = 9
Xb = 14

Step 3:
Ya = (71) ^ 9 mod 47 = 28
71⁹ mod 47 = 45848500718449031 mod 47 = 28
45848500718449031 / 47 roughly equals 975500015286149
975500015286149 * 47 = 45848500718449003
```

```
45848500718449031 - 45848500718449003 = 28
Send Ya.

Step 4:
Yb = (71) ^ 14 mod 47 = 42
71^14 mod 47 = 8272121069557032892770881 mod 47 = 42
8272121069557032892770881 / 47 roughly equals 176002575948021976441937
176002575948021976441937 * 47 = 8272121069557032892770839
8272121069557032892770881 - 8272121069557032892770839 = 42
Send Yb.

Step 5:
K = Ya^Xa mod p
28^9 mod 47 = 10578455953408 mod 47 = 27
10578455953408 / 47 roughly equals 225073530923
225073530923 * 47 = 10578455953381
10578455953408 - 10578455953381 = 27
Users A, Key = 27

Step 5:
K = Yb^Xb mod p
42^14 mod 47 = 53148384174432398229504 mod 47 = 27
53148384174432398229504 / 47 roughly equals 1130816684562391451691
1130816684562391451691 * 47 = 53148384174432398229477
53148384174432398229504 - 53148384174432398229477 = 27
Users B, Key = 27
```

Listing 4-6 shows that User A and User B derived the same secret key with only disclosing to each other a piece of their information.

Implementing the Diffie-Hellman key exchange

Listing 4-7 demonstrates the same calculation in Java. The example also demonstrates two more DH key generations with larger primes, one where the algorithm will choose p and g, and another where p and g are chosen and passed into the algorithm. See if the output in Listing 4-8 gives the same number for the first part, and observe the keys that DH will normally generate.

NOTE: This application uses the Java JDK 1.4. For more information go to the SUN JDK1.4 site at `http://java.sun.com/j2se/1.4/index.html`.

Listing 4-7: The `DHSimpleApp` class: A sample application generating keys

```
package com.richware.chap04;
import java.util.*;
import java.math.*;
import java.security.*;
import javax.crypto.spec.*;
```

```java
/**
 * Class DHSimpleApp
 * Description: This is an example of a
 * simple Diffie-Hellman
 *
 * Copyright:    Copyright (c) 2002 Wiley Publishing, Inc.
 * @author Rich Helton <rhelton@richware.com>
 * @version 1.0
 * DISCLAIMER: Please refer to the disclaimer at the beginning of this
book.
 */
public class DHSimpleApp
{
  public final static int pValue  = 47;
  public final static int gValue  = 71;
  public final static int XaValue = 9;
  public final static int XbValue = 14;
  /**
   * Method main
   * Description: Main Driver
   * @param args none
   *
   */
  public static void main(String[] args)
  {
    try
    {
      System.out.println();
      System.out.println(
        "DH Proving the algorithm*************************");

      /*
       * Step 1
       * Pick p and q
       */
      BigInteger p = new BigInteger(Integer.toString(pValue));
      BigInteger g = new BigInteger(Integer.toString(gValue));
      System.out.println("p = " + p);
      System.out.println("g = " + g);

      /*
       * Step 2
       * Select the random numbers
       */
      BigInteger Xa =
        new BigInteger(Integer.toString(XaValue));
      BigInteger Xb =
        new BigInteger(Integer.toString(XbValue));
      System.out.println("Xa = " + Xa);
```

```java
System.out.println("Xb = " + Xb);

/*
 * Step 3
 * Calculate Ya
 */
BigInteger Ya = g.modPow(Xa, p);
System.out.println("Ya = " + Ya);

/*
 * Step 4
 * Calculate Yb
 */
BigInteger Yb = g.modPow(Xb, p);
System.out.println("Yb = " + Yb);

/*
 * Step 5
 * User A calculates K
 */
BigInteger Ka = Ya.modPow(Xa, p);
System.out.println("Users A, K = " + Ka);

/*
 * Step 6
 * User B calculates K
 */
BigInteger Kb = Yb.modPow(Xb, p);
System.out.println("Users B, K = " + Kb);
DHSimpleApp app = new DHSimpleApp();
app.createKey();

/*
 * Generate a 512 bit Prime to pass as p and g
 */
int         bitLength = 512;  // 512 bits
SecureRandom rnd      = new SecureRandom();
System.out.println("BitLength : " + bitLength);
System.out
  .println("Selecting Prime Numbers..............");
p = BigInteger.probablePrime(bitLength, rnd);
g = BigInteger.probablePrime(bitLength, rnd);
System.out.println("P *********************");
System.out.println(p);
System.out.println("G *********************");
System.out.println(g);
app.createSpecificKey(p, g);
}
```

```
  /*
   * Catches
   */
  catch (Exception ex)
   {
    ex.printStackTrace();
   }
 }


 /**
  * Method createKey
  * Description: This is an example of
  * letting the algorithm choose
  * the values
  *
  */
 public void createKey()
  {
   try
    {
     System.out.println();
     System.out.println(
       "Diffie-Hellman letting the algorithm
choose******************");
     KeyPairGenerator kpg =
       KeyPairGenerator.getInstance("DiffieHellman");
     /*
      * A strong key uses 512 to 2048 bits
      * the bits must be multiples of 64
      */
     System.out.println("Provider =" + kpg.getProvider());
     kpg.initialize(512);
     KeyPair kp = kpg.generateKeyPair();
     /*
      * Read the keys
      * produced by the algorithm
      */
     System.out.println("Public Key ="
                       + kp.getPublic().getEncoded());
     System.out.println("Public Key Algorithm ="
                       + kp.getPublic().getAlgorithm());
     System.out.println("Public Key Format ="
                       + kp.getPublic().getFormat());
     System.out.println("Private Key ="
                       + kp.getPrivate().getEncoded());
     System.out.println("Private Key Algorithm ="
                       + kp.getPrivate().getAlgorithm());
     System.out.println("Private Key Format ="
                       + kp.getPrivate().getFormat());
```

```
    /*
     * Initialize the KeyFactory for DSA
     */
    KeyFactory kfactory =
      KeyFactory.getInstance("DiffieHellman");
    /*
     * Create the DH public key spec
     */
    DHPublicKeySpec kspec =
      (DHPublicKeySpec) kfactory
        .getKeySpec(kp.getPublic(), DHPublicKeySpec.class);
    /*
     * Print out public key values
     */
    System.out
      .println("Public Key Y **********************");
    System.out.println(kspec.getY());
    System.out
      .println("Public Key G **********************");
    System.out.println(kspec.getG());
    System.out
      .println("Public Key P **********************");
    System.out.println(kspec.getP());
  }
  /*
   * Catches
   */
  catch (java.security.NoSuchAlgorithmException ex)
    {
    ex.printStackTrace();
    }
  catch (Exception ex)
    {
    ex.printStackTrace();
    }
}

/**
 * Method createSpecificKey
 * Description: This is an example of
 * choosing e
 *
 */
public void createSpecificKey(BigInteger p, BigInteger g)
  {
  try
    {
      /*
       * Another provider specific to the signature instead of JSSE
```

```
      */
     System.out.println();
     System.out.println(
      "Diffie-Hellman Choosing the prime, must be at least 512
bits**********************");
     KeyPairGenerator kpg =
       KeyPairGenerator.getInstance("DiffieHellman");
     /* A strong key uses 512 to 2048 bits
      * the bits must be multiples of 64
      */
     System.out.println("Provider =" + kpg.getProvider());
     /*
      * Select the parameters
      */

     /*
      * Step 1
      * Pick p and q
      */
     DHParameterSpec param = new DHParameterSpec(p, g);
     kpg.initialize(param);
     KeyPair kp = kpg.generateKeyPair();
     /* Read the keys
      * produced by the algorithm
      */
     System.out.println("Public Key ="
                        + kp.getPublic().getEncoded());
     System.out.println("Public Key Algorithm ="
                        + kp.getPublic().getAlgorithm());
     System.out.println("Public Key Format ="
                        + kp.getPublic().getFormat());
     System.out.println("Private Key ="
                        + kp.getPrivate().getEncoded());
     System.out.println("Private Key Algorithm ="
                        + kp.getPrivate().getAlgorithm());
     System.out.println("Private Key Format ="
                        + kp.getPrivate().getFormat());
     /*
      * Initialize the KeyFactory for DSA
      */
     KeyFactory kfactory =
       KeyFactory.getInstance("DiffieHellman");
     /*
      * Create the DH public key spec
      */
     DHPublicKeySpec kspec =
       (DHPublicKeySpec) kfactory
         .getKeySpec(kp.getPublic(), DHPublicKeySpec.class);
     /*
```

```
        * Print out public key values
        */
    System.out
        .println("Public Key Y *********************");
    System.out.println(kspec.getY());
    System.out
        .println("Public Key G *********************");
    System.out.println(kspec.getG());
    System.out
        .println("Public Key P *********************");
    System.out.println(kspec.getP());
    }
    /*
     * Catches
     */
    catch (java.security.NoSuchAlgorithmException ex)
    {
      ex.printStackTrace();
    }
    catch (Exception ex)
    {
      ex.printStackTrace();
    }
  }
}
```

Listing 4-8: Listing 4-7 output

```
>java com.richware.chap04.DHSimpleApp
DH Proving the algorithm***************************
p = 47
g = 71
Xa = 9
Xb = 14
Ya = 28
Yb = 42
Users A, K = 27
Users B, K = 27

Diffie-Hellman letting the algorithm choose******************
Provider =SunJCE version 1.4
Public Key =[ B@7f1ba3
Public Key Algorithm =DH
Public Key Format =X.509
Private Key =[ B@ef8cf3
Private Key Algorithm =DH
Private Key Format =PKCS#8
Public Key Y *********************
```

```
21585330394772019139436320463228994785679401142303061584707349533775779673737061
45445273959429546042202620929288896891179157457484097068027153689230338237
Public Key G ***********************
78076742594159530111026742210073076301342044222176706354454368533398332414827022
40467339488425215533817947254553373198287585194733500616613932037121072779
Public Key P ***********************
11575309867515024649696400369831093493361458807573760616381819728787372352257166
904645891644283132883296560173559285063331655024682782209092633911135081389
BitLength : 512
Selecting Prime Numbers.............
P *********************
13030419426017202530031055547663367035273375888381324541437190761516268827501970
0
90099127670272133822527679980605050911269043560986613887496035881903082133
1
G *********************
10733750757590385308950336779149429606228026849083223135655759742518494982619853
8176781661273204318256161293005670493427210656553436743467874177036105083
81

Diffie-Hellman Choosing the prime, must be at least 512
bits*********************
***
Provider =SunJCE version 1.4
Public Key =[ B@8b819f
Public Key Algorithm =DH
Public Key Format =X.509
Private Key =[ B@eb017e
Private Key Algorithm =DH
Private Key Format =PKCS#8
Public Key Y ***********************
12527860659821222967624533874338971012796217323062458058513164947035276457931540
486555545177300397072927115804421228793021332981110882851978543144942240792
Public Key G ***********************
10733750757590385308950336779149429606228026849083223135655759742518494982619853
8176781661273204318256161293005670493427210656553436743467874177036105083
81
Public Key P ***********************
```

130304194260172025300310555476633670352733758838132454143719076151626882
75019700
900991276702721338225276799806050509112690435609866138874960358819030821
331

Listing 4-8 came up with the same calculations demonstrated in Listing 4-6. Listing 4-7 shows the code for that calculation, letting the algorithm choose p and g for you, and randomly choosing p and g for populating the DH algorithm. Passing the simple example of p with 47 and g as 71 would not have worked. The p and g that is passed in the algorithm must be 512 bits. Instead of trying to calculate a 512 prime number, it is much easier to let the `BigInteger` class solve these things. An interesting thing to note is that the DH algorithm is part of an engine class and will have an associated service provider. This is discussed in detail in the next chapter, but there are some interesting points in the code. In the second demonstration in the code, the keys were generated with Listing 4-9.

CROSS-REFERENCE: Chapter 5 discusses the Service Provider Interface in more detail.

Listing 4-9: Generating the DH key: An excerpt from Listing 4-7

```
KeyPairGenerator kpg =
    KeyPairGenerator.getInstance("DiffieHellman");

/*
 * A strong key uses 512 to 2048 bits
 * the bits must be multiples of 64
 */
System.out.println("Provider =" + kpg.getProvider());
kpg.initialize(512);
```

Listing 4-9 demonstrates that there is a choice in the key sizes. A key can be created with 512 bits to 2048 bits as long as the intervals in between are multiples of 64 bits. The engine class will call a service provider that will actually implement the algorithm; in this case, it was `SunJCE version 1.4` from the output produced. The code in the third calculation `DHParameterSpec param = new DHParameterSpec(p, g);` will pass the p and g variables into the algorithm. The p and g must be 512 bits because the algorithm is specified to use 512 bits in the `kpg.initialize(512);` code.

Understanding man-in-the-middle attacks

The DH algorithm was a landmark for calculating keys without passing the key itself, but it does have flaws. The biggest vulnerability that DH faces is the man-in-the-middle attack. The man-in-the-middle attack is possible because there is no authentication that User A or User B is actually User A and User B. A user could be communicating with both User A and User B and impersonating both of them. Call the user in the middle User M. User A could be passing User M his shared values, p, g, and Ya. User M could impersonate User B and return the correct values, while building the shared key for their use. User M could also be doing the same with User B, while impersonating User A. After User M has the correct keys from User A and User B, he could watch the messages from each in the network traffic and continue to impersonate the other user. It might be some time and many messages later that User A and User B discover that they have not actually communicated directly. Figure 4-7 demonstrates this attack.

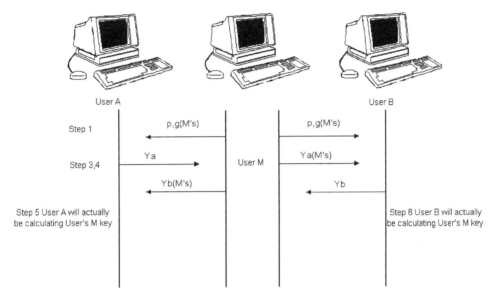

Figure 4-7: The man-in-the-middle attack

The man-in-the-middle attack is an impersonation of both users. The imposter, User M, will pass the correct the responses to each user while generating a secret key that will only work with the corresponding user. Listing 4-10 is an example output of such an attack.

Listing 4-10: An example output of a man-in-the-middle attack

```
>java com.richware.chap04.DHAgreement
M->Starting User....
A->Starting....

A-> Generating Keys....


A->G Value**********************
6867558896255424629130682254557735004760814180065118435942241926485327209
6450315
3024775568202156648810753262381970513924238964048989496299981143255533707
3

A->P Value**********************
```

```
121342879252870070401982768810332898164534958562066239078599729484086872
39636257
518379548669448217314594891252619981309038447645426521735635034139529123
263

A->Public Key**********************
[B@61d36b
B->Starting User....


M->A Public Key....
[B@61d36b
M->A's P....
121342879252870070401982768810332898164534958562066239078599729484086872
39636257
518379548669448217314594891252619981309038447645426521735635034139529123
263

M->A's G....
686755889625542462913068225455773500476081418006511843594224192648532720
96450315
302477556820215664881075326238197051392423896404898949629998114325553370
73
M->Generating a Key from A....

M->Sending fake B Public Key to A*********************
[B@69ca65

M->New p to B *********************
120907985973118437266700976647440042790231204195713579268540589413375372
40383708
944490845702553153976642382872825280210946033210850498023765243639783740
693

M->New g to B *********************
799275362637083479445764592093914331611444993546573758327869395318432202
21538632
646176500612903060198042258926433239611460988144417564622645106054964686
89

M->Generated a key to B....

M->Sending fake A Public Key to B*********************
[B@a37368
A->Got Public Key from B?.......
[B@69ca65


B->User A's Public?*********************
```

```
[ B@a37368
B->User A's G Value?**********************
7992753626370834794457645920939143316114449935465737583278693953184322022
21538632
6461765006129030601980422589264332396114609881444175646226451060549646868
9

B->User A's P Value?**********************
1209079859731184372667009766474400427902312041957135792685405894133753722
40383708
9444908457025531539766423828728252802109460332108504980237652436397837407
693

B->Public Key**********************
[ B@8916a2

M->B's Public Key....
[ B@8916a2

M->Got Cipher from A->How are you B?

M->Sending different Cipher to B->Are you sure that I am A?
B->Got Cipher->Are you sure that I am A?
```

Listing 4-10 demonstrates User M receiving the correct *p* and *g* from User A, and then generating a new *p* and *g* to User B. User M will associate his secret key with A, and a new secret key with B. User A and User B will have different secret keys, and User M will have a secret key for each user. User A then might pass a cipher message to User B such as "How are you, B?", which User M might intercept and change to "Are you sure that I am A?" and then send that message instead to User B. If User A actually received a response from User B without User M intervening and changing the keys, then User A would not be able to decrypt the message. User M would have to constantly act as redirector of messages and re-key the messages to both users to avoid getting caught. Listing 4-11 shows sample code for a multi-threaded man-in-the-middle attack. The output is displayed in Listing 4-10.

Listing 4-11: The DHAgreement class: Java code for the man-in-the-middle attack

```
package com.richware.chap04;
import java.math.*;
import java.security.*;
import java.security.spec.*;
import javax.crypto.*;
import javax.crypto.spec.*;
import javax.crypto.interfaces.*;

/**
 * Class DHAgreement
```

```
 * Description: This is an example of a
 * man in the middle attack
 *
 * Copyright:    Copyright (c) 2002 Wiley Publishing, Inc.
 * @author Rich Helton <rhelton@richware.com>
 * @version 1.0
 * DISCLAIMER: Please refer to the disclaimer at the beginning of this
book.
 */
public class DHAgreement implements Runnable
{
  byte                    userA[];  // Public Key from A
  byte                    userB[];  // Public Key from B
  byte                    userAfromM[];  // Public Key from A altered by
M
  byte                    userBfromM[];  // Public Key from B altered by
M
  boolean                 userAStarted = false;
  boolean                 userMStarted = false;
  byte[]                  ciphertext_from_A;
  byte[]                  ciphertext_from_M;  // CipherText from M
  public final static int bitLength = 512;  // The size of the key
  BigInteger              p, g;

  /**
   * Method run
   */
  public synchronized void run()
    {
    if (!userMStarted)
      {
      userMStarted = true;
      doUserM();
      }
    else if (!userAStarted)
      {
      userAStarted = true;
      doUserA();
      }
    else
      {
      doUserB();
      }
    }

  /**
   * Method main
   * Description: Main Driver
   * @param args none
```

```
 *
 */
public static void main(String[] args)
{
  try
    {
      DHAgreement test = new DHAgreement();
      new Thread(test).start();  // Starts User M
      new Thread(test).start();  // Starts User A
      new Thread(test).start();  // Starts User B
    }

  /*
   * Catches
   */
  catch (Exception ex)
    {
      ex.printStackTrace();
    }
}

/**
 * Method doUserA
 */
public synchronized void doUserA()
{
  try
    {
      System.out.println("A->Starting....");
      System.out.println();
      /*
       * User A generates a Key Pair
       */
      KeyPairGenerator kpg =
        KeyPairGenerator.getInstance("DH");
      /*
       * Initializes based on Key Length
       */
      kpg.initialize(bitLength);
      System.out.println("A-> Generating Keys....");
      System.out.println();
      KeyPair kp = kpg.generateKeyPair();
      /*
       * Create the DH public key spec
       */
      DHParameterSpec kspec =
        ((DHPublicKey) kp.getPublic()).getParams();
      /*
       * Get the G, P, and public key
```

```
 * to distribute
 */
g    = kspec.getG();
p    = kspec.getP();
userA = kp.getPublic().getEncoded();
/*
 * Print out public key values
 */
System.out.println();
System.out.println("A->G Value**********************");
System.out.println(g);
System.out.println();
System.out.println("A->P Value**********************");
System.out.println(p);
System.out.println();
System.out
  .println("A->Public Key**********************");
System.out.println(userA);
notifyAll();
/*
 * Do the KeyAgreement
 */
KeyAgreement ka = KeyAgreement.getInstance("DH");
ka.init(kp.getPrivate());
/*
 * Actually getting Key from M
 */
while (userBfromM == null)
 {
  wait();
}
System.out.println("A->Got Public Key from B?.......");
System.out.println(userBfromM);
System.out.println();
/*
 * Implement the Key Agreement
 */
KeyFactory        kf       =
  KeyFactory.getInstance("DH");
X509EncodedKeySpec x509Spec =
  new X509EncodedKeySpec(userBfromM);
PublicKey         pk       =
  kf.generatePublic(x509Spec);
ka.doPhase(pk, true);
/*
 * Implement the Key Agreement
 */
byte             secret[] = ka.generateSecret();
SecretKeyFactory skf      =
```

```
       SecretKeyFactory.getInstance("DES");
     /*
      * Send a DES Cipher to B
      * M will actually pick it up and translate it
      */
     DESKeySpec desSpec   = new DESKeySpec(secret);
     SecretKey  secretKey = skf.generateSecret(desSpec);
     Cipher     c         =
       Cipher.getInstance("DES/ECB/PKCS5Padding");
     c.init(Cipher.ENCRYPT_MODE, secretKey);
     ciphertext from A =
       c.doFinal("How are you B?".getBytes());
     notifyAll();
   }
  catch (Exception e)
    {
     e.printStackTrace();
    }
}

/**
 * Method doUserB
 */
public synchronized void doUserB()
 {
  try
    {
      System.out.println("B->Starting User....");
      System.out.println();
      while (userAfromM == null)
       {
         wait();
       }
      System.out.println();
      System.out
        .println("B->User A's Public?**********************");
      System.out.println(userAfromM);
      System.out
        .println("B->User A's G Value?*********************");
      System.out.println(g);
      System.out.println();
      System.out
        .println("B->User A's P Value?*********************");
      System.out.println(p);
      /*
       * Generate a Key Pair
       * based on the p and g received
       */
      KeyPairGenerator kpg    =
```

```
  KeyPairGenerator.getInstance("DH");
DHParameterSpec  dhSpec = new DHParameterSpec(p, g);
kpg.initialize(dhSpec);
KeyPair kp = kpg.generateKeyPair();
/*
 * Distribute Public Key
 */
userB = kp.getPublic().getEncoded();
System.out.println();
System.out
  .println("B->Public Key*********************");
System.out.println(userB);
notifyAll();
/*
 * Key Agreement
 */
KeyAgreement ka = KeyAgreement.getInstance("DH");
ka.init(kp.getPrivate());
/*
 * Secret Key Exchange
 * from M
 */
KeyFactory         kf          =
  KeyFactory.getInstance("DH");
X509EncodedKeySpec x509Spec =
  new X509EncodedKeySpec(userAfromM);
PublicKey          pk          =
  kf.generatePublic(x509Spec);
ka.doPhase(pk, true);
/*
 * Distribute Public Key
 */
byte secret[] = ka.generateSecret();
/*
 * Decrypt message, thought to be from A
 * Actually from B
 */
SecretKeyFactory skf          =
  SecretKeyFactory.getInstance("DES");
DESKeySpec        desSpec  = new DESKeySpec(secret);
SecretKey         secretKey = skf.generateSecret(desSpec);
Cipher            c           =
  Cipher.getInstance("DES/ECB/PKCS5Padding");
c.init(Cipher.DECRYPT_MODE, secretKey);
while (ciphertext_from_M == null)
 {
  wait();
 }
byte plaintext[] = c.doFinal(ciphertext_from_M);
```

```
      System.out.println("B->Got Cipher->"
                          + new String(plaintext));
    }
   catch (Exception e)
    {
      e.printStackTrace();
    }
  }

/**
 * Method doUserM
 */
public synchronized void doUserM()
 {
   try
    {
      System.out.println("M->Starting User....");
      /*
       * Wait for User A
       */
      while (userA == null)
       {
         wait();
       }
      System.out.println();
      System.out.println("M->A Public Key....");
      System.out.println(userA);
      System.out.println("M->A's P....");
      System.out.println(p);
      System.out.println();
      System.out.println("M->A's G....");
      System.out.println(g);
      /*
       * Generate a Key pair based on A
       */
      KeyPairGenerator kpg_from_A    =
        KeyPairGenerator.getInstance("DH");
      DHParameterSpec  dhSpec_from_A = new DHParameterSpec(p,
                                       g);
      kpg_from_A.initialize(dhSpec_from_A);
      System.out.println("M->Generating a Key from A....");
      KeyPair kp_from_A = kpg_from_A.generateKeyPair();
      userBfromM = kp_from_A.getPublic().getEncoded();
      System.out.println();
      System.out.println(
        "M->Sending fake B Public Key to A*********************");
      System.out.println(userBfromM);
      notifyAll();
      /*
```

```
 * Generate a 512 bit Prime to pass to B
 * with new  p and g
 */
SecureRandom rnd = new SecureRandom();
p = BigInteger.probablePrime(bitLength, rnd);
g = BigInteger.probablePrime(bitLength, rnd);
System.out.println();
System.out
  .println("M->New p to B *********************");
System.out.println(p);
System.out.println();
System.out
  .println("M->New g to B *********************");
System.out.println(g);
System.out.println();
/*
 * Generate a Key pair based on B
 */
KeyPairGenerator kpg to B    =
  KeyPairGenerator.getInstance("DH");
DHParameterSpec  dhSpec_to_B = new DHParameterSpec(p, g);
kpg_to_B.initialize(dhSpec_to_B);
System.out.println("M->Generated a key to B....");
KeyPair kp_to_B = kpg_to_B.generateKeyPair();
userAfromM = kp_to_B.getPublic().getEncoded();
System.out.println();
System.out.println(
  "M->Sending fake A Public Key to B*********************");
System.out.println(userAfromM);
notifyAll();
/*
 * Wait for B's distribution
 */
while (userB == null)
 {
  wait();
}
System.out.println();
System.out.println("M->B's Public Key....");
System.out.println(userB);
System.out.println();
/*
 * Key Agreement between A and M
 */
KeyAgreement ka_from_A = KeyAgreement.getInstance("DH");
ka_from_A.init(kp_from_A.getPrivate());
KeyFactory        kf from A      =
  KeyFactory.getInstance("DH");
X509EncodedKeySpec x509Spec_from_A =
```

```
   new X509EncodedKeySpec(userA);
PublicKey         pk_from_A      =
  kf_from_A.generatePublic(x509Spec_from_A);
ka_from_A.doPhase(pk_from_A, true);
byte secret_from_A[] = ka_from_A.generateSecret();
/*
 * Getting cipher text from A
 */
while (ciphertext_from_A == null)
 {
  wait();
}
/*
 * Decrypting A's Message
 */
SecretKeyFactory skf_from_A      =
  SecretKeyFactory.getInstance("DES");
DESKeySpec        desSpec_from_A =
  new DESKeySpec(secret_from_A);
SecretKey         key_from_A     =
  skf_from_A.generateSecret(desSpec_from_A);
Cipher            c_from_A       =
  Cipher.getInstance("DES/ECB/PKCS5Padding");
c_from_A.init(Cipher.DECRYPT_MODE, key_from_A);
byte plaintext[] = c_from_A.doFinal(ciphertext_from_A);
System.out.println("M->Got Cipher from A->"
                    + new String(plaintext));
/*
 * Key Agreement between B and M
 */
KeyAgreement ka_to_B = KeyAgreement.getInstance("DH");
ka_to_B.init(kp_to_B.getPrivate());
KeyFactory        kf_to_B        =
  KeyFactory.getInstance("DH");
X509EncodedKeySpec x509Spec_to_B =
  new X509EncodedKeySpec(userB);
PublicKey         pk_to_B        =
  kf_to_B.generatePublic(x509Spec_to_B);
ka_to_B.doPhase(pk_to_B, true);
byte secret_to_B[] = ka_to_B.generateSecret();

/*
 * M is sending B a cipher message
 */
SecretKeyFactory skf_to_B        =
  SecretKeyFactory.getInstance("DES");
DESKeySpec        desSpec_to_B =
  new DESKeySpec(secret_to_B);
SecretKey         key_to_B       =
```

```
      skf_to_B.generateSecret(desSpec_to_B);
   Cipher          c_to_B          =
      Cipher.getInstance("DES/ECB/PKCS5Padding");
   c_to_B.init(Cipher.ENCRYPT_MODE, key_to_B);
   System.out.println();
   System.out.println(
      "M->Sending different Cipher to B->Are you sure that I am A?");
   ciphertext_from_M =
      c_to_B.doFinal("Are you sure that I am A?".getBytes());
   notifyAll();
   }
 catch (Exception e)
   {
   e.printStackTrace();
   }
  }
}
```

Listing 4-11 demonstrates a multithreaded approach using the
`javax.crypto.KeyAgreement` class that will pass the shared secret key to the other user.
Network implementations of key exchange will be explored in a later chapter. Notice that User
M receives the *p*, *g*, and key information from User A and modifies it before sending it to User
B. The biggest weakness of the DH algorithm is the man-in-the-middle attack. To compensate
for it, another algorithm evolved, which is called the RSA algorithm, to prevent the man-in-
the-middle attack.

> **CROSS-REFERENCE:** Chapter 21 discusses network security in more detail.

The Rivest, Shamir, and Adleman Key Exchange

After the Diffie-Hellman key exchange, three young professors from MIT named Ron Rivest,
Adi Shamir, and Len Adleman published the *"Rivest, Shamir and Adleman"* algorithm at MIT
in 1978 as a method of exchanging keys. They created their own company named from the
initials of their last names, Rivest, Shamir, and Adleman, called *RSA Security*, which can be
found at `www.rsasecurity.com`. The RSA key exchange is also an asymmetric key
exchange and became very popular.

Understanding the RSA key exchange

The RSA public key algorithm depends on the calculation of five numbers: p, q, n, e, and d.
The numbers p and q are very large prime numbers. The n is the multiplication of p and q. The
e is the encryption key that is selected by the user. Finally, the d is the decryption key that is
calculated using the numbers.

The key agreement for RSA is as follows:

- First, pick two large prime numbers p and q.

  For example (I will demonstrate with very small numbers), $p = 47$, and $q = 71$.

- Multiply p and q to get n, the modulus.

  For the example, $n = p \times q = 47 \times 71 = 3337$.

- Then get $\phi(n)$ by multiplying $(p - 1)$ by $(q - 1)$.

  For the example, $\phi(n) = ((p - 1)(q - 1)) = 46 \times 70 = 3220$.

- Select a number e, for encryption, that is less than $\phi(n)$ and prime.

  For the example, $e = 79$.

- Then calculate a number for decryption, $d = e^{-1} \bmod \phi(n)$. That is, calculate a number d that satisfies the formula $de = 1 \bmod \phi(n)$.

  For the example, $d = 79^{-1} \pmod{3220} = 1019$.

- The public key is $\{n,e\}$ and the private key is $\{n,d\}$.

  For the example $\{n,e\} = \{3337, 79\}$ and $\{n,d\} = \{3337, 1019\}$.

For RSA, the public key is used to encrypt, which is depicted as the symbol e for encryption; the private key is used for decrypting, which is depicted as the symbol d for decryption. After p and q are used in the calculation, they should be thrown away or kept private because the encryption key e can be computed if p and q are found. One addition to RSA is to reuse the p and q in the *Chinese Remainder Theorem* (CRT) for faster computations. Because p and q are kept private, the CRT cannot be used for faster computations in decryption. Because the RSA private key supports CRT, the JDK 1.4 supports this functionality in the `java.security.interface.RSAPrivateCRTKey` interface.

CROSS-REFERENCE: Chapter 12 describes ciphers in more detail.

The RSA algorithm not only includes key exchange like the DH key exchange, but also goes beyond key exchanging by defining a cipher algorithm. Cipher algorithms are discussed later in the book. RSA will use the discrete logarithm and modular exponential to encrypt and decrypt messages. See Listing 4-12 as an example.

NOTE: Recall that the Chinese Remainder Theorem is:

1. Suppose that m_1, m_2, ..., m_r are pairwise relatively prime positive integers.

2. Let a_1, a_2, ..., a_r be integers.

Then the system of congruences, $x = a_i \pmod{m_i}$ for $1 <= i <= r$, has a unique solution modulo:

   $M = m_1 \times m_2 \times ... \times m_r$

which is given by: $x = a_1 M_1 y_1 + a_2 M_2 y_2 + ... + a_r M_r y_r \pmod{M}$,

where $M_i = M/m_i$ and $y_i = (M_i)^{-1} \pmod{m_i}$ for $1 <= i <= r$.

If you are interested in this theorem, there are many math books and WWW sites that explain it.

Listing 4-12: Encrypting/decrypting the RSA message

```
As an example, let's encrypt the number 43:
First, I will use the e and n from the example above.
CipherText = Message^encryption mod n = 43^79 mod 3337 = 1921
The encrypted message of 43 is 1921.

To decrypt the message, the same formula applies, except with the d and
n instead:
Message = Ciphertext^decryption mod n = 1921^1019 mod 3337 = 43
The decrypted message of 1921 is 43.
```

Listing 4-12 is a very simple demonstration of how the RSA algorithm works. Listing 4-13 is a sample output that verifies the results.

Listing 4-13: Verifying the RSA algorithm

```
p = 47
q = 71
n = 3337
phi = 3220
e = 79
d = 1019
Public Key {n,e} = { 3337,79}
Private Key {n,d} = { 3337,1019}
Encrypting value.....43
Ciphertext value = 1921
Decrypting value.....
Plaintext value = 43
```

Implementing the RSA key exchange

Like DH, the JDK 1.4 provides a `KeyPairGenerator` and service provider for implementing the RSA algorithm. To find out what keys are supported and which service providers are implemented on classes currently installed on your system environment, see the output of Listing 4-14 and its associated code in Listing 4-15.

Listing 4-14: Service providers installed

```
>java com.richware.chap04.GetProviderInfo
Providers installed on your system:
------------------------------------
[ 1] - Provider name: SUN
Provider version number: 1.2
Provider information:
SUN (DSA key/parameter generation; DSA signing; SHA-1, MD5 digests;
SecureRandom
; X.509 certificates; JKS keystore; PKIX CertPathValidator; PKIX
CertPathBuilder
; LDAP, Collection CertStores)
```

```
-----------------------------------
[ 2] - Provider name: SunJSSE
Provider version number: 1.4
Provider information:
Sun JSSE provider(implements RSA Signatures, PKCS12, SunX509 key/trust
factories
, SSLv3, TLSv1)
-----------------------------------
[ 3] - Provider name: SunRsaSign
Provider version number: 1.0
Provider information:
SUN's provider for RSA signatures
-----------------------------------
[ 4] - Provider name: SunJCE
Provider version number: 1.4
Provider information:
SunJCE Provider (implements DES, Triple DES, Blowfish, PBE, Diffie-
Hellman, HMAC
-MD5, HMAC-SHA1)
-----------------------------------
[ 5] - Provider name: SunJGSS
Provider version number: 1.0
Provider information:
Sun (Kerberos v5)
-----------------------------------
```

Listing 4-15: The `GetProviderInfo` class: Code for generating Listing 4-14

```java
package com.richware.chap04;
import java.security.*;
import java.util.*;

/**
 * Class GetProviderInfo
 * Description: This is an example of
 * retrieving providers
 *
 * Copyright:    Copyright (c) 2002 Wiley Publishing, Inc.
 * @author Rich Helton <rhelton@richware.com>
 * @version 1.0
 * DISCLAIMER: Please refer to the disclaimer at the beginning of this
book.
 */
class GetProviderInfo
{
   public static void main(String[] args)
   {
```

```
        System.out.println("Providers installed on your system:");
        System.out.println("----------------------------------");
        Provider[] providerList = Security.getProviders();
        for (int i = 0; i < providerList.length; i++)
        {
            System.out.println("[ " + (i + 1) + "] - Provider name: " +
providerList[ i].getName());
            System.out.println("Provider version number: " +
providerList[ i].getVersion());
            System.out.println("Provider information:\n" +
providerList[ i].getInfo());
            System.out.println("----------------------------------");
        }
    }
}
```

From Listing 4-14, the service providers for supporting RSA are found in both `SunJSSE` and `SunRsaSign`. To specify a particular service provider in code, the provider parameter can be passed in the `java.security.KeypairGenerator` class like `KeyPairGenerator kpg = KeyPairGenerator.getInstance("RSA", "SunRsaSign")`. If the provider name is not specified, the lookup for the first provider name will be used; in this case, it is the SunJSSE service provider interface for RSA.

Just as in the DH code example, after the service provider is selected for generating the keys, the `KeyPairGenerator` only requires a key size and it will generate the variables to use. The default for the public key exponent is 65537. The `java.security.spec.AlgorithmParameterSpec` interface can be used to pass in selectable RSA values to prime the RSA `KeyPairGenerator` class. The `AlgorithmParameterSpec` is algorithm specific. In the DH sample, the `javax.crytpo.spec.DHParameterSpec` class was used to pass in values *p* and *g*; and now for RSA, the keysize and the exponent *e* are the only values that can be entered in the `AlgorithmParameterSpec` as the RSA equivalent of a `java.security.spec.RSAKeyGenParameter` class. The key size must fall in the range of 512- to 2048-bit size and must be a multiple of 8. The default key size value is 1024. For an example of the calculations done in the explanation of the algorithm, letting the `KeyPairGenerator` choose the values for you, and choosing your own exponent, see Listing 4-16. Listing 4-17shows the associated output.

> **TIP:** Using `AlgorithmParameterSpec`, the RSA equivalent of a `java.security.spec.RSAKeyGenParameter` class, the key size must fall in the range of 512- to 2048-bit size and must be a multiple of 8. The default key size value is 1024.

Listing 4-16: The `RSASimpleApp` class: An RSA sample application

```
package com.richware.chap04;
import java.util.*;
import java.math.*;
```

```java
import java.security.*;
import java.security.spec.*;

/**
 * Class RSASimpleApp
 * Description: This is an example of a
 * simple RSA
 *
 * Copyright:    Copyright (c) 2002 Wiley Publishing, Inc.
 * @author Rich Helton <rhelton@richware.com>
 * @version 1.0
 * DISCLAIMER: Please refer to the disclaimer at the beginning of this
book.
 */
public class RSASimpleApp
{
  public final static int p       = 47;
  public final static int q       = 71;
  public final static int eValue = 79;
  public final static int mValue = 43;
  public final static int KEYSIZE_MIN     =  512;
  public final static int KEYSIZE_DEFAULT = 1024;
  public final static int KEYSIZE_MAX     = 2048;
  public final static int bitLength = KEYSIZE_DEFAULT; // KeySize
  /**
   * Method main
   * Description: This is a Sample JAAS application
   * @param args none
   *
   */
  public static void main(String[] args)
  {
    try
    {
      BigInteger c        = null;
      BigInteger d        = null;
      BigInteger phi      = null;
      BigInteger minusOne = null;
      BigInteger e        = null;
      BigInteger m        = null;
      System.out.println();
      System.out.println(
        "RSA Proving the algorithm*************************");

      /*
       * Step 1
       * Pick p and q
       */
      System.out.println("p = " + RSASimpleApp.p);
```

```
System.out.println("q = " + RSASimpleApp.q);

/*
 * Step 2
 * Calculate n = p * q
 */
BigInteger n = new BigInteger(Integer.toString(p * q));
System.out.println("n = " + n);

/*
 * Step 3
 * Calculate phi = (p - 1) * (q - 1)
 */
phi = new BigInteger(Integer.toString((p - 1)
                                    * (q - 1)));
System.out.println("phi = " + phi);

/*
 * Step 4
 * Select e a prime less than phi
 */
e = new BigInteger(Integer.toString(eValue));
if (e.intValue() < phi.intValue())
{
  System.out.println("e = " + e);
  minusOne = new BigInteger(Integer.toString(-1));

  /*
   * Step 5
   * Calculate d
   */
  d = e.modPow(minusOne, phi);
  System.out.println("d = " + d);

  /*
   * Step 6
   * Display private and public key
   */
  System.out.println("Public Key {n,e} = {" + n + ","
                    + e + "}");
  System.out.println("Private Key {n,d} = {" + n + ","
                    + d + "}");
  m = new BigInteger(Integer.toString(mValue));
  System.out.println("Encrypting value....." + m);
  c = m.modPow(e, n);
  System.out.println("Ciphertext value = " + c);
  System.out.println("Decrypting value.....");
  BigInteger plaintext = c.modPow(d, n);
  System.out.println("Plaintext value = " + plaintext);
```

```
    }
    else
     {
       System.out.println("e must be less than phi");
    }
    RSASimpleApp app = new RSASimpleApp();
    app.createKey();
    app.createSpecificKey();
  }

  /*
   * Catches
   */
  catch (Exception ex)
   {
     ex.printStackTrace();
   }
 }

/**
 * Method createKey
 * Description: This is an example of
 * letting the algorithm choose
 * the values
 *
 */
public void createKey()
 {
  try
   {
     System.out.println();
     System.out.println(
       "RSA letting the algorithm choose******************");
     KeyPairGenerator kpg =
       KeyPairGenerator.getInstance("RSA");

     /*
      * A strong key uses 512 to 2048 bits
      * the bits must be multiples of 8
      */
     System.out.println("Provider =" + kpg.getProvider());
     kpg.initialize(bitLength);
     KeyPair kp = kpg.generateKeyPair();

     /*
      * Read the keys
      * produced by the algorithm
      */
     System.out.println("Public Key ="
```

```
                                    + kp.getPublic().getEncoded());
      System.out.println("Public Key Algorithm ="
                            + kp.getPublic().getAlgorithm());
      System.out.println("Public Key Format ="
                            + kp.getPublic().getFormat());
      System.out.println("Private Key ="
                            + kp.getPrivate().getEncoded());
      System.out.println("Private Key Algorithm ="
                            + kp.getPrivate().getAlgorithm());
      System.out.println("Private Key Format ="
                            + kp.getPrivate().getFormat());


      /*
       * Initialize the KeyFactory for DSA
       */
      KeyFactory kfactory = KeyFactory.getInstance("RSA");


      /*
       * Create the RSA public key spec
       */
      RSAPublicKeySpec kspec =
        (RSAPublicKeySpec) kfactory
          .getKeySpec(kp.getPublic(), RSAPublicKeySpec.class);


      /*
       * Print out public key values
       */
      System.out.println("Public Key Modulus ="
                            + kspec.getModulus());
      System.out.println("Public Key Exponent ="
                            + kspec.getPublicExponent());
    }


  /*
   * Catches
   */
  catch (java.security.NoSuchAlgorithmException ex)
    {
      ex.printStackTrace();
    }
  catch (Exception ex)
    {
      ex.printStackTrace();
    }
}
/**
 * Method createSpecificKey
 * Description: This is an example of
 * choosing e
```

```
 *
 */
public void createSpecificKey()
{
  try
    {
     /*
      * Another provider specific to the signature instead of JSSE
      */
     System.out.println();
     System.out.println(
       "RSA Choosing the exponent*************************");
     KeyPairGenerator kpg =
       KeyPairGenerator.getInstance("RSA", "SunRsaSign");
     /* A strong key uses 512 to 2048 bits
      * the bits must be multiples of 8
      */
     System.out.println("Provider =" + kpg.getProvider());
     BigInteger e = new BigInteger(Integer.toString(eValue));
     System.out.println("e =" + e);


     /*
      * Select the exponent
      */
     RSAKeyGenParameterSpec param =
       new RSAKeyGenParameterSpec(bitLength, e);
     kpg.initialize(param);
     KeyPair kp = kpg.generateKeyPair();

     /* Read the keys
      * produced by the algorithm
      */
     System.out.println("Public Key ="
                     + kp.getPublic().getEncoded());
     System.out.println("Public Key Algorithm ="
                     + kp.getPublic().getAlgorithm());
     System.out.println("Public Key Format ="
                     + kp.getPublic().getFormat());
     System.out.println("Private Key ="
                     + kp.getPrivate().getEncoded());
     System.out.println("Private Key Algorithm ="
                     + kp.getPrivate().getAlgorithm());
     System.out.println("Private Key Format ="
                     + kp.getPrivate().getFormat());

     /*
      * Initialize the KeyFactory for DSA
      */
     KeyFactory kfactory = KeyFactory.getInstance("RSA",
```

```
                           "SunRsaSign");

    /*
     * Create the RSA public key spec
     */
    RSAPublicKeySpec kspec =
       (RSAPublicKeySpec) kfactory
         .getKeySpec(kp.getPublic(), RSAPublicKeySpec.class);

    /*
     * Print out public key values
     */
    System.out.println("Public Key Modulus ="
                        + kspec.getModulus());
    System.out.println("Public Key Exponent ="
                        + kspec.getPublicExponent());
  }


  /*
   * Catches
   */
  catch (java.security.NoSuchAlgorithmException ex)
    {
    ex.printStackTrace();
    }
  catch (Exception ex)
    {
    ex.printStackTrace();
    }
  }
}
```

Listing 4-17: Output for Listing 4-16

```
>java com.richware.chap04.RSASimpleApp

RSA Proving the algorithm*************************
p = 47
q = 71
n = 3337
phi = 3220
e = 79
d = 1019
Public Key {n,e} = { 3337,79}
Private Key {n,d} = { 3337,1019}
Encrypting value.....43
Ciphertext value = 1921
Decrypting value.....
```

```
Plaintext value = 43

RSA letting the algorithm choose******************
Provider =SunJSSE version 1.4
Public Key =[ B@50d89c
Public Key Algorithm =RSA
Public Key Format =X509
Private Key =[ B@f6f0bf
Private Key Algorithm =RSA
Private Key Format =PKCS8
Public Key Modulus
=16062945982618579666528081429124038312382864119892343625318190015105967600900993179379813518837953361152449071417557362065635231152737493397
2314666240736051405499460173153833176563844957125498513580090176620168124630240456357782570542459025554393662712254447788199547496264956561090877631097357422561127783459
Public Key Exponent =65537

RSA Choosing the exponent*************************
Provider =SunRsaSign version 1.0
e =79
Public Key =[ B@1cdeff
Public Key Algorithm =RSA
Public Key Format =X509
Private Key =[ B@d2068d
Private Key Algorithm =RSA
Private Key Format =PKCS8
Public Key Modulus
=12826130699258535966539595253944322004538652678011474063057897075847334312323840843970185943172795256148951870644419340640402958673921381081
5943357989407860321127928149794841840762406280614771712328422998505640156944532536111787318592712528672554936501568435238685663581311417565438997622399659613722180552193
Public Key Exponent =79
```

Using symmetric keys

So far the discussion has centered on the key pair algorithms. From Listing 4-14, there are several secret keys, or symmetric keys, that the standard service providers shipped with the JDK 1.4. Most noteworthy of the secret keys are *Data Encryption Standard* (DES), the oldest of all keys, and its replacement, *Triple-DES*.

> **CROSS-REFERENCE:** Chapter 12, Chapter 13, and Chapter 14 describe the implementation and the associated ciphers of DES and Triple-DES.

Understanding the Data Encryption Standard (DES) key

The *Data Encryption Standard* (DES) has been around since before the DH key exchange. It originally started out as Lucifer from IBM, which was bought by Lloyd's of London in 1973. Also in 1973, the National Bureau of Standards (NBS) was looking for a national encryption standard for encrypting unclassified documents, to be known as DES. The NBS eventually became the National Institute of Standards and Technology and published DES as the algorithm for encrypting unclassified information.

Lucifer started out as a 128-bit encryption. The National Security Agency (NSA) started the change over of Lucifer into DES and changed the key size to 64 bits. Of the 64-bit key, 8 bits are used for error correction in a parity check, which changes the key size to 56 bits. The 56-bit key makes the *brute-force attack* (to discover every key combination) possible since there are approximately 2^{56} key combinations, or approximately 7.2×10^{16} keys. DES encrypts and decrypts 64 bits (8 bytes) at a time and produces 64 bits of cipher text.

Because of the decrease in key size, there were many rumors that the NSA purposely weakened DES so that a brute-force attack could be easier. The NSA denies any wrongdoing, but many brute-force attacks in the mid-1990s were successful. Two of the biggest opponents of DES were Martin Hellman and Whitfield Diffie, who came up with the DH key agreement.

The *Electronic Frontier Foundation* (EFF) announced several successful DES attacks in 1997. By January 1999, the EFF was breaking DES within 24 hours. Many cryptographers and authors still suggest that DES is a viable algorithm and that the cost of the brute-force attacks outweigh the gain of decrypting the ciphertext. With the availability of computer power in the 21st century, and the ability to use idle computers from around the world for their processing power, I believe that this is a serious weakness. I will just reference the "Data Encryption Standard" from the National Institute of Standards and Technology, which you can find at `http://csrc.nist.gov/publications/fips/fips46-3/fips46-3.pdf`, and paraphrase: Use single DES for legacy systems where there isn't a choice, and whenever possible use Triple-DES. Other algorithms that were considered to replace DES are the SkipJack algorithm and the Clipper Chip.

Understanding the Triple-DES key

Because DES was a very popular algorithm, accepted and distributed by many, any substitution of DES in legacy systems would take time. In the mid-1990s many cracks and exposure of the DES weaknesses have become known.

> **TIP:** See The Electronic Frontier Foundation, "Cracking DES," Distributed by O'Reilly & Associates, `http://www.eff.org/descracker`, 1998, for further information.

A way of strengthening DES without changing the cipher was underway. The result became known as *Triple-DES* because of the use of three DES keys. For many, this algorithm also became known as DES EDE for DES Encrypt-Decrypt-Encrypt. The reasoning behind the EDE is that the Triple-DES key algorithm performs an encryption operation with one key, K_1, and decrypts with another key, K_2. At a minimum, Triple-DES must use two keys. Three keys can also be used. When Triple-DES decrypts with the K_2, it doesn't return the original plaintext, but a new ciphertext that has been changed through the decryption process by not using the original key K_1. A third key can be used, K_3, to encrypt again with the second encryption. Even if K_1 is used with the second encryption, it will still produce a unique output from the Encrypt-Decrypt because the ciphertext has already been modified by the decryption with a different key. The two-key implementation of Triple-DES uses a key, K_1, for both encryptions, and a second key for the decryption, as shown in Listing 4-18.

Listing 4-18: Triple-DES two-key implementation

```
A pseudo code example is as follows:
CipherText = Encrypt_K1 (Decrypt_K2(Encrypt_K1(PlainText)))

The first encryption uses K1:
CipherText_E1 = Encrypt_K1("Password");

The next step is an encryption with a different key K2:
CipherText_D1 = Decrypt_K2(CipherText_E1);

The next step is an encryption with the K1, but the input for the
plaintext is now a ciphertext returned by the decryption:
CipherText_E2 = Encrypt_K1(CipherText_D1);
```

Listing 4-18 describes the use of the Triple-DES two-key implementation. Now the algorithm not only has the strength of the two 56-bit keys, but also uses the same key to re-encrypt a new ciphertext. A typical strength of adding the two DES keys K_1 and K_2 would be $2^{56} + 2^{56}$ or 2^{122}. By using the keys multiple times, a different combination of encryption and decryption is achieved and the strength is greater.

The three-key implementation is also used in Triple-DES. The three-key implementation is used the same way as the two-key implementation, except that the second encryption doesn't use K_1. The second encryption uses a third key, K_3. See Listing 4-19 for an example of the implementation.

Listing 4-19: Triple-DES three-key implementation

```
A pseudo code example is as follows:
CipherText = Encrypt_K3 (Decrypt_K2(Encrypt_K1(PlainText)))

The first encryption uses K1:
CipherText_E1 = Encrypt_K1("Password");

The next step is an encryption with a different key K2:
```

```
CipherText_D1 = Decrypt_K2(CipherText_E1);

The next step is an encryption with the K_3, but the input for the
palintext is now a ciphertext returned by the decryption:
CipherText_E2 = Encrypt_K3(CipherText_D1);
```

Listing 4-19 describes the use of the Triple-DES three-key implementation. Now the algorithm has the strength of the three 56-bit keys. The typical strength of three DES keys would be 2^{56} + $2^{56} + 2^{56}$ or 2^{168}. The strength of 2^{168} would make any brute-force attack very time consuming. By supplying a higher key with the same algorithm, Triple-DES has increased the comfort level of using the DES algorithm.

The Future of Key Exchanges

Most key exchanges have been around since the 1970s, many with very little change. Key exchanges have evolved that form these basic algorithms into other protocols such as *Public Key Infrastructure* (PKI), where *Certificate Authorities* (CA) manage keys that store RSA key information in an X.509 certificate. Other keys such as DH agreement are done through secure networks; for example, the Simple Key Management for Internet Protocols (SKIP) that is used in Virtual Private Networks.

> **CROSS-REFERENCE:** Chapter 25 describes PKI in more detail. Chapter 24 describes the X.509 specification.

Proximity cards and smart cards

Still other means of key exchanging have evolved through physical mediums like proximity cards. *Proximity cards* are cards that are issued to people to provide entry into an area. The proximity card provides radio frequencies to activate the entryway or door. The user holds the proximity device, like a card, to a proximity reader to be granted access. The smart card is a similar concept, which contains a modem for I/O, a microprocessor, and some RAM. These cards are very similar in size and shape to a credit card. The smart card offers computational power, where records and keys can be manufactured and stored on the card. The smart card is placed in a smart card reader that might be attached to a computer terminal or desktop. The computer may require information such as a key set or the ability to perform a computation before the computer will even turn on. When the smart card is removed, the computer may turn off.

Other techniques that may be applied using a smart card are the Java buttons and biometric cards. A biometric card uses information that is associated with the medical industry. Medical information could be in the form of a fingerprint. The smart card reader could require a fingerprint record from the card, and next to the computer is a fingerprint scanner that will scan the user's fingerprint. The fingerprint from the card must match the user's fingerprint before access is granted into the system. The Java button can be embedded in a smart card, but also in a key ring, or any other device that is similar in shape and size to a small button. The

Java button can have the capability to process public keys in the form of a token. The issue with the DH key exchange is that a man-in-the-middle attack can occur if the messages are captured and resent. The device reader, while using a smart card or Java button, could be a hardware device between the desktop and connected directly to the desktop through an I/O device. Because of this direct hardware connection, there can be no man in the middle listening to the device. The device now uses a form of physical security and a close proximity to ensure that the user is authenticated.

> **CROSS-REFERENCE:** Chapter 14 provides a description of smart card basics.

Summary

There have been a lot of changes in key exchange methods, including the concept of smart cards. Many of these techniques and Java service providers still use the fundamental algorithms and ideas that were developed in the early 1970s.

This chapter offered a fundamental understanding of the basics of the key exchange. Keys provide a set of users the ability to encrypt and decrypt messages. Any compromise in securing the keys can compromise the integrity and confidentiality of the messages. The security of the messages depends on how keys are stored and exchanged. Throughout my lifetime, I have seen many organizations that were concerned about the strength of the cipher but stored the key on the Web server. The cipher doesn't have any strength if the key is available. Understanding how keys are managed is one of the most important aspects of security. The JDK 1.4 provides many fundamental service providers for key exchange, but more important, it provides the ability to implement your own service provider, as discussed in the next chapter.

## Chapter 5

Elliptic Curve Cryptography

In This Chapter

♦ Learning the need for key agreement

♦ Introducing mathematics for ECC key exchanging

♦ Understanding the importance of ECC

♦ Understanding how to implement your own key exchange through SPI

♦ Implementing the ECC through a Service Provider Interface

Introduction

Chapter 4 introduced exchanging keys using Diffie-Hellman and RSA. Both algorithms use Discrete Logarithms. Another algorithm that has become very important in cryptography is the elliptic curve. The elliptic curve is used for finding points on an ellipse and is used for *Elliptic Curve Cryptography* (ECC). The benefit of the ECC is that performance is faster, and it gives the same strength as RSA with a smaller key size. According to RSA Laboratory's findings (take a look at their site at www.rsasecurity.com/), the ECC key length of 192 bits has the same strength of the RSA key length of 1020 bits. Cracking a key that size with a brute force attack would take 114 computers with a total of 170 GB of memory and 3 million years. The principal attraction of ECC is the smaller bit size for the same strength as a larger RSA key bit size.

Just like the Diffie-Hellman and RSA algorithms, the ECC uses keys in the discrete range, meaning that only positive integers are used. All numbers must be finite and have a range of 0 to an agreed-upon number. As reviewed in Chapter 4, the exponential curve is somewhat straight after it reaches a certain point on the graph. The benefit of the elliptic curve is that various curves follow a curve formula with a discrete set of points, and finding a specific point on a curved line is more difficult.

The range of the elliptic curve could be from 0 to 23, a very low number, but the complexity of the curve, or the curviness, could generate many points on the curve. The complexity of the formula of the curve makes it difficult to guess at its sequence. The straighter the curve, the easier it is to guess at its sequence. Figures 5-1 and 5-2 illustrate the difference between some curves.

$$y^2 = x^3 - 3x + 5$$

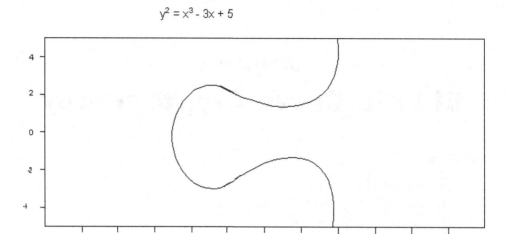

Figure 5-1: Curvier

$$y^2 = x^3 + x + 1$$

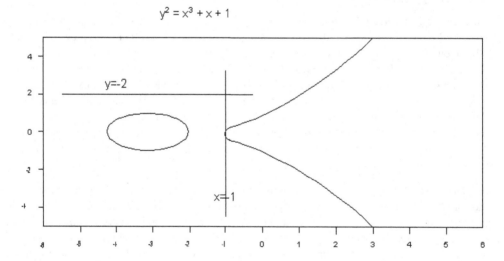

Figure 5-2: Less curvy

The elliptic curve uses points on the x,y coordinate system. For example, a point labeled P3 is described as (-1, -2). The x-coordinate is -1 units and the y-coordinate is -2 units. The coordinate is based on where the two lines intersect to form a point.

The special thing about elliptic curves is the unique characteristics that make up the points on the coordinate system. Unlike some other shapes, adding a point on an elliptic curve to another point on the curve results in a point on the curve that does not have any obvious pattern.

Another special property of elliptic curves is the scalar multiplication. For instance, multiplying a point times a number is called scalar multiplication and can only be performed one way, meaning that the original point cannot be derived from the result. For example, if the original point is *P0*, then *P1=2*P0* is the same as *P1=P0+P0* and *P2=3*P0* equals *P2=P0+P0+P0*; each of these points is different, and *P0* cannot be derived from either *P1* or *P2*.

Understanding the Mathematics of ECC

The mathematics behind *elliptic curves* has been around for at least 150 years. This concept is not new, but using ECC for exchanging keys has only been around for the last 10 years. One of the most noteworthy mathematicians who developed elliptic curves was Karl Weierstrass, a 19th century mathematician.

The ECC rests on solving the *Elliptic Curve Discrete Logarithm Problem* (ECDLP). An elliptic curve consists of all real numbers for the points *x*, *y*, *a*, and *b* in the *(x, y)* coordinate plane. The E_p *(a, b)* curve plane satisfies the following equation:

$$y^2 = x^3 + ax + b \pmod{p}$$

The prime number *p* sets the upper limits of the equation and is used for modulus arithmetic.

When using ECC, there are two types of arithmetic: the Cartesian coordinates for resolving the elliptic curve and modular arithmetic used for resolving the points along the coordinate system. For example, choosing $p = 23$ creates the elliptic curve $y^2 = x^3 + ax + b \pmod{23}$. Substituting $a = 1$ and $b = 1$ yields the following example equation #1:

$$y^2 = x^3 + x + 1$$

The example equation #1 creation is denoted by an elliptic group E_{23} *(1,1)*, where $p = 23$, $a = 1$, and $b = 1$. When a different *a* and *b* are chosen, the curve changes. The elliptic group in its raw form is denoted by E_p *(a, b)*.

The real number scale can now be solved for *y* by using all values of *x* that start with 0 and are less than *p*. The prime number *p* provides a limit of the points that can be found. So *y* can be solved for values 0 through 23. For instance, if $x = 0$ in $y^2 = 0^3 + 0 + 1 = 1$, then $y = 1$. The point is denoted as *(x, y)* or *(0, 1)*. All other points for *x* and *y* can be calculated in the same manner.

To represent the numbers in a binary form, *p* can take on the form of 2^m, which makes $E_2{}^m$ *(a, b)*. Also, the negative of a point is reflective of the shape across the x-axis. That is, if a $P = (0,1)$, the negative is the point $-P = (0, -1)$. In addition, the modulus equation can be used to find more points. Since *-1 mod 23 = 22*, the negative point *-P* of *P* = *(0,1)* can also be *(0,22)*. Listing 5-1 shows examples of the modulo operation.

> **TIP:** Recall from basic mathematics that *modulo* is the remainder. That is, $r = mod(x,p)$ if r is a number between 0 and p such that $x = q*p+r$ with integer q and imaginary parts ignored if they exist. Also, the *congruent modulo* is defined as $r \equiv x \ (mod \ p)$ if $[(r - x)/(p)]$ is an integer.

Listing 5-1: Modulo examples

```
Find r = mod(10,7): solve r=x - q*p so that r is between 0 and 7
so r = 3

Find r = mod(-10,7): solve r=x - q*p so that r is between 0 and 7
so r = 4

Find r = mod(10,-7): solve r=x - q*p so that r is between 0 and 7
so r = -4

Find 89 ≡ x mod 23:
89/23 roughly equals 3 so 3 * 23 = 69 and 89 - 69 = 20
so 89 ≡ 20 mod 23.
```

Modular arithmetic can also be applied to the equation of the curve to check the validity of a given point. Consider the E_{23} *(1, 0)*, which generates the curve $y^2 = x^3 + x$. To see if a point *P* *(9,5)* works on the curve, solve the "*mod 23*" for both sides as follows:

- First substitute the x and y parameters to have $5^2 = 9^3 + 9$.
- The highest degree to the equation is cubic, so the 9^3 is the greatest computation.
- Apply "*mod 23*" on both sides. That renders *25 mod 23 = 738 mod 23*.
- Now 25/23 = 1, 1*23 = 23, and 25 – 23 = 2 for the *y* side.
- Next solve the *x* side. 738/23 roughly equals 32. Multiplying 32 by 23 brings 736, and subtracting the closest difference is 738 – 736 = 2 for the *x* side.
- Since the *x* and *y* side equal each other, the *P (9,5)* is a valid point on the curve.

Modular arithmetic is also used for adding points. When adding points, usually a difference is taken on the curve to find the combination of the two points. The difference is denoted by the symbol lambda as λ. There are two possibilities:

- The two points are different. That is $P = (x_p, y_p)$, and $Q = (x_q, y_q)$ then $P + Q = (x_r, y_r)$ where (x_r, y_r) is the resulting point R. The difference is calculated $\lambda = (y_q - y_p)/(x_q - x_q)$ and the formulas for $x_r = (\lambda^2 - x_p - x_q)(mod \ p)$ and the formula for $y_r = (\lambda(x_p - x_q) - y_p)(mod \ p)$.
- The two points are equal. That is, you are doubling a point or adding the same point to it. There is no difference between the two points. The λ is calculated using $\lambda = 3x_p^2 + a / 2y_p$. After lambda is calculated, the point R representing (x_r, y_r) is calculated as 2P

instead of Q + P where (x_q, y_q) and (x_p, y_p) are now the same points. To calculate 3 times P, P can simply be added to itself 3 times using this equation.

Here is an example calculation, let $P = (3, 10)$, $Q = (9, -7)$ and E_{23} $(1, 1)$. Using these values, $P + Q = (x_r, y_r)$ for (x_r, y_r) and the curve $y^2 = x^3 + x + 1$.

♦ First calculate lambda

$\lambda = y_q - y_p / x_q - x_q = 7 - 10 / 9 - 3 = -3 / 6 = -1 / 2 \equiv 11 \bmod 23$.

TIP: You need to use the mod inverse of x to find 11. Here is a simple way of doing it:

(-1/2) = -1 * (1/2) so evaluate (1/2) (mod 23)

by trial and error get (12*2) ≡ 1 mod 23

from that (1/2) ≡ 12 mod 23

and therefore, -1 * 12 = -12 ≡ 11 mod 23

♦ Next calculate x_r

$x_r = (\lambda^2 - x_p - x_q)(\bmod p) = 11^2 - 3 - 9 = 109 \equiv 17 \bmod 23$ so $x_r = 17$.

♦ Then calculate y_r

$y_r = (\lambda(x_p - x_q) - y_p)(\bmod p) = 11(3 - (-6)) - 10 = 89 \equiv 20 \bmod 23$ so $y_r = 20$.

♦ The final result $R = (17,20)$.

NOTE: Multiplicative inverses are two numbers that multiplied together equal 1, for instance 11 and 1/11. Multipling by a modular inverse pair is just like multiplying by 1.

The ECCDH Key Exchange

One of the most common ways of passing ECC keys is to use a modified Diffie-Hellman using ECC (*ECCDH*) version. The idea is to pass a public key and then generate a shared secret key to use for a new public key. Just as in Diffie-Hellman, the key is produced from multiplication.

Understanding the ECC key exchange

The ECCDH public key algorithm depends on the calculation of an agreed-upon elliptic curve, the point on the curve as a starting point, deriving a random number for a private key, and sending other users the product of all these values. The receiving user, knowing the curve and starting point, can use the sender's product and derive a common product for both users to share as a key. The key agreement for ECCDH follows this sequence:

♦ First User A and User B select the elliptic curve by choosing prime numbers p, a, and b that satisfy the elliptic curve group $E_p(a,b)$. The elliptic curve equation is $y^2 = x^3 + ax + b \ (\bmod p)$.

For example, $p = 211$, $a = 0$, and $b = -4$ create the elliptic curve group E_{211} $(0, -4)$ and the elliptic curve $y^2 = x^3 - 4$.

♦ User A and User B select a common *(x,y)* coordinate point *P* on the elliptic curve $y^2 = x^3 - 4$ that is less than *p*.

For example, using *x = 2* will generate *y = 2*, so *P(2,2)*. The *P* point in this example is known as the *generator* or *G* in the Diffie-Hellman algorithm.

♦ User A selects a random number, *d*, less than *p*, that will be multiplied by the point *P* to retrieve a multiple point *Q* on the curve, *Q = dP*.

For the example *d = 203, Q = (203)(2,2) = (130,203)*.

♦ User A sends the public key *Q* to User B.

♦ User B selects a random number, *d*, less than *p* that will be multiplied by the point *P* to retrieve a multiple of point *Q* on the curve, *Q = dP*.

For the example *d = 121, Q = (121)(2,2) = (115,48)*.

♦ User B sends the public key *Q* to User A.

♦ User A can calculate a shared key by computing *S = dQ* with *Q* received from B.

For the example *d = 203, S = (203)(115,48) = (161,169)*.

♦ User B can calculate a shared key by computing *S = dQ* with *Q* received from A.

For the example *d = 121, S = (121)(130,203) = (161,169)*.

♦ Both users now contain share and public keys.

Understanding the Service Provider Interface (SPI)

There are two main layers that a developer using the JDK 1.4 must completely understand: the *Application Layer Interface* (API) and the *Service Provider Interface* (SPI). The API is the interface that the developer uses to load up algorithms and protocols. The SPI layer loads up the appropriate algorithms and protocols based on the parameters passed in through the API. The service providers maintain information in properties files. If the properties files are not defined correctly, the appropriate service may not be loaded, or worse, it may be loaded with a corrupted service. A simple issue can be that the classpath is not set correctly to the appropriate providers.

Implementing the ECC key exchange as an SPI

To build a service provider module, there are exact classes, interfaces, and entries into the properties files that must be accomplished. Building an SPI interface is a very structured interface for the JDK 1.4.

The interface that most developers will actually have to understand is the `java.security.Provider` class. To implement an asymmetric key interface, the `java.security.KeyFactory` and `java.security.KeyPairGenerator` must be implemented and an association must be provided in the Provider class implementation. See Listing 5-2.

Listing 5-2: The ECCProvider class: The Provider class

```
package com.richware.chap05;
import java.security.AccessController;
import java.security.PrivilegedAction;

/**
 * Class ECCProvider
 * Description: This is a example of a
 * simple ECC Provider
 *
 * Copyright:    Copyright (c) 2002 Wiley Publishing, Inc.
 * @author Rich Helton <rhelton@richware.com>
 * @version 1.0
 * DISCLAIMER: Please refer to the disclaimer at the beginning of this
book.
 */
public final class ECCProvider extends java.security.Provider
{
    private static final String INFO = "Rich's provider for ECC";

    public ECCProvider()
    {
        super("RichECC", 1.0, INFO);
        AccessController.doPrivileged(new PrivilegedAction() {
            public Object run()
            {
                put("KeyFactory.ECC",
"com.richware.chap05.ECCKeyFactory");
                put("KeyPairGenerator.ECC",
"com.richware.chap05.ECCKeyPairGenerator");
                return null;
            }
        });
    }
}
```

Listing 5-2 associates the com.richware.chap05.ECCKeyFactory and the com.richware.chap05.ECCKeyPairGenerator. It returns these instances when the "ECC" is passed in as the type for the KeyFactory's and KeyPairGenerator's getInstance methods. The name of the service provider is "RichECC", which is passed in the super class if a lookup is done by the service provider's name. The provider interface is supplied, but it will not be called unless the entry is added to the $JRE\lib\security\java.security file.

Listing 5-3 displays the added entry.

Listing 5-3: Adding the `ECCProvider` class

```
security.provider.1=sun.security.provider.Sun
security.provider.2=com.sun.net.ssl.internal.ssl.Provider
security.provider.3=com.sun.rsajca.Provider
security.provider.4=com.sun.crypto.provider.SunJCE
security.provider.5=sun.security.jgss.SunProvider
security.provider.6=com.richware.chap05.ECCProvider
```

Listings 5-2 and 5-3 give an example of configuring a provider. The developer should be familiar with this exercise. The developer should also be familiar with the API for calling the classes and methods to generate the keys. Listing 5-4 gives an example implementation of interfacing with the `KeyFactory` and `KeyPairGenerator`.

Listing 5-4: The `ECCSimpleApp` class: The sample application

```
package com.richware.chap05;
import java.util.*;
import java.math.*;
import java.security.*;
import javax.crypto.spec.*;

/**
 * Class ECCSimpleApp
 * Description: This is a example of a
 * simple ECC
 *
 * Copyright:    Copyright (c) 2002 Wiley Publishing, Inc.
 * @author Rich Helton <rhelton@richware.com>
 * @version 1.0
 * DISCLAIMER: Please refer to the disclaimer at the beginning of this
 book.
 */
public class ECCSimpleApp
{
  /**
   * Method main
   * Description: The Main test driver
   * @param args none
   *
   */
  public static void main(String[] args)
  {
    try
    {
      System.out.println();
      System.out.println(
        "ECC letting the algorithm choose randoms***************");
      KeyPairGenerator kpg =
```

```
       KeyPairGenerator.getInstance("ECC");

  /*
   * A strong key uses 512 to 2048 bits
   * the bits must be multiples of 64
   */
  System.out.println("Provider =" + kpg.getProvider());
  kpg.initialize(512);
  KeyPair kp = kpg.generateKeyPair();

  /*
   * Read the keys
   * produced by the algorithm
   */
  System.out.println("Public Key ="
                     + kp.getPublic().getEncoded());
  System.out.println("Public Key Algorithm ="
                     + kp.getPublic().getAlgorithm());
  System.out.println("Public Key Format ="
                     + kp.getPublic().getFormat());
  System.out.println("Private Key ="
                     + kp.getPrivate().getEncoded());
  System.out.println("Private Key Algorithm ="
                     + kp.getPrivate().getAlgorithm());
  System.out.println("Private Key Format ="
                     + kp.getPrivate().getFormat());

  /*
   * Initialize the KeyFactory for DSA
   */
  KeyFactory kfactory = KeyFactory.getInstance("ECC");

  /*
   * Create the DH public key spec
   */
  ECCPublicKeySpec kspec =
    (ECCPublicKeySpec) kfactory
      .getKeySpec(kp.getPublic(), ECCPublicKeySpec.class);

  /*
   * Print out public Public Q point public values
   * to be sent to the other user
   */
  System.out.println("Public Key QY =" + kspec.getQY());
  System.out.println("Public Key QX =" + kspec.getQX());
}

/*
 * Catches
```

```
   */
  catch (java.security.NoSuchAlgorithmException ex)
    {
    ex.printStackTrace();
    }
  catch (Exception ex)
    {
    ex.printStackTrace();
    }
  }
}
```

Listing 5-4 demonstrates initializing the ECC algorithm. The ECC algorithm needs to know the key size, and optionally the random generator. Like most algorithms, if the key size is not specified, it will default to 512-bit key size. The KeyFactory, ECCPublicKeySpec, and ECCPrivateKeySpec are used to pass key-specific parameters for initiation. The private key spec will be the d parameter, and the public key specifications will require the point for Q for x and y. These values were discussed earlier in this chapter.

The public key spec is needed to return the values of point Q in order to pass these values to the other user. Most implementations save the public key values to a file or a socket to pass them to the receiving user for developing a shared key. The key spec values are also useful for initializing the keys. The key spec values are extended for the java.security.spec.KeySpec interface.

The key specs are used to pass values to the actual keys, ECCPublicKey for an implementation of the public key and ECCPrivateKey for the private key. The public key is extended from the java.security.PublicKey interface. The private key is extended from the java.security.PrivateKey interface. The public key and private key interfaces mark the classes as serializable for saving key information and are used to identify in which class the key information is kept.

Other specifications in this implementation are the ECCParameterSpec and the ECCGenParameterSpec. Both of these spec classes are extended from the java.security.spec.AlgorithmParameterSpec interface. The ECCParameterSpec is used for passing cryptographic information between the keys in the generators and factories. The ECCGenParameterSpec is specific cryptographic information for generating the key pair. The ECCGenParameterSpec in the Listing 5-4 implementation contains the prime size p.

There are many benefits to using the API and SPI interfaces supplied by Java. By looking at the key and parameter spec, the parameters and high-level details of the algorithm can be understood without going into the minor details of the mathematics.

Listing 5-5 and Listing 5-6 show the ECCKeyFactory and ECCKeyPairGenerator classes, respectively.

> **TIP:** For more of the code and references to sites, see the companion Web site to this book at
> `www.wiley.com/extras.` Here are a few links to get you started:
>
> For cyptography and ECC information visit:
>
> `www.tcs.hut.fi/~helger/crypto/link/public/elliptic/`
>
> For information on security of elliptic curve cryptosystems visit:
>
> `www.certicom.com/research/wecc3.html`

Listing 5-5: The `ECCKeyFactory` class: The factory class

```
package com.richware.chap05;
import java.security.*;
import java.security.spec.*;
import javax.crypto.interfaces.*;
import javax.crypto.spec.*;

/**
 * Class ECCKeyFactory
 * Description: The factory class for
 * building and retrieving
 * keys based on spec.
 *
 * Copyright:    Copyright (c) 2002 Wiley Publishing, Inc.
 * @author Rich Helton <rhelton@richware.com>
 * @version 1.0
 * DISCLAIMER: Please refer to the disclaimer at the beginning of this
book.
 */
public final class ECCKeyFactory extends KeyFactorySpi
 {
  /**
   * Constructor ECCKeyFactory
   */
  public ECCKeyFactory() {}

  /*
   * Method engineGeneratePublic
   * Description: Builds public key
   * from spec info
   */
  protected PublicKey engineGeneratePublic(KeySpec keyspec)
        throws InvalidKeySpecException
    {
    try
      {
      if (keyspec instanceof ECCPublicKeySpec)
        {
        ECCPublicKeySpec eccpublickeyspec =
          (ECCPublicKeySpec) keyspec;
```

```
                 return new ECCPublicKey(eccpublickeyspec.getQY(),
                                   eccpublickeyspec.getQX());
        }
        else
         {
          throw new InvalidKeySpecException(
            "Inappropriate key specification");
        }
      }
      /*
       * Catches
       */
      catch (InvalidKeyException invalidkeyexception)
        {
          throw new InvalidKeySpecException(
            "Inappropriate key specification");
        }
    }

    /*
     * Method engineGeneratePrivate
     * Description: Builds private key
     * from spec info
     */
    protected PrivateKey engineGeneratePrivate(KeySpec keyspec)
            throws InvalidKeySpecException
    {
      try
        {
          if (keyspec instanceof DHPrivateKeySpec)
            {
              ECCPrivateKeySpec eccprivatekeyspec =
                (ECCPrivateKeySpec) keyspec;
              return new ECCPrivateKey(eccprivatekeyspec.getD());
            }
          else
            {
              throw new InvalidKeySpecException(
                "Inappropriate key specification");
            }
        }
        /*
         * Catches
         */
        catch (InvalidKeyException invalidkeyexception)
          {
            throw new InvalidKeySpecException(
              "Inappropriate key specification");
          }
```

```
}

/*
 * Method engineGetKeySpec
 * Description: Gets the spec info
 * based on key type
 */
protected KeySpec engineGetKeySpec(Key key, Class class1)
        throws InvalidKeySpecException
{
  try
    {
    if (key instanceof ECCPublicKey)
      {
      Class class2 = Class
        .forName("ECCPublicKeySpec");
      if (class2.isAssignableFrom(class1))
        {
        ECCPublicKey      eccpublickey      =
          (ECCPublicKey) key;
        ECCParameterSpec eccparameterspec =
          eccpublickey.getParams();
        return new ECCPublicKeySpec(eccpublickey.getQY(),
                                     eccparameterspec.getP());
        }
      else
        {
        throw new InvalidKeySpecException(
          "Inappropriate key specification");
        }
      }
    if (key instanceof ECCPrivateKey)
      {
      Class class3 = Class
        .forName("ECCPrivateKeySpec");
      if (class3.isAssignableFrom(class1))
        {
        ECCPrivateKey     eccprivatekey     =
          (ECCPrivateKey) key;
        ECCParameterSpec eccparameterspec1 =
          eccprivatekey.getParams();
        return new ECCPrivateKeySpec(eccprivatekey.getD());
        }
      else
        {
        throw new InvalidKeySpecException(
          "Inappropriate key specification");
        }
      }
    }
```

```
      else
       {
         throw new InvalidKeySpecException(
           "Inappropriate key type");
       }
     }
   )
   /*
    * Catches
    */
   catch (ClassNotFoundException classnotfoundexception)
   {
     throw new InvalidKeySpecException(
       "Unsupported key specification: "
       + classnotfoundexception.getMessage());
   }
  }

  protected Key engineTranslateKey(Key key)
       throws InvalidKeyException
  {
    try
     {
       if (key instanceof ECCPublicKey)
       {
         if (key instanceof ECCPublicKey)
          {
           return key;
          }
         else
          {
           ECCPublicKeySpec eccpublickeyspec =
             (ECCPublicKeySpec) engineGetKeySpec(key,
ECCPublicKeySpec.class);
           return engineGeneratePublic(eccpublickeyspec);
          }
       }
       if (key instanceof ECCPrivateKey)
        {
         if (key instanceof ECCPrivateKey)
          {
           return key;
          }
         else
          {
           ECCPrivateKeySpec eccprivatekeyspec =
             (ECCPrivateKeySpec) engineGetKeySpec(key,
ECCPrivateKeySpec.class);
           return engineGeneratePrivate(eccprivatekeyspec);
          }
```

```
    }
    else
    {
      throw new InvalidKeyException("Wrong algorithm type");
    }
  }
  /*
   * Catches
   */
  catch (InvalidKeySpecException invalidkeyspecexception)
  {
    throw new InvalidKeyException("Cannot translate key");
  }
}
```

Listing 5-6: The `ECCKeyPairGenerator` class

```
package com.richware.chap05;
import java.math.BigInteger;
import java.security.*;
import java.security.spec.AlgorithmParameterSpec;
import java.security.spec.InvalidParameterSpecException;
import javax.crypto.spec.DHGenParameterSpec;

/**
 * Class ECCKeyPairGenerator
 * Description: The generator for the
 * key pair for ECC
 *
 * Copyright:    Copyright (c) 2002 Wiley Publishing, Inc.
 * @author Rich Helton <rhelton@richware.com>
 * @version 1.0
 * DISCLAIMER: Please refer to the disclaimer at the beginning of this
book.
 */
public final class ECCKeyPairGenerator
       extends KeyPairGeneratorSpi
{
  private BigInteger   a;
  private BigInteger   b;
  private BigInteger   c;
  private BigInteger   d;
  private int          e;
  private int          f;
  private SecureRandom g;

  /**
```

```
 * Constructor ECCKeyPairGenerator
 */
public ECCKeyPairGenerator()
{
  e = 1024;
}

/**
 * Method initialize
 * Description: Initialiazes the
 * key bit size and random generator
 * @param i
 * @param securerandom
 *
 */
public void initialize(int i, SecureRandom securerandom)
{
  if ((i < 512) || (i > 1024) || (i % 64 != 0))
  {
    throw new InvalidParameterException(
      "Keysize must be multiple of 64, and can only range from 512 to
1024 (inclusive)");
  }
  else
  {
    e = i;
    f = 0;
    g = securerandom;
    return;
  }
}

/**
 * Method initialize
 * Description: Initialiazes the
 * key bit size and keys based on the
 * algorithm spec
 * @param algorithmparameterspec
 * @param securerandom
 *
 * @throws InvalidAlgorithmParameterException
 *
 */
public void initialize(
        AlgorithmParameterSpec algorithmparameterspec, SecureRandom
securerandom)
          throws InvalidAlgorithmParameterException
{
  if (!(algorithmparameterspec instanceof ECCParameterSpec))
```

```
    {
      throw new InvalidAlgorithmParameterException(
        "Inappropriate parameter type");
    }
    c = ((ECCParameterSpec) algorithmparameterspec).getP();
    e = c.bitLength();
    if ((e < 512) || (e > 1024) || (e % 64 != 0))
      {
        throw new InvalidAlgorithmParameterException(
          "Prime size must be multiple of 64, and can only range from 512
  to 1024 (inclusive)");
      }
    d = ((ECCParameterSpec) algorithmparameterspec).getG();
    f = ((ECCParameterSpec) algorithmparameterspec).getL();
    g = securerandom;
    if ((f != 0) && (f >= e))
      {
        throw new InvalidAlgorithmParameterException(
          "Exponent size must be less than modulus size");
      }
    else
      {
        return;
      }
  }


  /**
   * Method generateKeyPair
   * Description: Generates the key pair
   * @return the Key pair generated
   *
   */
  public KeyPair generateKeyPair()
  {
    KeyPair keypair = null;
    if (f == 0)
      {
        f = e - 1;
      }
    if (g == null)
      {
        g = new SecureRandom();
      }
    try
      {
        if ((c == null) || (d == null))
          {
            ECCGenParameterSpec    eccgenparameterspec    =
              new ECCGenParameterSpec(e);
```

```
      ECCParameterGenerator eccparametergenerator =
        new ECCParameterGenerator();
      eccparametergenerator.engineInit(eccgenparameterspec,
                                       null);
      AlgorithmParameters algorithmparameters =
        eccparametergenerator.engineGenerateParameters();
      ECCParameterSpec    ECCParameterSpec    =
        (ECCParameterSpec) algorithmparameters
          .getParameterSpec(ECCParameterSpec.class);
      c = ECCParameterSpec.getP();
      d = ECCParameterSpec.getG();
    }
    b = new BigInteger(f, g);
    a = d.modPow(b, c);
    ECCPublicKey  eccpublickey  = new ECCPublicKey(a, c, d,
                                  f);
    ECCPrivateKey eccprivatekey = new ECCPrivateKey(b, c, d,
                                  f);
    keypair = new KeyPair(eccpublickey, eccprivatekey);
  }
  /*
   * Catches
   */
  catch (InvalidAlgorithmParameterException
invalidalgorithmparameterexception)
    {
    throw new RuntimeException(
      invalidalgorithmparameterexception.getMessage());
  }
  catch (InvalidParameterSpecException invalidparameterspecexception)
    {
    throw new RuntimeException(invalidparameterspecexception
      .getMessage());
  }
  catch (InvalidKeyException invalidkeyexception)
    {
    throw new RuntimeException(invalidkeyexception
      .getMessage());
  }
  return keypair;
  }
}
```

Summary

This chapter discussed the benefits of and how to implement the ECC algorithm as a service provider. The mathematics were introduced into this chapter as simply as possible. For a more complex understanding of the modular arithmetic, there are many advanced mathematics books. In addition, this chapter discussed how to implement a key exchange and ECC using Java's Service Provider Interface (SPI).

When I worked on ECC, I wish I had had this chapter as a reference. As presented in this chapter, the mathematics of curves and modular arithmetic for ECC require only a handful of algorithms and functions to implement a key exchange. The ECCDH only requires a handful of steps to implement. ECCDH has a lot of promise, and I am surprised that DH and RSA are shipped with JDK 1.4, but not ECC. There are a few companies that are working to provide ECC such as `www.cryptix.com`. ECC is a hard-to-break algorithm and is lightning fast, so I would think that there would be more products using ECC.

Chapter 6

Key Management Through the Internet Protocol

In This Chapter

- ♦ Learning how to secure authentication through IP
- ♦ Introducing the protocols of IPSec and SASL
- ♦ Understanding the issues with exchanging keys through the Internet

Introduction

As mentioned in Chapter 4, there are many issues with exchanging keys, such as the man-in-the-middle attack. To ensure better protection in new versions of the *Internet Protocol* (IP) Ipv4 and Ipv6, the *Internet Engineering Task Force* (IETF) developed the *IP security protocol* (IPSec). The IPSec provides security services for authentication, message integrity, reply protection, confidentiality, and secure key exchange.

> **NOTE:** The Java implementation of IPSec can be found at the Jacob project at
> `http://sourceforge.net/projects/jacob.`

Another protocol that encapsulates keys and authentication is the *Simple Authentication and Security Layer* (SASL). The SASL is not part of the IPSec but is used as an authentication protocol for applications like *Lightweight Directory Access Protocol* (LDAP).

> **NOTE:** The Java implementation of SASL using the Cryptix implementation can be found at
> `http://sourceforge.net/projects/cryptix-sasl.` Sun provides information on SASL at
> `http://java.sun.com/products/jndi/tutorial/ldap/security/sasl.html.`

The Internet Protocol Security Protocol

IPSec was created simply to secure network packets when being transported for newer versions of the Internet Protocol such as Ipv4 and Ipv6. For more IPSec information, take a look at the `www.ietf.org/rfc/rfc2409.txt` site. IPSec makes up two main protocols, and at least two supporting protocols. The two main protocols are the *Authentication Header* (AH), found at `www.ietf.org/rfc/rfc2402.txt`, and *Encapsulating Security Payload* (ESP), at `www.ietf.org/rfc/rfc2406.txt`. In addition, there are two supporting protocols to exchange keys securely: the *Internet Security Association Key Management Protocol* (ISAKMP), found at `www.ietf.org/rfc/rfc2408.txt`, and the *Internet Key Exchange* (IKE), at `www.ietf.org/rfc/rfc2409.txt`.

Both AH and ESP support authentication, message integrity, and reply protection. ESP provides extra functionality for data confidentiality to protect the data in the network packet. Shared keys are needed to provide the authentication and encryption services and the capability to transmit the keys securely. The ISAKMP defines the communication process, the security level, and how the AH and ESP use the key exchange. The ISAKMP doesn't define the key exchange algorithms like DH and RSA; that definition is the purpose of the IKE. The IKE uses the ISAKMP to provide the keys to the AH and ESP. The relationships of the IPSec protocols are illustrated in Figure 6-1.

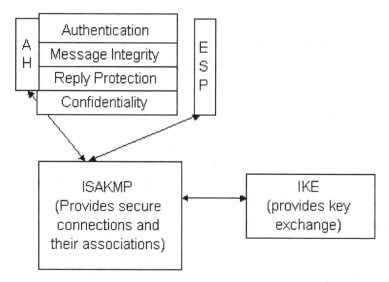

Figure 6-1: The IPSec protocol relationships

Figure 6-1 shows that the AH and ESP protocols provide some of the same functionality. Not only can they support some of the same functionality, but they also can be used in parallel. The ESP and AH headers can be used to add security in the network packet.

How the headers are defined determines some of the security features. The ESP header must be formatted before the data that it encrypts. The IPSec is a security mechanism defined for the *Internet Protocol* (IP). The ESP and AH headers are encapsulated by the IP header. The AH is merely a header and doesn't include the trailer. All the fields in the AH header are clear text.

The transport and tunnel modes

Another factor that defines the encapsulation of the headers is the operating mode of the IPSec. There are two operating modes of IPSec, the *transport mode* and the *tunnel mode*.

The *transport mode* is used to protect the next levels of encapsulation beyond IP such as the *Transmission Control Protocol* (TCP) and UDP. AH and ESP intercept the packets between the transport and network layers and provide the selected security.

The *tunnel mode* is used to protect the entire network packet. In tunnel mode, IPSec adds an IPSec header, called the *inner header*. The security device also adds an additional IPSec header — called the *outer header*. Nested tunnels, where you tunnel a tunneled packet, are also possible in IPSec. Listing 6-1 illustrates the operating modes of IPSec.

There are four possible combinations of modes: AH in transport mode, AH in tunnel mode, ESP in transport mode, ESP in tunnel mode. The AH and ESP header do not change between modes; the difference is basically whether the IP packet or the IP payload is being protected.

The AH and ESP headers are formatted differently based on the type of mode, either a tunnel mode or a transport mode. One of the biggest differences between the ESP and AH headers is that the ESP header requires an associated trailer. The data between the ESP header and the ESP trailer is the data encrypted to provide confidentiality by the ESP. The encrypted data could be an AH header that performs authentication by another host or router.

> **TIP:** The AH in tunnel mode protects the same data as the AH in transport mode and, therefore, is not used in practice.

Listing 6-1: The IPSec operation modes

```
An example of the transport mode header is
[ IP Header [ IPSec Header [ TCP Header [ Data]]]
An example of the tunnel mode header is
[ IP Header [ IPSec Header [ IP Header [ TCP Header [ Data]]]]]
```

Listing 6-1 shows examples of the network packets in the transport and tunneling mode. The tunneling mode contains extra IP headers that are added on by network devices like routers and hosts to provide the security services. For each tunnel, an extra IP header is added. A *tunnel* is a network connection between two intermediate endpoints that are embedded in two larger endpoints. An example of a tunnel is shown in Figure 6-2.

In Figure 6-2, the tunnel specified in the inner IP header would be the source address of router R1 and the destination address of R2. Tunnels are used when the originator didn't initialize the security such as in the *Virtual Private Networks* (VPNs) and as a means to provide intermediate security that is different.

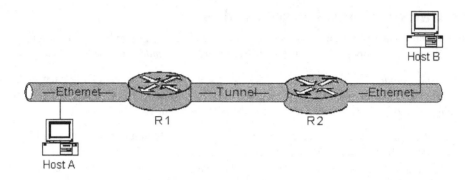

Figure 6-2: An example of a tunnel

> **TIP:** You may be wondering what the difference is between SSL and IPSec. SSL at the application layer. IPSec is a security mechanism of IP v 6.0 at the network or transport layer that your hardware must be aware of. Some applications may run on top of IPSec and not know it.

Security Associations

To establish any secure channel between two hosts or any routers, a *Security Association* (SA) must be created. There are many different types of SAs based on protocols. The IPSec SA contains the security association that uses ESP and AH protocols. The IPSec SA is the security parameters, policies, and key material between two peers. The SA is the security contract between the two peers. The SAs are maintained in a database of SA entries called the *SA Database* (SADB). A table in the SADB could be created for each protocol and each direction that the SA uses.

The ISAKMP SA initializes the IKE key exchange and is needed to provide a secure channel for doing the key exchange. The ISAKMP SA creates the IKE SA. The IKE SA creates the IPSec SA. The IKE SA is needed to pass the security parameters in a secure channel to start the IPSec SA.

The IPSec SA is unidirectional, meaning that SA only works in one direction to a host. For a multiplex or bidirectional connection traveling both directions to a host, two SA instances are needed. For an example, see Figure 6-3.

Figure 6-3 shows that two SAs are needed for the IPSec SA (SA_1 and SA_2) to establish messages in both directions to the hosts. SA associates the security services with the key, associates which network packets require security, and associates the security between the two peers. Each SA is uniquely identified by the *Security Parameter Index* (SPI); the index is in the IPSec protocol headers ESP and AH. The SPI is used to uniquely identify the SA and to determine which SA to communicate with.

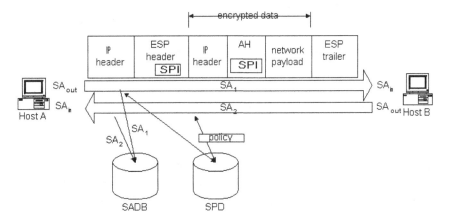

Figure 6-3: The SA example

Figure 6-3 also shows the ESP header and AH header in a tunnel mode. The IPSec network packet contains one tunnel because it contains one extra IP header. The IP header and AH header in this example are encrypted to ensure confidentiality. The inner IP header could be used between two routers in the middle of the two hosts to establish a tunnel. The outer IP header was built by the outbound host and is aware only of the source host, Host A, and the destination host, Host B.

The ISAKMP negotiates the key materials and cryptographic parameters that include the SPI for the IPSec SA. The IPSec SA contains the collection of the key materials and cryptographic material that was negotiated by the ISAKMP. The AH and ESP use the material supplied by the SA to establish authentication and a secure connection. The ISAKMP SA is used by the IKE to perform the key exchange.

Determining the security level

Before an SA is created, the IPSec must determine the level of security needed, if any. The IPSec determines the level of security and the security parameters based on the policy. The policy defines the security requirements for the IP packet. The policy is checked during the creation of an outbound packet and confirmed during the inbound packet to ensure that the security matches from host to host. The policies are stored in the *Security Policy Database* (SPD). The SA might already be created and, in that case, the SPD simply points toward the existing SA. If the SA wasn't created, a new SA must be instantiated. The IKE establishes the key exchange for the SA. The policy from the SPD determines the security of the packet.

The IKE protocol is a request-reply protocol. The request is called the *initiator* and the reply is called the *responder*. The initiator constructs an SA with the key exchanges specified by the policy. The key exchange started by the initiator must be exchanged with the responder. The IKE always uses the Diffie-Hellman (DH) key exchange. The key exchange depends on the mode specified by the policy for the IKE.

CROSS-REFERENCE: See Chapter 4 for a discussion of the Diffie-Hellman key exchange.

The two phases of the key exchange

The key exchange has two phases. *Phase 1* has two modes that can be used: the *Main* mode and *Aggressive* mode, described later in this chapter. *Phase 2* consists of one mode called the *Quick* mode for exchanging key material and parameters to other services beyond the SA key exchange.

The IKE uses the ISAKMP SA to communicate between the peers. The ISAKMP SA is bidirectional, which implements the request-reply created in phase 1. After phase 1, either peer can initiate the phase 2 Quick mode. Phase 1 establishes a secure channel between the two peers. Phase 2 extends the secure channel to negotiate more security services beyond the IKE, such as the rest of the protocols for IPSec.

The IKE uses ISAKMP to establish the SA. ISAKMP defines five different types of exchanges. Each of these exchanges has different goals, and they do not strictly belong to either phase 1 or 2 — rather, they are used for their specific goals.

- The **base exchange** minimizes the number of exchanges by allowing the key exchange and authentication information to be transmitted together. It uses four messages: the first two to provide cookies and establish an SA, the last two to exchange the key material and user identifications.

- The **identity protection exchange** expands the base exchange to protect the identity of the user. It uses four messages to establish the SA, the key exchange, and reply protection. Finally, the parties use two more messages to establish encrypted authentication to hide the identity of the peers.

- The **authentication only exchange** authenticates the peers using three messages and does not include a key exchange.

- The **aggressive exchange** minimizes the number of exchanges, but it does not povide identity protection.

- The **informational exchange** is a one-way communication that allows peers to send status and error messages. They are not acknowledged nor guaranteed to arrive.

The cookies are part of the ISAKMP header. The ISAKMP header contains the initiator cookie, the responder cookie, next payload, version, exchange type, flags, message ID, and total message length. Each cookie is unique to the remote peer and to the exchange in which it is defined. The cookies keep track of the state of the information and the ISAKMP exchange of information in progress. The cookies are exchanged in the ISAKMP header and provide some connection integrity. The first message sends a cookie to the responder from the initiator and the responder replies with a cookie. The cookies change states based on the message exchange and the current SA. For each message exchange, the protocol advances a state. After the state is advanced, the exchanges cannot rollback to the previous state.

The ISAKMP SA initializes as a connection pipe, but a policy must define and associate with both peers so that they can understand what the requirements of the ISAKMP SA are. The policy is exchanged. The policy defines the different parameters and payloads allowed in the ISAKMP SA.

The IKE defines the key exchange by executing the ISAKMP. The end result of the IKE is the IPSec SA. After the ISAKMP SA is established, the IKE starts phase 1. IKE first defines the phase 1 attributes of the SA that exchange the keys. Other security attributes, including phase 2, are defined using the *Domain of Interpretation* (DOI). For more information take a look at `www.ietf.org/rfc/rfc2407.txt`. Phase 1 must be done first to establish a secure channel to pass keys. The attributes, such as encryption and one-way hash algorithms, are referred to as a *protection suite*. The protection suite is agreed upon through the ISAKMP SA. After the ISAKMP SA has agreed on the parameters, the IKE SA must be created at the end of phase 1.

Phase 1 Two modes: Main and Aggressive

As previously mentioned, there are two modes that can be used to create the IKE SA, *Main* mode and *Aggressive* mode. The *Aggressive mode* is the fastest in execution. The *Main mode* uses all of the capabilities of the ISAKMP exchanges to ensure that the key exchange is secure and provides identity protection. Identity protection is important when the peers want to hide their identities and authentication is the key exchange algorithm. Authentication is important to avoid man-in-the-middle attacks. The Main mode uses six message exchanges. The first two messages are used to negotiate the policy for the IKE SA. The next two messages are used to exchange the DH key. The final two messages are used to authenticate the DH key exchange.

> **CROSS-REFERENCE:** See Chapter 4 for a discussion of the man-in-the-middle attack.

The Aggressive mode uses half the message exchanges that the Main mode does, which makes the key exchange faster but less secure. The first two messages are used to negotiate policy, exchange the DH keys, and authenticate the responder at the same time. The last message is used to authenticate the initiator. Because there are fewer messages being exchanged and more information in each packet, it is more prone to attacks.

The Quick mode, phase 2 only mode

After the IKE SA is generated, the next step is to generate the IPSec SAs for the ESP and AH. The IPSec SA is established through the phase 2 Quick mode exchange. The Quick mode exchange is used in the now secure IKE SA with a single key exchange. The Quick mode exchanges the security parameters and a new key set for the IPSec SA. The IKE SA protects the exchanges by encryption, authentication, and data integrity. The Quick mode is quick because it generates IPSec SAs simultaneously, and is not a complete exchange because it uses material from the IKE SA done in phase 1. After the Quick mode, the IPSec SA is ready to be used by the AH and ESP protocols.

Upon completion of a Quick mode, the previous IKE SA returns to a waiting state for further communication from the peer. The IKE SA stays active until it expires or is deleted. After the IPSec SA has been created, the AH and ESP can be used for securing the channel.

The Simple Authentication and Security Layer

The *Simple Authentication and Security Layer* (SASL) is a network protocol for exchanging keys using multiple authentication mechanisms. (For more information, reference the www.ietf.org/rfc/rfc2222.txt site.) *Lightweight Directory Access Protocol* (LDAP) servers have usually adopted SASL as the authentication mechanism, and when you access LDAP through a naming service such as Java Naming and Directory Interface (JNDI), it typically uses SASL.

Defining SASL

The SASL is a method for adding authentication support to connection-based protocols. A protocol includes a command for identifying and authenticating a user to a server and for optionally negotiating a security layer for subsequent protocol interactions. The first requirement is the argument for identifying the SASL mechanism such as "ANONYMOUS," "CRAM-MD5," "SRP," "DIGEST-MD5," "OTP," or "GSSAPI." These authentication mechanisms are passed in a field that can be no more than 20 characters long and must be registered with the Internet Assigned Numbers Authority (IANA). For more information, take a look at www.iana.org.

The client's authentication mechanism field is done in clear text and may be modified by an attacker. Any new SASL authentication mechanism must be designed with this in mind so that a weaker authentication mechanism cannot be selected instead. After an authentication mechanism is selected, it will provide the data integrity and key exchange information. The SASL defines the request-reply mechanics to the authentication mechanism. The strength of the authentication mechanism is dependent on which authentication mechanism is used.

> **TIP:** One idea to ensure that attackers cannot change clear text is to implement SASL with a secure transport protocol like SSL and TLS (discussed in Chapter 22). Initializing a secure transport layer can be done by adding commands to SASL, which is supported in the protocol.

If the server supports the SASL mechanism that is being requested, an authentication session is started; otherwise, an abort is returned. An authentication session lasts from when the client initiates the first request till when it has finished communicating with the SASL server. During an authentication session, only one full authentication can take place unless specified by the authentication mechanism's profile. Only one SASL security layer can be in effect at a given instance for authentication. So if multiple authentications are allowed simultaneously, the next authentication that is selected will replace the current security layer. If no security layer is selected, the original security layer remains in effect.

The command requires that you specify the name of the mechanism to use for authentication. An LDAP server such as the Netscape Directory Server might support the use of SASL mechanisms through server plug-ins. Many server plug-ins are extendable and can be written to support more authentication mechanisms as long as they are registered with IANA and the protocol is followed. SASL allows the same interface to support many authentication mechanisms. The authentication mechanism defines how the server will respond and accept responses.

> **NOTE:** In Java, pluggable authentication is provided by JAAS, GSS-API, and SASL. Additional support for securing communications across networks is provided by both the GSS and SASL after authentication has been completed. RFC 2222 specifies how GSS-API services can be used for SASL authentication and how they can be used to create a security layer for your application.

Server challenges and responses

A series of server challenges and responses will be executed based on the authentication mechanism. The form of the authentication messages will be in an octet binary token. The command may allow optional parameters for allowing the client to send ahead authentication information to avoid redundant challenges. The authentication mechanism will define whether optional parameters are allowed. If the server doesn't accept the optional principal and credential initially with the protocol, the server can request the authentication, and the client can send an empty response for the server to use the data previously sent.

After the server receives the commands from the client, the server may respond with an authentication challenge from the server, indicate a failure, or indicate that the authentication has completed based on the authentication mechanism.

When the client receives the authentication challenge from the server, the client may respond or abort the reply based on the authentication mechanism. The server and client can continue to issue a series of server challenges and client responses. During the challenges and responses, a "SUCCESS" is returned if the authentication is successful, and an error code such as "INVALID_CREDENTIALS" is returned if the authentication fails.

> **TIP:** The SASL is a plug-and-play protocol for communicating with authentication mechanisms. A Java implementation of a plug-and-play authentication mechanism is the Java Authentication and Authorization Service (JAAS) mentioned in Chapter 19, or IPSec mentioned in this chapter. It wouldn't be surprising that many SASL implementations are developed in JAAS.

During the authentication protocol exchange, the mechanism performs authentication and sets the principal credentials. The principal is normally set in the form of user identification. The principal and credentials could be set differently during or after authentication than the ones used during authentication to permit proxy server logins. If the authentication completes successfully, the client and server may agree on a security layer to protect the privacy of the session from that point on.

> **NOTE:** SASL mechanism registrations will be posted in the anonymous FTP

Directory at `ftp://ftp.isi.edu/in-notes/iana/assignments/sasl-mechanisms/`.

Summary

This chapter discussed the concepts of IPSec and SASL. IPSec is a set of protocols that are used to secure the Internet Protocol for VPNs, IP version 4, and IP version 6. No discussion of network security would be complete without discussing the standards that are used to protect the current version of the Internet Protocol. The IPSec has defined protocols for secure key exchanges and secure messaging through the network. IPSec also provides tunneling, which provides the capability to proxy through firewalls. I started this chapter by looking at the Simple Key Management for Internet Protocols (SKIP), which led me to the `www.skip.org`, RFC 2356, and Sun's SunScreen product.

Many references that led to the SKIP disappeared after 1996 and were replaced by ISAKMP. ISAKMP is just one of the protocols that are part of the IPSec. The IPSec covers securing the Internet Protocol and provides multiple protocols working together to make up the IPSec. The SKIP protocol is just one protocol that makes up the secure key exchange. I looked for a while for any implementation of SKIP and found several examples from other books. Most of them did not implement a CDR, header, or other components of SKIP.

The IPSec was created to be used with Ipv4 and Ipv6 and is handled by many services at the hardware and device driver level. It is also important when generating IP services that talk at the network transport level, such as applications that use Java sockets, that they can support these protocols if the security is high. There are many other protocols that can be used to some degree in place of IPSec, such as SSL, TLS, and GSS-API, but hardware devices like routers, that IPSec supports, do not support these protocols.

No discussion can happen about authentication with Java without SASL. SASL is heavily used for authenticating LDAP servers and is used with JNDI authentications. SASL is a protocol for key transfer and authentication that can use different pluggable authentication mechanisms. SASL doesn't define the implementation like JAAS, and JAAS can be used as the implementation for SASL. SASL doesn't have to be used just for JNDI or LDAP, but can be used as an authentication protocol for any client-server connection.

Chapter 7

Implementing Keys with Java

In This Chapter

♦ Understanding the key pair and symmetric key generation

♦ Generating a key

♦ Working with the `KeySpec` class

♦ Understanding the importance of `SecureRandom`

This chapter describes the process that JDK 1.4 uses to generate keys and how the security provider creates key generators. Generating keys is the fundamental process when working with other protocols, such as JSSE and GSS, for encrypting and decrypting data. In this chapter, you learn some of the fundamental principles of generating keys, such as generating a random number that will assist in key generation.

Introduction

Just to recap from other chapters, key material is any material used to generate or retrieve a public key. Before understanding SSL, JSSE, or any other protocol that uses key material, the first step in Java is to understand how Java generates and manages key material. Some keys are generated and then are used in JSSE. Other keys, such as *Password Based Encryption* (PBE), are generated from a password and *salted* with a pass phrase.

> **CROSS-REFERENCE:** For more detailed information on key algorithms, see Chapter 6.

The concept of a *salt* is to combine multiple inputs to generate a more complex key. For example, you salt a password by combining both the password and pass phrase, possibly in an XOR, to generate a more complex value to use as a key. A simple XOR algorithm (simple because it is easy to decrypt) is combining the bits to produce a different output.

> **TIP:** Recall that when combining two bits, XOR produces a one value when the bits are different, otherwise it produces a zero.

The more complex the algorithm is for generating a key, the harder it becomes to decipher the key. Once a key algorithm and key material is deciphered for an organization, keys from the organization can be replicated. The *key material* is the material outside of the key algorithm itself that is used to generate the key. In the example of a password and pass phrase, the key material was the password and pass phrase. Other examples of key material may be a username that is used to look up a certificate in a keystore to pass certificates to JAAS and JSSE.

> **CROSS-REFERENCE:** The keystore is demonstrated in Chapter 10.

Keys are needed for any type of encryption. They are combined with a cryptographic algorithm to encrypt and decrypt messages. *Cryptographic algorithms* work such that if hackers do not possess the key, they cannot decrypt or re-encrypt a secret message. Java supports two types of keys: *asymmetric* and *symmetric* keys. *Asymmetric* keys are a combination of public and private keys where one cannot work without the other. Sometimes these keys are called a *key pair* because a public key and private key can only work together.

The public key is useless without the private key, and the private key is useless without the public key. The public key works only with its particular private key, and the private key works only with its particular public key. The private key is used to encrypt the message and is kept private from users decrypting the message. The public key is used to decrypt the message and is given to all users who want to read the encrypted message. The keys are kept apart from each other because the messages cannot be compromised unless both keys are captured.

Each key is a product of the other, meaning that the private key is a logarithmic value of the public key and the public key is the inverse of the logarithmic method of the private key. *Symmetric* keys are normally called secret keys.

A *secret key* is one that is shared among everyone in a group for both encrypting and decrypting the same data message. Before a key can be used in an algorithm, it must first be generated. Java provides a framework for supporting many encryption and key generating algorithms.

Understanding DSA: The Digital Signature Algorithm

The *Digital Signature Algorithm* (DSA) was proposed to NIST and adopted as a U.S. Federal Information Processing Standard (FIPS) in early 1990s. It is described in FIPS Pub 186-1 "Digital Signature Standard," which was revised in 1998. See `http://www.itl.nist.gov/fipspubs/fip186.htm` as a reference for DSA.

> **CROSS-REFERENCE:** Chapter 11 describes the DSA algorithm in more detail and provides an implementation.

DSA takes advantage of the difficulty of computing discrete logarithms; here is a brief description of the algorithm based on the FIPS publication:

♦ p = a prime modulus, where $2^{L-1} < p < 2^{L}$ for $512 = < L = < 1024$ and L a multiple of 64

> **TIP:** This means a bit length between 512 and 1024 bits in increments of 64 bits.

♦ q = a prime divisor of p - 1, where $2^{159} < q < 2^{160}$

> **TIP:** This means a bit length of 160 bits.

♦ g = h$^{(p-1)/q}$ mod p, where h is any integer with $1 < $ h $ < p$ - 1 such that h$^{(p-1)/q}$ mod $p > 1$ (g has order q mod p)

> **TIP:** g has order q mod p means that g must be greater than 1.

♦ x = a randomly or pseudorandomly generated integer with $0 < x < q$. This parameter is the user's private key.

♦ y = g^x mod p. This paramater is the user's public key.

♦ k = a randomly or pseudorandomly generated integer with $0 < k < $ q. This parameter k must be regenerated for each signature.

The integers p, q, and g are public and can be common to a group of users. Parameters x and k are used for signature generation only and must be kept secret.

The user calculates r and s to create a signature:

♦ r = (g^k mod p) mod q

♦ s = [k^{-1}(H(M) + xr)] mod q, where H(M) is the SHA-1 hash of the message.

Verification is performed at the receiving end by testing $v = r'$, where r' is the received version of r and v is derived as follows:

♦ w = $(s')^{-1}$ mod q

♦ u1 = [H(M') w] mod q

♦ u2 = (r')w mod q

♦ v = [(g^{u1} y^{u2}) mod p] mod q

Where s', r' and M' are the received versions.

> **CAUTION:** DSA is only used for data validation, not for confidentiality.

Generating Key Pairs with Java

The symmetric key is used for both encrypting and decrypting the same data message. Unlike public and private keys, which are distributed as a pair, it is a single key. Algorithms that generate a single key are much simpler in design because they do not have to generate two keys that are dependent on each other.

> **TIP:** Using the secret key for both encrypting and decrypting is a higher risk because only one key does all of the work instead of a combination of two.

Because there are many differences between the secret key and the key pair, different classes are used in Java to generate them. The secret key is generated using the `javax.crypto.KeyGenerator` class. The secret key is returned as the `javax.crypto.SecretKey` object, which is described later. The key pair is generated with a different class, the `java.security.KeyPairGenerator`. The desired product is to get a `java.security.KeyPair` that represents both the public and private key. The `KeyPair` consists of two classes: `PublicKey` and `PrivateKey`.

> **NOTE:** All references to Java classes will be made using the JDK 1.4. This does not imply that the first definition of the class was defined in the JDK 1.4, but that it is currently used in the JDK 1.4.

The `PublicKey` class represents the public key interface, and the `PrivateKey` class represents the private key interface. The following list describes some of the methods of the `KeyPairGenerator`:

♦ Methods to create an instance of the `KeyPairGenerator`. Passing in the algorithm name is always mandatory, but to be more specific on the returned factory, the provider's name may also be passed in as a parameter. The provider is the organization that provides the algorithm and generation of the factory. For instance, one algorithm that ships with the JDK 1.4 is the *Digital Signature Algorithm* (DSA), which Sun provides. The methods for the `KeyPairGenerator` are as follows:

- `static public KeyPairGenerator getInstance( String algorithm, Provider provider)`
- `static public KeyPairGenerator getInstance( String algorithm, String provider)`

♦ Methods to initialize the algorithm. The method parameters may include the `SecureRandom` algorithm, which generates the random start of the keying algorithm; the key size, which describes the size of the key; or the `AlgorithmParameterSpec`, which defines values to initialize the cryptographic algorithm based on the values needed for the algorithm. For instance, as discussed at the beginning of the chapter, DSA uses p, q, and g values to generate the public and private key. The p, q, and g values are the values that are DSA-specific used by the algorithm to generate keys. The methods to intialize the parameters are as follows:

- `public void initialize (AlgorithmParameterSpec params)`
- `public void initialize (AlgorithmParameterSpec params, SecureRandom random)`
- `public void initialize (int keysize)`
- `public void initialize (int keysize, SecureRandom)`

♦ Methods to actually return the `KeyPair` class that contains both a private and public key. The keys that they generate are based on the algorithm that is specified for the `KeyPairGenerator` class:

- `public KeyPair generateKeyPair ( )`
- `public KeyPair genKeyPair ( )`

The `KeyPairGenerator` class does a `getInstance(  )` class to retrieve the instance of the `KeyPairGenerator` based on the algorithm passed in as a parameter. The service provider based on the algorithm creates the `KeyPairGenerator` class internally.

Implementation

Figure 7-1 demonstrates that the implementation that will be created depends on the algorithm. The implementation will be based on an association of the classes that are defined in the Java security file. A list of security providers is defined so that the lookup will match the algorithm to the class. The class that will be matched will be either a *Service Provider Interface* (SPI) class, an implementation of `KeyPairGeneratorSpi` that implements the underlying methods of the `KeyPairGenerator`, or a complete overwrite of the `KeyPairGenerator` class.

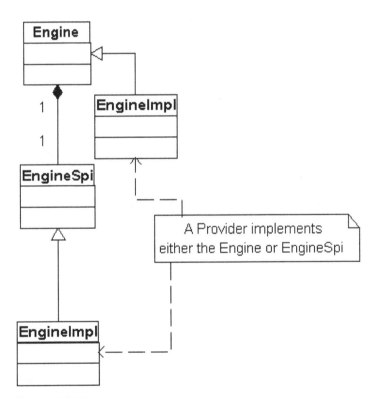

Figure 7-1: The engine class

Because a service provider like Sun implements the `KeyPairGenerator` class, it is called an *engine class*. An engine class is not created directly, but through lookup to a service provider that will create an engine for generating keys.

In the `EngineSpi` class, in this case the `KeyPairGeneratorSpi` class, a service provider will not directly overwrite the engine class, but rather the methods that the engine class will execute. For example, the code in Listing 7-1 demonstrates the `KeyPairGenerator` initialization for the DSA algorithm.

Listing 7-1: KeyPairGenerator creation

```
KeyPairGenerator keyGen = KeyPairGenerator.getInstance("DSA");
```

The `keyGen` object in this example is actually the implementation of the `DSAKeyPairGenerator` class without having to implement the algorithm or even understand it. The provider might do its implementation by overwriting the `KeyPairGenerator` class by implementing a new `KeyPairGeneratorSpi` that implements the internals of the `KeyPairGenerator` class. In Listing 7-1, the provider chose to overwrite the `KeyPairGenerator` class with the `DSAKeyPairGenerator` class. The purpose of the `KeyPairGenerator` is to find a matching interface to support the key algorithm.

To initialize a `KeyPairGenerator` class, or even the `KeyGenerator`, use the `getInstance()` method to pass in the algorithm type. Although the service provider hides much of the implementation, the algorithm must initialize the algorithm specifications and parameters into the engine class. The initialization specification for the cryptographic algorithm is passed in the class that is derived from the `AlgorithmParameterSpec` class.

The `AlgorithmParameterSpec` is a marker interface that contains no method or constants. *Marker interfaces* are used to mark the expectations that must be satisfied for the class implementation. The expectation in the `AlgorithmParameterSpec` class is that some parameters should be passed into the algorithm for type safety to initialize the algorithm. The `AlgorithmParameterSpec` class should be extended to define any variables that are used to calculate the algorithm.

By defining the variables in the `AlgorithmParameterSpec` class, type safety is enforced by centralizing the variable definitions to be used by other classes. The `AlgorithmParameterSpec` class can be used to reference the algorithm to any key generator.

An example of this interface is the `DSAParameterSpec` class, which is used to implement the Digital Signature Algorithm (DSA). As we discussed earlier, DSA requires three non-random parameters that are used in its calculation. These variables are p, q, and g. It follows that the `DSAParameterSpec` has the methods to get these variables in `getP( )`, `getQ( )`, and `getG( )`. Other variables that are required from the DSA algorithm are x, the private key, and y, the public key, which are generated from the p, q, g parameters and the `SecureRandom` class. The `DSAKeyPairGenerator` class generates the private and public key pair. Listing 7-2 shows an example of how to obtain a `KeyPair` and initialize the `SecureRandom` class.

Listing 7-2: Key pair generation

```
KeyPairGenerator keyGen = KeyPairGenerator.getInstance("DSA");
SecureRandom random = SecureRandom.getInstance("SHA1PRNG", "SUN");
random.setSeed(101L);
keyGen.initialize(1024, random);
KeyPair keypair = keyGen.generateKeyPair();
```

Searching for the service provider

As mentioned earlier, the first step in creating a `KeyPairGenerator` is to retrieve an instance of the engine class. The `keyGen` object is actually an instance of the `DSAKeyPairGenerator` class. The methods for `initialize()` and `generateKeyPair()` are implemented from the `DSAKeyPairGenerator` class. The `java.security.Security` class finds the `DSAKeyPairGenerator` class from the service providers listed in the `java.security` file. If the provider is not passed to the `KeyPairGenerator` class, the `KeyPairGenerator` searches through the entire service provider list until the algorithm is found. The list of service providers is found in the `java.security` file that is stored in the `$JRE/lib/security` directory. An entry for the Sun service provider in the `java.security` file appears as shown in Listing 7-3.

Listing 7-3: An entry for Sun

```
security.provider.1=sun.security.provider.Sun
```

The `security` class loads up the implementation of a provider class `Sun.class` in the package `sun.security.provider`. The Sun provider class is basically a set of `put()` methods that list the implementations for the specific class, `KeyPairGenerator` or `KeyPairGeneratorSpi`. Because the Sun service provider supports DSA, the method in Listing 7-4 has to implement the `sun.security.provider.Sun` class.

Listing 7-4: Associating the DSA algorithm to a class

```
put("KeyPairGenerator.DSA",
"sun.security.provider.DSAKeyPairGenerator");
```

Listing 7-4 shows that the when passing DSA in the `KeyPairGenerator` initialization, it will initiate and replace the `KeyPairGenerator` class with the `sun.security.provider.DSAKeyPairGenerator` class. To reference a different implementation for the DSA algorithm, the `put` method would have to be rewritten to reference a different class. Because the Sun provider is the first entry in the `java.security` file and has a DSA algorithm implementation, the `KeyPairGenerator` uses the Sun implementation.

If the `KeyPairGenerator` cannot find a `KeyPairGenerator` implementation, it looks for the `KeyPairGeneratorSpi` implementation. If the `KeyPairGenerator` can find neither implementation in the first entry for the service provider, it looks in the next entry for the service provider. The `KeyPairGenerator` continues the lookup process until it finds the implementation of DSA or runs out of service provider entries to search. If the KeyPairGenerator has exhausted the list of service providers and hasn't found a lookup for the DSA algorithm, a NoSuchAlgortihmException exception is thrown.

As mentioned earlier, the service provider's name can be passed to the getInstance( ) method. In the example given in the previous paragraph, passing in the "Sun" parameter would have just searched the Sun provider entry, which is given in Listing 7-3, to look up only in the Sun.class.

When searching through the service provider list, each provider entry is defined as a java.security.Provider object. The KeyPairGenerator class calls the java.security.Security class to search through the provider list. The description of the service provider is necessary not just to understand how to build them, but to understand how to lookup a key algorithm. Many things can go wrong when loading a service provider, and an understanding is needed on how the lookup process works to ensure that any lookup errors can be avoided. See Figure 7-2 for a diagram of the KeyPairGenerator sequence.

> **CAUTION:** Always check to make sure the service provider engines are in the classpath. Most of the engines are part of the rt.jar file, but others such as the SunJCE need to be explicitly set in the classpath from the sunjce_provider.jar.

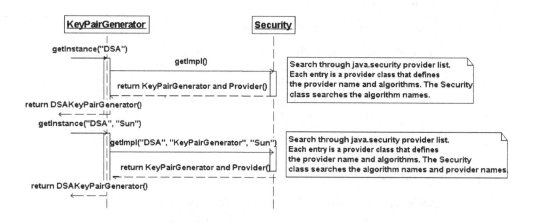

Figure 7-2: The KeyPairGenerator sequence diagram

Initializing the key with key material

After the KeyPairGenerator engine class is returned for the DSA algorithm, the keys require key material that is a random number to prime the keys. See Listing 7-2 for an example for the DSA algorithm. The key material primes the keys using the keyGen.initialize(1024, random); code statement in Listing 7-2. The key priming is accomplished with the `initialize( )` method for the `KeyPairGenerator` class. All key algorithms for the key pair require the `keysize`, `SecureRandom` class, or the `AlgorithmParameterSpec` class.

Initializing the key with a random number

Initializing the key with key material is very similar to salting a key. The purpose of the key material is to initialize a key with information that cannot be duplicated. The algorithms for keys, like DSA, are publicly available. The algorithms were built to avoid duplicating a key as much as possible; however, if the same parameters were passed for key material, the same algorithm will produce the same set of keys. By introducing an element of randomness that a hacker is unlikely to duplicate, unique key material can be introduced. If the hacker cannot produce the exact key material as the input to a key algorithm, he cannot produce the same set of keys. Understanding randomness is important to producing keys that cannot be duplicated. See `http://www.ietf.org/rfc/rfc1750.txt` as a reference for Randomness Recommendations for Security.

The more random an algorithm can be to generate random keys, the less likely the key material can be guessed. Many random generators contain some kind of pattern. To summarize a common concept in statistics, all properties being equal, when a coin is tossed in the air, it has a 50-50 chance of landing on heads or tails. If you throw the coin in the air an infinite number of times, it should fall on heads 50% of the time and tails 50% of the time.

Real-life variations

Hackers will try to guess at passwords that are based on the user's personal information or life experiences. As more administrators became aware of the hackers' techniques, administrators and secure protocols have required random numbers to be used with generating keys so that hackers cannot guess at a user's life experiences.

As protocols began to use random number generators from the operating system, numbers that are based on the milliseconds of a clock tick, or the number of hops to an Internet connection, the random generators from the operating systems began to show patterns. In order to counteract the patterns, most random generators require a *seed* to initialize the generator to avoid the pattern.

The importance of the seed

This seed is very important to generating the key. The seed to generate the random algorithm to avoid the pattern in the random number is very important, because the random number that is generated is used to avoid the pattern in the key. If there is a pattern in the seed, this pattern will propagate itself into the key. It can be very difficult to expose a pattern in the seed so, at most, thousands of numbers are generated and, if there is no pattern to be found, it is called *pseudo random*. Most out-of-the-box random number generators are considered *Pseudo-Random Number Generators* (PRNG).

> **NOTE:** The PRNG is considered a viable random number generator for most secure algorithms because if a pattern doesn't exist in thousands of numbers, it is computationally infeasible for a hacker to guess at the random seed.

To enhance the security of seeding, the `java.security.SecureRandom` class was distributed in Java to alter the seeding technique. The difference between the `SecureRandom` class and most other random number generators is that the `setSeed( )` method reseeds the algorithm. The *reseeding* process does not initialize the random generator with the seed, but rather adds the new seed to any existing seed. By adding the seed to the algorithm instead of initializing the algorithm with the seed, the seed in the algorithm becomes a new seed.

> **TIP:** Many programs use the same seed from the clock or some other input device, because using a static constant as a seed would invalidate the purpose of the seed. It is usually a system device because the input device should be automated to avoid human intervention every time a key needs to be generated. However, system devices were never built to seed random generators.

The `SecureRandom` class adds an algorithm to the seed initialization to avoid patterns. See Listing 7-5 to see what setting the seed twice to `101L` accomplishes; most other random generators would return `101L` as the seed.

Listing 7-5: The `RichSeed` class: Setting the seed twice

```
package com.richware.chap07;
import java.security.*;
import java.io.*;

/**
 * Class RichSeed
 * Description: A custom demonstration of
 * SecureRandom.
 *
 * Copyright:    Copyright (c) 2002 Wiley Publishing, Inc.
 * @author Rich Helton <rhelton@richware.com>
 * @version 1.0
 * DISCLAIMER: Please refer to the disclaimer at the beginning of this
book.
 */
public class RichSeed {
  /**
   * Method main
   * Description: The main driver to run the methods.
   * @param args (no arguments presently).
   *
   */
  public static void main(String args[]) {
    try {
      System.out.println("Seeding...This may take a minute...");
```

```
      SecureRandom ran = SecureRandom.getInstance("SHA1PRNG",
                                                  "SUN");

      ran.setSeed(101L);
      ran.setSeed(101L);
      byte[] seeds = ran.getSeed(24);
      for (int i = 0; i < seeds.length; i++) {
        System.out.println("Seed["+ i + "]:" + seeds[i]);
      }

      /*
       * Create the Serialized object
       */
    } catch (Exception e) {
      e.printStackTrace();
    }
  }
}
```

The output from the program in Listing 7-5 is shown in Listing 7-6.

Listing 7-6: Output from Listing 7-5

```
>java com.richware.chap07.RichSeed
Seed[ 0]:-22
Seed[ 1]:-79
Seed[ 2]:124
Seed[ 3]:-9
Seed[ 4]:106
Seed[ 5]:7
Seed[ 6]:-7
Seed[ 7]:4
Seed[ 8]:99
Seed[ 9]:-86
Seed[ 10]:86
Seed[ 11]:78
Seed[ 12]:102
Seed[ 13]:84
Seed[ 14]:-70
Seed[ 15]:21
Seed[ 16]:-52
Seed[ 17]:73
Seed[ 18]:-11
Seed[ 19]:49
Seed[ 20]:-90
Seed[ 21]:87
Seed[ 22]:-9
Seed[ 23]:18
```

The `SecureRandom` class is also an engine class similar to the lookup process in the `KeyPairGenerator` class. Just as the `KeyPairGenerator` class takes the input of the algorithm and provider in the `getInstance( )` method, so does the `getInstance( )` method of the `SecureRandom` class. When an algorithm name is passed in such as `SecureRandom random = SecureRandom.getInstance("SHA1PRNG");`, it implies that there is an underlying service provider providing the implementation algorithm that supports the SHA-1 message digest for PRNG.

Message digests are commonly used to generate random numbers. The SHA-1 uses 160 bits to increment a 64-bit counter every time the engine is called and return a random seed of 64 bits. The implementation is specified to "Appendix G.7 of IEEE standard 1363." To get the exact algorithm that is distributed from the Sun service provider, the code is now `SecureRandom random = SecureRandom.getInstance("SHA1PRNG","SUN");`. For the `SecureRandom` class, the `java.security` also gathers information from a defined random device that will establish greater entropy. Greater entropy represents a higher probability of chaos, which corresponds to more randomness. See Listing 7-7 for a definition of the random device for greater entropy.

Listing 7-7: Selecting the entropy source for the `SecureRandom` seed

```
#
# Select the source of seed data for SecureRandom. By default an
# attempt is made to use the entropy gathering device specified by
# the securerandom.source property. If an exception occurs when
# accessing the URL then the traditional system/thread activity
# algorithm is used.
#
securerandom.source=file:/dev/random
#
# The entropy gathering device is described as a URL and can
# also be specified with the property "java.security.egd". For example,
#   -Djava.security.egd=file:/dev/urandom
# Specifying this property will override the securerandom.source
setting.
```

There are many methods in the `SecureRandom` class for seed support. Some of the extended methods not found in most random generators are as follows:

- `public byte[] generateSeed ( int numbytes)`: This method generates a seeded byte array based on the size passed in as the parameter. The seed algorithm is the one that `SecureRandom` generates internally.

- `public void setSeed ( long seed)`: This method uses the eight bytes of the long type to reseed the current seed.

- `public void setSeed( byte [ ] seed)`: This method uses the incoming byte array to reseed the seed.

♦ `public void nextBytes ( byte [ ] bytes)`: This method returns the user-specified number of bytes that are passed in as a parameter. The array of bytes is filled with the random numbers.

♦ `public final int next( int numBits )`: This method generates the next reseed based on the input integer to define the number of bits to to be generated. The return is the number of bits that were generated.

Another example to show how more seed methods can be used to make the seed even more difficult to discern is shown in the sequence diagram in Figure 7-3. This implementation is for getting the instance, setting the seed, and getting the next set of random bytes.

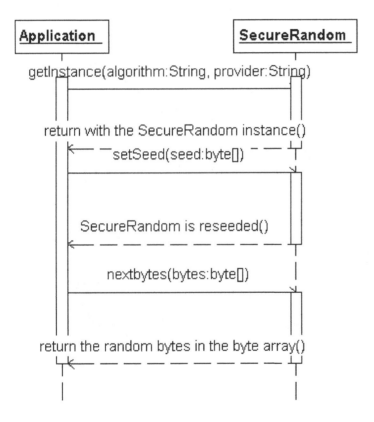

Figure 7-3: SecureRandom operation

To recap, the `SecureRandom` class has algorithms for changing the seed to generate the random number. By using the reseeding algorithm, the seeds that are used to initialize the random number generator are constantly changing. Random number generators are used to initialize the values for keys creation in the `KeyPairGenerator`. By seeding the random number generator with fewer patterns in the algorithm, it is less likely that a key can be guessed from the initialization parameters.

Initializing the key with key specifics

Keys are transferred and stored in various forms. Keys can be stored on hardware devices with the only association to the key being the key material. Some keys need to be identified from their key material. Different key algorithms use different key material, so the key material needs to be stored in a specific way. Storing the algorithm key to match the key algorithm specification is done in the `java.security.spec.KeySpec` interface.

Any key algorithms that are defined need to be extended and supported from the Java distribution and need to extend the `KeySpec` interface for use. The key material in the `KeySpec` is the variables in the algorithm that are used to create a specific key. For example, to build a public key using the DSA algorithm, the key-specific variables that are defined in the `java.security.spec.DSAPublicKeySpec` class have to be specified.

The variables y, p, q, and g are used to re-create the public key using the `DSAPublicKeySpec`. Listing 7-8 demonstrates generating a key, saving only the `DSAPublicKeySpec` to a `publicKeys` file, and then re-creating the same key from the `DSAPublicKeySpec`. The output of the example that demonstrates the re-creation of the public key is shown in Listing 7-9.

> **CROSS-REFERENCE:** I discussed the DSA algorithm earlier in this chapter. You can also reference Chapter 6 for the purpose of the variables y,p,q, and g for the DSA algorithm and Chapter 11 for a DSA implementation.

Listing 7-8: The `RichDSAKey` class: Writing and reading a `DSAPublicKeySpec`

```
package com.richware.chap07;
import java.security.*;
import java.security.spec.*;
import java.io.*;
import java.math.BigInteger;

/**
 * Class RichDSAKey
 * Description: A custom demonstration of
 * creating, writing, reading and
 * re-creating a DSA public key.
 *
 * Copyright:    Copyright (c) 2002 Wiley Publishing, Inc.
 * @author Rich Helton <rhelton@richware.com>
 * @version 1.0
```

```
 * DISCLAIMER: Please refer to the disclaimer at the beginning of this
book.
 */
public class RichDSAKey {

  /**
   * Method main
   * Description: The main driver to run the methods.
   * @param args (no arguments presently).
   *
   */
  public static void main(String args[]) {

    try {

      /*
       * Generate the key Pair
       */
      KeyPairGenerator keyGen =
        KeyPairGenerator.getInstance("DSA");
      SecureRandom       random =
        SecureRandom.getInstance("SHA1PRNG", "SUN");
      random.setSeed(101L);
      keyGen.initialize(1024, random);
      KeyPair keypair = keyGen.generateKeyPair();

      /*
       * Initialize the KeyFactory for DSA
       */
      KeyFactory kfactory = KeyFactory.getInstance("DSA");

      /*
       * Create the DSA public key spec
       */
      DSAPublicKeySpec kspec =
        (DSAPublicKeySpec) kfactory
          .getKeySpec(keypair
            .getPublic(), DSAPublicKeySpec.class);

      /*
       * Create the output stream
       */
      System.out.println("********Saving PublicKey*******");
      System.out.println(keypair.getPublic());
      FileOutputStream   fos =
        new FileOutputStream("publicKeys");
      ObjectOutputStream oos = new ObjectOutputStream(fos);

      /*
```

```
        * Write the Y,P, Q and G variables
        */
       oos.writeObject(kspec.getY());
       oos.writeObject(kspec.getP());
       oos.writeObject(kspec.getQ());
       oos.writeObject(kspec.getG());

       /*
        * Create the input stream
        */
       FileInputStream   fin =
         new FileInputStream("publicKeys");
       ObjectInputStream ois = new ObjectInputStream(fin);

       /*
        * Read the Y,P, Q and G variables
        */
       BigInteger Y = (BigInteger) ois.readObject();
       BigInteger P = (BigInteger) ois.readObject();
       BigInteger Q = (BigInteger) ois.readObject();
       BigInteger G = (BigInteger) ois.readObject();

       /*
        * Create the public key again
        */
       DSAPublicKeySpec keyspec = new DSAPublicKeySpec(Y, P, Q,
                                      G);
       PublicKey        pkey    =
         kfactory.generatePublic(keyspec);
       System.out.println("********PublicKey rebuilt*******");
       System.out.println(pkey);

       /*
        * Catches
        */
    } catch (Exception e) {
       e.printStackTrace();
    }
  }
}
```

Listing 7-9: Output for Listing 7-8

```
>java com.richware.chap07.RichDSAKey
********Saving PublicKey*******
Sun DSA Public Key
    Parameters:
    p:
```

     fd7f5381 1d751229 52df4a9c 2eece4e7 f611b752 3cef4400 c31e3f80
b6512669
     455d4022 51fb593d 8d58fabf c5f5ba30 f6cb9b55 6cd7813b 801d346f
f26660b7
     6b9950a5 a49f9fe8 047b1022 c24fbba9 d7feb7c6 1bf83b57 e7c6a8a6
150f04fb
     83f6d3c5 1ec30235 54135a16 9132f675 f3ae2b61 d72aeff2 2203199d
d14801c7
     q:
     9760508f 15230bcc b292b982 a2eb840b f0581cf5
     g:
     f7e1a085 d69b3dde cbbcab5c 36b857b9 7994afbb fa3aea82 f9574c0b
3d078267
     5159578e bad4594f e6710710 8180b449 167123e8 4c281613 b7cf0932
8cc8a6e1
     3c167a8b 547c8d28 e0a3ae1e 2bb3a675 916ea37f 0bfa2135 62f1fb62
7a01243b
     cca4f1be a8519089 a883dfe1 5ae59f06 928b665e 807b5525 64014c3b
fecf492a

  y:
     ab67aa43 9e8ea5c8 904b1afe 89ae185a 4ef595cf ca9b9114 f05373dc
193cddd3
     baefb0f8 8bd858ea d78632c2 6481c9e0 a4f56878 8f4b0f10 d505ee57
4b1c7d5d
     1196ddf0 1003578f 16272cb6 94f92796 57efd826 50287f9d b6f7e512
75fa4316
     5961aef6 ba663ab8 81c57606 554e4fb6 830b9a7b ce32d5a3 a708d09b
3b6aa8ff

********PublicKey rebuilt*******
Sun DSA Public Key
     Parameters:
     p:
     fd7f5381 1d751229 52df4a9c 2eece4e7 f611b752 3cef4400 c31e3f80
b6512669
     455d4022 51fb593d 8d58fabf c5f5ba30 f6cb9b55 6cd7813b 801d346f
f26660b7
     6b9950a5 a49f9fe8 047b1022 c24fbba9 d7feb7c6 1bf83b57 e7c6a8a6
150f04fb
     83f6d3c5 1ec30235 54135a16 9132f675 f3ae2b61 d72aeff2 2203199d
d14801c7
     q:
     9760508f 15230bcc b292b982 a2eb840b f0581cf5
     g:
     f7e1a085 d69b3dde cbbcab5c 36b857b9 7994afbb fa3aea82 f9574c0b
3d078267
     5159578e bad4594f e6710710 8180b449 167123e8 4c281613 b7cf0932
8cc8a6e1

```
    3c167a8b  547c8d28  e0a3ae1e  2bb3a675  916ea37f  0bfa2135  62f1fb62
7a01243b
    cca4f1be  a8519089  a883dfe1  5ae59f06  928b665e  807b5525  64014c3b
fecf492a

 y:
    ab67aa43  9e8ea5c8  904b1afe  89ae185a  4ef595cf  ca9b9114  f05373dc
193cddd3
    baefb0f8  8bd858ea  d78632c2  6481c9e0  a4f56878  8f4b0f10  d505ee57
4b1c7d5d
    1196ddf0  1003578f  16272cb6  94f92796  57efd826  50287f9d  b6f7e512
75fa4316
    5961aef6  ba663ab8  81c57606  554e4fb6  830b9a7b  ce32d5a3  a708d09b
3b6aa8ff
```

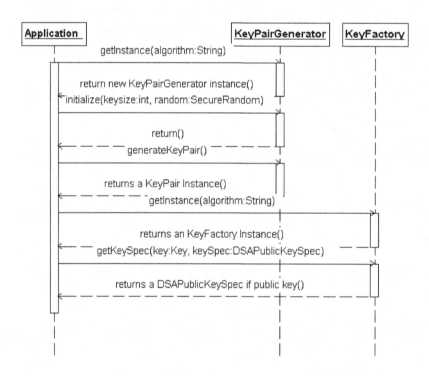

Figure 7-4: DSAPublicKeySpec

Listing 7-8 uses a `KeyFactory` interface to create and re-create the `KeySpec`. The `KeyFactory` class is another implementation of an engine class. The `KeyFactory` interface is an engine class just like the `KeyPairGenerator` class. The service providers and service provider lookup works in the same manner as the `KeyPairGenerator`. The only difference is that the `KeyFactory` name is passed in the security class lookup instead of the `KeyPairGenerator` name. The `KeyFactory` is overwritten for the DSA algorithm and returns a `sun.security.provider.DSAKeyFactory` implementation of the `KeyFactory` class. The `DSAKeyFactory` class generates the key algorithm specifics in the form of the `java.security.spec.DSAPublicKeySpec` class for the DSA public key and the `java.security.spec.DSAPrivateKeySpec` for the DSA private key. Generating the `DSAPublicKeySpec` from a `KeyFactory` is demonstrated in the sequence diagram in Figure 7-4.

Generating the Secret Key with Java

The secret key is a single key that is used for both encryption and decryption. The Java APIs in the Java Development Kit are very similar, so an understanding of the key pair API in this chapter is necessary. There are many similarities to generating the key pairs. Some of the differences are dependent on the secret key algorithms and the fact that there is only one key being generated instead of two keys in a key pair.

The `javax.crypto.KeyGenerator` class is used instead of `java.security.KeyPairGenerator` class to generate the secret key. Notice that the `KeyGenerator` comes from a different package, `javax.crypto`. The `KeyGenerator` comes from a different package because it uses a different service provider, the `SunJCE` service provider. The `SunJCE` service provider was originally a separate distribution in earlier Java Development Kits as the Java Cryptography Extensions (JCE) distribution. The `KeyGenerator` is an engine class just like the `KeyPairGenerator` and looks up the service provider and resolves the service provider from the `java.security` entry shown in Listing 7-10.

Listing 7-10: The SunJCE entry

```
security.provider.4=com.sun.crypto.provider.SunJCE
```

The service provider lookup follows the `com.sun.crypto.provider.SunJCE` class, which supports a `java.security.Provider` class and loads up the secret key algorithms. The example displayed in this section is the Data Encryption Standard (DES) secret key algorithm. The `KeyGenerator` service provider lookup resolves to the DES algorithm in the `SunJCE` provider. The `SunJCE` must have executed the `put` method defined in Listing 7-11 in order for the lookup to succeed.

Listing 7-11: The SunJCE put entry for DES

```
put("KeyGenerator.DES", "com.sun.crypto.provider.DESKeyGenerator");
```

After the `KeyGenerator` is overwritten with the `DESKeyGenerator` during the DES algorithm lookup, the key generator is initialized with a `SecureRandom` generated random number just as in the `KeyPairGenerator`. After the random number is initialized into the key generator, the `javax.crypto.SecretKey` object is generated from the key generator. The example shown in Listing 7-12 demonstrates generating a DES secret key, using the `KeySpec` to save it to the `secretKeys` file, and then reading it again into a `KeySpec`. The same key is re-created just from the saved `KeySpec` information. The DES secret key uses raw bytes as the key material, which is why the `KeySpec`'s key material is returned as a byte array. The output of the DES key demonstration showing that the keys are in fact equal is shown in Listing 7-13.

Listing 7-12: The `RichDESKey` class: A demonstration of the DES secret key

```
package com.richware.chap07;

/*
 * Different imports than RichDSAKey
 */
import javax.crypto.*;
import javax.crypto.spec.*;
import java.security.*;
import java.io.*;

/**
 * Class RichDESKey
 * Description: A custom demonstration of
 * creating, writing, reading and
 * re-creating a DES public key.
 *
 * Copyright:    Copyright (c) 2002 Wiley Publishing, Inc.
 * @author Rich Helton <rhelton@richware.com>
 * @version 1.0  01-FEB-2002
 * DISCLAIMER: Please refer to the disclaimer at the beginning of this
book.
 */
public class RichDESKey {

  /**
   * Method main
   * Description: The main driver to run the methods.
   * @param args (no arguments presently).
   *
   */
  public static void main(String args[]) {

    try {
```

```
/*
 * Generate the Secret key
 */
KeyGenerator keyGen = KeyGenerator.getInstance("DES");
SecureRandom random =
  SecureRandom.getInstance("SHA1PRNG", "SUN");
random.setSeed(101L);
keyGen.init(56, random);
SecretKey sKey = keyGen.generateKey();

/*
 * Initialize the KeyFactory for DSA
 */
SecretKeyFactory kfactory =
  SecretKeyFactory.getInstance("DES");

/*
 * Create the DSA public key spec
 */
DESKeySpec kspec = (DESKeySpec) kfactory.getKeySpec(sKey,
                      DESKeySpec.class);

/*
 * Create the output stream
 */
System.out.println("********Saving Secret Key*******");
System.out.println(sKey);
FileOutputStream    fos =
  new FileOutputStream("secretKeys");
ObjectOutputStream oos = new ObjectOutputStream(fos);

/*
 * Write the Key
 */
oos.writeObject(kspec.getKey());

/*
 * Create the input stream
 */
FileInputStream    fin =
  new FileInputStream("secretKeys");
ObjectInputStream ois = new ObjectInputStream(fin);

/*
 * Read the key variables
 */
byte[] kMaterial = (byte[]) ois.readObject();
```

```
    /*
     * Create the public key again
     */
    DESKeySpec keyspec = new DESKeySpec(kMaterial);
    SecretKey newKey = kfactory.generateSecret(keyspec);
    System.out.println("********SecretKey rebuilt*******");
    System.out.println(newKey);
    System.out.println("Do the keys equal :"
                        + newKey.equals(sKey));


    /*
     * Catches
     */
    } catch (Exception e) {
    e.printStackTrace();
    }

  }
}
```

Listing 7-13: Demonstration of the DES secret key: An output of Listing 7-12

```
>java com.richware.chap07.RichDESKey
********Saving Secret Key*******
com.sun.crypto.provider.DESKey@fffe792d
********SecretKey rebuilt*******
com.sun.crypto.provider.DESKey@fffe792d
Do the keys equal :true
```

One of the changes in Listing 7-12 is that the key factory for handling secret key specifications is the `javax.crypto.SecretKeyFactory` class. The secret key is developed in a manner similar to development of the key pairs. The difference is that there is a different Java API for handling secret keys, a different provider, different algorithms, and the secret key is a single key instead of a key pair. The similarities are that the classes are engine classes, there is service provider lookup to a provider of the algorithm using many of the same classes, and the `KeySpec` is used in a similar manner. The sequence diagram for generating the DES secret key is shown in Figure 7-5, which shows that the flow is similar.

> **NOTE:** There are many more keys interfaces and algorithms. Some of the keys that come standard with the JDK 1.4 that were not mentioned include the Diffie-Hellman (DH) key pair and the Rivest, Shamir, and Adleman (RSA) key pairs. Other secret keys that are included in the JDK 1.4 are the *Password Based Encryption* (PBE) and the Data Encryption Standard Encode-Decode-Encode (DES-EDE), commonly known as "Triple DES." These keys are fully supported by distributed service providers, key specifications, and all that is needed for key generation. Chapter 6 goes into detail of how these keys are different algorithmically.

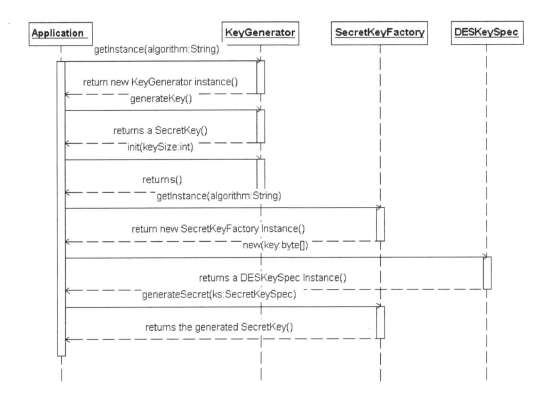

Figure 7-5: The UML of generating a DES secret key

Summary

This chapter discussed how Java implements key generation from the key generator engine classes. Several key sets for both key pairs and secret keys are supported by the out-of-the-box providers. The key generators have engine classes that perform the lookup for service providers. Keys have specific key parameters that can be saved to a stream and retrieved for later use.

An understanding is needed on how to look up the service provider to avoid any issues during the lookup, such as an incorrect classpath. The keys that are generated are the secret key and key pair. The key pair is used when two keys are required to encrypt and decrypt messages where the private key is always kept protected. The secret key is used for both encryption and decryption. With the secret key, the distribution is believed to be secure, meaning that the people and systems that get the key can be trusted.

Chapter 8

Java Implementation of Key Management

In This Chapter

♦ Understanding key stores

♦ Determining the difference between key stores and trust stores

♦ Learning how to build a key store

♦ Working with policy and key tools

♦ Working with engine classes

This chapter explores key stores, trust stores, trust managers, policy tools, and files. The SPI layer provides great flexibility for key management and the different tools provided by the JDK 1.4 provide a clear and interactive way to set properties.

Introduction

Key management deals with the generation and distribution of keys. These keys could be a `keypair` consisting of both a private and public key, or a secret key used as both a public and private key. According to the *FIPS 140-2, Security Requirements for Cryptographic Modules* from the National Institute of Standards and Technology (NIST), cryptographic management includes random-number and key generation, key establishment, key distribution, key entry/output, key storage, and key zeroization.

The JDK 1.4 supports these properties of cryptographic management by providing the ability to implement digital signatures, message digest algorithms, key generation algorithms, key factories, key store creation and management, algorithm parameter management, algorithm parameter generation, certificate factories, and *Pseudo-Random Number Generators* (PRNG). Each class is typically an engine class. It comprises a *Service Provider Interface* (SPI), in which at least one provider instance is distributed, and a factory that normally returns a `getInstance( )` method on the cryptographic class with the normal parameter to pass in as the type of algorithm for the creation of the object.

SPI Overview

Recall from Chapter 5 that the JDK 1.4 provides the *Service Provider Interface* (SPI) layer, which loads up the appropriate algorithms and protocols based on the parameters passed in through the *Application Layer Interface* (API). The provider implements the SPI layer, which is used by the abstract class for any of its implementations of the operations. Having an SPI layer gives organizations a layer to develop code that can still be used by the abstract class. An example is an organization that uses the JKS implementation and at later time decides to switch to a PKCS12 implementation for key stores because they want stronger security. Instead of changing all the implementation of the `KeyStore` (discussed in the next section of this chapter) functionality, they simply need to change the algorithm name that the `getInstance( )` is calling and the underlying implementation that is interfacing to the SPI API.

> **TIP:** Here is an example that demonstrates the importance of having an SPI layer: If we know the `KeyStore` comes with a `Java KeyStore` (JKS) implementation and we retrieve it using the `getInstance("JKS")` method, then with a little effort, we can extend the SPI interface for PKCS12 support. In addition, we can retrieve a `KeyStore` using a `getInstance("PKCS12")` method.

The following classes are considered the engine classes, and to fully support a new provider instance, all these classes should have an extended SPI implementation if the developer wants to fully utilize the key store, signature classes, and key generation of the new type of key. These classes are `Signature`, `MessageDigest`, `KeyPairGenerator`, `SecureRandom`, `KeyFactory`, `CertificateFactory`, `KeyStore`, `AlgorithmParameterGenerator`, and `AlgorithmParameters`.

The `KeyStore` class handles the management of keys; it stores the keys and certificates. How keys are stored and how they are accessed is just as important as the key itself. How many times have people saved confidential information to hard disk with access to it thinking that because it is physically nearby, it is safe? The `KeyStore` class, which usually saves information to a file, uses passwords and signatures to protect the information. This is discussed further later in this chapter.

> **CROSS-REFERENCE:** Chapter 12 provides an example of a SPI implementation for RSA, and Chapter 13 provides an implementation of a CipherSpi.

KeyStore

In SSL, a private key is used for encryption and public keys are used for decryption. Public keys and signatures are stored in certificates, so there must be a place in the organization to store these keys and certificates. The place to store keys is the `keystore`; a key store can be a flat file, a database, or an LDAP server that can store key material. With the capability to change the `keystore` type to a different provider, it is possible to implement different types of key stores.

> **CROSS-REFERENCE:** See Chapter 22 for more information about SSL.

To understand how keys are stored, you must understand how the `KeyManager` works. A `KeyManager` manages these key materials, and the `KeyManagerFactory` manages the `KeyManager` instance. A `TrustManager`, in turn, makes decisions about who to trust based on trusted material in the `truststore`. The `truststore` is part of the decision mechanism in that it contains trusted key material. If the certificate lives in that area, it is trusted. The `keystore` can contain several types of key material, such as the `keypair` used to decrypt and encrypt the messages and DSA and RSA key material.

> **CROSS-REFERENCE:** To further understand how these classes work together, see the examples in Chapter 23.

Each piece of key material is known as a *key entry* or a *trusted certificate entry*. The *key entry* is a public and private key pair. The *trusted certificate entry* can hold a set of trusted certificates when moved to a trusted store. When storing a key, there is a relationship between a key entry and a subject; this is normally called an *alias*. An example of an alias is `rich`, if the user `rich` has a key entry. These aliases are created with the key during its generation or import.

> **TIP:** To retrieve the key, you can look up the alias and get the corresponding key entry to that specific identity.

The `KeyStore` class is the interface that implements the provider's key store. One implementation shipped with the JDK 1.4 from the Sun provider is the Java `KeyStore` type called `JKS`, for `JavaKeyStore`. The `KeyStore` is an engine class and will find the provider using the `Security` class like the other engine classes. It will find an entry similar to the following:

```
put("KeyStore.JKS", "sun.security.provider.JavaKeyStore");
```

This will provide an overwritten implementation of the `JavaKeyStore` class in the `sun.security.provider` package when the following code is executed:

```
ks = KeyStore.getInstance("JKS");
```

This code example walks down the provider chain and maps the `JKS` algorithm for the key store to the `JavaKeyStore` implementation. This is the key store that is used by default and is also specified in the `java.security` file to be the default key store type, as in the following line:

```
keystore.type=jks
```

To understand how keys are stored, first examine the implementation of the `KeyStore` class. Some of the functions in the `KeyStore` class are as follows:

◆ KeyStore (KeyStoreSpi keyStoreSpi, Provider provider, String type): This is the KeyStore that takes in the provider's implementation, the provider itself, and the string type. This creates an instance of the of the KeyStore and is managed by the getInstance( ) function when a KeyStore is loaded through a store. The default store is file based, but could be expanded to use a database or LDAP just as the ACL. An example of a provider is Sun and a type is JKS; the default for the getInstance( ) method is JavaKeyStore (JKS). This is set by the keytool in the keystore.type field of the java.security configuration file. JKS is exportable and does not contain a strong encryption. The KeyManagerFactory typically initializes the KeyStore instance.

◆ The getInstance static functions get the instance of the KeyStore from a string, a string and Provider object, or a string of the type and provider. An example of getting a instance from the provider is KeyStore ks = KeyStore.getInstance("JKS");. An example from the string type and string provider is KeyStore ks = KeyStore.getInstance("JKS", "SUN");. To access the instance, the class must first be loaded. The getProvider( ) function can subsequently return the Provider class after the instance is received. There are three getInstance functions:

- public static KeyStore getInstance (String type)

- public static KeyStore getInstance (String type, Provider provider)

- public static KeyStore getInstance (String type, String provider)

◆ There are four functions that support the key entry. The string alias is used to name the entry, such as customer. It is very common to relate these aliases to principals. The password is used to password-protect the keys or certificates. If JKS is used to store the key, the format follows the PKCS #8 standard. These functions are used to store the KeyPair. The private key is passed in as an array of bytes. The public key is contained in the certificate. To check the aliases that are available, the aliases( ) function returns an enumeration of the available names. The deleteEntry deletes the key entry based on the name of the entry. The four functions are as follows:

- public void setKeyEntry (String alias, byte [ ] key, Certificate [ ] chain)

- public void setKeyEntry (String alias, byte [ ] key, char [ ] password, Certificate [ ] chain)

- public Key getKey (String alias, char[] password)

- public void deleteEntry (String alias)

> **TIP:** If the protected key is of type java.security.PrivateKey, it must be accompanied by a certificate chain certifying the corresponding public key. If the underlying keystore implementation is of type jks, key must be encoded as an EncryptedPrivateKeyInfo as defined in the PKCS #8 standard.

♦ There are five functions that support the Trusted Certificate Entry. The deleteEntry is also used to delete the Certificate based on its name. The setCertificateEntry passes in the Trusted Certificate Entry and its associated name. The isCertificateEntry( ) function is used to see if the Trusted Certificate Entry is in the Trusted store based on the Certificate's associated name. The getter functions can return the name, Certificate, or Certificate chain of both the Trusted Certificate Entry and the KeyEntry of the entire Certificate chain, from the current Certificate to the root Certificate that contains the chain of public keys. These functions are as follows:

- public Certificate getCertificate (String alias)

- public String getCertificateAlias (Certificate cert)

- public Certificate [ ] getCertificateChain (String alias)

- public boolean isCertificateEntry (String alias)

- public void setCertificateEntry (String alias, Certificate cert)

♦ In order to use any of the KeyStore, it must be loaded into memory as a storage device. By default, the functionality of File IO can be used to store and load the KeyStore from disk. The files are password protected to ensure some protection. However, these functions can be extended into an X.500 LDAP or database storage to improve security of the storage. There are two functions that provide this functionality:

- public void load (InputStream stream, char [ ] password)

- public void store (OutputStream stream, char [ ] password)

> **NOTE:** The KeyManagerFactory typically initializes the KeyStore so that the static getInstance( ) function is called to retrieve the KeyStore. By default, the KeyManagerFactory initializes everything to the SUNX509 provider type. This initializes the KeyManager, KeyManagerFactory, and JavaKeyStore to follow Sun's implementation for the X.509 protocol until something else is specified during one of the objects' startup.

The JavaKeyStore normally stores the keys in a flat file, which contains signatures for validity and is password protected. Loading the key store into memory requires that a password be authenticated through the KeyStore API. While the key store is loaded into memory, trusted applications can have access to it for gathering key information to other agents. Different implementations could change some of the operation of the key store, however extensibility is part of the API and the purpose of providing an SPI.

Although the JKS implementation comes out of the box from Sun Microsystems, there is nothing prohibiting the organization from increasing the protection of its resources for its own use. By using the signature and password to protect the keys, the key store exhibits the patterns of data integrity and data confidentiality. Keeping keys secure is crucial to the mechanics of security.

PKCS #12 KeyStore

The *Public Key Cryptography Standard* (PKCS) #12 specification defines the key container that is used to move keys from `keystore` to `keystore` without being compromised. These `keystores` could be used between different languages and different browsers such as Microsoft Internet Explorer and Netscape. This specification is used because there is no API to interface that all `keystores` implement. Instead the keys must be imported and exported to and from different `keystores`. The PKCS #12 doesn't define the transport mechanism but defines the wrapper of the key from a `keystore` to be sent to another `keystore`.

The transport itself can even be mail, sockets, files, or http. The PKCS #12 was designed as the transfer syntax for sharing keys. What this means is that PKCS #12 describes the transfer syntax between identities, including key and certificate information. This will help if one organization is using one kind of key store and another organization is using something different.

PKCS #12 provides a definition, or standard, on how the different transferring mechanisms can communicate to swap keys. Changing the implementation to a PKCS #12 algorithm instead of the Sun JKS algorithm is simply a matter of changing the implementing class by `KeyStore myKeyStore = KeyStore.getInstance("PKCS12");`. All other operations can be carried out in the same manner. That is the importance of having the implementation at the SPI layer instead of the top-level class layer. The `PKCS12` is a key store implementation that is developed by IBM as a security provider.

> **TIP:** Using the SPI layer, you can switch implementations with a simple class instantiation.

Truststore

The difference between `keystore` and `truststore` is in their purpose. Unlike the `keystore` that stores keys, the `truststore` verifies the client's certificate from the `keystore` or the certificate that is sent by the server that uses the `truststore`. The *Certificate Authority* (CA) signs the certificate with a digital signature to be trusted, and when the SSL client receives the certificate, it must authenticate it, which means it needs information from the CA's certificate. Because the CA's certificate is trusted, it is stored in a trusted store. In short, `keystores` are used to provide credentials to incoming requests for the organization to provide an authentication identity, whereas `truststores` are used for the organization to authenticate others. There are so many similarities between the two that it is easy to get them mixed up.

> **TIP:** The difference between `truststores` and `keystores` is that `truststores` are used for authenticating incoming requests, whereas `keystores` provide keys to show their authentication to others.

TrustManager

The `TrustManager` manages the `truststores`. The default `TrustManager` assumes the public certificates are held in `$JREHOME/lib/security/jssecacerts`. If that file doesn't exist, it assumes they are held in `$JREHOME/lib/security/cacerts`. These properties can be set in `javax.net.ssl.trustStore`. The `KeyTool` class manages the `truststore`, just like the `keystore`, and even further inherits the `KeyStore` class.

`TrustManager`s are initialized from the `TrustManagerFactory`. The `com.sun.net.ssl.TrustManagerFactory` has the same characteristics as the `KeyManagerFactory`. Just like the `KeyManagerFactory`, the `TrustManagerFactory` contains a static `getDefaultAlgorithm( )` method that returns the `sun.ssl.trustmanager.type` property defined in the `$JREHOME/lib/security/java.security` file. The `TrustManagerFactory` generates the instances of the `TrustManager`.

Keytool

The `keytool` utility distributed with the JDK 1.4 provides the capability to manage a `keystore`. A `keystore` is a container for two types of entries: the key entry and the trusted certificate entry. The *key entry* has a private and a public key. The private key is used with the corresponding public key from the certificate entry. The private key and the public key that it is related to make up a key pair. The *trusted certificate entry* is a certificate associated with a principal trusted to the organization to be used to decrypt and verify information from that specific principal. The certificates are used for ensuring integrity in their digital signatures, their public key for decrypting information, and their private key for encrypting data.

The `keytool` is an implementation of the Java `KeyStore` API designed for the management of *key entries*. A *key entry* consists of a private key and an X.509 certificate chain that authenticates the associated public key. The `keytool` does not provide support for secret keys but only for the certificates and key pairs. A trusted certificate entry is a certificate that authenticates the public key of another party.

The `keytool` offers a management of private and public keys in a secure format, which is X.509, and is encrypted also using X.509. Therefore, access to the X.509 certificate is limited to the individuals who can decrypt the public key, and the public key can be a password. The X.509 certificates are stored in an X.500 tree structure, which is similar to LDAP.

> **TIP:** The `keytool` can differentiate between trusted certificates and untrusted certificates.

If a certificate is trusted, it is assumed that the organization has authenticated the certificate; a trusted certificate can be used to establish other certificates that can also be trusted. A user could be part of a certificate so a user can also be authenticated in this manner. An organization's local private keys can also be stored in the `keystore` and managed by the `keytool`. This can be summarized by stating that the `keytool` has the following capabilities:

- ♦ Key pair generation
- ♦ Certificate generation
- ♦ Certificate signing request generation
- ♦ Management of key entries
- ♦ Management of trusted certificate entries
- ♦ Management of passwords
- ♦ Authenticating the X.509 certificate chains to the corresponding public keys

The `keytool` is a management utility to accompany this functionality. It provides the ability to manage `keypairs` and certificates. The `keystore` that is implemented by the `keytool` is using the `keystore` as a file.

The `keytool` loads and stores the keys that are specified in the `keystore`. The `keytool` defaults to the file named `.keystore` in the user's home directory. Otherwise, the `-keystore` parameter can be use to specify the location of the `keystore`'s file location. The `keystore` file is created whenever a key is generated or the `-identitydb` command is used to read the identity of the database.

The `keystore` uses aliases to associate the principals to the store. The aliases are not case sensitive, so `rich` and `Rich` are the same entry. The entry is specified when a key is generated with the `-genkey` command to generate a key pair (a public and private key) with a self-signed certificate or the `-import` command to import a trusted certificate. A self-signed certificate is when the certificate chain starts out with a single identity of the issuer and the subject being the same.

This is accomplished with the following command:

```
keytool -genkey -alias rich -keypass password
```

This command generates a public and private key for the principal `rich` and assigns the password `password` for the principal `rich` to use when accessing the private key (after a few questions are answered to develop the fields for the X.500 specification to fill the matching X.509 certificate). When not specifying the password with the command line, the user that is generating the key is prompted for the password at the command line. If the verification password does not match the initial password, an exception is thrown, as shown in the following code snippet:

```
D:\Working\SecurityBook\code>keytool -genkey -alias rich -keypass
password
Enter keystore password:  test
keytool error: java.io.IOException: Keystore was tampered with, or
password was incorrect
```

The questions that are asked when entering a matching password are needed for filling the X.500 specification. These entries are stored in the X.509 digital certificate for information in self-signing the certificate. The information is needed to fill both the identification of the issuer and the signer. The fields appear as the following:

♦ Common Name (CN): The common name of the issuer that consists of the first and last name of the alias.

♦ Organization Unit (OU): The small organization, or the department of an organization such as "Marketing."

♦ Organization Name (O): The organization or company name.

♦ Locality (L): The city name.

♦ State (S): The state name.

♦ Country (C): The country name.

The X.500 specification uses these fields for storing the directory structure, which is also used in LDAP. X.509 stores these fields on the certificate for certificate storage wherever the certificate will travel. These fields are discussed throughout various chapters of the book. The keytool utility inquires about these fields in the interaction in Listing 8-1.

Listing 8-1: Interaction with keytool

```
D:\Working\SecurityBook\code>keytool -genkey -alias richh -keypass
password
Enter keystore password:  password
What is your first and last name?
  [Unknown]:  Rich Helton
What is the name of your organizational unit?
  [Unknown]:  development
What is the name of your organization?
  [Unknown]:  richware
What is the name of your City or Locality?
  [Unknown]:  denver
What is the name of your State or Province?
  [Unknown]:  co
What is the two-letter country code for this unit?
  [Unknown]:  us
Is CN=Rich Helton, OU=development, O=richware, L=denver, ST=co, C=us
correct?
  [no]:  yes
```

To ensure that the entry was entered, the keytool -list command is used to print the keystore entries and to show how the key was stored, as shown in Listing 8-2.

Listing 8-2: Output of keytool -list

```
D:\Working\SecurityBook\code>keytool -list
Enter keystore password:  password
```

```
Keystore type: jks
Keystore provider: SUN

Your keystore contains 1 entry

richh, Nov 23, 2001, keyEntry,
Certificate fingerprint (MD5):
87:88:11:84:31:20:54:04:8F:CB:EE:C9:5D:5C:F0:B8
```

Certificates can be stored in either a binary format or a printable encoded format that is specified in the RFC 1421. RFC 1421 defines the Privacy Enhancement for Electronic Mail. This format is normally seen at the bottom of e-mails for digital certificate exchanges and is parsed out for authentication by applications that support *Privacy Enhanced Mail* (PEM), and other mail protocols such as *Pretty Good Privacy* (PGP). The keytool exports the program to a certificate file using the -export parameter and in the RFC 1421 format by using the -rfc command:

```
D:\Working\SecurityBook\code>keytool -export -rfc -alias richh -file
richcert.cer
Enter keystore password:  password
Certificate stored in file <richcert.cer>
```

The keytool utility always prompts the user for a password every time that it accesses a particular key to authenticate access to the key. The certificate that is generated with RFC 1421 looks like Listing 8-3.

Listing 8-3: RFC 1421-generated certificate

```
-----BEGIN CERTIFICATE-----
MIIDCDCCAsYCBDv+nBMwCwYHKoZIzjgEAwUAMGoxCzAJBgNVBAYMAnVzMQswCQYDVQQIDAJj
bzEP
MA0GA1UEBwwGZGVudmVyMREwDwYDVQQKDAhyaWNod2FyZTEUMBIGA1UECwwLZGV2ZWxvcGll
bnQx
FDASBgNVBAMMC1JpY2ggSGVsdG9uMB4XDTAxMTEyMzE4NTcyMloXDTAyMDIyMTE4NTcyMiow
ajEL
MAkGA1UEBgwCdXMxCzAJBgNVBAgMAmNvMQ8wDQYDVQQHDAZkZW52ZXIxETAPBgNVBAoMCHJp
Y2h3
YXJlMRQwEgYDVQQLDAtkZXZlbG9wbWVudDEUMBIGA1UEAwwLUmljaCBIZWx0b24wggG3MIIB
LAYH
KoZIzjgEATCCAR8CgYEA/X9TgR11EilS30qcLuzk5/YRtlI870QAwx4/gLZRJmlFXUAiUftZ
PYlY
+r/F9bow9subVWzXgTuAHTRv8mZgt2uZUKWkn5/oBHsQIsJPu6nX/rfGG/g7V+fGqKYVDwT7
g/bT
xR7DAjVUE1oWkTL2dfOuK2HXKu/yIgMZndFIAccCFQCXYFCPFSMLzLKSuYKi64QL8Fgc9QKB
gQD3
4aCF1ps93su8q1w2uFe5eZSvu/o66oL5V0wLPQeCZ1FZV4661F1P5nEHEIGAtEkWcSPoTCgW
E7fP
```

```
CTKMyKbhPBZ6i1R8jSjgo64eK7OmdZFuo38L+iE1YvH7YnoBJDvMpPG+qFGQiaiD3+Fa5Z8G
kotm
XoB7VSVkAUw7/s9JKgOBhAACgYAR9gX4fe5fkTNjGrvsHKRDbkEDOrJTFrq7RLtgk8eCjmJy
+VsC
seWdkPatbj2ByrJQuUXRxygpgA4Q0O9jcINmhcAP42edHOkOMI88u0mDimI74VrJAyJ0TOb7
GQzA
sxp7bJzwGWXAHAfXwsEq1OPPzdnECty8EP7uCZlmBDpwZjALBgcqhkjOOAQDBQADLwAwLAIU
SM9W
zM/EKrP2r5D58cGNXJdiwYYCFDc1v72BB3E4kAEVUFnGzYguKodD
-----END CERTIFICATE-----
```

The digital signature in Listing 8-3 is not very human readable. It is used to give to other users for authentication, validation, and to retrieve the public key to decrypt messages that can be sent in mail, data to be exchanged through SSL, or by many other applications. The digital certificate can be displayed through the `keytool` by using the `-printcert` parameter as shown in Listing 8-4.

Listing 8-4: Output of `keytool -printcert`

```
D:\Working\SecurityBook\code>keytool -printcert -file richcert.cer
Owner: CN=Rich Helton, OU=development, O=richware, L=denver, ST=co, C=us
Issuer: CN=Rich Helton, OU=development, O=richware, L=denver, ST=co,
C=us
Serial number: 3bfe9c13
Valid from: Fri Nov 23 11:57:23 MST 2001 until: Thu Feb 21 11:57:23 MST
2002
Certificate fingerprints:
        MD5:   87:88:11:84:31:20:54:04:8F:CB:EE:C9:5D:5C:F0:B8
        SHA1:
B7:85:C5:C6:8E:DB:C6:88:47:BE:9E:2A:C7:A9:5E:23:6D:7F:4A:E5
```

The `keytool` is a utility implemented with the `KeyStore` class. It has some of the same properties as the `KeyStore` class, such as using the `JKS` key store type by default and being able to be extended. To extend the `keytool`, you extend the `keystore` utility; this is done by extending the `KeyStoreSPI`. The JDK 1.4 comes with the `JKS` implementation for the `keystore` type, but if another `keystore` type is desired and retrieved, it can be specified in the implementation supported in the `{$JREHOME}/lib/security/java.security` file by setting the `keystore` property as follows:

```
#
# Default keystore type.
#
keystore.type=jks
```

This entry specifies the `keystore` type to use from the `jarsigner` and `keytool` utilities unless they explicitly use a different one in their command-line parameter. The `keystore.type` entry is retrieved by the following function:

```
KeyStore keyStore = KeyStore.getInstance(KeyStore.getDefaultType ( ) );
```

The `getDefaultType( )` function returns the `keystore` type defined in the `java.security` file. This function initializes the `keytool`. The `keytool` is a utility that extends the `KeyStore` class.

The `keytool` has the capability to generate the key and certificate entry. To accomplish this task, the `keystore` must be able to support multiple keying and encryption algorithms in order to be useful. By default, the `keytool` supports the DSA algorithm for the private key. When it uses DSA, the message digest will be SHA-1, and the public key will be stored in DSA. Another key algorithm that can be used is RSA, and the message digest will be MD5. The key sizes are by default 1024 bits, but it can support anywhere from 512 bits to 1024 bits at increments of 64 bits. Each algorithm, either the RSA or DSA, can be applied to both the key pair algorithm or the self-signed certificate. The key pair algorithm is defined with the `-keyalg` parameter, and the self-signed algorithm is defined with the `-sigalg` parameter.

The `keytool` is a rudimentary tool to store Java keys and to extract them from a file. It has the capability to use a lot of functionality through the policy files and command line. However, that might not be enough for some organizations that want to put everything in an LDAP system instead of using files. The `keytool` makes use of standard classes of the JDK 1.4 such as `KeyStore`, `X509Certificate`, and `X500Name` classes. In fact, when it generates a key pair, it performs a `setKeyEntry` method, passing in the X509Certificate array, the alias, the password, and the key of the alias. The `java.security.KeyStore` class demonstrates the `setKeyEntry` method.

> **CAUTION:** There are many undocumented classes that make up the `sun.security.tools.KeyTool` class to store certificates. One of the classes is the `sun.security.X509.X500Name` class.

The `X500Name` is set based on the fields passed in for `CN`, `OU`, `O`, `L`, `S`, and `C`. The `X509Certificate` is generated from the `X500Name`. The private key is generated and encrypted with the algorithm that is specified for the private key. These entries are set in the `KeyStore`'s `setKeyEntry` function along with a password to protect the entry in the `KeyStore`. The `KeyStore` supports loading and unloading of these entries, which are password protected for file access. To extend these entries without changing the `keytool`, a new implementation (instead of `JKS`) needs to be implemented with the `KeyStoreSpi` implementation and specified as the `keystore` type. To support an LDAP implementation, the `X500Name` already gives the directory naming structure variables; the LDAP extensions have to be implemented in the `KeyStoreSpi` and specified.

This type of implementation enables the developer to ignore a lot of the functionality of the `keytool` when extending it and to only focus on changing the SPI layer. The SPI layer redirects the actual store of the keys into any extension, such as LDAP, desired for the organization. The SPI extension gives the developers a lot of possibilities for extending interfaces without breaking the other interfaces or changing their behavior. Using the SPI to extend the functionality decouples the new implementation and its functionality from the rest of the interfaces that work together in the `keytool`. One popular extension that has been accomplished this way is the PKCS #12 implementation. The `keytool` can easily be extended for internal use in an organization.

Also, the `keytool` can be extended to design new security systems for an organization to implement, and this new implementation would not be made public to attackers. To help block attacks, an organization may use internal systems, which attackers have no knowledge of. These internal systems still support protocols to other organizations and customers. The `keytool` is a blueprint to store keys using the JDK 1.4. Organizations can extend this to further protect the access and management of keys. The `keytool` provides enough functionality out of the box to secure, generate, store, load, and manage keys.

> **TIP:** Security beyond the standard protocols can be implemented by using the SPI extensions designed for extending the functionality of the key management system.

Jarsigner

The `jarsigner` tool uses the `keystore` information to generate and verify digital signatures for *Java Archive* (JAR) files. When the JAR has been signed with a private key, the `jarsigner` tool verifies the digital signature block of the JAR. The `jarsigner` extracts the public key from the `keystore`. Then the digital signature is recomputed from the data using the principal's public key. This will allow the `jarsigner` to detect any modifications.

The concept comes from signing a contract. In a contract, two things are usually needed: the identity of the principal (a key) and the contract itself (the JAR). To read the JAR, the private key doesn't need to be used, but a public key, which is distributed by the principal, does. This is similar to a person giving someone else permission to read the document. One of the limitations of paper contracts is that they can be tampered with without knowledge of the person who signs. Unlike a contract, the integrity of each byte in the data can be rehashed, checked, and compared with the previous hash to ensure that no values are different. If any of the data has changed, it will produce a different hash result.

> **NOTE:** The public key cannot be forged because it requires the private key to be generated.

In order for a digital signature to be generated, a public and private key must be associated with the principal. A principal can be a user, group, or system. The `jarsigner` uses key and certificate information from the `keystore` to generate the digital signatures. The `keystore` may contain the key pair or the X.509 certificate. The X.509 certificate contains the public key to check the digital signature. The following steps are used for signing a JAR file:

1. Create the key pair using the `keytool` utility.
2. Use the `keytool` to export the public key into a file for others to access.
3. Create a JAR file with the `jar` utility for classes and resources to be distributed to others.
4. Sign the JAR file using the `jarsigner` and the private key created with the key pair.

The `keytool` has been described in developing a `keystore`. If multiple `keystores` are stored in the organization, the `-keystore` parameter can be used to stipulate the specific store by specifying its URL location. Using the default store from the previous examples, Listing 8-5 can be used to sign the JAR `Java2.jar`.

Listing 8-5: Signing the `Java2.jar`

```
D:\Working\SecurityBook\code>jarsigner -storepass password -verbose
Java2.jar richh
 updating: META-INF/MANIFEST.MF
   adding: META-INF/RICHH.SF
   adding: META-INF/RICHH.DSA
   adding: scjd/
 signing: scjd/instructions.html
   adding: scjd/starting/
   adding: scjd/starting/suncertify/
   adding: scjd/starting/suncertify/db/
 signing: scjd/starting/suncertify/db/Data.java
 signing: scjd/starting/suncertify/db/DataInfo.java
 signing: scjd/starting/suncertify/db/DatabaseException.java
 signing: scjd/starting/suncertify/db/FieldInfo.java
 signing: scjd/starting/suncertify/db/Data.class
 signing: scjd/starting/suncertify/db/DataInfo.class
 signing: scjd/starting/suncertify/db/DatabaseException.class
 signing: scjd/starting/suncertify/db/FieldInfo.class
 signing: scjd/starting/suncertify/db/db.db
```

In Listing 8-5, the alias `richh` was used from the `keystore` using the alias's password `password` with the `-storepass` command.

After the `jarsigner` has signed the JAR file, there will be two new files in the JAR for each alias. One file is the `.SF` file, or Signature File, which will have a set of signatures associated with each file in the JAR file. Each entry will contain the file name that it signed, the signature type (SHA-1 Digest in this example), and the digest value itself as shown in Listing 8-6.

Listing 8-6: Signature File example

```
Signature-Version: 1.0
Created-By: 1.4.0 (Sun Microsystems Inc.)
SHA1-Digest-Manifest: dfbEUpMl7mh66sLA/UFf0NZJ7E8=

Name: scjd/instructions.html
SHA1-Digest: XOeMFEQYda2AGXO/YKHzNMK/XGo=
```

The other file that is created by default is the `.DSA` file. DSA is the algorithm that the alias used to create the private key in the `keystore`. The `.DSA` file is the signature block that contains the certificate, or certificate chain, that is used to authenticate the public key. The signing was used with the corresponding private key from the alias. To verify that JAR has been signed correctly and to view the certifications, the -certs and -verify commands are used, as shown in Listing 8-7.

CROSS-REFERENCE: See Chapter 11 for a discussion on the Digital Signature Algorithm (DSA).

Listing 8-7: DSA file example

```
D:\Working\SecurityBook\code>jarsigner -certs -verify -verbose Java2.jar

        997 Sat Nov 24 01:15:30 MST 2001 META-INF/MANIFEST.MF
       1056 Sat Nov 24 01:15:36 MST 2001 META-INF/RICHH.SF
       1033 Sat Nov 24 01:15:36 MST 2001 META-INF/RICHH.DSA
          0 Fri Aug 04 13:38:14 MDT 2000 META-INF/
          0 Thu Aug 03 10:58:02 MDT 2000 scjd/
smk   22680 Fri Aug 04 13:36:52 MDT 2000 scjd/instructions.html
      X.509, CN=Rich Helton, OU=development, O=richware, L=denver,
ST=co, C=us (richh)
          0 Thu Aug 03 10:57:56 MDT 2000 scjd/starting/
          0 Thu Aug 03 10:57:56 MDT 2000 scjd/starting/suncertify/
          0 Fri Aug 04 08:53:58 MDT 2000 scjd/starting/suncertify/db/
smk   12482 Thu Aug 03 10:57:56 MDT 2000
scjd/starting/suncertify/db/Data.java

      X.509, CN=Rich Helton, OU=development, O=richware, L=denver,
ST=co, C=us (richh)
smk    3232 Thu Aug 03 10:57:56 MDT 2000
cjd/starting/suncertify/db/DataInfo.java
      X.509, CN=Rich Helton, OU=development, O=richware, L=denver,
ST=co, C=us (richh)
smk     188 Thu Aug 03 10:57:56 MDT 2000
scjd/starting/suncertify/db/DatabaseException.java
      X.509, CN=Rich Helton, OU=development, O=richware, L=denver,
ST=co, C=us (richh)
smk     933 Thu Aug 03 10:57:56 MDT 2000
scjd/starting/suncertify/db/FieldInfo.java
      X.509, CN=Rich Helton, OU=development, O=richware, L=denver,
ST=co, C=us (richh)
smk    5352 Thu Aug 03 10:57:56 MDT 2000
scjd/starting/suncertify/db/Data.class

      X.509, CN=Rich Helton, OU=development, O=richware, L=denver,
ST=co, C=us (richh)
smk    1565 Thu Aug 03 10:57:56 MDT 2000
scjd/starting/suncertify/db/DataInfo.class
      X.509, CN=Rich Helton, OU=development, O=richware, L=denver,
ST=co, C=us (richh)
smk     307 Thu Aug 03 10:57:56 MDT 2000
scjd/starting/suncertify/db/DatabaseException.class
```

```
         X.509, CN=Rich Helton, OU=development, O=richware, L=denver,
ST=co, C=us (richh)
smk      541 Thu Aug 03 10:57:56 MDT 2000
scjd/starting/suncertify/db/FieldInfo.class
         X.509, CN=Rich Helton, OU=development, O=richware, L=denver,
ST=co, C=us (richh)
smk      1646 Fri Aug 04 08:53:58 MDT 2000
scjd/starting/suncertify/db/db.db
         X.509, CN=Rich Helton, OU=development, O=richware, L=denver,
ST=co, C=us (richh)

  s = signature was verified
  m = entry is listed in manifest
  k = at least one certificate was found in keystore
  i = at least one certificate was found in identity scope

jar verified.
```

The `jarsigner` utility is useful for signing JAR files. It will ensure the integrity of the files that the JAR contains and stores. It provides the functionality to access `keystores` in case the application requires an authentication with the public key.

> **NOTE:** The `jarsigner` signs JARs from the specified `keystore` using trusted certificates. When a JAR file is received, one cannot verify the certificate unless the proper `keystore` is present. In addition, one cannot resign the JAR file unless one has access to the `keystore`.

The command to create a jar file is: `jar { ctxu}[ vfm0M] [ jar-file] [ manifest-file] [ -C dir] files ...` much as in the following code example.

```
jar cvf myjar.jar MyClass.class examples\MyOtherClass.class
```

This creates the `myjar.jar` file that make up the *payload* of the JAR packed into a copy of the original structure, and the directory `META-INF` with a `MANIFEST.MF` file. The manifest file (`MANIFEST.MF`) is created — by default — in the `META-INF` directory as per Sun specifications. The manifest file has details of the payload for the JAR, and there can be only one manifest in the JAR. The manifest file uses the RFC 822 ASCII format.

> **CAUTION:** Although you can manually edit the manifest, you must take great care to follow the syntax. A customized manifest can be added to the JAR file with the `m` or `M` option in the command line for the `jar` command.

As mentioned earlier, the JAR file can be signed. The signature file is also added to the `META-INF` directory (an example of a signature file is shown in Listing 8-6) and the digests (of the signature file) are created from the manifest file (and not from the payload). The signature file is in ASCII format. The signature block files are automatically created every time the JAR is signed. These signature block files are binary files and typically have a `.DSA` extension (since the DSA algorithm is usually used).

Policy File

A *policy file* is a file that contains a set of permissions and associates these permissions with a principal or a set of files. The policy file contains a class to associate to a resource. This class gives the permission to that file. For instance, to give a read permission to a file, a `FilePermission` class is used that allows read, write, execute, or delete permissions or any combination thereof. The `grant` keyword is used to grant permissions of a particular type to a specific resource. This is commonly known as a *grant entry*. Listing 8-8 shows a grant entry for giving read permissions to the `java.policy` file located under the Windows operating system path from the `$JRE` subdirectory.

Listing 8-8: Grant entry example

```
grant{  permission java.io.FilePermission "
D:\\jdk1.4\\jre\\lib\\security\\java.policy" "read";
}
```

To specify the type of permission, or permission entry, the `permission` keyword must be used to define the entry. In Listing 8-8, the `java.io.FilePermission` is known as the `permission_class_name` where the Java class is associated with the resource. The action is the action that the permission can exercise on the resource. The target resource name is referred to as the `target_name`. The `permission_class_name` contains a set of permissions that can be associated with the class to the resource, such as the action of reading a file. The `FilePermission` knows what this action means and how to operate on it. However, the class understands only the set of permissions that it can operate on. For example, the `FilePermission` does not understand a "connect" action because that is something specific to the `SocketPermission`. The behavior of using the policy file is similar to returning permission in code. For instance:

```
perm = new
java.io.FilePermission("D:\\jdk1.4\\jre\\lib\\security\\java.policy",
"read");
```

> **NOTE:** Double backslashes are used on Windows operating systems for special characters, but one forward slash can also be used to denote UNIX-like file structures.

The difference is that the policy file is giving access into the system versus a particular use in the code and hides the coding implementation. The `policytool` is designed to edit these files and does ensure that the file is formatted correctly. Many developers edit these by using text editors, but the `policytool` provides a GUI that lists the correct fields to input and other useful utilities.

The `FilePermission` class is a standard class that is distributed with the JDK 1.4, but this does not limit the developer to those that are distributed with the JDK 1.4. New permissions can be extended from the `java.security.Permission` class to develop any permission that the user may require.

The `signedBy` property can also be applied in the policy file to the target name. This property represents a certificate stored in a `keystore`. The public key within the certificate is used to authenticate the target and verify the digital signature of the code. A private key of the corresponding public key is used to sign the digital certificate. Multiple aliases from the `keystore` are comma-delimited.

For instance, a certificate from rich and richware are represented as "`rich,  richware`". This means that the target resource was signed by "`rich`" and "`richware`". If this field is omitted, it means that the authentication and validation can be any signer. It doesn't matter if the code is signed or not. Here is an example:

```
grant signedBy "rich,richware" (permission java.io.FilePermission
"/jdk1.4/jre/lib/security/java.policy", "read";
};
```

Two other properties that can be optionally set for the policy file are *codeBase* and the *principal*. The `codeBase` property indicates a code source location. The code is represented specifying the file using the slashes that are typically used in the UNIX operating system. An example that retrieves any JAR or class file in the JDK extensions directory is as follows:

```
grant codeBase "file:/D:/jdk1.4/lib/ext/*" (
    ...
    };
```

The *principal* property defines a principal that is associated with the authentication of the resource. The principal must be verified before accessing the resource. If the principal name is specified in the policy file, an X509 certificate must be retrieved from the `keystore` for authentication. The principal authentication follows the X500 authentication and is implemented using the `javax.security.auth.x500.X500Principal` class. If the certificate is ignored or cannot be authenticated, access to the target resource is denied. Here is an example:

```
grant principal javax.security.auth.x500.X500Principal "cn=rich" (
    permission java.io.FilePermission
"/jdk1.4/jre/lib/security/java.policy", "read";
    };
```

It is also possible to specify an additional policy file at runtime of an application. This is done by defining a `java.security.policy` system property using the `-Djava.security.policy` command. The security policy property is set to a URL that specifies the URL of a policy file. For example, the URL could be set to `www.richware.com/java.policy`.

The policy file can contain other entries besides the grant entries. Another entry that can be specified in the policy file is the `keystore` entry. The `keystore` must be specified in the policy file if any of the `signedBy` entries are specified so that the certification matching the signer of the grant entry may be retrieved from the specified `keystore`. Only the first keystore entry in the file is used. Other entries are ignored. The keyword keystore, the keystore URL, and the keystore type specify the format. The following example shows that the keystore file is being accessed from the root of the richware domain. The type of the keystore is the Sun Java KeyStore (JKS):

```
keystore "www.richware.com/.keystore", "JKS";
```

All the entries that have been mentioned so far are entries into a single file, but there might be a situation where a policy file is needed to run one application and another is used to run a different application. Instead of keeping all these policies in one policy file, a policy entry can be used to reference the file instead. This gives the environment the opportunity to have a system-wide file to reference all policy files that need to be referenced. This is done by listing all the other policy files as URLs in the main policy file, as the following two lines demonstrate:

```
policy.url.1=file:${java.home}/jre/lib/security/java.policy
policy.url.2=file:${user.home}/.java.policy
```

This example shows that the policy entry is referencing the default policy from the JDK 1.4 directory and the policy file from the user's home directory. These entries are defined in a single policy file that could be referenced from the -Djava.security.policy property.

Policytool

In JAAS, and many of the other engine classes, a security policy file is used to define the permissions for classes.

> **CROSS-REFERNCE:** Some of these permissions are described in Chapter 19.

The policytool utility is used so that the user need not edit the policy file in a text editor, but can edit it using a standardized menu to help the user understand the fields and check the validity of the policy file. When a Java Virtual Machine (JVM) is initialized to run a Java program, the JVM needs to check its local policy settings to understand the permission set that it uses to run the Java program. The JVM's java.policy is defaulted to the {$JREHOME}/lib/security/java.policy file. This file is commonly known as the "system" policy file that grants permissions to standard extensions and allows access to system properties and to nonprivileged ports.

In the following example, where the local Java Runtime Environment (JRE) is located in the D:\jdk1.4\jre directory, the policy tool will look like Figure 8-1.

The example policytool was started using the policytool -file D:\jdk1.4\jre\lib\security\java.policy command line. If no file name is specified during the startup of the policytool, it looks for the file called .java.policy under the user's home directory $HOME. Editing the policy file by hand is also possible;

however, the `policytool` will catch mistakes that editing it by hand will not. The `jdk1.4` policy file, which is distributed, contains the entries in Listing 8-9.

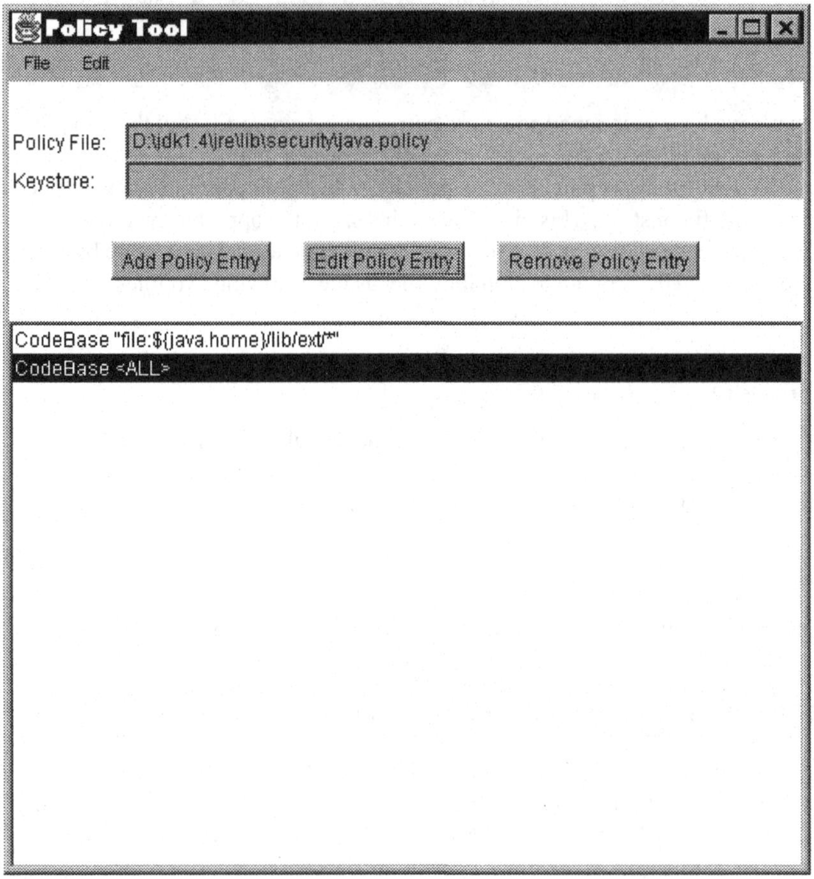

Figure 8-1: Policy tool loaded

Listing 8-9: `jdk1.4` policy file entries

```
// Standard extensions get all permissions by default

grant codeBase "file:${java.home}/lib/ext/*" {
    permission java.security.AllPermission;
};

// default permissions granted to all domains

grant {
```

```
// Allows any thread to stop itself using the java.lang.Thread.stop()
// method that takes no argument.
// Note that this permission is granted by default only to remain
// backwards compatible.
// It is strongly recommended that you either remove this permission
// from this policy file or further restrict it to code sources
// that you specify, because Thread.stop() is potentially unsafe.
// See "http://java.sun.com/notes" for more information.
permission java.lang.RuntimePermission "stopThread";

// allows anyone to listen on un-privileged ports
permission java.net.SocketPermission "localhost:1024-", "listen";

// "standard" properies that can be read by anyone

permission java.util.PropertyPermission "java.version", "read";
permission java.util.PropertyPermission "java.vendor", "read";
permission java.util.PropertyPermission "java.vendor.url", "read";
permission java.util.PropertyPermission "java.class.version", "read";
permission java.util.PropertyPermission "os.name", "read";
permission java.util.PropertyPermission "os.version", "read";
permission java.util.PropertyPermission "os.arch", "read";
permission java.util.PropertyPermission "file.separator", "read";
permission java.util.PropertyPermission "path.separator", "read";
permission java.util.PropertyPermission "line.separator", "read";

permission java.util.PropertyPermission "java.specification.version", "read";
permission java.util.PropertyPermission "java.specification.vendor", "read";
permission java.util.PropertyPermission "java.specification.name", "read";

permission java.util.PropertyPermission "java.vm.specification.version", "read";
permission java.util.PropertyPermission "java.vm.specification.vendor", "read";
permission java.util.PropertyPermission "java.vm.specification.name", "read";
permission java.util.PropertyPermission "java.vm.version", "read";
permission java.util.PropertyPermission "java.vm.vendor", "read";
permission java.util.PropertyPermission "java.vm.name", "read";
};
```

Notice that this policy file grants permissions to all users, but it does provide the `codebase` in the first policy entry. This file has two policy entries: `CodeBase` "`file:${java.home} /lib/ext/`" and `CodeBase<ALL>`. A `codebase` is the location of the code that requires the access permissions. It can be any type of URL, and because it is a URL, it requires forward slashes. The first entry specified in the policy file maps to the `codebase` for the java extension JARs. In this case, the `${java.home}` specifies the `D:\jdk1.4` java installation directory; therefore, the rest of the `codebase` will map to the `D:\jdk1.4\lib\ext\` directory for any Java extensions that are supplied for the library.

This entry grants all users all access to that subdirectory during the runtime of the JVM. The principal can be specified to grant a particular user access to the target resource. This can be added when editing a specific policy entry. Figure 8-2 shows how a principal entry can be added, edited, or removed.

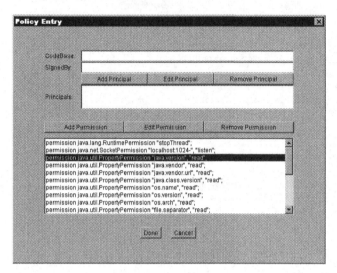

Figure 8-2: The principal entry

After you select a particular permission class, it can also be edited. One of the benefits of using the `policytool` is that it gives the editor the exact selections that are available without having to look them up in a permissions class. Figure 8-3 shows which actions are selectable for the `FilePermission`.

When the Edit/Change Keystore menu is selected, the Keystore entry, as shown in Figure 8-4, appears. The input that is needed in this window is the `keystore` URL and the `keystore` type, which will only allow the one entry into the policy file.

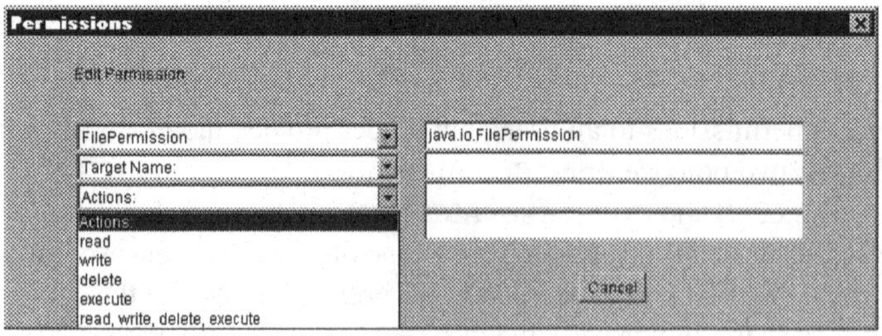

Figure 8-3: The Permission class

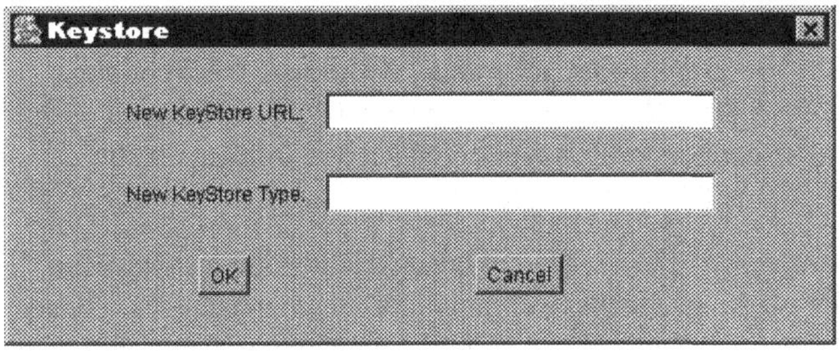

Figure 8-4: The Keystore entry

The `policytool` formats the policy file based on the rules of the policy file. It gives the editor direction on what is allowed into the policy file. This prevents the editor from making mistakes to the file. If the file already contains an error, the `policytool` displays a warning log if the severity is not too high, or it states the reason that the file cannot be parsed. It has been mentioned that many developers edit these files by hand, but then they may discover errors in the file only during runtime. The `policytool` guarantees the validity of the file before the execution of the application. This can save a lot of time and effort in troubleshooting an application.

You can use the `policytool` to grant permissions to local resources. For instance, you may want to grant an applet read/write access to a local directory or file. One way to accomplish this is to add a policy entry with a principal. Refer to Figure 8-2. You may want to require the code to be originated from a specific location (by using the CodeBase option in the policy tool). Also, you may require the code to be signed (by using the SignedBy text box in the policy tool). For example, you may want to require the code to be signed if you are interested in a trusted applet. To add a principal in the policy tool, you select the Add Principal button (in the Policy Entry dialog box) and select a principal type, such as `X500Principal`, which displays the complete principal type (like `com.sun.security.auth.X500Principal`). Next, you enter the principal name (such as `CN=TEST,OU=ORG,O=MYCOMPANY,C=US`). Finally, you must save your settings.

> **TIP:** In order for an applet to access a resource — or for that matter any application running with a security manager — the corresponding permission must be explicitly granted to the code attempting the access.

Summary

While the providers in the `keytool` and `jarsigner` utility can be rewritten at the SPI layer, great care must be taken to understand exactly which engine classes need to be overridden. The `keytool` utility obviously implements the `KeyStore` engine class with the algorithm that is set as the default type, or a different `storetype` is specified in the command line.

If the default is not used, a different provider's implementation should be fully tested. However, since it has to support all the functionality of the `KeyStoreSpi`, it will most likely work. Algorithms are also very specific to the `keytool` utility; it supports the DSA and RSA keying mechanisms. Because the `keytool` only supports these algorithms, there could be checks to ensure that the only the RSA or DSA is specified, and creating a different algorithm through a provider and passing in different algorithm types could cause problems in the `keytool` operation.

Re-implementing the `keytool` and `jarsigner` does not become a difficult task with the JDK 1.4 because most of the inner workings are just a combination of engine classes. To re-implement the keytool, obviously one uses the `KeyStore` in the implementation of the `JavaKeyStore`. Also, one would implement the `Signature` and `MessageDigest` engine classes, which would be implemented using their respective algorithms, such as DSA and MD5.

When you know that most of the engine classes are decoupled and the `keytool` is simply a matter of combining a set of engine classes, it becomes a matter of connecting interfaces to build a key store or `jarsigner`. These tools require nothing beyond the basic building blocks that are used to manage keys in code. These building blocks, the engine classes, make it easy for an organization to develop its own `keytool` or provider interface without breaking anything that is built using the standard JDK 1.4 security classes.

Part III

Data Integrity

Chapter 9: Ensuring Data Integrity

Chapter 10: Ensuring Message Authentication

Chapter 11: Signature Integrity

Chapter 9
Ensuring Data Integrity

In This Chapter

- ◆ Learning how to secure data through a message digest
- ◆ Understanding how to hash data
- ◆ Understanding the different message digests
- ◆ Implementing the supported message digests in the JDK

Introduction

Ensuring data integrity is a very important part of computer science, from the Web page to software that is being ordered off the Web. If files are not periodically checked, then viruses and Trojans can be inserted into the data without the organization's being aware of it. This can be very serious because if a customer buys the virused software from the organization, he or she may not be a repeat customer; also, the media reports stating that the software is virused could shut down an organization.

Another scenario where corrupt data could affect a company is in its communication with third-party vendors. For example, if an online mortgage company that looks for the best rates from banks receives a rate from one bank that is more than 200% higher than the others, a hacker might have altered the message. It is obvious that that bank will not be getting the business.

Protocols and software can be used to prevent thesesituations. The basic strategy to assist an organization is to establish security requirements, a policy for software, and steps to accommodate the plan. An organization should dedicate resources specifically for handling security issues and employ software architects and developers to specifically ensure the security of the organization. Many organizations are focused on getting the product finished, but if the product is deployed on an insecure framework, the entire product is compromised. Hackers spend their time knowing the market, and there have been many cases where a product was damaged before it reached the market.

> **NOTE:** See `http://www.richware.com/` for upcoming software and resources to assist organizations. If you require specific help or software, please e-mail me at `rhelton@richware.com`.

Understanding the Hash Function

The secure hash is an algorithm that takes a stream of data and creates a fixed-length digest from it. The digest is a fingerprint of the data. No message digest is perfect, but theoretically it should have a low collision rate, if any, and be a quick, secure algorithm that provides a unique fingerprint for every message. If even one single bit of data is changed in the message, the digest should change as well.

Notice, however, that there is a very remote probability that two different arbitrary messages can have the same fingerprint. When two or more messages can have the same fingerprint, it is known as a *collision*. When the same exact message is hashed twice, it should generate the same digest. These are just some of the requirements that the hash function is based on and they should be the criteria for which hash algorithm to choose.

The hash functions will generally fall into three types of algorithms based on their uses. There are hashes that don't require a key, those that require a secret key, and those that require a key pair. The algorithms that don't require a key are known as message digests. Those algorithms that require a secret key are known as message authentication codes, and those that require a key pair are known as digital signatures. All these algorithms and their differences are discussed in this chapter and the next two chapters. See Figure 9-1 for a breakdown of the algorithms.

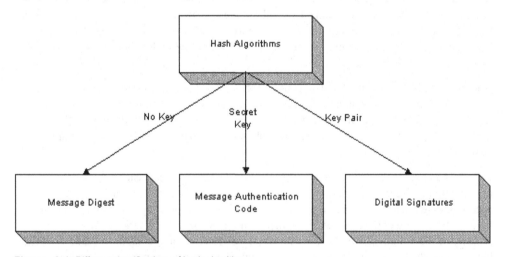

Figure 9-1: Different classifications of hash algorithms

Understanding the Message Digest

A *message digest* (MD) is an algorithm that uses a hash function to create a digest. The digest is simply the fingerprint of the original message. The digest is used to validate that the message has not been altered. In order to check the integrity of a digest, it must be compared against the original digest, which must be trusted by the receiver as being untampered with. For instance, if the message is M, and a message digest is used (MD), a digest (D) is produced. This is illustrated in the following equation.

$$MD_1(M)_1 = D_1$$

When the message needs to be validated again at a later time, the message is hashed to a new digest. If any data is changed in the message, even by one bit, the message digest must produce a different digest as illustrated in the next equation:

$$MD_2(M)_2 = D_2$$

Now the two digests are compared, and if there is a difference between the digests, D_2 is considered invalid or altered.

> **NOTE:** In the D_1 and D_2 comparison, D_1 must be trusted by the receiver as being the original digest and so it is up to the organization to keep it safe. One suggestion is to put D_1 in an LDAP server.

Encryption and digests

Another use of the digest is that it is encrypted in a message such as SSL or X.509 to be unencrypted by a public key and checked for corruption of the data. Since the private key is needed to encrypt the digest, only the owner of the private key can generate the digest. The owner of the private key is usually the initiator of the message, so this scenario works well. Any user that has a copy can decrypt the message, but cannot encrypt the message without a private key. This private-public key scenario is an example of a key pair.

> **CROSS-REFERENCE:** Key pairs and associated uses are discussed in Chapter 8. Chapter 24 discusses X.509, and Chapter 22 discusses SSL.

If you are familiar with Serial Communications and TCP/IP, this type of message integrity check may look familiar. In TCP/IP, there is a *Cyclic Redundancy Code* (CRC) to ensure that the receiver received the message in its entirety. If the receiver calculates the CRC and it doesn't match the message, the TCP/IP packet is retransmitted. The CRC code uses a 12-bit, 16-bit, or 32-bit CRC size. First, the CRC uses a polynomial calculation to sum the bits in the message into the desired bit-size CRC digest. Then, the CRC is used to detect errors in a transmission. The idea of using a digest for messages has been around for quite some time in other protocols; the algorithms have evolved over time.

Many algorithms can be used for checking the message digest, such as MD2, MD4, MD5, SHA-0, SHA-1, RIPEMD-160, Tiger, and many more. When testing the message, the tester must be aware of the algorithm that is being used. If the digest was hashed using MD5 and the message to be validated was hashed using SHA-1, then the digests is different even if the messages are the same. An organization needs to establish standards for which algorithms it uses for the MD.

> **TIP:** Using the Java JDK 1.4 limits the MD primarily to MD5 and SHA-1, two of the most popular algorithms; these algorithms are discussed later in this chapter.

Differentiating MDs

Many characteristics are used to differentiate MDs. Each MD usually has an initialization registers set of four or five values that will be the first values used in the hash. The registers were originally optimized for 32-bit processing machines and are the values that will initialize the registers. The initialization values are important to ensure that the input data is not the firstof the initialization variables, so that even less can be known about the input data. When the algorithm is initialized, buffers need to be zeroed out. When the digest is returned, the algorithm needs to be initialized again to start a new digest. Many algorithms use temporary buffers and have the capability to add input data through an update method.

One of the characteristics of the message digest is referred to as a *one-way hash*. A one-way hash means that the input data cannot be recovered by looking at the digest or hash. After the initialization of the message, data can be inputted for the algorithm to compute. The data must not exceed the message digest's maximum size. The message digest breaks down the input data into blocks. Most algorithms use a 512-bit block size, but the block size is algorithm-specific. If the data input is smaller than the block size, the algorithm must pad the data to reach the correct block size. Lengths are added inside many of the blocks to contain the length of the original message. After the input data is entered and formatted to the correct block size, each block will go through the algorithm's computations.

Breaking down the algorithm

The algorithm is normally broken down into *rounds* and *operations*. The *rounds* are a set of like operations performed on the data block. For example, SHA-1 has four rounds, and each round has 20 steps. The step is the number of times that the data is transformed. A *round* is the number of completely different transformations on the data. After the data has been hashed upon, the result needs to be compressed into a digest. The compression will take the 512-bit block and put it into a 160-bit digest in SHA-1; other algorithms have different sizes. An example of the padding, initialization, and updates for SHA-1 is displayed in Figure 9-2. Many of the message digests have different values, different operations in the computation, and several other factors; but the basic flow remains the same.

The initial variables in the five registers in SHA-1 are variables to initialize the chaining variables. The initial variables are hashed with the input message block. The result of the hash is used as initial variables in the next input message block that will be hashed. Then the result of that hash is used next as chaining variables, and this process continues until the final phase is called by the application to change the hash into the hash digest. The hash in SHA-1 has five integer registers until the final phase, and when the entering the final phase, the hash is converted to 20 bytes.

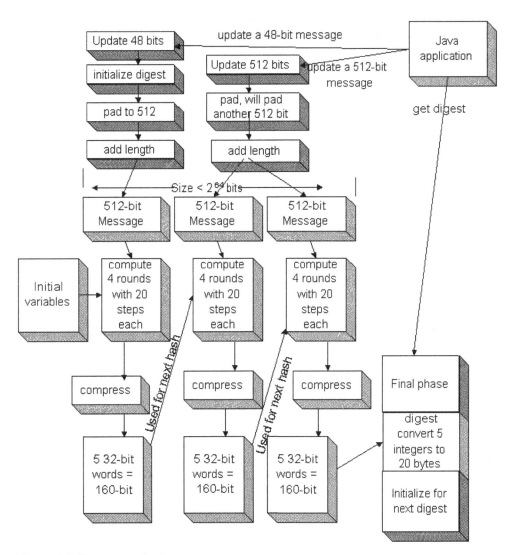

Figure 9-2: The message digest process

NOTE: The general steps of a message digest algorithm can be described as:

Step 1: Initialization.

Step 2: Break the data input into the appropriate block size, padding if necessary.

Step 3: Append the length.

Step 4: Pass each block through the algorithm's rounds and operations.

Step 5: Compress to digest the data.

Understanding the Different Message Digest Algorithms

The previous section mentioned that there are several parts that make up the message digest algorithm. These parts are initialization, message padding, appending length, computation parts (that include rounds and steps), and the compression to the digest size (that is usually based on the initialization registers). These parts of the message digest algorithm determine the outcome of speed, complexity, integrity, and security. The number of steps and how many operations there are in each step affect the speed of the computation. The size of the blocks and digest size may also affect the speed and security of the algorithm.

> **TIP:** When the digest has a higher bit size, the algorithm has a higher security and integrity.

A hash algorithm needs to have a *high collision resistance*, meaning that there should be a very low chance that two different messages can produce the same digest. The only guarantee that two messages can produce different digests is if the message itself is the digest. There is always a chance that a random message could produce the same digest. When different messages produce the same digest, the algorithm has *collisions*.

> **TIP:** The higher the bits for the digest, the lower the probability of producing the same digest.

MD algorithms

Ron Rivest, the "R" in RSA security, started many of the message digest algorithms. More information on Mr. Rivest can be found at `http://theory.lcs.mit.edu/~rivest/`. Rivest designed *MD2*, *MD4*, and *MD5* for message digest 2, message digest 4, and message digest 5.

> **NOTE:** These protocols can be studied in:
>
> RFC 1319: [RFC1319] Rivest, R. RFC1319 "The MD2 Message-Digest Algorithm," Internet Engineering Task Force, `http://www.ietf.org/rfc/rfc1319.txt`, 1992.
>
> RFC 1320: Rivest, R. RFC1320 "The MD4 Message-Digest Algorithm," Internet Engineering Task Force, `http://www.ietf.org/rfc/rfc1320.txt`, 1992.
>
> RFC 1321: [RFC1321] Rivest, R. RFC1321 "The MD5 Message-Digest Algorithm," Internet Engineering Task Force, `http://www.ietf.org/rfc/rfc1321.txt`, 1992.

Many subsequent protocols such as SHA-1 and RIPEMD-160 have been based on MD4. All three MD algorithms used a 128-bit digest size. The MD2 was the fastest, followed by MD4 and then MD5. Collisions have been detected in all three algorithms, and RSA's Laboratories' bulletin number 4 recommends that only MD5 be used when possible. The most collisions were found in the MD2 algorithm, followed by the MD4 algorithm, and then the MD5 algorithm.

The difference between these algorithms is the complexity of their computation. MD2 uses two rounds of 16 steps, MD4 uses three rounds of 16 steps, and MD5 uses four rounds of 16 steps. Thealgorithms with the lowest rounds and least complexity are the ones that are the fastest in computational time. There was also a difference in the initialization values. Only MD5 and MD4 use initialized registers. The initialization values for the MD5 and MD4 that are used as chaining variables are defined as follows:

A = 0x67452301;

B = 0xEFCDAB89;

C = 0x98BADCFE;

D = 0x10325476;

MD4 was designed specifically for implementations on 32-bit machines. Security concerns motivated the design for MD5 shortly thereafter. A 32-bit register is normally a hardware register that processes 32 bits at a time. Because of the breakdown into 32-bit registers, which maps to integers in Java, many algorithms have been modeled after MD4, including MD5. MD5 was designed to strengthen MD4 because it was thought that collisions might occur when using it. Even though collisions have been found, MD5 is widely used because the quickness of the algorithm far outweighs the calculation of the collision. Finding a collision in MD5 is almost as complex as finding the key for a DES cracker, and many believe that it would take a machine that costs $10 million (in 1996 dollars) 24 days to find a collision.

MD5 uses a 512-bit block. Sixty-four bits are used to describe the length of the block, leaving 448 bits for data. Padding is always added, even if the correct size was achieved by the input data. If the message size was originally 448 bits, which is the desired size, a pad must still be applied to add another 512-bit block. The number of padding bits can be anywhere from 1 to 512 bits.

The MD5 computation will execute four rounds with 16 steps each. Each 512-bit block will be executed in the four rounds instead of the MD4 three rounds. Because of the difference in computational power, MD5 is about 25% slower than MD4.

> **NOTE:** Here is a brief comparison of MD2, MD4, and MD5:
> 1. All use a 128-bit digest size.
> 2. They differ on the number of rounds:
> MD2 uses 2 rounds of 16 steps.
> MD4 uses 3 rounds of 16 steps.
> MD5 uses 4 rounds of 16 steps.
> 3. MD4 and MD5 use initialized registers (32-bit) and use chaining variables.
> 4. MD5 uses a 512-bit block: 64 bits for the length of the block, 448 bits for data.

The reference implementation given in the C language of MD5 is given in RFC 1321. Listing 9-1 gives my Java interpretation of the reference implementation.

Listing 9-1: The MD5 implementation

```
package com.richware.chap09;

import java.security.*;
/**
 * Class RichMD5
 * Description: This is an example
 * implementation of the MD5
 * algorithm.
 *
 * Copyright:    Copyright (c) 2002 Wiley Publishing, Inc.
 * @author Rich Helton <rhelton@richware.com>
 * @version 1.0
 * DISCLAIMER: Please refer to the disclaimer at the beginning of this
book.
*/
public class RichMD5
{
  public final static String[][] testData =
    {
    //    data string, md hex
    { "", "D41D8CD98F00B204E9800998ECF8427E" },      // A.5 1
    { "a", "0CC175B9C0F1B6A831C399E269772661" },      // A.5 2
    { "aa", "4124BC0A9335C27F086F24BA207A4912" },
    { "abc", "900150983CD24FB0D6963F7D28E17F72" },    // A.5 3
    { "aaa", "47BCE5C74F589F4867DBD57E9CA9F808" },
    { "bbb", "08F8E0260C64418510CEFB2B06EEE5CD" },
    { "ccc", "9DF62E693988EB4E1E1444ECE0578579" },
    { "message digest", "F96B697D7CB7938D525A2F31AAF161D0" },  // A.5 4
    { "abcdefg", "7AC66C0F148DE9519B8BD264312C4D64" },
    { "abcdefghijk", "92B9CCCC0B98C3A0B8D0DF25A421C0E3" },
    {                                                 // A.5 5
    "abcdefghijklmnopqrstuvwxyz",
    "C3FCD3D76192E4007DFB496CCA67E13B"
    },
    {                                                 // A.5 6
    "ABCDEFGHIJKLMNOPQRSTUVWXYZabcdefghijklmnopqrstuvwxyz0123456789",
    "D174AB98D277D9F5A5611C2C9F419D9F"
    },
    {                                                 // A.5 7
"12345678901234567890123456789012345678901234567890123456789012345678901
234567890",
    "57EDF4A22BE3C955AC49DA2E2107B67A"
    },
  };
  public static final char[] hexDigits =
    {
```

```
  '0', '1', '2', '3', '4', '5', '6', '7', '8', '9', 'A', 'B',
  'C', 'D', 'E', 'F'
};
private static final int    S11       = 7;
private static final int    S12       = 12;
private static final int    S13       = 17;
private static final int    S14       = 22;
private static final int    S21       = 5;
private static final int    S22       = 9;
private static final int    S23       = 14;
private static final int    S24       = 20;
private static final int    S31       = 4;
private static final int    S32       = 11;
private static final int    S33       = 16;
private static final int    S34       = 23;
private static final int    S41       = 6;
private static final int    S42       = 10;
private static final int    S43       = 15;
private static final int    S44       = 21;
private long                count;

/** 4 32-bit words (interim result) */
private int[] context = new int[ 4];

/** 512 bits work buffer = 16 x 32-bit words */
private int[] x = new int[ 16];
private byte  digestBits[];
private byte  buffer[];

/**
 * Constructor RichMD5
 */
public RichMD5()
{
  MD5Init();
}

protected void MD5Init()
{
  // initial values of MD5 i.e. A, B, C, D
  context[ 0] = 0x67452301;
  context[ 1] = 0xEFCDAB89;
  context[ 2] = 0x98BADCFE;
  context[ 3] = 0x10325476;
  buffer      = new byte[ 64];
  count       = 0L;
  digestBits  = new byte[ 16];
  for (int i = 0; i < digestBits.length; i++)
  {
```

```
    digestBits[ i]  = 0;
  }
}

/**
 * Method MD5Update
 * @param input
 * @param inputLen
 *
 */
public void MD5Update(byte[ ] input, int inputLen)
 {
  int k = 0;
  int j = inputLen;
  while (j > 0)
    {
    int l = (int) (count >>> 3 & 63L);
    if ((l == 0) && (j > 64))
      {
      count += 512L;
      MD5Transform(input, k);
      j -= 64;
      k += 64;
      }
    else
      {
      count    += 8L;
      buffer[ l]  = input[ k];
      if (l >= 63)
        {
        MD5Transform(buffer, 0);
        }
      k++;
      j--;
      }
    }
  }
}

/**
 * Method MD5Final
 * @return
 *
 */
public byte[ ] MD5Final()
  {
  byte abyte0[ ]  = new byte[ 8];
  for (int i = 0; i < 8; i++)
    {
    abyte0[ i] = (byte) (int) (count >>> i * 8 & 255L);
```

```
  }

  /* Pad out to 56 mod 64. */
  int index = (int) (count >> 3) & 0x3f;
  /*
   * Apply the padding
   */
  int  padLen  = (index >= 56)
                   ? 120 - index
                   : 56 - index;
  byte abyte1[ ] = new byte[ padLen];
  abyte1[ 0] = -128;
  MD5Update(abyte1, abyte1.length);
  MD5Update(abyte0, abyte0.length);
  for (int j = 0; j < 4; j++)
  {
    for (int i1 = 0; i1 < 4; i1++)
    {
      digestBits[ j * 4 + i1] = (byte) (context[ j] >>> i1 * 8
                                        & 0xff);
    }
  }

  /* Store state in digest */
  byte abyte2[ ] = new byte[ 16];
  System.arraycopy(digestBits, 0, abyte2, 0, 16);
  MD5Init();
  return abyte2;
}


protected void MD5Transform(byte[ ] block, int offset)
{
  /*
   * Decodes 64 bytes from
   * input block into an array of
   * 16 32-bit entities.
   * Decode function in reference
   */
  for (int i = 0; i < 16; i++)
  {
    x[ i] = (block[ offset++] & 0xFF)
          | (block[ offset++] & 0xFF) << 8
          | (block[ offset++] & 0xFF) << 16
          | (block[ offset++] & 0xFF) << 24;
  }
  int a = context[ 0];
  int b = context[ 1];
  int c = context[ 2];
  int d = context[ 3];
```

```
/* Round 1 */
a = FF(a, b, c, d, x[ 0], S11, 0xd76aa478);    /*  1 */
d = FF(d, a, b, c, x[ 1], S12, 0xe8c7b756);    /*  2 */
c = FF(c, d, a, b, x[ 2], S13, 0x242070db);    /*  3 */
b = FF(b, c, d, a, x[ 3], S14, 0xc1bdceee);    /*  4 */
a = FF(a, b, c, d, x[ 4], S11, 0xf57c0faf);    /*  5 */
d = FF(d, a, b, c, x[ 5], S12, 0x4787c62a);    /*  6 */
c = FF(c, d, a, b, x[ 6], S13, 0xa8304613);    /*  7 */
b = FF(b, c, d, a, x[ 7], S14, 0xfd469501);    /*  8 */
a = FF(a, b, c, d, x[ 8], S11, 0x698098d8);    /*  9 */
d = FF(d, a, b, c, x[ 9], S12, 0x8b44f7af);    /* 10 */
c = FF(c, d, a, b, x[10], S13, 0xffff5bb1);    /* 11 */
b = FF(b, c, d, a, x[11], S14, 0x895cd7be);    /* 12 */
a = FF(a, b, c, d, x[12], S11, 0x6b901122);    /* 13 */
d = FF(d, a, b, c, x[13], S12, 0xfd987193);    /* 14 */
c = FF(c, d, a, b, x[14], S13, 0xa679438e);    /* 15 */
b = FF(b, c, d, a, x[15], S14, 0x49b40821);    /* 16 */

/* Round 2 */
a = GG(a, b, c, d, x[ 1], S21, 0xf61e2562);    /* 17 */
d = GG(d, a, b, c, x[ 6], S22, 0xc040b340);    /* 18 */
c = GG(c, d, a, b, x[11], S23, 0x265e5a51);    /* 19 */
b = GG(b, c, d, a, x[ 0], S24, 0xe9b6c7aa);    /* 20 */
a = GG(a, b, c, d, x[ 5], S21, 0xd62f105d);    /* 21 */
d = GG(d, a, b, c, x[10], S22, 0x2441453);     /* 22 */
c = GG(c, d, a, b, x[15], S23, 0xd8a1e681);    /* 23 */
b = GG(b, c, d, a, x[ 4], S24, 0xe7d3fbc8);    /* 24 */
a = GG(a, b, c, d, x[ 9], S21, 0x21e1cde6);    /* 25 */
d = GG(d, a, b, c, x[14], S22, 0xc33707d6);    /* 26 */
c = GG(c, d, a, b, x[ 3], S23, 0xf4d50d87);    /* 27 */
b = GG(b, c, d, a, x[ 8], S24, 0x455a14ed);    /* 28 */
a = GG(a, b, c, d, x[13], S21, 0xa9e3e905);    /* 29 */
d = GG(d, a, b, c, x[ 2], S22, 0xfcefa3f8);    /* 30 */
c = GG(c, d, a, b, x[ 7], S23, 0x676f02d9);    /* 31 */
b = GG(b, c, d, a, x[12], S24, 0x8d2a4c8a);    /* 32 */

/* Round 3 */
a = HH(a, b, c, d, x[ 5], S31, 0xfffa3942);    /* 33 */
d = HH(d, a, b, c, x[ 8], S32, 0x8771f681);    /* 34 */
c = HH(c, d, a, b, x[11], S33, 0x6d9d6122);    /* 35 */
b = HH(b, c, d, a, x[14], S34, 0xfde5380c);    /* 36 */
a = HH(a, b, c, d, x[ 1], S31, 0xa4beea44);    /* 37 */
d = HH(d, a, b, c, x[ 4], S32, 0x4bdecfa9);    /* 38 */
c = HH(c, d, a, b, x[ 7], S33, 0xf6bb4b60);    /* 39 */
b = HH(b, c, d, a, x[10], S34, 0xbebfbc70);    /* 40 */
a = HH(a, b, c, d, x[13], S31, 0x289b7ec6);    /* 41 */
d = HH(d, a, b, c, x[ 0], S32, 0xeaa127fa);    /* 42 */
c = HH(c, d, a, b, x[ 3], S33, 0xd4ef3085);    /* 43 */
```

```
  b = HH(b, c, d, a, x[ 6], S34, 0x4881d05);    /* 44 */
  a = HH(a, b, c, d, x[ 9], S31, 0xd9d4d039);   /* 45 */
  d = HH(d, a, b, c, x[12], S32, 0xe6db99e5);   /* 46 */
  c = HH(c, d, a, b, x[15], S33, 0x1fa27cf8);   /* 47 */
  b = HH(b, c, d, a, x[ 2], S34, 0xc4ac5665);   /* 48 */

  /* Round 4 */
  a = II(a, b, c, d, x[ 0], S41, 0xf4292244);   /* 49 */
  d = II(d, a, b, c, x[ 7], S42, 0x432aff97);   /* 50 */
  c = II(c, d, a, b, x[14], S43, 0xab9423a7);   /* 51 */
  b = II(b, c, d, a, x[ 5], S44, 0xfc93a039);   /* 52 */
  a = II(a, b, c, d, x[12], S41, 0x655b59c3);   /* 53 */
  d = II(d, a, b, c, x[ 3], S42, 0x8f0ccc92);   /* 54 */
  c = II(c, d, a, b, x[10], S43, 0xffeff47d);   /* 55 */
  b = II(b, c, d, a, x[ 1], S44, 0x85845dd1);   /* 56 */
  a = II(a, b, c, d, x[ 8], S41, 0x6fa87e4f);   /* 57 */
  d = II(d, a, b, c, x[15], S42, 0xfe2ce6e0);   /* 58 */
  c = II(c, d, a, b, x[ 6], S43, 0xa3014314);   /* 59 */
  b = II(b, c, d, a, x[13], S44, 0x4e0811a1);   /* 60 */
  a = II(a, b, c, d, x[ 4], S41, 0xf7537e82);   /* 61 */
  d = II(d, a, b, c, x[11], S42, 0xbd3af235);   /* 62 */
  c = II(c, d, a, b, x[ 2], S43, 0x2ad7d2bb);   /* 63 */
  b = II(b, c, d, a, x[ 9], S44, 0xeb86d391);   /* 64 */
  context[ 0]  += a;
  context[ 1]  += b;
  context[ 2]  += c;
  context[ 3]  += d;
}

private static int F(int x, int y, int z)
 {
  return (z ^ (x & (y ^ z)));
 }

private static int G(int x, int y, int z)
 {
  return (y ^ (z & (x ^ y)));
 }

private static int H(int x, int y, int z)
 {
  return (x ^ y ^ z);
 }

private static int I(int x, int y, int z)
 {
  return (y ^ (x | ~z));
 }
```

```java
private static int FF(int a, int b, int c, int d, int k,
                      int s, int t)
{
  a += k + t + F(b, c, d);
  a = (a << s | a >>> -s);
  return a + b;
}

private static int GG(int a, int b, int c, int d, int k,
                      int s, int t)
{
  a += k + t + G(b, c, d);
  a = (a << s | a >>> -s);
  return a + b;
}

private static int HH(int a, int b, int c, int d, int k,
                      int s, int t)
{
  a += k + t + H(b, c, d);
  a = (a << s | a >>> -s);
  return a + b;
}

private int II(int a, int b, int c, int d, int k, int s,
               int t)
{
  a += k + t + I(b, c, d);
  a = (a << s | a >>> -s);
  return a + b;
}

/**
 * Method main
 * Description: This is a test driver
 * @param args none
 *
 */
public static void main(String[] args)
{
  try
    {
      /*
       * Create a new MD5 and test data
       */
      RichMD5 md5 = new RichMD5();
      /*
       * Create a JDK MD5 algorithm
       */
```

```
MessageDigest md5MD = MessageDigest.getInstance("MD5");
for (int index = 0; index < testData.length; index++)
{
  System.out.println("");
  System.out.println("MD5 Digesting...");
  System.out.println(testData[ index][ 0] );
  byte[] testBytes = testData[ index][ 0] .getBytes();

  /*
   * Update the digest with data
   * normally the data can be updated
   * at different times
   */
  System.out.println("Test Length :" + testBytes.length);
  md5.MD5Update(testBytes, testBytes.length);
  byte[] digest = md5.MD5Final();
  System.out.println("Trusted Digest :"
                     + testData[ index][ 1] );
  byte[] testDigest = testData[ 0][ 1] .getBytes();
  char[] buf       = new char[ digest.length * 2] ;
  int    j         = 0;
  int    k;
  for (int i = 0; i < digest.length; i++)
  {
    k         = digest[ i] ;
    buf[ j++] = hexDigits[ (k >>> 4) & 0x0F] ;
    buf[ j++] = hexDigits[ k & 0x0F] ;
  }
  String buffer = new String(buf);
  System.out.println("New Digest      :" + buffer);
}

/*
 *   Test the JDK Version
 */
for (int index = 0; index < testData.length; index++)
{
  System.out.println("");
  System.out.println("MD5 Digesting with JDK...");
  System.out.println(testData[ index][ 0] );
  byte[] testBytes = testData[ index][ 0] .getBytes();

  /*
   * Update the digest with data
   * normally the data can be updated
   * at different times
   */
  System.out.println("Test Length :" + testBytes.length);
  md5MD.update(testBytes, 0, testBytes.length);
```

```
        byte[] digest = md5MD.digest();
        System.out.println("Trusted Digest :"
                                + testData[ index][ 1 ] );
        byte[] testDigest = testData[ 0][ 1 ].getBytes();
        char[] buf        = new char[ digest.length * 2] ;
        int    j          = 0;
        int    k;
        for (int i = 0; i < digest.length; i++)
          {
            k         = digest[ i] ;
            buf[ j++] = hexDigits[ (k >>> 4) & 0x0F] ;
            buf[ j++] = hexDigits[ k & 0x0F] ;
          }

        String buffer = new String(buf);
        System.out.println("New Digest      :" + buffer);
      }
    }


  /*
   * Catches
   */
  catch (Exception ex)
    {
      ex.printStackTrace();
    }
  }
}
```

The output of Listing 9-1 demonstrates that the expected result is achieved. That is, the `Trusted Digest` and the `New Digest` values are the same for the same input, as the following fragment shows:

```
>java RichMD5
MD5 Digesting...
Test Length :0
Trusted Digest :D41D8CD98F00B204E9800998ECF8427E
New Digest     :D41D8CD98F00B204E9800998ECF8427E
MD5 Digesting...
a
Test Length :1
Trusted Digest :0CC175B9C0F1B6A831C399E269772661
New Digest     :0CC175B9C0F1B6A831C399E269772661
...........
```

The SHA-1 algorithm

Another algorithm that has become just as popular as the MD5 algorithm is the SHA-1 algorithm. In 1995, the *Federal Information Processing Standards* (FIPS) published publication 180-1 for the standard of the *Secure Hash Standard*.

> **NOTE:** For more information see FIPS 180-1 "Secure Hash Standard," Federal Information Publication Standards, http://www.itl.nist.gov/fipspubs/fip180-1.htm, 1995.

The algorithm from the 180-1 publication is defined as the *Secure Hash Algorithm number 1* (SHA-1). The National Institute of Standards (NIST) and the National Security Agency (NSA) developed the SHA-1 algorithm. SHA-1 is closely modeled after the MD4 algorithm. There is currently a draft by FIPS 180-2 publication to update the SHA-1 algorithm. The SHA-1 was designed for use with the *Digital Signature Algorithm* (DSA) in mind.

The algorithm can take the input of data of not more than 2^{64} bits and produce a digest of 160 bits. The input is broken down into 512-bit blocks and is processed individually. A 160-bit buffer is used to hold intermediate and final results of the hash function. The buffer can be represented by five 32-bit registers (A, B, C, D, and E). The initialization values for the SHA-1 are defined as follows:

A = 67 45 23 01

B = EF CD AB 89

C = 98 BA DC FE

D = 10 32 54 76

E = C3 D2 E1 F0

SHA-1 consists of four rounds of processing 20 operations. Each round will use a specific constant:

- ♦ Round 1 will use K_1 = 0x5a827999, which is equivalent to 2^{30} X $\sqrt{2}$.
- ♦ Round 2 will use K_2 = 0x6ed9eba1, which is equivalent to 2^{30} X $\sqrt{3}$.
- ♦ Round 3 will use K_3 = 0x8f1bbcdc, which is equivalent to 2^{30} X $\sqrt{5}$.
- ♦ Round 4 will use K_4 = 0xca62c1d6, which is equivalent to 2^{30} X $\sqrt{10}$.

All four rounds will be applied to each of the 512-bit blocks that are used for the input buffer. Because the complexity and collision resistance is higher in SHA-1, it is about 30% slower than MD5. See Listing 9-2 for an example implementation of the SHA-1 algorithm.

> **NOTE:** Some of the differences between the SHA-1 algorithm and the MD4 are:
> 1. The digest value for SHA-1 is 160 bits, and for MD4 it is 128 bits.
> 2. SHA-1 has 40 rounds of 20 steps each while MD4 has 3 rounds of 16 steps each.
> 3. SHA-1 has 5 chaining variables that are initialized with values while MD4 only has 4 registers.

Listing 9-2: An example SHA-1 algorithm

```java
package com.richware.chap09;
import java.security.*;

/**
 * Class RichSHA
 * Description: This is an example
 * implementation of the SHA-1
 * algorithm.
 *
 * Copyright:    Copyright (c) 2002 Wiley Publishing, Inc.
 * @author Rich Helton <rhelton@richware.com>
 * @version 1.0
 * DISCLAIMER: Please refer to the disclaimer at the beginning of this
book.
 */
public class RichSHA
 {
  /* Temoporary Buffer */
  public int W_[];

  /* counter for the bytes */
  private long count  = 0L;

  /* Initial Register Values */
  private int[] H_;

  /* Input buffer */
  private byte[] INPUT_;

  /*
   * The round constants
   */
  private final int round1_kt = 0x5a827999;
  private final int round2_kt = 0x6ed9eba1;
  private final int round3_kt = 0x8f1bbcdc;
  private final int round4_kt = 0xca62c1d6;

  /*
   * Trusted digests
   */
  public final static String[][] testData =
   {
    { "", "da39a3ee5e6b4b0d3255bfef95601890afd80709" },
    { "1", "356a192b7913b04c54574d18c28d46e6395428ab" },
    { "a", "86f7e437faa5a7fce15d1ddcb9eaeaea377667b8" },
```

```
{ "abc", "a9993e364706816aba3e25717850c26c9cd0d89d" },
{ "abcdefghijklmnopqrstuvwxyz",
  "32d10c7b8cf96570ca04ce37f2a19d84240d3a89" },
{ "abcdbcdecdefdefgefghfghighijhijkijkljklmklmnlmnomnopnopq",
  "84983E441C3BD26EBAAE4AA1F95129E5E54670F1" },

{ "Anyone got any SHA-1 test data?",
  "09b9e9c04a84ce274942048acf3a6f2ff4a8a39c" },
  { "Of cabbages and kings",
    "5f093d74a9cb1f2f14537bcf3a8a1ffd59b038a2" }
};

/*
 * For hex conversion
 */
public static final char[] hexDigits =
{
  '0', '1', '2', '3', '4', '5', '6', '7', '8', '9', 'A', 'B',
  'C', 'D', 'E', 'F'
};

/**
 * Constructor RichSHA
 * Description: The Main constructor
 */
public RichSHA()
{
  W_     = new int[ 80];
  H_     = new int[ 5];
  INPUT_ = new byte[ 64];

  initSHA();
}

/**
 * Method: initSHA
 * Description: Initialize the variables
 * for SHA
 */
protected void initSHA()
{
  // initial values of SHA i.e. A, B, C, D
  H [ 0] = 0x67452301;
  H [ 1] = 0xefcdab89;
  H [ 2] = 0x98badcfe;
  H [ 3] = 0x10325476;
  H [ 4] = 0xc3d2e1f0;

  for (int i = 0; i < 80; i++)
```

```
      {
        W_[ i]  =  0;
      }

      for (int i = 0;  i < 64;  i++)
      {
        INPUT [ i]  =  0;
      }

      count_  =  0L;
    }

/**
 * Method updateSHA
 * Description: Updates the SHA values
 * with a byte array
 * @param data the data to add
 * @param offset offset to add data
 * @param len length of bytes
 *
 */
public void updateSHA(byte data[], int offset, int len)
{
  if ((offset < 0) || (len < 0)
          || (offset + len > data.length))
  {
    throw new ArrayIndexOutOfBoundsException();
  }

  /*
   * SAVE Input and compute
   * when the block is done
   */
  for (int index = 0; index < len; index++)
  {
    INPUT_[ (int) count_ & 63] = data[ offset + index];

    if ((int) (count_ & 63) == 63)
    {
      computeSHA();
    }

    count_++;
  }
}

/**
 * Method digestSHA
 * Description: Calculates final digest
```

```
  * @return the byte array with final digest
  *
  */
 public byte[] digestSHA()
 {
   byte digest[] = new byte[ 20];
   try
    {
      pad();

      for (int i = 0; i < 5; i++)
       {
         digest[ 4 * i]     = (byte) ((H_[ i] >>> 24) & 255);
         digest[ 4 * i + 1] = (byte) ((H_[ i] >>> 16) & 255);
         digest[ 4 * i + 2] = (byte) ((H_[ i] >>> 8) & 255);
         digest[ 4 * i + 3] = (byte) (H_[ i] & 255);
       }

      initSHA();
    }

   /*
    * Catches
    */
   catch (Exception ex)
    {
      ex.printStackTrace();
    }

   return digest;
 }

 /**
  * Method computeSHA
  * Description: The SHA algorithm
  */
 private void computeSHA()
 {
   /* step a */
   for (int k1 = 0; k1 < 16; k1++)
    {
      W_[ k1] =
        (((((int) INPUT [ 4 * k1] & 255) << 8) + ((int) INPUT [ 4 * k1 +
1] & 255) << 8) + ((int) INPUT_[ 4 * k1 + 2] & 255) << 8)
        + ((int) INPUT_[ 4 * k1 + 3] & 255);
    }

   /* step b */
   /*
```

```
 * 32 bit Word values being derived
 * from the 512-bit Message
 */
for (int k2 = 16; k2 <= 79; k2++)
{
  int i = W_[ k2 - 3] ^ W_[ k2 - 8] ^ W_[ k2 - 14]
          ^ W [ k2 - 16];

  W_[ k2] = i << 1 | i >>> 31;
}

int a    = H_[ 0];
int b    = H_[ 1];
int c    = H_[ 2];
int d    = H [ 3];
int e    = H_[ 4];
int temp = 0;

for (int index = 0; index < 80; index++)
{
  /*
   * Round 1
   */
  if (index < 20)
  {
    temp = (a << 5 | a >>> 27) + (b & c | ~b & d) + e
           + W [ index] + round1 kt;
  }

  /*
   * Round 2
   */
  else if (index < 40)
  {
    temp = (a << 5 | a >>> 27) + (b ^ c ^ d) + e
           + W_[ index] + round2_kt;
  }

  /*
   * Round 3
   */
  else if (index < 60)
  {
    temp = (a << 5 | a >>> 27) + (b & c | b & d | c & d)
           + e + W_[ index] + round3_kt;
  }

  /*
   * Round 4
```

```
     */
    else if (index < 80)
     {
       temp = (a << 5 | a >>> 27) + (b ^ c ^ d) + e
            + W_[ index]  + round4_kt;
     }

    /*
     * All Rounds
     */
    e = d;
    d = c;
    c = b << 30 | b >>> 2;
    b = a;
    a = temp;
   }

  /*
   * Add the values back
   * to the registers
   */
  H_[ 0]  += a;
  H_[ 1]  += b;
  H_[ 2]  += c;
  H_[ 3]  += d;
  H_[ 4]  += e;
}

/**
 * Method pad
 * Description: Pads the bytes
 */
private void pad()
{
  int  i;
  long bitlength;
  bitlength                  = count_ << 3;
  INPUT_[ (int) count_ & 63] = (byte) 128;
  count_++;

  if ((int) (count_ & 63) >= 56)
   {
     for (i = ((int) count_ & 63); i < 64; i++)
      {
        INPUT_[ i] = 0;
        count_++;
      }
     computeSHA();
   }
```

```java
    for (i = ((int) count_ & 63); i < 56; i++)
    {
      INPUT_[ i] = 0;
    }

   INPUT_[ 56] = (byte) ((bitlength >>> 56) & 255);
   INPUT_[ 57] = (byte) ((bitlength >>> 48) & 255);
   INPUT_[ 58] = (byte) ((bitlength >>> 40) & 255);
   INPUT_[ 59] = (byte) ((bitlength >>> 32) & 255);
   INPUT_[ 60] = (byte) ((bitlength >>> 24) & 255);
   INPUT_[ 61] = (byte) ((bitlength >>> 16) & 255);
   INPUT_[ 62] = (byte) ((bitlength >>> 8) & 255);
   INPUT_[ 63] = (byte) (bitlength & 255);

   computeSHA();
}

/**
 * Method main
 * Description: This is a test driver
 * @param args none
 *
 */
public static void main(String[] args)
{
  try
  {
    /*
     * Create a new local SHA1 and test data
     */
    RichSHA sha = new RichSHA();

    /*
     * Create a JDK SHA aalgorithm
     */
    MessageDigest shaMD = MessageDigest.getInstance("SHA1");

    /*
     * Loop through the test data
     */
    for (int index = 0; index < testData.length; index++)
    {
      System.out.println("");
      System.out.println("SHA1 Digesting...");
      System.out.println(testData[ index][ 0]);
      byte[] testBytes = testData[ index][ 0].getBytes();

      /*
```

```
 * Update the digest with data
 * normally the data can be updated
 * at different times
 */
System.out.println("Test Length :" + testBytes.length);
sha.updateSHA(testBytes, 0, testBytes.length);
byte[] digest = sha.digestSHA();
System.out.println("Trusted Digest :"
                      + testData[ index][ 1] );

byte[] testDigest = testData[ 0][ 1] .getBytes();
char[] buf       = new char[ digest.length * 2];
int    j         = 0;
int    k;

for (int i = 0; i < digest.length; i++)
  {
    k        = digest[ i] ;
    buf[ j++] = hexDigits[ (k >>> 4) & 0x0F] ;
    buf[ j++] = hexDigits[ k & 0x0F] ;
  }

String buffer = new String(buf);
System.out.println("New Digest    :" + buffer);
}


/*
 *  Test the JDK Version
 */
for (int index = 0; index < testData.length; index++)
  {
    System.out.println("");
    System.out.println("SHA1 Digesting with JDK...");
    System.out.println(testData[ index][ 0] );
    byte[] testBytes = testData[ index][ 0] .getBytes();

    /*
     * Update the digest with data
     * normally the data can be updated
     * at different times
     */
    System.out.println("Test Length :" + testBytes.length);
    shaMD.update(testBytes, 0, testBytes.length);
    byte[] digest = shaMD.digest();
    System.out.println("Trusted Digest :"
                          + testData[ index][ 1] );
    byte[] testDigest = testData[ 0][ 1] .getBytes();
    char[] buf       = new char[ digest.length * 2];
    int    j         = 0;
```

```
    int    k;

    for (int i = 0; i < digest.length; i++)
    {
      k         = digest[ i];
      buf[ j++] = hexDigits[ (k >>> 4) & 0x0F];
      buf[ j++] = hexDigits[ k & 0x0F];
    }

    String buffer = new String(buf);
    System.out.println("New Digest     :" + buffer);
  }
}


/*
 * Catches
 */
catch (Exception ex)
{
  ex.printStackTrace();
}
  }
}
```

In Listing 9-2, the computeSHA method demonstrates the four rounds. The rounds are initialized with the K constants. Each round has much of the same functionality with slight differences in the b, c, and d logical operations. After the rounds are computed and the digest needs to be done, a compression of the digest takes place to shift the register values of A, B, C, D, and E into 20 bytes of digest represented in the H array. An example output of Listing 9-2 is given in Listing 9-3. Notice that the different input messages produce different digests. Also, a comparison is done with the JDK 1.4 SHA-1 message digest, and they match.

Listing 9-3: Output from Listing 9-2

```
SHA1 Digesting...

Test Length :0
Trusted Digest :da39a3ee5e6b4b0d3255bfef95601890afd80709
New Digest     :DA39A3EE5E6B4B0D3255BFEF95601890AFD80709

SHA1 Digesting...
1
Test Length :1
Trusted Digest :356a192b7913b04c54574d18c28d46e6395428ab
New Digest     :356A192B7913B04C54574D18C28D46E6395428AB

SHA1 Digesting...
```

```
a
Test Length :1
Trusted Digest :86f7e437faa5a7fce15d1ddcb9eaeaea377667b8
New Digest     :86F7E437FAA5A7FCE15D1DDCB9EAEAEA377667B8


SHA1 Digesting...
abc
Test Length :3
Trusted Digest :a9993e364706816aba3e25717850c26c9cd0d89d
New Digest     :A9993E364706816ABA3E25717850C26C9CD0D89D


SHA1 Digesting...
abcdefghijklmnopqrstuvwxyz
Test Length :26
Trusted Digest :32d10c7b8cf96570ca04ce37f2a19d84240d3a89
New Digest     :32D10C7B8CF96570CA04CE37F2A19D84240D3A89


SHA1 Digesting...
abcdbcdecdefdefgefghfghighijhijkijkljklmklmnlmnomnopnopq
Test Length :56
Trusted Digest :84983E441C3BD26EBAAE4AA1F95129E5E54670F1
New Digest     :84983E441C3BD26EBAAE4AA1F95129E5E54670F1


SHA1 Digesting...
Anyone got any SHA-1 test data?
Test Length :31
Trusted Digest :09b9e9c04a84ce274942048acf3a6f2ff4a8a39c
New Digest     :09B9E9C04A84CE274942048ACF3A6F2FF4A8A39C


SHA1 Digesting...
Of cabbages and kings
Test Length :21
Trusted Digest :5f093d74a9cb1f2f14537bcf3a8a1ffd59b038a2
New Digest     :5F093D74A9CB1F2F14537BCF3A8A1FFD59B038A2


SHA1 Digesting with JDK...

Test Length :0
Trusted Digest :da39a3ee5e6b4b0d3255bfef95601890afd80709
New Digest     :DA39A3EE5E6B4B0D3255BFEF95601890AFD80709


SHA1 Digesting with JDK...
1
Test Length :1
Trusted Digest :356a192b7913b04c54574d18c28d46e6395428ab
New Digest     :356A192B7913B04C54574D18C28D46E6395428AB


SHA1 Digesting with JDK...
a
```

```
Test Length :1
Trusted Digest :86f7e437faa5a7fce15d1ddcb9eaeaea377667b8
New Digest     :86F7E437FAA5A7FCE15D1DDCB9EAEAEA377667B8

SHA1 Digesting with JDK...
abc
Test Length :3
Trusted Digest :a9993e364706816aba3e25717850c26c9cd0d89d
New Digest     :A9993E364706816ABA3E25717850C26C9CD0D89D

SHA1 Digesting with JDK...
abcdefghijklmnopqrstuvwxyz
Test Length :26
Trusted Digest :32d10c7b8cf96570ca04ce37f2a19d84240d3a89
New Digest     :32D10C7B8CF96570CA04CE37F2A19D84240D3A89

SHA1 Digesting with JDK...
abcdbcdecdefdefgefghfghighijhijkijkljklmklmnlmnomnopnopq
Test Length :56
Trusted Digest :84983E441C3BD26EBAAE4AA1F95129E5E54670F1
New Digest     :84983E441C3BD26EBAAE4AA1F95129E5E54670F1

SHA1 Digesting with JDK...
Anyone got any SHA-1 test data?
Test Length :31
Trusted Digest :09b9e9c04a84ce274942048acf3a6f2ff4a8a39c
New Digest     :09B9E9C04A84CE274942048ACF3A6F2FF4A8A39C

SHA1 Digesting with JDK...
Of cabbages and kings
Test Length :21
Trusted Digest :5f093d74a9cb1f2f14537bcf3a8a1ffd59b038a2
New Digest     :5F093D74A9CB1F2F14537BCF3A8A1FFD59B038A2
```

The RIPEMD-160

Another algorithm that is very popular is the RIPEMD-160 (*Race Integrity Primitives Evaluation Message Digest for 160*). The RIPEMD-160 algorithm is also based on MD4. The "160" in RIPEMD-160 means that the algorithm produces a 160-bit digest. The computations are much more complex, and the speed of the algorithm is almost 25% slower than MD4.

The RIPEMD-160 has five rounds with 16 steps. The orders of the input words are processed and are modified along with the type of rotations on the words. There is also a parallel computation where the words are run twice through the computation differing only in the constants in the steps. Because of these differences, the algorithm makes it less prone to collisions and harder to break due to its complexity. The RIPEMD-160 uses five registers to initialize the hashing algorithm just like the SHA-1:

A = 67 45 23 01

B = EF CD AB 89

C = 98 BA DC FE

D = 10 32 54 76

E = C3 D2 E1 F0

The RIPEMD-160 extends five chaining registers just like SHA-1. The blocks are split into 512-bit blocks, and there is a 64-bit message length. There are many similarities between SHA-1 and RIPEMD-160, but the computation method and speed of the algorithm are different. The RIPEMD-160 is about 15% slower than SHA-1 because of the higher complexity of the algorithm of RIPEMD-160. RIPEMD-160 has a higher number of rounds, and each round rotates the hash left and then right using different constants.

- The left rotation constants for each round are 0, 2^{30} X $\sqrt{2}$, 2^{30} X $\sqrt{3}$, and 2^{30} X $\sqrt{5}$.
- The respective rounds for each on the right shift are 2^{30} X $\sqrt[3]{2}$, 2^{30} X $\sqrt[3]{3}$, 2^{30} X $\sqrt[3]{5}$, and 0.

The RIPEMD-160 is a much more complex algorithm than the other algorithms discussed so far. Because of its complexity, it is indeed the slowest of the algorithms. Some organizations, especially banks and brokerage companies, use it because its security and collision resistance is much higher, so being slower is acceptable.

Implementing the Different Message Digest Algorithms in Java

To understand which message digests are supported in Java, you can get a listing of the properties of the service providers.

> **CROSS-REFERENCE:** Refer to Listing 4-14 in Chapter 4 for an example in how to get provider information.

As you can see in Listing 4-14, the service providers in the JDK 1.4 for the message digests are the MD-5 and SHA-1. Listing 9-2 demonstrates the SHA-1 message digest code using a service provider as well as the algorithm from the specification. Listing 9-1 demonstrates the MD5 message digest code using a service provider as well as the algorithm from the specification. In Listing 9-1, the `getInstance` method from the `java.security.MessageDigest` class defines which algorithm to initialize. This example loads the "MD5" algorithm.

The update method of the `MessageDigest` class adds the input data to the algorithm. Multiple updates can be done to the message digest to be hashed. The final phase will not complete until the digest method is executed. The *variable chain* starts at the point of the `getInstance` or digest method and ends at the next digest method. What this means is that if the program does a `getInstance`, then does several updates, and finally a digest call, the digest is the total on all messages passed through the updates. Refer to Figure 9-2 to understand this better.

When the digest method is called, the variables and buffers will be reset to an initial state so that a new digest can start from that point on. Being able to provide multiple updates is one of the features that Java provides in addition to abstracting the algorithms. Another feature worth noting is the `java.security.DigestInputStream` class, which associates a message digest with an input stream. When data is read into the input stream, it is sent directly to the update of the message digest. Classes such as the `DigestInputStream` can alleviate several method calls that would be required to read and call the updates.

Summary

This chapter discussed the use of the message digest for ensuring message integrity. There are many message digest algorithms that can be used and more are evolving every day. Most of the modern-day algorithms are based on Ron Rivest's MD4. Some of the algorithms such as RIPEMD-160 have become much more complex in the computations of the hash, which means that the execution time of the algorithm is higher.

The algorithm that Ron Rivest designed after MD4 was MD5, the successor of MD4 because of MD4 collisions. Collisions occur when multiple messages can generate the same digest. MD5 is much faster than RIPEMD-160 but can also generate some collisions because the algorithm is not as complex as RIPEMD-160. In the middle of MD5 and RIPEMD-160 is SHA-1, which is faster than RIPEMD-160 but slower than MD5 because of its computational power. So there are several choices for the message digest algorithm. The algorithms supported by the Sun JDK 1.4 are MD5 and SHA-1.

Chapter 10
Ensuring Message Authentication

In This Chapter

♦ Learning how to secure data through message authentication

♦ Understanding how message authentication works

♦ Implementing the message authentication

Introduction

The previous chapter discussed the message digest. Recall that the original digest needs to be trusted to be valid in order for the receiver to validate its digest. Also, recall that I mentioned a way to protect the access to the original digest is to set up a secure database and allow minimum access to it. Another way to protect the digest is by using a secret key called the *message authentication code* (MAC), which is discussed in this chapter. A third way is to protect the digest by a key pair. Some of these methods can be used together. For instance, digests that are generated with a secret key could be stored in a secure file system and periodically verified with a secret key to check whether there has been tampering.

> **CROSS-REFERENCE:** The key exchange methods are discussed in Chapter 7.

Understanding the MAC

The message authentication code has the capability to authenticate that the message came from a group of users that have a secret key. A piece of the message, or code, is encrypted with a secret key. Only those users having a copy of the secret key can decrypt the same message, and if the correct code is decrypted, only a member with the secret key could have encrypted it. The MAC technique authenticates that a user of the secret key created the message. To pass the secret key to other users, a key exchange must take place.

> **CROSS-REFERENCE:** The key exchange methods are discussed in Chapters 4 and 5.

The key is passed in a one-way hash to build a *hash message authentication code* (HMAC). Only the users who have a copy of the secret key can generate the correct digest to compare the message. The digest can be changed, but anyone who generates the digest with a different key will generate a different digest. When a user passes in the correct secret key of an altered digest, the digests will validate differently.

An HMAC is useful for checking the integrity of a message over an unreliable medium such as a network. A form of a trusted medium is a digest stored in an LDAP server. If for any reason a form of trust is needed outside the LDAP server, protocols must be used to ensure trust. Users can share a secret key to check the validity of the message. Only those users with a copy of the secret key can check the message. If a hacker intercepts a secret key, he can alter the message digest. After the hacker alters the message, the digest can no longer be trusted. The trusted point for the HMAC is the secret key. The digest trust comes from the secret key that can generate it.

> **TIP:** The HMAC is described in RFC 2104, and it can be found at
> `http://www.ietf.org/rfc/rfc2104.txt.` [RFC2104].

The HMAC is hashed through message digest algorithms such as MD5 and SHA-1, as discussed in Chapter 9. The motivation behind the HMAC is to add functionality to the message digests without modifying the algorithms. Other motivations of the HMAC are not to degrade the performance of the message digests algorithms, to provide simple means of handling the secret keys, and to allow an upgradeable implementation for future message digests.

The HMAC requires a message digest and a secret key; the message digest is used to hash the digest and the secret key to encrypt the digest. The message digest iterates through 64-byte blocks and returns a 16-byte array for the MD5 digest and a 20-byte array for the SHA-1 digest. The secret key that is used for authentication can be any size that will not exceed the normal length of the input block.

> **NOTE:** The suggested length of the secret key is that it be the same as the size of the digest because having the key the same length as the digest makes a more secure hash. Having a secret key of greater length than the digest length does not increase the security of the hash. The secret key will be more secure if the key is randomly chosen to avoid any pattern.

The input block of the message digest is normally 64 bytes and can be denoted as B. B is then the size of the secret key length. If the secret key length is less than B, it is appended with zeros. If the secret key is greater than B, it is hashed and the key is replaced with the digest. After the secret key is cleaned up, the key is changed into an *inner pad*. The inner pad is the first piece to be digested, and the last pad is the *outer pad*.

The secret key is passed in the `init` method and is modified into an inner pad. The inner pad starts out as the secret key and is XORed with an array the size of B filled with 0x36 bytes. The size of B, in this case, is 64 bytes. The inner and outer pads are filled and XORed to add more levels of complexity into the key. Having both an inner and outer pad XORed produces different permutations of the key. Having these padded keys digested at different times adds more complexity to the key and is a means to add more security at the interface into the message digests. After the inner pad is formed, it is added to the `update` method of the message digest. During the operation of the `javax.crypto.Mac` class, updates of data can be added anywhere from the `init` to the `doFinal` methods. The update methods are similar to the update methods in the message digest; the difference is that the `doFinal` method is called in the end to add the final pad. When the `doFinal` method is called, a digest is created from the updates for temporary use. A new digest is then created with the outer pad and the temporary digest. The final result is the combination of the outer pad being XORed with a 64-byte array filled with 0x5C bytes.

Implementing the MAC

Listing 10-1 demonstrates an implementation of the MAC algorithm in Java code; it provides an example of the `init`, `doFinal`, and `update` methods. The following steps summarize the algorithm:

1. Initialization: If the key length is less than B, pad with zeros. If the key length is greater than B, hash it.

2. XOR the pads starting with the inner pad.

3. Create the outer pad.

4. Utilize the outer pad to create the final digest.

Listing 10-1: The `RichMAC` class a: MAC algorithm

```
package com.richware.chap10;

import java.security.*;
import javax.crypto.*;
import javax.crypto.spec.*;
import javax.crypto.interfaces.*;
import java.security.spec.*;
import java.math.BigInteger;

/**
 * Class RichMAC
 * Description: This is an example
 * implementation of the MAC
 * algorithm.
 *
 * Copyright:    Copyright (c) 2002 Wiley Publishing, Inc.
 * @author Rich Helton <rhelton@richware.com>
 * @version 1.0
 * DISCLAIMER: Please refer to the disclaimer at the beginning of this
book.
 */
public class RichMAC
 {
   /**
```

```
 * The algorithm used for the HMac. Usually SHA1 or MD5
 */

/* The algorithm name */
private String      algorithm_;
/* inner pad */
private static byte ipad_ = 0x36;
/* outer pad */
private static byte opad_ = 0x5c;
/* Digest Block Length */
private static int  B     = 64;

/* The Length */
protected int L_;

/* inner pad */
private byte[] ipad_key = new byte[ 64];

/* outer pad */
private byte[] opad_key = new byte[ 64];

/* The MAC key */
private byte[] macKey = new byte[ 64];

/* The Message Digest */
protected MessageDigest         md;
public final static String[][] testData =
 {
  //    data string, md hex
  { "", "D41D8CD98F00B204E9800998ECF8427E" },        // A.5 1
  { "a", "0CC175B9C0F1B6A831C399E269772661" },        // A.5 2
  { "aa", "4124BC0A9335C27F086F24BA207A4912" },
  { "abc", "900150983CD24FB0D6963F7D28E17F72" },      // A.5 3
  { "aaa", "47BCE5C74F589F4867DBD57E9CA9F808" },
  { "bbb", "08F8E0260C64418510CEFB2B06EEE5CD" },
  { "ccc", "9DF62E693988EB4E1E1444ECE0578579" },
  { "message digest", "F96B697D7CB7938D525A2F31AAF161D0" },   // A.5 4
  { "abcdefg", "7AC66C0F148DE9519B8BD264312C4D64" },
  { "abcdefghijk", "92B9CCCC0B98C3A0B8D0DF25A421C0E3" },
  {                                                   // A.5 5
   "abcdefghijklmnopqrstuvwxyz",
   "C3FCD3D76192E4007DFB496CCA67E13B"
  },
  {                                                   // A.5 6
   "ABCDEFGHIJKLMNOPQRSTUVWXYZabcdefghijklmnopqrstuvwxyz0123456789",
   "D174AB98D277D9F5A5611C2C9F419D9F"
  },
  {                                                   // A.5 7
```

```
"1234567890123456789012345678901234567890123456789012345678901234567890123456789 01
234567890",
    "57EDF4A22BE3C955AC49DA2E2107B67A"
  },
};
public static final char[] hexDigits =
  {
    '0', '1', '2', '3', '4', '5', '6', '7', '8', '9', 'A', 'B',
    'C', 'D', 'E', 'F'
  };

/**
 * Constructor RichMAC
 * @param algorithm
 *
 * @throws NoSuchAlgorithmException
 *
 */
public RichMAC(String algorithm)
        throws NoSuchAlgorithmException
  {
    algorithm_ = algorithm;
    md_        = MessageDigest.getInstance(algorithm_);
    L_         = md_.getDigestLength();
  }

/**
 * Method doFinal
 * Description : does the final calculations
 * and returns the digest
 * @return the digest
 *
 */
public byte[] doFinal()
  {
    byte[] hash1;
    byte[] hmac;

    /* Get the original digest */
    hash1 = md_.digest();
    md_.reset();
    /* Update with the outer pad */
    md_.update(opad_key);
    /* Update with the original hash */
    md_.update(hash1);

    hmac = md_.digest();
    return hmac;
```

```
}

/**
 * Method init
 * Description : does the initial calculations
 * with the secret key
 * @param key the Secret key
 *
 * @throws InvalidAlgorithmParameterException
 * @throws InvalidKeyException
 *
 */
public final void init(Key key)
        throws InvalidKeyException,
                InvalidAlgorithmParameterException
{
    init(key, null);
}

/**
 * Method init
 * Description : does the initial calculations
 * with the secret key and algorithm spec
 * @param key the secret key
 * @param params the key parameters
 *
 * @throws InvalidAlgorithmParameterException
 * @throws InvalidKeyException
 *
 */
public void init(Key key, AlgorithmParameterSpec params)
        throws InvalidKeyException,
                InvalidAlgorithmParameterException
{
  byte[]            keyBytes;

  /*
   * convert the secret key into a bytearray.
   */
  if (key instanceof SecretKey)
  {
    keyBytes = key.getEncoded();
  }
  else
  {
    throw new InvalidKeyException();
  }
```

```
/*
 * If the key is greater than B,
 * the key has to be hashed.
 * If the key is less than B
 * the key must be extended with zeros.
 */
int n = B - keyBytes.length;

/*
 * If the key is less than B,
 * fill up to B size with zeros
 */
if (n > 0)
{
  System.arraycopy(keyBytes, 0, macKey, 0,
                   keyBytes.length);
  for (int i = 0; i < n; i++)
  {
    macKey[ keyBytes.length + i] = 0;
  }
}
/*
 * if the key size is greater than B,
 * the key has to be hashed and the
 * digest is retrieved
 */
else
{
  if (n < 0)
  {
    md.update(keyBytes);
    macKey = md.digest();
  }
}

/* Copies the MAC Key into the ipad_key */
System.arraycopy(macKey, 0, ipad_key, 0, B_);
/* Copies the MAC Key into the opad_key */
System.arraycopy(macKey, 0, opad_key, 0, B_);

for (int j = 0; j < B_; j++)
{
  /* XOR the ipad key with the ipad */
  ipad_key[ j] = (byte) (ipad_key[ j] ^ ipad_);
  /* XOR the opad key with the opad */
  opad_key[ j] = (byte) (opad_key[ j] ^ opad_);
}

/* Digest the ipad_key */
```

```
  md.update(ipad_key);
}

/**
 * Method reset
 * Description : Resets the values for a new digest
 */
public void reset()
{
  md.reset();
}

/**
 * Method update
 * Description : Updates the input data
 * @param input the input data
 *
 */
public void update(byte[] input)
{
  md.update(input, 0, input.length);
}

/**
 * Method update
 * Description : Updates the input data
 * with the offset and data length.
 *
 * @param input the input bytes
 * @param offset the offset of the input
 * @param len the length of the input
 *
 */
public void update(byte[] input, int offset, int len)
{
  md.update(input, offset, len);
}

/**
 * Method update
 * Description : Updates the input data
 * with the offset and data length.
 * @param input byte
 *
 */
public void update(byte input)
{
  md.update(input);
}
```

```
/**
 * Method getMacLength
 * @return the length of message digest
 *
 */
public int getMacLength()
{
  return L_;
}


/**
 * Method main
 * Description: This is a test driver
 * @param args none
 *
 */
public static void main(String[] args)
{
  try
    {
    /*
     * Create a password for the file
     */
    char[] password = new char[4];
    password[0] = 't';
    password[1] = 'e';
    password[2] = 's';
    password[3] = 't';

    /*
     * Create a new local MD5 and test data
     */
    RichMAC local_m = new RichMAC("MD5");

    /*
     * Test the JDK version
     */
    javax.crypto.Mac m =
      javax.crypto.Mac.getInstance("HmacMD5");

    /*
     * Build the key
     */

    // Use the char array to create a PBEKeySpec
    PBEKeySpec keySpec = new PBEKeySpec(password);

    // Create a SecretKeyFactory for the PBE key
```

```
SecretKeyFactory keyFactory =
  SecretKeyFactory.getInstance("PBEWithMD5AndDES");

// Generate the key from the key spec
SecretKey srKey = keyFactory.generateSecret(keySpec);

// Convert the key to a byte buffer
byte[] keyBuffer = srKey.getEncoded();

m.init(srKey);
local m.init(srKey);
byte[] testBytes = testData[1][0].getBytes();

/*
 * Update the digest with data
 * normally the data can be updated
 * at different times
 */
System.out.println("Test Length :" + testBytes.length);
System.out.println("Test String :" + testData[1][0]);
m.update(testBytes);
local_m.update(testBytes);

byte[] digest  = m.doFinal();
byte[] digest2 = local_m.doFinal();
char[] buf     = new char[digest.length * 2];
char[] buf2    = new char[digest2.length * 2];
int    j       = 0;
int    k;

for (int i = 0; i < digest.length; i++)
 {
  k        = digest[i];
  buf[j++] = hexDigits[(k >>> 4) & 0x0F];
  buf[j++] = hexDigits[k & 0x0F];
 }

String buffer = new String(buf);
System.out.println("JDK New Digest       :" + buffer);
j = 0;

for (int i = 0; i < digest2.length; i++)
 {
  k        = digest2[i];
  buf[j++] = hexDigits[(k >>> 4) & 0x0F];
  buf[j++] = hexDigits[k & 0x0F];
 }

String buffer2 = new String(buf);
```

```
        System.out.println("Local New Digest      :" + buffer2);
    }


    /*
     * Catches
     */
    catch (Exception ex)
    {
       ex.printStackTrace();
    }
  }
}
```

Listing 10-2 demonstrates its output. The example also uses the MAC classes in the JDK to verify that it works correctly.

Listing 10-2: The output of Listing 10-1

```
>java com.richware.chap10.RichMAC
Test Length :1
Test String :a
JDK New Digest      :146304F265F9D40E5192933CB29C6CAD
Local New Digest    :146304F265F9D40E5192933CB29C6CAD
```

Listing 10-1 demonstrates the HMAC algorithm. If a different password is passed in the init method, different digests are produced. Notice that the program does not have to re-invent the message digest algorithm, but is simply a wrapper around the message digest. The modifications around the message digest are used to handle the secret key through inner and outer padding. The RichMAC class, a demonstration, is simply a wrapper of a generic interface into the message digest. To know which message digest to use, the algorithm name must be passed in the constructor. After the class is constructed, it will wrap an instance of a message digest created with the algorithm name. Most of the methods simply call the message digest interface. The only real work done is the manipulation of the secret key.

Listing 10-1 also demonstrates how to implement the MAC through the JDK's javax.crypto.Mac class. The Mac class supports the init, update, and doFinal methods. The Mac class is an engine class, meaning that it doesn't create the constructor of the algorithm directly. The class of the algorithm is returned through a getInstance method. The algorithms that can be returned are the ones supported through the underlying service providers as shown in Chapter 4.

> **TIP:** The javax.crypto.interfaces.PBEKey interface is for handling Password Based Encryptions (PBE), where the key is based on a password. The PBEKey interface can create a secret key from a password and be used like any other secret key algorithm. See Chapters 4 and 7 for more details on PBE.

Summary

This chapter presented a discussion on how a message can be authenticated and the data in the message verified. The validation is done through the combination of a secret key and a message digest. The secret key is digested in between the actual message input. Only those users who pass in the same secret key can get the same digest, otherwise the data is considered compromised. If different data or a different key is passed in, the digest produced is different. Some algorithms discussed in the previous chapter do produce collisions. Collisions occur when multiple messages can produce the same digest. MD5 is known to produce collisions, but is still considered by most as a valid algorithm to use. The algorithms used should be considered carefully. The HMAC classes are wrappers around a generic interface into the message digest that will use a secret key as part of the digest.

Chapter 11
Signature Integrity

In This Chapter

- ◆ Learning the benefits of using a digital signature
- ◆ Understanding the Digital Signature Algorithm
- ◆ Understanding the Digital Signature Standard
- ◆ Implementing the digital signatures in Java

Introduction

A digital signature serves many purposes. It doesn't just validate data, but is truly a fingerprint from the sender. The digital signature depends on the key pair, the data of the message, and a signature. All these elements are mapped to each other so that if any item changes, the signature does not pass verification. The originator of the data hashes the data with his or her private key to create a signature. A specific public key that is generated from the private key can be used to verify the signature. Verifying the signature matches the data, signature, and public key.

If the signature passes verification, it is guaranteed that the message has not changed and that the public key used came from the user who generated the signature. The exchange of the private and public key becomes the crucial point in identifying the user. A person might deny that his or her private key encrypted the message and assert that someone else sent you the public key. If the exchange can be guaranteed and the message signature is verified, it is relatively easy to prove that a specific user sent the message and hard for the user to deny sending the message.

Because of this type of verification and the need to ensure authenticity of messages for legal reasons, state legislatures and many legal organizations have been looking at digital signatures to provide a means of identifying a message. Because more and more contract agreements are being handled electronically, many organizations need a way to verify the origin of a message from a person or an organization.

With the threat of hackers and others manipulating data, it becomes difficult to prove that a message originated from a specific user. Digital signatures offer a solution. Many companies are specializing in digital signatures for these reasons. The digital signature can be combined with other protocols such as *Public Key Infrastructure* (PKI) and the X.509 certificate.

> **CROSS-REFERENCE:** X.509 certificates are discussed in Chapter 24, and PKI is discussed in Chapter 25.

The RSA Security Company, which provides the RSA key exchange algorithm, was one of the first vendors to provide digital signatures. While many vendors were working with RSA on a digital signature, the *National Institute of Standards and Technology* (NIST) decided to provide a standard for the community. The NIST published a proposed Federal Information Processing Standard (FIPS) for the *Digital Signature Standard* (DSS) in August 1991.

At the time of its conception, the DSS received a lot of criticism from RSA, simply because RSA was already trying submit its own proposal for a digital signature standard using the RSA key exchange. The NIST did not adopt the RSA key exchange but instead introduced a new keying algorithm that was part of the *Digital Signature Algorithm* (DSA). A lot of companies at the time, such as IBM and Sun, invested a lot of time and money into the RSA Digital Signature Algorithm. The NIST received a lot of criticism because during this time, in January 1992, the NIST also invented the SHA-1 message digest to support the DSS. The criticism came from the fact that the SHA-1 was based on the MD4 algorithm, and now it seemed as though the DSS was being based on some of the work from RSA.

> **CROSS-REFERENCE:** RSA and DSA are described in Chapter 4. Chapter 9 discusses SHA-1 and MD4.

More criticism came from the fact that the *National Security Agency* (NSA) also worked with NIST to develop the algorithm, that it was a suggested public standard, and that the original key length was 512 bits. As with many other collaborations from the NSA, many organizations felt that the NSA had a crack for the algorithm so that it could maintain surveillance of data. There is still a lot of paranoia that the use of a public key and public variables can be used in combination to break the signature. Because some of the key exchanges, such as the RSA and Elliptic Curve key exchange, appear stronger, the NIST has added these algorithms to the DSS. Figure 11-1 shows the signature algorithms approved by FIPS in the FIPS186-2.

> **NOTE:** You can find FIPS186-2 at
> `http://cscr.nist.gov/publications/fips/fips186-2/fips186-2-`
> `change1.pdf` the FIPS 186-2-Change1 "Digital Signature Standard (DSS)," Federal Information Publication Standards, 2000.

Even though there is paranoia surrounding some of the history of DSS, the DSS provides a global standard for exchanging signatures and for how the DSA works. Because of the DSS, many protocols such as X.509, *Privacy Enhanced Email* (PEM), and *Pretty Good Privacy* (PGP) have evolved. The digital signature, like so many other aspects of security, is not an entity unto itself but is used with several other building blocks of security.

> **TIP:** The digital signature provides an organization the capability to protect itself with the combination of all the other building blocks mentioned throughout the book.

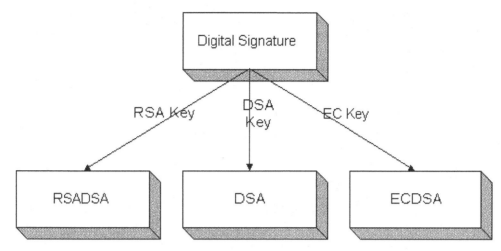

Figure 11-1: The FIPS approved digital signatures

Understanding the Digital Signature Algorithm (DSA)

The *Digital Signature Algorithm* is the algorithm specified for the DSS (http://www.itl.nist.gov/fipspubs/fip186.htm). The DSA's objective is to provide a signature and verify it in the form of two variables, r and s. A private key is needed in order to sign the data. In order to verify the signature, the public key is needed. There are generally three major steps that must be accomplished before signing data or verifying the signature:

♦ The private and public keys must be available.

♦ The parameters must be initialized (for DSA, they are called DSA parameters).

♦ Before signing and verifying, the data must be passed through the update methods.

Figure 11-2 illustrates these steps.

> **NOTE:** Recall from Chapter 7 that the DSA algorithm uses three integers, p, q, and g, and the signature variables r and s.

The first step in the algorithm is to initialize the DSA parameters p, g, and q along with the private key x and the public key y. The public variables p, q, and g are needed to compute and verify the signature. These variables are used to help compute the hash value with the private key and to verify the hash value with the public key. If the computation for verification does not work with the public variables p, q, and g, the public key y, the signature variables r and s, or the integer value representing the hash, the data is non-trustworthy. The public variables p, q, and g are considered public because they can be distributed to an entire group without compromising the algorithm. The signature variables *r* and *s* need the public variables plus the hash value and a randomly generated *k* value that is generated specifically for every signature. The private variable *k* must always be newly generated for each signature, and the hash value is taken from the data that is updated for the SHA-1 digest. Figure 11-3 shows the association of the signature generation variables.

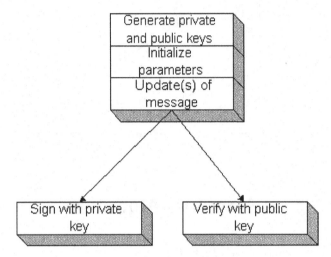

Figure   11-2: Digital signature steps

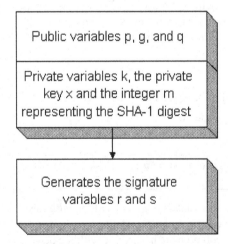

Figure   11-3: Signature generation variables

Listing 11-1 (later in the chapter) demonstrates the algorithms for generating the variables. There are some things that must be emphasized. One thing to note is that there are many papers, algorithms, and specifications that list algorithms for *probabilistic primality testing —*

used to generate and test for a prime number. The `java.math.BigInteger` class uses the `isProbablePrime` method to test the number for its primeness to a degree of specified certainty. The `java.security.SecureRandom` class will also generate a prime number guaranteed to the specified primeness. The higher the degree of certainty, say 90%, the longer the algorithm takes to ensure the number is prime. Many encryption algorithms require prime numbers or the algorithms will not work.

The p, g and q must satisfy the following requirements:

- The public variables p and q must be prime numbers.
- The q number is a randomly generated prime divisor, and p is its associated prime modulus.
- The p must be a number with the length between 512 and 1024 bits. Most algorithms will denote the length by the letter l.
- The q must fall between 2^{159} and 2^{160}.
- The p and q numbers must have an association in which they can generate an integer g in the form $g = h^{(p-1)/q} \bmod p$. The variable h is normally a randomly generated integer between 0 and $p - 1$.

The sample program tries many combinations until the numbers can fit into the preceding restrictions. Many algorithms generate the public variables when the keys are generated and pass them through the public and private key classes. After the public variables are generated, the public and private keys can be generated. The private key, represented by x, is a randomly generated integer greater than 0 and less than q. The public key y is generated by the equation

$$y = g^x \bmod p$$

The public key is a product of the private key and forms a relationship where only x can be associated with y and vice versa. After the keys and public variables are formed, a message can be signed. The verification and signing of the message cannot be accomplished without most of these variables. The verification requires the public variables and the public key y. The signing of the message requires the public variables and the private key x. The message signature and verification are dependent on one other variable besides the public variables and keys, and that is the message itself. The signature is an r and s variable. The r variable is calculated from the equation

$$r = (g^k \bmod p) \bmod q$$

These are the public variables and a randomly generated integer k. The s variable is calculated by the using the message hash with the SHA-1 message digest in *SHA(M)* and the private key x as in the following equation:

$$s = (k^{-1} (SHA(M) + xr)) \bmod q$$

The verification of the message fails without the correct private key and the correct message digest. The goal of the signature verification is to generate a verification value represented by *v* and to compare it to the variable *r* of the signature. If they are not equal, the verification fails. See Figure 11-4 for the verification generation variables.

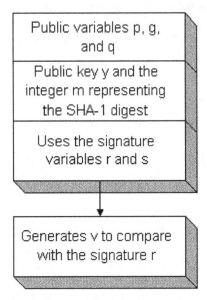

Figure 11-4: Verification generation variables

The variable *v* does not need the private variable *k* and the private key that were used to generate the digital signature. The associated public key and the message digest, generated again by the SHA-1 algorithm with the message, are the only new variables needed. The calculation of *v* is quite lengthy and is broken down into multiple steps.

♦ The first step is to compute the variable *w*, which is from the signature *s* variable from the equation $w = (s)^{-1} \bmod q$.

♦ The next step is to use the message digest to calculate the *u1* variable in the equation $u1 = ((SHA(M))\ w)\ mod\ q$, which is used to verify the message digest.

♦ The next equation is used to add the signature *r* in the calculation to produce the *u2* variable with the equation $u2 = ((r)w)mod\ q$.

♦ Finally, all these calculations, including the public variables and the public key, are used to calculate the *v* variable with the equation from the previous steps with $v = (((g)^{u1}(y)^{u2})mod\ p)mod\ q$.

The variable *v* is checked against the signature variable *r,* and they should be equal unless something has been altered or used incorrectly, such as the associated public key. If the variable *v* matches the variable *r*, the correct digest and public key were used in the calculation. If the correct public key was used in the calculation, the matching private key was used to generate the signature. By knowing that the public key matches a specific user's private key, there is a guarantee that the message came from that user.

If the message digest computed from the data checks — that is, it validated — there is a guarantee that the data has not changed. The only piece missing from DSA is the guarantee that the key came from a specific user, but that is the purpose of the key exchange. The DSS may embed the public key in a message, such as in *Pretty Good Privacy* (PGP) or many other means. For this reason, the NIST has updated the DSS to include the RSA digital signature and ECDSA with their appropriate key exchanges (`http://cscr.nist.gov/publications/fips/fips186-2/fips186-2-change1.pdf`).

Understanding the RSA Digital Signature Algorithm

The latest FIPS186-2 now lists the *RSA digital signature* (RSA ds) as one of the three recommended algorithms for digital signatures. The FIPS186-2 simply says to see the ANSI x9.31 for documentation. The RFC 2437 (`http://www.ietf.org/rfc/rfc2437.txt`) also describes the RSA digital signature, the RSA key exchange, and more, and is freely available. Those who need to understand any differences between the RFC 2437 and the ANSI X9.31 can reference the paper "Differences between ANSI X9.31 and RSA PKCS#1" (`http://www.corsec.com/copy/pdf/X931_PKCS1.pdf`).

Recall from the key agreement algorithm in Chapter 4 that RSA had three public variables called p, q, and the modulus n. The public key is represented by *{n,e}* and the private key is *{n,d}*. If the private key *{n,d}* is not available, it will have to be computed from the p, q, dP, dQ, and $qInv$ variables with the *Chinese Remainder Theorem* (CRT) key.

CROSS-REFERENCE: The Chinese Remainder Theorem was introduced in Chapter 4.

If the CRT key is used, the variable s can be generated from the following equations:

◆ $s2 = m^{dQ}$ mod q.

◆ $h = qInv(s1 - s2)$ mod q.

◆ $s = s2 + hq$.

When the signature is generated, a digest is computed for the data and returned as the variable m. The signature s is computed from the following equation:

$$s = m^d \bmod n$$

To verify the message, the algorithm will need the public key *{n,e}*, the capability to recompute the same digest from the data as m, and the signature s. The message digest is recomputed as the test variable a. The b variable will be generated using the following equation from the signature and the public key:

$$b = s^e \bmod n$$

The variables a and b match if the signature, keys, and data are valid. The a value is computed as the integer returned as the message digest. Unlike the DSS algorithm, the RSA algorithm may use the MD2, MD4, MD5, or SHA-1 digest. In order to account for the possibility of different message digests, the message digest algorithm identifier is returned as part of the signature information block.

> **CROSS-REFERENCE:** Chapter 9 introduced MD2, MD4, MD5, and SHA-1.

Other variables that are included in the format of the signature are block type, encryption-block formatting, and a padding block. RSA not only has a key algorithm and signature algorithm, but also an encryption algorithm. Since RSA includes an encryption algorithm, the signature block may also be encrypted with the RSA cipher.

> **TIP:** In order to format the signature block, the PKCS#1 includes a padding string and algorithm to ensure the correct format size when hashing and using the RSA encryption.

Understanding the Elliptic Curve Digital Signature Algorithm

Just like the RSA, the *Elliptic Curve Digital Signature Algorithm* (ECDSA) has been added to the FIPS186-2 (http://cscr.nist.gov/publications/fips/fips186-2/fips186-2-change1.pdf).

> **CROSS-REFERENCE:** The ECC for key exchange was discussed in Chapter 4. The ECC provides a key exchange for the key pair.

The ECDSA generates a signature with a private key and verifies the signature with a public key. The ECDSA starts by selecting an integer value k to be multiplied by a Point $P = (x_1, y_1)$ along the elliptic curve. Just like the DSS algorithm, an r and s variable is calculated and saved for the signature. Since x_1 is an integer point on the x coordinate system, r can be computed by the following equation:

$$r = x_1 \bmod n$$

The variable s is calculated by the SHA-1 hash on the message represented by $h(m)$ and the private key d. The s equation becomes

$$s = k^{-1} (h(m) + dr) \bmod n$$

The signature is the r and s variable. To verify the signature, the ECDSA needs the r, s, the message for the digest, and the public key *(E, P, n, Q)*. The `verify` method is initialized with the public key. Then the message needs to be passed through the algorithm's `update` method to store the hashed message. The `verify` method is then called, passing in the signature containing the r and s. The `verify` method hashes the message and converts the digest into an integer m. Just like the DSA algorithm the ESDSA contains multiple calculations. The next variable after m to be calculated is the variable w, which is calculated using the equation

$$w = s^{-1} \bmod n$$

The next two variables are *u1* and *u2* calculated by

$$u1 = mw \ mod \ n \text{ and } u2 \text{ is } u2 = rw \ mod \ n$$

The point along the elliptic curve is computed from these calculations. Taking the public key variables *P* and *Q*, the additive property is used from *u1* and *u2* to form *u1P* + *u2Q*. The point from *u1P* + *u2Q* is computed in the x-y coordinate system as the point (x0, y0). The *x0* coordinate along the x-axis is used to find the result in *v* = *x0 mod n*. If the variable *v* in the verify method equals the variable *r* in the signature generator, the message and keys used are valid.

Some of the equations between the ECDSA and DSA appear similar because both algorithms are based on the ElGamal signature algorithm by signing the equation

$$s = k^{-1} \ \{h(m) + dr\} \ mod \ m$$

Both the ECDSA and DSA use the SHA-1 message digest as the defined digest to use. The ECDSA uses public variables from the public key *(E, P, n, Q)* that are used to compute the intermediate variables *w*, *u1*, and *u2*. Looking at DSA, similar calculations were accomplished using public variables *p*, *q*, and *g*. These values are needed to produce the algorithms without the private key. Both of these algorithms share the complexity of trying to generate the checks with just the public variables. The biggest difference that exists between these two algorithms is the type of equations. The ECDSA is elliptical and uses geometric properties. In other words, checks consist of checking if points fall on a curve as opposed to checking if the values are greater than 0 and less than *q,* as in the DSA.

> **NOTE:** The DSA is easier from a computational standpoint in that numbers can be checked to be less than, greater than, or equal to. The computational complexity of ECDSA makes the algorithms more secure. Also, because the numbers that can be used in ECDSA are limited to the points along a curve (versus the DSA using prime numbers that must fit together), the ECDSA is computationally faster.

Implementing the Digital Signature Algorithm (DSA)

The JDK 1.4 supports only the DSA and RSA out of the box for providing service providers. The JDK 1.4 is easily extensible to add more service providers from other vendors or to build a custom one for algorithms such as the ECDSA. The ECDSA is a very popular algorithm, and there are service providers for the algorithm from companies such as Certicom and Cryptix. For many organizations, using the DSA and RSA signatures is sufficient. An example of the DSA algorithm is shown in Listing 11-1 using both the JDK 1.4 and an implementation demonstrating the DSA algorithm.

The first step in using the JDK 1.4 framework is to generate a key pair using the java.security.KeyPairGenerator class's getInstance method. By passing in the variable DSA, a key pair for the DSA algorithm is created. If RSA is passed in as the parameter, a pair of RSA keys is generated. Likewise, the java.security.Signature class's getInstance method initializes the signature class by passing in a SHA1withDSA parameter. To generate RSA signatures, the MD5withRSA, MD2withRSA, and SHA1withRSA parameters can be used depending on which message digest needs to be implemented. Whether the signature is being used for generating the signature or verifying the signature will determine which key, public or private, will be initialized into the algorithm.

> **TIP:** All signature algorithms require that the data be passed through the update method for both verifying and generating the signature. After the message data has been updated, a signature can be returned from the sign method, or a signature can be verified by passing it in the verify method.

One of the features found in the JDK 1.4 is the java.security.SignedObject class. The SignedObject class is created with a digital signature passed into it and a serialized object. The purpose of the SignedObject class is to protect the runtime object with an associated signature. If the integrity of the object is compromised, then the signature detects it and an exception is thrown. The SignedObject provides a deep copy of the serialized object so a digest can be created and the integrity checked. Features like this one and the capability to use a DSA and RSA signature out of the box make Java a powerful programming language. Listing 11-1 shows the RichDSA class, which is a sample application that demonstrates these concepts.

Listing 11-1: The RichDSA class: The DSA Signature sample application

```
package com.richware.chap11;

import java.security.*;
import javax.crypto.*;
import javax.crypto.spec.*;
import javax.crypto.interfaces.*;
import java.security.spec.*;
import java.math.BigInteger;
import java.io.*;

/**
 * Class RichDSA
 * Description: This is an example
 * implementation of the DSA
 * algorithm.
 *
 * Copyright:    Copyright (c) 2002 Wiley Publishing, Inc.
 * @author Rich Helton <rhelton@richware.com>
 * @version 1.0
 * DISCLAIMER: Please refer to the disclaimer at the beginning of this
book.
 */
public class RichDSA
{
  /* the key length */
  private int l_ = 1024;
```

```
/* the private key */
private BigInteger x_;

/* the public key */
private BigInteger y_;

/* the DSA parameters, see spec */
/* h is used to generate g */
private BigInteger h_;
private BigInteger p_;
private BigInteger q_;
private BigInteger g_;

/* q bit length */
int qBitLength  = 160;

/* the SHA1 message digest */
private MessageDigest md_;

/* To debug or not to debug */
private final boolean DEBUG = false;

/* The certainty, that the generated numbers are prime. */
private final int CERTAINTY = 80;

/* The secure random generator */
private SecureRandom secureRandom ;

/* BigInteger Constants */
private static final BigInteger ZERO =
  BigInteger.valueOf(0L);
private static final BigInteger ONE  =
  BigInteger.valueOf(1L);
private static final BigInteger TWO  =
  BigInteger.valueOf(2L);

/**
 * Constructor RichDSA
 *
 *
 */
public RichDSA()
{
  initKeys();
}

/**
 * Method initKeys
 */
```

```java
public void initKeys()
{
  BigInteger x, c, qMultTwo;
  try
    {
      md_ = MessageDigest.getInstance("SHA1");
      if (secureRandom  == null)
       {
         secureRandom_ = new SecureRandom();
       }
      int      counter     = 0;
      boolean primesFound = false;
      while (!primesFound)
       {
         counter = 0;

         /*
          * Calculate Q
          */
         q_ = new BigInteger(qBitLength_, CERTAINTY,
                             secureRandom_);
         while ((counter < 4096) && (!primesFound))
          {
            /*
             * q must be a divisor of p
             * h ^ ((p-1) / q) mod p
             * and p being prime are a
             * must. X will be shifted to try
             * another random and tested for prime.
             * See DSA Spec.
             * Appendix 2 and 3.
             */
            x        = reseedX();
            qMultTwo = q_.multiply(TWO);
            c        = x.mod(qMultTwo);

            /*
             * Calculate P
             */
            p_ = x.subtract(c.subtract(ONE));

            /*
             * If P is long enough and is prime,
             * use it
             */
            if (p_.bitLength() >= (l_))
             {
               if (DEBUG)
                {
```

```
        System.out.println("Counter :" + counter);
    }

    /*
     * P must be prime to quit
     */
    if (p .isProbablePrime(CERTAINTY))
    {
      primesFound = true;
    }
  }

  counter++;
  }
}

/*
 * Calculate H
 */
boolean hFound = false;
while (!hFound)
{
  h_ = new BigInteger(1 , secureRandom );
  if ((h_.compareTo(ONE) > 0)
        || (h_.compareTo(p_.subtract(ONE)) < 0))
  {
    hFound = true;
  }
}

/*
 * Generate G, the generator
 */
BigInteger pMinusOneOverQ = p_.subtract(ONE).divide(q_);
boolean    gFound        = false;
while (!gFound)
{
  g_ = h_.modPow(pMinusOneOverQ, p_);

  if (g_.compareTo(ONE) > 0)
  {
    gFound = true;
  }
}

/*
 * Generate X, the private key
 */
x_ = new BigInteger(qBitLength_ - 1, secureRandom_);
```

```
      while ((x_.compareTo(BigInteger.ZERO)) == 0)
       {
         x  = new BigInteger(qBitLength  - 1, secureRandom );
       }

       /*
        * Generate Y, the public key
        */
       y_ = g_.modPow(x_, p_);

       /*
        * If DEBUG, print the results
        */
       if (DEBUG)
        {
          System.out.println();
          System.out.println("p_  :" + p_);
          System.out.println();
          System.out.println("q   :" + q );
          System.out.println();
          System.out.println("x_  :" + x_);
          System.out.println();
          System.out.println("y   :" + y );
          System.out.println();
          System.out.println("g_  :" + g_);
          System.out.println();
          System.out.println("h   :" + h );
        }
     }

     /*
      * Catches
      */
     catch (Exception ex)
      {
        ex.printStackTrace();
      }
   }

/**
 * Method reseedX
 * Description reseed X by shifting
 *
 * @return a new random X
 *
 */
private BigInteger reseedX()
 {
   byte[] shiftBytes = new byte[(l_ / 8)];
```

```
   secureRandom_.nextBytes(shiftBytes);
   shiftBytes[0] = (byte) (shiftBytes[0] | 128);
   return (new BigInteger(1, shiftBytes));
}

/**
 * Method sign
 * Description: return the
 * signature
 * @return mostly r and s
 *
 */
public byte[] sign()
{
  try
   {
    /*
     * Calculate the digest, number
     */
    byte[]      digest = md_.digest();
    BigInteger m       = new BigInteger(1, digest);

    /*
     * Generate k, a random number
     * 0 < k < q
     */
    BigInteger k = new BigInteger(qBitLength  - 1,
                                      secureRandom_);
    while (k.compareTo(q_) >= 0)
     {
       k = new BigInteger(qBitLength  - 1, secureRandom );
     }

    /*
     * Inverse of K
     */
    BigInteger kInv = k.modInverse(q_);

    /*
     * r =  (g ^ k mod p) mod q
     */
    BigInteger r = (g_.modPow(k, p_)).mod(q_);

    /*
     * s =  (k ^ -1(SHA(M) +xr)) mod q
     */
    BigInteger s =
      kInv.multiply((m.add(x_.multiply(r)))).mod(q_);
```

```
/*
 * If DEBUG, print the results
 */
if (DEBUG)
{
  System.out.println();
  System.out.println("sign:r :" + r);
  System.out.println();
  System.out.println("sign:s :" + s);
  System.out.println();
  System.out.println("sign:m :" + m);
}

/*
 * Put r and s in a buffer
 * with some magic numbers
 * to check for corruption
 */
byte[] rdata = r.toByteArray();
byte[] sdata = s.toByteArray();
byte[] data  = new byte[6 + rdata.length + sdata.length];
int    i     = 0;

/*
 * Put first magic number
 */
data[i++] = 0x40;

/*
 * Put in length
 */
data[i++] = (byte) (data.length - 2);

/*
 * Put in Separator
 */
data[i++] = 0x02;

/*
 * Put in r length
 */
data[i++] = (byte) (rdata.length);

/*
 * Put r in buffer
 */
for (int j = 0; j < rdata.length; j++)
{
  data[i++] = rdata[j];
```

```
    }

    /*
     * Put in sepaerator
     */
    data[ i++]  = 0x02;

    /*
     * Put in s length
     */
    data[ i++]  = (byte) (sdata.length);

    /*
     * Put s in buffer
     */
    for (int j = 0; j < sdata.length; j++)
    {
      data[ i++]  = sdata[ j] ;
    }

    return data;
  }

  /*
   * Catches
   */
  catch (Exception ex)
  {
    ex.printStackTrace();
  }

  return null;
}

/**
 * Method update
 * Description : uppdate the hash
 *
 * @param b the bytes
 * @param offset the offset
 * @param len the length
 *
 * @throws SignatureException
 *
 */
public void update(byte[] b, int offset, int len)
        throws SignatureException
{
  md_.update(b, offset, len);
```

```
   if (DEBUG)
    {
     System.out.println();
     System.out.println("update:Length:" + len);
    }
}

/**
 * Method verify
 * @param data
 *
 * @return
 *
 */
public boolean verify(byte[] data)
 {
  try
   {
    int i = 0;

    /*
     * Check for the first
     * magic number,
     * the length
     * and separator
     */
    if ((data[ i++]  != 0x40)
            || (data[ i++]  != data.length - 2)
            || (data[ i++]  != 0x02))
     {
      throw new SignatureException(
        "Corrupted signature data");
     }

    /*
     * Check r length
     */
    byte len = data[ i++];
    if (len > 21)
     {
      throw new SignatureException(
        "Corrupted signature data");
     }

    /*
     * Get the r buffer
     */
    byte[] rdata = new byte[ len];
    for (int j = 0; j < len; j++)
```

```
  {
    rdata[ j]  = data[ i++];
  }

  /*
   * Check separator
   */
  if (data[ i++]  != 0x02)
  {
    throw new SignatureException(
      "Corrupted signature data");
  }

  /*
   * Check s length
   */
  len = data[ i++];
  if (len > 21)
  {
    throw new SignatureException(
      "Corrupted signature data");
  }

  /*
   * Get the s buffer
   */
  byte[ ] sdata = new byte[ len];
  for (int j = 0; j < len; j++)
  {
    sdata[ j]  = data[ i++];
  }

  /*
   * Get r and s from Buffer
   */
  BigInteger r = new BigInteger(rdata);
  BigInteger s = new BigInteger(sdata);

  /*
   * reject the signature, if r or s >= q
   */
  if ((r.compareTo(q_) >= 0) || (s.compareTo(q_) >= 0))
  {
    return false;
  }

  /*
   * Get the hash value,number
   */
```

```
byte[]    digest = md_.digest();
BigInteger m      = new BigInteger(1, digest);

/*
 * w = (S^-1) mod q
 */
BigInteger w = s.modInverse(q_);

/*
 * u1 = ((SHA(M)w) mod q
 */
BigInteger u1 = m.multiply(w).mod(q_);

/*
 * u2 = ((r)w) mod q
 */
BigInteger u2 = r.multiply(w).mod(q_);

if (DEBUG)
 {
  System.out.println();
  System.out.println("verify:r :" + r);
  System.out.println();
  System.out.println("verify:s :" + s);
  System.out.println();
  System.out.println("verify:m :" + m);
  System.out.println();
  System.out.println("verify:w :" + w);
  System.out.println();
  System.out.println("verify:u1 :" + u1);
  System.out.println();
  System.out.println("verify:u2 :" + u2);
  System.out.println();
  System.out.println("verify:g :" + g_);
  System.out.println();
  System.out.println("verify:p :" + p_);
  System.out.println();
  System.out.println("verify:q :" + q_);
  System.out.println();
  System.out.println("verify:y :" + y_);
 }

BigInteger gu1 = g_.modPow(u1, p_);
BigInteger yu2 = y_.modPow(u2, p_);

/*
 * v = (((g)^u1 (y) ^u2 ) mod p) mod q
 */
BigInteger v = gu1.multiply(yu2).mod(p_).mod(q_);
```

```
      return v.equals(r);
  }

  /*
   * Catches
   */
  catch (Exception ex)
   {
     ex.printStackTrace();
   }

  return false;
}

/**
 * Method main
 * Description: This is a test driver
 *
 *
 * @param args none
 *
 */
public static void main(String[] args)
 {
   try
    {
      String localDirectory  = System.getProperty("user.dir");
      System.out.println("Changing directory to Chapter 11");
      System.setProperty("user.dir",localDirectory +
"\\com\\richware\\chap11\\");
      localDirectory  = System.getProperty("user.dir");
      String localFile  = localDirectory + args[0];
      System.out.println("Openining Chapter 11 plus the file as an
argument: " + localFile);
      System.out.println("Initializing Keys... This could take several
minutes....");

      /*
       * Start the homegrown signer
       * it automatically
       * generates the keys
       */
      RichDSA dsa = new RichDSA();
      /*
       * Start the JDK version
       */

      /*
       * Generate the Keypair
```

```
 * get the private Key
 * get the public Key
 */
KeyPairGenerator kpg =
  KeyPairGenerator.getInstance("DSA");
SecureRandom     r   = new SecureRandom();
kpg.initialize(1024, r);
KeyPair    kp     = kpg.genKeyPair();
PrivateKey privKey = kp.getPrivate();
PublicKey  pubKey  = kp.getPublic();

/*
 * Construct a sign
 * and verify Signature
 * If the same Signature
 * class is used for both
 * sign and verify in the same context
 * might cause some problems
 */
Signature dsaSign   =
  Signature.getInstance("SHA1withDSA", "SUN");
Signature dsaVerify =
  Signature.getInstance("SHA1withDSA", "SUN");

/*
 * Init a sign
 * with private Key
 * and verify with
 * a public Key
 */
dsaSign.initSign(privKey);
dsaVerify.initVerify(pubKey);

/*
 * Open a File
 * and read the text
 */
File              inputTextFile =
  new File(localFile);
FileInputStream     fis         =
  new FileInputStream(inputTextFile);
BufferedInputStream bis         =
  new BufferedInputStream(fis);
byte[]              buff        =
  new byte[(int) inputTextFile.length()];
int               len;

/*
 * Loop through the File
```

```
 * pass the date through
 * update method for
 * hashing
 */
while (bis.available() != 0)
{
  len = bis.read(buff);

  dsa.update(buff, 0, len);
  dsaSign.update(buff, 0, len);
}

/*
 * Close the file
 */
bis.close();
fis.close();

/*
 * Get the signatures
 * the signature and public Key bytes
 * are normally written to file
 */
byte[] text_signature = dsa.sign();
byte[] jdk_signature   = dsaSign.sign();

/*
 * Open a File
 * and read the text
 */
inputTextFile = new File(localFile);
fis           = new FileInputStream(inputTextFile);
bis           = new BufferedInputStream(fis);
buff          = new byte[(int) inputTextFile.length()];

/*
 * Loop through the File
 * pass the date through
 * update method for
 * hashing
 */
while (bis.available() != 0)
{
  len = bis.read(buff);

  dsa.update(buff, 0, len);
  dsaVerify.update(buff, 0, len);
}
```

```
        /*
         * Verify with hash
         * public key and
         * signatures
         */
        boolean verifies      = dsa.verify(text_signature);
        boolean jdk_verifies = dsaVerify.verify(jdk_signature);

        System.out.println("RichDSA Verify : " + verifies);
        System.out.println("JDK Verify     : " + jdk_verifies);

        /*
         * Close the file
         */
        bis.close();
        fis.close();
      }

      /*
       * Catches
       */
      catch (Exception ex)
      {
        ex.printStackTrace();
      }
    }
  }
```

If I run Listing 11-1 with the following input string:

```
testing the Signature
```

The output looks like the following string:

```
q*ù°•M Ô|òæ€ >fN€%õ÷îE
```

Summary

The essence of the digital signature is to provide a key pair that can verify a digest and generate a signature for verification. If the data, signature or key doesn't match, then the message is corrupted. The public key that can validate the message can only come from the specific person who signed the message using his or her private key. If a different public key is used, then the signature will not verify. The signature on the message, in most cases, will be unique and can easily verify whether changes have been made to the message in transit. Because the validation on the sender's private key, data, and signature can be accomplished, it is normally assumed that it can be guaranteed that the message came from a specific user.

Part IV

Data Hiding

Chapter 12: Understanding Ciphers

Chapter 13: Extending New Ciphers with the JDK

Chapter 14: Applying Ciphers

Chapter 12
Understanding Ciphers

In This Chapter

- ♦ Understanding the basic cipher
- ♦ Implementing the asymmetric cipher
- ♦ Learning about the symmetric block cipher
- ♦ Understanding the symmetric stream cipher

Introduction

Ciphers have been used as far back as the Emperor Julius Caesar, who used a rudimentary cipher to send messages to his commanders. If a messenger was captured, the enemy couldn't read the message unless he was trained in the algorithm. A cipher is basically an algorithm that gives a selected group the ability to read a message. Wartime has always brought about the evolution of ciphers, such as the enigma machine used during War World II. The enigma machine, though primitive, brought about a new evolution. The enigma machine rotated the algorithm, unlike many ciphers that could be deciphered by anyone who knew the algorithm. The enigma machine did not execute the exact same cipher over and over again, but rather executed a set of ciphers and rotated them when needed. The allied forces were confused on many occasions simply because the algorithm was able to modify, or rotate, itself.

> **TIP:** The basic principle of any cipher is to confuse hackers and never to establish a pattern that can be broken.

The enigma machine broke the pattern of using the same cipher algorithm constantly. Once it was taken, understood, and the finite set of rotations mapped, the enigma machine became useless. What was needed was a larger set of variables that could alter the cipher algorithm. Over time, and with the help of Diffie-Hellman and other algorithms, the key to lock and unlock a cipher algorithm evolved.

The evolution brought about the secret key that could be used for locking and unlocking the cipher. The secret key is used for *symmetric ciphers*, which use the same key for both . encryption and decryption. The algorithm that evolved from the symmetric algorithm was the *asymmetric cipher*, which uses separate keys for encryption and decryption. The idea of having two keys is to allow only the decryption key to be made public to other users, and to keep the encryption key secure. If the enemy captures the decryption key, the messages can be read but not written, which prevents the enemy from writing new messages after the interception. If the enemy captures the secret key, he or she could read the message and also rewrite a different message to confuse the others that use the secret key.

The security of the cipher keys gives the ability to lock and unlock the messages by encrypting and decrypting them. Digital keys should be guarded to protect information, just as physical keys are guarded to protect physical property. The information transported in messages is informational property. Even though some information could be thought of as trivial, such as e-mails to various people in customer service, those e-mails could be monitored to get information about servers. That information could then be used to guess at passwords, for example.

> **TIP:** Keys should not be saved on the hard disk on a computer without being in a secure storage and encrypted to avoid copying.

Some break-ins to some of the most secure systems start out with the most trivial information. It is important to try to secure as much information as possible. The war that industry fights now is one against industrial espionage. Just as the enigma machine was broken during WWII, so are the coding algorithms of organizations broken today. Just as the plans of U-boat attacks were being read, so is the code of a new software release.

The best advice that can be offered to organizations is to have a security department for handling digital protection. The organization should staff the security department with trained professionals and establish protocols and requirements for handling multiple contingencies.

> **TIP:** Always plan to upgrade and use as many levels of security as possible.

An example from past experience is what I call just blocking entry. One organization used badges and VPNs to block access into the organization, but once inside there were no cameras and very few monitoring tools. The organization had issues with people stealing things overnight, and the best advice that I could give was to have multiple levels of security inside as well as at the entry into the organization. The same advice applies to encryption. Not only should organizations have firewalls, but also their data and e-mails should be encrypted when possible.

> **CROSS-REFERENCE:** See Chapter 4 for more information on keys.

Understanding Symmetric Ciphers

The *symmetric cipher* uses the same key for both encryption and decryption. In the *asymmetric cipher*, separate keys are used for encryption and decryption. When using an asymmetric cipher, the operation is dependent on the key used. In the symmetric cipher, the algorithm needs to be instructed — via a parameter, for example — whether it is encrypting or decrypting.

There are two types of symmetric algorithms: stream and block algorithms. A *stream* algorithm can encrypt a single bit or byte. The stream algorithm may even XOR it to the next byte. The operation is similar to a message digest. The stream algorithm doesn't have the same fixed-length limitations that the message digests have and uses a key to apply to the algorithm. Since the stream is one byte at a time, it eliminates the need for padding and doesn't need to work with a message block other than being encrypted or decrypted a byte size.

For algorithms where the current byte will be applied to the encryption of the next byte, the decryption will have to read in reverse. For example, the starting byte B_1 . . .B_3, where B_1 will be encrypted first and B_3 encrypted last, will be decrypted starting with B_3 first and B_1 last. Since the cipher is encrypted a byte at a time, it is difficult to calculate the pattern that will emerge 64 bytes later.

> **TIP:** If a pattern arises, the algorithm can be compromised. Patterns should be avoided because they may offer some insight into how the algorithm is behaving. If the hex number x05 shows up every few bytes in the message, and the hacker knows that the letter "e" appears in every other word in the first sentence, it might be a good guess that the pattern continues for the letter "e." For this reason, and the fact that block ciphers can be used as stream ciphers, there are a lot more block ciphers than stream ciphers.

To help with the repetition of bytes in the stream, a key stream is used to encrypt and decrypt each byte. The key generator changes a block of a key into a key stream. The key stream matches the plaintext, or ciphertext stream, in a byte-by-byte ratio. When P_1 is being encrypted with the cipher algorithm, it has a matching key called k_1. The next byte, P_2, uses P_1 as material. The next key in the stream, k_2, uses k_1 as a material to generate itself. The combination of P_2 and k_1 is used to generate C_2 and so on. For generating the plaintext, the ciphertext (C_1, C_2, C_3, and so on) works similarly with the key stream to produce the previous plaintext. The key stream is needed for keeping out any patterns and protecting the data. This process is illustrated in Figure 12-1.

The *block* cipher works with block of data at a time. The key stream is important for keeping patterns out of the ciphertext. The block cipher is dependent on the input size. The objective of the cipher is to permutate the data with the key and to to reverse the process to restore the original data. The key can be permutated in a process called whitening. *Whitening* is the technique of XORing key material before the first round and after the last round. The cipher algorithm will perform a number of like operations. These operations are called *rounds* and have been demonstrated with the message digest.

> **CROSS-REFERENCE:** The message digest is discussed in Chapter 9.

The round operation is denoted by the function *f* in mathematical terms. The function *f* uses the key *k* and the plaintext *p* to build a ciphertext *c*. A cipher such as DES could be expressed in a mathematical function:

$$16f(kp) = c$$

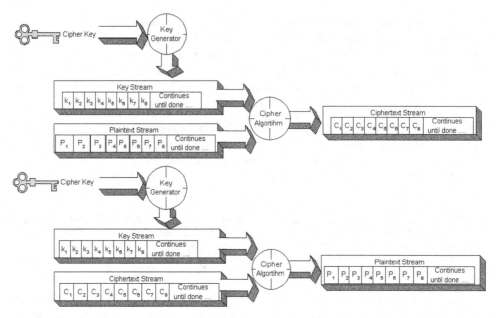

Figure   12-1: The key stream

The DES algorithm executes the function f 16 rounds, or times. Each round executes the function on the key and plaintext to form the ciphertext. If the key was permutated with the whitening process w, the key could be expressed as $w(k) = k_w$. Each cipher needs to have the capability to be expressed in mathematical formula so that it may be studied, understood, and analyzed. The function and keys can be broken down so that an analysis can find any weaknesses.

For example, the function for DES includes the breakdown of the plaintext into a right side and a left side. The right side could be expressed as r_1 and the left side as l_1. The next piece of the function may shift the l_1 through an S-box.

> **NOTE:** Recall that an S-box is a substitution box. Ever since DES and Lucifer, S-boxes have been used to describe the substitution operations. Most block ciphers use S-boxes. An example of how DES uses S-boxes is that DES takes 48 of the 56 bits of plaintext, and splits the 48 bits into a right half and a left half. The right half and left half expand the 24 bits into 48 bits and split the 48 bits into 6-bit sets. Each 6-bit set is passed into an S-box.

Before the shift, l_1 can be represented in hex as `0x9Ab37uIt`. After the shift operation with the S-box, $S_1(l_1) = So_1$, the output data may become `0Xccv899oD`. The operations are analyzed and studied for any patterns. If patterns or weaknesses are found in the algorithm, the algorithm can be fixed and upgraded. Unless you can express the algorithm in mathematical terms and to analyze the operations, the algorithm becomes difficult to express.

By looking at the algorithm and how the plaintext and ciphertext propagate through the rounds, cryptologists are able to analyze the differences through the algorithm. This is known as *differential cryptanalysis*. Differential cryptanalysis is the ability to take pairs of ciphertext, while looking at their plaintexts, and examine their differences for weaknesses.

There are eight S-boxes for this operation because 6 bits × 8 S-boxes = 48 bits. The result of the 48 bits after passing through the S-box set is 32 bits. S-boxes normally have a different number of bits coming in and going out. The ratio of bits going in and coming out is known as the *S-box size*. The size of the S-box is the number of bits that the S-box can handle. The designation of the inputs is normally n and the designation of the outputs is normally m. The size of the S-box is $n \times m$. The size of the S-box just described for DES is a 6 × 4 S-box. Each DES S-box will have 6 bits going in and 4 bits coming out. Because there are 8 S-boxes, the total input will be 48 bits and the total output will be 32 bits.

The operation that S-box offers is a substitution cipher by mapping the bit substitution. The DES S-box reads the 6-bit input number and, based on the number, it maps the number to a row and column in the substitution table. Based on the mapping in the substitution table, it modifies the number specified in the table. An example of the S-box substitution can be seen in Figure 12-2.

In that example, the result is 11 from 51. If the digit 11 was expanded again by being wrapped with ones, 1(1011)1, the result would be 55. Passing 55 through the same S-box would yield a different result. For decryption, the return path could be done in reverse to establish the original message by using the table lookups. The tables themselves have sometimes evolved over time. Some are generated randomly and tested to see if they are weak. Others are designed using mathematical principles through statistics to avoid patterns. Depending on the means used to create the S-box table, the table can add strength or weakness to the cipher.

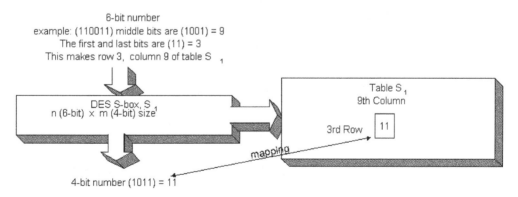

Figure 12-2: The S-box substitution

DES has been the cornerstone of discussion with the S-box. Many block ciphers have evolved from using DES as a foundation. For the message digest, MD4 serves the same purposes.

Because the types and levels of security for different people and organizations are very diverse, block ciphers must cover a wide variety of uses. To do so, block ciphers use four modes of operation. These modes of operation are based on the DES four modes of operation: *Electronic CodeBook Mode* (ECB), *Cipher Block Chaining* (CBC), *Cipher Feedback* (CFB), and *Output Feedback* (OFB).

The first mode of operation is ECB. The ECB is the simplest form of the operation modes. The ECB offers a one-to-one relationship between a block of plaintext and ciphertext. DES has a 64-bit size. In ECB mode, each 64-bit block is encrypted with the same key producing the same 64-bit ciphertext. If the input to the cipher is not 64-bit, the cipher algorithm will apply a pad to ensure that input fits the correct block size. If the message is longer than 64 bits, then it is broken down into 64-bit blocks. The encryption and decryption of each block is independent of the other blocks.

The reason that the ECB is called the codebook mode is because the same plaintext will always produce the same ciphertext. Theoretically, but not practically, it is possible to establish a codebook of all the possible combinations of plaintext and ciphertext to avoid calculations. That is also the weakness of the ECB. Because the same plaintext will produce the same ciphertext, a pattern could be found and the cipher could be cracked. If you know that the string "ABC" will always produce the output "0xOis6rtsr" for a given key, the next time you see the ciphertext "0xOis6rtsr" (and the key has not changed), you know the input was "ABC." See Figure 12-3 for an example of the ECB.

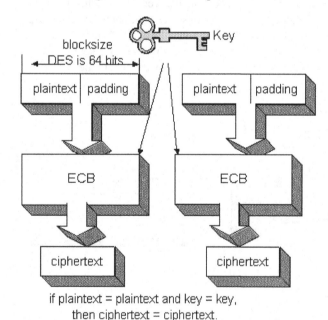

if plaintext = plaintext and key = key,
then ciphertext = ciphertext.

Figure 12-3: The ECB mode

The ECB cipher producing the same ciphertext for the same key has been seen as a deficiency on the operational mode. To compensate for this deficiency, the CBC has evolved. The CBC repeats the same plaintext, and the key produces a different ciphertext. It accomplishes this task by chaining the cipher block. The cipher block is the ciphertext that is the output of the encryption algorithm. The output of one algorithm block is used to permutate the input of another block so that when a second block contains the same plaintext, it produces a different ciphertext. The ciphertext from the first block is XORed with the plaintext of the next block. Hashing the input with an output alleviates patterns for the same plaintext to become the same ciphertext. For every plaintext, there is an accompanying ciphertext to be XORed with in order to mask the plaintext.

To ensure that the first round works the same as the other rounds, an *initialization vector* (IV) is used. Since the first round of plaintext doesn't have a previous ciphertext block to work with, the IV is used to simulate a block of ciphertext for the first round. For DES, the IV would be a 64-bit block of random data to simulate a block of ciphertext. The random data cannot be randomly generated data on-the-fly because the data is needed for encrypting and decrypting the same data. If one DES engine uses one set of data for the IV and another uses a different set of data for IV, the encryption and decryptions will not work. The IV gives the algorithm the same security as an extra key.

If an organization fears that its ciphertexts have been compromised, it could decrypt its messages, change the IV, and re-encrypt all the messages, making sure that every trusted party uses the same IV. If the organization rotates the IV, the crackers that don't have the IV will be kicked out of the decryption and have to find the new IV data set. The weakness of the CBC is that some block ciphers such as DES, which is 64 bits or 8 bytes, do not have enough randomness within the blocks. The blocks are small, and there is not enough change in the data by an XOR to ensure no patterns are established. If the blocks were much larger, the XOR of larger values would have the probability to produce more of a change in data.

Another issue is that the ciphertext can be determined, and an attacker can take into consideration that the ciphertext is XORed with plaintext to compensate for the chaining. Just as the chaining is used to XOR the plaintext for the next ciphertext, any cracker intercepting the first ciphertext can use it as part of the cracking mechanism. While the CBC has the capability to chain the plaintext with ciphertext and produce a different ciphertext for the same plaintext block, it does this chaining at a very rudimentary level. This makes a crack possible for those who can intercept pieces of the ciphertext and use it to piece back the plaintext. See Figure 12-4 for an overview of CBC.

The CFB mode can force a block cipher to act like a stream cipher. The CFB has the capability to work with sizes that are smaller than the block size. For DES, it can work with a block smaller than 64 bits. The CFB could encrypt 1 byte (8 bits) or even 1 bit at a time. Encrypting 8 bits at a time is referred to as CFB8. Since the CFB acts like a stream cipher, padding is not required. Figure 12-5 shows an overview of CFB8.

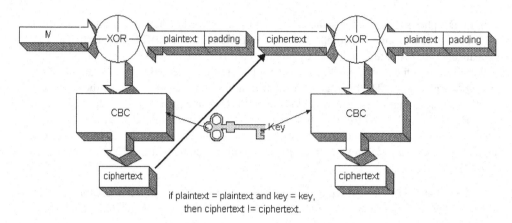

Figure   12-4: A CBC overview

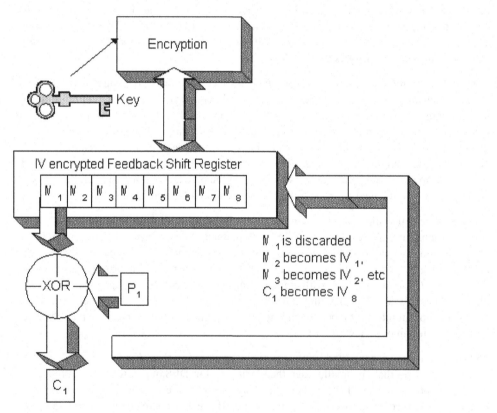

Figure   12-5: Overview of the CBC8

To start the algorithm, the IV is initialized and encrypted. Each byte will be XORed with the plaintext one byte at a time. The first byte to be XORed will be the first byte in the shift register labeled IV_1 to the first byte of plaintext labeled P_1. The result of the two elements produces the ciphertext C_1. IV_1 will be discarded and all the other entries in the IV register will shift one byte to take its place. When all bytes shift to the beginning of the queue, one byte will be left empty on the end of the register that was labeled IV_8. A copy of the ciphertext C_1 will fill the gap and replace IV_8. The ciphertext is fed back into the VI shift register. The entire 64 bits of the IV shift register block will be encrypted again. This process continues until all the plaintext has been encrypted. The encryption algorithm is also used during decryption. The difference between encryption and decryption is that during decryption, the ciphertext byte is XORed with the IV register instead of the plaintext byte. Because the IV shift register is encrypted every time the register is shifted, the CFB mode is a lot slower than the previous two modes. In this example, the entire block of 8 bytes will be encrypted for every one byte that is added to the register.

The OFB is another example of a block cipher that can be used like a stream cipher. The OFB works just like the CFB except that ciphertext does not feed back into the IV shift register, but rather the IV shift register feeds back into itself. When all the IV entries shift to replace the IV_1 entry, the IV_1 entry will move into the IV_8 position. The plaintext and ciphertext will not actually be encrypted. They will be XORed with the values in the IV that are encrypted. The encryption will happen again every time the IV entries are shifted. Because the ciphertext is no longer in the equation, if any corruption errors occur in the ciphertext, they will not be propagated to the plaintext. Because the IV is used for encrypting data, instead of the ciphertext, the IV shift register could be susceptible to attacks to crack the plaintext or corrupt the message. This is illustrated in Figure 12-6.

The symmetric cipher algorithms can be classified and categorized based on key size, block size, number of S-boxes, number of rounds, and other factors that describe the algorithm. To understand the weaknesses and strengths of a cipher, the mathematics, substitutions, and modes must be understood. The mathematics describes the process of the algorithm in a common language.

The constructs, like the modes and substitutions, can be used to walk through the process of the algorithm and conceptualize the weaknesses and strengths of the algorithms. It is up to the individual and the organization to understand the algorithm's weaknesses and strengths to ensure that they are using the correct algorithms. If users understand the characteristics that make up the symmetric algorithms, such as key size, the ability to differentiate between the different algorithms can be offered.

NOTE: An organization must know and understand the export laws for a very large key size. This can influence the decision about which algorithm to use. For instance, an organization may not use a specific algorithm if the organization frequently sends messages overseas.

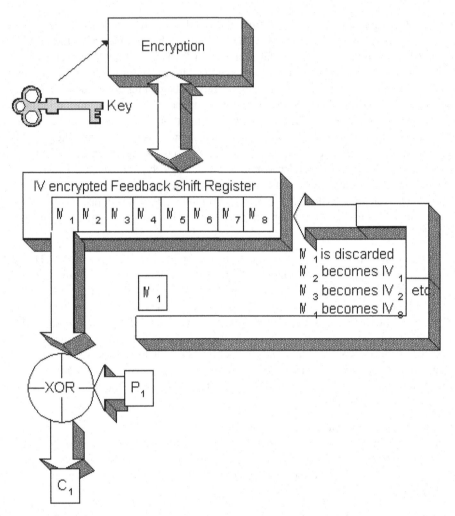

Figure   12-6: The OFB mode

Implementing RSA Public Key Encryption

The RSA encryption has been described in earlier chapters. This chapter shows an implementation of the RSA algorithm. There are really two parts in developing a cipher *Service Provider Interface* (SPI): understanding how to implement the SPI layer with the `javax.crypto.CipherSpi` class and understanding the cipher algorithm. The RSA algorithm is described in detail in its PKCS#1 documentation (http://www.rsasecurity.com/rsalabs/pkcs/pkcs-1/index.html).

CROSS-REFERENCE: See Chapter 4 for more on RSA.

The RSA algorithm was followed step-by-step in implementing the private methods such as RSADP, which performs the decryption of an integer that was encrypted with the RSA algorithm. I am not going step-by-step through the algorithm, simply because the code is exactly documented in each method following the PKCS#1, and an overview of RSA has already been provided. The example is a tested version for the readers to implement their own RSA encryptions.

> **CAUTION::** The RSA algorithm has been patented by RSA. RSA released the patent on September 6, 2000. It is up to the user to check if any other patents apply before using the algorithm.

The difference between the implementation in Listing 12-1 and other RSA algorithms that are provided by other *Java Cryptography Extensions* (JCE) is that the RSAPublicKey, RSAPrivateKey, and other RSA components that the JDK 1.4 supports can still be used. The implementation simply extends the JDK 1.4 to provide an RSA cipher. The JDK 1.4 already has support for RSA signature algorithms and RSA keys. The example code that tests the cipher, the javax.crypto.CipherSpi class, and the java.security.Provider class that loads the cipher as an SPI layer will be discussed in detail in the next chapter with other cipher algorithms. The purpose of the algorithm in this chapter is to demonstrate some of the differences between symmetric and asymmetric ciphers.

One of the differences is the constant testing of the key. In the RSA case, the RSAPrivateKey is always associated and tested with the decryption mode. The RSAPublicKey is always associated with the encryption mode. In the symmetric key ciphers, there is only one key for all these methods. Another difference to note is that while the example is dictated to be ECB mode, it is different from other block ciphers. The engineGetBlockSize and engineGetOutputSize are associated with the key size. In most symmetric key algorithms, the cipher block size is different from the key size. A symmetric block size is related to the S-box, which might look more like a static 64-bit block.

The RSA algorithm also has a padding string that adds delimiters to define where the pad begins and ends. An S-box in a symmetric algorithm will produce a ciphertext of a fixed size. The pad in this implementation will be of PKCS1_V1_5 type. The PKCS1_V1_5 is an older pad. This pad will put a padding string in the message to fill the pad to reach the key size. The padding string is just random bytes that act as a filler. A more secure pad evolved in the more current versions of RSA for padding as the *Optimal Asymmetric Encryption Padding* (OAEP). The OAEP will XOR the plaintext. For the padding, it will apply a message digest and a *mask generation function* (MGF). The MGF will mask the pad so that it is difficult to tell what is pad and what is data for encryption. The OAEP prevents parsing from the delimiters that can be looked at to determine what is message and what is pad.

Simply put, because the asymmetric algorithm is very key-size–centric, it must pad differently than the block ciphers. Many of the block ciphers will pad using PKCS#5 of the RSA documentation. The PKCS#5 padding will pad a number at the end that describes the number of padded bytes before encryption. If 8 bytes need to be padded at the end of the plaintext, the algorithm will input the number 8 in the last 8 byes. See Figure 12-7 for a comparison. Which key is used in the asymmetric algorithm decides whether the encryption mode or decryption mode is set. The asymmetric cipher depends on the discrete logarithm problem, mentioned in previous chapters, and works with integers instead of a pure S-box implementation.

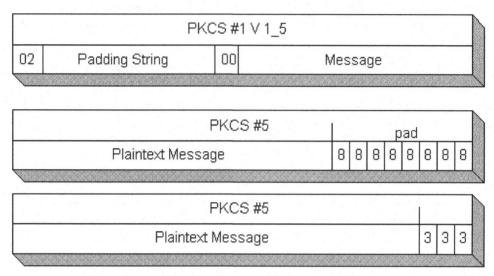

Figure 12-7: Padding in ciphers

Listing 12-1: The `RichRSACipher` class: An RSA cipher implementation

```
package com.richware.chap12;

import java.io.*;
import java.math.BigInteger;
import java.security.*;
import java.security.interfaces.*;
import java.security.spec.*;
import javax.crypto.*;
import sun.misc.*;

/**
 * Class RichRSACipher
 * Description: This is an example of a
 * simple RSA Encryption
 * RSA information is from PKCS#1v2.0
 * a publication from RSA Security
 *
 * Copyright:    Copyright (c) 2002 Wiley Publishing, Inc.
 * @author Rich Helton <rhelton@richware.com>
 * @version 1.0
```

```
 * DISCLAIMER: Please refer to the disclaimer at the beginning of this
book.
 */
public final class RichRSACipher extends CipherSpi
{
  private RSAKeyGenParameterSpec params_;
  private SecureRandom           random ;
  private final static boolean   DEBUG = true;
  private int                    opmode_;
  private Key                    key_;
  private byte[]                 internal buffer ;

  /**
   * Constructor RichRSACipher
   */
  public RichRSACipher() {}

  /**
   * Method engineDoFinal
   * Description: See CipherSpi
   */
  protected byte[] engineDoFinal(
         byte[] input, int inputOffset, int inputLen)
            throws IllegalBlockSizeException,
                   BadPaddingException
  {
    byte[] output = engineUpdate(input, inputOffset, inputLen);
    internal_buffer_ = null;
    return output;
  }

  /**
   * Method engineDoFinal
   * Description: See CipherSpi
   */
  protected int engineDoFinal(
         byte[] input, int inputOffset, int inputLen, byte[] output,
int outputOffset)
            throws ShortBufferException,
                   IllegalBlockSizeException,
                   BadPaddingException
  {
    byte[] buffer;
    buffer = engineDoFinal(input, inputOffset, inputLen);
    if (output.length - outputOffset < buffer.length)
     {
       throw new ShortBufferException(
         "Output longer than buffer");
     }
```

```
     System.arraycopy(buffer, 0, output, outputOffset,
                       buffer.length);
     return buffer.length;
}

/**
 * Method engineGetBlockSize
 * Description: See CipherSpi
 */
protected int engineGetBlockSize()
  {
   if ((opmode_ == Cipher.ENCRYPT_MODE)
          || (opmode_ == Cipher.WRAP_MODE))
    {
     return params_.getKeysize();
    }
   else
    {
     return params_.getKeysize() - 1;
    }
  }

/**
 * Method engineGetIV
 * Description: See CipherSpi
 */
protected byte[] engineGetIV()
  {
   return null;  // If not supported
  }

/**
 * Method engineGetKeySize
 * Description: See CipherSpi
 */
protected int engineGetKeySize(Key key)
        throws InvalidKeyException
  {

   /*
    * Get the key size based on bit length
    */
   if (key instanceof RSAPrivateKey)
    {
     RSAPrivateKey k = (RSAPrivateKey) key;

     return k.getModulus().bitLength();
    }
   else if (key instanceof RSAPublicKey)
```

```
      {
      RSAPublicKey k = (RSAPublicKey) key;

      return k.getModulus().bitLength();
   }

   throw new InvalidKeyException("Unsupported RSA key!");
}

/**
 * Method engineGetOutputSize
 * Description: See CipherSpi
 */
protected int engineGetOutputSize(int inputLen)
{
  if ((opmode_ == Cipher.ENCRYPT_MODE)
         || (opmode_ == Cipher.WRAP_MODE))
   {
     return params_.getKeysize();
   }
   else
    {
     return params_.getKeysize() - 1;
   }
}

/**
 * Method engineGetParameters
 * Description: See CipherSpi
 */
protected AlgorithmParameters engineGetParameters()
{
  return null;
}

/**
 * Method engineInit
 * Description: See CipherSpi
 */
protected void engineInit(
       int opmode, Key _key, AlgorithmParameterSpec params,
SecureRandom _random)
         throws InvalidKeyException,
               InvalidAlgorithmParameterException
{
  // Check for valid key
  if ((!( key instanceof RSAPublicKey))
        && (!(_key instanceof RSAPrivateKey)))
    {
```

```java
    throw new InvalidKeyException("Unsupported RSA Key!");
}

// Check for valid Parameter Spec
if ((params != null)
        && (!(params instanceof RSAKeyGenParameterSpec)))
{
  throw new InvalidAlgorithmParameterException(
    "Unsupported RSA AlgorithmParameterSpec!");
}

// Initialize the params
if (params != null)
{
  params_ = (RSAKeyGenParameterSpec) params;
}
else
{
  int        keysize   = 0;
  BigInteger publicExp = null;
  if (_key instanceof RSAPublicKey)
  {
    publicExp = ((RSAPublicKey) _key).getPublicExponent();
    int modulusLength =
      ((RSAPublicKey) _key).getModulus().bitLength();
    keysize = (modulusLength + 7) / 8;
  }
  else if (_key instanceof RSAPrivateKey)
  {
    int modulusLength =
      ((RSAPrivateKey) _key).getModulus().bitLength();
    keysize = (modulusLength + 7) / 8;
  }
      if(DEBUG){
        System.out.println("RichRSACipher:engineInit:keysize:" +
keysize);
      }
  params_ = new RSAKeyGenParameterSpec(keysize, publicExp);
}
random_ = _random;
// Check for valid types of opmode
if ((opmode == Cipher.DECRYPT_MODE)
        || (opmode == Cipher.ENCRYPT_MODE)
        || (opmode == Cipher.UNWRAP_MODE)
        || (opmode == Cipher.WRAP_MODE))
{
  if (((opmode == Cipher.DECRYPT_MODE) || (opmode == Cipher
        .UNWRAP_MODE)) && (_key instanceof RSAPublicKey))
  {
```

```
         throw new InvalidKeyException(
            "Unsupported: Decrypt/UnWrap mode must use RSAPrivateKey");
      }
      if (((opmode == Cipher.ENCRYPT_MODE) || (opmode == Cipher
             .WRAP_MODE)) && (_key instanceof RSAPrivateKey))
       {
         throw new InvalidKeyException(
            "Unsupported: Encrypt/Wrap mode must use RSAPublicKey");
       }
      if(DEBUG){
         if ((opmode == Cipher.DECRYPT_MODE) || (opmode ==
Cipher.UNWRAP_MODE)){
            System.out.println("RichRSACipher:engineInit:DECRYPT_MODE");
         }else{
            System.out.println("RichRSACipher:engineInit:ENCRYPT_MODE");
         }
       }
    }
    else
     {
      throw new InvalidKeyException("Unsupported opmode!");
     }
    opmode_ = opmode;
    key_ = _key;
 }

 /**
  * Method engineInit
  * Description: See CipherSpi
  */
 protected void engineInit(
        int opmode, Key _key, AlgorithmParameters params, SecureRandom
_random)
          throws InvalidKeyException,
                 InvalidAlgorithmParameterException
  {

   /*
    * Note  key is used instead of Key, because Key is a class.
    * Random is also a class.
    */
   engineInit(opmode, _key, (AlgorithmParameterSpec) null,
             _random);
 }

 /**
  * Method engineInit
  * Description: See CipherSpi
  */
```

```
protected void engineInit(
        int opmode, Key _key, SecureRandom _random)
          throws InvalidKeyException
{
  try
    {
      engineInit(opmode,  key, (AlgorithmParameterSpec) null,
                _random);
    }
  catch (InvalidAlgorithmParameterException ex)
    {
      throw new InvalidKeyException(ex.getMessage());
    }
}

/**
 * Method engineSetMode
 * Description: See CipherSpi
 */
protected void engineSetMode(String mode)
        throws NoSuchAlgorithmException
{
  if (!mode.equalsIgnoreCase("ECB"))
    {
      throw new NoSuchAlgorithmException(
        "RSA supports only ECB mode");
    }
}

/**
 * Method engineSetPadding
 * Description: See CipherSpi
 */
protected void engineSetPadding(String s)
        throws NoSuchPaddingException
{
  // Only accepts avaliable padding
  if (!s.equalsIgnoreCase("PKCS1_V1_5"))
    {
      throw new NoSuchPaddingException("Unknown padding: "
                                        + s);
    }
}

/**
 * Method engineUpdate
 * Description: See CipherSpi
 */
protected byte[] engineUpdate(byte[] input, int inputOffset,
```

```
                              int inputLen)
{
 try
  {
   if (inputOffset > 0)
    {
     int    outputSize = inputOffset + inputLen;
     byte[] tmp        = new byte[ outputSize];
     System.arraycopy(input, inputOffset, internal_buffer_,
                      internal_buffer_.length, inputLen);
     if ((opmode  == Cipher.ENCRYPT_MODE)
            || (opmode_ == Cipher.WRAP_MODE))
      {
       return (encrypt(internal_buffer_));
      }
     else
      {
       return (decrypt(internal_buffer_));
      }
    }
   else
    {
     internal_buffer_ = new byte[ inputLen];
     System.arraycopy(input, 0, internal_buffer_,0, inputLen);
     if ((opmode_ == Cipher.ENCRYPT_MODE)
            || (opmode_ == Cipher.WRAP_MODE))
      {
       if(DEBUG){
        System.out.println("RichRSACipher:engineUpdate:encrypting");
       }
       return (encrypt(internal_buffer_));
      }
     else
      {
       if(DEBUG){
        System.out.println("RichRSACipher:engineUpdate:decrypting");
       }
       return (decrypt(internal_buffer_));
      }
    }
  }

 /*
  * Catches
  */
 catch (Exception ex)
  {
   ex.printStackTrace();
  }
```

```
      return null;
  }

  /**
   * Method engineUpdate
   * Description: See CipherSpi
   */
  protected int engineUpdate(
          byte[] input, int inputOffset, int inputLen, byte[] output,
int outputOffset)
          throws ShortBufferException
  {
    byte[] buffer;
    buffer = engineUpdate(input, inputOffset, inputLen);
    if (output.length - outputOffset < buffer.length)
    {
      throw new ShortBufferException(
        "Output longer than buffer");
    }
    System.arraycopy(buffer, 0, output, outputOffset,
                     buffer.length);
    return buffer.length;
  }

  /**
   * Method I2OSP
   * Description: Integer to Octet String Primitive
   * See PKCS#1
   */
  private byte[] I2OSP(BigInteger x, int l)
          throws IllegalBlockSizeException
  {
    /*
     * Section 4.1 of PKCS#1v2.0
     * I2OSP converts a nonnegative integer to an octet string
     * of a specified length. I2OSP (x, l)
     * Input: x nonnegative integer to be converted
     * l intended length of the resulting octet string
     * Output: X corresponding octet string of length l; or
     * integer too large
     * Steps:
     */

    /*
     * 1. If x = 256l, output  "integer too large " and stop.
     */
    int j = (x.bitLength() + 7) / 8;
    if (l == -1)
    {
```

```
    l = j;
  }

  if ((j > l) || (x.signum() == -1))
  {
    throw new IllegalBlockSizeException("Block too large");
  }

  /*
   * 2. Write the integer x in its unique l-digit representation
   * base 256: x = xl- 1 256^ (l- 1) + xl -2 256 256^(l -2) + ...& +
xl 256 + x0
   * where 0 = xi < 256 (note that one or more leading digits
   * will be zero if x < 256^ (l- 1)).
   */
  byte[] C = x.toByteArray();

  /*
   * remove the leading zeros
   */
  int index = 0;
  for (; (index < C.length) && (C[ index] == 0); index++);
  if (index > 0)
  {
    byte[] temp = new byte[ C.length - index];
    System.arraycopy(C, index, temp, 0, temp.length);
    C = temp;
  }
  else if (C.length > 1)
  {
    throw new IllegalBlockSizeException("Block too large");
  }

  /*
   * 3. Let the octet Xi have the value xl -i for 1 = i = l.
   * Output the octet string X = X1 X2 & ... Xl.
   */
  if (C.length == l)
  {
    return C;
  }

  /*
   * C is not long enough
   */
  byte[] result = new byte[ l];

  System.arraycopy(C, 0, result, l - C.length, C.length);
```

```java
      return result;
  }

  /**
   * Method encrypt
   * Description: Encrypt with pad
   * See PKCS#1
   * @param M the plaintext message
   */
  private byte[] encrypt(byte[] M)
        throws IllegalBlockSizeException
  {
    /*
     * RSA Steps according to PKCS #1 v 2.0 pg 15 for encryption:
     * 1. Apply the EME-PKCS1-v1 5 encoding operation (Section 9.1.2.1)
     * to the message M to produce an encoded message EM of length k-1
     * octets: EM = EME-PKCS1-V1_5-ENCODE (M, k-1)
     * If the encoding operation outputs  "message too long,   ," then
output
     * message too long  and stop.
     */
    int   k  = params_.getKeysize();
    byte[] EM = EME_PKCS1_V1_5_ENCODE(M, k - 1);

    /*
     * 2. Convert the encoded message EM to an integer message
     * representative m:  m = OS2IP (EM)
     */
    BigInteger m = new BigInteger(1, EM);

    /*
     * 3. Apply the RSAEP encryption primitive (Section 5.1.1) to the
     * public key (n, e) and the message representative m to produce
     * an integer ciphertext representative c: c = RSAEP ((n, e), m)
     */
    BigInteger c = RSAEP((RSAPublicKey) key_, m);

    /*
     * 4. Convert the ciphertext representative c to a ciphertext C of
     * length k octets: C = I2OSP (c, k)
     */
    byte[] C = I2OSP(c, k);

    /*
     * 5. Output the ciphertext C.
     */
    return C;
  }
```

```
/**
 * Method decrypt
 * Description: Decrypt with pad
 * See PKCS#1
 * @param M the ciphertext message
 */
private byte[] decrypt(byte[] C)
       throws BadPaddingException, IllegalBlockSizeException
{
  /*
   * RSA Steps according to PKCS #1 v 2.0 pg 16 for decryption:
   * 1. If the length of the ciphertext C is not k octets, output
   * decryption error  and stop.
   */
  int k = params .getKeysize();

  if (k != C.length)
   {
    throw new IllegalBlockSizeException("decryption error");
   }

  /*
   * 2. Convert the ciphertext C to an integer ciphertext
   * representative c: c = OS2IP (C)
   */
  BigInteger c = new BigInteger(1, C);

  /*
   * 3. Apply the RSADP decryption primitive to the private
   * key (n, d) and the ciphertext representative c to produce
   * an integer message representative m: m = RSADP ((n, d), c)
   * If RSADP outputs  ciphertext out of range,  then output
   * decryption error  and stop.
   */
  BigInteger m = RSADP((RSAPrivateKey} key , c);

  /*
   * 4. Convert the message representative m to an encoded message
   * EM of length k-1 octets: EM = I2OSP (m, k-1)
   * If I2OSP outputs  integer too large,  then output  decryption
   * error  and stop.
   */
  byte[] EM = I2OSP(m, k - 1);

  /*
   * 5. Apply the EME-PKCS1-v1_5 decoding operation to the encoded
   * message EM to recover a message M: M = EME-PKCS1-V1 5-DECODE(EM)
   * If the decoding operation outputs  decoding error,  then output
   * decryption error and stop.
```

```
    */
  byte[] M = EME_PKCS1_V1_5_DECODE(EM);

  /*
   * 6. Output the message M.
   */
  return M;
}

/**
 * Method EME PKCS1 V1 5 ENCODE
 * Description: Pad encoding
 *
 * @param M the ciphertext message
 * @param emLen the length of encr message
 *
 * @return encoded pad
 *
 * @throws IllegalBlockSizeException
 *
 */
private byte[] EME_PKCS1_V1_5_ENCODE(byte[] M, int emLen)
        throws IllegalBlockSizeException
{
  /*
   * Section 9.1.2.1 of PKCS#1v2.0
   * 1. If the length of the message M is greater than emLen    10
   * octets, output  message too long  and stop.
   */
  if (M.length > emLen - 10)
    {
    throw new IllegalBlockSizeException("message too long");
    }

  /*
   * 2. Generate an octet string PS of length emLen-||M||-2
   * consisting of pseudorandomly generated nonzero octets.
   * The length of PS will be at least 8 octets.
   */
  byte[]              PS  =
    new byte[(emLen - M.length - 2)];

  // Fill the padding string with random non-zero bytes
  for (int i = 0; i < PS.length; i++)
    {
    PS[i] = (byte) (random_.nextInt(255) + 1);
    }

  /*
```

```
   * 3. Concatenate PS, the message M, and other padding to
   * form the encoded message EM as EM = 02 || PS || 00 || M
   */
  byte[] EM = new byte[emLen];
  int index = 0;
  EM[index++] = (byte) 0x02;
  for (int i = 0; i < PS.length; i++)
  {
    EM[index++] = PS[i];
  }
  EM[index++] = (byte) 0x00;
  for (int i = 0; i < M.length; i++)
  {
    EM[index++] = M[i];
  }

  /*
   * 4. Output EM.
   */
  return EM;
}

/**
 * Method EME_PKCS1_V1_5_DECODE
 * Description: Pad decoding
 *
 * @param EM the encrypted message
 *
 * @return pad
 *
 * @throws BadPaddingException
 *
 */
private byte[] EME_PKCS1_V1_5_DECODE(byte[] EM)
        throws BadPaddingException
{
  /*
   * Section 9.1.2.2 of PKCS#1v2.0
   * 1. If the length of the encoded
   * message EM is less than 10, output  decoding error
   * and stop.
   */
  if (EM.length < 10)
  {
    throw new BadPaddingException("message too short");
  }

  /*
   * 2. Separate the encoded message EM into an octet string PS
```

```
 * consisting of nonzero octets and a message M as
 * EM = 02 || PS || 00 || M. If the first octet of EM is not 02,
 * or if there is no 00 octet to separate PS from M,
 * output  decoding error  and stop.
 */
if (EM[0] != (byte) 0x02)
{
  throw new BadPaddingException(
    "message not formatted properly");
}

// Need to start by looking for the first non-zero byte
int start = 0;
while (EM[start] != (byte) 0x00)
{
  start++;
  if (start >= EM.length)
  {
    throw new BadPaddingException("bad padding");
  }
}

start++;  // Ignore the first 00

/*
 * 3. If the length of PS is less than 8 octets,
 * output  decoding error  and stop.
 */
if (start < 10)
{
  throw new BadPaddingException("bad padding");
}
byte[] M = new byte[EM.length - start];
System.arraycopy(EM, start, M, 0, M.length);

/*
 * 4. Output M.
 */
return M;
}

/**
 * Method RSEAP
 * Description: Performs the encryyrption
 *
 * @param publicKey the RSA public key
 * @param m the plaintext integer
 *
 * @return the ciphertext integer
```

```
 *
 * @throws IllegalBlockSizeException
 *
 */
private BigInteger RSAEP(RSAPublicKey publicKey, BigInteger m)
        throws IllegalBlockSizeException
{

  /*
   * RSAEP ((n, e), m)
   * Input: (n, e) RSA public key
   * m message representative, an integer between 0 and n-1
   * Output: c ciphertext representative, an integer between 0 and
   * n-1; or message representative out of range
   * Assumptions: public key (n, e) is valid
   */
  BigInteger e = publicKey.getPublicExponent();
  BigInteger n = publicKey.getModulus();

  /*
   * 1. If the message representative m is not between 0 and n-1,
   * output  message representative out of range  and stop.
   */
  BigInteger nMinusOne = n.subtract(BigInteger.ONE);

  /*
   * m > 0 and m < n-1
   */
  if (m.compareTo(BigInteger.ZERO) < 0)
  {
    throw new IllegalBlockSizeException(
      "Ciphertext too small");
  }

  if (m.compareTo(nMinusOne) > 0)
  {
    throw new IllegalBlockSizeException(
      "Ciphertext too large");
  }

  /*
   * 2. Let c = me mod n.
   */
  BigInteger c = m.modPow(e, n);

  /*
   * 3. Output c.
   */
  return c;
```

```
}

/**
 * Method RSADP
 * Description: Performs the decryption
 *
 * @param K the RSA Private Key
 * @param c an integer representing
 * the cipher
 *
 * @return the plaintext integer
 *
 */
private BigInteger RSADP(RSAPrivateKey K,
                         BigInteger c)
{

  /*
   * RSADP (K, c)
   * Input: K RSA private key, where K has one of the following
   * forms: a pair (n, d)
   *    a quintuple (p, q, dP, dQ, qInv)
   * c ciphertext representative, an integer between 0 and n-1
   * Output: m message representative, an integer between 0 and n-1;
or
   *   ciphertext representative out of range
   * Assumptions: private key K is valid
   * Steps:
   * 1. If the ciphertext representative c is not between 0 and n-1,
   * output  ciphertext representative out of range  and stop.
   */

  /*
   * 2.1 Let m = cd mod n.
   * PKCS #1 V2.0: RSA CRYPTOGRAPHY STANDARD 9
   * Else, if the second form (p, q, dP, dQ, qInv) of K is used:
   */
  if (!(K instanceof RSAPrivateCrtKey))
  {

    BigInteger d = K.getPrivateExponent();
    BigInteger n = K.getModulus();

    BigInteger m = c.modPow(d, n);

    return m;
  }

  /*
```

```
 * 2. If the first form (n, d) of K is used:
 */
RSAPrivateCrtKey privateCrtKey =
  (RSAPrivateCrtKey) K;
BigInteger        p              = privateCrtKey.getPrimeP();
BigInteger        q              = privateCrtKey.getPrimeQ();
BigInteger        dP             =
  privateCrtKey.getPrimeExponentP();
BigInteger        dQ             =
  privateCrtKey.getPrimeExponentQ();
BigInteger        qInv           =
  privateCrtKey.getCrtCoefficient();

/*
 * 2.2 Let m1 = cdP mod p.
 */
BigInteger m1 = c.modPow(dP, p);

/*
 * 2.3 Let m2 = cdQ mod q.
 */
BigInteger m2 = c.modPow(dQ, q);

/*
 * 2.4 Let h = qInv ( m1   m2 ) mod p.
 */
BigInteger h = m1.subtract(m2);

h = h.multiply(qInv);
h = h.mod(p);

/*
 * 2.5 Let m = m2 + h q.
 */
BigInteger m = h.multiply(q);

m = m.add(m2);

/*
 * 3. Output m.
 */
return m;
}
}
```

TIP: Listing 12-1 is based on the PKCS#1 v2.1, the RSA Cryptography Standard (http://www.rsasecurity.com/rsalabs/pkcs/pkcs-1/index.html). The code in Chapter 13 uses this listing; make sure to import it or that they belong to the same package.

Some Security Suggestions

Looking at ciphers and their dependencies on keys gives many ideas regarding the security of an organization. Since keys play a vital role, and changing the keys changes the results of the messages, rotating the keys can keep a hacker guessing. Many attacks on algorithms are considered brute-force attacks. A *brute-force* attack is not analyzing the cryptographic algorithm, such as in a cryptanalysis attack, but trying many permutations of keys until some information is recovered from the plaintext. If a hacker is trying the brute-force attack and the keys have changed in the middle of the attack, the hacker needs to start again. Rotating keys can add to the confusion for an attacker.

> **TIP:** A rule of thumb is simply to keep the attacker guessing. For very sensitive data, the data should periodically change with a new key set. However, rotating keys too much can also be problematic because an attacker could be waiting to intercept the key. Only a key rotated through secure means is worth rotating.

Messages can use session keys that are created during a communication session to ensure that the keys are not stagnant. There are many layers in security that have been mentioned, and it is important to make sure that they are all implemented.

The only way to ensure that the different layers are implemented is to test. One of the organizations that I consulted for would have a down day to test the security. A team of network and system administrators would have all their tools monitoring the network. Then they would run all the servers and application servers while the organization was connected to the Internet. Another team of engineers would spend its time trying to hack in to see if it could be stopped. During these tests, there was always a router that could be turned off to cut off the organization from the Internet, and all software was backed up. Many holes in the network were found during these routine tests.

> **TIP:** Make sure to consider how hackers try to break your organization's security and keep the attackers guessing.

One fruitful suggestion is simply to know the software and hardware. Ensure that people are always getting trained and occasionally bring in consultants to test out the systems and check the installation of equipment. Most attacks that I have witnessed occurred when somebody didn't set up the firewall correctly, or left a back door to a server or machine by not taking the time to delete files or double-checking the setup. Know the security of the applications and application servers.

Note that there are some J2EE servers that will use message digests to save passwords to databases. The passwords are normally six or eight characters long. Spending day in and day out looking at a set of six-character passwords that MD5 produces the same resulting hash for, makes it possible for several passwords to be guessed. The attack is simply based on the fact that using the same six-digit password will always produce the same digest. A pattern emerges, and it produces a pattern attack. Always avoid patterns. Using keys to encrypt the password instead of a digest would eliminate the pattern.

> **TIP:** Avoid patterns, especially in passwords. Patterns can be mitigated with the use of encryption.

Another attack is the chaotic attack. In software, there is the *monkey test*; the monkey test is based on the theory that if you have a certain number of monkeys randomly pushing keys for an amount of time, one of them is bound to type something meaningful, just by accident. While everything works with the Web site or application when I follow procedure, what happens when I randomly push keys? Pushing function keys has led to back doors.

One time, in the chaotic scenario, I was FTPing an expensive application in beta, and I wondered what would happen if I changed the directory to a home directory with one of the developer's names as a subdirectory. Next thing I knew, I saw the source to the application. Test the security — not just how is should work, but how it shouldn't work. Test to see if the login is working securely. What happens if I login as "guest" or don't enter a password?

> **TIP:** The best way to know the degree of your organization's security is to test, test, and test. Not only test how it should work, but also how it should not.

Summary

This chapter provided the basis for understanding the symmetric ciphers. An implementation of an RSA algorithm was given to show some of its characteristics and the differences between asymmetric and symmetric algorithms. Cipher algorithms can be described in both mathematics and its constructs. The mathematics describes the algorithm by assigning operations and variables and executing them in a function so you understand the complexities and issues surrounding an algorithm in a common language.

The constructs, like the substitutions in an S-box, are used to understand the process and how a physical form of the algorithm would be processed. The characteristics of the cipher algorithms can be used to differentiate and classify the different cipher algorithms. The speed of an algorithm might mean that it is not complex. The complexity of the algorithm might mean that there are many dependencies within the algorithm. Understanding these properties and concepts provides an introduction to using the cipher algorithms for solving security problems.

Chapter 13

Extending New Ciphers with the JDK

In This Chapter

♦ Understanding the benefits of a stream cipher

♦ Learning how to implement new ciphers

♦ Investigating how to implement a stream cipher

Introduction

In order to implement a cipher algorithm in the JDK 1.4 and to provide it as a framework to be used by other developers, you use the service provider framework. The service provider framework for ciphers is part of the *Java Cryptography Extension* (JCE), which normally makes up the `javax.crypto` package of the JDK 1.4. The JCE before JDK 1.4 was a separate, distributed package that has recently been integrated into the JDK. The service provider framework and interfaces provide a common framework and a means to hide the implementation of the cipher algorithms themselves.

When you use the Service Provider Interface, a `Provider` class provides a mapping for a specific algorithm to a class that implements the algorithm. By using a mapping as a service provider in this way, an algorithm can be made to point to a different service provider with very little work and very few changes to the system environment. The RSA algorithm and some code from the previous chapter is used. The stream algorithm is also used to demonstrate how a cipher engine can be built to add new cipher algorithms to be extended into the JDK.

Implementing a CipherSpi

The previous chapter showed an RSA algorithm extended using a `javax.crypto.CipherSpi` class. The `CipherSpi` class is used to add ciphers inside the JCE. To be extended, the cipher must be implemented in the methods of the `CipherSpi` class in order for these methods to be accessed by the client. Some of the methods may not be implemented; they simply return a null or throw an exception, such as `engineGetIV` and `engineGetParameters`, which are algorithm-specific.

Some ciphers may not require the *Initialization Vector* (IV) or parameters like *p*, *q*, and *g* to have variables initialize key parameters. The RSA cipher requires two keys: a public key and a private key. The key that is initialized in the cipher will determine whether the RSA is encrypting or decrypting. The RSA algorithm is a special case because many ciphers will use the symmetric key, which is a single key for both encrypting and decrypting. Because the cipher engine may not know if it is in an encrypting or decrypting mode, the mode must be passed in during the initialization of the cipher engine.

Another element that is always required during the initialization of the cipher engine is the key or certificate. An X.509 certificate contains public keys and can be used by some algorithms instead of the `java.security.Key` class. Many cipher keys, like the RSA public key and RSA private key, are extended from the `Key` class. The key is normally extended into a `java.security.KeyPair` for the asymmetric key or `javax.crypto.SecretKey` class for the symmetric key. All ciphers require some kind of key for operation.

> **CROSS-REFERENCE:** See Chapter 4 for information on key generation.

The key generation must always be accomplished before initializing the cipher because a key must be passed in during initialization. The same service provider may write both the key engine and cipher engine to ensure integration. If you follow specifications and algorithms exactly, you can mix and match keys and cipherengines. The cipher engine that I produced in the previous chapter uses the RSA public key and RSA private key that come standard with the JCE, which is now included in the JDK 1.4.

> **HINT:** To execute an addition to the JCE, you must store the `CipherSpi` and `Provider` classes as a JAR file in the `$JRE/lib/ext` directory for access to Java extension. The JAR file must be signed by a trusted certificate stored in the local `KeyStore`. The JAR file must also be in the `CLASSPATH` for execution. These measures help limit tampering to JCE files and changing ciphers. A trusted certificate can be inserted into the `KeyStore`. See Chapter 8 for information on the `KeyStore`.

Listing 13-1, later in the chapter, shows the test example. To get the instance of the key pair generator, the `KeyPairGenerator.getInstance("RSA")` method is called to retrieve the first key algorithm available from a service provider. The service provider that is loaded is of no consequence as long as it loads a valid RSA key pair. There is no RSA cipher that is shipped with the JCE part of the JDK 1.4, so one had to be extended using the cipher SPI layer.

> **CROSS-REFERENCE:** Chapter 4 provides information on key service providers.

After the keys are created using the `javax.crypto.KeyGenerator`, `java.security.KeyPairGenerator`, `java.security.KeyFactory`, or `javax.crypto.SecretKeyFactory` packages, the cipher engine can be initialized.

> **TIP:** Notice that the asymmetric keys use the `java.security` package, and the symmetric key uses the `javax.crypto` package.

The key to initializing the cipher engine is the implementation of the associated `java.security.Provider` class. The associated provider implementation is given in Listing 13-2. The provider is needed to load the cipher engine. When the `Cipher.getInstance("RSA", "RichWare")` method is executed, an instance of the cipher engine needs to be created. If everything is created correctly, calling the method `cipher.init(Cipher.ENCRYPT_MODE, publKey, _random)`, from Listing 13-1, will call the `RichRSACipher` SPI's `engineInit` method. To get to this point, the JCE will have to successfully do the following:

♦ Find the RichWare provider class `RichProvider`

♦ Find the successful association of RSA

♦ Successfully load the associated class `com.richware.RichRSACipher` (dicussed in Listing 12-1) to use as the SPI interface

When the `getInstance` method is called from the Java application, the `javax.crypto.Cipher` class will call JCE methods to search down the SPI chain, find the cipher property for the `RSA` mapping, and load the associated class specified in the `Provider` class as `com.richware.RichRSACipher`.

The JCE internal code is more restrictive than other SPI interfaces. The JCE will check to see if the proper security settings are set for cipher engines. The JCE does this extra work to avoid interceptions and corruptions of cipher algorithms. A good point of attack for any hacker is to monitor the cipher engine for plaintext, or try to modify it to send plaintext to a pickup location. The JCE must ensure that the provider and cipher engine classes are signed in a JAR file by a trusted certificate. Basically, this means that the cipher jar can be trusted.

For simplicity, the JAR file can be copied into the `$JRE/lib/ext` subdirectory. The `$JRE/lib/ext` subdirectory is a subdirectory that is normally used for extending the JDK 1.4. The extending subdirectory is given special permissions from the default `java.policy` file that is normally called by the Java virtual machine. The following code demonstrates how to grant permissions to the `$JRE/lib/ext` subdirectory:

```
grant codeBase "file:${java.home}/lib/ext/*" {
  permission java.security.AllPermission;
};
```

Figure 13-1 demonstrates the mapping of the `CipherSpi` and `Provider` classes. In the example in Listing 13-1, the `RichWare` provider is added to the SPI chain in the second entry by using the `Security.insertProviderAt(new com.richware.RichProvider(), 2)` method. The cipher's `getInstance` method will pass in the entry to be searched in the `RichProvider` class. The entry in the provider class is `Cipher.RSA` to define that it is an RSA implementation of the `CipherSpi`. The `getInstance` method looks up the `RichWare` provider that is initialized as `RichWare` in the `RichProvider` class because it is passed as one of the parameters.

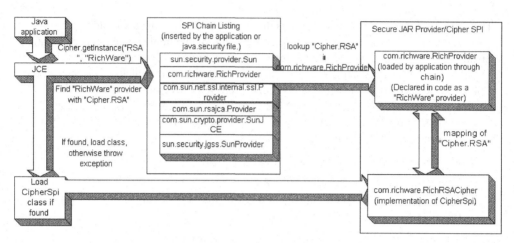

Figure 13-1: The Provider and CipherSpi mapping

The getInstance method may be more defined than just specifying the RSA algorithm lookup for the cipher. There may be multiple RSA algorithms in the CipherSpi, or multiple CipherSpis that define different types of the RSA algorithms. The question becomes how to find the correct algorithm other than by using the algorithm name and provider name. The answer requires a further examination of the CipherSpi interface.

The previous chapter showed that when selecting a cipher algorithm, the operation mode (like ECB), and the padding (such as PKCS1_V1_5), parameters are used to define the algorithm. These parameters can be used when creating the cipher instance. The mapping in the provider can include a specific association of Cipher.RSA/ECB/PKCS1_V1_5 to map to a different CipherSpi implementation class. The getInstance method can include the operation mode, or both the operation mode and padding to map to a specific implementation of the algorithm.

> **TIP:** Because JCE extensions are little more discrete, not passing the getInstance method the provider name may cause problems when extending the ciphers in the JCE.

If the provider does not include the padding and operation mode, but the getInstance method has specified a specific implementation, the loader will set the cipher engine to use the padding and operation mode specified. If the getInstance method specifies the padding and operation mode of the algorithm, the loader will create the cipher engine and then execute the engineSetPadding and engineSetMode methods. The loader will pass the desired padding in the engineSetPadding method. If the cipher engine does not support the padding type, it will throw a NoSuchPaddingException. The loader will pass the desired operation mode in the engineSetMode method. If the cipher engine does not support the operation mode, it will throw a NoSuchAlgorithmException.

> **CROSS-REFERENCE:** See Chapter 12 for the types of operation modes and paddings.

Some algorithms may also require the IV vector implementation, the
`java.security.AlgorithmParameters` implementation, the
`java.security.spec.AlgorithmParameterSpec` implementation, and the
`java.security.SecureRandom` classes. Using these classes is highly dependent on the
algorithm of the cipher. For example, Blowfish uses an IV.

> **TIP:** The SPI layer requires a discrete operation to be implemented from the application. All the methods must be implemented from the `CipherSpi` class even though some of them return nulls. The developer has limited control on the operation of the SPI. For most implementations, it will simply be a matter of providing the `java.security.Provider` interface to add the algorithm into the SPI chain and to put the cipher algorithm in the `CipherSpi` class that the JCE will load.

A service provider also provides the `AlgorithmParameters` class because the algorithm
parameters are closely tied to the ciphers and the keys. Using the `IVParameterSpec`, I could
generate the IV to initialize the Blowfish cipher. IV is similar to a second key that will change
the output of the cipher. Another example of using the algorithm parameter could be a matrix
of points along an ECC curve to avoid computations. For RSA, an algorithm parameter may be
the p, q, and g to use the Chinese Remainder Theorem for faster RSA calculations.

> **CROSS-REFERENCE:** Chapter 5 describes ECC, and Chapter 4 describes the RSA algorithm.

The purpose of the algorithm parameters is to initialize a cipher engine. The
`AlgorithmParameterSpec` class will define how the algorithm parameters are constructed.
The only other class that may apply during initialization is the
`java.security.SecureRandom` class. If the users of the algorithm wish to initialize a
random class with special seeds to ensure more of a pure randomization, they may pass that
class to the cipher algorithm for when the cipher engine generates any randomized numbers.

By using any combination of these classes for initialization of cipher engines, the cipher
engine could start with predefined variables that have been groomed by an organization
without changing the cipher engine. Many cipher engines may not support these algorithms;
the user must check with the service provider to see what parameters it is supporting for the
cipher engine.

> **CROSS-REFERENCE:** The Blowfish cipher is discussed in detail in Chapter 14.

All the work that has been done thus far is to get the initialization of the cipher engine started.
The `opmode` of the initialization, not the creation of the `Cipher` class, will determine whether
the cipher engine is encrypting or decrypting. The `opmode` parameter for the `init` method
tells the cipher engine whether it is encrypting or decrypting.

> **TIP:** The `opmode` in this case is not the operation mode of the algorithm, but the operation mode of the cipher engine.

After the cipher has been fully initialized and knows if it is encrypting or decrypting, a byte
array can be passed in the cipher engine to be encrypted or decrypted. The `opmodes` are

defined as `Cipher.DECRYPT_MODE` and `Cipher.UNWRAP_MODE` for decryption and `Cipher.ENCRYPT_MODE` and `Cipher.WRAP_MODE` for encryption. To perform the operation, either encryption or decryption, with the cipher engine, the `update` and `doFinal` methods are used. The `update` method of the `Cipher` class will call the `engineUpdate` method of the `CipherSpi` implementation. The `doFinal` method of the `Cipher` class will call the `engineDoFinal` method of the `CipherSpi` implementation.

> **TIP:** In Listing 13-1, the `sun.misc.BASE64Encoder` class is used for representing an array of bytes as ASCII characters.

The difference between the two methods is that the `doFinal` method is used when the last piece of the message needs to be operated. The `update` method can be used to partially encrypt or decrypt pieces of the message sequentially. Listing 13-1, as I mentioned earlier in this chapter, provides the `TestRSACiphers` class, which is a test example for `com.richware.RichRSACipher` that provides the SPI interface. The `com.richware.RichRSACipher` class was described in Chapter 12. In addition, the `TestRSACiphers` class uses the `com.richware.RichProvider`, which is included in Listing 13-2.

Listing 13-1: The `TestRSACiphers` class: RSA test for the cipher

```
package com.richware.chap13;

import java.io.*;
import java.math.BigInteger;
import java.security.*;
import java.security.interfaces.*;
import java.security.spec.*;
import javax.crypto.*;
import sun.misc.*;

/**
 * Class TestRSACiphers
 * Description: This is an example to
 * test the RSA cipher.
 *
 * Copyright:     Copyright (c) 2002
 * Company:       HungryMinds
 * @author Rich Helton <rhelton@richware.com>
 * @version 1.0
 * DISCLAIMER: Please refer to the disclaimer at the beginning of this
book.
 */
public final class TestRSACipher
{
  /**
   * Constructor TestRSACipher
   */
```

```
public TestRSACipher() {}

/**
 * Method main
 * Description: This is a Sample JAAS application
 * @param args none
 *
 */
public static void main(String[] args)
{
  try
   {
    String      message = "This is a test, hackers beware.";
    SecureRandom _random = new SecureRandom();

    /*
     * Generate the RSA Keys
     */
    KeyPairGenerator kpg =
      KeyPairGenerator.getInstance("RSA");
    kpg.initialize(1024);
    System.out.println("Generating a key pair...");
    KeyPair keyPair = kpg.generateKeyPair();
    System.out.println("Done generating keys.\n");

    /*
     * Get the public and private keys.
     */
    PublicKey  publKey = keyPair.getPublic();
    PrivateKey privKey = keyPair.getPrivate();

    /*
     * Create a base-64 encoder for displaying binary data.
     */
    BASE64Encoder encoder = new BASE64Encoder();

    /*
     * Register the provider.
     */
    Security
      .insertProviderAt(new RichProvider(), 2);

    /*
     * Create a byte array from the message.
     */
    byte[] messageBytes = message.getBytes("UTF8");

    /*
     * Create the cipher algorithms
```

```
 * cipher is formatted algorithm/mode/padding or algorithm
 */
Cipher cipher  = Cipher.getInstance("RSA", "RichWare");
/*
 * Create an algorithm for decryption
 */

Cipher cipher2 = Cipher.getInstance("RSA/ECB/PKCS1_V1_5",
                                    "RichWare");


/*
 * Encrypt the message with the public key.
 */
cipher.init(Cipher.ENCRYPT_MODE, publKey, _random);

byte[] encryptedMessage =
   cipher.doFinal(messageBytes, 0, messageBytes.length);
System.out.println("Encrypted message:\n"
                   + encoder.encode(encryptedMessage));


/*
 * Decrypt the message with the private key.
 */
cipher2.init(Cipher.DECRYPT_MODE, privKey, _random);
byte[] decryptedMessage      =
   cipher2.doFinal(encryptedMessage, 0,
                   encryptedMessage.length);
String decryptedMessageString =
   new String(decryptedMessage, "UTF8");
System.out.println("\nDecrypted message: "
                   + decryptedMessageString);


/*
 * Check that the decrypted message and the original
 * message are the same.
 */
if (decryptedMessageString.equals(message))
 {
   System.out.println("\nTest succeeded.");
 }
else
 {
   System.out.println("\nTest failed.");
 }
}

/*
 * Catches
 */
```

```
catch (Exception ex)
  {
    ex.printStackTrace();
  }
  }
}
```

Listing 13-1 requires a provider, which is Listing 13-2, `RichProvider`. In order for the client (in this case `TestRSACipher`) to find its provider (`RichProvider`) the following steps need to happen:

1. Get a Code-Signing Certificate:
   - Use `keytool` to generate a DSA keypair
   - Use `keytool` to generate a certificate signing request
   - Send the CSR, contact information, and other required documentation to the JCE Code Signing Certification Authority
   - Use `keytool` to import the certificates received from the CA

2. JAR the `RichProvider` code

3. Sign with a trusted certification `RichProvider`

> **CROSS-REFERENCE:** Chapter 8 explains the the `keytool` utility and the `jarsigner` utility.

4. Install `RichProvider`

   You have two choices:
   - You can install the signed jar file as a bundle extension
   - You can add the signed jar file in your CLASSPATH

5. Register `RichProvider`

   You have two choices to register a provider:
   - Statically: add the provider to your list of approved providers by editing the security properties file
   - Dynamically: this registration is not persistent and can only be done by code

6. Set `RichProvider` Permissions

7. Run `TestRSACiphers` Program

> **TIP:** Steps 1 through 3 create a trusted jar file before you to install the provider. You can find a signed `RichProvider` at www.richware.com.

The list of service providers is found in the `java.security` file that is stored in the `$JRE/lib/security` directory as described in Chapter 7.

The above information is found in the JDK 1.4 documentation and is critical in order for you to be able to run the sample code. Listing 13-2 is the provider implementation for Listing 13-1.

Listing 13-2: The `RichProvider` class: The Provider implementation

```
package com.richware.chap13;

import java.security.*;

/**
 * Class RichProvider
 * Description: This is an example to
 * load a provider for ciphers.
 *
 * Copyright:    Copyright (c) 2002 Wiley Publishing, Inc.
 * @author Rich Helton <rhelton@richware.com>
 * @version 1.0
 * DISCLAIMER: Please refer to the disclaimer at the start of this book.
 */
public final class RichProvider extends java.security.Provider
{
  private static final String NAME    = "RichWare";
  private static final double VERSION = 1.0;
  private static final String INFO    = "RichWare Ciphers";


  /**
   * Constructor RichProvider
   */
  public RichProvider()
  {
    super(NAME, VERSION, INFO);
    /*
     * Need to execute as a PrivilegedAction
     * for security reasons.
     */
    AccessController.doPrivileged(new PrivilegedAction()
    {
      public Object run()
      {
        put("Cipher.RSA", "com.richware.chap12.RichRSACipher");
        put("Cipher.RC4", "com.richware.chap13.RichRC4Cipher");
        put("KeyGenerator.RC4",
"com.richware.chap13.RichRC4KeyGenerator");
        return null;
      }
    });
  }
}
```

Implementing the RC4 Stream Cipher

So far there has been a lot of discussion surrounding the block and asymmetric ciphers. The asymmetric cipher uses a key pair, while the block and stream ciphers use a secret key. The block ciphers encrypt a block and may require padding if the message is smaller than the block. The stream cipher doesn't require the padding because it may encrypt a bit or byte at a time.

One of the more popular stream encryptions is *RC4*, which is discussed in this section. RC4 is a trademark of RSA, but the algorithm was made public on the Internet by an anonymous donor on the Cypherpunks mailing list in 1994. The discussion here is for educational purposes only to demonstrate what makes up a stream cipher. RC4 actually stands for Ron's Code number 4 (or Rivest's Cipher 4, Ron being Ron Rivest, the "R" in RSA).

> **CAUTION:** RC4 is used here for educational purposes only to demonstrate stream ciphers. Any commercial use of the algorithm must be arranged through RSA Data Security, Inc. at www.rsa.com. RC4 was made public on the Internet in 1994, and the algorithm has been distributed freely. This author wishes merely to demonstrate RC4 as a stream cipher for non-commercial purposes and educational purposes of understanding stream ciphers. It is the responsibility of the reader to arrange through RSA any use of RC4 for an organizational or personal use. RC4 is a trademark of RSA.

One of the characteristics of a stream cipher is not only the block size of 1 byte, but that one block will affect the encryption of the next block. A stream cipher is simply when one byte is XORed into the next byte, which is XORed into the next byte, and so on until the entire stream is encrypted. See Figure 13-2 for an example of an XORed byte stream.

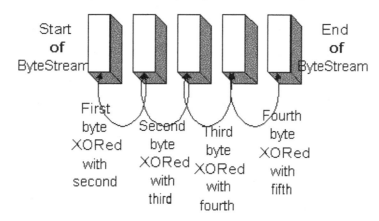

Figure 13-2: An XORed byte stream

> **CROSS-REFERENCE:** It is common for streams to have bytes XORed into the next byte in a stream cipher algorithm. See Chapter 3 for more information on XOR.

The previous discussion has given enough information to understand the basics of implementing a stream cipher as a service provider. The difference is that the block size will be 1 byte, and the padding and cipher operation mode will be null since a stream cipher does not have the same properties as a block cipher. Because the `CipherSpi` has already been discussed in detail, I will only mention some of the differences in this section. The biggest of these differences is the code that was published on the on the Cypherpunks mailing list. The RC4 algorithm is given in Listing 13-3.

> **TIP:** The examples from this book will be available at the companion Web site (`www.wiley.com/extras`).

Listing 13- 3: The RC4 algorithm

```
/**
 * Method rc4
 * Description: performs encryption
 * and decryption
 *
 * @param in the in buffer
 * @param inOffset any in offset
 * @param inLen the length of the in buffer
 * @param out the out buffer
 * @param outOffset any out offset
 *
 */
protected void rc4(byte[] in, int inOffset, int inLen,
               byte[] out, int outOffset)
{

    /*
     * The byte is XORed with the plaintext to produce the ciphertext
     * The byte is XORed with the ciphertext to produce the plaintext
     * The algorithm is symmetric, meaning this function will work for both
     * encryption and decryption
     */
    int xorIndex, temp;

    for (int i = 0; i < inLen; i++)
    {
        x                   = (x + 1) & 0xFF;
        y                   = (sBox[ x] + y) & 0xFF;
        temp                = sBox[ x] ;
        sBox[ x]            = sBox[ y] ;
        sBox[ y]            = temp;
        xorIndex            = (sBox[ x] + sBox[ y] ) & 0xFF;
        out[ outOffset++] = (byte) (in[ inOffset++]
                                 ^ sBox[ xorIndex] );
```

```java
    }
}

/**
 * Method prepare_key
 * Description: initializes the key
 *
 *
 * @param key the key that will set the S-box.
 *
 * @throws InvalidKeyException
 *
 */
protected void prepare_key(Key key) throws InvalidKeyException
{

  /*
   * Fill the S-box with the key
   * Key Setup
   */
  byte[] userkey = key.getEncoded();

  if (userkey == null)
   {
     throw new InvalidKeyException("Null user key");
   }

  int len = userkey.length;

  if (len == 0)
   {
     throw new InvalidKeyException(
       "Invalid user key length");
   }

  /*
   * Reset x and y
   */
  x = y = 0;

  for (int index = 0; index < 256; index++)
   {
     sBox[index] = index;
   }

  int index1 = 0, index2 = 0, temp;

  for (int counter = 0; counter < 256; counter++)
   {
```

```
    index2 =
      ((userkey[ index1] & 0xFF) + sBox[ counter] + index2)
      & 0xFF;

    /*
     * Swap the byte
     */
    temp          = sBox[ counter] ;
    sBox[ counter] = sBox[ index2] ;
    sBox[ index2] = temp;
    index1        = (index1 + 1) % len;
  }
 }
}
```

Listing 13-3 lists the methods for the RC4 stream cipher algorithm. There are two main parts to the algorithm: the `prepare_key` that will set the S-boxes based on the key, and the RC4 method that will perform encryption and decryptions. An S-box is a substitution box, as discussed in Chapter 12. The RC4 does not do anything different for the encryption versus the decryption. The only difference is the input data. The key must remain the same for the encryption and decryption. The key for RC4 is a random byte array. To implement the key to the cipher engine as a service provider, a SPI implementation of the `javax.crypto.KeyGeneratorSpi` will have to be implemented that returns a `javax.crytpo.SecretKey` instance.

The `SecretKey` will be the key that is passed in the initialization of the engine cipher to be used for encryption and decryption. The key size of RC4 is variable. The key size can be from 1 byte to 256 bytes to match the S-boxes. The exporting regulations of the U.S. define that the maximum key size for exporting RC4 should not exceed 40 bits. The `opmode` that is normally passed in to determine whether the cipher engine is encrypting or decrypting wouldn't make a difference in this algorithm, because the only difference for encrypting and decrypting in RC4 is the input data.

When the key is passed into the RC4 engine cipher, it will be used to create the S-box. The S-box is an integer array containing 256 integers. The S-box offers 256 substitutions. These substitutions are permutations of the numbers 0 through 255. The permutations go through two steps. The first is to initialize the S-box 0 through 255, where S-Box[0] = 0, S-Box[1] = 1, and so on. After the S-boxes are initialized, they will be traversed again. A temporary value will be taken from an S-box that will be executed from 0 to 255. The key value is indexed from the length of the key. The S-box indexed from the counter will be swapped with the S-box indexed from the temporary value. The swapping will happen until all the S-boxes are walked through from 0 to 255.

CROSS-REFERENCE: The S-boxes are discussed in Chapter 12.

Like most stream algorithms the encryption and decryption will be XORed through the byte stream. The text is processed one byte at a time. The RC4 method will work for both encrypting and decrypting. The RC4 method will generate to indexes. In Listing 13-3, the variables x and y are used for these indexes. Some algorithms will describe these variables as i and j. The x index is generated by adding to itself and finding the modulus; the y index is done the same way and adds the S-box. The S-boxes that are indexed by x and y are swapped and then an XOR index value is found by adding the values in the S-boxes. The XOR index is used as an index for the S-box that will be XORed with the input byte. If the input byte is plaintext, it will return ciphertext. If the input byte is ciphertext, it will return plaintext.

> **TIP:** See `http://www.ncat.edu/~grogans/main.htm` for further information on RC4.

Summary

This chapter discussed the `CipherSpi` class that is used to provide a cipher as a service provider. The Service Provider Interface gives Java applications the capability to use the cipher algorithm without your having to understand the details of the algorithm. Special security considerations have to be taken into account when working with a cipher service provider. If the algorithm was corrupted or compromised, the plaintext could be intercepted.

Regardless of the type of cipher algorithm, be it an asymmetric cipher or stream cipher, the cipher SPI works the same. The differences are algorithm specific. These specifics include the padding types and cipher modes. The cipher engine is initialized with a key. The key could be a secret key or one of the keys in the key pair. The point is that all initializations require a key. The cipher Service Provider Interface provides a common framework for all ciphers regardless of the algorithm. The algorithm will change in the internal workings on how the bytes and keys are manipulated.

Chapter 14

Applying Ciphers

In This Chapter

- Learning the different ciphers out of the box
- Deciding which ciphers to use out of the box
- Implementing ciphers out of the box
- Exploring different ways to use ciphers
- Understanding smart cards

Introduction

Chapter 4 gave an introduction to the DES and Triple-DES algorithms. Simply put, the *Data Encryption Standard* (DES) is the cipher algorithm referenced for most modern-day algorithms. The DES algorithm has been broken, so Triple-DES was invented. Triple-DES does not change the cipher algorithm itself, except that it uses a combination of three keys to encrypt-decrypt-encrypt (EDE) the data. DES and Triple-DES are not the only ciphers supported by the JDK 1.4; this chapter introduces a few more.

Understanding PBE

One of the algorithms supported by the JDK 1.4 actually works on top of DES and Triple-DES. The algorithm known as *Password Based Encryption* (PBE) is described in the RSA documentation PKCS#5 from RSA.

> **NOTE:** The RSA reference to Password Based Encryption can be found at
> `http://www.rsasecurity.com/rsalabs/pkcs/pkcs-5/index.html.`

PBE works on top of DES and Triple-DES and simply provides the ability to use a password to generate an encryption key. The password used to generate the key could be anything meaningful to a user or even a random value. After the key is generated, the cipher can encrypt or decrypt the message using DES or Triple-DES. The differences in the parameters are `PBEWithMD5AndDES` for DES and `PBEWithMD5AndTripleDES` for Triple-DES.

The PBE is based on creating a key generated from the password. The same password generates the same data in the key. When the key is passed in the cipher, the key needs an iteration count and salt. The iteration count is used for the number of iterations to pass through the message digest. The *salt* is a random number of bytes that will be hashed into the password to randomize the password.

> **NOTE:** Salting the password makes the password more random to avoid patterns in the key.

After the password is salted, the cipher passes the password through a message digest, in this case MD5, and digests the salted password based on the number of times given by the iteration count. After the password is salted and digested the given number of times, the resulting key is used in DES like a normal key. The PBE specification specifies that the PBE algorithm must be done in the CBC mode and PKCS5Padding for the message for 64-bits. See Figure 14-1 for an example of these key combinations.

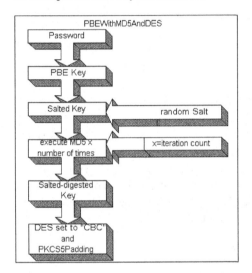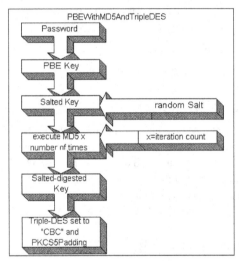

Figure 14-1: The PBE key for DES and Triple-DES

By default, the DES and Triple-DES PBE algorithms set the iteration count to 10. The PBE specification recommends setting the iteration count to 1000. To bypass the defaults of the cipher, the `javax.crypto.spec.PBEParameterSpec` class or the algorithm parameters that were created with the `PBEParameterSpec` class can be passed in. The `PBEParameterSpec` class takes in two parameters, a byte array containing the salt and an integer that represents the iteration count. The password is a character array passed in the `javax.crypto.spec.PBEKeySpec` class to create the key. Whatever is used by the cipher engine as the salt and iteration count, both must match the encryption and decryption. The salt could be considered as an extra subkey, like the *initialization vector* (IV).

> **NOTE:** Recall from Chapter 12 that since the first round of plaintext doesn't have a previous ciphertext block to work with, an initialization vector is used to simulate a block of ciphertext for the first round.

The iteration count controls the number of iterations of the digest. When the same password is salted and then digested x number of times, it produces the same results.

The purpose of the algorithm is to provide a cryptographically secure key that can be generated from a password and to duplicate the same key given the same parameters. If the encryption and decryption are used in different applications, a decision has to be made on how to pass the salt and iteration count to both applications, or to use the default. Listing 14-1 demonstrates a sample application for PBE, the key; using MD5, the digest; and using DES, the cipher.

Listing 14-1: The `TestPBECiphers` class: PBE cipher testing

```
package com.richware.chap14;

import java.io.*;
import java.math.BigInteger;
import java.security.*;
import javax.crypto.interfaces.*;
import javax.crypto.spec.*;
import javax.crypto.*;
import sun.misc.*;


/**
 * Class TestPBECiphers
 * Description: This is an example to
 * test the PBE ciphers.
 *
 * Copyright:    Copyright (c) 2002 Wiley Publishing, Inc.
 * @author Rich Helton <rhelton@richware.com>
 * @version 1.0
 * DISCLAIMER: Please refer to the disclaimer at the beginning of this
book.
 */
public final class TestPBECiphers
{
  /**
   * Constructor TestPBECiphers
   */
  public TestPBECiphers() {}

  /**
   * Method main
   * Description: This is a main test driver.
   *
   *
   * @param args none
   *
   */
  public static void main(String[] args)
```

```
{
  try
  {
    /*
     * Message to encrypt/decrypt
     */
    String message = "This is a test, hackers beware.";

    /*
     * Set the password
     */
    char[] Password = new char[ 8] ;
    Password[ 0] = 'P';
    Password[ 1] = 'a';
    Password[ 2] = 's';
    Password[ 3] = 's';
    Password[ 4] = 'M';
    Password[ 5] = 'e';
    Password[ 6] = '2';
    Password[ 7] = '1';

    /*
     * Create the key from the password
     */
    PBEKeySpec keySpec = new PBEKeySpec(Password);

    /*
     * Form the secret key factory
     * for secretKey generation
     */
    SecretKeyFactory keyfactory =
      SecretKeyFactory.getInstance("PBEWithMD5AndDES");

    /*
     * Generate the secret key
     */
    SecretKey secretkey = keyfactory.generateSecret(keySpec);
    /*
     * Create a base-64 encoder for displaying binary data.
     */
    BASE64Encoder encoder = new BASE64Encoder();

    /*
     * Create a byte array from the message.
     */
    byte[] messageBytes = message.getBytes("UTF8");

    /*
     * Create the cipher algorithms
```

```
 * cipher is formatted algorithm/mode/padding or algorithm
 */
Cipher cipher  = Cipher.getInstance("PBEWithMD5AndDES");
Cipher cipher2 = Cipher.getInstance("PBEWithMD5AndDES");

/*
 * Encrypt the message with the secret key.
 */
cipher.init(Cipher.ENCRYPT_MODE, secretkey);
byte[] encryptedMessage =
  cipher.doFinal(messageBytes, 0, messageBytes.length);
System.out.println("Encrypted message:\n"
                   + encoder.encode(encryptedMessage));

/*
 * retrieve parameters generated by underlying cipher
 * implementation
 */
AlgorithmParameters algParams = cipher.getParameters();
Class               PBEClass =
  Class.forName("javax.crypto.spec.PBEParameterSpec");

/*
 * get the PBEParameterSpec
 * to read the salt and IterationCount
 */
PBEParameterSpec spec =
  (PBEParameterSpec) algParams
    .getParameterSpec(PBEClass);

/*
 * Get the salt and iteration generated by the cipher
 * implementation
 */
System.out.println("Salt:"
                   + encoder.encode(spec.getSalt()));
System.out.println("IterationCount:"
                   + spec.getIterationCount());

/*
 * Decrypt the message with the secret key.
 * PBE Decryption requires algorithm parameters
 * The algorithm parameters include Salt and iteration
 */
cipher2.init(Cipher.DECRYPT_MODE, secretkey, algParams);
byte[] decryptedMessage       =
  cipher2.doFinal(encryptedMessage, 0,
                  encryptedMessage.length);
String decryptedMessageString =
```

```
        new String(decryptedMessage, "UTF8");
      System.out.println("\nDecrypted message: "
                      + decryptedMessageString);


      /*
       * Check that the decrypted message and the original
       * message are the same.
       */
      if (decryptedMessageString.equals(message))
      {
        System.out.println("\nTest succeeded.");
      }
      else
      {
        System.out.println("\nTest failed.");
      }
    }


    /*
     * Catches
     */
    catch (Exception ex)
    {
      ex.printStackTrace();
    }
  }
}
```

Understanding Blowfish

One of the most common symmetric block ciphers that I have seen implemented in Java is *Blowfish*. Blowfish and Twofish (Twofish is the version after Blowfish) were invented by one of the most famous cryptography authors, Bruce Schneier. The JDK 1.4 supports Blowfish, which is a non-patented and free algorithm to use.

> **NOTE:** Ron Rivest has been mentioned constantly throughout this book. Another legend of cryptography is Bruce Schneier, who invented Blowfish and Twofish. Bruce Schneier is the CEO of Counterpane Technologies (see `http://www.counterpane.com`). He is also the author of *Applied Crytography*, which is a good source of his algorithms and more.

A block cipher

Blowfish is a block cipher that takes a variable-length key from 32 bits to 448 bits. Since the key can be varied from a low to a high range, it is ideal for exporting at the low range and using the high range of keys in the United States. Blowfish can be executed in all 4-cipher modes of "ECB," "OFB," "CBC," and "CFB." The algorithm can execute in a pure block mode or a stream mode with the "CFB" and "OFB." The padding scheme that Blowfish can use when some is required is the "PKCS5Padding." When Blowfish is executing in "CFB8" mode and no padding is needed, the algorithm can be used in a no-padding mode executed as "NoPadding."

CROSS-REFERENCE: Blowfish can operate in "ECB," "OFB," "CBC," and "CFB" modes. see Chapter 13 for more on these modes.

Blowfish will execute 16 rounds on every block. The 16 rounds are the exact same operations for every block that is normally in a `for` loop. There are 4 S-boxes that are used of the size 8 x 32, which means 8 bits in and 32 bits out. The S-boxes are used in the function f of the cipher. Another variable that is important to the algorithm is 18 32-bit subkeys that are designated as the variable p, which is an array of 18 integers and is known as a subkey. A *subkey* is a permutation of the original key used to help eliminate patterns in the encryption results. The Blowfish algorithm uses 64-bit blocks as input to generate a 64-bit output, when not using a stream mode.

Generating subkeys and S-boxes

When the Blowfish algorithm initializes, it generates the subkeys and S-boxes. The P-array and S-boxes will be initialized with fractional pieces of π. The subkeys in the P-array are XORed with the byte array containing the key. The key is a byte array generated from a Blowfish `javax.crypto.KeyGenerator` class. The `KeyGenerator` returns a `javax.crypto.SecretKey` class. The `SecretKey` class contains an array of random bytes. The size of the random bytes is based on the size passed in the `KeyGenerator`'s `init` method. The `SecretKey`'s `getEncoded` method returns the key byte array. After the P-array is updated, an initial block of zeros will be encrypted with the current S-boxes and subkeys. The encrypted block will be updated into the S-boxes and subkeys. After the P-array and S-boxes are permutated, the algorithm is ready for encryption or decryption.

Figure 14-2 demonstrates the encryption process, and Figure 14-3 demonstrates the decryption process. The only difference between the two processes is the indexing of the P-array subkeys. Encrypting will be XORed with the subkeys going in a positive sequence, and the decryption will do the reverse.

NOTE: Like most block ciphers, the function f executes the S-boxes and performs an arithmetic function of the results.

Many ciphers break apart the 64-bit block into a left and a right side and XOR the results together. The basic operation is executed 16 times and is mostly a matter of the left block being XORed into the subkey, and the right side having the function executed on it with the S-boxes and then being XORed with itself. The left block and right block are swapped, and the same operation happens a total of 16 times. When the rounds are complete, there are two arrays of the subkeys that haven't been used yet, and they will be XORed into the blocks. The two 32-bit blocks will then be combined to form the 64-bit block, and the encryption or decryption has been accomplished.

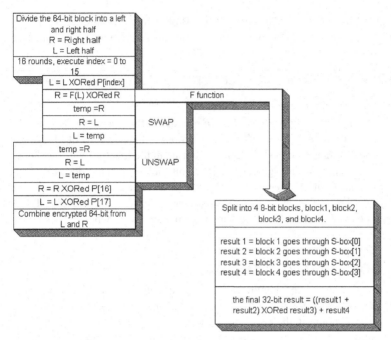

Figure 14-2: Blowfish encryption

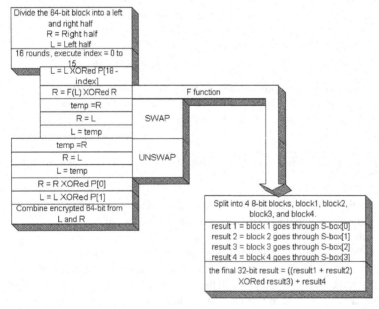

Figure 14-3: Blowfish decryption

Reading a plaintext file

Listing 14-2 demonstrates the Blowfish algorithm reading a plaintext file and encrypting it into a ciphertext file. The JDK 1.4 provides a `javax.crypto.CipherInputStream` and `javax.crypto.CipherOutputStream`. The `CipherInputStream` will combine the `FileInputStream` with the functionality of the `Cipher` class. When reading a file, the input data can be encrypted or decrypted while being read. The stream will be decrypted or encrypted based on the cipher instance that the `CipherInputStream` was initialized with during its creation. The cipher itself does not change; the stream is just given the functionality of the cipher without making extra calls to decrypt or encrypt after reading the file. The `CipherOutputStream` can execute the cipher functionality while writing to a file. The cipher engine is not changed at all; it doesn't become a stream cipher, it merely executes on the file I/O.

Listing 14-2 also comments on the four operational modes that Blowfish supports. The cipher modes of operation are "Blowfish/CFB/NoPadding," "Blowfish/OFB/NoPadding," "Blowfish/ECB/PKCS5Padding," and "Blowfish/CBC/PKCS5Padding." If only "Blowfish" is passed in, the default mode is "Blowfish/ECB/PKCS5Padding." The OFB and CFB use an *initialization vector* (IV) for operation and, when these modes are used, the IV needs to be maintained. If the IV is generated at random, and the key is generated at random, these two variables need to be saved in a secure location to be able to decrypt the file.

Listing 14-2: The `TestBFCipher` class: A Blowfish example

```
package com.richware.chap14;

import java.io.*;
import java.math.BigInteger;
import java.security.*;
import java.security.interfaces.*;
import java.security.spec.*;
import javax.crypto.*;
import sun.misc.*;

/**
 * Class TestBFCipher
 * Description: This is an example to
 * test the Blowfish cipher.
 *
 * Copyright:    Copyright (c) 2002 Wiley Publishing, Inc.
 * @author Rich Helton <rhelton@richware.com>
 * @version 1.0
 * DISCLAIMER: Please refer to the disclaimer at the beginning of this
book.
 */
public final class TestBFCipher
```

```
{
  /**
   * Constructor TestRSACipher
   */
  public TestBFCipher() {}

  /**
   * Method main
   *
   * @param args none
   *
   */
  public static void main(String[] args)
  {
    try
    {
      String localDirectory = System.getProperty("user.dir");
      System.out.println("Changing directory to Chapter 11");
      System.setProperty("user.dir",localDirectory +
"\\com\\richware\\chap11\\");
      localDirectory = System.getProperty("user.dir");
      if((args[0] == null) || (args[1] == null){
        System.out.println("This application requires an input file and
output file");
        System.out.println("as arguments");
      }
      String localInputFile = localDirectory + args[0];
      System.out.println("Openining Chapter 14 plus the input file as an
argument: " + localInputFile);
      String localOutputFile = localDirectory + args[1];
      System.out.println("Openining Chapter 14 plus the output file as
an argument: " + localOutputFile);

      /*
       * Generate a Blowfish Key
       */
      System.out.println("Generating a Blowfish key...This could take
several minutes");

      KeyGenerator keyGenerator =
        KeyGenerator.getInstance("Blowfish");

      /*
       * Set the key Size
       * Blowfish can be from 32 bits to 448 bits
       */
      keyGenerator.init(128);

      Key secretKey = keyGenerator.generateKey();
```

```
    System.out.println("Done generating the key.");

    /*
     * Blowfish modes       .
     * Blowfish/CFB/NoPadding
     * Blowfish/OFB/NoPadding
     * Blowfish/ECB/PKCS5Padding
     * Blowfish/CBC/PKCS5Padding
     */

    // Create a cipher using that key to initialize it
    Cipher cipherOut =
      Cipher.getInstance("Blowfish/CFB/NoPadding");

    cipherOut.init(Cipher.ENCRYPT_MODE, secretKey);

    /*
     * Create a base-64 encoder for displaying binary data.
     */
    BASE64Encoder encoder = new BASE64Encoder();

    /*
     * When the CFB or OFB is used
     * IV needs to passed as well as key
     * Unless it is hardcoded in the algorithm
     */

    /*
     * Get IV
     * if not in CFB or OFB,
     * returns null
     */
    byte iv[] = cipherOut.getIV();
    if (iv != null)
    {
      System.out
        .println("Initialization Vector of the Cipher:\n"
                + encoder.encode(iv)};
    }

    /*
     * Get the Input File Stream
     */
    FileInputStream fin = new FileInputStream(localInputFile);
    /*
     * Start that CipherOutputStream
     * The Stream will encrypt while
     * writing
```

```
     */
      FileOutputStream    fout  =
        new FileOutputStream(localOutputFile);
      CipherOutputStream cout  = new CipherOutputStream(fout,
                                      cipherOut);
      int                input = 0;

      while ((input = fin.read()) != -1)
        {
        cout.write(input);
        }

      fin.close();
      cout.close();
    }

    /*
     * Catches
     */
    catch (Exception ex)
      {
      ex.printStackTrace();
      }
    }
}
```

A test run with the input file as

```
Blowfish Cipher Engines are great.
```

gives an out put that looks like

```
‹ RⱡOÀt=mIÉ‡__'_ìù^T Z e!ùÜY¿c, "1N
```

Some Implementations in Ciphers

The purpose of using ciphers is simply to provide confidentiality of data. The data that needs to be kept private could be stored on a hard disk or be transported through a network. The data is kept private to most people, but can be viewed by some other users (people or systems) that possess the key to decrypt the information. The key needs to always be kept in a secure location, accessed by only a select few. The problem with many systems is their inability to hide the implementations. For example, if a key is kept in a database and an application server accesses the database, the application server must also be secure. If the application server saves the password and user ID in a readable configuration file, such as XML, as some do, now the key's security is based on the security of the configuration file.

Proprietary information and security

There are a multitude of strategies and ways that organizations have tried to hide keys and mask the operations of ciphers. One clever way in the days of floppy disks was to cut a track and look for the cut in the track before granting access to software. Other ideas have been to mask the key or the password to retrieve the key in the offset of a device driver. Some ideas range from the complex to the very complex. Ciphers are simply a means of adding mathematical complexities to data. If everyone understood the complexities in great detail, another strategy would have to be formed. One strategy to avoid hackers has always been to implement software and only let a select few know how it is implemented. The term *proprietary information* has been derived from this notion.

The same tactics need to be well thought out and applied to the security world. *Security* is simply a means of protecting one's information and assets. Another complexity of confusion that is added to cipher, in many cases, is to abstract out the operations of the data. By using Operating System internals to add to the complexity of ciphers, only those that understand these internals can understand where to get the keys and access to the ciphers. Before the Internet was popular, this scheme was quite secure because no one knew how to access it, but as people discovered how to access it, it became less and less secure. The lesson is that to keep something secure, simply don't let anyone know about it.

There has been a lot of work in native libraries, Operating Systems, and device drivers to secure data with ciphers and accessing the data through the devices. This chapter talked a little about a `CipherInputStream`, but stream drivers and stream development with ciphers have been around for a long time; ciphers are used to encrypt data. The critical point always becomes the key storage. The X.509 certificate offers a way to protect keys by using third parties called *Certificate Authorities* (CA) to provide authentication to access the key in the certificate.

> **TIP:** There is also an initiative called OpenCA to provide frameworks for authenticating certificates. See `http://www.openca.org/`.

The idea behind X.509

Public Key Infrastructure (PKI) is the idea behind the X.509, and the concept becomes to organize the entire company, or Internet, around security concepts. The cipher is just one component in the security concepts. Throughout the book I have mentioned several others, but the cipher is used to wrap data specifically for privacy. There are basically two storage mediums where data has the potential to be wrapped: the *file system* and the *network system*. You can consider (for security purposes) any data that can be stored on a hard drive, including databases and applications, as a file system. Any data that is communicated between two or more machines, again for security purposes, can be thought of as a network system. Some ways to secure data through a network are to use JSSE, OpenSSL, or even to provide an SPI layer using native libraries.

Many organizations have issues implementing security techniques because people don't want to take the time to implement them. The organizations can make the security invisible to the user or provide a network interface that is invisible to the user. Figure 14-4 demonstrates a possibility to put a cipher layer in between applications and the network card. Another way to do this is to make sure that all the network applications are using JSSE and to have a JSSE infrastructure set up throughout the organization.

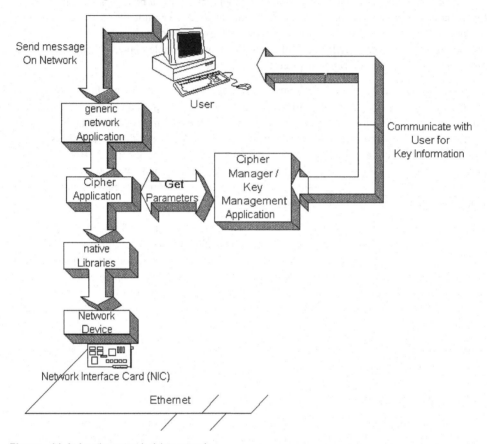

Figure 14-4: A native network cipher example

CROSS-REFERENCE: Chapter 16 describes Kerberos, and Chapter 17 presents the GSS-API.

To provide data security on hard disks, a secure network file system could be used as displayed in Figure 14-5. The example in Figure 14-5 demonstrates a centralized server where sensitive information could be stored and managed. LDAP would be prime candidate for managing data in an organization in this manner. Protocols for authentication such as Kerberos and the Java GSS-API could be used to manage the authentication. The idea that I am trying to express is that the cipher is only as secure as the keys and the infrastructure. Use all of the security components together to complement the ciphers, and the ciphers can be managed to fulfill their roles and keep data private. The application of a cipher in most scenarios is not just a method call, but an infrastructure. One of the components used in Java to help keep the data private is the smart card.

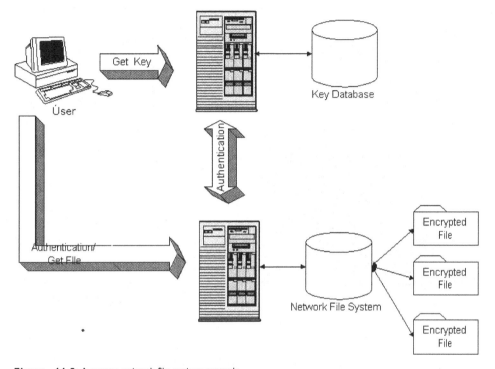

Figure   14-5: A secure network file system example

Java Smart Card Basics

The *Java smart card* is a means to authenticate, store keys, or to even operate cipher algorithms. DES and Triple-DES are normally used in smart cards and can be used to wrap keys. Wrapping is a way to encrypt a key. Applications can use the card to check for keys. In addition, applications can run off of the card. In the Blowfish example, an OFB mode could be used; however, the IV and key would be needed to encrypt and decrypt data. The Java smart card could be used to provide the IV and key to an application on a laptop to encrypt and decrypt all the sensitive data on that laptop. The key benefit is that if the laptop were stolen, the thief would need the smart card to get the sensitive data from the laptop.

Figure 14-6 shows a smart card. The smart card consists of a smart card chip, which is the heart of the card.

NOTE: Java smart cards are a product that can be found at
`http://java.sun.com/products/javacard/index.html`. The discussion follows from
the JavaCard 2.2 specifications.

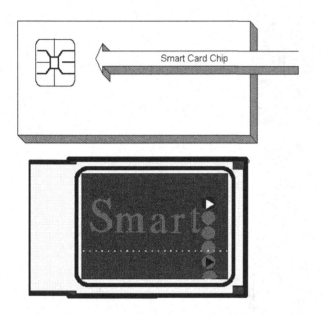

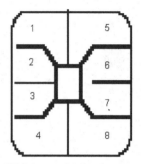

Pin Number	Description
1	VCC (+ 5VDC)
2	RESET
3	CLOCK
4	Not Connected
5	Ground
6	Not Connected
7	Input/Output
8	Not Connected

Figure   14-6: The smart card

TIP: The physical and operational characteristics of the smart card must conform with the ISO 7816.

In order for a card to operate, there are several characteristics that have to be taken into
account. For instance, a card is not going to have a hard disk or full operating system. Instead,
a smart card will have an *Electrically Erasable Programmable Read Only Memory*
(EEPROM) for burning in programs.

A computer in your wallet

To put it simply, a smart card is a miniature computer that can be kept in a wallet. A full
instance of hardware, operating system, or the Java language is not going to be supported. A
subset for basic use that is deemed important is the target for support. It follows that smart
cards are used for securing a larger computer or applications, and the smart card is the key for
doing it. The smart card will have only a little memory to work with, such as 1K of RAM (a
typical smart card doesn't have more than 512 bytes of RAM) so the application must be
optimized for memory. Therefore, the Java smart card will not support the normal JVM, JRE,

or Java API, but will support a subset of each with features for the smart card. This is called the *Java Card Virtual Machine* (JCVM), the *Java Card Runtime Environment* (JCRE), and the *Java Card Application Programming Interface* (JCAPI), respectively. Each one of these packages must take into account the memory and processing limitations of the smart card.

Because the Java language supports the Java smart card, many features of Java must still be implemented, such as the use of classes, encapsulation, and data hiding. The garbage cleanup will also have to be supported. Many larger features of Java that use a large overhead in memory will not be supported. Some of these features are Strings, Threads, Serialization, Cloning, and many more.

Previous chapters have demonstrated what is needed for keys and ciphers, and many of the primitives such as integers, bytes, and many of the calculations are supported. In other words, an EJB cannot be supported in a Java smart card, but an RSA encryption can be supported. The supported JCAPI provides classes such as `javacard.security.RSAPrivateKey`, `javacard.security.RSAPublicKey`, and `javacard.security.ECKey` (Elliptic Curve), and uses the Remote Method Invocation (RMI), `javacardx.rmi.RMIService` class, and services for communications to clients and servers. Any communication done to chip and card itself is done through serial communications on the serial bus. An encapsulation is done to the serial communication to provide the I/O to applications through the *Application Protocol Data Unit* (APDU). The JCRE will pass the APDU to the application to process any I/O request to the card itself from the card reader or writer.

These limitations do not affect the API itself but do affect the development environment. Since the smart card is limited by processing power and memory, the source code is not compiled and debugged on the smart card itself. The Java code is developed on a desktop in a JCVM interpreter. The code can be compiled, debugged, and simulated to some degree. A constraint would be an application that could be simulated on a desktop machine with 512 KB of memory and may work fine; however, it may not work on a card with 1 KB of memory.

When the program is ready to be transported to the smart card, it must be converted into a *Converted Applet* (CAP). The CAP file is equivalent to a Java class file, except it is specific for Java smart cards. The CAP is processed in a *Java Archive* (JAR), just like normal Java class files. After the CAP files are created from the converter, they must be written to the smart card for execution. A smart card device kit is used with a card reader that will also provide the development kit for simulation and debugging on the development desktop. The application that is used to verify the structure of the Java code for smart card support and export the code into a CAP file is called an *Off-Card Verifier*.

The Off-Card Verifier

The Off-Card Verifier will provide the debugging capabilities on the development desktop. The Off-Card Verifier is a special instance of the JCVM to debug and build the CAP of the development desktop. A thinner JCVM will be used by the Java smart card for executing the virtual machine for running the CAP.

The Java smart card development environment

See Figure 14-7 for an example of the Java smart card development environment. The Java card installer will work with the card writer to install the application files, or CAP files. The CAP files are generated from the `capgen` utility from the Java smart card development kit. To dump the CAP file into a readable form for understanding, a `capdump` utility can be used. The Java card installer will be used to write the CAP files into the smart card.

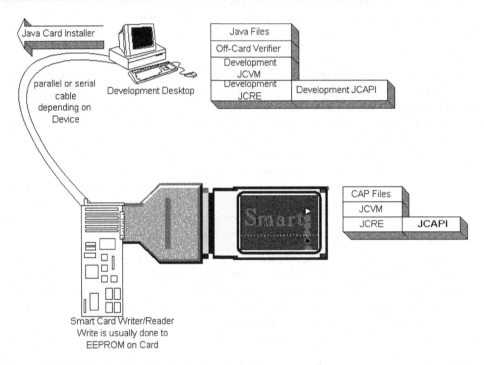

Figure 14-7: The Java smart card development environment

Besides the class files, export files are used to define the scope of which packages to use when generating the CAP files. The export files are used during generation but are not loaded on the Java smart card. The export file lists the methods and fields that are available for applications to use. It works very much like a header file in the C programming language.

The export file is used during the link time of the CAP application. The export file will list the available methods and fields that can be used by public packages. The available methods from the `javacard.framework` package are listed in the `framework.exp` file. The export files are used to specify which methods and fields should be used in generating the CAP and to limit the scope.

Application and Resource Identifiers

The identification of the package in the CAP file is called an *Application Identifier* (AID) and must follow the ISO 7816-5 specification. When the Java files are converted to CAP files, an AID must be used to identify the file. Instead of parsing out names through an environment, a JCRE will use AID-based Naming. The AID uses two fields: a *Resource Identifier* (RI) and a *Proprietary Identifier Extension* (PIX). The RI is a 5-byte identification that is assigned by the ISO organization to identify the company of the package.

A package that is identified as `com.richware` will require an ISO identifier assigned to the richware.com company. The PIX is a 0- to 11-byte field that uniquely identifies the package itself. If the package were named `com.richware.mytest`, the `mytest` package would require a unique identification. The PIX is assigned by the organization that is doing the development.

The JCRE will use the AID to identify the Java application. In order for a Java application to be implemented on the smart card, the application will extend the `javacard.framework.Applet` package. The Java application in a smart card will process the requests from the JCRE. The application will not start the requests.

The Java application that will be loaded in a Java smart card will need to extend the `javacard.framework.Applet` interface and implement the `install`, `select`, `deselect`, and `process` methods. The `install` method will be the first method that the JCRE calls to initialize the Java application.

The `install` method is called to initialize any variables and register the application into the JCRE. The `install` method will create the instance of the application. In order for the application to register itself into the JCRE, it must call one of the `Applet.register` methods. When the `register` method is implemented, the application will be fully associated with the AID.

The applications in the smart card are single threaded. There might be many applications that need processing power at the same time. The JCRE will select which application to use by calling the application's `select` method. When the application is being deselected from the active channel, the JCRE will call the application's `deselect` method. When the application is being deselected, it needs to perform any cleanup work because the application will be removed from the active channel.

Any APDU data will be processed from the JCRE into the application's `process` method. It is up to the application to process the data. The data will be passed to the application to be processed.

See Figure 14-8 for an example of the interface.

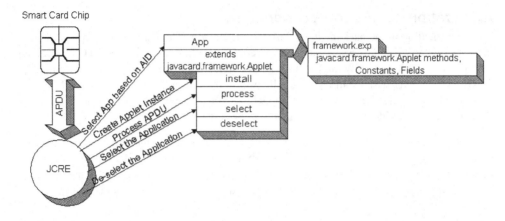

Figure 14-8: The Java smart card interface

Summary

The purpose of this chapter was not to add ciphers, algorithms, or keys to the JDK, but to understand how existing interfaces to ciphers and frameworks can be used. An infrastructure for how ciphers can be used was introduced, along with the smart card, which is a device that uses keys and ciphers to hide keys.

The smart card is a portable device that can be used to protect a larger device. For example, a laptop with the correct application and smart card reader could require the smart card before startup or otherwise it won't start up. By having the smart card reader tied directly in the laptop through a serial port, a new form of physical security is used. The key cannot be sniffed off of the laptop, because the key could be stored on the smart card. The key cannot be sniffed off of the network because the key only travels through the serial cable. If the laptop is stolen, the missing piece needed to start the laptop should be kept in the user's wallet.

Other concepts that were introduced in this chapter were the PBE, which is a method to turn a non-secure password into a secure key by salting it and iteratively digesting it. Blowfish was introduced in this chapter because it is one of the most popular ciphers. PBE and Blowfish come out of the box in the JDK 1.4 and can be used free of charge with very little work.

Part V

Resource Access Using Java

Chapter 15: Securing Enterprise Resources

Chapter 16: Java Authentication and Authorization Through Kerberos

Chapter 17: Securing Messages with the Java GSS-API

Chapter 18: Java Access: The Security Manager

Chapter 19: Java Authentication and Authorization Service

Chapter 15

Securing Enterprise Resources

In This Chapter

- Learning about the Common Criteria effort
- Exploring how to define your security needs
- Investigating some of the technologies available to meet common security objectives

This chapter presents the *Common Criteria* (CC), an effort by the international community to define a standard set of evaluation criteria for IT security, and then it presents a starting point for you to explore and gather your application's security needs. I present a set of questions to guide you on the definition of security objectives, which is the basis for defining your security requirements. Finally, this chapter introduces some of the technologies that are addressed in subsequent chapters and that are designed to address common security requirements and needs.

Common Criteria for Security Systems

The *International Organization for Standardization* (ISO) approved (in 1999) standard criteria to evaluate security within the computing industry in a document known as the *Common Criteria* (CC). A good reference for CC is the www.commoncriteria.org site.

Origins of the Common Criteria

The Common Criteria is the result of the international community's efforts to create criteria to evaluate IT security. In the United States, the *Trusted Computer System Evaluation Criteria* (TCSEC) was developed in the 1980s and was the basis for efforts in Europe and Canada. In addition, in 1990 ISO began to develop standard evaluation criteria of standardized security.

In 1991, the European Commission (after a joint development by France, Germany, the Netherlands, and the United Kingdom) published the *Information Technology Security Evaluation Criteria* (ITSEC) v 1.2. In 1993, a combination of ITSEC and TCSEC was created as the *Canadian Computer Product Evaluation Criteria* (CTCPEC) v 3.0. Shortly after, in the United States, the draft Federal Criteria for Information Technology Security v 1.0 was published as a combination of both North American and European efforts. Finally, in 1999 the ISO adopted a set of common criteria for security evaluation in the CC document that brought all these efforts together.

Common Criteria building blocks

The Common Criteria defines a set of security functional requirements that are grouped into classes. A class is the most general grouping, and all members of the class share security objectives although they may differ in emphasis. CC is also composed of assurance requirements, which in turn are grouped into classes.

The Common Criteria is intended as standard evaluation for security in products. Utilizing these criteria to describe an end-to-end security solution and using them for comparison is difficult because solutions do not use these terms uniformly and combine them in a complex way. However, CC provides a model for security evaluation and an acceptance as a standard security requirement definition. In addition, understanding these criteria may guide you through the selection of security solutions, implementations, and even requirement gathering.

Functional Requirements

The functional requirements are based on the specific requirements to support security, and they define the desired behavior. There are 11 classes of functional requirements that are further divided into families and component criteria. The 11 classes as described in the Common Criteria for Information Technology Security Evaluation documentation are as follows:

- **Communication:** This class is concerned with assuring the identity and non-repudiation of parties in a communication or data exchange.

- **Component access:** This class specifies the requirements for controlling the establishment of a user's session such as session locking and access history.

- **Cryptographic support:** This class provides support for the life-cycle management of cryptographic keys. In addition, it defines requirements for cryptographic key generation, distribution, access, and destruction.

- **Identification and authentication:** This class specifies requirements for functions to establish and verify a user's identity, which is required to ensure that users are associated with the proper security attributes such as roles and groups.

- **Security management:** This class specifies the management of several aspects such as management of data, security attributes (such as Access Control Lists), and security roles.

- **Privacy:** This class describes the requirements used to satisfy the user's privacy needs and still provide the system flexibility for controls over the operation of the system. Users' privacy can span from complete anonymity to different degrees of accountability.

- **Protection of security functions:** This class addresses the functional requirements related to the integrity and management of security functions and integrity of system data. This is very similar to the user data-protection requirements. The main difference is that the protection of security functions is focused on the system data rather than the user's.

♦ **Resource utilization:** This class addresses the support for and the availability of required resources such as processing capability. For instance, fault tolerance and priority of services are addressed by this class.

♦ **Security audit:** This class involves recognizing, recording, storing, and analyzing information related to security-relevant activities.

♦ **Trusted path or channel:** This class addresses requirements for trusted communication paths between users and the system. These requirements include providing assurance that the user is communicating with the correct system. It also addresses requirements for trusted channel between the system and other systems such as third-party applications.

♦ **User data protection:** This class specifies the requirements for security functions and policies to protect user data such as access control policies, stored data integrity, and data authentication.

Assurance Requirements

Assurance requirements specify that each operation (or function) needs to meet a minimum level or metric. For example, logging in to a system may require a high level of security. The security assurance requirements are grouped into eight classes. The eight classes as described in the Common Criteria for Information Technology Security Evaluation documentation are as follows:

♦ **Configuration management:** This class addresses the means for establishing that the functional requirements and specifications are realized in the implementation of the system while controlling changes that occur during development.

♦ **Delivery and operation:** This class addresses the requirements for correct delivery, installation, generation, and start-up of the system.

♦ **Development:** This class defines requirements for the stepwise refinement down to the actual implementation of security functions and provides information to determine whether the functional requirements have been met.

♦ **Guidance documents:** This class addresses the requirements for user and admininstrator guidance documentation.

♦ **Life-cycle support:** This class addresses the discipline and control in the process of refinement of the system during development and maintenance phases. It includes development security and flaw remediation.

♦ **Tests:** This class addresses the need to guarantee and verify that the security functional requirements are met. It includes independent tests and functional tests.

♦ **Vulnerability assessment:** This class addresses the existence of exploitable covert channels, the possibility of misuse or incorrect configuration, and exploitable vulnerabilities (introduced during development and/or operation) of the system.

♦ **Assurance maintenance:** This class addresses requirements that are aimed to assure the system continues to meet the security requirements after the system or its environment changes. These changes include the discovery of new threats, changes in user requirements, and correction of bugs.

Each of these assurance classes contains families, which share objectives. Each family contains a hierarchy of one or more components. However, the degree of assurance may change for a set of functional requirements. For example, the development process and requirement gathering for a solution impact the degree of severity of potential security vulnerabilities.

Also, the assurance level to which the security objectives are satisfied can be measured from the confidence level that the implementation of security functions is correct and that it actually satisfies the security objectives.

Understanding Your Security Needs

There are many different reasons why you need security in your solution. The reasons typically include objective and subjective motivations to the selection or definition of the secure solution. Here are a few motivating questions:

- How do you manage authorization?
- Only those users with the correct credentials can acccess the system resources (data, network, and the like). What levels of user privacy are required?
- How do you manage availability? How do you keep the system resources reachable?
- How do you enforce accountability? You need to identify who did what and when.
- How do you control access consistent with roles, reponsibilities, and policies? Can you deny access based on user identity, clearance level, membership in a role and/or user integrity level?
- How do you protect messages and data integrity during transmission? How are you going to protect data integrity in the overall system? Do all resources have the same importance? Is there a priority of services based on the protection level of resources?
- How do you protect and react to attacks? Is it prudent to have separated security domains? What is to be done when an attack is discovered?
- How do you ensure the correct and reliable function of components and services?
- How do you deploy your solution securely?
- How do you manage recovery? Define what is meant by minimal recovery; define the different types of failures. You need to understand if there is an acceptable loss of data and information.
- What level of auditing is required? What type of logs and data are necessary? What type of audit functions are necessary? What type of response is necessary in the case of a violation? What is the basic threshold for potential violations of the system?
- Is non-repudiation necessary? Do you need non-repudiation of origin and/or receipt? What services are required?
- How do you protect user data and to what extent? Are you allowing revocation of security attributes? Are they going to expire? Are you going to establish a user session? For how long? Are you going to limit the number of concurrent user sessions?

Once you have addressed these questions (and all the others that are specific to your needs), you are ready to understand your security risks, specify your security objectives, and finally, state your security requirements. After your security requirements are clearly specified, you can start the selection of the technologies that best address your needs. This process is summarized in Figure 15-1.

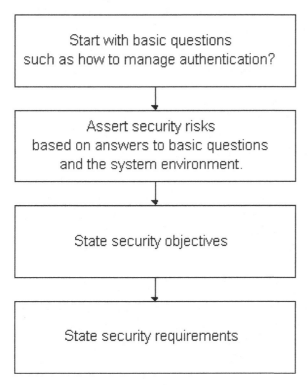

Figure   15-1: Understanding your security needs

Asserting your security risks

Once you understand how your system is required to address the security needs of the solution, you are ready to assert the possible security risks by analyzing your security requirements (derived from answering your basic questions) and the security environment in which the solution will exist.

You need to define the risks to your solution and define the measures necessary to manage these risks to an acceptable level. To aid you in this definition you can analyze the possible threats and determine which ones apply to your solution. For instance, do you need to protect against loss of confidentiality? How about protecting against loss of integrity — damage through unauthorized access?

Once you define the risks to your solution, you may want to understand the likelihood that the attack may be successful and the consequence the attack will have on your system. After this assertion, you are ready to clearly state the security objectives of your application.

Stating your security objectives

Your organization probably has security policies and assumptions — if it does not, it should! You must be consistent with these policies when stating your solution's security objectives. The security objectives address the security concerns and requirements of the overall system.

The security objectives are generated based on the following:

♦ **Experience.** Have you seen a need or risk before?

♦ **Engineering judgment.** Does it make sense?

♦ **Security policies.** Is it required, for example, to have three levels of logins?

♦ **Risks acceptance decisions.** Is it acceptable to have certain data compromised?

♦ **Economics.** Is it affordable?

The objectives can be satisfied by the solution itself or by the environment in which the solution will reside. After you have clearly stated the security objectives, they are refined into security requirements. The system meets the security objectives if it correctly and effectively implements all the security requirements.

Fulfilling Your Security Requirements

Once you have clearly defined your security requirements, you need to choose how to satisfy them. For instance, you may select to use a third-party security application, or integrate some of the available technologies and implement custom security functionality.

You may want to consider the following suggestions:

♦ Use firewalls and De-Militarized Zones (DMZs) as appropriate. It is a bad idea to connect your system directly to the Internet and open it to attacks. In addition, be careful with what you download to your system.

> **CROSS-REFERENCE:** Chapter 21 provides a discussion on firewalls and DMZs.

♦ Since security is in constant evolution and security holes are often addressed in new releases, always use the most current versions of third-party applications and network software.

♦ Perform audits frequently and investigate all anomalies.

♦ Keep current on security issues by looking into sites such as CERT (`www.cert.org`) that announce potential and actual security breaches.

♦ Consider your vulnerability to security breaches such as attacks that can

- Alter system resources. This is a serious attack that compromises data, and probably affects your level of service. The good news is that this type of attack is — in practice — difficult to achieve in most Java environments.

- Compromise a user's privacy. This is another serious attack that annoys users and has the potential to modify messages and e-mail. Using a combination of technologies gives you strong protection against this type of attack.

- Cause denial of service. This is a moderate attack and one of the most common. A denial of service attack can be accomplished by exhausting system resources such as consuming CPU cycles and allocating all available memory. Java does not provide a way to defend against this type of attack. Recovery may be as simple as rebooting the system — although you may lose some customers in the process.

> **CROSS-REFERENCE:** Chapter 2 provides a discussion on different attacks and security vulnerabilities.

The following sections describe some of the available Java technologies that you may consider.

Considering communication and trusted path or channel

As part of the CC, communication is the functional requirement that guarantees the identity of the parties during data exchange. This is a concept called *non-repudiation*. The most popular technologies are digital signatures and message digests. The trusted path or channel functional requirements address the need for trusted communication between the system and its users (including third-party applications).

> **CROSS-REFERENCE:** Chapter 9 discusses message digests, and Chapter 11 describes digital signatures.

Message digests are used to verify that the contents of a message have not been altered. Message digests, however, do not verify the message came from the supposed sender. Since algorithms for the digests are public, anyone can create a message, generate the digest, and then say it came from anyone in the world. In order to authenticate a message and its sender, you need to use digital signatures.

Digital signatures are a way to label messages or objects so that the creator of that message or object can be positively identified to the recipient or user. They also verify that the contents have not been altered.

> **TIP:** If you would like a third party for public key cryptography, products such as JSAFE, J/Crypto, and Cryptix are available. JSAFE offers support for RSA, DES, Triple-DES, RC2, RC4, and RC5. You can find JSAFE information at the `www.rsasecurity.com/products/bsafe/index.html` site. J/Crypto information can be found at `www.baltimore.com/products/jcrypto/index.html`. J/Crypto includes X.509 certificates, RC4, Triple-DES, hashes, and key exchange algorithms. Cryptix information can be found at `www.cryptix.org` and also provides RSA public key cryptography, among others.

The *Java Secure Socket Extension* (JSSE) is now integrated with the J2SDK v 1.4. It enables secure Internet communications by providing a framework and an implementation for a Java version of the *Secure Sockets Layer* (SSL) and *Transport Layer Security* (TLS) protocols. Some of the functionality included in JSSE is for data encryption, message integrity, and server and client authentication. You can use JSSE to secure data transmission between client and server using any application protocol, such as HTTP or Telnet.

> **CROSS-REFERENCE:** Chapter 23 discusses the JSSE framework.

Considering component access

Component access is the functional requirement that controls a user's session, session locking, and access history. Some of the Java technologies that control component access include the class loader, the sandbox architecture, Java protected domains, the byte code verifier, and the different containers (such as the EJB container and the Web container).

When you design a component, you must think about the access rights necessary to access the component. You can specify security roles based on these access rights, and use these roles during deployment Once the component is deployed, the administrator of the J2EE server maps the roles to the users or groups of the default realm — this can be accomplished by using the `deploytool`.

> **NOTE:** J2EE has roles and groups that represent a logical grouping of users. A J2EE role is a category of users specific to an application and a group is a category of users for the entire J2EE server.

Java-protected domains allow multiple and unique permissions for applications by enabling the use of permissions or preconfigured settings.

Considering cryptographic support

The cryptographic support requirements address the life-cycle management of cryptographic keys and their access, distribution, and destruction. The Java 2 SDK v 1.4 provides cryptographic services in the `java.security` and `java.net` packages.

The *Java Cryptography Architecture* (JCA) is a framework for cryptographic capabilities in Java programs. These capabilities include support for RSA, digital signatures, and message digests. JCA allows these security components to have implementation independence and, if possible, algorithm independence. Other security components in the Java 2 platform include the *Java Cryptography Extension* (JCE) that provides key generation and cipher support, and the JSSE API discussed earlier.

> **NOTE:** The JCE also provides support for encrypted streams; therefore, there are JCE export restrictions.

Considering identification and authentication

The identification and authentication functional requirements address the need to establish and verify the identity of a user. Java Authentication and Authorization (JAAS), Java GSS-API, and Kerberos are some of the Java technologies that address this functional requirement.

> **TIP:** As discussed in previous chapters, there are a several technologies that address the need for identification and authentication, such as digital signatures and certificates for authentication. Also, the security manager and Java-protected domains are used for authorization.

Kerberos v 5 is used for authentication and secure communication of client and server applications, and it is the basis for many authentication systems. The purpose of the Kerberos system is to authenticate one principal to another.

> **CROSS-REFERENCE:** Chapter 16 discusses Kerberos.

The Java Authentication and Authorization Service (JAAS) is a set of packages that implements the standard Pluggable Authentication Module (PAM) framework and services to authenticate users (determine who is executing the code) and to authorize (enforce access controls to) users. JAAS is now integrated into the Java 2 SDK v 1.4.

> **CROSS-REFERENCE:** Chapter 19 discusses JAAS.

The Java GSS-API is used to secure the exchange of messages between applications. It contains the Java bindings for the Generic Security Services Application Program Interface (GSS-API), which defines a uniform API to security services including Kerberos. The GSS-API is defined in RFC 2853 (found at the `www.ietf.org/rfc/rfc2853.txt` site).

> **CROSS-REFERENCE:** Chapter 17 discusses the Java GSS-API.

Considering security audits

This functional requirement addresses the need to recognize, store, and analyze information about security activities in the system. Auditing is important because it provides a history of events that help identify what happens during an attack or security breach. The revelation of security breaches are usually discovered through audit trails, which flag unauthorized access, indicate variations from normal operations, and help detect violations to the security guidelines and policies.

> **TIP:** Because audit information is very important to your system, protect audit records at the highest level. Auditing has limited support in Java provided by the `SecurityManager`. There are plans to define a set of standard auditing functionalities for the future.

The security manager component is part of the core Java security architecture. It is responsible for determining whether certain requests to access particular valued resources are to be allowed.

> **CROSS-REFERENCE:** Chapter 18 provides a discussion on the security manager.

You can extend the `SecurityManager` by using the `policytool` program and setting additional functionality. If you wish to monitor security access, you can set the `java.security.debug` system property.

> **NOTE:** There are several concepts related to auditing that you should consider in your system, such as:
>
> Monitoring, for intrusions and violations.
>
> Security auditing, such as internal and external auditors that look for backup controls, contingency plans, and standards.
>
> Audit trails, which keep records of transactions, events, and logs.

Considering user privacy and user data protection

The functional requirement for privacy addresses the need to satisfy the user's privacy needs and is usually satisfied via encryption. Sun's *Simple Key Management Internet Protocol* (SKIP) allows parties in a communication to agree on an encryption scheme to ensure privacy.

> **CROSS-REFERENCE:** Chapter 6 discusses SKIP.

The functional requirement for user data protection specifies the requirements for security functions and policies to protect user data such as access control policies, stored data integrity, and data authentication. The `java.security.acl` package defines support for access control lists. These can be used to restrict access to resources in any manner desired. The package consists of interfaces (and exceptions). The actual implementations, within Sun's JDK, are provided in the `sun.security.acl` package.

Summary

Security is not static. You need to have specific and clear security goals and requirements, understand the different technologies available, and use the most adequate for your needs. The Common Criteria effort was developed by the international community to evaluate security IT solutions and can be used as a roadmap to understand and derive your security objectives as well as to evaluate third-party security solutions.

In addition, the Java Security Model gives a flexible security model that can be used to satisfy your security requirements. You can use Java technologies to create secure and trustworthy applications. These technologies include the Java Cryptography Architecture (JCA), Java Cryptography Extension (JCE), Java Secure Socket Extension (JSSE), Java Authentication and Authorization (JAAS), and the Java GSS-API. These technologies are described in the next few chapters.

However, there is still an ongoing process, and new refinements and capabilities are to be expected in the future.

Chapter 16

Java Authentication and Authorization Through Kerberos

In This Chapter

♦ Understanding the role that Kerberos plays in authentication and authorization

♦ Learning about the differences and similarities between Kerberos versions 4 and 5

♦ Working with Kerberos using Java

♦ Understanding the role of configuration files

The Kerberos Authentication System has been around for more than 20 years and is the basis for many authentication systems. In order to understand security in general and JAAS security in particular, you must understand its underlying layers, of which Kerberos is one. The goal of this chapter is to present to you the major elements behind Kerberos and give you an understanding of its services and how they affect security including Java.

Introduction to Kerberos

In 1983, the Massachusetts Institute of Technology (MIT), Digital Equipment Corporation (DEC), and IBM teamed up to create project Athena. The purpose of the project was to prevent unwanted users from accessing the services on workstations and to give the services to the trusted users. Two of the projects that came out of this cooperation were the Kerberos Authentication System and the X Windows System. The name *Kerberos* is taken from the Greek mythological three-headed dog that guards Hades. Just as the dog guards Hades, the Kerberos System guards the organization's services against attackers. The three heads of the dog represent authentication, authorization, and accounting. The requirements of Kerberos were that it must be:

♦ **Secure:** To block a network eavesdropper from impersonating a user.

♦ **Reliable:** To make Kerberos always available, so that the target service is always available.

♦ **Transparent:** To provide a method so that the user will not be aware of the Kerberos System except for entering a password.

♦ **Scalable:** To be able to support a large number of users and target services.

In 1987, version 4 (v4) was released to be freely distributable across the world. Some of the encryptions are too strong to be distributed outside of the United States, so a version is also available without the encryptions, which is known as the Bones, for bare bones, of the distribution. Version 5 (v5) was released to make up for the deficiencies in v4.

> **TIP:** The distribution of Kerberos can be found at `ftp://athena-dist.mit.edu/pub/kerberos/`.

The Kerberos System uses a principal store. The *principal* can represent a user, a computer service, a computer resource, or a group. The purpose of the Kerberos System is to authenticate one principal to another, such as a user to a computer service like a *Network File System* (NFS). The principals authenticate each other through the use of a *Key Distribution Center* (KDC). The KDC is composed of two other servers called the *Authentication Server* (AS) and the *Ticketing Granting Server* (TGS). The AS is used for authentication and the TGS is used for supplying tickets after authentication. This chapter discusses v4 in detail since it is still widely used and also discusses the differences between v4 and v5.

Principal Names and Key Distribution Center

The KDC uses a *Principal Database* (PD) to store the principal's information. The principal is identified by the principal name. The principal name consists of three parts to identify the principal: primary name, instance, and realm. The *primary name* is the client's name or service trying to access the server, such as rich or rcmd; the rcmd is a remote command. The *instance* is the current instance of the server specified in the *Fully Qualified Name* (FQN) form, or a special group that the user belongs to, such as `root`. For instance, in the FQN of `security.richware.com`, the server is `security`. The *realm* is the domain of the local Kerberos instance such as `richware.com`.

The *Key Distribution Center* (KDC) is used to authenticate an identity. Once the identity is authenticated, it becomes a *principal*. In most cases Kerberos is used to authenticate the client to a server, or for mutual authentication. *Mutual authentication* is used to authenticate the client to the server and the server to the client. The authentication can be used on an open network, without depending on the operating system, relying on hardware devices, or using physical security involved in using special routers.

> **CROSS-REFERENCE:** Chapter 1 introduced the concept of authentication as one of the pillars of security.

Differences between Kerberos v4 and v5

There were many weaknesses in v4 of Kerberos. To make up for these issues, MIT started working on v5 in 1989. In 1993, v5 was developed and the specification was documented in RFC 1510. In this section, I describe the functionality of Kerberos and the difference between Kerberos versions 4 and 5, which include:

- Modifications to encryption support
- Modifications to TGS
- Modifications to principal name representation
- Modifications to the requesting process of the TGS ticket
- Modifications in requesting Service ticket
- Modifications to the client/server authentication process
- Modifications to tickets

Modifications on encryption support

One of the biggest issues with v4 was that it only implemented DES for encryption. The v5 uses the *Generic Security Services Application Programming Interface* (GSS-API) to support many encryption algorithms; v5 is a layer on top of GSS-API so that it may take advantage of everything that the GSS-API has to offer.

> **CROSS-REFERENCE:** The GSS-API is discussed in detail in Chapter 17.

In addition, in Kerberos version 5, the ticket is updated to include a start date and end date for when the ticket is active. This is needed for scheduled clients to execute without human interaction at scheduled times.

Modifications to the TGS

Another limitation of v4 was that *everything* was authenticated within the same realm, which meant that the user or client had to be local. In v5, the client can access many realms across the Internet; this is possible because TGS was modified to send and accept tickets to other TGSs. The principal can access a realm, which can communicate to another realm, which in turn can communicate with yet another realm, and so on, until the client's principal gets a ticket from the target service if the realm trusts the realm of the client's target realm.

Modifications to the principal name representation

In v4, you have the primary name, the instance, and the realm name for the representation of a principal name. In v5, the principal name can append multiple names, such as `rich/admin`, so that instance is just a name appended to the first name. This gives the v5 format as multiple names and the realm.

The format of the principal name, in v4, is `name.instance@realm`. For example, if `name = rich`, `instance = admin` and the `realm = richware.com`, then the principal name is `rich.admin@richware.com`. In this example, `rich` is the root user. Another principal name example is `rcmd.security@richware.com`, which is used to run the `rcmd` command in the rcmd server on `richware.com`.

In Kerberos version 5, the principal takes on the form of `name/name/domain` so the above example becomes `rich/admin/richware.com`.

Modifications to the TGS ticket request process

When a user logs into a service that is protected by Kerberos, the user passes his principal's primary name as part of the input. The Kerberos client requests a ticket from the AS for access to a target service on a server. This TGS ticket has been modified to enhance some of the issues from version 4.

Requesting the TGS Ticket in v4

When the Kerberos client requests a ticket from the AS (to access a target service) the request that is being sent to the AS does not contain a password. The user's password is not exposed, but the principal's primary name is sent to the AS. This request also passes the TGS ID to request the ticket from the appropriate TGS and the timestamp of the ticket. This request is called the `KRB_AS_REQ`. The AS then looks up the principal from the PD. The password of the principal is used to encrypt the ticket's response stored in the PD.

When an error happens, the `KRB_ERROR` message is sent to show that there is an error, otherwise the encrypted `KRB_AS_REP` message is sent as a response.

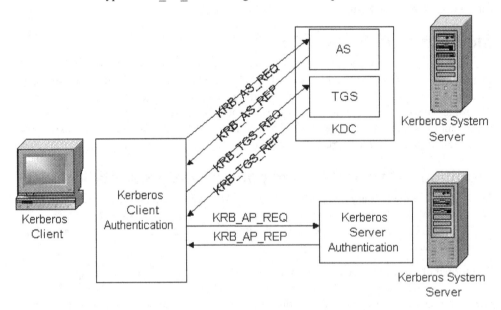

Figure 16-1: Kerberos messaging

The `KRB_AS_REP` message will have a new randomly generated session key for temporary use from the client to the TGS. This message will contain the timestamp of the issue from the

AS, the lifetime of the ticket, and the ticket to be used by the client to the TGS. When the client receives this ticket, the principal is prompted for its password, which is used to decrypt the `KRB_AS_REP` message. If the password doesn't decrypt the message, it is not considered a valid password. The principal's password from the PD is always the valid password. If the event decryption fails, the process may start again to get a valid decryption. After a valid decryption, the client now has an encrypted TGS ticket, a session key, and other information in the `KRB_AS_REP`. Figure 16-1 illustrates this Kerberos messaging.

> **NOTE:** The response includes such information as a reply message or an error message (for example, that the principal is not found in the PD or that there is more than a five-minute difference from the AS).

Requesting the TGS ticket in v5

One of the main differences between v4 and v5 is that v5 supports multiple realms outside the local realm. V5 also uses a start time and an end time for running jobs at a later time without human interaction. v5 passes messages the same way as v4; however, the structure of these messages is somewhat different since messages for v5 include the above-mentioned enhancements.

In v5, just as in v4, a client logs in to the Kerberos client and transmits the principal's name and makes a request to the AS. v5 supports the principal's primary name, but it doesn't use the instance name; instead it treats regular names as instance names. Previously in the principal's primary name, the client might use `rich.admin@richware.com`, where `admin` is an instance name. In v5, the same principal name is `rich/admin/richware.com`, where the `admin` is a name of the group that `rich` belongs in. It is done this way because going across realms may need the support of a list of names.

In v5 `KRB_AS_REQ`, the Kerberos AS request message contains the primary principal's name, the *options*, the client's realm, the *times*, and the *nonce*.

The *options* are flags set to instruct the servers on what options are available in the protocol. The client uses the following flags to instruct the servers: The `RENEWABLE-OK` and `ENC-TKT-IN-SKEY` can set two flags. The `RENEWABLE-OK` option indicates that the client will accept a renewable ticket if a ticket with the requested life cannot otherwise be provided. If a ticket with the requested life cannot be provided, the KDC may issue a renewable ticket with a `renew-till` field equal to the requested end-time. The value of the `renew-till` field may still be adjusted by site-determined limits or limits imposed by the individual principal or server.

The `ENC-TKT-IN-SKEY` option is honored only by the ticket-granting service; it indicates that the to-be-issued ticket for the end server is to be encrypted in the session key from the additional ticket-granting ticket provided with the request.

The *times* section contains the from-time (which is the desired start time of the target service), the till-time (which is end-time of the tickets), and the rtime (which requests the ticket renewal times).

The *nonce* is a randomly generated number passed around the messages used to validate that no other client is trying to impersonate the source client.

The return message from the AS has the INITIAL flag set to state that the message was returned from the AS protocol and not from the TGS. One of the reasons this flag is needed is because in v5, the AS can return the KRB_TGS_REP directly after a valid authentication. The PRE-AUTHENT and HW-AUTHENT flags provide additional information about the initial authentication; these flags are carried forward from the ticket-granting ticket. The PRE-AUTHENT flag indicates that during initial authentication, the client was authenticated by the KDC before the ticket was issued. The HW-AUTHENT indicates that the protocol employed for initial authentication required the use of hardware expected to be possessed solely by the named client. Figure 16-2 shows the v5 flags.

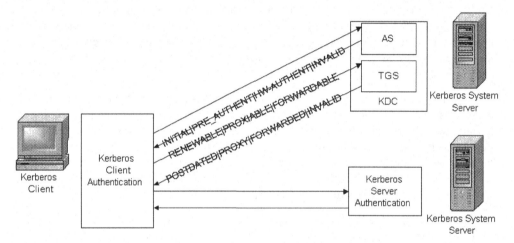

Figure   16-2: The v5 flags

Modifications to the Service ticket request process

After the client receives the TGS ticket from the AS, it must request the Service ticket from the TGS to access the target service. The client initiates this after decrypting the TGS ticket. Kerberos version 5 improves on the way version 4 requests the Service ticket.

Requesting the Service ticket in v4

When the client initiates the Service ticket request, it sends the KRB_TGS_REQ message, which contains the target service ID, the TGS ticket, and the client's authenticator. The client generates the *authenticator* with the client's ID, the client's address, and a new timestamp from the client. The authenticator is encrypted with the session key and is used to verify that the client, not an attacker, received the message. If the authenticator is ever reused, it will be rejected by the TGS. TGS then checks the timestamps to ensure that the session hasn't timed out.

After checking the PD and verifying that the principal has access or permissions to the target server, the TGS replies with the KRB_TGS_REP response message if everything was successful; if there was an error, it responds with KRB_ERROR. The KRB_TGS_REP contains the new ticket for the target service encrypted by the service's password that was in the PD. Also, the KRB_TGS_REP has a new timestamp (generated by the TGS), the service's ID, and a random session key (generated by the TGS for the client and server to use when communicating). The message is encrypted in the previous session key for the client and TGS to communicate.

Requesting the Service ticket in v5

The v5 message operates similarly to the v4 message. Like v4, it includes an authenticator, a ticket, and the name of the requested service. The addition to version 5 includes the requested time and the nonce field mentioned in the previous message. In addition, the authenticator in v4 is very similar in v5; the flags are the difference again. One of the flags, the FORWARDABLE flag, is used by the TGS.

When this flag is set, it tells the ticket-granting server that it is okay to issue a new ticket-granting ticket with a different network address based on the presented ticket. The FORWARDED flag is set by the TGS when the client sets the FORWARDABLE flag initially. When the FORWARDED flag is set, it indicates that the ticket has either been forwarded or was issued based on authentication involving a forwarded ticket-granting ticket.

The PROXIABLE flag is another flag that is only interpreted by the TGS. This flag is similar to the FORWARDABLE flag, except that it tells the ticket-granting server that only non-ticket-granting tickets may be issued with the different network addresses. When the ticket is returned, the PROXY flag is set to state that the ticket is a proxy.

One of the new features in v5 is the capability to set times beforehand for batch jobs. To implement this functionality, the client obtains tickets that will be used at a later time. By using the POSTDATED flag, the client can obtain these tickets at the job submission time and then leave them dormant for further validation at job execution time. The client issues the MAY-POSTDATE flag in the ticket to the TGS to tell the TGS that a postdated ticket may be issued based on this ticket-granting ticket. The TGS responds with the POSTDATED flag to indicate that the ticket has been postdated.

The RENEWABLE flag may also be used to indicate that a ticket may be valid for a long period of time. However, keeping a ticket around longer can expose the credential to be broken for a longer period of time. When the RENEWABLE flag is set, the ticket contains two expiration times. The first is when the current instance of the ticket expires, and the second is the latest permissible time for the expiration. During the time, the ticket must occasionally renew itself to the KDC to stay active. If there are any issues with the ticket, it may set the INVALID flag stating that the ticket is INVALID and must be authenticated with the KDC again before use.

Modifications to the client/server authentication process

After the client receives the ticket to the target service, the client then needs to access the service. The client creates a new authenticator, and the authenticator is encrypted within the new session key for the client and service to use when communicating. Again, Kerberos version 5 improves on the authentication process of Kerberos version 4.

Client/server authentication in v4

The client sends the authenticator and the server's ticket in the form of a KRB_AP_REQ message. The server decrypts the ticket with its password and checks the authenticator to ensure that client matches for a validation.

If the client requires mutual authentication, then one authentication is added to the timestamp and is encrypted with the session key of the client and server communication. If the client decrypts it and sees that an authentication was added to the timestamp, the server is also validated. If the client doesn't require mutual authentication, once the server authenticates the client, it gives the client access to its resources.

Client/server authentication in v5

Some of the features that have evolved over the years to improve the authentication protocol include the choice for authentication key. As mentioned before, v4 was limited to DES; in v5, the client has a choice for the type of authentication key. This field can be defaulted to the standard key. An optional sequence number may be used to keep track of the iteration of the message to avoid replay attacks.

Modifications to tickets

There are ticket changes between the two versions. This was done to address some of the issues that version 4 did not address. However, in both versions the ticket of the TGS is encrypted for security reasons.

Tickets in v4

The ticket of the TGS is encrypted with the TGS's password and contains the session key, the client's ID, the IP address of the client, the TGS's ID, the timestamp from the AS, and principal's lifetime that is specified in the PD.

The TGS ticket contains the following fields:

♦ **Client ID:** This field contains the client's principal name.

♦ **TGS ID:** This field contains the server's realm, which is configured local to the server, and the server's instance name.

♦ **Address:** This field contains the network address of the client starting the request.

♦ **Timestamp:** The field contains the time that the KDC issued the ticket and is based on the KDC clock.

- **Lifetime:** This field contains the life of the ticket. The lifetime is represented in five-minute increments, and it is eight bits long. Therefore, the maximum lifetime can be 255 (8-bits) x 5 minutes = 1,275 minutes or 21.25 hours.
- **TGS Key:** This field contains the TGS's password.

These fields combined make up the ticket as:

$$(\{T_{tgs}\}Key_{tgs}) = \{client, server, address, timestamp, lifetime, Key_{client,server}\}\ Key_{tgs}$$

The Key_{tgs} means that the entire ticket is encrypted with the services' principal secret key. This ticket may be reused any number of times from the client as long as the lifetime is still active.

The Service ticket is the same, except that now a ticket to the target server is also included with a session key encryption from the client to the server. The server ticket also includes identification to the client.

Tickets in v5

The ticket of the TGS is encrypted with the TGS's password and contains the session key, the flags, the IP address of the client, the realm of the client, and the times requested by the user.

The TGS ticket fields contain the following:

- **Flags:** This field contains the flags that instruct the client what is happening, such as `INITIAL`, `PRE-AUTHENT`, `HW-AUTHENT`, and `INVALID`.
- **TGS Key:** This field contains the TGS's password.
- **Client Realm:** This field contains the client's realm. Using realm values gives the capability to use multiple-realm authentications.
- **Client ID:** This field contains the client's principal name.
- **Client Address:** This field contains the network address of the client starting the request.
- **Times:** This field contains a set of times when jobs can start and stop for the use of batch jobs.

These fields combined make up the ticket as:

$$(\{T_{tgs}\}Key_{tgs}) = \{client, server, address, timestamp, lifetime, Key_{client,server}\}\ Key_{tgs}.$$

The Key_{tgs} means that the entire ticket is encrypted with the services' principal secret key. This ticket may be reused any number of times from the client as long as it falls within the times specified.

The Service ticket is almost completely different. It includes a subkey for the encryption scheme, a sequence number to identify the message, the client identification, the timestamp, and the client realm. These fields are needed to change the realms and encryptions. Further security is added by specifying specific times of use and sequence numbers to avoid replay attacks.

The Kerberos Authenticator

The authenticator is used to prove the credential from the client to the server. Unlike the ticket, it can only be used during one session to the server. The authenticator is manufactured by the client instance of Kerberos. This method assures the TGS that the ticket presenter to TGS is the same client that the ticket was issued to from the AS. It has a very limited life to prevent replay attacks from other clients.

The authenticator is represented by:

$$\text{Authenticator}_{\text{client}} = \{\text{client, address, timestamp}\}\ \text{Key}_{\text{client,server}}$$

The client is the client's full principal, the address is the client's network address, and the timestamp is the client's current time of the creation of the authenticator. The client sends this along with the ticket to the target service, and the service compares address -to address and principal-name to principle-name to validate the client's credential. The timestamp contains the client's current time to the millisecond to avoid an impersonation with the same authenticator at a later time, and to prevent the client from sending duplicate authenticators to the target service.

The $\text{Key}_{\text{client,server}}$ is the random session key that the KDC generates and can only be read by the client's secret key. Sometimes mutual authentication is necessary. Mutual authentication is when the client requires mutual authentication to avoid an impersonation of the target service to collect client information. When the client has sent the authenticator and ticket to the target server and requires mutual authentication, the server must respond with its authenticator and ticket pair.

The authenticator of the server is the client's timestamp + 1 millisecond that is encrypted in the key as the client. This proves that the target server was able to decrypt the timestamp from the client. Because there is so much time synchronization between clients and servers, the Kerberos System allows the machines to have a five-minute difference; otherwise it becomes a time-out-of-bound error.

The Kerberos Principal Database

The v4 Principal Database (PD) is local data store used by the KDC that contains principal information in it. All target servers and users must be entered in the PD as principals. The following are the fields that each row includes:

- **Primary name and instance:** This field is the name and instance of the client. The local realm is retrieved during runtime.

- **Cryptographic key:** This field is the secret key shared between the principal and the KDC. In v4, this is a 56-bit DES key seeded from the password. A master key that is only viewed by the administrator is used to encrypt and decrypt them from the database to ensure that they cannot be viewed in cleartext.

- **Key version number:** This field is the version of the current secret key. If a secret key is updated, then the version number is incremented to keep track of changes in the secret key.

- **Expiration date:** This field specifies the last day that the principal can request tickets from the Kerberos System.

- **Last modification date:** This field specifies the last time that these fields have been modified. It is used for auditing purposes if anything is questionable with the record.

- **Principal that last modified this record:** This field specifies the principal that modified the record. It is used to check who has modified the record.

- **Maximum ticket lifetime:** This field specifies the maximum lifetime of the principal's ticket. It is used in five-minute intervals and is usually set for 255, which is 21.25 hours.

The v4 of the Principal Database is normally implemented in DBM, which is a low-end database distributed with most UNIX systems. One of the limitations of using this database is that only 35,000 principals can be allocated. In v5, these fields are extended to include the client realm, the encryption type, and times of use.

> **NOTE:** The database can be further extended to follow an LDAP schema and include permission and principal sets that are used in Java.

Commands

There are several commands outside of the Kerberos API with a human interfacing into the Kerberos System. The following is a list of user or client commands:

- `kinit`: This command is used for logging in to the Kerberos System.

- `kdestory`: This command is used for logging out of the Kerberos System. It destroys the tickets in the user's cache.

- `klist`: This command displays the contents of the user's ticket cache.

- `ksu`: This command can change the current user to a root user, if the current user has root access.

- `kpasswd`: This command is used to change the current user's password.

The `kinit` command is used for logging in to the Kerberos server. An example for user "rich" to log into the host of `security.richware.com` is in Listing 16-1, which includes the password input.

Listing 16-1: The `kinit` command

```
% kinit rich
Welcome to rich's security site
Kerberos Initialization for "rich"
Password: password
```

After logging in to the Kerberos System, if the user desires to log out, he simply destroys the tickets in the cache by calling the `kdestroy` command. The `klist` command is used to display the contents of the user cache. An example of executing the `kpasswd` command is shown in Listing 16-2.

Listing 16-2: The `kpasswd` command

```
% kpasswd
Old password for rich: Old Password
New password for rich: New Password
Verifying, please re-enter New Password for rich: New Password
Password changed.
```

One of the services running as a daemon, or background service, is the `kadmind`. This service is accessible to the remote administrator for administration purposes of the Kerberos System. Some of the administration commands are as follows:

- `kdb_init`: This command creates the PD. It prompts the administrator for the master key that will be used to encrypt and decrypt fields from the PD, and the administrator will need it to access administration functionality.

- `kdb_destroy`: This command destroys the PD.

- `kstash`: This command relays the Kerberos master key to the KDC software.

- `kdb_edit`: This command gives the administrator the ability to add and modify principals to the PD.

- `ext_srvtab`: This command creates a `srvtab` on the target service for Kerberos.

- `ksrvutil`: This command is used to add keys to the `srvtab`.

- `kdb_util`: This command is a utility for administrating the PD. It has several sub-commands for accomplishing this task:

  - `dump`: This command dumps the DBM into an ASCII format.

  - `load`: This command can rebuild the database from an ASCII dump.

  - `slave_dump`: This command dumps the DBM into an ASCII format for use in all KDCs, including non-administration KDC.

  - `new_master_key`: This command encrypts all the principals with the master key.

- `kadmin`: This is the client program for the kadmind server to remotely administrate a specific principal in the database. This command has several subcommands for accomplishing this task:

  - `cap`: This command changes the administration password.

- `get`: This command gets a specific principal's maximum ticket lifetime and expiration date.
- `cpw`: This command changes a principal's password.
- `ank`: This command adds a new principal to the database.

Configuration files

On UNIX systems, the tickets usually are stored in the temporary directory `/tmp/` and the user's ticket directory that is appended with the user's ID `/tmp/tkt${ UID}`. This can be overridden with the `KRBTKFILE` environment variable.

The `/etc/services` file defines the service ports that can be used with Kerberos. The Kerberos v4 uses port 750; other entries for v5, including tools and utilities can be seen in Listing 16-3.

Listing 16-3: Kerberos commands and tools

```
kerberos       88/tcp     krb5 kerberos-sec      #Kerberos
kerberos       88/udp     krb5 kerberos-sec      #Kerberos
kpasswd        464/tcp                       # Kerberos (v5)
kpasswd        464/udp                       # Kerberos (v5)
klogin         543/tcp                       #Kerberos login
kshell         544/tcp    krcmd              #Kerberos remote shell
kerberos-adm   749/tcp                       #Kerberos administration
kerberos-adm   749/udp                       #Kerberos administration
kpop           1109/tcp                      #Kerberos POP
knetd          2053/tcp                      #Kerberos de-multiplexor
```

The `krb.conf` is the Kerberos configuration file and is usually located under `/etc/athena` to represent the athena configuration files. In v5, it is stored as `/etc/krb5/krb5.conf`, and in WinNT, it is stored as `C:\WINNT\krb5.ini`. In this file you find the realm name, the KDC, and administration server (identified in the above file on port 749). This Kerberos server is identified as the administration server by "admin server" in the configuration file. Other Kerberos servers may be identified in this configuration file; however, only one administrator server to be accessed by the `kadmin` command can be specified. An example of the file with the main realm, an administrator server, and a non-administration server are seen in the following:

```
RICHWARE.COM
RICHWARE.COM admin-kerberos.richware.edu admin server
RICHWARE.COM Kerberos.richware.com
```

For every target service that is employing Kerberos, there must be a `srvtab`. The `srvtab` file contains the server keys. This file may also be stored in `/etc/athena/` server. The server keys are used for the target servers to share keys with the KDC. The administrator should ensure that only the root, or administrator, has access rights to these files or else attackers can modify the files for control of the Kerberos System. The server keys can also be viewed in the `klist` command by specifying the `/etc/srvtab` file, as seen in Listing 16-4.

Listing 16-4: The /etc/srvtab file

```
rich# klist -file /etc/srvtab -srvtab
Server key file: /etc/srvtab
Service      Instance      Realm                       Key Version
kpop         rich          RICHWARE.COM                          1
rcmd         rich          RICHWARE.COM                          1
```

Java Kerberos

The Kerberos System is an integral part of the Java Authentication and Authorization Service (JAAS).

> **CROSS-REFERENCE:** Chapter 19 provides a description and introduction to JAAS.

Kerberos can be used in the `LoginModule` of the JAAS. The Kerberos class in Java is specified as `com.sun.security.auth.module.Krb5LoginModule`. When this is set in the `jaas.conf` as the `LoginModule` to use, the Kerberos protocol is used for authentication in the JAAS. As mentioned in earlier chapters, a *subject* is a user or other type of principal before it is authenticated. After it is authenticated, it becomes a *principal*, in this case, a `KerberosPrincipal`. The subject's private credentials will then be set with the `KerberosTicket` that will contain the keys, tokens, and other information that ensure the credentials of the principal.

This authentication is completed when the `commit` function is completed in the `Krb5LoginModule`. If the `storeKey` is set to true in the JAAS configuration file, the `Krb5LoginModule` stores the `KerberosKey` also as a private credential. If the `useFirstPass` is set in the JAAS configuration file, the `LoginModule` retrieves the username and password from the module's shared state using the `javax.security.auth.login.name` and the `java.security.auth.login.password` classes as the username and password keys.

If the authentication fails, there is no attempt for a retry and failure is reported. If the `tryFirstPass` is set to true, it operates like the `useFirstPass` except that if the authentication fails, the `LoginModule` uses the `CallBackHandler` to retrieve a new username and password. If it fails again, then a failure is reported back to the calling application. If the `storePass` is used, the username and password are stored even after authentication; otherwise if the `clearPass` is set, after authentication, the username and password are cleared. These are just some of the ways that the `Krb5LoginModule` class can use the client process for Kerberos.

The `KerberosTicket` class is the client class that sets up the ticket to communicate to the AS and TGS. To understand the fields and methods in this class, see the v5 ticket structure.

The `KerberosPrincipal` class structures the name of the principal name; it takes the form of `rich/admin/richware.com` as described for v5.

In the JAAS framework, just like the specification itself, Kerberos uses the GSS-API. In Java, it uses the Java GSS-API. These are all included in the 1.4 JREs that also support the Sun `LoginModule` of Kerberos. To run the Sun implementation, the `krb5.conf` and KDC must be set up correctly. These settings are used to set up the realm. The realm can also be set in the following properties: `java.security.krb5.realm` and `java.security.krb5.kdc`. If you set one of these properties, you must set them both. The property `java.security.krb5.conf` is used to define the location of the `krb5.conf` to the Java application.

Like all `LoginModules` in JAAS, there is the process of authentication. The Kerberos `LoginModule` is very popular for authentication. In order to log in using a username and password, a principal must be represented as soon as the subject logs in. The `javax.security.auth.Kerberos.KerberosPrincipal` class in Java implements this representation in both Java and Kerberos. The naming of this key is defined in RFC 1964.

When a key is available in the Kerberos `keytab`, the `LoginModule` reads it from Kerberos and uses it as the secret key. The Java class to support this functionality is the `javax.security.auth.Kerberos.KerberosKey` class as part of the private credential set for using a key for the login of the principal. Using this functionality in a non-Java GSS (JGGS) implementation requires the use of the `PrivateCredentialPermission` from Java. Otherwise, when using JGSS, it will require the JAAS `ServicePermission`.

Another class that is used by the JAAS Kerberos `LoginModule` is the `javax.security.auth.Kerberos.KerberosTicket` class that is used to authenticate the principal to the KDC. The `KerberosTicket` is a wrapper around the Kerberos ticket mentioned in the Kerberos protocol and is used in both the requests and replies to and from the KDC. If using the JGSS, it also uses a `ServicePermission` that sets the permissions of the user based on the Kerberos PD from the KDC. Otherwise, the `PrivateCredentialPermission` of JAAS must be used to set the permissions of the principal because if JGSS is not being used to interface into the CSS-API, the KDC cannot set the principal's permission set using JASS.

Summary

The Kerberos System has been around for almost 20 years now, and many systems that have been developed in UNIX have used it for more than a decade for authentication. In Windows 2000, support Dynamic Link Libraries for Kerberos are part of the operating system distribution. It has predated, survived, and has been modeled over many other authentication systems. Examining JAAS services cannot be done without some knowledge of Kerberos. It is an integral part of the common implementation of JAAS, its history, and what JAAS is trying to achieve. JAAS is easy to set up and use. It hides much of the complexity of what is needed to achieve a secure system.

Knowing how the underlying layers of JAAS and any security works is a must for understanding the level of security that an organization needs, as well as the weaknesses and strengths of the system. If a security leader for an organization assumes that he can just set up JAAS and it will protect everything, the assumptions are incorrect. JAAS provides a simple means to work with Kerberos and get it working in a timely manner. However, to fully understand the benefits and weaknesses of Kerberos, an examination of the protocol must take place. Attackers spend countless hours studying the weaknesses of protocols, and we recommend the same for anyone who wants to ensure that his organization is secure.

Chapter 17

Securing Messages with the Java GSS-API

In This Chapter

♦ Understanding the GSS Security components

♦ Learning how to use the GSS initiator

♦ Understanding how to use the GSS acceptor

♦ Working with sending messages securely with GSS

Introduction

The *Generic Security Services Application Programming Interface* (GSS-API) provides a generic security API for generalized security services. The GSS-API uses generalized security services that can be used for authentication, encryption, decryption, and message integrity. The authentication mechanism is generally Kerberos, which uses a secret key exchange.

Other authentication schemes could be done through public key exchange mechanisms such as *Simple Public Key GSS-API Mechanism* (SPKM). Another mechanism that provides both secret key and public key mechanisms is the *Secure European System for Application in Multi-vendor Environment* (SESAME). The service provider hides the detailed implementation of the selected authentication mechanism. The GSSManager class is an engine class used to implement the service provider. Like all service providers, it supports the Provider and Security classes and must have a provider implementation specified in a security file.

> **CROSS-REFERENCE:** See Chapter 7 for information on service providers.

The GSS-API is similar to the JSSE in that it is used to transmit and receive secure messages; however, the GSS-API is not limited to TCP/IP. The GSS-API can encrypt and decrypt any message through a byte array and Java input streams. The JSSE does not use cipher suites that GSS-API supports, like Kerberos. The GSS-API has the only Java class that is shipped with the JDK 1.4 that supports Kerberos directly. Kerberos is one of the pluggable authentication modules supported by JAAS for pluggable authentication. The GSS-API provides the implementation for the Kerberos authentication and message confidentiality.

CROSS-REFERENCE: See Chapter 23 for information on JSSE.

The Java GSS-API is a token-based API that relies on the application to do the communication. This means that the application can use TCP sockets, UDP datagrams, or any other channel that will allow it to transport GSS-API-generated tokens. If the application has varying protocol needs, then Java GSS-API might be more appropriate than JSSE because JSSE is limited to TCP/IP and UDP/IP. The GSS-API can read and write its tokens using input and output streams. Because the messages are selectively encrypted and decrypted per message, using the GSS-API can allow an application to encrypt some messages but not all that would allow both plaintext and ciphertext messages.

Overview of GSS-API

The GSS-API classes and methods are found in the `org.ietf.jgss` package. The GSS-API provides a generic service for encapsulating messages and tokens in a security context. Unlike the JSSE implementation, the socket calls themselves for network communications are kept separate from the GSS-API. For that reason, the GSS-API does not have to be a mechanism established on top of TCP/IP; however, GSS-API passes messages though a stream or byte array as long as the client and server share the same security context.

Because the GSS-API does not have to be a client/server application program, the terms that are used to describe the different peers are initiator and acceptor. The *initiator* is similar to a client in TCP/IP in that it is the process that is initiating the communication. The communication mechanism in the GSS-API is the security context. The *acceptor* is similar to the server in the TCP/IP paradigm, in that it is accepting or rejecting the communication from the initiator.

Implementing the interaction

Implementing the interaction between the initiator and acceptor is a four-stage process. The four stages are:

♦ Credentials acquisition

♦ Context establishment

♦ The per-message service

♦ Context completion

The credentials acquisition is the initiator acquiring the principals and credentials of a user who wants to authenticate or access a resource through a Kerberos service, or any supported authentication of GSS-API.

The credential is dependent on the authentication mechanism that is currently loaded in the GSS-API. The credential entry can contain multiple credential elements, each representing one of the authentication mechanisms. The GSS-API can support multiple authentication mechanisms for use of the JAAS mechanisms that may be executing in front of the GSS-API initiator.

After the initiator establishes the credentials, possibly from JAAS, it must pass the principals and credentials to the acceptor. The mechanism for passing messages could easily be through TCP/IP using Java sockets. The purpose of sending the principal and credentials to the acceptor is so that the acceptor can authenticate the initiator. The initiator may request an authentication from the acceptor to validate the acceptor's identity. When the acceptor must also validate itself to the initiator, it is a mutual authentication. When only the initiator must authenticate itself to the acceptor, it is a one-way authentication.

After the acceptor, and possibly the initiator, accepts the other's principal and credential, they each create a security context. The security context is a pair of GSS-API data structures that contain shared information and individual state information. These data structures are used in order that per-message security services may be provided between the initiator and acceptor. The shared state in the security context may be cryptographic keys and message sequence numbers. For the security context to establish and maintain the shared state, the security context returns a token structure. The token structure is an opaque data type that may contain cryptographically protected data.

Token communication

The initiator and acceptor are responsible for the transferring of the token, or token communication. When one of the communication peers receives the token, the peer application is responsible for passing the token to the correct GSS-API routine that will decode the token, extract the information, and update the security context. There are two types of tokens: context and message. A *context* token is exchanged during context establishment. A *message* token is used over the security context to provide protection for each message. The first token is for establishing the authentication mechanism that will contain the OID name of the authentication mechanism. All other token formats are authentication-mechanism specific.

After the security context is established between the initiator and the acceptor, messages can be encrypted, decrypted, authenticated, and validated through message integrity. The security context may detect messages that were not sent in order using the unwrap and verifyMIC methods. The out-of-sequence protection is added during the security context's wrap and getMIC methods.

The getMIC method calculates the encrypted message's checksum and passes the checksum in the token. The sender must pass the encrypted message and token to the receiver of the message. The receiver can then use the verifyMIC message to ensure that the checksum is correct. The encrypted message is encrypted with the security context's wrap method. The wrap method can also calculate the checksum of the encrypted message and pass the checksum and message in the same token. The application sends the token to the receiver, which decrypts the message and checks the checksum using the unwrap method. If there is a duplication of messages or the messages are out of sequence, then either method may detect it. The MessageProp class is used to detect if there were any inconsistencies with the encrypted messages. Message protection operations can occur in both directions concurrently.

After all the messages are completed between the initiator and the acceptor, the security context is no longer needed. In Java, there is no explicit delete function; however, any communication and connections must be closed when they are no longer needed, and the `dispose` method is used from the security context to release any system resources such as the cryptographic keys. Figure 17-1 provides a GSS-API overview.

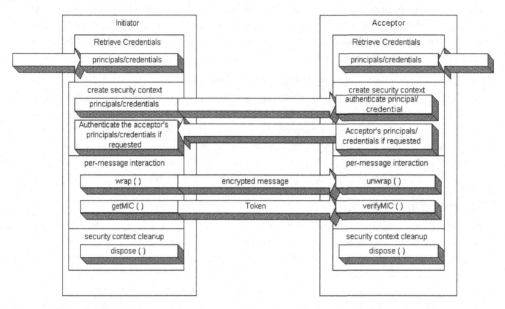

Figure 17-1: GSS-API overview

Benefits of GSS

The GSS-API provides the security services API for initiator and acceptors to act as secure agents through tokens to each other using an underlying authentication mechanism like Kerberos. The GSS-API provides an API for authentication, encryption and decryption of messages, and message integrity. The GSS-API has several authentication protocols and keying mechanisms such as Kerberos, SPKM, SESAME, and SASL that it can implement while hiding the complexity of the authentication mechanisms themselves. The authentication mechanisms are pluggable between the two peers, the initiator and the acceptor.

CROSS-REFERENCE: See Chapter 16 for information on Kerberos.

Another feature of the GSS-API is the capability to delegate the principal's rights and credentials to be applied to another application. Delegation gives the acceptor the capability to act on behalf of the initiator by using the initiator's principals and credentials. The acceptor can impersonate the initiator and any permission needed to access resources. The GSS-API is limited to the functionality provided by the underlying authentication mechanisms because many authentication mechanisms do not provide support for the anonymous authentication.

For those authentication mechanisms that allow it, the GSS-API will be able to use it through its API set. The anonymous authentication gives access to anonymous principals that do not wish to give a name. A reason could be that they want to check out a catalog before registering at a Web site. The security context may check to see if it is an anonymous identity by using the `isAnonymous` method.

Several other benefits are guaranteed by using the GSS-API for a secure message mechanism. The messages that are sent between the peers' security contexts can check the integrity of the message to see if has been tampered with, check to see if the messages were sent out of sequence, ensure that duplicate messages were not resent, and encrypt/decrypt the messages through keys that were exchanged.

The GSS-API is tightly integrated to the underlying security mechanism that the security context is initialized to support. The GSS-API was developed to generalize the supported authentication mechanisms. The token format is dependent on the initialized authentication module, as well as the type of *Quality of Protection* (QOP) that is supported by the authentication module. The QOP offers the strength and level of protection that can be offered to each message for a specific authentication module.

GSS API component model

The GSS-API is made up of several components. The components can be categorized into four components:

♦ Management components
♦ Naming components
♦ The security context
♦ The message components

The management component initializes the other classes through the use of naming an authentication service provider. The naming component names the principals, host name, service name, anonymous, and authentication mechanism name. The security context is responsible for establishing the security state of the application and any shared cryptographic information between peers. The last of the components are for message manipulation that encrypt/decrypt messages and validate the integrity of the messages.

Management components

The GSS-API uses the `org.irtf.jgss.GSSManager` as the management class. The `GSSManager` serves as a factory to create other GSS-API classes such as `GSSName`, `GSSCredential`, and `GSSContext`. The `GSSManager` provides methods for querying the available authentication mechanisms. The `GSSManager` creates a default manager when a `getInstance` method is executed. From the instance of the `GSSManager` object that is created, the security context is created using the `createContext` method. The `createContext` method can set the authentication module by naming the OID of the authentication type or by adding the provider through the manager. The `GSSManager` class is responsible for finding the service provider through the lookup based on the service provider named mechanism.

> **TIP:** When you add a provider through the manager, you can add it at the beginning or the end of the list of authentication modules, to be used if no other authentication module is explicitly named.

A service provider lists its support for a mechanism by defining a mapping from the mechanism to a `Provider` class that implements that mechanism. A provider can support more than one mechanism. For an application to use a provider, the `Provider` class must be defined in the `java.security` file. An application can update and manipulate the ordering of the runtime provider list through the `GSSManager` interface. At runtime, GSS-API searches the list of providers for the first provider that supports the mechanism to be used.

One way to choose a mechanism is to start out with the *Simple And Protected GSS-API Negotiation Mechanism* (SPNEGO). SPNEGO is a pseudo-mechanism that negotiates an actual mechanism between the two peers. Some other ways the two peers can decide on a mechanism can be found at `http://www.ietf.org/rfc/rfc2744.txt`. Listing 17-1 demonstrates the lookup of the service provider. The service provider is looked up by passing the OID in the `createContext` method.

Listing 17-1: The `RichGSSService` class: An example in creating the security context

```
package com.richware.chap17;

import java.security.*;
import java.io.*;
import java.net.*;
import org.ietf.jgss.*;

/**
 * Class RichGSSService
 * Description: A custom demonstration of
 * the acceptor/initiator of the GSS-API.
 *
 * Copyright:    Copyright (c) 2002 Wiley Publishing, Inc.
 * @author Rich Helton <rhelton@richware.com>
 * @version 1.0
 * DISCLAIMER: Please refer to the disclaimer at the beginning of this
book.
 */
public class RichGSSService {
  /*
   * Port number for connection
   */
  public final static int localPort = 6000;

  /*
   * true if acceptor, false if initiator
```

```
 * this will distinguish the two in code
 */
public boolean isAcceptor;

/*
 * the Server name to connect
 */
public final static String hostname = "localhost";

/**
 * Method main
 * Description: The main driver to run the methods.
 *
 *
 * @param args (no arguments presently).
 *
 */
public static void main(String args[]) {
  DataInputStream  inStream     = null;
  DataOutputStream outStream    = null;
  Socket           localsocket  = null;

  try {
    RichGSSService service = new RichGSSService();
    if(args[ 0] != null){
      if(args[ 0].equalsIgnoreCase("Server")){
        service.isAcceptor = true;
        System.out.println("Starting Server");
      }
    }

    /*
     * Establish the socket connection
     * For the server, the application is just collecting the
     * first socket connection
     */
    if (service.isAcceptor) {
      ServerSocket ss = new ServerSocket(service.localPort);
      localsocket = ss.accept();
    } else {
      localsocket = new Socket(service.hostname,
                               service.localPort);
    }
    /*
     * Establish the streams from the socket connection
     */
    inStream =
      new DataInputStream(localsocket.getInputStream());
    outStream =
```

```
         new DataOutputStream(localsocket.getOutputStream());
      System.out.println("Connected to server "
                          + localsocket.getInetAddress());
      /*
       * Create the GSS Manager instance
       */
      GSSManager manager = GSSManager.getInstance();
      /*
       * Create the security context
       */
      System.out.println("Creating Security Context....");
      /*
       * Create the context from the manager
       */
      GSSContext context =
        service.createContext(manager, service.hostname,
                              service.isAcceptor);
      if (context == null) {
        System.out.println("..creation failed");
      }
      /*
       * Loop until a security context is established
       * through tokens
       */
      service.contextLoop(context, service.isAcceptor,
                          inStream, outStream);
   /*
    * If mutual authentication did not take place, then only the
    * client was authenticated to the server. Otherwise, both
    * client and server were authenticated to each other.
    */
  if (context.getMutualAuthState()){
      System.out.println("Mutual authentication took place!");
  }
      /*
       * In this example, the initiator writes the message
       * and the acceptor reads the message
       */
      if(service.isAcceptor){
       String message = service.readMessage(context,inStream);
       System.out.println("Message Read :" + message);
       }else{
       String message = "GSS Rules";
       System.out.println("Writing Message :" + message);
       service.writeMessage(context,message,outStream);
       }
      /*
       * Cleanup
       */
```

```
      context.dispose();
      localsocket.close();
      /*
       * Catches
       */
    } catch (IOException e) {
      e.printStackTrace();
    } catch (Exception e) {
      e.printStackTrace();
    }
  }
}


/**
 * Method createContext
 * Purpose: to start the security context by
 * defining the authentication mechanism
 * principals and credentials.
 *
 *
 * @param manager the GSSManager
 * @param hostname the hostname to connect
 * @param isAcceptor is an acceptor or not
 *
 * @return the security context created
 *
 */
public GSSContext createContext(GSSManager manager,
                                String hostname,
                                boolean isAcceptor) {

  GSSContext context = null;
  try {
    Oid krb5Mechanism          =
      new Oid("1.2.840.113554.1.2.2");
    Oid krb5PrincipalNameType =
      new Oid("1.2.840.113554.1.2.2.1");

    /*
     * Create a GSSName out of the server's name.
     * If a null is passed in the nametype,
     * the underlying mechanism will try to
     * parse it as the default syntax that it chooses.
     * If the krb5PrincipalNameType is passed in,
     * then it will be parsing it in the kerberos
     * name type.
     */
    GSSName serverName = manager.createName(hostname, null);

    /*
```

```
 * Create a security context for the initiator
 */
if (!isAcceptor) {
  /*
   * Identify who the client wishes to be
   */
  GSSName userName =
    manager.createName("rich", GSSName.NT_USER_NAME);


  /*
   * Acquire credentials for the user
   */
  GSSCredential userCreds =
    manager
      .createCredential(userName, GSSCredential
        .DEFAULT_LIFETIME, krb5Mechanism, GSSCredential
        .INITIATE_ONLY);


  /*
   * Create a GSSContext for mutual authentication with
   * the server.
   *      - serverName is the GSSName
   * that represents the server.
   *      - krb5Mechanism is the Oid for
   * the kerberos 5 authentication mechanism.
   *      - the credentials for the user
   *      - DEFAULT_LIFETIME lets the mechanism
   * decide how long the
   *         context can remain valid.
   * Note: If using a ull for the credentials,
   * the GSS-API will use the default
   * credentials. This means that the mechanism
   * will look among the credentials stored
   * in the current Subject to find the
   * right kind of credentials that it needs.
   */
  context =
    manager.createContext(serverName, krb5Mechanism,
                          userCreds,
                          GSSContext.DEFAULT_LIFETIME);


  /*
   * Set the desired optional features on
   * the context. set the mutual authentication,
   * confidentiality and integrity
   */
  context.requestMutualAuth(true);
  context.requestConf(true);
  context.requestInteg(true);
```

```
    /*
     * Create a security context for the acceptor
     */
    } else {

      /*
       * Acquire credentials for the server
       */
      GSSCredential serverCreds =
        manager
          .createCredential(serverName, GSSCredential
            .DEFAULT_LIFETIME, krb5Mechanism, GSSCredential
            .ACCEPT_ONLY);

      /*
       * Instantiate and initialize a security
       * context that will wait for an
       * establishment request token from the client
       */
      context = manager.createContext(serverCreds);
    }
    /*
     * Catches
     */
  } catch (org.ietf.jgss.GSSException e) {
    e.printStackTrace();
  } catch (Exception e) {
    e.printStackTrace();
  }

  return context;
}

/**
 * Method contextLoop
 * Purpose: to loop until the context is
 * established from the tokens
 *
 *
 * @param context the intitialized token
 * @param isAcceptor is the acceptor or not
 * @param inStream the input stream
 * @param outStream the output stream
 *
 */
public void contextLoop(GSSContext context,
                        boolean isAcceptor,
                        DataInputStream inStream,
                        DataOutputStream outStream) {
```

```
byte[] token = null;
try {
  while (!context.isEstablished()) {
  /*
   * Finish a security context for the acceptor
   * Read the token and accept it
   */
    if (isAcceptor) {
      token = new byte[ inStream.readInt()];

      System.out
        .println("Will read input token of size "
                  + token.length
                  + " for processing by acceptSecContext");
      inStream.readFully(token);

      token = context.acceptSecContext(token, 0,
                                       token.length);
  /*
   * Else , finish a security context for the initiator
   * pass a empty token to initialize the context
   */
    } else {
token = new byte[ 0];
      /*
       * token is ignored on the first call
       */
      token = context.initSecContext(token, 0,
                                     token.length);
    }

    /*
     * Send a token to the peer if one was generated by
     * initSecContext
     */
    if (token != null) {
      System.out.println("Will send token of size "
                          + token.length
                          + " from initSecContext.");
      outStream.writeInt(token.length);
      outStream.write(token);
      outStream.flush();
    }

    /*
     * The initiator has an extra read of the token
     * from the acceptor
     *
     */
```

```
      if ((((!context.isEstablished()) && (!isAcceptor)))) {
        token = new byte[ inStream.readInt()];

        System.out
           .println("Will read input token of size "
                    + token.length
                    + " for processing by initSecContext");
        inStream.readFully(token);
      }
    }

    System.out.println("Context Established! ");
    System.out.println("Client is " + context.getSrcName());
    System.out.println("Server is " + context.getTargName());
    /*
     * Catches
     */
  } catch (org.ietf.jgss.GSSException e) {
    e.printStackTrace();
  } catch (IOException e) {
    e.printStackTrace();
  } catch (Exception e) {
    e.printStackTrace();
  }
}


/**
 * Method readMessage
 * Purpose: reads a input stream from the socket
 *
 * @param context the current security context
 * @param inStream the input stream
 *
 * @return the string read from the input
 *
 */
public String readMessage(GSSContext context,
                          DataInputStream inStream) {
  String str = null;
  try {
    /*
     * Create a MessageProp which unwrap will use to
     * return information such as the
     * Quality-of-Protection that was applied to
     * the wrapped token, whether or not it was
     * encrypted, etc. Since the initial
     * MessageProp values are ignored,
     * just set them to the defaults of 0 and false.
     */
```

```
      MessageProp prop = new MessageProp(0, false);

      /*
       * Read the token. This uses the same token byte array
       * as that used during context establishment.
       */
      byte[] token = new byte[ inStream.readInt()];

      System.out.println("Will read token of size "
                          + token.length);
      inStream.readFully(token);
      byte[] bytes = context.unwrap(token, 0, token.length,
                                    prop);
      str = new String(bytes);
      System.out.println("Received data \"" + str
                         + "\" of length " + str.length());
      System.out.println("Confidentiality applied: "
                         + prop.getPrivacy());

      /*
       * Catches
       */
    } catch (org.ietf.jgss.GSSException e) {
      e.printStackTrace();
    } catch (IOException e) {
      e.printStackTrace();
    } catch (Exception e) {
      e.printStackTrace();
    }

    return str;
  }

  /**
   * Method writeMessage
   * Purpose: writes the output stream to the socket
   *
   * @param context the current context
   * @param message the message to write to the output
   * @param outStream the output stream
   *
   */
  public void writeMessage(GSSContext context, String message,
                           DataOutputStream outStream) {
    try {
      byte[] messageBytes = message.getBytes();

      /*
       * The first MessageProp argument is 0 to request
```

```
        * the default Quality-of-Protection.
        * The second argument is true to request
        * privacy (encryption of the message).
        */
      MessageProp prop = new MessageProp(0, true);

      /*
        * Encrypt the data and send it across.
        * Integrity protection is always applied,
        * irrespective of confidentiality (i.e., encryption).
        * You can use the same token (byte array) as that
        * used when establishing the context.
        */
      byte[] token = context.wrap(messageBytes, 0,
                            messageBytes.length, prop);
      System.out.println("Will send wrap token of size "
                      + token.length);
      outStream.writeInt(token.length);
      outStream.write(token);
      outStream.flush();

      /*
        * Catches
        */
    } catch (org.ietf.jgss.GSSException e) {
      e.printStackTrace();
    } catch (IOException e) {
      e.printStackTrace();
    } catch (Exception e) {
      e.printStackTrace();
    }

  }
}
```

Naming components

The GSS-API can be used in conjunction with JAAS. JAAS uses the concept of a subject, using a named subject in the form of the principal and associated credentials to prove the identity.

CROSS-REFERENCE: See Chapter 19 for information on JAAS.

For the GSS-API, there are two classes that make the principal and credentials: the
`org.ietf.jgss.GSSName` interface to handle principal entities and the
`org.ietf.jgss.GSSCredential` interface to encapsulate the credentials for the entity. The
`GSSName` contains many representations of the principal and underlying mechanisms that need to
be named. Some of the names can consist of the host name, the user name, an anonymous name,
and machine name.

The mechanism name is specified by a matching OID that defines the mechanism. Listing 17-1 demonstrates the Kerberos 5 OID `1.2.840.113554.1.2.2` that is defined in the Kerberos RFC 1964 (`http://www.ietf.org/rfc/rfc1964.txt`). The mechanism name can be used in the `GSSName` interface to define the name of the authentication mechanism. The different types of `GSSNames`, such as the anonymous name type, are predefined in the `GSSName` interface as an OID to be passed in the `createName` method. The anonymous name type is an OID defined as the `NT_ANONYMOUS` name type in the `GSSName`. The purpose of the `GSSName` is to define a name construct to be passed to other GSS-API methods.

> **CROSS-REFERENCE:** See Chapter 16 for information on Kerberos.

The `GSSCredential` interface encapsulates the credentials for an entity. A credential contains all the necessary cryptographic information to enable the creation of a context on behalf of the entity that it represents. A named entity, such as a user defined in a `GSSName`, can have multiple credentials. The GSS-API and other mechanisms communicating to it, such as JAAS, can have multiple authentication mechanisms to authenticate the same principal. To authenticate through multiple types of authentication mechanisms, different types of credentials are required.

There would have to be a credential per authentication mechanism. The Kerberos v5 authentication module requires a Kerberos credential. The same principal could be used throughout in many cases because the name of the user does not change; however, in some cases the type of the principal name may change when being transported across multiple protocols like GSS-API to JSSE. Using the GSS-API requires a Kerberos naming type in almost all conditions, so the principal name type does not need to change. Setting the credentials for both the initiator and acceptor peers of the GSS-API service is shown in Listing 17-1.

Security context components

The `org.ietf.jgss.GSSContext` is the interface that encapsulates the GSS-API security context and provides security services such as the `wrap`, `unwrap`, `getMIC`, and `verifyMIC` methods to encrypt, decrypt, and check the validity of messages.

> **TIP:** The security context is established between peers using the peers' acquired credentials. Multiple contexts may exist simultaneously between a pair of peers.

Before the context establishment phase is initiated, the context initiator may request specific characteristics desired of the established context such as the initiator requesting mutual authentication. The request methods in the security context are used to set the properties of the security context and request operations from the authentication module. To request mutual authentication from the security context to the authentication mechanism, the `context.requestMutualAuth(true)` method is used in Listing 17-1. The request is made to the authentication mechanism.

The authentication mechanism may or may not support some of these operations. For handling the mutual authentication, nothing else needs to be accomplished in the GSS-API outside the normal transfer of tokens to transfer for the security context. If there are no acceptor credentials, and the initiator is expecting a specific set of credentials, a `GSSException` will be thrown stating that the authentication was denied from the acceptor with the `NO_CRED` constant field thrown. The `NO_CRED` constant field is defined as no credentials in the `org.ietf.jgss.GSSException` class.

Besides requesting the operations in the security context, the security context can check if the state was set by the underlying security context with the `GSSContext`'s get methods. To check on the acceptor peer if the initiator requested mutual authentication and there was support from the authentication mechanism, the `context.getMutualAuthState` method is used to return true if mutual authentication was requested.

The context establishment phase begins with the first call to the `initSecContext` method by the context initiator. During this phase, the `initSecContext` and `acceptSecContext` methods produce the GSS-API authentication tokens that the calling application needs to send to its peers. The `initSecContext` initiates the token from the initiator, and the `acceptSecContext` method accepts the token from the acceptor. If no exceptions are thrown, the peer application has established the security context connections between the tokens. After the security context is established, the peer can call the `isEstablished` method to see if the context is established. The peer can call `isProtReady` to determine the actual characteristics and services of the established context.

To see if the initiator requires delegation, the acceptor's security context can use the `getCredDelegState` method to check the state. If delegation is required, the acceptor can use the `getDelegCr` method to retrieve the `GSSCredentials` from the initiator as its credentials to use instead of the server's principals and credentials. In order for the Kerberos authentication mechanism to delegate the credentials, the `DelegationPermission` in the policy file must be set to allow the Kerberos server to delegate the credentials.

Encryption and decryption components

After the security context has been established, messages and tokens can be passed from peer to peer. In most cases, the initiator will send the first message to the acceptor. The peer communications is similar to a client sending a message to a server through sockets, except that message encryption, decryption, and message integrity takes place. The initiator usually starts sending a message because it normally initiates the message exchange. To encrypt the message, the security context's `wrap` method is used to encrypt a byte array. The `wrap` method also can take an input stream to define where the message will be sent. The term "wrap" is defined in GSS-API as wrapping the security around the message.

When the message is received on the corresponding peer, such as the acceptor, the message needs to be unwrapped. The security context uses the `unwrap` method to transform the ciphertext back into plaintext. Following the token that the message is wrapped in are also any message properties such as the message integrity checksum. Most of the message properties are returned in the `org.ietf.jgss.MessageProp` class that is sent with the `wrap` method and retrieved with the `unwrap` method. The message property is the property of a specific message, and not global to all the messages. Some of the properties that can be retrieved include information about whether the token is duplicated, if there is a gap between tokens, if the token is out of sequence, and the level of quality of protection.

> **NOTE:** The message property can set the level of quality of protection. The QOP is authentication-mechanism dependent.

Other message methods are the `getMIC` and `verifyMIC`. The `getMIC` method generates a message integrity code to be passed to the peer to check the validity of the message. The `verifyMIC` method checks the message integrity that it received from the peer. Listing 17-2 displays the code for establishing the security context, the `wrap` method, and `unwrap` method.

Listing 17-2: The context loop, wrap, and unwrap methods

```
/**
 * Method contextLoop
 * Purpose: to loop until the context is
 * established from the tokens
 *
 *
 * @param context the intitialized token
 * @param isAcceptor is the acceptor or not
 * @param inStream the input stream
 * @param outStream the output stream
 *
 */
public void contextLoop(GSSContext context,
                        boolean isAcceptor,
                        DataInputStream inStream,
                        DataOutputStream outStream) {

  byte[] token = null;
  try {

    while (!context.isEstablished()) {
      /*
       * Finish a security context for the acceptor
       * Read the token and accept it
       */
      if (isAcceptor) {
        token = new byte[ inStream.readInt()];

        System.out
          .println("Will read input token of size "
              + token.length
              + " for processing by acceptSecContext");
        inStream.readFully(token);
```

```
                token = context.acceptSecContext(token, 0,
                                                 token.length);
        /*
         * Else , finish a security context for the initiator
         * pass an empty token to initialize the context
         */
        } else {
token = new byte[ 0];

            /*
             * token is ignored on the first call
             */
            token = context.initSecContext(token, 0,
                                           token.length);
        }

        /*
         * Send a token to the peer if one was generated by
         * initSecContext
         */
        if (token != null) {
          System.out.println("Will send token of size "
                             + token.length
                             + " from initSecContext.");
          outStream.writeInt(token.length);
          outStream.write(token);
          outStream.flush();
        }

        /*
         * The initiator has an extra read of the token
         * from the acceptor
         *
         */
        if (((!context.isEstablished()) && (!isAcceptor))) {
          token = new byte[ inStream.readInt()];

          System.out
            .println("Will read input token of size "
                     + token.length
                     + " for processing by initSecContext");
          inStream.readFully(token);
        }
    }

    System.out.println("Context Established! ");
    System.out.println("Client is " + context.getSrcName());
    System.out.println("Server is " + context.getTargName());
```

```java
    /*
     * Catches
     */
    } catch (org.ietf.jgss.GSSException e) {
        e.printStackTrace();
    } catch (IOException e) {
        e.printStackTrace();
    } catch (Exception e) {
        e.printStackTrace();
    }
}


/**
 * Method readMessage
 * Purpose: reads a input stream from the socket
 *
 * @param context the current security context
 * @param inStream the input stream
 *
 * @return the string read from the input
 *
 */
public String readMessage(GSSContext context,
                          DataInputStream inStream) {

    String str = null;

    try {

        /*
         * Create a MessageProp which unwrap will use to
         * return information such as the
         * Quality-of-Protection that was applied to
         * the wrapped token, whether or not it was
         * encrypted, etc. Since the initial
         * MessageProp values are ignored,
         * just set them to the defaults of 0 and false.
         */
        MessageProp prop = new MessageProp(0, false);

        /*
         * Read the token. This uses the same token byte array
         * as that used during context establishment.
         */
        byte[] token = new byte[ inStream.readInt() ];

        System.out.println("Will read token of size "
                        + token.length);
        inStream.readFully(token);
```

```
        byte[] bytes = context.unwrap(token, 0, token.length,
                                      prop);

        str = new String(bytes);

        System.out.println("Received data \"" + str
                          + "\" of length " + str.length());
        System.out.println("Confidentiality applied: "
                          + prop.getPrivacy());

        /*
         * Catches
         */
    } catch (org.ietf.jgss.GSSException e) {
        e.printStackTrace();
    } catch (IOException e) {
        e.printStackTrace();
    } catch (Exception e) {
        e.printStackTrace();
    }

    return str;
}

/**
 * Method writeMessage
 * Purpose: writes the output stream to the socket
 *
 * @param context the current context
 * @param message the message to write to the output
 * @param outStream the output stream
 *
 */
public void writeMessage(GSSContext context, String message,
                         DataOutputStream outStream) {

    try {
        byte[] messageBytes = message.getBytes();

        /*
         * The first MessageProp argument is 0 to request
         * the default Quality-of-Protection.
         * The second argument is true to request
         * privacy (encryption of the message).
         */
        MessageProp prop = new MessageProp(0, true);

        /*
```

```
     * Encrypt the data and send it across.
     * Integrity protection is always applied,
     * irrespective of confidentiality (i.e., encryption).
     * You can use the same token (byte array) as that
     * used when establishing the context.
     */
    byte[] token = context.wrap(messageBytes, 0,
                                 messageBytes.length, prop);

    System.out.println("Will send wrap token of size "
                        + token.length);
    outStream.writeInt(token.length);
    outStream.write(token);
    outStream.flush();


    /*
     * Catches
     */
} catch (org.ietf.jgss.GSSException e) {
    e.printStackTrace();
} catch (IOException e) {
    e.printStackTrace();
} catch (Exception e) {
    e.printStackTrace();
  }

 }
}
```

Implementing the GSS with Initiators and Acceptors

Listings 17-1 and 17-2 contain the code for both the initiator and acceptor. There are two major differences between the initiator and acceptor in the listings: the credential set and the peer that is initiating the security context. The credential set is different simply because the initiator will use the credentials of the client or other initiating authentication such as JAAS. The acceptor credentials could be a delegation of the initiator's credentials, or the server's principal and credentials, depending on the resources' permissions. Server principals are normally needed when the client principals are restrictive, such as when accessing an organization's database.

As mentioned before, it is up to the application to use any additional functionality to transport the messages such as Java sockets. The GSS-API handles the following, but not the transport mechanisms other than byte arrays and Java streams:

♦ Establishing the authentication mechanism

♦ Establishing the principals and credentials in the form of the authentication mechanism

♦ Establishing the security context of peers through tokens transported in streams or transported in byte arrays, which establishes the security material

♦ Wrapping and unwrapping each message with the security material in the form of streams and byte arrays

♦ Supporting further checks and quality of protection with the message property (`MessageProp`) class

♦ Supporting the MIC for alternative message integrity other than the wrap and unwrap

♦ Finally disposing of any system resources when completed

The preceding is the basic functionality of the GSS-API, and the how the Java stream or byte array is transported is independent of the GSS-API itself. The GSS-API could be transported through files, sockets, or even JSSE.

> **TIP:** The difference between the initiator and the acceptor is how they establish the security context.

The initiator starts the security context by establishing the user's credential, the server's name for identification, and the authentication mechanism for creating the security context. After the security context is created, the context tokens must be passed between the initiator and the acceptor, which is normally accomplished in a context loop. The initiator creates an initialization token with the `initSecContext` method and writes the token to the acceptor. The acceptor, in turn, reads the token and checks to see if the token is acceptable with the `acceptSecContext` method.

If the token is not acceptable, a `GSSException` is thrown. If the token is acceptable from the acceptor, the `acceptSecContext` method modifies the token with the server's credentials and the acceptor sends the token back to the initiator to confirm initialization. After the token has been processed by the initiator and the acceptor methods for initializing and accepting the token, the `isEstablished` flag in both security contexts is set to true to state that the security context has authenticated and is ready to wrap and unwrap messages.

Once the security context has been authenticated, only the security context between the peers can wrap and unwrap the messages. In other words, only the security contexts that are authenticated can access, or unwrap, the encrypted message. Once a message is wrapped, the token with the message in it is passed to the peer. Part of the wrap is not only the message but also information about the message and the security's context passed between peers. Only the established peers can unwrap the message. By providing the confidentiality, the GSS-API provides authorization for authenticated security contexts to access the plaintext message after it is wrapped.

Authenticating with JAAS

Up till now in this chapter, passing credentials through the Kerberos authentication mechanism have been coded directly in the `GSSNames`. The Kerberos login module has been set up from Chapter 16. In order to use the Kerberos login module, you need the Kerberos realm, the Kerberos Key Distribution Center that is part of the server, and the configuration file for the Kerberos login module.

The basic configuration file defines the Kerberos login module to be used for authentication and gives parameters on how to load the Kerberos module. The `com.sun.security.jgss.initiate` entry is the parameters for the Java GSS initiator's authentication mechanism and the `com.sun.security.jgss.accept` entry is for the acceptor's authentication mechanism. The accept entry specifies the `storeKey=true` that indicates that the Kerberos secret key will be generated from the Kerberos password and stored in the Kerberos private credential set. The basic configuration file is needed by the underlying GSS-API for startup information for the Java GSS's matching authentication mechanisms and is given in Listing 17-3.

Listing 17-3: Basic configuration file

```
/**
 * Login Configuration for JAAS.
 */

com.sun.security.jgss.initiate {
  com.sun.security.auth.module.Krb5LoginModule required;
};

com.sun.security.jgss.accept {
  com.sun.security.auth.module.Krb5LoginModule required storeKey=true;
};
```

The same type of configuration parameters can be applied directly to the initiator and acceptor. If the `RichGSSService.java` file was broken out into two files, one for the initiator `RichGSSInitiate.java` and the acceptor kept as the `RichGSSService.java`, the configuration file could be updated just for the client and the server in a `csLogin.conf` in Listing 17-4.

Listing 17-4: Client/server configuration file

```
/**
 * Login Configuration for JAAS.
 */

RichGSSInitiate{
  com.sun.security.auth.module.Krb5LoginModule required;
};

RichGSSService{
  com.sun.security.auth.module.Krb5LoginModule required storeKey=true
principal="rich@richware.com";
};
```

In Listing 17-4 the service principal is defined in the client/server configuration file as "`rich@richware.com`" to define access to the server for any service interaction.

The rest of this section describes changing the implementation to set up JAAS. Once JAAS becomes enforced, the security manager and access controller are now defined. When the security manager is defined, permissions to sockets and services must become explicit in security policies. The best way to differentiate between the client and the server is to codebase them.

By codebasing the client and server, each class is put into a separate jar file, and the jar file references each grant entry. The `RichGSSIntitiate.jar`, which contains the `RichGSSInitiate.class`, references the entry for the initiator and the `RichGSSService.jar`, which contains the `RichGSSService.jar` file, references the entry acceptor.

CROSS-REFERENCE: See Chapter 19 for information on grant entries.

The initiator's policy file will now need to grant socket connect permissions and service permissions to access the socket protocol and Kerberos realm. See Listing 17-5.

Listing 17-5: RichGSSInitiator's policy file

```
grant CodeBase "file:./Login.jar" {
        permission java.security.AllPermission;
};
grant CodeBase "file:./RichGSSInitiator.jar",
 Principal javax.security.auth.kerberos.KerberosPrincipal
  "rhelton@richware.com" {

 permission java.net.SocketPermission "*", "connect";

 permission javax.security.auth.kerberos.ServicePermission
  "krbtgt/richware.com@richware.com",
  "initiate";

 permission javax.security.auth.kerberos.ServicePermission
  "rich@richware.com",
  "initiate";
};
```

NOTE: The username is that defined in the policy file in Listing 17-5 as "`rhelton@richware.com`" and must be used as the principal in the `RichGSSInitiator.jar` to access the policy's resources that are defined.

Listing 17-5 defines the initiator jar to give access to Kerberos user principal `rhelton@richware.com` to allow a socket connection and initiate the GSS for the Kerberos mechanism at `richware.com` with the Kerberos service principal of `rich@richware.com`. The grant entry gives access to initiate and connect through a socket to the Kerberos acceptor at `richware.com`. The `Login.jar` contains the `Login.class` file that contains the callback handlers and login functionality for the JAAS login.

The reason that access must now be given by the grant entry by Kerberos and the sockets is because a security manager is defined when JAAS is set up. If a security manager was defined in the JVM during runtime and JAAS was not being set up, these permissions would still need to be defined to explicitly access resources.

CROSS-REFERENCE: See Chapter 18 for information on the security manager.

The acceptor's policy file will now need to grant socket accept permissions and service permissions to access the socket protocol and Kerberos realm. See Listing 17-6.

Listing 17-6: RichGSSService's policy file

```
grant CodeBase "file:./Login.jar" {
        permission java.security.AllPermission;
};
grant CodeBase "file:./RichGSSService.jar"
 Principal javax.security.auth.kerberos.KerberosPrincipal
  "rich@richware.com" {

 permission java.net.SocketPermission "*", "accept";

 permission javax.security.auth.kerberos.ServicePermission
  "rich@richware.com", "accept";
};
```

Listing 17-6 gives the functionality to the `RichGSSService.jar` to accept incoming socket calls and act as a Kerberos acceptor for Kerberos initiators.

The last step for changing the `RichGSSService.java` code to support JAAS is to provide the `Login.java`. An example of a `Login.java` is given in Chapter 19. Since the initiator previously had hard coded principals, the Login code simply passes the JAAS principals and credentials, given as a JAAS Subject object, to the `RichGSSInitiator.class` to define the Kerberos username and password to authenticate through the GSS-API. The modules now appear as shown in Figure 17-2.

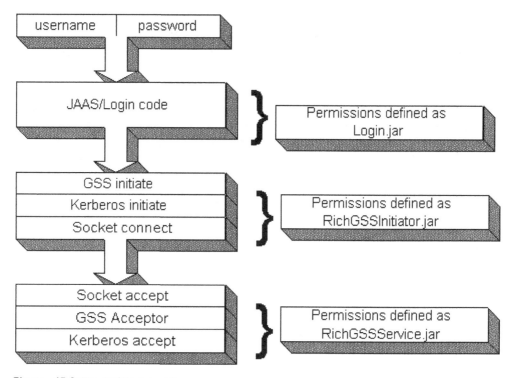

Figure 17-2: The JAAS implementation

> **TIP:** You can find tutorials on GSS at
> `http://java.sun.com/j2se/1.4/docs/guide/security/jgss/tutorials/`,
> which contains examples and detailed information about the GSS API.

Summary

Security products are based on keying mechanisms and authentication techniques in a variety of forms and different authentication mechanisms. The GSS-API provides a generic mechanism for defining authentication that is not bound by any specific network protocol or specific authentication mechanism. Kerberos is the most widely used authentication mechanism, but many more are supported such as SASL, which is an authentication mechanism used with LDAP servers. The GSS-API provides authentication, message confidentiality, and message integrity. JAAS, which is a pluggable authentication and authorization service that uses login modules, can work with the GSS-API to provide authentication and secure messages across different modes of communications, such as TCP/IP.

The GSS-API by definition is generic and uses OIDs to define the authentication mechanisms that it will use to authenticate. Standards and the service providers that the GSS-API will load when initializing define which OIDs are available. Since the OID is generic, code does not have to be changed when loading up a new authentication mechanism; only the OID needs to define a new mechanism and policy files for permission support. The GSS-API by itself is not an authentication mechanism. The GSS-API is simply an interface to use other authentication mechanisms such as Kerberos.

The GSS-API is not a transport mechanism like JSSE, because the GSS-API is not required to use sockets. The GSS-API is also not as pluggable as JAAS. It may require code changes for OIDs, and is not strictly used for authentication and authorization like JAAS because GSS-API is used for secure messaging. GSS-API is an interface and API mechanism for authentication, secure messaging, and key exchange that works with authentication mechanisms. GSS-API serves a different purpose than other Java APIs and provides secure functionality that is generic and can be extended to support many purposes such as secure messaging in the same machine.

## Chapter 18

Java Access: The Security Manager

In This Chapter

♦ Understanding the Java 2 sandbox

♦ Discovering the security manager

♦ Understanding the access controller

♦ Leaning about guarded objects

♦ Understanding the signed object

♦ Working with the policy

♦ Learning about the permission collection

Introduction

In Java 1.1, there was security to prevent Java Applets from accessing local system resources such as the local area network and the local file system. As time progressed, Java 2 needed to treat remote applications like Java Applets and local applications in a similar manner because local applications also needed the same security precautions. The Java architecture needed a means to change the permissions on applications dynamically without changing code. There arose the need for a security policy file for the application that could be changed similar to a properties file with a set of permissions to protect the domain.

The protection domain is a specific set of permissions. As time progressed and the security manager utility managed permissions, there arose the need to modify and extend permissions for a more robust protection domain to fine-tune the permissions. The security manager was permission-specific and had individual `checkXXX ( )` methods per each permission operation. An access controller was added to check any class derived from the `Permission` class so that permissions could be extended without changing Java code. This made up the Java 2 security sandbox. The Java security sandbox begins at the time that a class is loaded into a JVM.

For a class file to load up in the *Java virtual machine* (JVM), there are many checks that must be performed to ensure that the Java application functions properly. A class file is a runnable Java file. The basic flow of a class file is that it first must be loaded by a JVM. The JVM loads a class file using the java.lang.ClassLoader class. The class loader first checks the byte stream to ensure that the class file is a valid Java class file. An example of what it will check for is the 0xCAFEBABE (Café Babe) magic number at the beginning of the class file. After it ensures that the class is structured and follows a valid class format, it loads up the reference classes and fields. Then the JVM checks to see if a SecurityManager is defined for the class file, and if so, it checks the permissions and operations against any defined system resources.

If the security manager is set, and the application tries to access a system resource that is not defined for access in the protection domain, the security manager throws a SecurityException. The security manager uses an access controller to check the permissions that are defined in a protection domain. The protection domain is a set of permissions and their associated system resources. Figure 18-1 displays the basic interaction. If no security manager is defined, then the application can access any system resource. Java Applets automatically have a security manager defined, so they have limited access to the local system.

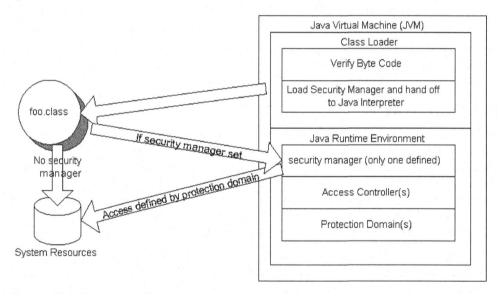

Figure 18-1: The basic class flow

The Class Loader

The class loader is simply an object that is responsible for loading and verifying a Java class. The class loader checks for imported classes that are referenced in the class by searching through the CLASSPATH. The class loader also checks for any security manager and, after the class is loaded, the class is handed off to the Java Runtime Environment (JRE) for execution.

The `java.lang.ClassLoader` is the base class that creates the class loader object. The `ClassLoader` class is an abstract class because it returns the current instance when calling the `Class.getClassLoader ( )` method. All Java classes can call the `Class.getClassLoader ( )` method to retrieve the reference to the executing class loader that will load itself. The class could be as simple as an `Array` class and execute the `Class.getClassLoader ( )`, and it will return the class loader that loaded the `Array` class.

Some applications may implement subclasses of the `ClassLoader` class to extend operations when loading a class. Several come deployed with Java 2. Figure 18-2 displays the extended classes that are also deployed in JDK 1.4.

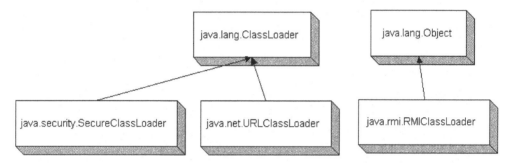

Figure   18-2: Some ClassLoader extension classes

A class loader is any class that adheres to the `ClassLoader` interface. These interfaces include the following:

- `java.lang.ClassLoader`: This class loader represents the base class loader from which all other class loaders will be derived.

- `java.security.SecureClassLoader`: This class loader was introduced in Java 2 to provide the capability to associate classes with permissions and the code source. The permissions are retrieved by the system policy by default.

- `java.net.URLClassLoader`: This class loader was introduced in Java 2 to provide the capability to load classes from a list of URLs.

- `java.rmi.server.RMIClassLoader`: This class loader was introduced in Java 1.1 to provide RMI applications during marshaling and unmarshaling of classes passed as parameters. The `RMIClassLoader` loads classes from the network using a list of URLs.

The Security Manager

The security manager component of the core Java security architecture is responsible for determining whether certain requests to access particular valued resources are to be allowed. It is up to the security manager to determine which operations are allowed or rejected. In Java 2, some of the work for checking the permissions and comparing with the resources are offloaded to the access controller. The security manager will not be used unless it is explicitly defined. The application will be used when specifying the `-Djava.security.manager` option when running the application.

> **TIP:** By default, Java Applets will have an installed security manager to prevent access from local networks and local file access.

The security manager provides the mechanism to validate if the class has access to a system resource. If access is denied, a `java.lang.SecurityException` is thrown. If access is permitted, the call proceeds as normal. Each Java virtual machine process instance allows only one security manager to be installed at a given time. If a security manager is installed, access is required for resources loading up into the class. An example is the source code for initializing a `FileInputStream`. The source from Java for the `FileInputStream` can be displayed as shown in Listing 18-1.

Listing 18-1: The `FileInputStream`

```
public FileInputStream(String name) throws   FileNotFoundException {
 SecurityManager security = System.getSecurityManager();
 if (security != null) {
     security.checkRead(name);
 }
 fd = new FileDescriptor();
 open(name);
}
```

The `security.checkRead(name)` method, in turn, calls the `java.security.AccessController.checkPermission(perm)` passing in a runtime permission for reading the file descriptor. There are many methods in the security manager commonly starting with `check` and the operation to validate, such as the `checkConnect  ( )` method, and they call the `AccessController` class in a similar manner. The reason that the `AccessController` is not called directly is because it is used for backward capability with Java 1.1.

The `SecurityManager` becomes a wrapper around the `AccessController`. The `AccessController` works with several other classes to look up the permission set from a grant entry in a policy file. Each permission entry works only with operations specified for the particular `Permission` class. This is discussed in more detail in the following sections; however, the point is that actual checking of the permission and the control of the access is handed off to the `AccessController` from the `SecurityManager`.

The Access Controller

The history of the access controller started with Java 2 and provided the default implementation of the security manager. The class for implementing the access controller is `java.security.AccessController`. The constructor of the access controller is private so that it cannot be instantiated because the use of the class is dependent on its static methods like `checkPermission ( )`. The `checkPermission ( )` method checks the permission of an object. The permission is associated with a protection domain for each method on the stack. The protection domain is associated with a single grant entry. An example of a grant that would appear in a policy file can be seen in Listing 18-2.

Listing 18-2: Grant entry

```
grant {
  permission java.util.PropertyPermission "java.version", "read";
};
```

Listing 18-2 shows a basic grant entry in a policy file. Each grant entry has a set of permissions that it will apply to a protection domain. Each class with the protection domain will have the permission checked for each method on the stack. In this grant entry example, any class in the protection domain can have access to read the system property of the Java version number being used in the JRE. Each permission entry in the grant entry requires the `Permission` class type, in this case `PropertyPermission`, and the parameter and operation based on the permission type. For the property permission, the system property name of `java.version` and the `read` operation are acceptable.

There are always exceptions to the rules, and they must be accounted for in the protection domain. The issue could arise in the protection domain because only a class can go beyond what is defined in the grant entry. It might be necessary to bypass the grant entry in only one method while all the other methods follow the grant entry. An example comes from the `KeyStore.java` file that is distributed with the JDK 1.4. If the `KeyStore` type is not `jks`, then a get system property is performed to get the current `keystore` type. The reading of the `keystore.type` might not be set in the grant entry, so the privileged action demonstrated bypasses the security mechanism.

The `doPrivileged ( )` methods on the `AccessController` can be used to perform specific actions as a privileged caller. When a `checkPermission` method does reach the privileged action with the `doPrivileged` method, the `checkPermission` will not check the permission of the privileged action. Privileged actions are bypassed from the `checkPermission` method and will not be denied access for any reason from an `AccessController`. Listing 18-3 shows an example of the `doPrivileged` action.

Listing 18-3: A doPrivileged action

```
public final static String getDefaultType() {
  String kstype;
  kstype = (String)AccessController.doPrivileged(new  PrivilegedAction()
{
     public Object run() {
   return Security.getProperty(KEYSTORE_TYPE);
     }
```

```
});
if (kstype == null) {
    kstype = "jks";
}
return kstype;
}
```

The `AccessController` checks each of the threads in the current thread's given context. Each `AccessController` call checks a specific thread's context, not taking into account the parent thread. It would be a lot easier if the thread just inherited the parent's thread security context. Every time a new thread is created, the parent's security context is passed down to the newly created thread. To pass the parent's security context, the `checkPermission ( )` method calls would have to take into consideration the parent's context. The `AccessControlContext` class takes into consideration both the parent's context and the current thread being executed.

The `AccessControlContext`'s `checkPermission` method is a transitive method in that it takes into account the parent's and even the grandparent's security context. The `AccessControlContext` takes into account the thread's current context, while the `AccessControl` class checks throughout the thread's current context. Using the same permission set during the thread's current context ensures that all the subsequent threads will have the same access control. However, the permission set should not be used when it is assumed that the permissions are not to be changed throughout the threads that are created from the application. The `AccessControl` class should be used if the threads that are created by the application have different access and permissions. To execute the `AccessControlContext`'s `checkPermission` method, the current context of the `AccessControl` can be returned with Listing 18-4.

Listing 18-4: Code fragment to get the context

```
AccessControlContext context = AccessController.getContext();
```

The method in Listing 18-4 returns the current thread's context from the `AccessController`. Subsequent children threads can then use the returned `AccessControlContext` to perform a `checkPermission` on child threads that will use the same permission set. The `AccessControlContext` can be executed in more than one `ProtectionDomain`. A `ProtectionDomain` encapsulates the permission set with a single grant entry. The `ProtectionDomain` stores the permission set as a `PermissionCollection` object, the array of `Principal` objects, and the `CodeSource` object. The `CodeSource` is made up of the optional `CodeBase` entry and possibly many `SignedBy` entries. The `CodeBase` object encapsulates the code update location mapped in a URL. The `SignedBy` entries are an array of `Certificate` objects. The array of `Principal` objects are the users or groups that have access to the permissions. Figure 18-3 shows a diagram of the Protection Domain/grant entry.

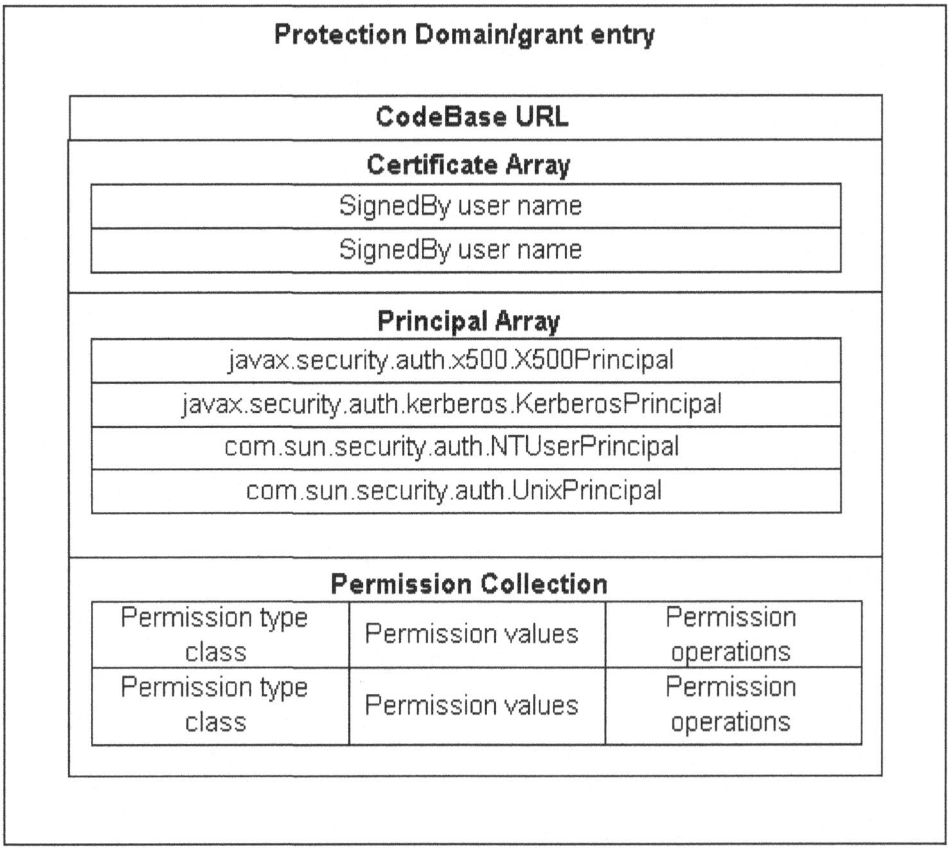

Protection Domain/grant entry

CodeBase URL

Certificate Array
SignedBy user name
SignedBy user name

Principal Array
javax.security.auth.x500.X500Principal
javax.security.auth.kerberos.KerberosPrincipal
com.sun.security.auth.NTUserPrincipal
com.sun.security.auth.UnixPrincipal

Permission Collection		
Permission type class	Permission values	Permission operations
Permission type class	Permission values	Permission operations

Figure 18-3: The Protection Domain

Guarded objects

The notion of an access controller is an object encapsulating access of resources of other objects in the current thread creating a new thread context. The access control context is an object that encapsulates access of resources of other objects throughout the thread context. The guarded object is used to protect the object from another object. There are three pieces to understanding the guarded object: the guard, the protected object, and the requesting object. The guarded object uses the java.security.GuardedObject class.

The constructor of the guarded object uses two parameters: the protected object and the guard. The protected object is the object that is being protected by the guard. The guard is a class from the Permission class such as the FilePermission class. The requesting object is the object that will try to access the protected object by calling the getObject ( ) method. The object that is created by a guarded object is constructed but cannot be retrieved until a `getObject ( )` method is performed to retrieve the newly created object. When the `getObject ( )` method is called, the guarded object performs a `checkGuard ( )` operation against the guard and if the protected object can be accessed by the definition of the guard, then access is granted. Listing 18-5 demonstrates this functionality.

Listing 18-5: The `RichGuard` class: An example of a guarded object

```
package com.richware.chap18;
import java.security.*;
import java.io.*;

/**
 * Class RichGuard
 * Description: A custom demonstration of
 * guarding an object. This code is the requestor.
 *
 * Copyright:    Copyright (c) 2002 Wiley Publishing, Inc.
 * @author Rich Helton <rhelton@richware.com>
 * @version 1.0
 * DISCLAIMER: Please refer to the disclaimer at the beginning of this
book.
 */
public class RichGuard {

  /**
   * Method main
   * Description: The main driver to run the methods.
   *
   *
   * @param args (no arguments presently).
   *
   */
  public static void main(String args[]) {
    try {
      /*
       * Combine the userdirectory + package name + input file
       * to find the file and where its location should be
       */
      System.out.println("Starting RichGuard....");
      String localDirectory  = System.getProperty("user.dir");
      System.out.println("Changing directory to Chapter 11");
      System.setProperty("user.dir",localDirectory +
"\\com\\richware\\chap18\\");
      localDirectory  = System.getProperty("user.dir");
      String localInputFile  = localDirectory + args[ 0];
      System.out.println("Openining Chapter 14 plus the input file as an
argument: " + localInputFile);

      /*
```

```
 * Create the protected object
 * as a FileInputStream object
 */
FileInputStream protectedObject =
  new FileInputStream(localInputFile);

/*
 * Create the guard object
 * as a FilePermission for
 * what is needed to access the object.
 */
FilePermission guard = new FilePermission(localInputFile,
                                                "read");

/*
 * Create the guarded object
 * which is an association between the
 * requestor, guard and protected object
 */
GuardedObject guardedObject =
  new GuardedObject(protectedObject, guard);

/*
 * get the object so this is
 * the requestor object
 * this will call the checkGuard
 * and Permission.checkPermission()
 */
Object o = guardedObject.getObject();

System.out.println("Got access to object");

/*
 *    catches.
 */
} catch (AccessControlException e) {
e.printStackTrace();
} catch (Exception e) {
e.printStackTrace();
}
}
}
```

The guarded object uses the `FilePermission` object as the guard that is set for read access on the `temp.txt` file. If the application doesn't have read permission on `temp.txt`, then a `SecurityException` is thrown. The permission will be validated with a defined security manager that will look up the permission set through the protection domain.

If no security manager is present, the `SecurityException` will not be thrown. The check for the permission will be called by the guard's `Permission.checkGuard ( )` method during the requestor's call to the `getObject ( )` method.

An example output looks like the following code fragment:

```
>java com.richware.chap18.RichGuard temp.txt
Starting RichGuard....
Changing directory to Chapter 11
Opening Chapter 14 plus the input file as an argument:
C:\RICH\com\richware\chap18\temp.txt
Got access to object
```

The purpose of guarded objects is slightly different from that of the access controller, but it does make significant use of the `Permission` class, security manager, and protection domain just as the access controller does. The concept of the guarded object is to validate the permission of the protected object with the protection domain before retrieving the object in the requesting object. The requesting object cannot access the object itself until the defined protection domain grants access.

If a security manager defines no protection domain, then permission is granted. The biggest difference between the access controller and the guarded object is that in the guarded object, the access is checked outside of the defined or guarded object; whereas in the access controller, the access method `checkRead ( )` is performed in the `FileInputStream` object when there is an attempt to read the file.

The signed object

Another concept that was introduced in Java 2 is the concept of a signed object. A signed object is used to apply a digital signature to a serialized object when it is written to disk. The digital signature is used to check the integrity of the saved serialized object to ensure that no one has tampered with the serialized object. The digital signature of the serialized object is signed with a private key and verified with the matching public key.

A serializable object uses the `readObject ( )` and `writeObject ( )` methods to read and write the object to Java streams using the `java.io.Serializable` interface. The serializable object is passed in the creation of the `java.security.SignedObject` along with the private key and signature algorithm.

When the creation of the `SignedObject` is executed, the `writeObject ( )` method of the serializable object is encapsulated internally to the signed object. When the `verify ( )` method is executed, the object is read back out and if the verification succeeds, the object can be retrieved with the `getObject ( )` method. Listing 18-6 demonstrates the functionality just described.

Listing 18-6: The `RichSign` class: A signed object example

```
package com.richware.chap18;
import java.security.*;
import java.io.*;

/**
 * Class RichSign
 * Description: A custom demonstration of
 * signing an object.
 *
 * Copyright:    Copyright (c) 2002 Wiley Publishing, Inc.
 * @author Rich Helton <rhelton@richware.com>
 * @version 1.0
 * DISCLAIMER: Please refer to the disclaimer at the beginning of this
 book.
 */
public class RichSign {

  /**
   * Method main
   * Description: The main driver to run the methods.
   *
   *
   * @param args (no arguments presently).
   *
   */
  public static void main(String args[]) {
    try {
      System.out.println("Starting RichSign....");
      /*
       * Create the Serialized object
       */
      String str = "I am verified";

      /*
       * Create the KeyPair
       */
      KeyPairGenerator keyGen =
        KeyPairGenerator.getInstance("DSA");

      /*
       * Create the signature
       */
      Signature sign    = Signature.getInstance("SHA1withDSA");
      KeyPair   keyPair = keyGen.generateKeyPair();
      System.out.println("Creating signed object ...");

      /*
```

```
       * Create the Signed object
       */
      SignedObject so = new SignedObject(str,
                                         keyPair.getPrivate(),
                                         sign);

      System.out.println("\nVerifying signature ...");

      /*
       * verify the Signed object
       * print the results
       */
      if (so.verify(keyPair.getPublic(), sign)) {
        System.out.println(so.getObject());
      } else {
        System.out.println("Signature NOT verified!");
      }
    } catch (Exception e) {
      e.printStackTrace();
    }
  }
}
```

An run of Listing 18-6 gives the following:

```
>java com.richware.chap18.RichSign
Starting RichSign....
Creating signed object ...

Verifying signature ...
I am verified
```

The Policy

It has been mentioned that a protection domain has the grant entry. The grant entry is mapped from a security policy that takes the form of Listing 18-7.

Listing 18-7: The grant entry structure

```
grant [ SignedBy "signer_names"] [ , CodeBase "URL"]
    [ , Principal [principal_class_name] "principal_name"]
    [ , Principal [principal_class_name] "principal_name"] ... {
  permission permission_class_name [ "target_name" ]
            [ , "action"] [ , SignedBy "signer_names"];
  permission ...
};
```

The format of the policy file can contain multiple grant entries, as shown in Listing 18-7, as long as they have a different CodeSource. The CodeSource differentiates one grant entry from another in the same file. The only other way to separate grant entries is to have them defined in different files. The Principals, SignedBy, and CodeBase make up the CodeSource associated with the grant entry. The CodeSource, if defined, specifies a URL to download updated class or JAR files for the application. The signedBy, if defined, contains a list of names. The CodeBase searches the keystore entries for matching names and, for each one found, it returns the matching X.509 certificate. When the code base is downloaded, the CodeSource checks the signatures of the class files and JARs to ensure that the individuals in the signedBy list signed the files. See Listing 18-8 for a signedBy example.

Listing 18-8: signedBy example

```
grant signedBy "Rich" {
  permission java.io.FilePermission "/tmp/*", "read";
  permission java.util.PropertyPermission "user.*";
};
```

This example will grant the permission set to code only signed by the individual "Rich" after comparing the certificate from the keystore with the signed code. Another example, CodeBase from www.richware.com, is shown in Listing 18-9.

Listing 18-9: CodeBase example

```
grant codeBase "http://www.richware.com/*", signedBy "Rich" {
    permission java.io.FilePermission "/tmp/*", "read";
    permission java.io.SocketPermission "*", "connect";
};
```

This example will grant the permission set only to code signed by "Rich" and downloaded from www.richware.com. An individual can also sign individual permission types to validate any new permission code.

The third part of the CodeBase is the principal name. The principal name can be any principal name derived from the java.security.Principal class such as the javax.security.auth.x500.X500Principal class. The purpose of the principal entries is to define the users that are allowed to access the permission when the code is executing. Listing 18-10 shows an example of the executing code.

Listing 18-10: Principal example

```
grant principal javax.security.auth.x500.X500Principal "cn=Rich" {
  permission java.io.FilePermission "/", "write";
};
```

Checking the permission set will only work if the security manager is defined with the –
Djava.security.manager system property; however, the policy file is always set. By
default, the policy file will be called by the JRE subdirectory
${JRE}/lib/security/java.policy file unless otherwise set with the –
Djava.security.policy system property. Listing 18-11 demonstrates the java.policy
that is set by default. The example selects the protection domain without the signedBy and
CodeBase entry. Selecting the grant entry is defined by which policy file is currently active in
the system properties and then selecting the specific grant entry out of the policy file by
defining a CodeSource. Listing 18-12 demonstrates an example of getting the policy and the
permission collection from the current policy in the system properties.

Listing 18-11: The `RichPolicy` class: A policy example code

```
package com.richware.chap18;
import java.security.*;
import java.io.*;

/**
 * Class RichPolicy
 * Description: A custom demonstration of
 * printing out default policies.
 *
 * Copyright:    Copyright (c) 2002 Wiley Publishing, Inc.
 * @author Rich Helton <rhelton@richware.com>
 * @version 1.0
 * DISCLAIMER: Please refer to the disclaimer at the beginning of this
 book.
 */
public class RichPolicy {
  /**
   * Method main
   * Description: The main driver to run the methods.
   * @param args (no arguments presently).
   *
   */
  public static void main(String args[]) {
    try {
      System.out.println("Starting RichPolicy.....");
      /*
       * Get the Policy
       */
      Policy localPolicy = Policy.getPolicy();
      /*
       * Get the CodeSource
       * Shown here is an empty CodeSource
       */
      CodeSource codesource = new CodeSource(null,null);
```

```
    /*
     * Get the Permission Collection
     * from the CodeSource
     */
    PermissionCollection permissioncollection =
localPolicy.getPermissions(codesource);
    /*
     * Get the current ClassLoader
     */
    ClassLoader loader = ClassLoader.getSystemClassLoader();
    /*
     * Get the ProtectionDomain
     * from the CodeSource & Permission Collection
     */
    ProtectionDomain protectiondomain = new
ProtectionDomain(codesource, permissioncollection);
    /*
     * Get the current Security Manager
     */
    SecurityManager sm = System.getSecurityManager();
    System.out.println("********Security Manager*********");
    System.out.println(sm);
    System.out.println("********CodeSource*********");
    System.out.println(codesource);
    System.out.println("********ClassLoader*********");
    System.out.println(loader);
    System.out.println("********Protection Domain********");
    System.out.println(protectiondomain);
    System.out.println("********Permissions*********");
    System.out.println(permissioncollection);
    } catch (Exception e) {
    e.printStackTrace();
    }
  }
}
```

By default, the outcome of running the JDK 1.4 distribution will produce Listing 18-12.

Listing 18-12: Policy example code output

```
>java com.richware.chap18.RichPolicy
Starting RichPolicy.....
********Security Manager*********
null
********CodeSource*********
(null <no certificates>)
********ClassLoader*********
sun.misc.Launcher$AppClassLoader@bac748
```

```
********Protection Domain********
ProtectionDomain  (null <no certificates>)
 null
 <no principals>
 java.security.Permissions@3c5982 (
 (java.util.PropertyPermission java.specification.vendor read)
 (java.util.PropertyPermission java.vm.specification.vendor read)
 (java.util.PropertyPermission path.separator read)
 (java.util.PropertyPermission java.vm.name read)
 (java.util.PropertyPermission java.class.version read)
 (java.util.PropertyPermission os.name read)
 (java.util.PropertyPermission java.vendor.url read)
 (java.util.PropertyPermission java.vendor read)
 (java.util.PropertyPermission java.vm.vendor read)
 (java.util.PropertyPermission file.separator read)
 (java.util.PropertyPermission os.version read)
 (java.util.PropertyPermission java.vm.version read)
 (java.util.PropertyPermission java.version read)
 (java.util.PropertyPermission line.separator read)
 (java.util.PropertyPermission java.vm.specification.version read)
 (java.util.PropertyPermission java.specification.name read)
 (java.util.PropertyPermission java.vm.specification.name read)
 (java.util.PropertyPermission java.specification.version read)
 (java.util.PropertyPermission os.arch read)
 (java.lang.RuntimePermission stopThread)
 (java.net.SocketPermission localhost:1024- listen,resolve)
)




********Permissions********
java.security.Permissions@3c5982 (
 (java.util.PropertyPermission java.specification.vendor read)
 (java.util.PropertyPermission java.vm.specification.vendor read)
 (java.util.PropertyPermission path.separator read)
 (java.util.PropertyPermission java.vm.name read)
 (java.util.PropertyPermission java.class.version read)
 (java.util.PropertyPermission os.name read)
 (java.util.PropertyPermission java.vendor.url read)
 (java.util.PropertyPermission java.vendor read)
 (java.util.PropertyPermission java.vm.vendor read)
 (java.util.PropertyPermission file.separator read)
 (java.util.PropertyPermission os.version read)
 (java.util.PropertyPermission java.vm.version read)
 (java.util.PropertyPermission java.version read)
 (java.util.PropertyPermission line.separator read)
 (java.util.PropertyPermission java.vm.specification.version read)
```

```
(java.util.PropertyPermission java.specification.name read)
(java.util.PropertyPermission java.vm.specification.name read)
(java.util.PropertyPermission java.specification.version read)
(java.util.PropertyPermission os.arch read)
(java.lang.RuntimePermission stopThread)
(java.net.SocketPermission localhost:1024- listen,resolve)
)
```

Notice in Listing 18-12 that, by default, there is no security manager defined and that the grant permission set is opened up for property and socket permissions from the `java.policy` file.

The Permission Collection

The permission collection is basically a set of permissions that is defined in the protection domain and stored in a `java.security.PermissionCollection` class. The permission collection can be returned from the `java.security.Policy` class or `java.security.ProtectionDomain` class. The policy class returns the permission collections that are defined in the policy file.

Setting permissions

When setting permissions, it is important to know how the permissions work, their purpose, and their parameters. For instance, in Listing 18-13, the `FilePermission` is set to allow read access from all files in the `/tmp` directory. The `FilePermission` takes the name value of a file name and the operations can be read, write, execute, and delete.

Listing 18-13: FilePermission example

```
grant {
  permission java.io.FilePermission "/tmp/*", "read";
};
```

All permissions are derived from the `java.security.Permission` class. The immediate derived classes are illustrated in Figure 18-4.

Extending permissions

There are many more permissions than are shown here. These are the main permissions that immediately derive from the `Permission` class. To give an idea how many more permissions are extended, the classes derived from `java.security.BasicPermission` are:

♦ `java.sound.sampled.AudioPermission`

♦ `javax.security.auth.AuthPermission`

♦ `java.awt.AWTPermission`

- ◆ javax.security.auth.kerberos.DelegationPermission
- ◆ java.util.logging.LoggingPermission
- ◆ java.net.NetPermission
- ◆ java.util.PropertyPermission
- ◆ java.lang.reflect.ReflectPermission
- ◆ java.lang.RuntimePermission
- ◆ java.security.SecurityPermission
- ◆ java.io.SerializablePermission
- ◆ java.sql.SQLPermission
- ◆ javax.net.ssl.SSLPermission.

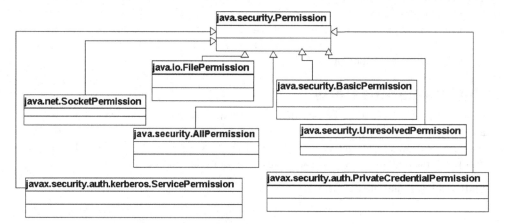

Figure 18-4: Immediate java.security.Permission derived classes

Many permissions need to be supported and, instead of extending the security manager for every extension, the access controller checks all permissions that are derived from the Permission class.

Summary

This chapter introduced the concept of what is needed to access system resources from the JRE. Permissions were extended to support many types of access to system resources. The Java 2 SDK had to be extended to support generic permissions instead of specific permissions.

There are several ways to look up the permission set, such as an access controller and guarded object. The use of permissions needed changing without changing code so the concept of a protection domain was used that accessed policy files.

The policy files are structured to support `CodeSource` for getting signed and unsigned code updates, principals to check access during runtime, and permission sets. The permissions use name values and operations to pass in the specifics of resources and the operation to check access before execution. In short, there are several ways to extend and use the Java 2 SDK to provide limited access to almost any system resource.

## Chapter 19

Java Authentication and Authorization Service

In This Chapter

♦ Learning common definitions and components

♦ Understanding different interfaces for authentication and authorization

♦ Working with policies, subjects, principals, permissions, and credentials

♦ Learning about Access Control Lists

♦ Understanding how JAAS provides a common model for security

Java provides support for authentication and authorization through the *Java Authentication and Authorization Service* (JAAS) framework. JAAS provides an interface in Java that hides the complexities of the underlying authentication and authorization mechanisms. This chapter presents the common terms, definitions, and interfaces for JAAS.

What Is JAAS?

Java Authentication and Authorization Service is a framework for providing authentication and authorization to runtime resources. JAAS provides an interface to pluggable authentication mechanisms for authentication, and a framework to require users to have explicit permissions to perform runtime operations in an application.

> **NOTE:** JAAS uses a dynamic security policy to define permissions instead of placing the permissions in code.

These permissions normally identify the user, the permissions to the resource, and the name of the resource itself. For example, an application may have the user `rich` with the `write` permission to a resource called `file1`. In this example, `rich` has the right to execute a write to `file1`. *Authentication* is the ability to give a user access through the application, and *authorization* ensures that the user has access to resources. Users may be authenticated but not authorized until they try to access the resource. JAAS provides a two-step process, one for authentication and one for authorization.

> **NOTE:** All code and references have been made using the JDK 1.4 distribution.

When JAAS runs, it creates a subject that contains a principal, which represents a named user, and credentials that represent private and public keys. The subject, containing the principal and credentials, gets authentication and authorization based on the login modules and permissions. The authentication and authorization are based on the principal, and the credentials are proof of the identity of the principal. Basing the authentication and authorization on the principal is called principal-based access control, which is discussed in the next section.

> **CROSS-REFERENCE:** For definitions of authentication and authorization, see Chapter 1.

Using Authentication

JAAS authentication is done using principal-based access control and pluggable authentication. JAAS can also be used in conjunction with Java Servlets, *Java Server Pages* (JSPs), and *Enterprise Java Beans* (EJBs). The authentication part of JAAS provides the capability to reliably and securely maintain client identity.

Understanding principal-based access control

Java 2 provides the ability to load the `SecurityManager` to enforce access to system resources. When JAAS is loaded, the `SecurityManager` should also be loaded for privileged actions. To use the `SecurityManager`, a policy file must be maintained, which follows the format of all policy files that use the Java 2 `SecurityManager`. The `SecurityManager` enforces the permissions based on the principal entries. Each permission entry protects a defined system resource. A permission set is called a grant entry. There could be many grant entries in a file or just one. When there are several grant entries in a file, there must be another defining entry, such as principal, codebase, or signed by, that gives a grant entry its uniqueness so that the `SecurityManager` can uniquely define several grant entries in the same policy file. Because the grant entry defines the principal, either explicitly or implicitly, to protect system resources, this form of access control is called *Principal-Based Access Control*.

Before accessing a resource, the principal of the resource must be defined. The principal must be authenticated to guarantee its authenticity. *Authentication* is the matching of the principal with its associated credentials through the authentication mechanism to validate the principal's authenticity.

> **NOTE:** The authentication mechanism is any authentication module that a service provider distributes for Java, such as the standard Kerberos, NT, UNIX, JNDI, and keystore that Sun ships with the JDK 1.4.

Sun is the service provider for these authentication modules. A service provider is any organization that distributes the authentication module that supports the JAAS API. After the principals and credentials have been authenticated through an authentication mechanism, through an encapsulating class called the *subject*, the JAAS can process the authorization. The principal can be a person, service, process, or group. When the subject is being authenticated, it is populated with `Principal` classes. The subject can have a collection of principals. The principal is a set of identities that separates it from other subjects.

The Principal-Based Access Control defines access to a resource based on the policy file's principals. Only authorized principals can access the resources. To explicitly define the principal for the grant access, the principal follows the `grant` entry. The principal can take on many principal naming forms, such as Kerberos names, X.500 names, Solaris names, and Windows NT names. Different forms of the principal are needed to format the principal for particular authentication mechanisms. For example, the X.500 name is used when the principal is used with digital certificates.

Listing 19-1 is an example of a grant entry. The grant entry, in this case, is a non-principal example that implicitly allows all principals and updates code from `http://richware.com`. This code is signed by the user `rich` for all principals to access (read) the resource (the `cdrom`). Notice the use of the `grant  Codebase` element instead of `grant  Principal` element in the policy file. The user `rich` must be in the local keystore to verify the signature of the files in Listing 19-1.

Listing 19-1: Grant entry

```
// Java 2 codesource-based policy
grant Codebase "http://richware.com", Signedby "rich" {
  permission java.io.FilePermission "/cdrom/-", "read";
}
```

NOTE: The files will have the signature of `rich` regardless of who executes it.

Listing 19-2 shows a policy file that specifies a principal using JAAS.

Listing 19-2: Grant entry with principal

```
// Java 2 codesource-based policy
grant Principal com.sun.security.auth.UnixPrincipal "rich" {
  permission java.io.FilePermission "/cdrom/-", "read";
}
```

In this example, only a user associated with the `UnixPrincipal` principal type and associated with the name `rich` can have access to the `cdrom`. The `com.sun.security.auth.UnixPrincipal` is a Sun principal for a UNIX user.

Recall that a subject is the source of the request to a resource, and that it is authenticated before it is authorized. A subject may have security-related attributes known as *credentials*. Credentials are security attributes that can be shared among subjects. An example of a credential is a public key that some subjects may share that is used to validate their principals. One of the easiest ways to execute the subject is to use the static method `doAs`, which associates a method with a `javax.security.auth.Subject` class. Listing 19-3 shows how the `doAs` method is used for access control.

Listing 19-3: The doAs method

```
class ExampleAction implements java.security.PrivilegedAction {
  public Object run() {
    java.io.File f = new java.io.File("/cdrom/-");
    // the following call invokes a security check
    if (f.exists()) {
      System.out.println("cdrom exists");
    }
    return null;
  }
}

public class Example1 {
  public static void main(String[] args) {
    // Authenticate the subject, "rich".
    // This process is described in the
    // LoginContext section.
    Subject rich;
    ....
    // perform "ExampleAction" as "rich"
    Subject.doAs(rich, new ExampleAction());
}
```

The code in Listing 19-3 checks whether it can read the cdrom as the user rich. The line cdrom exists is printed out if the user rich is authenticated using the UNIX principal and is authorized with the permission set in a policy file in Listing 19-2.

Understanding the Pluggable Authentication Module standard

Many types of authentication mechanisms are available that organizations can implement. Some may be proprietary, and others may be standards such as RSA, Kerberos, and smart cards. JAAS was built with the idea of it being able to plug in to different authentication and keying mechanisms. The *Pluggable Authentication Module* (PAM) framework is a plug-and-play technology for using authentication mechanisms.

Because many different technologies can be used to enter a system, new versions of authentication mechanisms are updated to an organization's authentication system, and new authentication modules are added inline for security enhancements. PAM technology is significant to understanding the pluggable authentication modules of JAAS and how they are configured.

Before PAM, most authentication mechanisms were operating-system–specific, proprietary, or could not be changed, such as rlogin in UNIX or Kerberos authentication using a C language Software Development Kit (SDK), where the needed implementation is specific to the authentication mechanism. PAM allows an organization to use multiple, different authentication mechanisms and switch among them without code changes. The system administrator simply plugs in a new authentication module without modifying any coding in the services. The PAM model defines configuration modifications to change authentication mechanisms.

The authentication mechanisms are pluggable in PAM, so the methods calling the authentication mechanisms must also become pluggable in order for the mechanisms to be dynamic. For instance, if the authentication mechanism is switched to Kerberos, the user's password and username should remain the same as it was before the switch of technology. In reality, there might be many authentication mechanisms throughout the underlying system that are hidden from the user, which perform the principals and credentials transformation. An extra authentication layer may be needed, for example, to provide the administration of permissions to access system resources.

These resources, for instance, can be databases and property files. Some legacy systems have passwords that may be hard coded into the system. Making passwords and usernames static throughout a system creates a security risk and destroys the capability to change passwords dynamically. These passwords can be observed if an attacker of the system has the ability to desource the source code into readable form. PAM helps alleviate these issues and the gives the capability to layer authentications and allows a pluggable model to dynamically enhance a system.

However, PAM does not address all the authentication issues, such as the single-sign-on problem of securely transferring the identity of the caller to a remote site. This issue arises when a user of an e-commerce system logs in once and its credentials are distributed throughout the system. The organization needs to distribute the credentials through an enterprise system using a form of delegation. What PAM does provide is the capability for the system administrator to install multiple authentication protocols for each application. PAM allows users to be authenticated from multiple protocols without retyping the password. The architecture provides a pluggable model for system authentication and related tasks such as password, account, and session management.

> **NOTE:** PAM is independent of the operating system and the network protocol.

Figure 19-1 shows the PAM architecture and the `pam.config` file that is used to store and configure the authentication modules. The example shows the ftp, telnet, and login applications using Kerberos, UNIX authentication, and S/Key authentication mechanisms. There are four possible attributes in PAM that can be configured independently: authentication, password, session, and account.

For instance, the system administrator may add a Kerberos and password module and reuse the same session and account modules. Just as PAM uses a configuration file to plug in different login modules, JAAS uses a policy file to specify the modules and permissions. Other classes that assist in using the authentication and authorization are the

`javax.security.auth.login.LoginContext` and
`javax.security.auth.spi.LoginModule` classes.

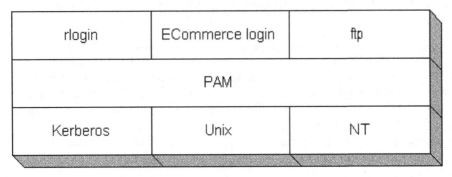

Figure   19-1: The Pluggable Authentication Module

Implementing the LoginContext and LoginModule

As mentioned earlier, PAM provides the pluggable interface standard. PAM provides the
underlying layer for pluggable authentication. That means that PAM is a separate protocol
from JAAS; it is not a requirement that PAM be written in the Java language. In JAAS, the
`LoginContext` class and `LoginModule` class represent the Java implementation of the
PAM framework. The `LoginContext` class uses a configuration file, for which modules are
configured to determine the `LoginModule`.

A `LoginModule` can best be described as a wrapper around an authentication service
provider such as Kerberos. JAAS client applications write to the `LoginContext` API, while
authentication service providers implement the `LoginModule` interface. It is this
`LoginModule` implementation that the configuration file calls to be used with the
`LoginContext` so that multiple `LoginModules` can be plugged under the same application
without modifications to the application. Only the configuration file needs to be changed.
Listing 19-4 shows the `LoginContext` class and the `LoginModule` interface.

Listing 19-4: The LoginContext class

```
public final class LoginContext {
  public LoginContext(String name) { }
  public void login() { }          // two phase process
  public void logout() { }
  public Subject getSubject() { } // get the authenticated
}

public interface LoginModule {
  public void initialize(Subject subject,
                    CallbackHandler callbackHandler,
                    Map sharedState,
```

```
                          Map options);
    boolean login();      // 1st authentication phase
    boolean commit();     // 2nd authentication phase
    boolean abort();
    boolean logout();
}
```

The `LoginContext` is responsible for reading the configuration file and installing the correct `LoginModules`. Each `LoginContext` has a subject that represents the subject currently being authenticated and is updated with the proper credentials if the authentication succeeds.

For logging in, the `LoginContext`'s `login` method is invoked, which in turn invokes the appropriate `LoginModule`'s `login` method. The `login` method is dependent on which login modules the configuration loads. The `login` method executes the appropriate login procedure, such as adding principals and credentials to the subject and checking the password and principal.

For logging out, the `LoginContext`'s `logout` method is invoked, which in turn invokes the `LoginModule`'s `logout` method. This `logout` method is executed from the `LoginModule` class that performs the `logout` procedure, such as removing principals and credentials from a subject and invalidating the login session. The login modules include many variations such as `NTLoginModule`, `KeyStoreLoginModule`, `Krb5LoginModule`, `UnixLoginModule`, and `JNDILoginModule` in the `com.sun.security.auth.module` package.

The `LoginContext` class is an API that applications interface with to provide authentication. This authentication implements the `LoginModule` interface. Service providers that are technology vendors, such as Sun, provide many login modules. The modules are initialized based on the `javax.security.auth.login.Configuration` class that retrieves information from a configuration file. The configuration file in Listing 19-5 shows that the `UnixLoginModule` is always used, and the `Krb5LoginModule` is provided when a ticket is present.

Listing 19-5: The login configuration file

```
Login {
    com.sun.security.auth.module.UnixLoginModule  required;
    com.sun.security.auth.module.Krb5LoginModule  optional
                useTicketCache="true"
                ticketCache="${user.home}${/}tickets";
};
```

Not only does this technology provide pluggable authentication, but it also supports the notion of *stacked authentication*. This means that a single `LoginContext` can use multiple `LoginModules` in an authentication chain. In the Listing 19-5, the `LoginContext` could use both UNIX and Kerberos. The `javax.security.auth.login.Configuration` interface is used to read this configuration file and pass the specifics to the `LoginContext`. The `Configuration` interface uses an array of `javax.security.auth.login.AppConfigurationEntry` classes. In Listing 19-5, the `AppConfigurationEntry` contains two entries, one for the `UnixLoginModule` and one for the `Krb5LoginModule`.

The `AppConfigurationEntry` array loads the `LoginModules` in the `Configuration` class. The `javax.security.auth.login.ConfigFile` is the default implementation of the `Configuration` interfaces. The `ConfigFile` interface looks for the `java.security.auth.login.config=` or `java.security.auth.login.config==` from the system properties. If the `java.security.auth.login.config==` is defined as the system property, then the `ConfigFile` ignores all other configuration files except for the one defined with this property. If the `java.security.auth.login.config=` is defined, other configuration files may still be used in conjunction. Listing 19-6 demonstrates defining the `ConfigFile` to read the configuration files and the configuration files defined by the `login.config.url.1` that are URLs given sequentially. The excerpt is from the $[JRELIB] `/security/java.security` file. The `ConfigFile` loops through the sequence of login URLs and loads up the defined login files in these login configurations from the `login.config.url.X` entries.

Listing 19-6: Defining the `ConfigFile` for reading login configurations

```
#
# Class to instantiate as the javax.security.auth.login.Configuration
# provider.
#
login.configuration.provider=com.sun.security.auth.login.ConfigFile


#
# Default login configuration file
#
#login.config.url.1=file:${ user.home} /.java.login.config
```

Using the configuration file in this manner allows the login modules to be updated and changed without any modifications to the code itself. When a JAAS application is initialized, the login configuration file is defined using the `java.security.auth.login.config` system property. The entry in the login configuration for the login modules is defined when creating the `LoginContext`. The `LoginContext` loads the login modules when it is constructed through an internal `init` method, but it interfaces to the login modules directly through the `javax.security.auth.callback.CallbackHandler` interface. Listing 19-7 demonstrates the runtime definitions when running the JAAS application, and Listing 19-8 demonstrates JAAS application code.

Listing 19-7: Runtime definitions

```
java -Djava.security.manager -
Djava.security.auth.login.config=jaas.config -
Djava.security.policy=jaasapp.policy com.richware.chap19.JAASApp
```

Listing 19-8: The JAASApp class: A JAAS application

```
package com.richware.chap19;

import java.security.*;
import java.util.*;
import javax.security.auth.*;
import javax.security.auth.login.*;

/**
 * Class JAASApp
 * Description: This is a Sample JAAS application
 *
 * Copyright:    Copyright (c) 2002 Wiley Publishing, Inc.
 * @author Rich Helton <rhelton@richware.com>
 * @version 1.0
 * DISCLAIMER: Please refer to the disclaimer at the beginning of this
book.
 */
public class JAASApp
 {
  /**
   * Method main
   * Description: This is a Sample JAAS application
   * An example of running
   * java -Djava.security.manager
   *    -Djava.security.auth.login.config =jaas.config
   *    -Djava.security.policy=jaasapp.policy
   *
   * @param args none
   *
   */
  public static void main(String[] args)
   {
    LoginContext loginContext = null;
    try
     {
      loginContext =
        new LoginContext("RichJAAS",
                         new RichCallbackHandler());
      loginContext.login();
      System.out.println("\nLogin succeeded");
     }
    catch (LoginException le)
     {
      le.printStackTrace();
      System.out.println("\nLogin failed");
     }
    try
```

```
    {
      // Now we're logged in, so we can get the current subject.
      Subject subject = loginContext.getSubject();

      // Perform the example action as the authenticated subject.
      subject.doAs(subject, new JAASAction());
    }
    catch (Exception ex)
    {
      ex.printStackTrace();
    }
  }
}
```

The `LoginContext` initializes the `LoginModules` based on the entry in the configuration file and the type of `CallbackHandler`. If the `CallbackHandler` is not used, the parameters for the login module need to be defined in the login configuration file. Listing 19-9 shows the login configuration file for the JAAS application example.

Listing 19-9: The JAAS login configuration

```
RichJAAS {
   com.sun.security.auth.module.KeyStoreLoginModule required
keyStoreURL="file:///C:/.keystore";
};
```

The `RichJAAS` entry is defined in the JAAS application's `LoginContext` when created. The `RichCallbackHandler` is an implementation of the `CallbackHandler` interface for the login module to get the input information for username, passwords, any text, and confirmations. The `LoginContext` could also pass in the username and password through the `CallbackHandler` to be grabbed by the login module at a later time. Listing 19-10 shows the `RichCallbackHandler` class.

Listing 19-10: The `RichCallbackHandler` class: An example of runtime definitions

```
package com.richware.chap19;

import java.io.*;
import java.security.*;
import javax.security.auth.*;
import javax.security.auth.callback.*;

/**
 * Class RichCallbackHandler
 * Description: This is a Sample Callback Handler
 *
 * Copyright:    Copyright (c) 2002 Wiley Publishing, Inc.
 * @author Rich Helton <rhelton@richware.com>
```

```
 * @version 1.0
 * DISCLAIMER: Please refer to the disclaimer at the beginning of this
book.
 */
public class RichCallbackHandler implements CallbackHandler
{
  /**
   * Constructor RichCallbackHandler
   */
  public RichCallbackHandler() {}

  /**
   * Method handle
   * Description: Retrieve or display the information requested in the
   * provided Callbacks.
   *
   *
   * @param callbacks - an array of Callback objects provided by an
underlying
   * security service which contains the information requested to be
retrieved
   * or displayed.
   * @throws IOException  - if an input or output error occurs.
   * @throws UnsupportedCallbackException - if the implementation of
this
   * method does not support one or more of the Callbacks specified in
the
   * callbacks parameter.
   *
   */
  public void handle(Callback[] callbacks)
         throws IOException, UnsupportedCallbackException
  {
    for (int i = 0; i < callbacks.length; i++)
    {
      if (callbacks[ i] instanceof TextOutputCallback)
      {
        /*
         * Display the message according to the specified type
         */
        TextOutputCallback toc =
          (TextOutputCallback) callbacks[ i];
        switch (toc.getMessageType())
        {
        case TextOutputCallback.INFORMATION :
          System.out.println(toc.getMessage());
          break;

        case TextOutputCallback.ERROR :
```

```
        System.out.println("ERROR: " + toc.getMessage());
        break;

      case TextOutputCallback.WARNING :
        System.out.println("WARNING: " + toc.getMessage());
        break;

      default :
        throw new IOException("Unsupported message type: "
                              + toc.getMessageType());
      }
    }
    else if (callbacks[ i] instanceof NameCallback)
    {
      // Prompt the user for the username
      NameCallback nc = (NameCallback) callbacks[ i];
      System.err.print(nc.getPrompt());
      System.err.flush();
      nc.setName(
        (new BufferedReader(
          new InputStreamReader(System.in))).readLine());
    }
    else if (callbacks[ i] instanceof PasswordCallback)
    {
      /*
       * Prompt the user for the username
       */
      PasswordCallback pc = (PasswordCallback) callbacks[ i];
      System.err.print(pc.getPrompt());
      System.err.flush();

      /*
       * Note: JAAS specifies that the password is a char[] rather
than a String
       */
      String tmpPassword =
        (new BufferedReader(new InputStreamReader(System
          .in))).readLine();
      int    passLen     = tmpPassword.length();
      char[] password    = new char[ passLen];

      for (int passIdx = 0; passIdx < passLen; passIdx++)
      {
        password[ passIdx] = tmpPassword.charAt(passIdx);
      }
      pc.setPassword(password);
    }

    /*
```

```
   * Confirmation callbeack for KeyStore
   */
  else if (callbacks[ i] instanceof ConfirmationCallback)
  {
    // Prompt the user for the username
    ConfirmationCallback nc =
      (ConfirmationCallback) callbacks[ i];
  }
  else
  {
    throw new UnsupportedCallbackException(
      callbacks[ i], "Unrecognized Callback");
  }
 }
}
}
```

Using the `KeyStore` login module, as defined in Listing 19-9, the login module requests
information that it needs to log in a user using the `RichCallbackHandler`. The
`RichCallbackHandler` prompts the user for the information that it requires. Listing 19-11
demonstrates the interaction for the alias `richh` and `rich3` with the callback handler
interaction.

Listing 19-11: Callback handler interaction

```
>ECHO ENSURE that richjaas.jar and jaasaction.jar are in the CLASSPATH
ENSURE that richjaas.jar and jaasaction.jar are in the CLASSPATH

>ECHO ENSURE that the keystore file is in the root drive of C:\
ENSURE that the keystore file is in the root drive of C:\

>java -Djava.security.manager -
Djava.security.auth.login.config=jaas.config -
Djava.security.policy=jaasapp.policy com.richware.chap19.JAASApp
Please login to keystore
Keystore alias: richh
Keystore password: password
Private key password (optional): password

Login succeeded
JAAS has many secrets. There is much to know.
```

In Listing 19-11, the alias `richh` from the keystore is allowed to log in and access the file
`secretinfo.txt`. The alias `rich3` from the keystore receives a
`java.security.AccessControlException` when trying to access the
`secretinfo.txt` file, but is allowed to log in because the alias is listed in the keystore. If

the alias were not in the keystore, a
`javax.security.auth.login.FailedLoginException` would occur.

> **CROSS-REFERENCE:** See Chapter 8 for more on the `keystore` and `policytool`.

The user `richh` is allowed to access the resources because the permissions for the common name in the keystore are given access in Listing 19-12.

Listing 19-12: The permissions

```
/* AUTOMATICALLY GENERATED ON Sun Feb 03 23:56:54 MST 2002*/
/* DO NOT EDIT */

grant codeBase "file:./richjaas.jar" {
  permission java.security.AllPermission;
};


grant codeBase "file:./jaasaction.jar",
      principal javax.security.auth.x500.X500Principal "CN=Rich
Helton,OU=development,O=richware,L=denver,ST=co,C=us" {
  permission java.security.AllPermission;
};
```

The policy file in Listing 19-12 is generated with the `policytool` utility. The security policy is defined at runtime in the system property –
`Djava.security.policy=jaasapp.policy`. The principal is defined to have access to all system resources. The alias `richh` maps to the principal
`javax.security.auth.x500.X500Principal` entry and allows the permission to all resources. Any other principal does not allow any permission to access any resources in the `jaasaction.jar` where the JAAS privileged action is defined.

The privileged action contains the authorization components of JAAS that are executed by a subject. A subject is the implementation of the `javax.security.auth.Subject` class. The subject class is created with the associated principals, such as the username or the `X500Principal` in this example, and any credentials whether they are public or private. Public credentials are public keys such as the password for the user, and private credentials are the private keys such as the private key in the X.509 certificate in the keystore. The subject is created in the login module after a successful login has completed, and it is used by the login context to execute any privileged action using the subject's information. In the examples given so far, the login context uses the `getSubject` method to retrieve the subject from the login module and executes privileged code with the `doAs` method.

The `LoginContext` completes a two-phase authentication process in order to create a subject. A *two-phase authentication process* means that after the `login()` method is initialized, either a `commit()` or `abort()` method is invoked. A `commit()` method finishes any processing after a valid login, and the `abort()` method performs cleanup after a login is invalid and the module needs to be returned to an initialized state. Since the `LoginModules` are stackable, the `LoginContext` looks for a valid commit from all the modules to ensure that valid authentication takes place. Also, the higher module doesn't commit until the bottom module commits, so that if an abort happens for the last authentication, the `LoginContext` aborts the previous modules.

After a valid authentication succeeds, the module populates the subject, and the `LoginContext` can now access the subject with the `getSubject()` method. This gives the `LoginContext` a valid subject to use for authorization. If a valid authentication has not succeeded, there is no subject for the `LoginContext` to use for the next phase of security in authorization. Figure 19-2 shows this class interaction.

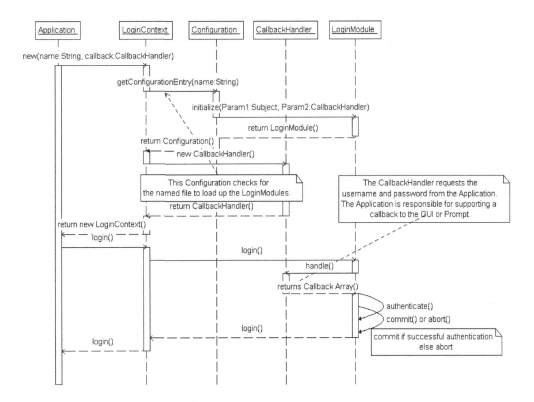

Figure 19-2: Java Authentication Class interaction

NOTE: The subject assigned to `LoginModule` is a placeholder to pass principal and credential information. It does not associate the principal names and credentials until the authentication is completed. In the example, the principal is the `X500Principal` string and the credentials are the X509 certificate that is retrieved from the keystore. The alias and passwords for the keystore are authentication information and not the subject.

More detail for the CallbackHandler and Callbacks

The JAAS `Callback` is how information, such as username and password, is passed between the application and `LoginModule`. The list of `Callbacks` contains the information, and the `CallbackHandler` is the mechanism for passing the `Callback` information. When the `LoginModule` gets the `login` method, it requests the login and may request information such as the username and the password, from the `CallbackHandler`'s `handle` method that is defined in the login context. The requesting information is dependent on the login module that is defined.

For instance, in the `KeyStoreLoginModule` there was a request for an alias name, a password for the keystore, a password for the alias, and a confirmation. Many other login modules may only require the username and password. The alias name and username were prompted for and sent back in the `NameCallback`. The passwords were prompted for and returned in the `PasswordCallback`. Listing 19-13 shows another example to populate the callback list. These callbacks are passed through an array of `Callbacks`; the array contains the various pieces of information to pass to the application depending on what is required from the `LoginModule`.

Listing 19-13: Populating the callback list

```
/*
 * Populate callback list
 */
Callback[] callbacks = new Callback[2];

callbacks[0] = new NameCallback("username: ");
callbacks[1] = new PasswordCallback("password: ", false);

try {

    /*
     * Prompt for username and password
     */
    callbackHandler.handle(callbacks);

    /*
     * Retrieve username
     */
    username = ((NameCallback) callbacks[0]).getName();

    /*
     * Retrieve password, converting from char[] to String
     */
    char[] charPassword =
    ((PasswordCallback) callbacks[1]).getPassword();

    if (charPassword == null) {
```

```
    /*
     * Treat a NULL password as an empty password, not NULL
     */
    charPassword = new char[ 0] ;
    }

    password = new String(charPassword);
}
```

Following are several callback types that you can use:

♦ `javax.security.auth.callback.ChoiceCallback` is used to give a user, through the application, a set of choices to select from for the `LoginModule`.

♦ `javax.security.auth.callback.ConfirmationCallback` is the callback that allows the `LoginModule` to prompt the application for extra authentication. This information is in the form of a question where a yes/no, yes/no/cancel, or similar answer is processed. There are possible options that are passed to the application with the selection index used to understand which one was selected from the user. A message should normally be prompted to the user, through the application, in the form of a `String`.

♦ `javax.security.auth.callback.LocaleCallback` is the callback needed if the `LoginModule` needs locale information from the application to determine country and language information for the user. The information is passed to the `LoginModule` in the form of the Java's `Locale`.

♦ `javax.security.auth.callback.NameCallback` is the callback object used to pass a name to the `CallbackHandler`. The the name is in the form of a `String`.

♦ `javax.security.auth.callback.PasswordCallback` is the password object to support the `CallbackHandler`. The password is stored in the form of an array of characters.

♦ `javax.security.auth.callback.TextInputCallback` allows the login modules to retrieve arbitrary text from the application. This data is in the form of a `String`.

♦ `javax.security.auth.callback.TextOutputCallback` allows the `LoginModule` to send informational or warning information to the application. This takes the form of a `String` message and a message type. The type of message matches one of these static values of `INFORMATION`, `WARNING`, or `ERROR`.

More on the configuration file setup

The JAAS login configuration file defines the login modules to be used, and the entries to be used are defined in the creation of the `LoginContext` objects. The configuration file is defined by the property settings of the system environment in the `java.security.auth.login.config` definition. The associated login module class defines each login module in the configuration.

Listing 19-14 defines an example configuration where two `LoginModules` are required to be used for the underlying login. This contains a list of login modules used for that application. The authentication proceeds down the list in the exact same order as the modules that have the `REQUIRED` field set.

Listing 19-14: A configuration file example

```
Login{
  com.sun.security.auth.SampleLoginModule REQUIRED debug=true;
  com.sun.security.auth.NTLoginModule REQUIRED debug=true;
}
```

There are four flags to define when the associated login module is to be used: They are the `REQUIRED`, `REQUISITE`, `SUFFICIENT`, and `OPTIONAL` flags.

- ◆ `REQUIRED`. The login module is required to succeed. The authentication proceeds to the next login module down the chain regardless of whether it succeeded or failed. All required login modules must succeed in order for the authentication to succeed.

- ◆ `REQUISITE`. The login module is required to succeed. The authentication returns immediately to the application if the authentication fails; otherwise, it returns to the next login module down the chain. All requisite login modules must succeed in order for the authentication to succeed.

- ◆ `SUFFICIENT`. The login module is not required to succeed. If it succeeds, it returns immediately to the application without proceeding down the chain; otherwise, it proceeds down the chain.

- ◆ `OPTIONAL`. The login module is not required to succeed. The authentication proceeds to the next login module down the chain regardless of whether it succeeded or failed.

At least one of the `OPTIONAL` or `SUFFICIENT` modules must succeed in order for an authentication to succeed.

Understanding JAAS Authorization

Authentication is used to verify an authentication mechanism. It validates an entity by associated credentials that provide identification for the entity, very much like a driver's license is used to verify a person. After an identity has been verified, the entity becomes a subject with principals and credentials. The principal can now try to access system resources such as a file, device, other process, and more.

Just because a user has been validated does not mean that the user has permissions to access the system resources. The next phase of JAAS must check permissions of the system resource. The permissions are stored in a security policy file, and JAAS will use the Java 2 security manager to check the permissions of the principal to ensure authorization to the system resource.

CROSS-REFERENCE: See Chapter 18 for more on the security manager and security policy file.

Authorization regulates, by defined security policies, that the subjects only access their permissions and perform actions based on those permissions. Any subject without specific permissions should not be allowed system resources. All systems have users and the system role responsible for assigning the permissions to specific subjects, which sometimes is called root or admin. Accessing resources in this way is dated back to the beginning of the UNIX operating system, and since there are specific permissions associated to a subject and there is discretion as to which subjects get which permissions. This type of security is called the *Discretionary Access Control* (DAC) model.

The DAC model specifies that the owner of each file can determine who else can access it by setting the file's permission bits, and it is the reason why the DAC model is sometimes called the owner-based model. One of the issues with this model is that anyone who has read access to a file can copy the file and give it to another user.

In the JAAS model, the security manager is the root process that may check permissions to determine if the principal has access to the system resource. JAAS is the specification that is now part of using the JDK 1.4, and the access is no longer dependent on the operating system. Listing 19-8 demonstrates the subject requesting permission to access a privileged action using the doAs method. Listing 19-15 demonstrates the privileged action.

Listing 19-15: The `JAASAction` class: A privileged action example

```
package com.richware.chap19;

import java.security.*;
import java.util.*;
import javax.security.auth.*;
import javax.security.auth.login.*;
import javax.security.auth.x500.*;
import java.io.*;

/**
 * Class JAASAction
 * Description: This is a Sample PrivilegedAction implementation
 * to read the secretinfo.txt file.
 *
 * Copyright:    Copyright (c) 2002 Wiley Publishing, Inc.
 * @author Rich Helton <rhelton@richware.com>
 * @version 1.0
 * DISCLAIMER: Please refer to the disclaimer at the beginning of this
book.
 */
public class JAASAction implements PrivilegedAction
{
  /**
    * Method run
    * Description: Run the printing of secret info
```

```
 *
 *
 * @return the running object
 *
 */
public Object run()
{
  try
   {
     printSecretText();
     return this;

     /*
      * Catches
      */
   }
  catch (Exception ex)
   {
     ex.printStackTrace();
   }

  return null;
}

/**
 * Method printSecretText
 * Description: Print the secret text from a file
 */
public void printSecretText()
{
  try
   {
     FileReader in   = new FileReader("secretinfo.txt");
     char[]     buff = new char[ 50];
     int        nch;
     while ((nch = in.read(buff, 0, buff.length)) != -1)
      {
        System.out.println(buff);
      }
     in.close();
   }
  catch (Exception ex)
   {
     ex.printStackTrace();
   }
 }
}
```

Listing 19-15 demonstrates the privileged action that is called in the JAAS application from Listing 19-8. The privileged action is called privileged because any time that a system resource is being accessed, the security manager does a permission lookup to see if the principal has the required permissions. In the example in Listing 19-15, no system is accessed until the read of the file `secretinfo.txt`. The `secretinfo.txt` file is a system resource.

When accessing a file, the permission `java.io.FilePermission` must be defined for the principal. An operation must also be defined for the permission. The read action on the `secretinfo.txt` file must be specified for access to read the file. Listing 19-12 gave the `X500Principal` access for all permissions, so the alias for `richh` may read the file. If the principal does not match the user in this case, then the principal will have no access to system resources. Figure 19-3 gives a sequence overview of the subject and privileged action.

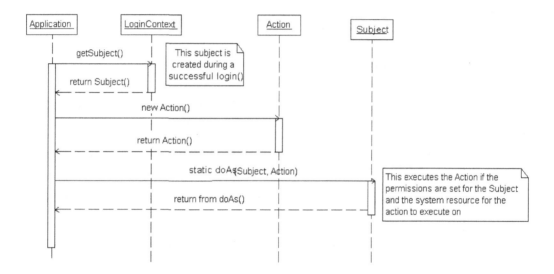

Figure 19-3: Java Authorization Class interaction

Understanding the subject

To understand the how to implement a subject, a configuration identifying the resources that must be accessed by the principal must be defined. If no principal is explicitly defined, then it is implicit that all principals have access to the permission set. To use the subject for accessing the system resource, the security manager must be defined. To explicitly use a particular subject, the `Subject`'s class `doAs()` and `doAsPrivileged()` methods can be used to execute a privileged action. Once a subject is instantiated and authenticated, it provides the facilities to store a set of principals, private credentials, and public credentials.

Principals and credentials

After a user logs in to a system, a name is attached to the user, and each specific name attached to the subject as identification is a *principal*. A *credential* is a token for security access, such as a password or Kerberos certificate. The principal is the name of the subject trying to access a system resource, and the credential is the security token for verifying that subject's principal. A single subject to authenticate and authorize through multiple authentication mechanisms and authorization systems may use multiple principals and credentials. In an enterprise system, the subject may be passed through many authorization systems.

The credential can be either public or private key type. The key is a private key for the *private credential*, and for the *public credential*, the key acts like a public key. Credentials are a security token associated with a principal meant to give the user access to the resource. Credentials may include passwords, Kerberos tickets, and data related to authentication throughout the system. The subject only becomes a principal after a successful authentication into the system. The subject also maintains a set of principals because a user might take on many names throughout an enterprise system on the different tiers of authentication.

Initiating and caller principals

These resources cannot only be static, such as a file, but also dynamic such as a running process. The *initiating principal* can be turned over to a *caller principal*. An example of an initiating principal is when a user logs in to an e-commerce system. An example of the caller principal is when a principal is trying to access a system resource. In some cases, these principals may be the same, but in others they may be different.

An example of when they are different is when a customer logs in to a Web site but needs to access the database to get his or her record. The customer does not have access to most organizations' databases directly, so the customer is masked as a user that has the rights to the database for access. The customer, in this case, is the initiating principal and the user that has the access to the database is the caller principal. The caller principal could be a role or group that the customer is assigned to once he is authenticated.

Groups

A *group* refers to a subject containing a set of principals that are managed equally. The group could be an identity that contains multiple identities. The reason for the group concept is because the access across the system may change from resource to resource, and it is difficult to set the accesses to each resource individually.

Therefore, when a set of principals is created, each principal in the set is managed in the same way. The principal is a named identifier of groups and users to authorize a system resource. A principal can be a user, group, computer resource, or a computer component. Figure 19-4 shows a diagram of the Java subject.

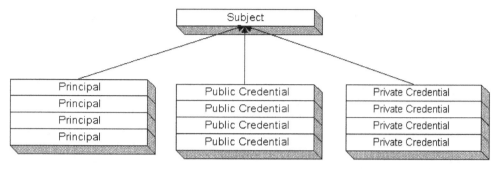

Figure 19-4: The Java subject

As mentioned, principals can be people, organizations, daemon threads, or even smart cards. Once a principal is established in a subject, the principal's name is immutable, meaning it cannot change once initialized. Using the subject's principal and credential sets can further authorize and authenticate throughout multiple systems. Figure 19-5 demonstrates these concepts with an extended Java subject.

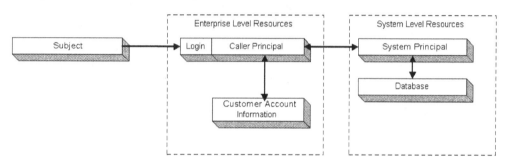

Figure 19- 5: The Java subject extended

Many different classes of principals and credentials come distributed in the JDK 1.4. Some of these principals, like the `NTUserPrincipal`, are specific to the WinNT operating system. Others, like the `X500Principal`, are specific for support of a protocol, in this case the X.500 Directory Protocol. Many of these can be found in the `com.sun.security.auth` package.

Understanding groups

Because there could be many users accessing a system, in some systems thousands and even hundreds of thousands, it can be very time consuming to manage the users individually, so groups are needed. A *group* is a set of users that have the same permissions. Groups allows many principals to be associated with a set of permissions and associated system resources.

For instance, if an administrator wants to give access to many users at once, the administrator creates a group that consists of all the users. Since a group itself is a principal, groups can present a hierarchy of principals, meaning that one of the entries in a group can be another group. The concept of hierarchical groups makes it possible for some "user" groups to belong to an admin group. The group class is defined in java.security.acl.Group as shown in Figure 19-6.

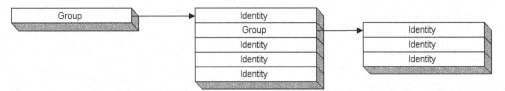

Figure 19-6: The Java group

Understanding permissions

The java.security.acl.Permission class is an abstract class representing a system resource and the desired actions for the system resource. For instance, a subject might want to access a file resource and read from it, so the action would be a read, and the system resource would be a particular file. However, system resources can have a wide range of actions, and they can vary based on the system resource. For example, a file could be executed using the execute permission, but a Socket doesn't understand what execute means.

There are many extensions to the base Permission class, specific to a system resource, to ensure that the appropriate actions and other attributes, such as how files are named, are associated with the correct permission. Some of these permissions are for File, Socket, Property, Runtime, AWT, Net, Security, Serializable, and Reflection classes. An association for a permission is also between the resource type, operation, and resource name. Listing 19-16 shows a permission association allowing the user's home directory to be read.

Listing 19-16: A permission entry

```
//Allow the user's home directory to be read
permission java.io.FilePermission "${user.home} /-", "read";
```

Listing 19-16 demonstrates a java.io.FilePermission. The file permission has the actions of read, write, execute, and delete. FilePermission formats for naming the file information is platform dependent. Listing 19-16 specifies the macro for the user.home in a UNIX format. Some of the Permission classes from Java exist in the following formats:

♦ java.security.BasicPermission. This is the permission base class for most of the Permission classes, such as SocketPermission, PropertyPermission, RuntimePermission, AWTPermission, and others. It extends the Permission class to include actions and simply allows or blocks permission. There are no other operations for the permission to support.

♦ java.net.SocketPermission. Actions are accept, listen, connect, and resolve. This class represents access to the network through the socket API. The access is dependent on the host name, through a DNS name, or an IP address is specified with the range of port numbers. The port or port range is optional. The following example gives access for connection to a client and accepting connections from a server for the local machine for the port 1024 and above:

```
//Allow the user's home directory to be read
permission java.net.SocketPermission "localhost:1024/-",
"connect,accept";
```

- ◆ `java.util.PropertyPermission`. Actions are read and write. This class provides access for getting local or system properties defined in the environment. Access can be denied for the read permission, for the `System.getProperty` method, and write permission, for the `System.setProperty` method. An example to grant the user `testUser` the read permission for the `java.home` directory is as follows:

```
grant codebase "file:./sample_action.jar",
 Principal SamplePrincipal "testUser" {

  permission java.util.PropertyPermission "java.home", "read";
};
```

- ◆ `java.lang.RuntimePermission`. There are no actions in this policy. There are no target names involved because you either have the permissions or you do not. In the following example, the first entry shows accessing the specified package name "*", meaning any package, via a class loader's `loadClass` method. The second entry shows accessing all declared members of a class. The third field gives access to create a class loader. The last field can be a large security risk because it gives the applications the capability to load their own rogue class loaders that, in turn, can load their own rogue classes into the system.

```
grant codebase "file:./sample_action.jar",
 Principal SamplePrincipal "testUser" {
  permission java.lang.RuntimePermission "accessClassInPackage.*";
  permission java.lang.RuntimePermission "accessDeclaredMembers.*";
  permission java.lang.RuntimePermission "createClassLoader";
};
```

- ◆ `java.awt.AWTPermission`. There are no actions in this policy. It gives the user to a specific AWT resource, such as accessing the Clipboard. The following example grants the user `testUser` access to the event queue and Clipboard:

```
Grant codebase "file:./sample_action.jar",
 Principal SamplePrincipal "testUser" {
  permission java.awt.AWTPermission "accessClipboard";
  permission java.awt.AWTPermission "accessEventQueue";
};
```

- ◆ `java.security.SecurityPermission`. There are no actions; the following example shows how `SecurityPermission` is used:

```
Grant codebase "file:./sample_action.jar",
 Principal SamplePrincipal "testUser" {
```

```
permission java.security.SecurityPermission "getPolicy";
permission java.security.SecurityPermission "setPolicy";
};
```

♦ `java.lang.reflect.ReflectionPermission`. This is the `Permission` class
for reflective operations that are part of introspection. *Introspection* is the capability of a
class to examine itself to understand what type of object it belongs in and get data based
on its members. There are no targets because it gives access to all classes or it does not.
There are also no actions because all that exists is the `Permission` descriptor to give
all access in the `suppressAccessChecks` or not to give all access. This policy could
be a security risk as it no longer relies on the classes' encapsulation and gives access for
reflective programs to access protected and private members. Here is an example:

```
grant codebase "file:./sample_action.jar",
 Principal SamplePrincipal "testUser" {
  permission java.lang.reflect.ReflectPermission "suppressAccessChecks";
};
```

♦ `java.security.AllPermission`. This `Permission` class gives all or no access to
a user. The following example gives the user `testUser` all permissions:

```
Grant codebase "file:./sample_action.jar",
 Principal SamplePrincipal "testUser" {
  permission java.security.AllPermission;
};
```

♦ `java.security.AuthPermission`. This `Permission` class gives all
authentications or no authentication to a user. The following lines give the user
`testUser` all permissions:

```
Grant codebase "file:./sample action.jar",
 Principal SamplePrincipal "testUser" {
   permission javax.security.auth.AuthPermission
"createLoginContext.Sample";
   permission javax.security.auth.AuthPermission "doAs";
};
```

Understanding ACLs

The DAC model has also been enhanced over the years, from the structure of UNIX files and
directories. The Java 2 security manager model implements the DAC model and is a standard
interface shipped with the JDK v1.4. The DAC model can further store entries outside of
configuration files in the form of *Access Control Lists* (ACL). The ACL is a data structure for
security objects, such as the ones mentioned earlier (permissions, groups, and principals).

So far, the discussion has been centered on the security policy file that stores the principal,
permissions, and resource entries. The ACL data structure can form relationships with other
permission sets, groups, principals, and resources. The ACL is a named object that represents
the system resource. Because this model is very generic, it can easily suit access control
requirements for any system.

Each `ACL` has a list of `AclEntry` objects. An `AclEntry` associates an implemented principal, such as `NTUserPrincipal` having the name of `rich`, with a permission object, such as read. Permissions normally have a plus sign associated with them to allow the permission and a minus sign to deny permissions. The `AclEntry` accommodates this by having a boolean flag set to true if it is a negative, or minus, permission. Figure 19-7 demonstrates the Java `ACL` and `AclEntry` objects.

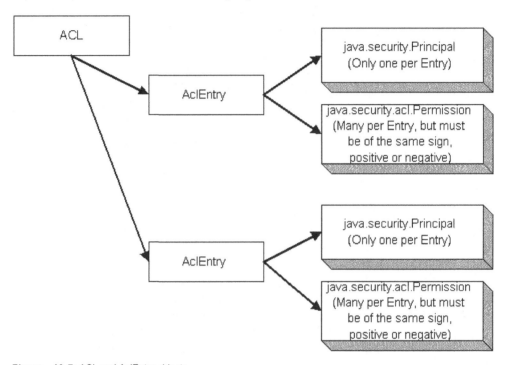

Figure 19-7: ACL and AclEntry objects

The ACL and its associated `AclEntry` lists have several objects that have relationships. These relationships can be formed in a relational database of the LDAP server. The advantages of this architecture include its relationship nature and the capability to decouple the individual objects from the list when needed. Storing these objects in a centralized area also promotes having all the security information, permissions, subjects, and resources in a centralized data store. An LDAP server is an implementation of an organization's security realm.

A *security realm* is the central location for storing information across an enterprise system. Figure 19-8 gives an example of a database relationship.

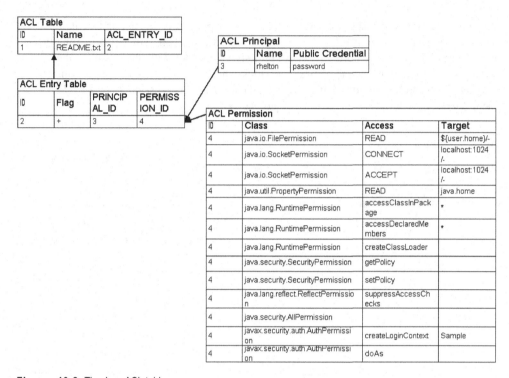

ACL Table

ID	Name	ACL_ENTRY_ID
1	README.txt	2

ACL Entry Table

ID	Flag	PRINCIPAL_ID	PERMISSION_ID
2	+	3	4

ACL Principal

ID	Name	Public Credential
3	rhelton	password

ACL Permission

ID	Class	Access	Target
4	java.io.FilePermission	READ	${user.home}/-
4	java.io.SocketPermission	CONNECT	localhost:1024 /-
4	java.io.SocketPermission	ACCEPT	localhost:1024 /-
4	java.util.PropertyPermission	READ	java.home
4	java.lang.RuntimePermission	accessClassInPackage	*
4	java.lang.RuntimePermission	accessDeclaredMembers	*
4	java.lang.RuntimePermission	createClassLoader	
4	java.security.SecurityPermission	getPolicy	
4	java.security.SecurityPermission	setPolicy	
4	java.lang.reflect.ReflectPermission	suppressAccessChecks	
4	java.security.AllPermission		
4	javax.security.auth.AuthPermission	createLoginContext	Sample
4	javax.security.auth.AuthPermission	doAs	

Figure 19-8: The Java ACL table

Using a table like the one in Figure 19-8 centralizes all the security resources in a centralized table. A centralized data store provides a convenient management facility with all security information in the same location and in the same form. Centralizing the security material into one location can help the user understand and modify the security resources more easily.

Summary

JAAS provides a set of specific implementations of authentication and authorization that can be changed without changing code. JAAS provides the ability to plug in different and stacked login modules to provide authentication mechanisms. Another important feature of the JAAS interface is the capability to use different interfaces for authentication and authorization.

An example is the `LoginModule` for Kerberos, which can use Kerberos keys and tickets for authentication while the authorization remains the same. To provide authentication, a subject is created that is used to further provide authorization. The authorization part of JAAS uses permissions, principals, and associated system resources to define how resources can be accessed. JAAS provides a common implementation and set of definitions when developing Java systems.

In the early networking days, it was very difficult for network engineers to communicate with each other about different protocols and extend an existing protocol because there was no common model that was protocol independent. The network OSI model was developed to supplement this type of communication. Chapter 21 mentions more on this subject, but the point is that a common model is needed to really make progress in a particular discipline in computer science. JAAS has created a common model for authentication and authorization in Java.

Part VI

Enterprise Data Security

Chapter 20: Working with Database Security

Chapter 20
Working with Database Security

In This Chapter

♦ Connecting to your database

♦ Learning about the requirements for JDBC and JDBC drivers

♦ Using the Connector API to connect to a database

♦ Understanding the need to encrypt your data at the database level

Applications typically divide their functionality across multiple tiers, each of which has a specific purpose. This division makes it easier to understand and maintain an architecture that allows existing and future integration of different systems.

The J2EE environment divides these tiers into the Client tier, Web tier, the Enterprise JavaBeans tier, and the *Enterprise Information Systems tier* (EIS). The *Client tier* is where the user interacts with the J2EE application. The *Web tier* makes an application available on the World Wide Web.

The *Enterprise JavaBeans tier* provides portable, available, scalable access to data and business rules. EJB components reside in an EJB container that manages security, transactions, and concurrent data access.

The *Enterprise Information Systems tier* allows the J2EE application to integrate with other enterprise information systems such as databases, enterprise resource planning systems, and legacy systems. A discussion of the EIS tier is beyond the scope of this book. This chapter addresses database security, however, because it is an integral security need of an enterprise solution.

> **CROSS-REFERENCE:** The Client and Web tiers are addressed in Chapter 27. The Enterprise JavaBeans tier is discussed in Chapter 28.

Introduction

The access of database systems can be divided into two types:

♦ **EIS-tier databases:** Database systems that are accessed via the Java DataBase Connectivity (JDBC) API.

♦ **Non-EIS-tier databases:** Database systems that are not accessed via the JDBC API. These databases are accessed via the vendor's proprietary protocols and APIs, the J2EE Connector Extensions, or CORBA.

Relational Database Management Systems (RDBMS) are typically used for enterprise data storage, and many providers use either JDBC 2.0 or 3.0 APIs. JDBC has two parts: a *client-level* API (to access the RDBMS) and a *standard system-level* contract for connection pooling and transaction implementation used by the vendors. The standard system-level API, in JDBC 3.0, is the same as the Connector architecture system contracts.

Connecting Your Database through JDBC

JDBC drivers enable clients to perform database connections, database queries, stored procedures, and other operations. JDBC drivers implement the JDBC API that allows for the interaction to the database server. Sun has divided the JDBC drivers into four types: 1, 2, 3, and 4. Types 1 (JDBC-ODBC bridge) and 2 (JDBC-Native API) use additional software, such as a C dynamic link library, that needs to be installed on the client. Types 3 (100% Java JDBC-Network) and 4 (100% Java) are Java implementations that do not require additional software installations. Figure 20-1 shows the difference among the different types of JDBC drivers.

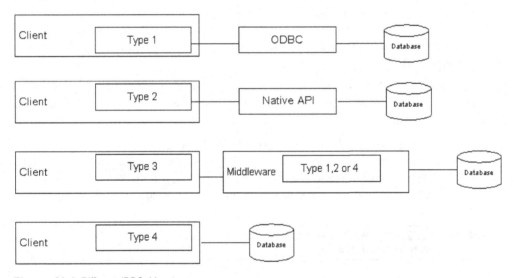

Figure 20-1: Different JDBC driver types

Getting a connection to a database resource (and for that matter, any resource) is called a *resource sign-on*. The user requests a connection, which is established based on that user's *security context*. As you may recall, the security context has information such as the user's authorization level and access rights. The application provider can choose to let the container manage the database sign-on or may choose to manage it at the application code. Regardless of which you choose, the following three steps are performed:

1. Obtain a JNDI context.
2. Obtain a connection factory using a JNDI lookup.
3. Obtain a connection through the factory.

Using the *container-managed sign-on* allows principals to be mapped across security domains and adds flexibility to the process. The deployer sets up the resource sign-on and user authorization and authentication information required for database access. Listing 20-1 shows the steps to follow, and Listing 20-2 shows the deployment descriptor for container-managed sign-on.

Listing 20-1: Container-managed sign-on

```
// Step 1. Obtain a JNDI context.
  Context ctx = new InitialContext();

// Step 2. Obtain a connection factory using a JNDI lookup.
javax.sql.DataSource ds = (javax.sql.DataSource) ctx.lookup(
    theDatabaseJNDIname);

// Step 3. Obtain a connection through the factory.
// Note: The deployer gives the security information so you
//       do not need to pass it in.
java.sql.Connection dbcx = ds.getConnection();
```

Listing 20-2: Deployment descriptor for container-managed sign-on

```
<resource-ref>
 <description>description</description>
 <res-ref-name>jdbc/MyDatabase</res-ref-name>
 <res-type>javax.sql.DataSource</res-type>
 <res-auth>Container</res-auth>
</resource-ref>
```

Using the *application-managed sign-on* means that you must implement the resource sign-on at the code level. The difference is in step 3: You pass in the security information at the connection request method of the `javax.sql.DataSource`. Listing 20-3 shows an example for application-managed sign-on.

Listing 20-3: Application-managed sign-on

```
// Step 1. Obtain a JNDI context.
Context ctx = new InitialContext();

// Step 2. Obtain a connection factory using a JNDI lookup.
```

```
javax.sql.DataSource ds = (javax.sql.DataSource)ctx.lookup(
    theDatabaseJNDIname);

// Step 3. Obtain a connection through the factory.
// Note: You need to pass in the the security info
java.sql.Connection dbcx = ds.getConnection(userName,userPsswrd);
```

NOTE: In Listing 20-3 the username and user password are passed as clear text. You probably want to secure your database connection, which can be done with SSL, cryptography, and digital signatures to enable privacy and authenticity of network communication.

In addition, you can control access to the application components declaratively or programmatically. When you use *declarative* access, you describe in a deployment descriptor the rights a user must have to access the methods or system data. You can use security roles to define the access of a user. When you *programmatically* control access, you check in your code whether the user has the proper rights to access the components. For instance, if you use EJBs, you can use `getCallerPrincipal` and `isCallerInRole` to get the caller's security context.

CROSS-REFERENCE: Chapters 27 and 28 demonstrate the use of the `getCallerPrincipal` and `isCallerInRole` methods.

The management of JDBC is typically performed by the `Driver` class. For security reasons, the JDBC management layer keeps track of the class loader provided by the driver. The `DriverManager` class keeps a list of `Driver` classes that have registered (by calling the `Driver.Manager.registerDriver`). A `Driver` class may do so by:

♦ explictly loading the driver class with a call to the `Class.forName` method.

Or

♦ the `DriverManager` class loads a list of class names from the `java.lang.System` property called `jdbc.driversfs`.

When the `DriverManager` class opens a connection, it uses only those drivers that come from the local file system or the same class loader as the code issuing the request for the connection.

TIP: When you select your database driver, make sure that it is a secure one that protects shared connections, file access, and meets your security needs.

Connecting Your Database through the Connector Architecture

The J2EE Connector API provides a generic framework to map data from *Enterprise Application Integration* (EAI) systems and EIS systems. A good site for information is the J2EE Connector architecture discussion in the `java.sun.com/j2ee/connector/` site, on which some of this discussion is based. Some of the benefits of the Connector API include *connection management*, *security management*, and *transaction management*. The J2EE Connector architecture defines the following three system-level contracts (between an application server and EIS):

♦ A *Connection Management contract*, which allows an application to have server pool connections — for reuse without the delay of connection instance allocation and deallocation — to an underlying EIS, and lets application components connect to an EIS.

♦ A *Transaction Management contract*, which lets an application server use a transaction manager to manage transactions across multiple resource managers. This contract also supports transactions that are managed internal to an EIS resource manager without the necessity of involving an external transaction manager. Data manipulation requires transactional integrity to ensure that rollbacks and commits can be supported, and so transaction management is important.

♦ A *Security contract,* which enables a secure access to an EIS. This contract provides support for a secure application environment to reduce security threats to the EIS.

The J2EE Connector architecture defines a *Common Client Interface* (CCI) for EIS access that defines a standard client API for application components. The purpose of the CCI is to provide a generic Connector implementation independent of the application server. This connection is not aware of the security management, the transaction management, or the connection management. Figure 20-2 shows where the CCI is used.

> **CAUTION:** Security management (as well as transaction and connection management) is not automatically provided for you just because you use the CCI.

In the example code of Listing 20-3, I used the JDBC `javax.sql.DataSource` and `java.sql.Connection` interfaces for database connections. The connection and connection factory are defined for the CCI with the interfaces `javax.resources.cci.ConnectionFactory` and `javax.resources.cci.Connection`. The `ConnectionFactory` creates (or finds in a pool) a `ManagedConnection` that has an associated transaction.

> **NOTE:** The Connector API does not define a standard format and requirements for security mechanisms for specific credentials, but it does offer a `GenericCredential` interface to wrap Kerberos credentials.

The authentication is specified in the `<authentication-mechanism-type>` tag of resource adapter's deployment descriptor, which allows the resource adapter to get the information about the credential. As with JDBC, the security context is propagated and principals are passed through the subject during the `getConnection`.

> **CROSS-REFERENCE:** Chapter 19 describes credential, principals, and subject concepts.

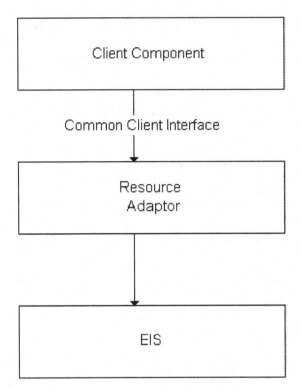

Figure 20-2: The Common Client Interface

As noted earlier, the communications between the EIS and the application server are subject to attacks. These threats include data modification and man-in-the-middle attacks. Therefore, securing the communication is important and can be done with SSL, and some EISs can support the GSS-API. The GSS-API is the *Generic Security Services Application Programming Interface*. The application server uses the `createManagedConnection` when it requests a resource adapter to create a new connection. It can pass in the subject by using either the application-managed sign-on (the application component passes the subject to the resource) or container-managed sign-on (application server fills in the subject).

A subject represents a grouping of related information for a single entity. This information includes the subject's identity, passwords, and cryptographic keys. A subject may have multiple identities, which are the principals within the subject. A subject may have credentials that are the security-related attributes; the sensitive credentials are stored within a credential set. Credential sets can be public (intended to be shared) or private.

For sign-on:

♦ The application server provides one-to-many `PasswordCredentials` in the `Subject` class. The resource adapter uses this information to sign on to the EIS. The

`PasswordCredentials` are set in the private credential set. The resource adapter extracts the username and password and uses this information for EIS sign-on.

♦ The application server provides one-to-many `GenericCredentials` in the `Subject` class. The resource adapter uses this information as private or public keys, which could be Kerberos keys. The resource adapter extracts these credentials, and if Kerberos is selected as the authentication mechanism type, it gets this information out of the private credential as Kerberos-based keys.

♦ By passing a null subject, the application server does not provide any security information. In this case the application component is responsible for the security. The security can be placed in a `ConnectionRequestInfo` for component information; however, the application server cannot read this information because the `ConnectionRequestInfo` is a data structure for the resource adapter to pass information for its own data in the connection request. If the resource adapter does not find information in the `ConnectionRequestInfo`, it uses the default security configuration.

> **CROSS-REFERENCE:** Chapter 16 discusses Kerberos. Chapter 17 discusses the GSS-API.

Securing Enterprise Data in the Database

Sometimes protecting the communication channel to the database is not enough, and you may want to protect the data in the database itself. You can accomplish this protection by encrypting the data. There are two possibilities: symmetric encryption and asymmetric encryption.

> **CROSS-REFERENCE:** Chapter 4, Chapter 12, and Chapter 13 discuss symmetric and asymmetric concepts.

Symmetric encryption uses a key stored in the application to access the database and its data. This way if the database itself is compromised, the information is not available. The main requirement for this type of database encryption is that the application itself is secured. If the application is compromised, the attacker is able to obtain the symmetric key to decrypt the data. *Asymmetric encryption* uses both public and private keys. You use this method when you need to protect your data from both the database and the application being compromised.

Using encryption is expensive — the data needs to be decrypted before it is processed. This removes some of the advantages of using a database, such as being able to use SQL statements to perform searches. Setting database permissions goes a long way to protect your data from undesired requests.

In addition, you have the option to create a read-only or write-only database. For instance, many online stores use write-only databases to store credit card information.

> **TIP:** You can establish levels of access in your database to prevent a user from accessing information that is restricted; a database *view* is commonly used for this. A view is a virtual relation that combines information from other relations.

The connection management to the database is frequently left to the application server. Chapter 29 presents some frequently used application servers and their security.

Summary

This chapter addressed the need to secure your enterprise data. There are basically two ways to accomplish this: Secure the connection and secure your data at the source. Depending on your needs, you can implement either or both of these methods.

Securing the connection involves ensuring that the data is not modified or compromised in transit. There are two mechanisms that you can use to connect to your database: JDBC and the Connector architecture. Actually, the mechanisms to secure the connection are the same: Let the container manage the connection or manage the connection at the application level. These connections can be established using SSL, and you have the option to use Kerberos-based authentication.

Securing your data at the source involves making sure that your database is secure against break-ins. You can accomplish this by encrypting your data at the database level — denying access to certain data by creating a read- or write-only database. In addition, setting and managing the permissions at the database system is an important security step to prevent your data from being compromised.

Part VII

Network Access

Chapter 21: Network Security Architecture

Chapter 22: SSL and TLS

Chapter 23: Java Secure Socket Extension

Chapter 21
Network Security Architecture

In This Chapter

- ◆ Understanding network security
- ◆ Learning about network concepts such as IP addresses, TCP and UDP, and routing
- ◆ Understanding firewalls
- ◆ Learning about DMZs
- ◆ Discovering the OSI model
- ◆ Working with Java Sockets

Using networks as a security measure is a common practice to protect the organization at a network level of security that can be applied over and over again throughout the organization. The security level involves selected hardware, software, and internally developed programs to monitor and manipulate packets. Blocking packets that appear questionable can keep hackers at bay. However, various organizations that I have consulted for have come to the realization, over and over again, that the only guarantee to ensure that attackers will never enter an organization is to simply cut the network cable from the organization to the Internet. Some highly visible organizations have done that to ensure their privacy. However, not being connected to the Internet does limit an organization's effectiveness in doing business.

Even today, when many organizations are connected to the Internet, there is very little understanding of using network security to understand and block questionable packets. Some organizations have network engineers that truly understand TCP/IP at a network level, but very few can afford the expense of having developers who can develop customization to ensure a strong security image. Many organizations solve these issues through third-party software and hardware. However, inexperienced engineers who administrate the third-party devices incorrectly can limit the usefulness of these devices.

There have been many incidents when hundreds of thousands of dollars have been spent on third-party devices and a very minimally skilled person has set them up. Later it is discovered that some of the updates or security features were never turned on. It is just as important to have someone who truly understands networking develop the perimeters of an organization as it is to have quality equipment. A discussion of security is intrinsically coupled with networks and network security. This chapter introduces concepts of networking and network security to provide a basis for future chapters. It discusses the importance of protocols and how they manage security, the importance of the OSI model, and it includes a section on Java Sockets along with Java source code to aid in the understanding and implementation of the discussed concepts.

Understanding Network Security

To understand network security, you need to understand networking. Networks provide a means to transport packets either by *Local Area Network* (LAN), *Metropolitan Area Network* (MAN), or *Wide Area Network* (WAN). For the purpose of most security discussions, security can easily be broken down into the organization's *enterprise domain* and the Internet. The organization's enterprise domain is a LAN because it is local to the organization's internal users, and the organization's enterprise domain is a WAN to the users who are not trying to access the organization's domain locally. If users only need to access the domain locally, the only security issue is the trust it places in those users because external connections to the LAN can be prohibited.

The LAN for the organization usually contains a single domain. If more domains are registered for the organization, there are more LANs for that organization. Many services operate a LAN, such as FTP, Telnet, and *Domain Name Service* (DNS); through the years, protocols have been established to specify how these services communicate with each other. These services manage the domain and they know how to interpret the various packets from the network based on the connection information and data in the packet. These services act as listeners on the remote machine to accept connections from a client. A *client* is a process that wishes to start the communication, such as a user starting an FTP session to move files. The *service* is the process to retain the files and accept the communication if it believes that the client matches the protocol.

Network Concepts Overview

This section provides a brief overview of some network protocols; many books and RFCs are maintained on the subject. Many protocols have had security issues because messages can be piggybacked and protocol services can be faked out into doing something insecure. There is no shame in having a system compromised; the difficulty arises when a system is broken into and no one knows about it. In addition, network protocols provide very important aspects of security; for example, knowing how a packet is transmitted inside a LAN from an outside source is valuable information to determine if the packet is valid, and whether the packet should be stored locally (in a trusted domain). The next sections provide information on some basic concepts and prepare you for the more advanced topics addressed later in this chapter, which are building blocks to subsequent chapters on network security.

IP addresses

The *IP address* is the logical address of a specific machine based on the format of the Internet Protocol. The IP address is based on a subnet mask; it is this mask that specifies what parts of the address are viable for use. The *subnet mask* can tell the routers which IP addresses make up the segment or LAN. For instance, using 255.255.255.0 tells the router and machine that all addresses except the last digit live on the same segment. So addresses 169.169.169.0 through 169.169.169.255 make up the same segment. The router keeps a routing table. The router uses the routing table to direct all packets to the available machines under the router's segment.

NOTE: Recall that there are different classes of network addresses: A, B, C, D, and E. The first four bits of an address identify the class as follows:

Class A has initial bits 0xxx

Class B has initial bits 10xx

Class C has initial bits 110x

Class D has initial bits 1110

Class E has initial bits 1111

Organizations with classes A and B, typically, have complex networks. These networks use *subnets* to partition the address space in a convenient manner and the size of the subnet is the responsibility of the organization that owns that part of the address. In order for routers and hosts to recognize the subnet the *subnet mask* parameter is used.

Figure 21-1 shows two LANs with routers and using IP addresses.

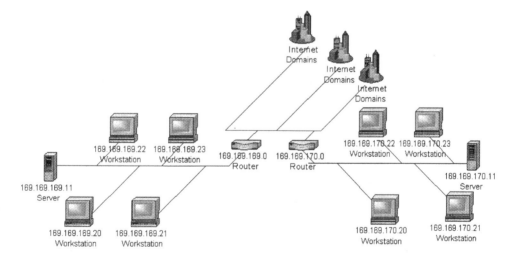

Figure 21-1: Two LANs by address

These address segments are not arbitrarily assigned. The Network Information Center, which registers protocol ports, IP addresses, and domains for the Internet, also registers these addresses. Although IP addresses accurately describe the relationships within the domain, their format is problematic for administrators and users. To overcome this limitation, the domain and resources within the domain can be managed using a DNS.

The purpose of DNS is to resolve a human-readable address to an IP address for specific machines; these human-to-machine mappings are entered through the DNS's services table. This adds another layer of logical names to the addresses. Figure 21-2 shows how the introduction of DNS names affects the two LANs from Figure 21-1; each workstation now has a logical name, there is a DNS server, and the DNS table maps the logical names to the address.

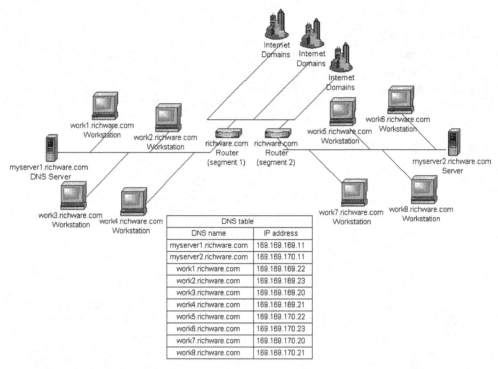

DNS table	
DNS name	IP address
myserver1.richware.com	169.169.169.11
myserver2.richware.com	169.169.170.11
work1.richware.com	169.169.169.22
work2.richware.com	169.169.169.23
work3.richware.com	169.169.169.20
work4.richware.com	169.169.169.21
work5.richware.com	169.169.170.22
work6.richware.com	169.169.170.23
work7.richware.com	169.169.170.20
work8.richware.com	169.169.170.21

Figure 21-2: Two LANs by domain name

The creation of DNS tables simplifies the process of looking for a particular machine and knowing the logical topology for humans. The network does not understand these tables until they are resolved through the DNS. Until that point, the packets are still transported through their IP addresses from a source to a destination. The IP header that contains the addresses is a wrapper for the higher layer protocol, such as *Transmission Control Protocol* (TCP) and *User Datagram Protocol* (UDP).

Figure 21-3 shows the structure of an *IP packet*. The packet is an individual unit of data that is being transmitted. These units of work contain many more protocols; the protocols identify how the data is to be sent across the networks. The packet across the network takes the form of an IP packet. An IP packet contains information that makes the delivery possible, such as the destination (the IP address to send the packet to) and the source (the IP address that sent the packet). Many of the other fields in an IP packet describe the packet metadata information, such as packet size, IP version, and time before the packet times out (the TTL, or Time To Live). The IP packet is normally created in a device driver; the device driver knows that it will be using IP to communicate across the Internet.

NOTE: The data packaged in the IP packet is normally another packet, such as a TCP or UDP packet.

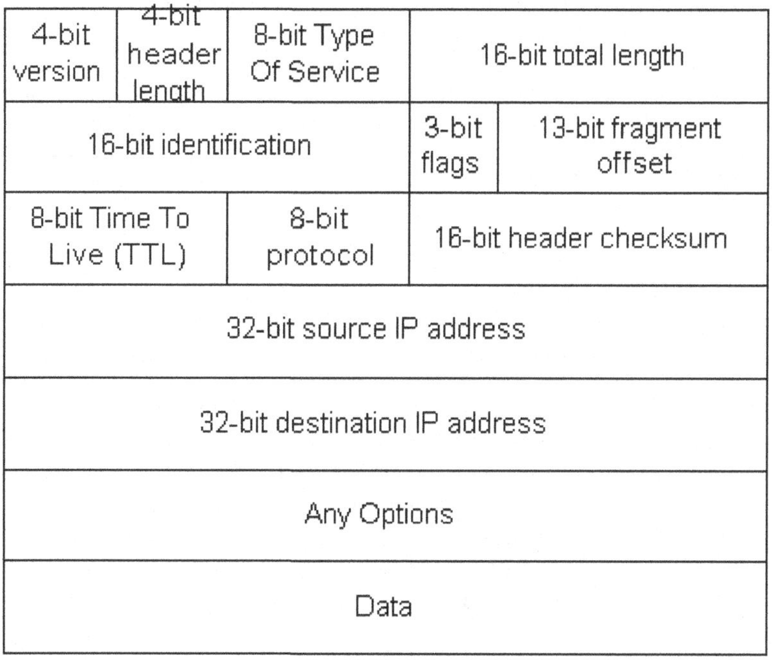

4-bit version	4-bit header length	8-bit Type Of Service	16-bit total length	
16-bit identification			3-bit flags	13-bit fragment offset
8-bit Time To Live (TTL)		8-bit protocol	16-bit header checksum	
32-bit source IP address				
32-bit destination IP address				
Any Options				
Data				

Figure 21-3: IP packet

An IP packet contains an IP address that is a logical address for routing the IP packets. This is not a physical address, but one configured for the machine's and the network's configuration. In fact, the *MAC* address, which is part of the network card used for a physical connection, is the closest thing to a physical address. The network card's manufacturer assigns the MAC addresses, which must contain different numbers. The networks are connected in tree-like segments, where the router moves packets based on the destination address. A *network topology* is the mapping of machine addresses. Figures 21-2 and 21-3 give examples of network topologies.

Although I have discussed how addresses are resolved for a given packet, I have not tackled the port number and its resolution. The *port* is the location of the service on the machine. The *port number* is a logical location for the connection of that process.

TIP: Recall that many port numbers are protocol specific. The *Internet Assigned Numbers Authority* (IANA) (`ftp://ftp.isi.edu/in-notes/iana/assigments/port-numbers`) provides a list of port numbers assignments. There are three types:

Well-known ports that are ports in the range of 0 through 1023, which are controlled and assigned by IANA. Examples of well-known ports are port 21 for Telnet, port 21 for FTP, port 80 for HTTP, port 53 for DNS, and port 443 for SSL.

Registered ports that are ports in the range of 1024 through 49151. These ports are not controlled by IANA but they are registered with it.

Private ports that are ports in the range of 49152 through 65535. These ports are not controlled or registered with IANA.

Protocols use tables that can usually be found in a services file. The port numbers are not part of the IP packet, so they must be part of the packet that the IP wraps, such as TCP and UDP.

NOTE: All ports below 1024 are predefined to match a protocol.

TCP and UDP

TCP is normally referred to as a connection-oriented protocol. In contrast, because UDP is used for broadcasting and multicasting, and a full connection is not required for the sending and receiving of packages, *UDP* is normally referred to as a connectionless protocol.

A typical use of UDP is a stock ticker, where a service broadcasts stock information but there is no guarantee by the protocol that the message is received. Figure 21-4 shows the structure of a UDP packet; you can see that the UDP packet is simple and straightforward. It contains a source port and destination port, a checksum to ensure the integrity of the data, the length of the data, and the data itself. There is no guarantee in what sequence the data will come in. It could be that the start of the stream arrives after the middle of the stream. For the example of a stock ticker, each stock should be a separate and independent packet.

16-bit source port number	16-bit destination port number
16-bit UDP Length	16-bit UDP Checksum
Any Data	

Figure 21-4: UDP packet

NOTE: Recall that a connection-oriented protocol provides a reliable communication between the end points such as a file transfer over TCP. The term *connectionless* refers to a protocol or communication that does not establish a reliable, long-term relationship between the client and server.

The *TCP packet* is a bit more complex because the protocol itself guarantees the delivery. There are six 1-bit flags that help with fulfilling the connection. The flags of the TCP packet are very important, as explained in the following list:

♦ The URG flag means that the urgent pointer is in use. If the URG flag is set, then the data is interpreted to be urgent. The pointer is a positive offset and is added to the sequence number field to give the last byte of urgent data.

♦ When set, the SYN flag (which stands for synchronize) means that the packet is an initial connection. The service will reply with the ACK set and SYN set saying that it has acknowledged the connection.

♦ When ACK is set, it is acknowledging that something has been sent. When 1024 bytes are received and there is no issue, the response is 1024 bytes in the acknowledge number and ACK set. This can happen both from the client and the service because TCP is full duplex, meaning that both sides can send data. If the next sequence is 2049, missing the sequence 1025-2048, the ACK will not be sent because it is out of sequence. The receiver waiting for the 1025-2048 acknowledgements will resend the data until the correct sequence is received or the service has timed out. When both ACK and SYN are set, the protocol knows that this is the beginning of a data packet defined for that protocol. For the HTTP protocol, the service looks for the beginning of the HTTP header in the data.

♦ The PSH flag tells the receiver to push all available data and to avoid buffering the data.

♦ The RST, or reset flag, resets the receiving connection because there could be errors in the connection.

♦ The FIN, or finish flag, means that all data has been sent.

The window size is the number of bytes that can be sent to the receiver beyond the bytes being acknowledged. This byte count is not the total number of bytes allowed in this field, but the number of bytes allowed on top of the acknowledged size; this is the reason why that number needs to be added to the acknowledged size. Figure 21-5 shows a TCP packet.

A *socket* or connection refers to the combination of port number and IP address. The term "socket" is a semaphore to a power cord connecting into a wall socket. A *socket pair* refers to the combination of port number and IP address pairs for both source and destination. It is called a socket pair because it connects at both ends. The term *Sockets* commonly refers to the socket wrapped into an API. Up to this point, the transportation and the protocol headers managed the data.

The content of the data, besides size and checksum, is really unknown to the lower protocols. The lower protocols' responsibility is to transport data reliably regardless of what the data contains.

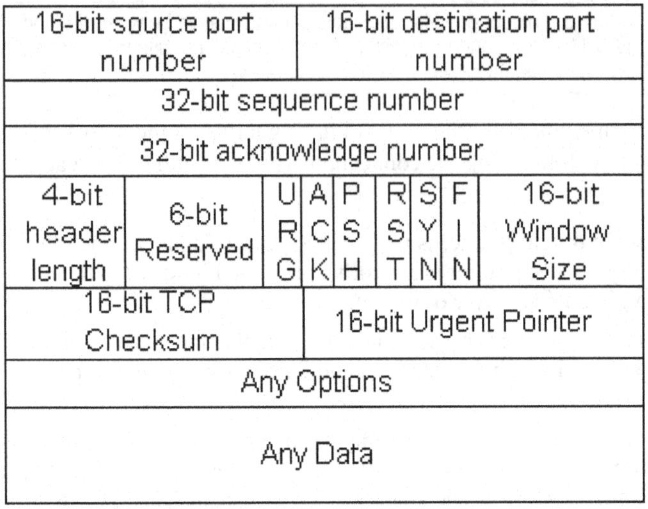

16-bit source port number	16-bit destination port number						
32-bit sequence number							
32-bit acknowledge number							
4-bit header length	6-bit Reserved	URG	ACK	PSH	RST	SYN	FIN	16-bit Window Size
16-bit TCP Checksum	16-bit Urgent Pointer						
Any Options							
Any Data							

Figure 21-5: TCP packet

The lower protocols handle the data generically and some of the packetizing of the data is handled at the device-driver level communicating directly to the network card. To communicate to the device driver, the developer uses the Socket API; this API provides a standard way to specify whether the protocol is UDP or TCP, which ports and addresses to use, and to translate the data into the protocol.

The Open Systems Interconnection (OSI) has developed a model to show the different protocols that wrap the network transportation of data. Figure 21-6 shows the OSI model and demonstrates that there are several protocols that wrap the data from the physical network.

The hardware also follows standards such as the *Carrier Sense Multiple Access/ Carrier Detection* (CSMA/CD) protocol. The CSMA/CD listens for a carrier signal on the wire, and if one is not there, it believes that the wire is clear to send a packet. If a collision happens while sending a signal, it is re-sent.

From this point, a packet contains Ethernet frames to signal the beginning and end of digital data and to indicate whether collision signals are detected at signal thresholds. The digital data is the IP information that wraps either TCP or UDP, and the devices will unwrap the protocol (either TCP or UDP) based on the protocol header.

The protocol header is defined in the wrapped IP. If the TCP header is used, the device driver knows to respond to the connection and to guarantee the delivery; otherwise, if the header is UDP, the device driver will know not to respond. The device driver and underlying layers may communicate to the protocol services through the socket API. The Socket API is supported in Java in the `java.net` package.

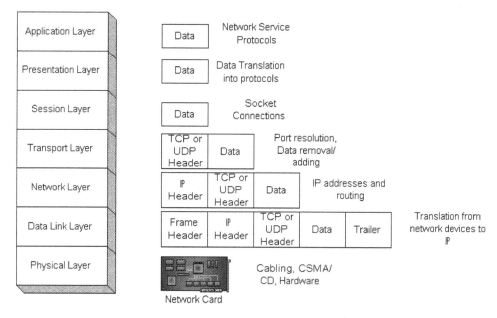

Figure 21-6: The OSI model

Listing 21-1 gives the `SocketServer` example: a typical example of a listener that receives a connection, sends some data, and prints what it receives. The start of the work can be seen in the `ServerSocket` initialization. The initialization in the `LOCAL_ONLY` block shows a listener being created to receive connections only from the local machine. The other initialization receives connections from any machine on port 2000. The `accept()` method waits for the client to connect to the listener and returns a reference to the client socket to read and write as a stream. This sample will create a thread to read and write to the client socket.

Listing 21-1: The `SocketServer` class: A socket listener example

```
package com.richware.chap21;

import java.io.*;
import java.net.*;

/**
 * Class SocketServer
 * Description: Demonstrates a listener for connections.
 *
 * Copyright:    Copyright (c) 2002 Wiley Publishing, Inc.
 * @author Rich Helton rhelton@richware.com
 * @version 1.0
 * DISCLAIMER: Please refer to the disclaimer at the beginning of this
book.
```

```
*/
public class SocketServer extends Thread {
  protected Socket socket;

  /**
   * Port number is set to 2000 to avoid the protocols below 1024.
   */
  final static int PORT_NUM = 2000;

  /**
   * True to only accept connections from the local machine.
   */
  final static boolean LOCAL_ONLY = false;

  /**
   * Constructor SocketServer
   * Description: Creates a new Server for Sockets.
   *
   * @param socket, the client socket to run.
   */
  SocketServer(Socket socket) {
    this.socket = socket;
  }

  /**
   * Method run
   * Description: A thread to send some data and read a response.
   *
   */
  public void run() {
    try {
      /**
       * For exiting the server
       */
      boolean isExit = false;
      /**
       * The in receives the data from the client
       */
      InputStream in = socket.getInputStream();
      /**
       * The out sends the data to the client
       */
      OutputStream out = socket.getOutputStream();
      System.out.println("Sending Some Data...");
      out.write("Send Some Data\r\n".getBytes());
      byte[] buffer = new byte[1024];

      int    read;
      while (((read = in.read(buffer)) >= 0) && !isExit) {
```

```
            String readString = new String(buffer);
          System.out.println("Read Data:" + new String(buffer));
          /**
           * Reset the contents of the buffer
           */
          for(int i = 0; i < 1024; i++){
             buffer[ i] = 0;
          }
          if(readString.equalsIgnoreCase("Exit")){
             isExit = true;
          }
          System.out.println("Exiting Client Connection");
       }
    } catch (IOException ex) {
          ex.printStackTrace();
    } finally {
       try {
          socket.close();
       } catch (IOException ignored) {}
    }
}

/**
 * Method main
 *
 *
 * @param args the standard arguments for a main driver.
 *
 * @throws IOException to propagate from the any IO exceptions for
sockets.
 *
 */
public static void main(String[] args) throws IOException {
    ServerSocket server = null;
    System.out.println("Starting SocketServer....");

    /**
     * If local, only receive connections from the local host
     */
    if (LOCAL_ONLY) {
       InetAddress address = InetAddress.getLocalHost();
       server = new ServerSocket(PORT_NUM, 10, address);
    } else {
       server = new ServerSocket(PORT_NUM);
    }
    System.out.println("SocketServer Listening....");
    while (true) {
       System.out.println("Waiting for Connection....");
       /**
```

```
     * Accept a new client
     */
    Socket client = server.accept();
    /**
     * Start the current class;
     */
    SocketServer socketServer = new SocketServer(client);
    /**
     * Start the Thread
     */
    socketServer.start();
    }
  }
}
```

Listing 21-2 shows a corresponding SocketClient example that creates the connection to the awaiting listener. It needs to know the port number and address of the listener for the connection.

Listing 21-2: The SocketClient class: A socket client example

```
package com.richware.chap21;

import java.io.*;
import java.net.*;

/**
 * Class SocketClient
 * Description: Demonstrates a client connection to a Socket Server.
 *
 * Copyright:    Copyright (c) 2002 Wiley Publishing, Inc.
 * @author Rich Helton <rhelton@richware.com>
 * @version 1.0
 * DISCLAIMER: Please refer to the disclaimer at the beginning of this
book.
 */
public class SocketClient extends Thread {
    protected Socket socket;
    /**
     * Port number is set to 2000 to avoid the protocols below 1024.
     */
    final static int PORT_NUM = 2000;

    /**
     True to only accept connections from the local machine.
     */
    final static boolean LOCAL_ONLY = true;
```

```
    /**
     * Constructor SocketClient
     * Description: Creates a new Socket to communicate with the Server.
     *
     */
    SocketClient() {}

    /**
     * Method main
     *
     *
     * @param args the standard arguments for a main driver.
     *
     * @throws IOException to propagate from the any IO exceptions for
sockets.
     *
     */
    public static void main(String[] args) throws IOException {
        Socket socket = null;
        System.out.println("Starting SocketClient....");
        /**
         * If local, only receive connections from the local host
         */
        if (LOCAL_ONLY) {
            /**
             * Communicate with the local server at port 2000.
             */
            InetAddress address = InetAddress.getLocalHost();
            socket = new Socket(address, PORT_NUM);
        } else {
            /**
             * Communicate with the server on myserver1 at port 2000.
             */
            InetAddress address =
                InetAddress.getByName("myserver1.richware.com");
            socket = new Socket(address, PORT_NUM);
        }

        /**
         * The in receives the data from the client
         */
        InputStream in    = socket.getInputStream();
        OutputStream out = socket.getOutputStream();
        byte[]       buffer = new byte[1024];
        int          read;
        if ((read = in.read(buffer)) >= 0) {
            System.out.println("Socket Read:" + new String(buffer));
        }
```

```
    /**
     * The out sends the data to the client
     */
    System.out.println("Sending Data");
    out.write("Received Data\r\n".getBytes());
    /**
     * The out sends the data to the client
     */
    System.out.println("Sending Exit Server");
    out.write("EXIT".getBytes());

    /**
     * Close the socket
     */
    socket.close();
  }
}
```

The connections are in the Session Layer because they require a reference to each other to communicate. The client output looks like the following lines:

```
>java com.richware.chap21.SocketClient
Starting SocketClient....
Socket Read:Send Some Data

Sending Data
Sending Exit Server
```

The matching server output looks like the following:

```
>java com.richware.chap21.SocketServer
Starting SocketServer....
SocketServer Listening....
Waiting for Connection....
Waiting for Connection....
Sending Some Data...
Read Data:Received Data
EXIT

Exiting Client Connection
```

The layers above the Session Layer are protocols that manipulate the data. If the connection is at port 80, the defined port for HTTP, there should be an HTTP service responsible for managing the information. The HTTP service should then look at the data and ensure that it meets the proper format.

> **TIP:** In Java, by passing the encoding scheme in, the `getBytes(encoding method)` function can be used to ensure the right format. The HTTP can get the `InputStream` and parse out the "`GET /`", which is the beginning of an HTTP request.

After this point, the service protocol parses out and manipulates data according to the HTTP specification. I have now completed all the layers of the OSI model and taken a trip through some samples of wrappers that might encapsulate the various protocols and specifications. Many books have been written on this topic because there are many more specifications and protocols — (Token Ring, FDDI, ATM, Sonet, and ISDN are some examples) that encompass this area and could be addressed here.

However, our discussion for all these protocols would follow the OSI model I have used so far: If supporting TCP/IP, the IP header remains the same, the TCP header remains the same, and the sockets and application protocols remain the same. The difference resides in the network card, the framing in the Data Link Layer, and the signaling of the carrier wave. If, instead of HTTP, I use FTP, and the port number and the data change, additional layers of connection may be required to move ports around for commands versus passing of data, but a connection of sockets for TCP and UDP still works in the same manner.

> **NOTE:** Recall that the Application Layer handles the details of the application. TCP/IP has several common applications that most implementations provide. These applications include Telnet for remote login, File Transfer Protocol (FTP), the Simple Mail Transfer Protocol (SMTP), and the Simple Network Management Protocol (SNMP).

The different OSI layers communicate at the different peers; however, some routing is still involved to reach the destination of the LAN system. The router passes the packet into the organization's LAN and drops the packet, but the security behind it can be increased.

Routing basics

As described in the previous section, the router's responsibility is to examine the packet and check whether it should be passed to the organization's LAN. The router reads the IP address out of the IP packet and, if the IP address is for a machine registered on the LAN, the router sends the packet there. The router is responsible for the support of the lower three layers of the OSI model, as Figure 21-7 shows.

The router maintains a table to know whether the registered machine exists on the LAN; in order to accomplish this task, the router must follow the *Address Resolution Protocol* (ARP) specified in RFC 826. ARP handles the translation of the 32-bit IP addresses, in the IP header, into the hardware address, in the network card. The *hardware address* is a 48-bit address that follows the network card.

The *Routing Information Protocol* (RIP) is another protocol that the router uses. RIP gives routers the capability to periodically broadcast to the networks that they are aware of to find out their distance.

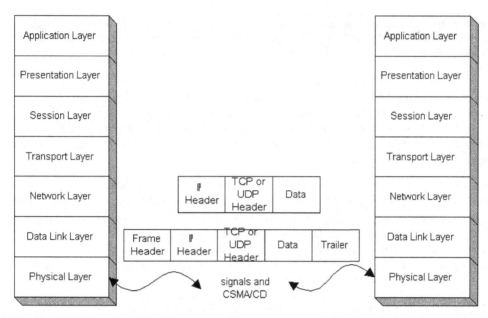

Figure 21-7: The routing OSI model

The ping and traceroute protocols give insight to RIP because RIP is very similar to sending a ping, getting a return echo, and keeping track of the shortest distance to the networks. RIP is used for discovering dynamic addresses across a network that occasionally changes, such as machines configured with dynamic addresses when they register themselves to the domain. The network ping concept can be traced to a submarine ping: A submarine can send a high-pitched noise to find nearby ships by the echo of the signal. The network ping is part of the *Internet Control Message Protocol* (ICMP). The ICMP packet can be used instead of the TCP and UDP packet in the Transport Layer. Figure 21-8 shows the structure of ICMP packets.

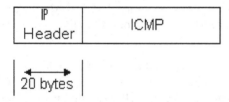

Figure 21-8: ICMP packet

The ICMP protocols have multiple types of services for querying information about a machine or network: 0 for ping reply, 3 for a destination unreachable, 5 for redirect, 8 for ping request, 9 for router advertisement, and 10 for router solicitation. Message Types 9 and 10 of ICMP are part of RFC 1256, which is the ICMP Router Discovery Message. This message is used for discovering the different static addresses across the network; machines with static addresses change with less frequency and require less work for router tables. Since static addresses don't change, they must be dedicated to a machine.

This scheme gives little address re-use to other machines that could be using the address when the machine (associated with the static address) is down. A machine that has a static IP address is also more susceptible to attacks because, when it is alive, an attacker can find the same machine over and over again with the same address. Based on the type of service in ICMP, a code is returned: For example, for type 3, code 0 means that the network was unreachable and a code 7 means that the host is unknown. These packets change based on the type of the service. Figure 21-9 shows the ICMP packet with type and code.

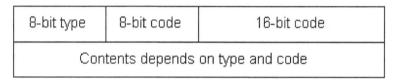

Figure 21-9: The ICMP packet with type and code

Listing 21-3 gives an example ping program run.

Listing 21-3: Ping output

```
C:\>ping ftp-dom.earthlink.net

Pinging ftp-dom.earthlink.net [ 207.217.111.93] with 32 bytes of data:

Reply from 207.217.111.93: bytes=32 time=241ms TTL=247
Reply from 207.217.111.93: bytes=32 time=230ms TTL=247
Reply from 207.217.111.93: bytes=32 time=221ms TTL=247
Reply from 207.217.111.93: bytes=32 time=240ms TTL=247

Ping statistics for 207.217.111.93:
    Packets: Sent = 4, Received = 4, Lost = 0 (0% loss),
Approximate round trip times in milli-seconds:
    Minimum = 221ms, Maximum =  241ms, Average =  233ms
```

The ping program uses an IP record route (RR) in the IP header. The RR can be seen from the next example of ping in Listing 21-4. What makes the use of this ping special is that it allows the RR to record 9, which was specified at the command; it represents the hops that it took to reach the destination and back again.

In the preceding example, it went to the addresses 209.247.8.235, 209.247.8.242, 209.245.88.33, 207.217.1.125, 207.217.2.34, 207.217.111.5 before reaching the destination of 207.217.111.93, which is the host specified.

Listing 21-4: Ping showing an IP record route

```
C:\>ping -r 9 ftp-dom.earthlink.net

Pinging ftp-dom.earthlink.net [207.217.111.93] with 32 bytes of data:

Reply from 207.217.111.93: bytes=32 time=231ms TTL=248
    Route: 209.247.8.235 ->
           209.247.8.242 ->
           209.245.88.33 ->
           207.217.1.125 ->
           207.217.2.98 ->
           207.217.111.5 ->
           207.217.111.93 ->
           207.217.2.62 ->
           207.217.1.108
Reply from 207.217.111.93: bytes=32 time=230ms TTL=248
    Route: 209.247.8.235 ->
           209.247.8.242 ->
           209.245.88.33 ->
           207.217.1.125 ->
           207.217.2.34 ->
           207.217.111.5 ->
           207.217.111.93 ->
           207.217.2.126 ->
           207.217.1.44
Reply from 207.217.111.93: bytes=32 time=221ms TTL=248
    Route: 209.247.8.235 ->
           209.247.8.242 ->
           209.245.88.33 ->
           207.217.1.125 ->
           207.217.2.98 ->
           207.217.111.5 ->
           207.217.111.93 ->
           207.217.2.30 ->
           207.217.1.11
Reply from 207.217.111.93: bytes=32 time=220ms TTL=248
    Route: 209.247.8.235 ->
           209.247.8.242 ->
           209.245.88.33 ->
           207.217.1.125 ->
           207.217.2.34 ->
           207.217.111.5 ->
           207.217.111.93 ->
           207.217.2.30 ->
           207.217.1.75


Ping statistics for 207.217.111.93:
    Packets: Sent = 4, Received = 4, Lost = 0 (0% loss),
```

```
Approximate round trip times in milli-seconds:
    Minimum = 220ms, Maximum =  231ms, Average =  225ms
```

For all ICMP hosts, the support for the RR in the IP header is optional; however, it is supported by most router systems. Another issue with the support of RR is the size limitation in the IP header, which only allows 39 bytes for this option. Figure 21-10 shows the RR IP address header.

1-byte type	1-byte len	1-byte ptr	4-byte IP addr #1	4-byte IP addr #2	.....	4-byte IP addr #9

Figure 21-10: The RR IP address header

Here is an example of how ICMP can be used to map routes: Traceroute (a similar program to ping) sends a UDP at a very high port, such as 30,000, that should not exist. This causes the destination host's UDP service protocol to generate an ICMP "port unreachable" error. Then three more UDP messages are sent with a *Time To Live* (TTL) field set to one. This causes the first router on the path to return an ICMP message reporting that the TTL has expired. Next, three more UDP messages are sent with the TTL set to 2, which causes the second router to return that the TTL has expired. This process continues, and the routers are mapped while collecting the return addresses of the routers that are reporting expiration.

Now that you understand how addresses can be checked, the next thing to understand is how to maintain a routing table. The routing table is maintained by checking the default entries of the host or router for the host address, its matching network address, and its default entry that is its gateway. The service protocol utility `netstat  -rn` supports this functionality on most platforms. Performing the `netstat  -rn` command on a Windows 2000 machine connecting directly to a direct connection yields the results in Listing 21-5; gateways usually end with the address of 0, but not always.

Listing 21-5: `netstat  -rn` run on a Windows 2000 machine

```
C:\>netstat -rn

Route Table
==================================================================================
===
Interface List
0x1 ........................ MS TCP Loopback interface
0x1000003 ...00 00 86 56 f5 97 ...... FE575 Ethernet Adapter
0x2000004 ...00 53 45 00 00 00 ...... WAN (PPP/SLIP) Interface
==================================================================================
===
==================================================================================
===
```

```
Active Routes:
Network Destination          Netmask            Gateway            Interface
Metric
           0.0.0.0           0.0.0.0       64.156.32.172       64.156.32.172
1
    64.156.32.172    255.255.255.255         127.0.0.1           127.0.0.1
1
   64.255.255.255    255.255.255.255     64.156.32.172       64.156.32.172
1
         127.0.0.0          255.0.0.0         127.0.0.1           127.0.0.1
1
    209.247.23.216   255.255.255.255     64.156.32.172       64.156.32.172
1
         224.0.0.0          224.0.0.0     64.156.32.172       64.156.32.172
1
   255.255.255.255   255.255.255.255     64.156.32.172             1000003
1
Default Gateway:        64.156.32.172
==========================================================================
===
Persistent Routes:
  None

C:\>
```

To initialize the routing table, a route command is used. These are normally routes to hosts or networks that are not directly connected, usually an address that is currently not in the local segment and requires more than one hop. An example of adding to the routing table on the Windows 2000 machine is shown in Listing 21-6.

Listing 21-6: Adding to the routing table

```
> route PRINT
> route ADD 157.0.0.0 MASK 255.0.0.0  157.55.80.1 METRIC 3 IF 2
        destination^        ^mask      ^gateway      metric^      ^
                                                              Interface^
  If IF is not given, it tries to find the best interface for a given
  gateway.
> route PRINT
> route PRINT 157*          .... Only prints those matching 157*
> route DELETE 157.0.0.0
> route PRINT
```

To get the information to fill the routing table through RIP is a little more complicated. RIP's version 1 has had a lot of security issues because the client usually accepts any data that is sent. The packages have been able to send not just routes but logging information about hosts. Information about the first version can be found in RFC 1058. To avoid these security issues, the second version uses MD5 authentication of passwords for authenticating the requester; information on the second version can be found in RFC 1388. RIP works by computing a distance vector for the hops. Each hop has a cost, and the total metric distance for a path is the sum of the hops cost. Therefore, RIP knows the distance by adding the cost of each hop and summing the total.

RIP is a message wrapped by the IP/UDP packet. RIP can keep track of 25 routes because the packet size is 20 bytes, and it must maintain the packet less than 512 bytes. RIP operates on the router port, which is port 520. The router knows the cost to its neighbor on the path toward the destination address; that router knows the cost to the next neighbor and so on until all the metrics are calculated. The router broadcasts its routing table, or a part of it, to its neighbor every 30 seconds to update its neighbor's routing table.

If something special happens, such as a metric for a route changes in the table, it might trigger a new update of the table immediately to tell the neighboring router of the change. These notifications of changes in metrics give the neighbor the capability to know the cost of its closest neighboring router.

In 1998, a protocol to replace RIP was started by the Internet Engineering Task Force called the *Open Shortest Path First* (OSPF) Interior Gateway Protocol. OSPF is public. The OSPF standard describes *networks* (which are actually subnets) and *areas* (which are sets of networks).

OSPF is designed to scale well because routers only need information about the area that the router serves. A router keeps information on the area (called a *database*), and when a change happens the information is propagated through the area. Every router in an area keeps an identical database of the network. When a node is initiated, it gets the information from its network and after that only changes must be propagated. OSPF supports traffic splitting across multiple paths, routing based on type of service, and authentication for routing update messages.

> **NOTE:** For more information on OSPF visit
> `http://www.ietf.org/rfc/rfc2178.txt?number=2178`.

Firewalls

The purpose of a firewall is to provide a single choke point to block out unwanted packets from possible attackers of an organization's system. A *choke point* is where many packets must enter to get routed into the organization's LANs. In most cases, a firewall is an addition to the gateway, or entry router, into an organization's network systems. The best way to understand an organization's network topology is to understand that there may be many choke points into a system. An organization's topology with three routers might look like the one in Figure 21-11.

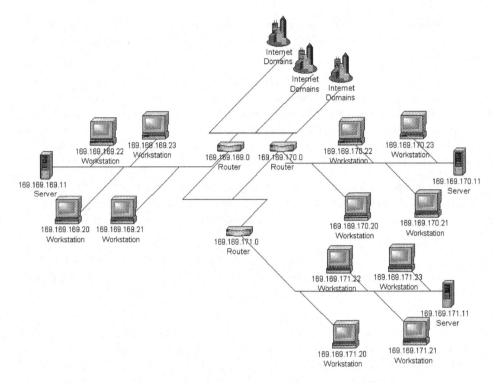

Figure 21-11: A organization's LAN example

Notice in Figure 21-11 that there are three routers and there is no single choke point. In this example, there is nothing to prevent rogue packets from getting routed to the appropriate machines if the port and address matches for the services running the protocols.

In this scenario, the only way to prevent hackers from accessing the services is the security of the services themselves. For instance, the authentication in FTP prevents the hacker from logging in.

However, one issue with the FTP service is that if the "anonymous" user is accessible and the security is relaxed on the files on that machine, then those files are easily attainable. In addition, the operating system running on each individual box is also susceptible to intrusion for any security that is not tightly managed.

To avoid this security issue, establish a single choke point that all packets must enter. Figure 21-12 illustrates a firewall as a single point of contact that all packets must enter and exit into the untrusted Internet. All the packets that now work with the routers are assumed to be trusted and not a threat to attack the machines in the organization's domain.

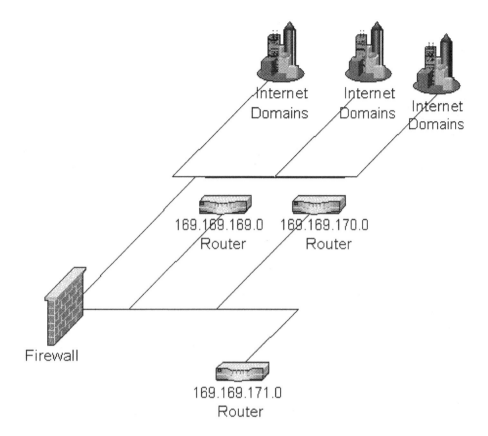

Figure   21-12: Firewall

The firewall that communicates directly with the outside Internet is normally termed a *Bastion Host*. Because the Bastion Host is exposed to the Internet, its security must be kept high. Many Bastion Hosts are administered remotely by telneting into them and configuring the internal files. The operating system and any administration tools must be accessible only by the administrators in the organization or the Bastion Host becomes a security concern. The firewall can protect the internal domain by filtering and blocking packets that may be questionable. There are three ways in which a firewall can filter out unwanted attacks: by acting as a circuit-level gateway, by acting as an application-level gateway, and through packet filtering. These concepts are discussed in the following sections.

Circuit-level gateway

The purpose of *circuit-level gateways* is to relay TCP connections, and they act as a proxy at the Transport Layer. The sender connects to a TCP port on the gateway, which connects to some destination on the other side of the gateway. During the operation, the circuit-level gateway program moves the data bytes back and forth between endpoints. The gateway is called circuit based because it behaves as a circuit, relaying bytes back and forth as if it was hardware.

A circuit-level gateway can be a standalone system or it can be a function performed by an application-level gateway for certain applications. A circuit-level gateway does not permit an end-to-end TCP connection; rather, the gateway sets up two TCP connections, one between itself and a TCP user on an inner host, and one between itself and a TCP user on an outside host. Once the two connections are established, the gateway typically relays TCP segments from one connection to the other without examining the contents. The security function consists of determining which connections will be allowed.

A typical use of circuit-level gateways is a situation in which the system administrator trusts the internal users. The gateway can be configured to support application-level or proxy service on inbound connections and circuit-level functions for outbound connections. In the configuration, the gateway can incur the processing overhead of examining incoming application data for forbidden functions but does not incur that overhead on outgoing data.

The protocol described here is designed to provide a framework for client-server applications in both the TCP and UDP domains to conveniently and securely use the services of a network firewall. The protocol is conceptually a "shim-layer" between the Application Layer and the Transport Layer, and as such does not provide network-layer gateway services, such as forwarding of ICMP messages.

Circuit gateways operate at the Network Transport Layer. Again, connections are authorized based on addresses. Like filtering gateways, they (usually) cannot look at data traffic flowing between one network and another, but they do prevent direct connections between one network and another.

Application-level gateway

Another type of firewall is having special-purpose code for each application. This handles traffic at the Application Layer. An application gateway, also called a proxy server, acts as a relay for application-level traffic. The user contacts the gateway using a TCP/IP application, such as Telnet or FTP, and the gateway asks the user of the remote host to be accessed. When the user responds and provides valid user and authentication information, the gateway contacts the application on the remote host and relays TCP segments containing the application data between the two endpoints. If the gateway does not implement the proxy code for a specific application, the service is not supported and cannot be forwarded across the firewall. Further, the gateway can be configured to support only specific features of an application that the network administrator considers acceptable while denying other features.

Application-level gateways tend to be more secure than packet filters. Rather than trying to deal with the numerous possible combinations that are allowed and forbidden at the TCP and

IP level, the application-level gateway need only scrutinize a few allowable applications. In addition, it is easy to log and audit all incoming traffic at the application level.

A prime disadvantage of this type of gateway is the additional processing overhead on each connection. In effect, there are two spliced connections between the end users, with the gateway at the splice point; and the gateway must examine and forward all traffic in both directions.

Packet filtering

Packet filtering can normally be encompassed as part of a router. The purpose of packet filtering is simply to block questionable packets. The router can sniff these by the IP header, TCP header, UDP header, ICMP header, and more. *Packet sniffing* is the process of examining the packet to see what it contains. The formats of the IP header and the rest of the headers are well known. The data can also be read if it is not encrypted, and what the packet is trying to accomplish can be understood.

Since the packet has to get routed to the organization's domain, it can be intercepted through a program and examined. Installing a Bastion Host centralizes where the interception can be done before entering the organization's domain. Some of the fields that can be easily examined are ports and addresses, and any data that is plaintext can also be examined to try to understand the protocol. Common parenting software works this way by examining the data and ensuring that anything containing "XXX" will be blocked.

Organizations can easily sniff the data to learn what their employees are surfing the Web for, and many people might consider this an invasion of privacy. However, packets that are being transported across the Internet could be sniffed at any point during transport. For example, by looking at the data and the SYN flag of the TCP packet, a firewall can examine the "GET /index.html" and assume that the protocol is HTTP; next the firewall verifies that the destination port is port 80. If the destination address is any address except the domain's HTTP server, the firewall can deny that packet.

The sender of the packet receives a "destination unreachable" or a "Communication with destination host is administratively forbidden" message in a formatted ICMP reply packet depending on the configuration and the firewall. The same rules apply for the organization's internal domain. A user in the domain could try to reach a host that the organization deems untrustworthy. The firewall can deny a connection by sniffing the destination address for outgoing packets and returning a deny to the user. Most firewalls should be configured to log discrepancies to know whether an attacker is trying to access the system.

The users of the domain can also get logged at the firewall; using this strategy, a person within the organization accessing a competitor's system or sending them e-mails could be logged. To understand how a packet filter might be set up to deny service for an HTTP service, look at the configuration shown in Figure 21-13. In this example, any inbound TCP packets originating outside the firewall above port 1023 directed to a machine in the domain using port

80 as an initial SYN, meaning no ACK, will be denied. Also, any originating TCP packets from the domain on port 80 going out the firewall to a port above 1023 with an ACK, meaning a reply, will be denied.

Packet Direction	Source Address	Destination Address	Protocol	Source Port	Destination Port	ACK	Action
Inbound	External	Internal	TCP	>1023	80	NO	Deny
Outbound	Internal	External	TCP	80	>1023	Yes	Deny

Figure   21-13: Firewall configurations

These configurations are just some ways, without even examining the data, to deny access to any HTTP server from the domain to the Internet that works on port 80. The configuration denies any service that meets the rules specified for the configuration. If you want a single machine to have an HTTP server, you could specify to allow packets specific to that destination address within the domain.

This situation does resolve a lot of issues, however in enterprise computing the concept exists that enterprise data must go through the appropriate services to initiate requests. This concept chains a request through more than one firewall and is commonly known as a *de-militarized zone* (DMZ).

De-Militarized Zones (DMZs)

The *De-Militarized Zone* is a concept that comes from war; the concept of a no man's land, meaning that at some point a person must be viewed as an ally or an enemy when they cross a certain boundary. In a firewall boundary, it is a combination of firewalls in which an internal firewall filters the Bastion Host firewall. Figure 21-14 shows the concept of a DMZ.

The purpose of the *DMZ* is to separate the services that communicate to the Internet on a server, or set of servers such as a Web farm, from all the other machines. The HTTP server can communicate to databases or enterprise systems through a secondary firewall. The internal firewall will only accept packets from the organization's designated HTTP server and usually in the form of HTTP; however, it will send and receive on designated ports that are not HTTP. The Bastion Host will only allow packets for the HTTP protocol into the HTTP server. All other packages will be blocked; this scheme keeps all packets narrowed into one protocol and coming from one machine, or a set of machines. In this case, the HTTP server acts as a dual-homed host.

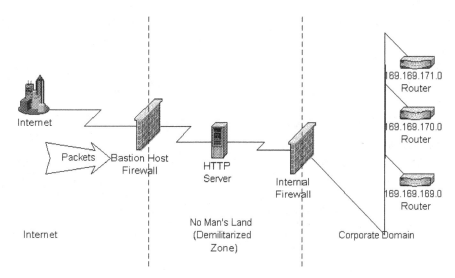

Figure 21-14: DMZ

A *dual-homed host* acts as a router between the Internet and the organization's domain. The packets on the Internet can communicate with the server, and the packets on the organization's domain can communicate with the server, however neither can communicate directly. The Bastion Host, in this case, is there to ensure that no packets from the Internet can communicate to any other host except the dual-homed host. In addition, the internal firewall is there to ensure that communication from the organization's domain can only communicate with a separate port specified from the dual-homed host. Even if a hacker does IP spoofing, the response from the organization's domain will only be routed to the dual-homed host. The attacker would have to intercede for the router and route the packets to a different machine to try to bypass the dual-homed host.

Another tactic to further confuse possible attackers is to build a fake dual-homed host as a secondary firewall. This host could be further separated by firewalls and given less security so that an attacker would spend his time trying to attack a machine with nothing proprietary on it. This approach is sometimes referred to as the "sacrificial lamb approach" because a machine is sacrificed for the purpose of saving the domain. In this approach, logging is heavily guarded to study the attacker's techniques to be ready for when he moves his attack to the rest of the domain.

Proxies can also be used to hide the true identity of the dual-homed host. A *proxy* gives a host the capability to look like another host and process its request without the user discovering the difference. The proxy can create further security and examine the request; if it appears questionable, the proxy can disregard it. If the request appears valid, the proxy forwards it to the real host and responds to the sender as the actual host. A package called SOCKS is used to help in such deception. *SOCKS* is an API that helps support proxy-aware servers and clients.

SOCKS is considered a circuit-level gateway to allow selected TCP/IP connections through firewalls.

> **NOTE:**The RFC for SOCKS is RFC 1928
> (http://www.ietf.org/rfc/rfc1928.txt?number=1928).

Understanding Proxying Firewalls

Before the rise of application servers, distributed objects were deployed in a distributed environment across an organization's enterprise systems. An example of these objects is RMI, CORBA, and DCOM. These objects are not governed by a set of a few application servers, but can be distributed across many machines. Naming servers are required for distributed objects to resolve their location and interfaces. There can be multiple backups across an enterprise in case one of the naming servers goes down. For enterprise beans, the *Java Naming and Directory Interface* (JNDI) resembles a naming server. See Figure 21-15 for an example.

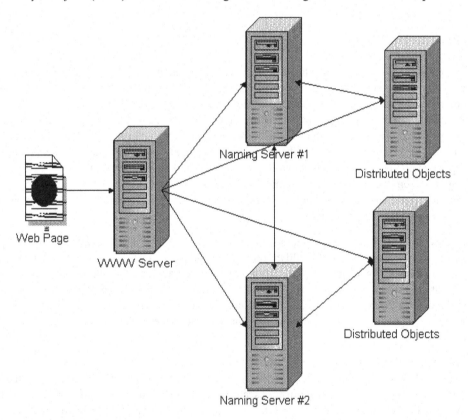

Figure 21-15: Distributed objects

Figure 21-15 illustrates a Web server connecting to the distributed object after doing a lookup on the naming server. When distributed objects are created, they may require a new port. A newly created port is used as a location of the distributed object on a machine. The use of distributed object prohibits the use of a backend firewall because it may block a newly created port when an object is dynamically created. To counteract the issue, many application servers and distributed systems may have plug-ins for Web servers and proxy devices for firewalls.

The purpose of many plug-ins is to act as an intermediate device between the Web server, the naming server, and the distributed objects. CORBA uses the *General Inter-ORB Protocol* (GIOP) proxy for tunneling through firewalls. The GIOP protocol resolves the objects into eight basic messages. GIOP works as the underlying message architecture that transports the objects on top of TCP/IP. See Figure 21-16 for an example of a GIOP proxy.

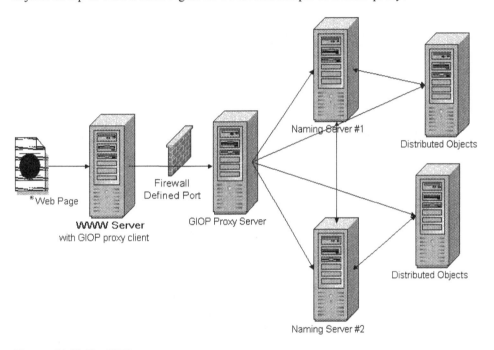

Figure 21-16: The GIOP proxy

The figure displays a CORBA plug-in on the WWW server that will act as the CORBA naming server and distributed objects messaging to a GIOP server. The GIOP server will use the messages and act as the client communicating to enterprise environment. When the naming server or Object Request Broker (ORB) responds to the GIOP proxy server, the GIOP proxy server will pass these objects as messages through return path of the firewall, and the GIOP client proxy will respond to the WWW server as the naming server and objects.

A more generic proxying device is to transmit a SOAP structure message through a firewall using HTTPS. The *Simple Object Access Protocol* (SOAP) provides a mapping of objects to XML. SOAP was built on top of XML for RPC, but XML for RPC provided the XML interface to methods instead of objects. The SOAP interface requires a client that maps the object calls into a SOAP message and a server side that will execute the distributed objects from the SOAP message and respond with the results. See Figure 21-17 for a SOAP proxy.

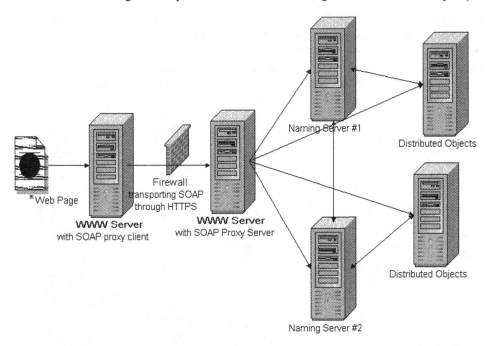

Figure   21-17: The SOAP proxy

By using the SOAP proxy, instead of a GIOP messaging structure, the SOAP XML stream can be passed between two Java Servlets using HTTPS. Using Java Servlets can make the development cycle easier than defining a protocol. HTTPS could be used to provide extra security to ensure that the message derived from the SOAP proxy client and that the SOAP proxy server is authenticated. The SOAP document would have to be parsed out by the servlet and execute the distributed objects. The servlet would act a controller pattern to execute the correct objects based on the SOAP stream.

Many application servers are shipped with proxy plug-ins for tunneling through firewalls. They may incorporate a multitude of means in order to narrow the ports through a firewall. If an application server executes only on a selected port, then the job of proxying is an easier task. Some plug-ins may require extra authentication such as HTTPS to ensure that a hacker is not simulating the client and server. If the enterprise system is not supporting a backend firewall, then any process being executed from the Web server farm may potentially access any port in the enterprise system. Limiting the traffic to only selected ports narrows the possibilities for potential attacks.

> **TIP:** Java provides automatic support for SOCKS with the system properties `socksProxyHost` and `socksProxyPort`.

HTTP Tunneling

As mentioned before, the firewall's function is to block ports to force an attacker to use specific ports that are monitored, for example to force the attacker to use port 80 for HTTP. *Port filtering* is the concept of allowing certain network ports, but not others, to be visible to the outside world. Ensuring that the only protocol entering the port is the protocol permitted by the firewall is called *protocol filtering*.

For instance, firewalls may employ an HTTP protocol filter to allow only HTTP connections; however, HTTP filtering restricts the access so that other "friendly" protocols, such as RMI, are not allowed either. These friendly protocols can be "wrapped" within the allowed protocol; in the case of HTTP, this is called *HTTP tunneling*. HTTP tunneling allows these wrapped packets to be treated as HTTP packets by the firewall and let through. The recipient of the tunneled packets must recognize them and unwrap them. Figure 21-18 shows a diagram of how HTTP tunneling works.

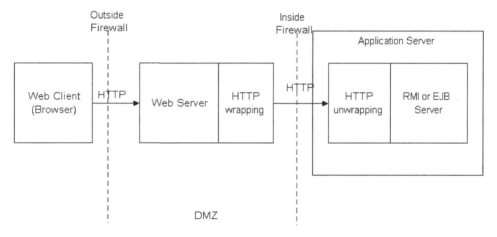

Figure 21-18: HTTP tunneling

The Java package `java.rmi.server` provides classes that implement HTTP tunneling. For RMI, there are two forms of HTTP tunneling: http-to-port and http-to-cgi. Using the http-to-port tunneling, RMI attempts an HTTP post request to an `http:` URL directed at the host name and port number of the target machine. If the firewall accepts it, the request is forwarded to the listening machine, which unwraps the request and sends an HTTP reply through the same firewall.

However, the firewall may not accept requests to unusual port numbers and so http-to-cgi may be used. In the case of http-to-cgi, the URL has the form of `http://intendedserver:80/cgi-bin/java-rmi.cgi?port=intendedportx;` the intended server must be listening on port 80 to run the `java-rmi.cgi` script that forwards the request to the RMI server listening on the `intendedportx`. The `java-rmi.cgi` script can be found in the JDK.

> **CAUTION:** Using http-to-cgi will redirect any incoming request to any port, creating a security hole on the server.

Java Sockets

So far, you have seen how networks work; in this section you learn about the interface that programs use to communicate with the network. The operating system uses network drivers to communicate with the *Network Interface Card* (NIC), and the device driver may provide other Dynamic Link Libraries, or native libraries, for other applications and libraries to communicate to the operating system. These native libraries act as wrappers around the device driver to provide an interface that abstracts the low-level details of developing the TCP/IP and UDP/IP packets. The native libraries themselves can take time to implement a protocol like FTP and Telnet to production. The quickness from design to production is one of the reasons Java has become so popular.

Java Sockets were also developed to implement protocols like FTP in a quick and non-complicated manner. One of the features that I liked about Java Sockets when they were first introduced was their capability to use a buffered stream that would pass a stream of information through a socket instead of breaking up pieces into individual records. Other enterprise products, such as Enterprise JavaBeans (EJB) and CORBA, have far surpassed the Socket programming interface by providing additional features and services out of the box. However, for simple tasks and implementing enterprise products, knowing how Sockets work is crucial. Figure 21-19 shows Sockets in the OSI model.

The obvious way to identify a client or a server is by the IP address and port number; this address can be associated with a logical name identified by the host name. An example of a host name is `security.richware.com`. The `java.net.InetAddress` class is used to wrap, or encapsulate, the IP address, host name, and port number information. The `InetAddress` class does not contain a constructor but can be created by calling a static method on the `InetAddress` class itself. For example, the function `InetAddress.getAllByName()` returns an array of `InetAddresses` that contains all the IP addresses of the host (by its name) passed in as the parameter. Another example is the `InetAddress.getLocalHost()`, which returns the local host.

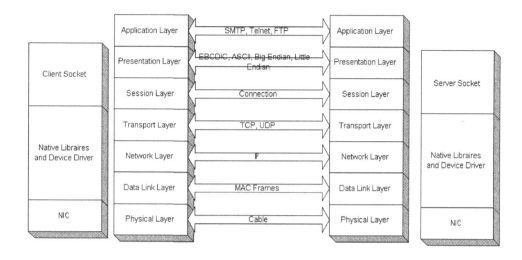

Open Systems Interconnection (OSI) Model

Figure   21-19: The Sockets in the OSI model

To create a connection between two network endpoints, an interface is established. The interface hides the complexity of the devices and the MAC frames and allows multiple protocols, such as IPX, to be used with just a change in the devices. In Java the interface is established with the `java.net.Socket` class for the client, and the `java.net.ServerSocket` for the server. An example of a client connecting to a server is included in Listing 21-7.

Listing 21-7: The `Client_Socket` class: An example of a client for Listing 21-8

```
package com.richware.chap21;

import java.io.*;
import java.net.*;
import java.util.*;

/**
 * Class Client_Socket
 * Description: An example client
 *
 * Copyright:    Copyright (c) 2002 Wiley Publishing, Inc.
 * @author Rich Helton <rhelton@richware.com>
 * @version 1.0
 * DISCLAIMER: Please refer to the disclaimer at the beginning of this
book.
 */
```

```
public class Client_Socket{
    public static void main(String args[]) {
        try {
            /*
             * Create a socket on the local machine using port 9000
             */
            System.out.println("Starting Client Server....");
            Socket m_socket = new Socket(InetAddress.getLocalHost(), 9000);


            /*
             * Serialize the Credit Card Number, Example only, no security
             */
            OutputStream out = m_socket.getOutputStream();
            ObjectOutput cc = new ObjectOutputStream(out);
            System.out.println("Sending Credit Card Number....");
            cc.writeObject("My Credit Card Number");
            cc.writeObject("4444-4444-4444-4444");
            cc.flush();
            cc.close();
            /*
             *  Catches
             */
        } catch (Exception e) {
            e.printStackTrace();
            System.exit(1);
        }

    }
}
```

The connection is established by the creation of the Socket instance for a waiting ServerSocket. The accepting ServerSocket will return the Socket object of the client. Both the client and server can get the BufferedInputStream and BufferedOutputStream objects from the Socket object. The client output looks like the following:

```
>java com.richware.chap21.Client_Socket
Starting Client Server....
Sending Credit Card Number....
```

and the matching server output is as follows:

```
>java com.richware.chap21.Server Socket
Starting Server_Socket....
My Credit Card Number
4444-4444-4444-4444
```

Using these InputStreams, the client and server can read and write data to each other. They can read files, mpegs, and other formats. The running application programs, which execute the

Socket objects, are responsible for the formatting and unformatting of the data. The
ServerSocket is initialized to listen on a specific port for the client connection. The
accept() function waits until the client establishes a connection. Listing 21-8 shows the
Server_Socket class that matches the Client_Socket class in Listing 21-7.

Listing 21-8: The Server_Socket class: An example of a server for Listing 21-7

```
package com.richware.chap21;

import java.io.*;
import java.net.*;
import java.util.*;

/**
 * Class Server Socket
 * Description: An example server
 *
 * Copyright:    Copyright (c) 2002 Wiley Publishing, Inc.
 * @author Rich Helton rhelton@richware.com
 * @version 1.0
 * DISCLAIMER: Please refer to the disclaimer at the beginning of this
book.
 */
public class Server_Socket {

    /**
     * The main driver, no args used.
     */
    public static void main(String args[]) {
      System.out.println("Starting Server_Socket....");
      ServerSocket  m server = null;
      Socket  m_socket = null;
      try {
      /*
       * Listen to port 9000.
       */
      m_server = new ServerSocket(9000);
      /*
       * This will wait for a connection is made from the client.
       * It returns the client socket.
       */
      m_socket = m_server.accept();
      InputStream in = m socket.getInputStream();
      ObjectInput cc = new ObjectInputStream(in);
      String m_header = (String) cc.readObject();
      String m_number = (String) cc.readObject();
      cc.close();

      // print out what has been  just received
```

```
        System.out.println(m_header);
        System.out.println(m_number);
        /*
         * Catches
         */
        } catch (Exception e) {
                e.printStackTrace();
        System.exit(1);
        }
    }
}
```

As with any typical client/server scenario, for everything to work there must be a matching server for each client. In addition, both client and server information, as well as data formats, need to match each other. However, besides the port and address, much of the connection work can be hidden. In the BSD sockets, a bind and listen function also has to be defined on the server side; the bind sets up the address, and the listen prepares the socket to listen so that the `accept()` function works appropriately. Much of this work is now hidden and buffered so that streaming can be implemented easily, as described in Figure 21-20.

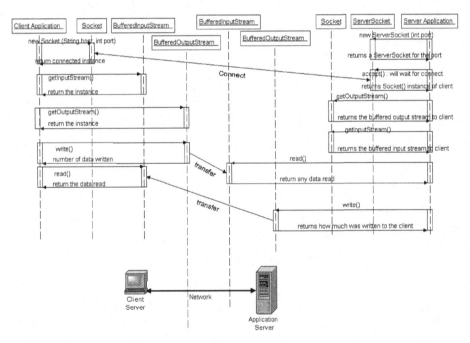

Figure   21-20: Streaming implementation

When a Socket is constructed, it installs a default `SocketImpl`. The default instance of the `SocketImpl` is created though the `PlainSocketImpl`:

```
Socket(String host, int port) {
        . . .
        }
```

If the default `SocketImpl` is not desired, an extended implementation of the `SocketImpl` can be passed in, as a parameter, to the constructor to be defined in the socket class:

```
protected Socket(SocketImpl impl) {
        this.impl = impl;
        }
```

It is a protected constructor because it does create the connection of the socket. The `SocketImpl` class is the protocol implementation of the `Socket` class. A `SocketImpl` can be passed in to support IPX; then the `Socket` class can be used, as previously discussed, except that instead of supporting TCP/IP, it supports IPX. The `SocketImpl` class is extremely helpful when extended to support transparent proxy connections like SOCKS. In addition, a `SocksSocketImpl` can be passed in the same way to support SOCKS, and change the `Socket` interface into a protocol to support the proxying of firewalls. The `SocksSocketImpl` class gives Java applications the capability to support most firewalls, satisfying the capability to implement the SOCKS protocol for firewalls.

> **NOTE:** The `SocketImpl` class only affects a subclass of the `Socket` class so that much of the original `Socket` function and functionality remains the same.

The `ServerSocket` must also provide support for the `SocketImpl` class. Functionality is needed for the support of the server accepting the client connection, which is implementing the `SocketImpl` class. In order to do this, the `ServerSocket` must create an instance of its own `SocketImpl` during the `ServerSocket` construction. Since most of the `Socket` functionality remains the same, only the `accept()` function needs overwriting. Sockets that don't implement the `SocketImpl` on the client need not implement the `implAccept()` on the server end, as shown in the following lines of code:

```
public class ServerSocket {
        . . .
        protected final void implAccept(Socket s) throws IOException {
            . . .
            // on return from this call s will be connected to a client
        }
        . . .
```

Most of the discussion has been dedicated to connection-oriented `Socket`s, normally TCP/IP. *Connection-oriented* means that a client `Socket` is fully guaranteed a connection to the server `Socket`. When there is an interruption in the network connection, both client and server are aware of it. Recall that a TCP connection also guarantees delivery because there are flags in the packet to set an acknowledgement. Since the `Socket` interface supports the connection-oriented protocol, a separate interface needs to support the connectionless protocol.

The reason for a separate interface is that the means of connection needs to be kept separate; to keep them separate, the connectionless protocol (UDP) can be implemented with the `java.net.DatagramSocket`. The `DatagramSocket` is used for sending UDP packets. Each packet is individually addressed and routed, and can be received by a machine in any order. There are many similarities between a `Socket` and `DatagramSocket`. For instance, the connections of the server and client communicate on the same port, and if on a different machine, the address must be specified. If the port is in use by another application, another port has to be found in order to communicate. The following line establishes the port in the `DatagramSocket`:

```
socket = new DatagramSocket(9000);
```

However, there are many differences between the two protocols. The `Socket` class can support a stream because it can receive bytes in order, because it is connection-oriented and establishes a connection to send and receive on. The `DatagramSocket` can only receive or send packets from the class `java.net.DatagramPacket` and is bound to a port; the port is normally on the local machine and just receives packets. In the `DatagramSocket` scenario, there is no server listening for a connection like a `ServerSocket`. There are simply two `DatagramSocket`s; one might use the `send()` function passing in the packet, and the other one might use a `receive()` function to receive the packet. A receiving packet may look like the following:

```
byte[] buf = new byte[256];
DatagramPacket packet = new DatagramPacket(buf, buf.length);
socket.receive(packet);
```

In this example, the receiving socket, previously defined on port 9000, is receiving up to 256 bytes worth of data. It cannot receive more than that in the packet. The `getLength()` function of the `DatagramPacket` returns how much data was received. The `packet` is a class created and filled in by the `receive` method. In order to fill the data from the `receive` method, there must be a corresponding `send` method initiated as follows:

```
InetAddress address = Socket.getLocalAddress();
int port = 9000;
packet = new DatagramPacket(buf, buf.length, address, port);
socket.send(packet);
```

The difference between a `send` and `receive` is that `send` always is routed to the machine based solely on the port and address defined in the `DatagramPacket`. When the packet is received, the information can be retrieved with the following two lines:

```
InetAddress address = packet.getAddress();
int port = packet.getPort();
```

The `getAddress` and `getPort` functions return the host that sent the message. The port and address are always associated with the remote host when dealing with the `DatagramPacket`. The remote host is the one to send to or to receive from. There are many issues to take into consideration when working with the `DatagramSocket`; the biggest one is that if two messages are sent one after the other, the receiver can receive the messages in any order. However, the `DatagramSocket` has many advantages for sending a broadcast to many machines or sending messages for which no guarantee is warranted; the reason is that the `DatagramSocket` requires no synchronizing between a client and server. It is simply an application sending messages and another receiving them. Examples of applications include a mail application, a stock ticker, and broadcasting log information on a system whose purpose is to apprise an administrator about the health of another system. `DatagramSocket` buys simplicity and speed in moving packets around.

Java SOCKS

One of the implementations needed to proxy through firewalls is SSL, and the SOCKS protocol needs to also proxy through firewalls. The Java Sockets support the v4 and v5 SOCKS for TCP proxy mechanisms. The system properties that set the SOCKS proxy in the `Socket` and `ServerSocket` are the `socksProxyHost` and the `socksProxyPort`. To specify the location of the proxy server, the `socksProxyHost` can be an IP address or host name. The `socksProxyPort` specifies the port number to establish the connection; the default port is 1080. SOCKS cannot proxy without valid authentication of the username. The SOCKS protocol needs authentication to tunnel and uses the Java network authentication to authenticate the user and password.

The `java.net.Authenticator` class is used to obtain authentication for a network connection. When authentication is required, the system will invoke the method on the subclass `getPasswordAuthentication()`. The support is completely for supporting client connections to a Java proxy server; there are several Java proxy servers on the market today. Since the definitions are at the `Socket` level, applications like FTP and Telnet (built on top of the `Socket` level) can take advantage of the SOCKS protocol by the setting of the system properties. When the properties are set, the factory is set from the `SocketImpl`; and it becomes a `SocksSocketImpl` used as a proxy connection.

Channel

The concept of a *channel* represents an open connection for hardware devices, files, socket connections, or program components that perform reading and writing. The channel is either open or closed; it is open on creation, and when it is closed, it remains closed. The `isOpen()` function checks whether the channel is open or closed.

There is little difference between a `Socket` and the blocking, or synchronous, `SocketChannel`, but the non-blocking, or asynchronous, mode of `SocketChannel` has no equivalent in the `Socket` class. To implement the synchronous `SocketChannel`, use the following code:

```
SocketChannel channel = SocketChannel.open();
channel.connect(socketAddress);
```

The java.nio.channels.SocketChannel can be created by using the static SocketChannel.open() function. The open() function will subsequently create a corresponding Socket instance. The channel handles all the I/O operations; but the protocol-specific information, such as port numbers, host names, and the connection, is the responsibility of the Socket implementation. The SocketChannel, which makes up part of the Socket class, can be a returned Socket instance or the ServerSocket instance with the getChannel() method.

It is not possible to associate the channel to a Socket that already exists. If the Socket is not connected, invoking an I/O operation on the channel causes an exception because the Socket is not yet connected. The SocketChannel can invoke the connect() method, which establishes a client connection to the server. The finishConnect() method is used to finish the connection later. An isConnected() function can be called to determine if the client is already connected, and an isConnectionPending() is called if the connection operation is in progress. Unlike the other Socket classes, the SocketChannel requires multiple steps to get a connection to the server. The following lines show how to establish the asynchronous SocketChannel:

```
String host = "www.richware.com";
InetSocketAddress socketAddress =
                new InetSocketAddress(host, 80);
channel = SocketChannel.open();
channel.configureBlocking(false);
channel.connect(socketAddress);
```

The SocketChannel can be either asynchronous or synchronous. Passing in a false in the configureBlocking(false) function sets the SocketChannel to non-blocking. If the channel is non-blocking or asynchronous, it can continue operation without waiting for a response from the server. If it is blocking, or synchronous, it must wait for a response from the server before continuing. When a SocketChannel is in blocking mode, it can do a timeout on the read operations by calling a setSoTimeout(int) to specify the timeout period. It cannot do a timeout during non-blocking, or asynchronous mode, because the read is not waiting for a corresponding write operation.

Unlike the Socket, which can retrieve the InputStream and OutputStream at any time, the SocketChannel can only open and close once. The beginning of the SocketChannel is when the channel is open with input and output, and it is closed when the stream is closed; in contrast, the life cycle of Socket is usually open when the connection starts and ends when the connections ends. The SocketChannel shuts down the input side of the channel with the shutdownInput() function and the output side of the channel with the shutdownOutput() function. The SocketChannel supports every function asynchronously, even shutdown. An example of an asynchronous shutdown is a read (or write) that could be in progress during a shutdown, and once these functions have been notified of a shutdown in progress, they will stop reading (or writing) and return that there is nothing to read (or write).

> **NOTE:** SocketChannels are safe for use across multiple concurrent threads.

The SocketChannel is extended from the AsbstractSelectableChannel that gives the SocketChannel the capability to be a SelectableChannel. A SelectableChannel can register itself to a selector in the following way:

```
Selector selector = Selector.open();
channel.register(selector,
SelectionKey.OP_CONNECT);
```

The SelectableChannel works with a Selector. The purpose of a Selector is to notify the channel when an event has occurred. The event is based on the SelectionKey. The SelectionKey defines the keys that have a selected interest. To find out the available keys, the SocketChannel can use the method validOps(), which returns the keys OP_READ, for reading data; OP_WRITE, for writing data; and OP_CONNECT, for a connection interest.

The isRegistered() function can be used to return true to check if the channel is registered, as the following line shows.

```
channel.isRegistered();
```

After the selector is registered to the channel, the select() method of the selector is called to see if one of the specified operations has occurred. The select() methods are blocking, meaning that when called, the thread of execution will wait until there is a selection key available, a wakeup call from a another thread, or a timeout in the select(int timeout) method. The keys() or selectedKeys() functions will return a set of selection keys when they are available. Instead of comparing if the key is SelectionKey.OP_CONNECT, the isConnectable() function on the key will return if it is indeed a connection operation. Listing 21-9 shows the completion of a connection using the selection key of a SocketChannel.

Listing 21-9: SocketChannel connection completion

```
if (selector.select() > 0){
    // If the selector has a registered key in queue
    for (Iterator i = sel.selectedKeys().iterator(); i.hasNext();) {
        //Retrieve the next key and remove it from the set
        SelectionKey sk = (SelectionKey)i.next();
        i.remove();
        // Retrieve the target and the channel
        Target t = (Target)sk.attachment();
        SocketChannel sc = (SocketChannel)sk.channel();
        // Attempt to complete the connection sequence if Connecting
        if(sk.isConnectable()){
```

```
       try {
            if (sc.finishConnect()) {
             sk.cancel();
             t.connectFinish = System.currentTimeMillis();
             sc.close();
             printer.add(t);
            }
       } catch (IOException x) {
             sc.close();
             t.failure = x;
             printer.add(t);
       }
       }
    }
}
```

The New I/O (NIO) API performs asynchronous operations like never before. Each routine can be broken down, such as the `connect()` and `finishconnect()`, to fine-tune when operations should be executing. It might appear overly complicated to perform simple tasks such as communicating from a client to a server, but for very complex business logic, it is a must.

An example is a client logging in and starting to perform some tasks. While the client is in midstream of reading some of the data, the server must perform another task, such as a scheduled update of many of the client's records. After the server performs those operations, it finds out that the client's subscription has expired. At this point, the server can respond to the client with an error on his current subscription. The purpose of asynchronous communication and operations is to give the applications the capability to accomplish multiple tasks without waiting to finish a specific task.

Summary

The importance of the OSI model, DMZs, Java Sockets, HTTP tunneling, and firewalls was introduced and discussed in this chapter. I also presented important network concepts and investigated how security is handled at the network level. You should have an understanding of asynchronous communications, TCP, UDP, and routing and be able to run, understand, and write Java-code implementing sockets, channels, TCP, and UDP concepts.

To understand network security, you must understand common network principles and be able to apply them over and over again in different organizations to block attackers. Firewalls and router security are just some of the tools that are available, but using these products in unison to provide robust security and understanding is only one fraction of securing an organization. Having a secure organization, and hence a secure network, should be the goal of every organization. Thus, having a dual-homed host should be a minimum, not a maximum. Having a monitor device and a network engineer who can read the packets coming across a network should also be a minimum in the organization's overall security scheme.

There are many organizations that have secure doors going in o the buildings, but the network is like an open door without a key. So I ask, what is the purpose of having a locked door, when the biggest door, the network, is unsecure? Security is an everyday requirement, and a discipline that should be practiced by the organization's best people. If an organization doesn't wish to protect its resources through secure means, the organization should question what resources they have that are not publicly available. What information makes that organization special?

Using network security, understanding networks and blocking of questionable packets, is a practice that has been around since the ARPANET. Some of the RFCs that are still in use today date back to the 70s and 80s. With the information being available to both organizations and attackers for so long, it is surprising to see how few people can read a packet or truly look at network practices. From our experiences, I have known many people with the network engineer responsibilities who do not know what a firewall is, have called a DMZ a system with one firewall and do not understand the need for another firewall. In contrast I have also met people who could read information across a network as easily as many people read a newspaper. You can imagine what would happen if people like these turn to hacking.

This chapter was an introduction, and I hope you start the down the path of examining more information, and encourage your organization to employ true network engineers. I suggest to any organization interested in securing its systems that it employ staff with many years of network experience, enforce its network systems, ensure that it has proper security equipment, and test these systems by practicing mock attacks to check whether its systems are vulnerable.

Chapter 22
SSL and TLS

In This Chapter

♦ Understanding the handshake protocol

♦ Learning the key generation process

♦ Reviewing the SSL record structure

♦ Understanding the data transfer process

♦ Learning about WLS

Secure communications are important in the enterprise. The *Secure Socket Layer* (SSL) was developed to make secure communications available in the World Wide Web, and the Internet. SSL has evolved into the *Transport Layer Security* (TLS) and now *Wireless TLS* (WLS). This chapter explores the concepts behind these technologies, and how they provide confidentiality, message integrity, and end-point authentication.

The Secure Socket Layer (SSL)

The Secure Socket Layer (SSL) was designed for secure communications. Secure communications have three properties: *confidentiality*, *message integrity*, and *end-point authentication*. *Confidentiality* means that your message is kept secret from unintended listeners — usually called *eavesdroppers*. *Message integrity* means that you can identify whether your message has been tampered with — you want to be sure you receive the same message you were sent. *End-point authentication* means that you can be confident of the person who sent you the message.

Two important goals of SSL are to provide confidentiality between client and server and to ensure that only the correct end-points can transfer data. The API goals of SSL are to mimic the Socket API as closely as possible to provide an easy way to move code from Sockets to SSL.

This section first explores some of the history behind SSL and TLS. It then describes *digital signatures* and *message digests*, which along with *symmetric ciphers* and *public key ciphers* are the four fundamental types of algorithms used in SSL.

History

In the early 90s, using BSD Sockets, the Socket Application Program Interface was used to develop network protocols in the C language on UNIX; later it was the basis for the NT operating system using WinSock. At the time, there were no standards, just Cipher libraries. Therefore, there was not a standard way for clients and servers to exchange keys, and there was no way to ensure other client vendors used the same package. This made the support for network protocol cumbersome at best.

In 1994, Netscape created the Secure Socket Layer (SSL v1.0) as a wrapper for the Socket API; version 2 was released initially in November 1994 and deployed in Netscape 1.1 in March 1995. Also in 1995, Microsoft released *Private Communications Technology* (PCT), which (among other things) improved performance and included a non-encrypted mode. In late 1995, SSL v3 was released. SSL v3 is a complete rewrite of SSL; it added ciphers, such as *Digital Signature Standard* (DSS) and *Diffie-Hellman* (DH), and added support for a closure handshake.

> **CROSS-REFERENCE:** Chapter 4 introduced Diffie-Hellman, and Chapter 7 introduced the Digital Signature Standard.

SSL is a layered protocol that sits on top of TCP, as Figure 22-1 shows.

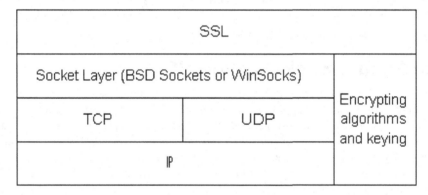

Figure 22-1: SSL layering

In 1996, the *Internet Engineering Task Force* (IETF) initiated the *Transport Layer Security* (TLS) working group to create a standard SSL-like protocol (that is, merge/standardize PCT and SSL v3). Because of some obstacles and complexity, it was not until January 1999 that TLS was published as RFC 2246.

Digital signatures

Digital signatures are based on the same concept as a person signing a document. For example, assume a bank sends a person a document to be signed and requires the document to be returned. Once the bank receives the document back, how does it know it has a valid signature? The bank may have the person's signature on file and compare it to the document, and if the signatures appear the same, the bank accepts the document. However, there are people who can forge signatures very easily. Another solution is to require the person to present identification verified from a trusted third party; but sometimes more than this type of authentication is needed, such as when it is possible to forge the document and/or identification.

Direct digital signatures

There are two types of digital signatures: *direct digital signatures* and *arbitrated digital signatures*. The *direct digital signature* is just between the sender and receiver; it uses a key to decrypt the message. If there are only two people in the group that share the key, trusting that it came from the other person who has the secret key can be somewhat valid. Once the group grows beyond two people, copies could start to appear and managing the digital signature becomes an issue.

One method of ensuring who encrypted a message is by applying the key pair algorithm. Consider the following example: A person receives a message from Jane, and if the message decrypts with Jane's public key using the key pair algorithm, the receiver can somewhat trust that Jane used her private key to encrypt the message and that, therefore, the message is valid. However, the integrity of the message can be compromised if the secret key or the private key is stolen.

Arbitrated digital signatures

An *arbitrated digital signature* involves a sender, a trusted third party, and a receiver. The trusted third party, such as a *Certificate Authority* (CA) in the Authentication Principle, ensures authenticity and acts as an arbitrator. The idea is that every signed message between the sender and receiver goes through an arbitrator, which all parties must trust. The arbitrator receives the message from the sender, validates that the message came from the sender, signs it saying that it was verified, and forwards it to the receiver. Since the receiver trusts the arbitrator, the message is accepted.

One way the message verification may work is to establish a secret key between the arbitrator and the sender and another secret key between the arbitrator and the client. The arbitrator decrypts the sender's message using his secret key, then encrypts the message using the other key, and sends the newly encrypted message to the receiver.

> **TIP:** With arbitrated digital signatures an attack is more difficult because the attacker requires both secret keys and must identify the arbitrator.

Message digest

A message digest is simply a function that takes as input an arbitrary-length message and outputs a fixed-length string. Two important properties of a message digest are irreversibility and collision resistance. *Irreversibility* means that it should be extremely hard to compute a message given its digest. *Collision resistance* means that it should be difficult for the same digest to be produced from two distinct messages. Message digests are used for the computation of digital signatures and *message authentication codes* (MACs).

A MAC is similar to a digest algorithm that incorporates a key into the computation. This makes the MAC dependent on both the key being used and the message being MACed. The MAC is an authentication code added to the message to validate that the message is reliable; it is typically a one-way hash and is rehashed to ensure that the hashes compare. Usually, the MAC consists of the packet's sequence number, type of packet, and data.

> **CROSS-REFERENCE:** Chapter 10 discusses the MAC in more detail.

The SSL Layers

The *Secure Socket Layer* protocol enables private communications over the Internet and was designed as a programming interface for network protocols. It basically creates a secure channel between the two machines; this channel is *transparent*, meaning that the data is unchanged while it passes through it. SSL is designed to prevent eavesdropping, tampering, or message forgery.

A connection has two phases: the handshake and the data transfer. The *handshake* phase authenticates the server and allows the client and server to agree on the algorithm(s) to be used to protect the data. It also allows the client and server to establish a set of cryptographic keys to protect the data; optionally, the client may also be authenticated in this phase. The *data transfer* phase consists of breaking the data and transmitting it as a series of records.

Following are some of the properties of SSL:

♦ Message confidentiality

♦ Handshaking, which may be done by using the key pair algorithm, for end-point authentication

♦ Encryption, which may be done by using a secret key

♦ Message transport, which includes message integrity

♦ Support of digital signatures such as MD5 and SHA

This makes SSL a very powerful instrument in the arsenal against attackers; the main advantage of SSL (and TLS) is that it is protocol independent. SSL is composed of two layers: the SSL Handshake Protocol and the SSL Record.

The Handshake Protocol

The *SSL Handshake Protocol* allows client and server to authenticate each other and to negotiate the keys before the data is transmitted and received. To understand the handshake phase, you need to understand the key generation process. In TLS key generation, the client first computes a `pre_master_secret` — a secret string produced using a *pseudo-random function* (PRF). Then the `pre_master_secret` is combined with a client random and a server random to generate another secret called the `master_secret`, which is used to produce all cryptographic keys to protect the data. The `master_secret` then is used for the cryptographic keys (for encryption and MAC algorithms).

The process is very similar for SSL v3; however, the PRF is replaced with a series of functions based on the combination of MD5 and SHA-1. Figure 22-2 illustrates this process, where Function stands for either the PRF or the combination of MD5 and SHA-1.

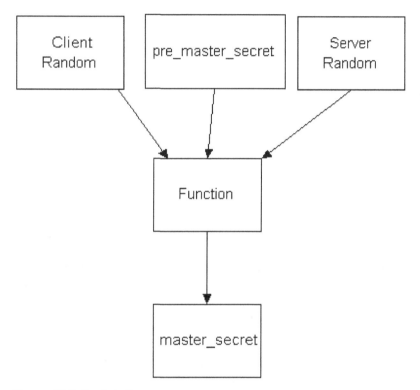

Figure 22-2: Key derivation process

CROSS-REFERENCE: Chapter 9 describes the message digest MD5 and SHA-1 in more detail.

Now that you understand the key generation process, we can continue to explore the handshake process. Think of it as the client saying hello to the server. The server answers with a hello and a certificate, and then the client returns a `master_secret` and sends a `Finished` message that is answered by the server with a `Finished` message. Figure 22-3 illustrates this process.

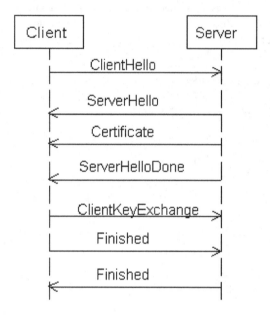

Figure 22-3: Basic SSL Handshake Protocol

As Figure 22-3 illustrates, the client initiates the handshake with a ClientHello message, which contains the supported ciphers and the client random. This message is to communicate the client preferences to the server for version, cipher algorithms, and compression algorithms. The client then waits for the server to send the acceptable parameters based on what the client has presented in the ClientHello message. The server responds with its algorithm preferences and the server random in the first ServerHello message. The client treats any other message returned by the server, except for the hello request, as a fatal error. The ServerHello message has the same format as the ClientHello message. The difference is that the client offers a list and the server responds with a selection from that list. The server may also respond with a session_id for the client to re-use a session on the established keys if the server supports it. Otherwise a zero-length session_id is returned. If the server doesn't support any of the choices in the list that the client has sent in the ClientHello message, the session fails. This is a bit difficult for client implementers since the server decides on which keys and algorithms it will use.

The server normally sends a Certificate message after the ServerHello message, so it can be authenticated. The certificate is a sequence of X.509 certificates and has the server's public key and its identity. The certificate is particular to the selected cipher suite's key exchange algorithm. For instance, a modified X.509 will be used for Fortezza. The sequence has a particular order: The first certificate is the one for the server; the next contains the key for the first certificate; the next certificate contains the key for the previous certificate, and so on until a root certificate is reached. The root certificate contains the last key. In some cases, only one certificate is sent as a test certificate to test out the system.

> **CROSS-REFERENCE:** Chapter 25 describes the X.509 specification.

Because there could be other messages after the certificate, the server signals that it is done with this step in the process with an empty `ServerHelloDone` message. This is a marker interface to complete the certificates. If the server sends no certificates, or not enough certificate information, the `ServerKeyExchange` message is used for additional parameters to complete some of the keys. These keys include `RSA_EXPORT`, `DHE_DSS`, `DHE_DSS_EXPORT`, `DHE_RSA`, and `DHE_RSA_EXPORT`.

The client then sends a `ClientKeyExchange` that contains the `pre_master_secret`, which was computed using the server's public key. It sets the key exchange for the server. For RSA, it will set an `EncryptedPreMasterSecret` message; for Diffie-Hellman, it will set a `ClientDiffieHellmanSecret` message; and for Fortezza, it will set a `FortezzaKeys` message. At this point both server and client have the client random, server random, and `pre_master_secret`, all of which are used to calculate the encryption and MAC keys. The client sends a `Finished` message that contains a MAC of all the previous messages and the server responds with its `Finished` message.

> **NOTE:** TLS and SSL v3 are very similar but incompatible. The differences are few: They include the hashing fuction, the `ClientKeyExchange` message, and the cryptographic key generation (TLS uses HMAC keyed message authentication v.s. SSL v3's keyed MAC function). In addition, TLS does not provide Fortezza support.

So far the handshaking has been established and keys have been exchanged. The point of using SSL is to translate the data into ciphertext. The purpose of the initial handshaking is to set up keys and a `SYN` state, similar to TCP, to synchronize the states in preparation for data transfer. This transfer is accomplished using the SSL Record Protocol.

An example of the cipher algorithm is "`TLS_RSA_WITH_IDEA_CBC_SHA`," which means the message will use an RSA key exchange, an `IDEA_CBC` encryption algorithm, and a `SHA` message digest for the MAC. There are 32 cipher suites.

The SSL Record

The SSL Record is at the lowest level to handle the transport of data; the data stream is broken into fragments and the MAC is computed and appended to the fragment. The combination of MAC and data fragment is encrypted; the encrypted combination of fragments and MAC is referred to as the *encrypted payload*. A header is attached to the payload to form a *record*. As the receiver gets each record, it decrypts and verifies the record; the records are reassembled at the receiving end in plaintext, after validation, to make up the data stream.

This approach is mirrored after TCP. The header contains the *content type, the length*, and the *SSL version*; it is similar to the TCP packet header since it provides the necessary information for processing the payload into data. Figure 22-4 shows the record header.

Header (content type + length + ssl version)	Encrypted Payload (Data fragment + MAC)

Figure 22-4: SSL record

The *content type* identifies the type of message. These messages depend on the current state of the SSL server and client. SSL supports four content types:

- ◆ `application_data`: All data is transmitted as `application_data`, including the ciphertext that is transferred from the sender to the receiver.
- ◆ `alert`: Usually used to transport errors from one peer to another to signal that an error condition has occurred and to provide some level of detail to describe the issue. Some of the conditions could be that the connection is about to close, errors with the handshaking, error with validation of the MAC, and more.
- ◆ `handshake`: Used to carry handshake messages.
- ◆ `change_cipher_spec`: Used to change the algorithm on the encryption and authentication of records. It also signals that the set of keys that was established in the handshaking is ready to be used for application data.

The *length* field is the length of more bytes to read off the receiver before processing the message; it is required for a stream message so that the receiver knows when it has the complete stream before decryption. The *version number* identifies the SSL version number to use; so far there are three versions. For SSLv3, the version's major will be set to 3 and the version's minor will be set to 0. For TLS, the major will be 3 and the minor will be 1. The server may respond with a lesser version. If the server responds with a lesser version and the client does not wish to use that version, the client needs to terminate the connection to the server.

The size of the record header is 5 bytes: 1 byte for the content type, 2 bytes for the protocol version, and 2 bytes for the length.

When the client is finished working with the server, it sends a `close_notify` alert message to signal the server that the connection is going to close. The TCP's `FIN` flag being set in the TCP packet follows this message. The server also responds with the TCP's `FIN` flag being set. These flags being set signify the closing of the connection.

According to the RFC, data fragments can be done in stream or block form depending on the format of the message. There are four cryptographic operations that SSL supports: *digital signing, stream cipher encryption, block cipher encryption,* and *public key encryption*.

There is the one-way hash function of SHA and MD5 for use in *digital signing*; in RSA, a 36-byte MD5 or SHA structure is used for the message digest. In DSS, the 20-byte SHA is used through the digital signing algorithm. In *stream cipher encryption*, the plaintext is exclusively ORed. In the *block cipher encryption*, the message is encrypted in block sizes; it is necessary to pad out the non-used characters, usually with zeros.

SSL Sessions and Connections

SSL makes a distinction between a connection and a session. A *session* represents the negotiated algorithm and the `master_secret`; that is, a session is established every time the `master_secret` is negotiated. A *connection* is the specific communications channel along with the associated keys, cipher choices, and so on.

> **NOTE:** Multiple connections can be associated with a session.

SSL allows a way to circumvent the handshake, since it is expensive (in CPU time and the number of round trips), if the client and server have already communicated once. Client and server are allowed to establish a new connection using a `master_secret` from the previous handshake, and each connection has a different set of keys because it is achieved by combining the old master secret with a random number.

The first time the client interacts with the server, both the client and server create a session and a connection. The server sends a `session_id` in the `ServerHello` message and caches the `master_secret` for later reference. When the client initiates a new connection with the same server, it uses the `session_id` in the `ClientHello` message, and the server resumes the session using the `session_id` in the `ServerHello`. The rest of the handshake is skipped; this is much faster because it re-uses previously processed key material.

So far you have seen how the server is authenticated; however, SSL allows the authentication of the client as well, which is described in Figure 22-5. The server initializes the authentication by requesting a certificate (via the `CertificateRequest` message). The client sends a `Certificate` message and a `CertificateVerify` message (with the private key associated with the certificate) to identify itself. If the client has no certificate, a `Certificate` message with no certificates should be sent, the server may then decide to continue without authentication, or with other means of authentication; otherwise, the server sends a fatal `handshake_failure`.

The SSL session is *stateful*, meaning that the client and server have synchronized states between each other. SSL performance is slow, especially compared to TCP connections. The main factor is the cryptography because it is computationally expensive and it affects the performance because each data fragment is encrypted. Therefore, fragmenting the data into small pieces decreases performance and if the data to be transmitted is large, cryptography is the main factor affecting performance. Also, the choice of the algorithms used during the handshake phase affects performance; you have to choose between a fast algorithm and a strong one. For example, RSA with 1024 bits is about four times slower than the one with 512 bits.

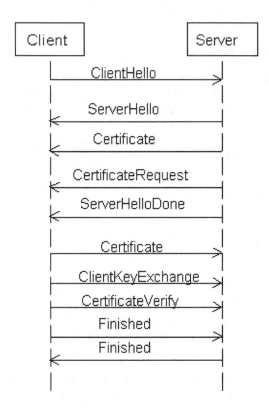

Figure 22-5: SSL Handshake with client authentication

TIP: For sessions that do not have large amounts of data, the handshake becomes the main factor affecting performance.

SSL/TLS modes

When SSL was designed, U.S. export regulations restricted the size of keys that could be used by applications exported from the U.S. Therefore, SSL was designed to have 1024-bit and 512-bit key exchanges to allow the option of strong cryptography providing maximum security while still remaining exportable. SSL v3 and TLS incorporate *Ephemeral RSA* for communication to an exportable client. The server generates a 512-bit key and associates it with its strong key; for domestic clients it just uses the strong key. The Ephemeral RSA mode has the `ServerKeyExchange` message to transmit the signed RSA key, and the client verifies the server's signature.

The other mode for SSL v3 and TLS is the *Server Gated Security* (Microsoft's Server Gated Cryptograph [SGC] or Netscape's Step-Up). Exceptions to the export regulations were allowed so that exportable clients could communicate with secure servers when absolutely necessary — such as in financial applications. The server has a certificate; this certificate identifies the server as able to engage in strong cryptography with exportable clients. Very few trustworthy *Certificate Authorities* (CAs), such as Verisign, issue this certificate. During the handshake, the client offers weak ciphers, and the server presents its certificate. The client verifies the server and confirms that more secure communication is appropriate; the client initiates a second handshake by offering strong ciphers in the `ClientHello` message.

Therefore, SSL v3 and TLS have two modes: Ephemeral RSA and Server Gated Security.

SSL and authentication

So far we have discussed RSA because it is the dominant public algorithm, but SSL v3 supports a number of other ciphers such as DSS and DH, both of which are mandatory in TLS. The TLS standard specifies DH/DSS key exchange and less-used cipher suites that use Elliptic Curves, Kerberos, and Fortezza algorithms. Unlike RSA, which can be used for digital signature and key agreement, DH can only be used for key agreement and DSS for digital signatures. So, DSS and DH are typically used together.

One way that DSS and DH are used together is for the server to generate a temporary DH key, sign it with DSS key, and transmit the signed key using the `ServerKeyExchange` message. The client uses the DH key for key agreement. Another way to use the DSS/DH combination is to use DH keys as fixed keys: The server has a certificate signed with DSS and that contains the DH key; the client uses the DH key in the certificate for key agreement.

For the key agreement, the client and server must be able to compute the shared DH secret. For that, they need their own DH key and the other side's public key. For this to happen, the client gets the server's DH key and generates a DH key in the same family — unless it already has one. The client then sends its public key in the `ClientKeyExchange` message. The DH secret is used as the `pre_master_secret,` and the rest of the connection is the same as with RSA.

Elliptic Curve (EC) ciphers use points in an elliptic curve but no cipher suites — so far — have been standardized. Kerberos is a symmetric key authentication system. It uses a central server trusted by the entities in the system, and the ticket is used to encrypt the `pre_master_secret`. The `ClientKeyExchange` contains both the ticket and the encrypted `pre_master_secret`. The server extracts the shared key from the ticket and decrypts the `pre_master_secret`. The process continues as in the previous cases.

CROSS-REFERENCE: Chapter 5 describes elliptic curves, and Chapter 16 explains Kerberos in more detail. Chapters 4 and 11 discuss RSA.

The Fortezza card is a U.S.-government-designed cryptographic token that uses *Key Exchange Algorithm* (KEA) for the key agreement and SKIPLACK (a block cipher) for the block encryption algorithm. Fortezza cards were specified in SSL v3 but removed for TLS.

Security and Attacks

As discussed, the server is always authenticated, and SSL allows for the client to also be authenticated. SSL provides for secure notification of exceptional conditions, error, and connection closure — assuming that keys are correctly generated and kept secure. As of this writing, no good attacks are known on SSL itself, but there are a few on specific implementations. Each cipher suite has algorithms for key establishment, digital signatures, data encryption, and message digest. The SSL security depends on the security of the cipher used. Also, the random (both client and server) is used to generate the other keys and thus affects the SSL implementation security. Therefore, select your random number generator carefully.

Recall that the client and server share the client random and server random elements and so, if an attacker knows the `master_secret`, all the other keys may be derived; the attacker can decrypt the records or compute the MAC keys. This is very significant because the attacker can change records (decrypting the record and changing the message), although to avoid lots of work, he may not want to change the record length.

> **CAUTION:** The selection of the client and server random affects the SSL implementation.

The attacker could even intercept the connection, behave as one of the end points (the server, for example), establish another connection with the other end point (the client), and control the exchange — this is known as a man-in-the-middle attack. SSL provides a check on the handshake precisely to avoid this type of attack, but because the `master_secret` has been compromised, it could be possible.

The `master_secret` may be acquired if the key establishment algorithm is compromised. In addition, if the key establishment algorithm is compromised for a CA, the attacker can impersonate all entities that trust the CA.

SSL uses digital signatures to authenticate the certificates, to sign the Ephemeral keys, and to sign the `CertificateVerify` messages. Therefore, if the algorithm used for digital signatures is compromised, it affects all these uses and makes SSL vulnerable. For instance, if the server's key is compromised, the attacker can pose as the server; or if the client key is compromised, the attacker can pose as the client. The server key is a valuable key to attack and a *timing cryptanalysis* attack can be used. The attacker using the timing cryptanalysis attack times the victim while it uses the private key and with enough samples, the attacker can recover the entire key. In 1996, Paul Kocher publicized details on this attack and examples using RSA, DH, and DSS.

> **TIP:** A countermeasure to the timing cryptanalysis attack is to slow down operations by a random amount of time, or to make the operations take the same amount of time.

There is a wide range of data encryption algorithms used to encrypt the message; SSL supports a variety of algorithms from the strong 3DES to 40-bit RC4. The selection of data encryption algorithm depends on the data you are transmitting.

Another attack is the million-message attack, usually used with RSA with PKCS #1. The attacker uses the encrypted `pre_master_secret` to generate a series of messages (roughly a million). The victim's server is then probed with these messages and the responses examined until the original message is determined. This is a simplistic explanation and the exact details are beyond the scope of this book.

One countermeasure is, if the server detects an error during the handshake (there are errors in the message), to continue with the handshake by sending a message filled with a `pre_master_secret` with random data. Another counter attack is to use a padding algorithm sensitive to alterations to the plaintext since all messages used by the attacker will be rejected automatically.

HTTPS: HTTP over SSL

Because SSL acts so much like TCP, and there are so many protocols that run over TCP, securing these protocols by creating an SSL channel is a common implementation. The implementation usually is one of two schemes. One is to use separate ports for the secure and non-secure protocols. The alternative is called *upward negotiation*: The application is modified to support a message to indicate that either the client or the server wants to upgrade to SSL; if the other side agrees, the SSL handshake begins.

In HTTP, a TCP connection is established and the client sends requests to the server, which in turn sends a response (a document). Using SSL, the client establishes a TCP connection and then (on top) an SSL channel. The HTTP requests are sent over the SSL channel; the server responds over the SSL connection. The server lets the client know that SSL should be used. The URL begins with `https` rather than `http`. HTTPS is a secure communication mechanism between an HHTP client and an HTTP server pair.

From the Session Layer, this is also a socket pair. By using TLS/SSL, HTTPS can offer a wide range of combinations between keying, cipher algorithms, and message digests. HTTPS provides symmetric capabilities for both client and server, meaning that requests and replies are both encrypted. This is accomplished by synchronizing the preferences of the client and server while following the application protocol of HTTP. HTTPS does not require client-side public key certificates to support this symmetric property of HTTP, so it is helpful in allowing users to connect to a secure sight without having to set up any notion of a public key from the client's perspective.

WLS

TLS has Wireless TLS for wireless support and is supported by the WAP Forum. Wireless devices are slowly becoming predominant for receiving and transmitting information without the use of a laptop or desktop, and handheld devices are used to transfer stocks and receive e-mails, all of which requires security. Security is also needed for the information to and from Web servers. Wireless Transaction Protocol was invented to transfer secure messaging at the Transport Layer. However, there are many differences in the protocol stack.

WAP

There is complexity involved in the Physical Layer of the *Wireless Application Protocol* (WAP). An example is WAP that supports UDP instead of TCP. Compression is applied to many of the packets, and a WAP gateway is used to translate application protocols from one medium to the next. WAP is used to transmit the information over a low-bandwidth wireless environment, and unlike a LAN wire, various frequencies and hops are applied through the transmission of *radio frequencies* (RFs).

Many electronics are used to minimize the noise across the line, and in *Personal Communication Systems* (PCS) the signal is distributed within the noise to hide the digital signals. The digital encoding is exposed by different digital shifting techniques and centering on the frequency that is specific for the bandwidth. Echoes of this center frequency can also introduce harmonics.

Changing the physical medium

Before PCS, scanners could easily pick up wireless phone conversations. Going through the Protocol Gateway does change the physical medium, but other translations are needed through the protocol layers to ease the protocol-to-protocol match. The HTTP and FTP protocols must communicate from the IP to the WAP world exactly so that the Internet protocols may be used from one medium to the next with only minor changes. Some of these changes are text sizes, the number of lines displayed, and amount of graphics transported.

In this model the transmission is done in the RF up to the Bearers. The Bearers are the different underlying protocols that a mobile device can use to communicate with the wireless network. The Bearer bares the frames on top of the RF and translates them into the UDP packets. As mentioned previously, datagrams are a connectionless protocol; this means that there is no guarantee that the message will reach the receiver. Some protocols, such as SMTP, are also connectionless.

When an e-mail is sent, there is no guarantee that the receiver will receive it. However, acknowledgements can be built on top of the datagrams. This is accomplished with the *Wireless Transaction Protocol* (WTP) that provides the reliability of the messages. This will establish packets that are connection-oriented or like TCP. Figure 22-6 shows the WAP protocol stack.

Internet OSI	Internet Example	WAP
Application Layer	SMTP, Telnet, FTP	Wireless Application Layer
Presentation Layer	EBCDIC, ASCII, Big Endian, Little Endian	
Session Layer	Connection	Wireless Session Protocol
Transport Layer	TCP, UDP	Wireless Transaction Protocol Wireless Datagram Protocol
Network Layer	IP	Bearers (SMS, CSD)
Data Link Layer	MAC Frames	Digital Frames
Physical Layer	Cable	RF

Figure 22-6: WAP protocol stack

WSP

The Bearer Services normally support protocols like *Short Message Service* (SMS) or *Circuit Switched Data* (CSD). SMS sends lots of short messages to the mobile device. CSD is like a modem being connected to a laptop that interacts directly with an *Internet service provider* (ISP). The *Wireless Session Protocol* (WSP) handles session management just like in sockets. The difference is the commands such as an S-Connect; the client and server scenario is still used as in the Internet Protocol stack.

WTLS

The *Wireless Transport Layer Security* (WTLS) goals are to provide privacy, server authentication, client authentication, and data integrity. For WTLS to be supported, TLS must also be in place at both the client and the server. This security is needed in order to connect to secure systems such as online banking. The client and server are both authenticated, the message is encrypted, and the message is signed using a one-way hash to ensure that the message has not been intercepted and tampered with (as in the man-in-the-middle attacks).

Summary

SSL was developed for confidentiality, message integrity, and end-point authentication. There have been several versions of SSL and version 3 is the current one. Based on SSL v3, TLS was created to address some of SSL's weaknesses. The handshake and data phases are the phases in data connections. These phases divide the two layers of SSL: the SSL handshake and the SSL record. An SSL session is created every time a new master_secret is negotiated and may have one or more connections. SSL allows for client verification as well as server verification.

The purpose of the SSL handshake is threefold. First, the client and the server need to agree on a set of algorithms that will be used to protect the data. Second, they need to establish a set of cryptographic keys that will be used by those algorithms. Third, the handshake may optionally authenticate the client. So far, there are no known attacks to SSL, but several SSL implementations are vulnerable to some attacks such as the man-in-the-middle attack and the million-message attack.

This chapter also briefly discussed wireless principles such as *Wireless Transport Layer Security* (WTLS), *Wireless Session Protocol* (WSP), and *Wireless Application Protocol* (WAP).

Chapter 23

Java Secure Socket Extension

In This Chapter

♦ Understanding the JSSE API

♦ Working with `SSLContext`, `KeyManager`, and `TrustManager`

♦ Understanding how to use the socket factory and listener

♦ Learning about the underlying layers beneath the JSSE standard API

The *Secure Sockets Layer* (SSL) is a popular means for encrypting traffic between client and servers. SSL sessions are encrypted using server-side certificate information and can also require clients to authenticate themselves. The *Java Secure Socket Extension* (JSSE) provides a standard API for encapsulating the SSL protocol for use by SSL clients and servers. JSSE providers plug their specific SSL implementations beneath the JSSE standard API. By using JSSE in your Java applications, you can better insulate your applications to vendor-specific SSL API mechanisms. Although this is generally true, a vendor-specific method for configuring socket factories and authentication information is still required for JSSE v1.0.

JSSE Architecture

The *Java Secure Socket Extension* (JSSE) is an extension of Java Sockets to provide extended functionality for SSL and *Transport Layer Security* (TLS). Sockets derive their name from wall sockets, where electricity is provided through a connection from the wall into an electric device. Like the connection of electricity, a socket provides a connection of data.

Just as the session of electricity has a beginning and ending of electric current that it provides to the electric device, there is a session of connectivity from the client to the server and back. During this session, encryptions are passed along with other information that changes state between the connections. The state and information that is exchanged between the client and server are based on the protocol, in this case SSL version 3.0 or TLS version 1.0, and so it is critical to understand the different protocols.

The TLS and SSL protocols provide functionality for data encryption, server authentication, message integrity, and client authentication. The JSSE interface, just like the socket interface, works on the Session Layer. The parent applications that operate at the application level, such as HTTPS, FTP, and Telnet, are meant to use sockets to handle the TCP (or UDP) communications and handshaking.

These applications deal with the support of application protocols that require multiple connections and sessions. Some of the applications that use HTTPS require JSSE for some connections and Java Sockets for other connections, depending on whether the application requires a secure or non-secure connection during an implementation of the current process. Just as Java Sockets hide the Ethernet implementations of session and connection, the JSSE protocol hides those layers as well as the handshaking of keys and implementations of the cipher suites. The *connection* is the general transport mechanism, and *session* is state-specific information shared between the peers.

The *socket connection* provides a transport between the two peers, client and server, just as a power cord provides a connection between an appliance and the power source. The OSI layering model provides the definitions of the packets.

The *socket session* is the instance and state between a specific client and server. It includes the handshake protocol, keys, security parameters, and any specific information between the client and server. The JSSE encapsulates socket implementation, encryption, and the TCP/IP stack, as shown in Figure 23-1.

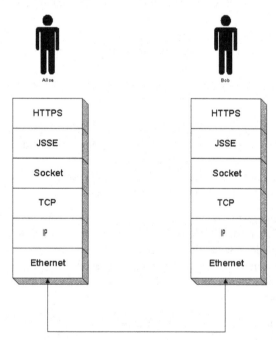

Figure 23-1: JSSE encapsulates sockets and TCP/IP layers

CROSS-REFERENCE: Chapter 21 describes the OSI model.

In addition to the JSSE being a standard API for SSL and TLS, it also supports an API to the *Transport Layer Security* (TLS) secure socket protocol. The JSSE supports SSL versions 2 and 3 and TLS version 1. The JSSE v1 is available from `http://java.sun.com/products/jsse`. A close look at the API shows that, just like the Java Sockets, the JSSE forms wrappers around the regular socket layers around Java; it is just an extension of Java Sockets.

The following packages comprise the JSSE v1.0 architecture:

◆ `java.net.ssl`: This package contains the core classes and the interfaces for the JSSE API.

◆ `javax.net`: This package is the socket support needed for client and server socket factory functionality.

◆ `javax.security.cert`: This package is needed to support basic certificate management functionality.

The JSSE architecture is primarily useful for its encapsulation of SSL Sockets, SSL server socket objects, and factories. SSL session handles can also be useful. Finally, the SSL binding and handshake event and listener APIs are also provided. The following list describes the role of each major API class or interface in the JSSE architecture:

◆ `SSLSocket`: A socket that supports SSL, TLS, and WTLS secure socket protocols.

◆ `SocketFactory`: A factory for socket objects. Factories create the instance of the class for the socket. The factory object can be re-used for new sockets.

◆ `SSLSocketFactory`: A factory of `SSLSocket` objects.

◆ `SSLServerSocket`: A server socket that supports the SSL, TLS, and WTLS secure socket protocols.

◆ `ServerSocketFactory`: A factory for `ServerSocket` objects.

◆ `SSLServerSocketFactory`: A factory for `SSLServerSocket` objects.

◆ `SSLSession`: An interface to an object encapsulating an SSL session (exposing standard session attributes, peer identity, peer host, and cipher suit name).

NOTE: Recall that a session shows information on a relationship between endpoints (such as a server and client).

◆ `SSLSessionContext`: An interface to an object encapsulating a collection of SSL sessions identified with a session ID.

◆ `SSLBindingEvent`: An event class encapsulating SSL session binding and unbinding events.

NOTE: Listener objects can be bound and unbound to an SSL session, and objects that implement `SSLBindingListener` receive `SSLBindingEvents`.

- ◆ SSLBindingListener: A listener interface. Objects wanting to be made aware of SSL session binding and unbinding events implement this interface.

- ◆ HandshakeCompletedEvent: An event class encapsulating the fact that an SSL handshake has completed.

- ◆ HandshakeCompletedListener: A listener interface. Objects wanting to be made aware of SSL handshake completion events implement this interface.

The basic JSSE architecture is rather simple, yet it provides a core suite of API abstractions necessary for tapping the functionality of SSL from within the Java applications. Figure 23-2 describes how a client and server communicate using the JSSE API; the client and server communicate through sockets. The server has an instance of an SSLServerSocket from an SSLServerSocketFactory, and the SSLSession (used to access all state information) is created in the SSLServerSocket. Likewise, the client has an instance of an SSLSocket acquired from the SSLSocketFactory and contains an SSLSession.

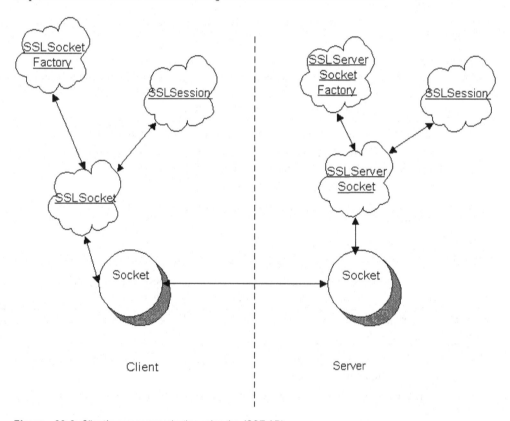

Figure 23-2: Client/server communication using the JSSE API

For a connection to be completed, two peers must establish an acceptance of each other at both ends. One end is normally called a *client*, characterized because it initiates the request, and the other end is a receiver, the server, that listens for the initiating request for connection. In normal Java Sockets, the server has a listening socket called the `ServerSocket` that is generated in `ServerSocketFactory`.

In the JSSE API the interaction is similar; however, `SSLServerSocketFactory` initiates the `SSLServerSocket,` and the `SSLSocketFactory` generates the client's `SSLSocket`. You use the `getDefault()` method, which uses the default `SSLContext`, to retrieve these factories. The property provider defined in the `JRE_HOME\lib\security\java.security` file during runtime defines the SSL factories as the following lines of code show:

```
ssl.ServerSocketFactory.provider = com.richware.ssl.ServerSocketFactory
ssl.SocketFactory.provider = com.richware.ssl.SocketFactory
```

Additionally, there are vendor-specific ways to obtain the handles for the `SSLServerSocketFactory` by using the `SSLContext`. The JSSE reference implementation provides a reference implementation of the `com.net.ssl.SSLContext` class to handle concrete implementations and proper initialization of the `SSLServerSocketFactory`. To initialize the `SSLContext`, at least a `KeyManager` or `TrustManager` must be used to retrieve the collection of the server certificates and keys.

> **CROSS-REFERENCE:** Chapter 8 describes `KeyManagers` and `TrustManagers`.

After a JSSE-specific collection of key managers is created, using the JCA `Keystore` object, the key managers are initialized in the `SSLContext` as the set of keys that are used during the SSL authentication process.

After an SSL server socket has been created, the SSL server listens for the client connection similar to the way the Java Sockets listen to the client connection. This is done by explicitly calling the `ServerSocket`'s `accept` method, or by implicitly calling the `createServerSocket()` function. If the server needs the `SSLSocket` class for interaction, a cast can be done to accept the socket. Listing 23-1 illustrates how these calls are used.

Listing 23-1: Server socket creation

```
try {
  /*
   * Get the server socket factory
   */
  SSLServerSocketFactory ssf =
    (SSLServerSocketFactory)
    SSLServerSocketFactory.getDefault();
  /*
   * Get the server socket
```

```
  */
  SSLServerSocket server
=(SSLServerSocket)ssf.createServerSocket("25001");
  /*
   * Get the client socket
   */
  SSLSocket sock = (SSLSocket)server.accept();
  /*
   * Get the stream
   */
  OutputStream out = sock.getOutputStream();
  InputStream in = sock.getInputStream();
  /*
   * Do the protocol here through the streams
   */
}
catch(IOException e) {
  e.printStackTrace();
}
```

You can expose special SSL-related socket manipulation operations to the SSL server socket by casting the `javax.net.ssl.SSLSocket` subclass of `Socket`. The need for clients to authenticate themselves to SSL servers can also be established on the server side. SSL servers use the `SSLServerSocket.setNeedClientAuth(boolean flag)` method call to indicate whether clients must supply certificates during the creation of new connections to the server. The `SSLServerSocket.getNeedClientAuth()` call returns a `boolean` value indicating whether client authentication is required after such a value has been set.

If the client authentication is required, the SSL client has to provide certificate information to the SSL server. When using JSSE on the client side, the client authentication steps are accomplished primarily using vendor-specific means. This is similar to the SSL server obtaining the socket handles.

After a client obtains an `SSLSocketFactory`, it can then use one of the few simple means for creating a handle to a `javax.net.ssl.SSLSocket` object; a `javax.net.Socket` object is returned using one of four calls defined at the base `SocketFactory` level, as described in the following list:

- `createSocket (String host, int port)` is used for creating a remote host and port number.
- `createSocket (InetAddress host, int port)` is used for creating a remote host and port number.
- `createSocket (String host, int port, InetAddress clientHost, int clientPort)` is used for creating a remote host and port number in addition to a client-side host and port number.

♦ createSocket (InetAddress host, int port, InetAddress clientHost, int clientPort) is used for creating a remote host and port number in addition to a client-side host and port number.

An SSL session represents a communications session between two endpoints. Data communicated between such entities engaged in an SSL session can be exchanged over different physical connections during the lifetime of the session. Likewise, an SSL connection might allow more than one session to utilize the established SSL connection.

> **NOTE:** Due to import control restrictions, the JSSE implementation provided in JDK 1.4 release includes the strong cipher suites, but does not allow the default SSLSocketFactory and SSLServerSocketFactory to be replaced.

JSSE providers

The JSSE uses standard JCA mechanisms for configuring the JDK when running a JVM instance. That is, a JSSE provider can be configured for use with a JVM instance through an entry in the [JRE_HOME] \ lib\ security\ java.security file; the entry security.provider.x can be modified or added to reference a particular security provider. For example, you might have the following line:

```
Security.provider.1 = com.richware.security.SSLProvider
```

Similarly, a security provider might also be configured for use with a JVM instance from within a static method call to the java.security.Security class as exemplified in the following lines:

```
//Add new instance of JSSE Provider
java.security.Provider provider = new
com.sun.net.ssl.internal.ssl.Provider();
java.security.Security.addProvider(provider);
```

The provider class name used for this example is simply the default SSL provider that comes equipped with the downloaded JSSE reference implementation. The end-to-end SSL client and server example that is built up throughout this chapter, in fact, assumes that your SSL client and SSL server have established the default security provider during startup as shown in the preceding code.

The default provider implementation packaged with the JSSE reference implementation provides support for SSL v3 and TLS v1. The default implementation also provides support for RSA encryption used in generating signatures, support for PKCS 12 key store, X.509 key management functionality for loading authentication keys from a key store, and X.509 trust management functionality for chaining of certificates.

SSLContext

The first piece that makes up the SSL API is the `TrustManager` and `KeyManager` that maintain the keys. These interfaces are discussed in other chapters. The interface into the SSL from the keys and managers consists of the `SSLContext`.

Interactions

The `SSLContext` interacts with `TrustManager` and `KeyManager` to use the keys and certificates when the default implementation of the `SSLContext` is not supplied. By default, the JSSE can utilize default `TrustManagers` and `KeyManagers`. However, if any customization is involved, or any default options are changed, the new instance of an `SSLContext` must be used.

The class that defines the `SSLContext` in JSSE is the `com.sun.net.ssl.SSLContext` class. The `SSLContext` provides a context for communicating with the `SecureRandom` algorithm, `KeyManagers`, and `TrustManagers`. Without the `SSLContext`, only default settings may be applied to these algorithms. This means that any access to a non-defaulted `KeyStore`, keying mechanism, `TrustStore`, or `SecureRandom` and their accompanying managers will be denied. The `SSLContext` is the interface for these mechanisms, as shown in Figure 23-3.

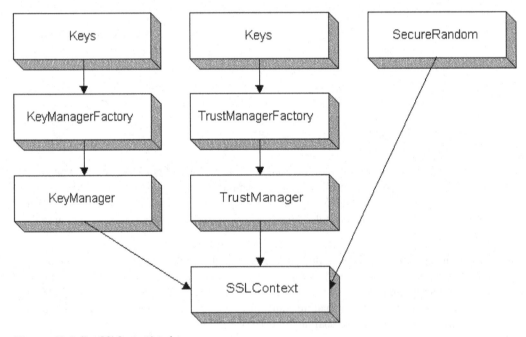

Figure 23-3: The SSLContext interface

The SSLContext

The SSLContext holds the state information across sockets. An instance of this class acts as a context factory for the SocketFactory. The session state is used for the handshaking of the client and server SSLSocket. SSLSockets that are created under the same context can share and re-use the cache sessions. The SSLContext initializes the managers. These managers provide the support for key agreement and authentication. The following protocols are supported in the SSLContext:

- **SSL:** For support of other versions of SSL
- **SSLv2:** Supports version 2 or higher
- **SSLv3:** Supports version 3
- **TLS:** For support of other versions of TLS
- **TLSv1:** Supports version 1

The purpose of SSLContext is to set up the KeyManager, TrustManager, and SecureRandom to the factories of the server and client sockets on what key mechanisms to use for the handshaking. Listing 23-2 displays the server setup for a KeyManager; it is an example of X509-based key managers using the com.sun.net.ssl.KeyManager class. A TrustManager uses the com.sun.ssl.TrustManager package to implement the trusted remote process decisions used during the SSL authentication.

The standard JCA java.security.SecureRandom class is used for generating a random seed value that is used for the SSLContext. After getting the handle to the KeyManager objects, the TrustManager objects, and the SecureRandom object, the SSLContext object can be created and initialized. These objects are used during the initialization of the SSLContext object that will be used subsequently to initialize the security and operational qualities of the SSLServerSocketFactory.

Listing 23-2: X509-based key manager

```
/**
 * Method getServerSocketFactory
 * @param type is the support of TLS.
 * @return the ServerSocketfactory created with the context.
 */
public static ServerSocketFactory getServerSocketFactory(String type) {
  if (type.equals("TLS")) {
SSLServerSocketFactory ssf = null;
try {
  /*
   * set up key manager to do server authentication
   */
  SSLContext    ctx;
```

```
KeyManagerFactory kmf;
KeyStore     ks;
/*
 *   passphrase is the password for the store
 */
char[] passphrase = "passphrase".toCharArray();
/*
 *   Use TLS
 */
ctx = SSLContext.getInstance("TLS");
/*
 *   Get an instance of the X509
 */
kmf = KeyManagerFactory.getInstance("SunX509");
/*
 *   Get the default Java KeyStore
 */
ks = KeyStore.getInstance("JKS");
/*
 *   Open the keystore that is a file called testkeys and the password
 */
ks.load(new FileInputStream("testkeys"), passphrase);
/*
 *   Initialize the KeyManager with the KeyStore
 */
kmf.init(ks, passphrase);
/*
 *   Initialize the SSLContext with the keyManager
 */
ctx.init(kmf.getKeyManagers(), null, null);
/*
 *   Initialize the ServerSocketFactory with the SSLContext
 */
ssf = ctx.getServerSocketFactory();
return ssf;
} catch (Exception e) {
e.printStackTrace();
}
} else {
return ServerSocketFactory.getDefault();
}
return null;
}
```

Another way to look at the calling of these methods is in a UML sequence diagram, as shown in Figure 23-4.

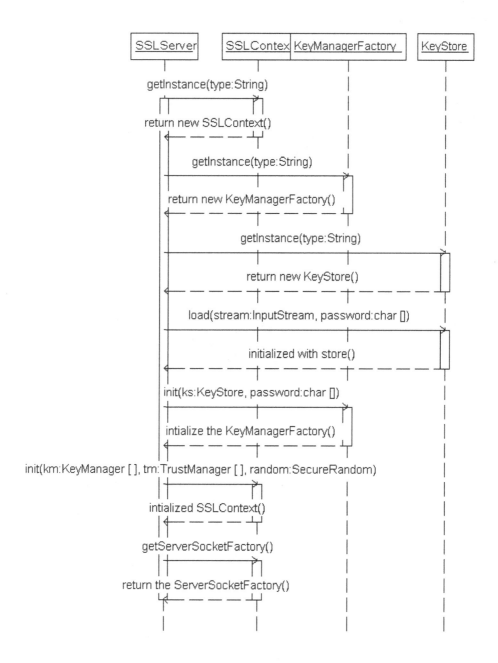

Figure   23-4: SSLServer, SSLContext, KeyManager,and KeyStore UML sequence

SSLSession

A `javax.net.ssl.SSLSession` represents a security context negotiated between the client and the server. Once a session is created, it is used between the same connections of the client and server. The session contains the cipher suite, connection information, and management information that will be used over the secure socket connection. The session also can be seen as means to retrieve key information from a socket connection. One of the items that can be retrieved is the session ID that identifies a particular session. Other items include the creation time of the session, the certificates, the cipher suite name, and the `SSLSessionContext`, as shown in Listing 23-3.

Listing 23-3: Getting the `SSLSession`

```
/*
 * Get the SSLSession and print some of the session info
 */
SSLSession session = socket.getSession();
System.out.println("Peer Host :" + session.getPeerHost());
System.out.println("Name of the cipher suite :" +
session.getCipherSuite());
/*
 *   Get the certificate Chain
 */
X509Certificate[] certificates = session.getPeerCertificateChain();
/*
 * Print the distinguished Principal's name
 */
System.out.println("DN :" + certificates[0].getSubjectDN().getName();
```

An `SSLSession` is associated with getting information from a given connection. However, a client and server can contain many connections and peers to those connections. To encapsulate a set of `SSLSessions`, an `SSLSessionContext` is used that contains the server's or client's set of `SSLSessions` that are associated with the connection. An individual `SSLSession` can be retrieved by the `getSession()` on a particular client socket. Also, the `SSLSessionContext` that is retrieved from the `SSLSession` contains a set of more `SSLSessions` that may be part of the socket entity.

For example, when a `ServerSocket` has many client sessions, the `ServerSocket` can retrieve the `SSLSessionContext` that contains all the sets of `SSLSessions` related to all of the client sessions. The `SSLSessionContext` is a set of `SSLSessions` that belong to either client or a server that maintains many connections, and correspondingly many `SSLSessions`. The set is stored in an enumeration data type that is looked up by the `SSLSession`'s identification. The `SSLSessionBindingEvent` handles any notification of events to the `SSLSession`. Attackers can easily intercept data that is open across a network.

When the data includes private information, such as passwords and credit card numbers, steps must be taken to hide the data to make the data unintelligible except to the intended parties. You must ensure these parties are authentic, that they are who they say they are; and ensure that the data has not been modified during transport; therefore, a form of data integrity must be enforced. TLS and SSL were designed to protect the privacy and integrity of data during transport. Each instance creates a trust and key manager, if any are needed for the authentication in the SSLSession.

JSSE SSLServerSockets

Creating SSL server sockets can be as simple as creating regular Java TCP/IP server sockets. SSL server socket abstractions provide additional hooks, however, to manipulate the security and SSL-related operation characteristics of SSL socket connections. SSL cipher parameters, authentication properties, and handshaking management are also exposed by the SSL abstractions.

Although standard APIs exist for creating SSL server sockets using standard SSL server socket factories, the means by which handles to SSL server socket factories are obtained can be JSSE provider-specific. The SSLServerSocket is obtained through the SSLServerSocketFactory that creates the instance of the SSLServerSocket. The javax.net.ssl.SSLServerSocketFactory extends the javax.net.ServerSocketFactory class. Once the SSLContext of the SSLServerSocketFactory is defined, an unlimited supply, depending on resources, of ServerSockets can be created containing the same SSLContext information. The factory provides the capability to create instances depending on the SSLContext specified for the factory.

Obtaining an SSL server socket factory

The JSSE uses the concept of socket factories to create handles to SSL sockets. The javax.net.ServerSocketFactory class is an abstract class used to create generic server sockets. The javax.net.ssl.SSLServerSocketFactory abstract class is used to create SSL server socket handles and subclasses javax.net.ServerSocketFactory. The default server socket factory class name is identified in the [JRE_HOME] \ lib\ security\ java.security file for your Java runtime environment using ssl.ServerSocketFactory.provider property name. Additionally, JSSE providers often provide vendor-specific ways to obtain handles to SSLServerSocketFactory objects so that server authentication information can be provided.

For example, the JSSE reference implementation provides a com.sun.net.ssl.SSLContext class that can be used to obtain handles to concrete SSLServerSocketFactory implementation objects after proper initialization. Before you can use the reference implementation's SSLContext object to obtain such an SSL server socket factory, you must first take a number of steps to configure the SSL server socket with particular security and operational properties.

The standard JCA `java.security.KeyStore` object is first used to obtain a handle to a stored collection of server certificates and keys. For example, you first obtain a handle to a stored collection of server certificates and keys via a `KeyStore` object. Also, you create a `KeyStore` object using the JCA-provided LKS keystore type with a `testKeys` keystore file name; it is loaded using a `passphrase` password.

A special JSSE reference implementation-specific collection of key managers is then created using the JCA `KeyStore` object. This object is used to manage the keys employed during the SSL authentication process. For example, you create a collection of X509-based key managers using the `com.sun.net.ssl.KeyManager`. `TrustManagers` and `SecureRandom` can also be initialized with non-default implementations and passed inside the `SSLContext`.

Now that you have handles to `KeyManager` objects, `TrustManager` objects, and a `SecureRandom` object, you can create and initialize the `SSLContext` object. Such objects used during initialization of the `SSLContext` object are also used subsequently to initialize the security and operational qualities of the `SSLServerSocketFactory`. The creation and initialization of the JSSE reference implementation-specific `SSLContext`.

Creating SSL server sockets

You can create handles to SSL server sockets using the `SSLServerSocketFactory` object in one of three ways. The `SSLServerSocketFactory` object's base `ServerSocketFactory` class has three standard `createServerSocket()` methods defined. These return handles to `java.net.ServerSocket` objects. When you are using a `SSLServerSocket` subclass, the returned server sockets will actually be subclasses of the abstract `javax.net.ssl.SSLServerSocket` class. Listing 23-4 shows an example that creates an SSL server socket.

Listing 23-4: The `SSLServer` class: An example for creating SSL server sockets

```
package com.richware.chap23;

import java.io.*;
import java.net.*;
import java.security.*;
import javax.net.*;
import javax.net.ssl.*;
import javax.security.cert.*;

/**
 * Class SSLServer
 * This example demonstrates a JSSE server with context creation.
 *
```

```
 * Copyright:    Copyright (c) 2002 Wiley Publishing, Inc.
 * @author Rich Helton <rhelton@richware.com>
 * @version 1.0
 * DISCLAIMER: Please refer to the disclaimer at the beginning of this
book.
 */
public class SSLServer extends Thread
{
  private final static int port = 25001;
  Socket                 sock;
  String                 docroot = "C:\\";
  final static String    debug   = "none";

  /**
   * Method main
   * The main driver for the server.
   *
   * @param args none needed
   *
   * @throws Exception if there is an issue.
   *
   */
  public static void main(String[] args) throws Exception
  {
    try
    {
      System.out.println("Starting SSLServer....");

      /*
       * Pass in the argument of the keystore file
       * It will be opened in the same directory as the application
       */
      if (args[0] == null)
      {
        System.out.println(
          "This application requires an input file for the location of
the keystore");
      }

      String localDirectory = System.getProperty("user.dir");
      System.out.println("Changing directory to Chapter 23");
      System.setProperty("user.dir",
                      localDirectory
                      + "\\com\\richware\\chap23\\");
      localDirectory = System.getProperty("user.dir");

      /*
       * Get the local keystore that contains a trusted certificate
       */
```

```java
        String localInputFile = localDirectory + args[ 0];

    System.out.println(
      "Openining Chapter 23 plus the input file as an argument: " +
localInputFile);

    /*
     * Set the SSL internal debugger to none
     * Set it to all for all connections
     */
    System.out.println("Setting SSL debugging to :" + debug);
    System.setProperty("javax.net.debug", debug);

    ServerSocketFactory ssf =
      SSLServer.getServerSocketFactory("TLS",
                                        localInputFile);
    ServerSocket         ss = ssf.createServerSocket(port);
    ((SSLServerSocket) ss).setNeedClientAuth(true);

    /*
     * Keep accepting Socket Connections and starting them on a thread
     */
    while (true)
    {
      System.out
        .println("Waiting for client connection....");
      new SSLServer(ss.accept()).start();
    }
  }
  catch (Exception e)
  {
    e.printStackTrace();
  }
}


/**
 * Method getServerSocketFactory
 *
 *
 * @param type is the support of TLS.
 * @param filename
 *
 * @return the ServerSocketfactory created wuth the context.
 *
 */
public static ServerSocketFactory getServerSocketFactory(
        String type, String filename)
{
  if (type.equals("TLS"))
```

```
{
  SSLServerSocketFactory ssf = null;
  System.out.println("Starting TLS Exchange....");
  try
  {
    /*
     * set up key manager to do server authentication
     */
    SSLContext          ctx;
    KeyManagerFactory   kmf;
    TrustManagerFactory tmf;
    KeyStore            ks;

    /*
     *  passphrase is the password for the store
     */
    char[] passphrase = "passphrase".toCharArray();

    /*
     *  Use TLS
     */
    ctx = SSLContext.getInstance("TLS");

    /*
     *  Get an instance of the X509
     */
    kmf = KeyManagerFactory.getInstance("SunX509");

    /*
     *  Get an instance of the X509
     */
    tmf = TrustManagerFactory.getInstance("SunX509");

    /*
     *  Get the default Java KeyStore
     */
    ks = KeyStore.getInstance("JKS");

    /*
     *  Open the keystore that is a file called testkeys and the
password
     */
    ks.load(new FileInputStream(filename), passphrase);

    /*
     *  Initialize the KeyManager with the KeyStore
     */
    kmf.init(ks, passphrase);
    tmf.init(ks);
```

```
      System.out.println("Opened KeyStore");

      /*
       *   Initialize the SSLContext with the keyManager
       */
      ctx.init(kmf.getKeyManagers(), tmf.getTrustManagers(),
              null);
      /*
       *   Initialize the ServerSocketFactory with the SSLContext
       */
      ssf = ctx.getServerSocketFactory();
      return ssf;
    }
    catch (Exception e)
     {
      e.printStackTrace();
     }
  }
  else
   {
    return ServerSocketFactory.getDefault();
   }
  return null;
}

/**
 * Constructor SSLServer
 * Initializes the client socket when acceptance.
 *
 * @param s the client socket.
 *
 */
public SSLServer(Socket s)
 {
   sock = s;
 }

/**
 * Method run
 * This method is a thread that is accepting an input socket
 *
 */
public void run()
 {
   try
    {
      System.out.println("Received client connection....");
      /*
       *   Get the Input and Output Socket Streams
```

```
     */
    PrintWriter    out = new PrintWriter(
      new BufferedWriter(
        new OutputStreamWriter(sock.getOutputStream())));
    BufferedReader in  =
      new BufferedReader(new InputStreamReader(sock
        .getInputStream()));
    String         inputLine;

    /*
     * Read until all input is read
     */
    if ((inputLine = in.readLine()) != null)
    {
      System.out.println(inputLine);
    }

    out.println("Post HTTP/1.1");
    out.flush();

    /*
     * Close the stream and connection
     */
    in.close();
    out.close();
  }
  /*
   * Print any errors
   */
  catch (IOException ex)
  {
    System.out.println("Error: " + ex.getMessage());
    ex.printStackTrace();
  }
  finally
  {
    try
    {
      System.out.println("Closing Client Socket......");

      /*
       * Close the Socket Connection
       */
      sock.close();
    }
    catch (IOException e) {}
  }
}
}
```

SSL server socket listener

After an SSL server socket has been created, the `SSLServerSocket` listens for the SSL client requests in the same way that regular server sockets listen for socket client requests. That is, the `SSLServerSocket` class's `accept()` method is used to block for client requests and returns an instance of a `java.net.Socket` object representing the socket connection with the requesting client. By casting this object to the `java.net.ssl.SSLSocket` abstract subclass of `Socket`, special SSL-related socket manipulation operations are exposed to the SSL server socket.

Then the thread handler may handle client requests using socket calls from the `java.net` package and I/O stream handling from the `java.io` package as usual without any cognizance of SSL specifics.

Client authorization

The need for clients to authenticate themselves to SSL servers can also be established on the server side. SSL servers use the `SSLServerSocket.setNeedClientAuth(boolean flag)` method call to indicate whether clients must supply certificates during the creation of new connections with the server. The `SSLServerSocket.getNeedClientAuth()` call returns a `boolean` value indicating whether client authentication is required after such a value has been set. If client authentication is required, the SSL client has to provide certificate information to the SSL server.

> **NOTE:** When using JSSE on the client side, the client authentication steps are accomplished primarily using vendor-specific means. The vendor-specific means for providing such information will most likely be similar to the means that JSSE SSL servers use to obtain handles to JSSE SSL server socket factories.

JSSE SSL client sockets

The creation of SSL sockets from client to server is also a very simple task using JSSE. Clients must first obtain handles from the SSL socket factories. The handles, which are obtained in the same manner as SSL servers, obtain handles to the SSL socket factories. Creation of SSL client sockets is then accomplished using one of a few very simple creation calls. SSL sockets are then used much as regular Java Socket objects are used to communicate with a remote server. This section describes how to obtain SSL socket factory objects and how to create SSL socket objects using JSSE.

Obtaining an SSL socket factory

Akin to the way in which SSL servers obtain handles to SSL server socket factories, SSL clients obtain handles to SSL socket factories. The abstract `javax.net.ssl.SSLSocketFactory` class extends the `javax.net.SocketFactory` class to return SSL socket handles for clients. JSSE providers might provide vendor-specific mechanisms for obtaining `SSLSocketFactory` handles, or a client might obtain a handle to the default `SSLSocketFactory` configured for that client's environment.

The vendor-specific way for obtaining an `SSLSocketFactory` handle using the JSSE reference implementation is nearly identical to the creation of `SSLServerSocketFactory` handles. The only key difference is that the client initiates the request and doesn't have to listen and wait for the request to be initiated. Listing 23-5 demonstrates this process.

Listing 23-5: The `SSLClient` class: An example usage of `SSLSocketFactory`

```
package com.richware.chap23;

import java.io.*;
import java.net.*;
import java.security.*;
import javax.net.*;
import javax.net.ssl.*;
import javax.security.cert.*;

/**
 * Class SSLClient
 * This example demonstrates a JSSE client with context creation.
 *
 * Copyright:   Copyright (c) 2002 Wiley Publishing, Inc.
 * @author Rich Helton <rhelton@richware.com>
 * @version 1.0
 * DISCLAIMER: Please refer to the disclaimer at the beginning of this
book.
 */
public class SSLClient
{
  private final static int    port  = 25001;
  private final static String host  = "127.0.0.1";
  final static String         debug = "none";

  /**
   * Method main
   * This method is the main driver for the client.
   *
   * @param args none needed, later can put in host and port.
   *
   * @throws Exception if there is an issue.
   *
   */
  public static void main(String[] args) throws Exception
  {
    try
```

```
    {
    System.out.println("Starting SSLClient....");
    /*
     * Pass in the argument of the keystore file
     * It will be opened in the same directory as the application
     */
    if (args[ 0] == null)
    {
      System.out.println(
        "This application requires an input file for the location of
the keystore");
    }

    String localDirectory = System.getProperty("user.dir");
    System.out.println("Changing directory to Chapter 23");
    System.setProperty("user.dir",
                       localDirectory
                       + "\\com\\richware\\chap23\\");
    localDirectory = System.getProperty("user.dir");

    /*
     * Get the local keystore that contains a trusted certificate
     */
    String localInputFile = localDirectory + args[ 0];
    System.out.println(
      "Openining Chapter 23 plus the input file as an argument: " +
localInputFile);

    /*
     * Set the SSL internal debugger to all
     */
    System.out.println("Setting SSL debugging to :" + debug);
    System.setProperty("javax.net.debug", debug);

    /*
     * Get a TLS socket factory
     */
    SSLSocketFactory socketFactory =
      SSLClient.getClientSocketFactory("TLS",
                                        localInputFile);

    /*
     * Get the client socket instance
     */

    //    SSLSocket    socket    =
    //       (SSLSocket) socketFactory.createSocket("www.richware.com",
    //                  25001);
    SSLSocket sock =
```

```
     (SSLSocket) socketFactory.createSocket(host, port);

  /*
   * send http request
   *
   * Before any application data is sent or received, the
   * SSL socket will do SSL handshaking first to set up
   * the security attributes.
   *
   * The only way to tell there was an error is to call
   * PrintWriter.checkError().
   */
  System.out.println("Socket : " + sock);
  sock.startHandshake();
  System.out.println("Handshake finished");

  /*
   * Get the SSLSession and print some of the session info
   */
  SSLSession session = sock.getSession();
  System.out.println("Peer Host :"
                     + session.getPeerHost());
  System.out.println("Name of the cipher suite :"
                     + session.getCipherSuite());

  /*
   *  Get the certificate Chain
   */
  X509Certificate[] certificates =
    session.getPeerCertificateChain();

/*
 * Print the distinguished Principal's name
 */
  System.out
    .println("DN :"
             + certificates[0].getSubjectDN().getName());

  /*
   * Get the output stream
   */
  PrintWriter out = new PrintWriter(
    new BufferedWriter(
      new OutputStreamWriter(sock.getOutputStream())));

  /*
   * Send the Get method
   */
  out.println("GET HTTP/1.1");
```

```
    out.println();
    out.flush();

    /*
     * Make sure there were no issues
     */
    if (out.checkError())
    {
      System.out
        .println("SSLClient:  java.io.PrintWriter error");
    }

    /*
     * Read any responses
     */
    BufferedReader in =
      new BufferedReader(new InputStreamReader(sock
        .getInputStream()));
    String        inputLine;

    /*
     * Read until all input is read
     */
    while ((inputLine = in.readLine()) != null)
    {
      System.out.println(inputLine);
    }

    /*
     * Close the stream and connection
     */
    in.close();
    out.close();
    sock.close();
  }
  catch (Exception e)
  {
    e.printStackTrace();
  }
}

/**
 * Method getClientSocketFactory
 *
 *
 * @param type is the supported TLS type.
 * @param filename
 *
 * @return the SocketFactory created with the context.
```

```
 *
 */
public static SSLSocketFactory getClientSocketFactory(
        String type, String filename)
{
  if (type.equals("TLS"))
  {
    SSLSocketFactory factory = null;
    System.out.println("Starting TLS Exchange....");
    try
    {
      /*
       * set up key manager to do server authentication
       */
      SSLContext        ctx;
      KeyManagerFactory   kmf;
      TrustManagerFactory tmf;
      KeyStore          ks;

      /*
       *  passphrase is the password for the store
       */
      char[] passphrase = "passphrase".toCharArray();

      /*
       *  Use TLS
       */
      ctx = SSLContext.getInstance("TLS");

      /*
       *  Get an instance of the X509
       */
      kmf = KeyManagerFactory.getInstance("SunX509");

      /*
       *  Get an instance of the X509
       */
      tmf = TrustManagerFactory.getInstance("SunX509");

      /*
       *  Get the default Java KeyStore
       */
      ks = KeyStore.getInstance("JKS");

      /*
       *  Open the keystore that is a file called testkeys and the
password
       */
      ks.load(new FileInputStream(filename), passphrase);
```

```
      /*
       *   Initialize the KeyManager with the KeyStore
       */
      kmf.init(ks, passphrase);
      tmf.init(ks);
      System.out.println("Opened KeyStore");

      /*
       *   Initialize the SSLContext with the keyManager
       */
      ctx.init(kmf.getKeyManagers(), tmf.getTrustManagers(),
               null);

      /*
       *   Initialize the SocketFactory with the SSLContext
       */
      factory = ctx.getSocketFactory();
      return factory;
    }
    catch (Exception e)
      {
      e.printStackTrace();
      }
    }
    else
      {
      return (SSLSocketFactory) SSLSocketFactory.getDefault();
      }

    return null;
  }
}
```

Alternatively, a default SSLSocketFactory, which can be configured for the client's environment, is the [JRE_HOME] \ lib\ security\ java.security file's ssl.SocketFactory.provider property as follows:

```
ssl.SocketFactory.provider=com.assuredtech.ssl.SocketFactory
```

The output for the client looks like the following:

```
>java com.richware.chap23.SSLClient testkeys
Starting SSLClient....
Changing directory to Chapter 23
Openining Chapter 23 plus the input file as an argument: C:\
\com\richware\chap23\testkeys
```

```
Setting SSL debugging to :none
Starting TLS Exchange....
Opened KeyStore
Socket : ac2f9c[ SSL_NULL_WITH_NULL_NULL:
Socket[ addr=127.0.0.1/127.0.0.1,port=25
001,localport=1244]]
Handshake finished
Peer Host :127.0.0.1
Name of the cipher suite :SSL_RSA_WITH_RC4_128_SHA
DN :CN=Duke, OU=Java Software, O="Sun Microsystems, Inc.", L=Cupertino,
ST=CA, C=US
HTTP/1.0 200 OK
Post HTTP/1.1
```

and the corresponding server output is as follows:

```
>java com.richware.chap23.SSLServer testkeys
Starting SSLServer....
Changing directory to Chapter 23
Openining Chapter 23 plus the input file as an argument: C:\
com\richware\chap23\testkeys
Setting SSL debugging to :none
Starting TLS Exchange....
Opened KeyStore
Waiting for client connection....
Waiting for client connection....
Received client connection....
Wait for input
Received input
GET HTTP/1.1
Closing Client Socket......
```

Creating SSL client sockets

After an `SSLSocketFactory` is obtained, a client can then use one of the few simple means
for creating a handle to a `javax.net.ssl.SSLSocket` object. A
`java.net.Socket.object` is returned using one of four calls defined in the base
`SocketFactory` level as follows:

- ◆ `createSocket( String host, int port)`: Creates a socket given a remote host
  and port number.

- ◆ `createSocket( InetAddress host, int port )`: Creates a socket given a
  remote host and port number.

- ◆ `createSocket (String host, int port, InetAddress clientHost,
  int clientPort)`: Creates a socket given a remote host and port number in addition
  to a client-side host and port number.

◆ createSocket(InetAddress host, int port, InetAddress clientHost, int clientPort): Creates a socket given a remote host and port number in addition to a client-side host and port number.

Additionally, the SSLSocketFactory subclass of SocketFactory defines another createSocket() method that creates a socket wrapped around an existing socket. In addition to an existing socket handle, a remote server host String, a remote port number, and a boolean value are provided to indicate whether to close the wrapped socket when the newly created socket is closed. The signature of this method is createSocket(Socket wrappedSocket, String host, int portNumber, boolean autoClose).

> **NOTE:** When you are creating SSLSocket objects, they must be cast from the signature java.net.Socket type.

Here is an example of how to create an SSLSocket object:

```
// Set remote host and port number
String host = "111.111.111.111";
String portNumber = 9000;
// Create an SSLSocket to a remote server
SSLSocket sslSocket = (SSLSocket) sslSocketFactory.createSocket(host,
portNumber);
```

Then the use of the SSLSocket objects on the client side proceeds as usual with the base Socket class. All encryption and decryption via SSL occur transparently to the client when InputStream and OutputStream objects are used to receive and send data, respectively.

An SSL session represents a communications session between two endpoints. Data communicated between such entities engaged in an SSL session can be exchanged over different physical connections during the lifetime of the session. Likewise, an SSL connection might allow more than one session to utilize the established SSL connection. To get the different SSLSessions, the SSLSessionContext class is used to retrieve the set of SSLSessions.

In the server side, the capability to create SSL sessions associated with an SSL server socket can be established using the SSLServerSocket.setEnabledSessionCreation(boolean flag) method. The boolean value passed into such a method, of course, indicates true if SSL sessions are allowed to be created on the server socket connection. The SSLServerSocket.getEnabledSessionCreation() method call returns a boolean value to determine whether the SSL server socket enables session creation.

The same two methods exist on the SSLSocket object as well. In addition to such methods, the SSLSocket object also provides a getSession() method to return an SSLSession object used by the current connection. The SSLSession.invalidate() method is used to invalidate sessions and, thus, prevent other connections from using the current SSL session.

The `javax.net.ssl.SSLSession` interface provides a means by which objects can be bound to a session; this interface uses a `String` name for removing and retrieving such objects via the following methods:

♦ `void putValue( String name, Object value)`: Binds the named object to the session.

♦ `void removeValue ( String name )`: Removes the bound named object from the session.

♦ `Object getValue ( String name)`: Returns a handle to an object bound with an associated name to this session.

♦ `String [] getValueNames ( )`: Returns a collection of `String` names for those objects bound to this session.

Additionally, `SSLSession` defines a number of other getters related to attributes of the SSL session; here is a list of these methods:

♦ `byte [ ] getID ( )`: Returns the session ID.

♦ `String getPeerHost ( )`: Returns the host name for the remote session peer.

♦ `X509Certificate [ ] getPeerCertificateChain ( )`: Returns a chain of certificates associated with the remote peer of this session.

♦ `String getCipherSuite ( )`: Returns a name for the SSL cipher suite used by this session.

♦ `long getCreationTime ( )`: Returns a long value representation of when the session was created, measured in milliseconds since January 1, 1970.

♦ `long getLastAcessedTime ( )`: Returns a long value representation of when the session was last used, measured in milliseconds since January 1, 1970.

♦ `SSLSessionContext getSessionContext ( )`: Returns a handle to the context for the session.

The `javax.net.ssl.SSLSessionContext` interface simply serves as a collection of `SSLSession` objects that are associated with a particular entity. The `SSLSessionContext` interface defines the `getIDs ( )` method to return an enumeration of all session IDs associated with the SSL context. The `SSLSessionContext` interface also defines a `getSession (byte [ ] sessonID)` method to return an `SSLSession` identified by the session ID byte array.

The client and server

To establish the two peer sessions of both the client and the server, a server must be listening for the client to request upon. The server must be using a `KeyManager` or `TrustManager` that the client can accept. The client initiates the request to the server for an SSL connection. The client tells the server which cipher suites it can accept. The server responds with which SSL cipher suites it supports. By default, SSL supports eight cipher suites based on key exchange, encryption, and one-way hash. These are:

- SSL_DHE_DSS_EXPORT_WITH_DES40_CBC_SHA

- SSL_DHE_DSS_WITH_3DES_EDE_CBC_SHA

- SSL_DHE_DSS_WITH_DES_CBC_SHA

- SSL_RSA_EXPORT_WITH_RC4_40_MD5

- SSL_RSA_WITH_3DES_EDE_CBC_SHA

- SSL_RSA_WITH_DES_CBC_SHA, SSL_RSA_WITH_RC4_128_MD5

- SSL_RSA_WITH_RC4_128_SHA

Here is an example of how to read this: SSL_RSA_WITH_RC4_128_SHA means that the keys are using an RSA key exchange using the RC4 algorithm at 128 bits and the SHA one-way hash.

After the client and the server negotiate which algorithm suite to use, the server responds with a certificate to verify the server identity. This initiates a key exchange by the keys that are contained in the X.509 certificate. The client completes the key exchange of public and private keys to the server after verifying the certificate, which includes checking the validity of the keys with the message digest of SHA or MD5. Based on the type of key exchange, RSA or Diffie-Helman, the client makes a final recommendation on the rest of the cipher suite. The server may accept the recommendation and accept the exchange.

The SSL protocol handles most of the interaction. The developer in JSSE selects the keys, can set the type of cipher suite to use, and establishes the manager of the keys or trust. The developer initiates the entries that are needed for the SSL and TLS protocol, but does not need to worry about most of the internal exchanges. The developer does have access to look at any part that is going on in the session by the SSLSession class.

HTTPSURLConnection

Because SSL became popular because of its use on the Internet over HTTP, it is natural to think about how JSSE can be used with Web-enabled applications. On the Web-client side, the built-in SSL functionality of your Web browser will most likely be utilized when the need for a Web-enabled SSL client arises. However, signed Java applets may also take advantage of JSSE. Homegrown Web clients may also utilize the standard Java URL, java.net, and java.io libraries to implement Web-based clients over HTTPS.

However, if the developer uses the standard Java URL libraries, a vendor must provide a java.net.URLStreamHandler implementation, and you must configure such an implementation with the JVM using the java.protocol.handler.pkgs system property. Additional arguments that can be defined in this system property are the https proxy host, proxy port, and cipher suite.

The HttpsUrlConnection encapsulates both the SSLSocketFactory class and the HostnameVerifier class. These are the classes that are needed to complete an HTTPS connection. HTTPS (Secure HTTP) is one of the primary uses of SSL and TLS. The

`HttpsUrlConnection` supports the HTTP protocol and using SSL or TLS as the underlying layers that handle the handshaking, confidentiality, and integrity. The `HostnameVerifier` is used to ensure that the host name in the certificate matches the URL that the HTTPS is requesting the connection from.

If the two host names do not match, then a false is returned and the connection should not be allowed. Encapsulating these classes gives a developer and architect the ability to build a HTTPS client while using many of the defaults of SSL and TLS without having to explicitly set up the socket interfaces. Specifying the URL and not explicitly assigning a port and host establishes the connection.

Summary

JSSE hides a lot of the complexities of SSL and TLS, but provides the security of either protocol. SSL and TLS provide integrity between data connections, a means of transferring keys, and encryption to the data sent between the connections for confidentiality. To accomplish the work that JSSE provides would require an in-depth knowledge of both the TCP/IP and UDP/IP protocols to extend the Java Socket layer as well as the ability to implement the SSL and TLS protocol. Using the input and output streams enables the developer to work with just the data and not decipher each block of data and maintain the session keying in the protocol itself. There is a great deal of complexity that is hidden from the developer of JSSE. However, using SSL and TLS on the Internet is a must for providing any level of security.

This chapter provided an introduction to JSSE, and steps must be taken in the future to enhance the security wherever possible. There are many places that the developer must anticipate attacks. The `KeyStore` and `TrustStore` must be secure, as well as any access to the code. Each endpoint must be examined to ensure that there are no security issues at a package and coding level. Some extra precautions can be established to combine other techniques.

An example is using a `KeyStore` and certificates from the LDAP interface and taking advantage of the security of LDAP. Another is using the `SSLPermissions` and security manager of the server and client to provide only local initialization of the server through a JAAS authentication so that only an authenticated user can start and stop the `SSLServer`. These are just a couple of examples of enhancing applications. The developer and architect should understand a multitude of protocols and algorithms and provide their own combination that seems reasonable. The security measures described are just building blocks. The architect should provide a robust and steady way to combine the blocks.

Part VIII

Public Key Management

Chapter 24: Java Digital Certificates

Chapter 25: PKI Management

Chapter 24
Java Digital Certificates

In This Chapter

♦ Understanding the purpose of the digital certificate

♦ Exploring the format of the digital certificate

♦ Learning how to build a digital certificate

♦ Working with format of the digital certificate

♦ Understanding how a digital certificate is revoked

♦ Working with the format of a Certificate Revocation List (CRL)

This chapter explores the digital certificate, which is the format used to manage public keys. The sample code included demonstrates the different fields in all three versions of the digital certificates using JDK 1.4. Some of the classes that are used are not documented in the JavaDocs, and the sample code is meant for demonstration purposes only.

There are two parts to the digital certificate: the *digital certificate message* and the *management of transferring the digital certificate*. This chapter takes an in-depth look at the digital certificate message format. The "Internet x.509 Public Key Infrastructure Certificate and CRL Profile" contains information about the X.509 specification, and for further analysis, the digital certificate format can be found at
`http://www.ietf.org/rfc/rfc2459.txt`.

Introduction to Digital Certificates

The purpose of a digital certificate is to provide a mechanism for transmitting a public key to a subject to use in decrypting a message. The *subject* has three characteristics: First, he is the receiver of the message; second, he is the receiver of the public key; and finally, he wants to decrypt a message. The transferring of a public key doesn't sound very complicated, but there are many issues that can arise in the process. For example, how do you know that the public key originated from the person who sent the message, and how do you know that the public key hasn't been tampered with?

To understand the digital certificate, there are three basic protocols that you need to understand. The first is the key pair algorithm. In that algorithm, a private key encrypts, and a public key decrypts what the private key encrypted. The public and private keys are mapped to each other, which means that these keys are generated from each other and only those two combinations can work together.

> **CROSS-REFERENCE:** Refer to Chapter 7 for information on key pairs.

The next protocol you must understand is the *X.509* specification. X.509 describes the format of digital certificates and some of the common management techniques used because of the format. This chapter addresses the X.509 specification. Part of the X.509 specification identifies the issuer and the subject with a *distinguished name* (DN) that belongs to the X.500 specification. The X.500 is used to identify the issuer and subject, and can also be used as a directory tree structure to save the certificate in a repository such as the *Java KeyStore* (JKS).

> **CROSS-REFERENCE:** Chapter 8 defines the Java KeyStore (JKS).

The X.509 specification has a definition in the name itself. The "X" part of the specification means that it is part of the data networks and open system communications. Any specification that falls between X.500 and X.599 means that it is a directory specification. X.509 is a directory specification because it is built to store security keys into a directory structure. The directory structure entries are stored in the certificate using the X.500 protocol that was introduced as the *Data Communication Network Directory*. Later, version 1 of X.500 was enhanced to become version 2, which is commonly known as the *Lightweight Directory Access Protocol* (LDAP).

Organizations that use digital certificates are known to have an infrastructure that supports public keys, which is commonly known as *Public Key Infrastructure* (PKI). The format of the digital certificate provides information on who issued the key, along with the public key and the signature to validate all the information. Some commercial organizations pick up the responsibility of managing and authenticating the digital certificate. Such an organization is known as a *Certificate Authority* (CA).

> **NOTE:** You can create your own CA to control the certificates in your organization. The function of a CA is that, if a CA says the public key in the certificate belongs to a certain organization, the receiving entity can be assured the public key is indeed of that organization.
>
> Typically, you send a certificate signing request (CSR) to the CA and you may also submit some information describing or proving your identity. If the CA grants your request; it then provides a public and private key pair. In addition, CAs keep a Certificate Revocation List (CRL), which is a list of certificates that have been revoked before their expiration dates.
>
> A common CA is VeriSign (`www.verisign.com`) and tools (like Web browsers) often are preconfigured with certificates of many common CAs.

A Quick Overview of X.500

Although you can find a more detailed explanation of the X.500 specification in Chapter 25, a short introduction must be given here to discuss the benefits involved with using the X.509 format and X.500 fields. The X.509 specification uses the identity and naming techniques of

X.500 to develop a distinguished name for the issuer and subject. A *distinguished name* is a name that uniquely identifies the subject or issuer. The issuer, or subject, of the certificate could be an organization, group, or individual. The DN is comprised of many pieces, such as *common name* (CN) and *organizational unit* (OU), which is used to distinguish one user from another.

Here is an example to help you understand these concepts. Assume that there is an organization named `RichWare,LLC`. `RichWare` that has only one user in the Development department named `Rich Helton in Denver, CO`. Because there is only one individual who meets those requirements, the user is distinguished from everyone else in the organization.

The organization `RichWare,LLC` can be mapped to `www.richware.com` for direct access into the organization's servers. The user can be identified in the organization, and the organization can be found on the Internet. Therefore, the user can be found from the Internet, thus mapping the identity from an X.500 name format to an exact individual on the Internet. Figure 24-1 depicts this structure. Do not worry about understanding all the details; they are discussed later in this chapter.

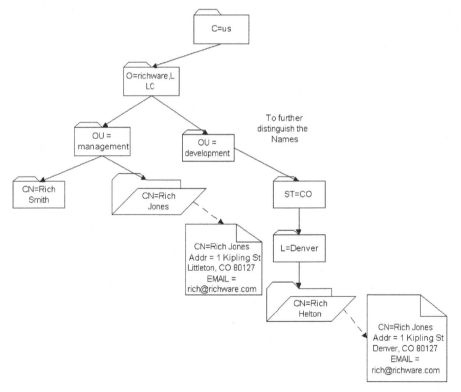

Figure 24-1: The organization of X.500

The X.509 Specification

Digital certificates are taken from the X.509 specification. As mentioned before, the X.509 specification is an integrated extension to the X.500 specification. X.500 builds a directory structure in the shape of a tree based on the organization name, common names, distinguished names, and organizational unit. The X.509 was built to store the keying information. Using a tree that hides the keys and transports them through the Internet helps in this task.

The LDAP service

The transfer of public keys should happen without the fear that whoever accesses them can break the private key or change the digital certificate information. The directory structure can interface with a set of distributed servers, or a single server, for maintaining a data structure of information for an organization. The *LDAP service* (X.500 service before LDAP) assists an organization in keeping records of the users inside the organization in a tree-like directory structure similar to the one just described.

The information defined in the directory structure could be certificates, users, or keys, just to name a few. An LDAP service could be used as a repository to store the digital certificates following the directory structure from the X.500 entries in the digital certificate. When an organization starts working with certificates, the architecture should establish a plan for managing and distributing the X.509 certificates using either a Java `keytool` utility or extending the utility to interface with the LDAP service. The architect can start by understanding the `keytool` utility concepts.

> **CROSS-REFERENCE:** The `keytool` was introduced in Chapter 8.

You can find the reference used to understand the X.509 specification in the RFC 2459 at `http://www.ietf.org/rfc/rfc2459.txt` "Internet x.509 Public Key Infrastructure Certificate and CRL Profile." This is my main reference besides the code used in the JDK 1.4 distributions for this chapter.

To understand the capabilities of the X.509 use and specification, you must have an in-depth understanding of the elements of the X.509. Each field in the X.509 specification has a specific use for transfer and use of the digital certificate. One of the elements of the X.509 is the signature. The *signature* of the certificate is a one-way hash function, such as MD5 or SHA-1, which is used for validating the fields in the X.509 certificate. The signature field is used to validate the information of the digital certificate. The signature field is just one example of why understanding the fields in the X.509 digital certificate is important.

The elements inside a digital certificate are used to generate a digital signature. After receiving the digital certificate, the organization validates the elements by validating the digital signature. This ensures that no elements were tampered with. When studying certificates, it is important to note that a developer can generate certificates using the Java utility `keytool`.

> **CROSS-REFERENCE:** Chapter 8 describes how to extend the `keytool` utility.

This chapter goes into detail with some of the Java code used to generate the X.509 fields. You could accomplish the extension of all X.509 protocols using Java with a combination of the information presented on key storage and transference in Chapter 7, this chapter (Chapter 24), and Chapter 8.

A self-signed certificate

When you generate a digital certificate using the `keytool` utility, the certificate is a self-signed certificate. A *self-signed certificate* is a root certificate, meaning that the certificate was not passed through a CA or even multiple CAs. After the certificate information is signed, it is encrypted with the issuer's private key. Only the issuer's public key can decrypt the signature to verify the validity of the certificate. The public key is also included in the digital certificate. The certificate is considered to be from a trusted location.

Sometimes a certificate will go through several trusted locations, each trusting and validating each other. If there is any question as to the authenticity of the digital certificate, the certificate will be added to the *Certificate Revocation List* (CRL) to be revoked for subsequent uses. The digital certificate can be questioned and verified through multiple trusted sources.

The combination of these trusted sources for a specific certificate is known as the certificate's chain. The *certificate chain* is a chain of responsibility asking if the certificate can be trusted until the subject reaches a trusted source that is unquestionable to the subject. The certificate chain does not exist for a self-signed certificate, because the certificate is at its originating source. When a certificate is generated with the `keytool`, it has originated locally and has not been requested through a CA.

> **CROSS-REFERENCE:** Chapter 25 goes into a lot more detail on the transferring of digital certificates. I added a brief introduction for understanding why the digital certificate is constructed in an X.509 format.

X.509 also defines alternative authentication protocols based on the use of public key certificates. The importance of X.509 is that it defines the structure of digital certificates and the related protocols, such as TLS, which are used in PKI. The X.509 specification was originally created in 1988, the second version was updated in 1993, and the current version, (the third) was drafted in 1995. There are many algorithms for encrypting and for public key exchange. Standard algorithms are recommended, however, very much like the ones specified for TLS. The digital signatures require a one-way hash algorithm such as SHA-1 or MD5.

Some of the certificate entries were first developed in version 1 of the X.509, such as version number and signature. Version 2 of the certificate included the Unique Identifier of both the issuer and the subject. Version 3 included extensions that follow a name/value pair like Key Usage. Version 2 and version 3 entries will be discussed in detail later in this chapter. Version 1 entries are discussed in detail first. Many of the methods used to retrieve the certificate entries are displayed in Figure 24-2 along with the basic form of the X.509 certificate.

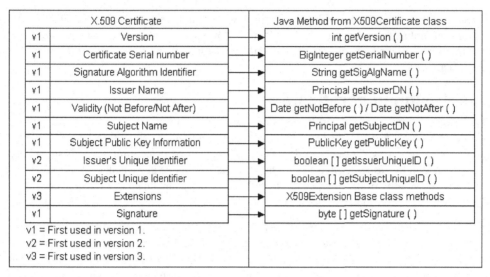

X.509 Certificate		Java Method from X509Certificate class
v1	Version	int getVersion ( )
v1	Certificate Serial number	BigInteger getSerialNumber ( )
v1	Signature Algorithm Identifier	String getSigAlgName ( )
v1	Issuer Name	Principal getIssuerDN ( )
v1	Validity (Not Before/Not After)	Date getNotBefore ( ) / Date getNotAfter ( )
v1	Subject Name	Principal getSubjectDN ( )
v1	Subject Public Key Information	PublicKey getPublicKey ( )
v2	Issuer's Unique Identifier	boolean [ ] getIssuerUniqueID ( )
v2	Subject Unique Identifier	boolean [ ] getSubjectUniqueID ( )
v3	Extensions	X509Extension Base class methods
v1	Signature	byte [ ] getSignature ( )

v1 = First used in version 1.
v2 = First used in version 2.
v3 = First used in version 3.

Figure   24-2: Certificate basic structure

Let's start by printing out the version 1 entries using code. Listing 24-1 provides the code for importing a version 1 certificate. This code imports the file, basically by opening a certification file and initializing the X509Certificate class with the contents of the file. Using the version 1 methods from the X509Certificate class, the code retrieves the data and prints it out to the screens. The CertificateFactory initializes the type of certificate that is created in the program. The CertificateFactory is an engine class described in Chapter 8.

Listing 24-1: The RichCertificate class: Importing X509Certificate version 1 in Java

```
package com.richware.chap24;

import java.security.PublicKey;
import java.security.Principal;
import java.security.cert.X509Certificate;
import java.security.cert.CertificateException;
import java.security.cert.CertificateFactory;
import java.io.FileInputStream;
import java.io.FileNotFoundException;

/**
 * Class RichCertificate
 * Description: A custom demonstration of the certificate.
 *
 * Copyright:    Copyright (c) 2002 Wiley Publishing, Inc.
```

```
 * @author Rich Helton <rhelton@richware.com>
 * @version 1.0
 * DISCLAIMER: Please refer to the disclaimer at the beginning of this
book.
 */
public class RichCertificate
{
  /**
   * Method main
   * Description: The main driver to run the methods.
   *
   *
   * @param args (no arguments presently).
   *
   */
  public static void main(String args[])
  {
    try
      {
      System.out.println("Starting RichCertificate....");

      /*
       * Pass in the argument of the keystore file
       * It will be opened in the same directory as the application
       */
      if (args[0] == null)
        {
        System.out.println(
          "This application requires an input file for the location of
the certificate");
        }

      String localDirectory = System.getProperty("user.dir");

      System.out.println("Changing directory to Chapter 24");
      System.setProperty("user.dir",
                         localDirectory
                         + "\\com\\richware\\chap24\\");
      localDirectory = System.getProperty("user.dir");

      /*
       * Get the local keystore that contains a trusted certificate
       */
      String localInputFile = localDirectory + args[0];
      System.out.println(
        "Openining Chapter 24 plus the input file as an argument: "
        + localInputFile);

      /*
```

```
       * Import the certificate
       */
      RichCertificate myCertificate  = new RichCertificate();
      X509Certificate newcertificate =
        myCertificate.importCertificate(localInputFile);
      myCertificate.printVersion1(newcertificate);


      /*
       *  catches.
       */
    }
  catch (Exception e)
    {
     e.printStackTrace();
    }
}


/**
 * Method importCertificate
 * Description: Import the certificate.
 *
 * @param filename is the file to import.
 *
 * @return the certification.
 *
 */
public X509Certificate importCertificate(String filename)
  {
  X509Certificate cert = null;
  try
    {
    CertificateFactory cf =
      CertificateFactory.getInstance("X509");

    /*
     * Get the File I/O of the Certificate
     */
    FileInputStream fr = new FileInputStream(filename);

    /*
     *  Construct the certificate based on the import
     */
    cert = (X509Certificate) cf.generateCertificate(fr);

    /*
     *  catches.
     */
    }
  catch (CertificateException e)
```

```
    {
      e.printStackTrace();
    }
    catch (FileNotFoundException e)
    {
      e.printStackTrace();
    }
    return cert;
}


/**
 * Method printVersion1
 * Description: Print version 1 information of the Certificate.
 *
 *
 * @param cert is the certification to read from.
 *
 */
public void printVersion1(X509Certificate cert)
{

  try
  {
    /*
     *  Get the information of the certificate.
     */
    System.out.println(
      "Certificate->Version Number*****************");
    System.out.println(cert.getVersion());
    System.out.println(
      "Certificate->Serial Number******************");
    System.out.println(cert.getSerialNumber());
    System.out.println(
      "Certificate->Signature Algorithm Identifier*");
    System.out.println(cert.getSigAlgName());
    System.out.println(
      "Certificate->Issuer Name********************");
    System.out.println(cert.getIssuerDN());
    System.out.println(
      "Certificate->Not Before Validity************");
    System.out.println(cert.getNotBefore());
    System.out.println(
      "Certificate->Not After Validity*************");
    System.out.println(cert.getNotAfter());
    System.out.println(
      "Certificate->Subject Name*******************");
    System.out.println(cert.getSubjectDN());
    System.out.println(
      "Certificate->Subject Public Key Information*");
```

```
    System.out.println(cert.getPublicKey());
    System.out.println(
      "Certificate->Signature*********************");
    System.out.println(cert.getSignature());

    /*
     *  catches.
     */
  }
  catch (Exception e)
    {
    e.printStackTrace();
    }
  }
}
```

The output of Listing 24-1 is included in Listing 24-2. The output is totally dependent on how the digital certificate was generated.

Listing 24-2: Output for Listing 24-1

```
>java com.richware.chap24.RichCertificate rich.cer
Starting RichCertificate....
Changing directory to Chapter 24
Openining Chapter 24 plus the input file as an argument:
C:\com\richware\chap24\rich.cer
Certificate->Version Number******************
1
Certificate->Serial Number*******************
1006541843
Certificate->Signature Algorithm Identifier*
SHA1withDSA
Certificate->Issuer Name********************
CN=Rich Helton, OU=development, O=richware, L=denver, ST=co, C=us
Certificate->Not Before Validity************
Fri Nov 23 11:57:23 MST 2001
Certificate->Not After Validity*************
Thu Feb 21 11:57:23 MST 2002
Certificate->Subject Name*******************
CN=Rich Helton, OU=development, O=richware, L=denver, ST=co, C=us
Certificate->Subject Public Key Information*
Sun DSA Public Key
    Parameters:DSA
        p:      fd7f5381 1d751229 52df4a9c 2eece4e7 f611b752 3cef4400
c31e3f80 b6
512669
    455d4022 51fb593d 8d58fabf c5f5ba30 f6cb9b55 6cd7813b 801d346f
f26660b7
```

```
    6b9950a5 a49f9fe8 047b1022 c24fbba9 d7feb7c6 1bf83b57 e7c6a8a6
150f04fb
    83f6d3c5 1ec30235 54135a16 9132f675 f3ae2b61 d72aeff2 2203199d
d14801c7
       q:      9760508f 15230bcc b292b982 a2eb840b f0581cf5
       g:      f7e1a085 d69b3dde cbbcab5c 36b857b9 7994afbb fa3aea82
f9574c0b 3d
078267
    5159578e bad4594f e6710710 8180b449 167123e8 4c281613 b7cf0932
8cc8a6e1
    3c167a8b 547c8d28 e0a3ae1e 2bb3a675 916ea37f 0bfa2135 62f1fb62
7a01243b
    cca4f1be a8519089 a883dfe1 5ae59f06 928b665e 807b5525 64014c3b
fecf492a

  y:
    11f605f8 7dee5f91 33631abb ec1ca443 6e41033a b25316ba bb44bb60
93c7828e
    6272f95b 02b1e59d 90f6ad6e 3d81cab2 50b945d1 c7282980 0e10d34f
63708366
    85c00fe3 679d1ce9 0e308f3c bb49838a 623be15a c9032274 4ce6fb19
0cc0b31a
    7b6c9cf0 1965c01c 07d7c2c1 2ad4e3cf cdd9c40a dcbc10fe ee099966
043a7066

Certificate->Signature***********************
[ B@aaa14a
```

The certificate that was imported was generated and exported using the keytool. The generated certificate is shown in Listing 24-3.

Listing 24-3: The generated certificate

```
-----BEGIN CERTIFICATE-----
MIIDCDCCAsYCBDv+nBMwCwYHKoZIzjgEAwUAMGoxCzAJBgNVBAYMAnVzMQswCQYDVQQIDAJj
bzEP
MA0GA1UEBwwGZGVudmVyMREwDwYDVQQKDAhyaWNod2FyZTEUMBIGA1UECwwLZGV2ZWxvcG1l
bnQx
FDASBgNVBAMMC1JpY2gqSGVsdG9uMB4XDTAxMTEyMzE4NTcyMloXDTAyMDIyMTE4NTcyMlow
ajEL
MAkGA1UEBgwCdXMxCzAJBgNVBAgMAmNvMQ8wDQYDVQQHDAZkZW52ZXIxETAPBgNVBAoMCHJp
Y2h3
YXJlMRQwEgYDVQQLDAtkZXZlbG9wbWVudDEUMBIGA1UEAwwLUmljaCBIZWx0b24wggG3MIIB
LAYH
KoZIzjgEATCCAR8CgYEA/X9TgR11Ei1S30qcLuzk5/YRt1I870QAwx4/gLZRJmlFXUAiUftZ
PY1Y
+r/F9bow9subVWzXgTuAHTRv8mZgt2uZUKWkn5/oBHsQIsJPu6nX/rfGG/g7V+fGqKYVDwT7
g/bT
```

```
xR7DAjVUE1oWkTL2dfOuK2HXKu/yIgMZndFIAccCFQCXYFCPFSMLzLKSuYKi64QL8Fgc9QKB
gQD3
4aCF1ps93su8q1w2uFe5eZSvu/o66oL5V0wLPQeCZ1FZV4661F1P5nEHEIGAtEkWcSPoTCgW
E7fP
CTKMyKbhPBZ6i1R8jSjgo64eK7OmdZFuo38L+iE1YvH7YnoBJDvMpPG+qFGQiaiD3+Fa5Z8G
kotm
XoB7VSVkAUw7/s9JKgOBhAACgYAR9gX4fe5fkTNjGrvsHKRDbkEDOrJTFrq7RLtgk8eCjmJy
+VsC
seWdkPatbj2ByrJQuUXRxygpgA4QO09jcINmhcAP42edHOkOMI88u0mDimI74VrJAyJ0TOb7
GQzA
sxp7bJzwGWXAHAfXwsEq1OPPzdnECty8EP7uCZlmBDpwZjALBgcqhkjOOAQDBQADLwAwLAIU
SM9W
zM/EKrP2r5D58cGNXJdiwYYCFDc1v72BB3E4kAEVUFnGzYguKodD
-----END CERTIFICATE-----
```

Some of the X.500 features of the certificate can be seen in the Issuer Name and Subject Name sections that define the organization, location, state, common name, and organizational unit. Many protocols, such as LDAP and X.500, use this information for building a directory tree for storage of the certificate. Another form of tree structure is the Internet. The organization could be treated as a domain name, such as www.richware.com. The organizational unit (OU), common name (CN), location (L), state (ST), and country (C) are used to store the certificate by different organizations that need it for storage and transportation. You may want to refer to Figure 24-1 because it is discussed in more detail now.

Other organizations will receive the certificate to get the public key. The issuer organization keeps the private key that is used to encrypt the certificate. The CA also manages and stores the certificates. The X.500 information is needed by all these organizations to define how to store the certificate. The X.500 information could also be used to map to the exact location from the issuer and to the receiver (the subject). Most certificates are generated by a CA and tracked by the CA in an X.509 directory structure. A copy could also be kept by the organization for additional verification. The X.500 directory structure provides access to the certificates. The version 1 certificate normally includes the following:

♦ **Version number:** This specifies the version number of the X.509 of this certificate. The default is 1, but can be set as 2 or 3. Based on the certificate version, the format of the certificate changes.

♦ **Certificate's Serial Number:** The integer value that is unique to each certificate during creation. The CA normally generates this value. The example in Listing 24-2 shows

```
1006541843
```

♦ **Signature Algorithm Identifier:** The algorithm and parameters used to sign the certificate. This could be SHA-1 or MD5. The example in Listing 24-2 shows SHA1withDSA. This field is also repeated in the Signature field at the end of the certificate.

♦ **Issuer Name:** The X.500 name of the CA or user that created the certificate. With the combination of these entries, it makes up a distinguished name. The distinguished name is something that uniquely identifies the issuer. It may consist of the address or the individual machine that the issuer uses. The example in Figure 24-1 shows the following:

The CN element is the common name of the issuer. It is normally the proper name of the issuer.

```
CN=Rich Helton
```

The C element stands for the two-letter country code of the country where the certificate was created.

```
C=us
```

The L element stands for the locality code of the city where the certificate was created.

```
L=Denver
```

The ST element is the state where the certificate was issued.

```
ST=co
```

The O element is the organization code for the organization in which the certificate was created. This could also be the domain name.

```
O=richware,LLC
```

The OU element is the organizational unit code for the unit in which the certificate was created.

```
OU=development
```

♦ **Period of Validity:** This field contains two dates of validation: the date for when the certificate becomes active and the date when the certificate is de-activated. If the current date does not follow within these two dates, the certificate is not valid.

```
Not Before: Fri Nov 23 11:57:23 MST 2001

Not After: Thu Feb 21 11:57:23 MST 2002
```

♦ **Subject Name:** The X.500 name of the end-entity. The end-entity can be a Web server, an organization, or an individual. This is the holder of the key pair. The subject could be organization that is encrypting the data, and the issuer is the CA who manages the certificate. The combination of these entries makes up a distinguished name. The distinguished name is something that uniquely identifies the subject. This field must have an entry unless a version 3 extension is used. The example in Listing 24-2 shows

```
CN=Rich Helton, OU=development, O=richware, L=denver,
ST=co, C=us
```

♦ **Subject's public-key Information:** This field contains the subject's public key information, such as the value of the key, the algorithm used, and any parameters for the algorithm. This field must always have at least one entry. The example shown in Listing 24-2 is the DSA key.

♦ **Signature:** This field contains the hash code that verifies that the data in the certificate has not changed. It is encrypted with the CA's public key and decrypted with the subject's public key. The example in Listing 24-2 is a one-way hash in SHA-1. This field must always have an entry and is used to ensure that the data in the certificate has not changed. The example shown is

```
[ B@ded0fd
```

Version 2 unique identifier fields

As mentioned before, in 1993, the X509 certificate was updated for version 2. The reason for the new version was that some DNs were not being kept unique enough from the registration. For example, when generating the certificate, I might have entered the organization code in the certificate as `richware` instead of `richware, LLC`. There are at least two `richware` organizations.

In version 1, there is no way to uniquely identify the two organizations. Version 2 suggested having a string of bits to keep the organizations separate. That way a CA may know to send to `richware` with a bit string of `00000010` to my organization instead of another. It was not long before version 3 offered other alternatives, and many organizations and CAs don't support unique identifiers; therefore, unique identifiers are not recommended. An alternative in X509 version 3 is to add the `URIName` of `www.richware.com`. This way users of the certificate know that it came from my `RichWare, LLC` and not another organization.

The two main fields for identification are the subject and issuer, and the unique identifier fields support both the Issuer Unique Identifier and a Subject Unique Identifier. To retrieve the Issuer Unique Identifier, the `getIssuerUniqueID ( )` method of the `X509Certificate` class is used to return an array of `booleans`. Each `boolean` entry represents a bit.

To retrieve the Subject Unique Identifier, the `getSubjectUniqueID ( )` method of the `X509Certificate` class is used to return an array of `booleans` as a bit string. These are optional fields. Not all applications check these fields and there is no way to keep them unique. So you should use the fields in version 3 if there is any ambiguity to the DN, or simply to ensure that the DN is unique.

Version 3 key extensions

In the earlier versions of X509, there were issues with the key information that required extensions. One of the questions asked was, "What if the private key has different validity dates than the public key?" Other questions were, "If there are multiple subject public keys, which one do I use?" and "What was the intended purpose of the public key: for the CA to verify the digital signature or the subject?" When the digital certificate became more common, the answer to those questions was to extend the format of the X.509 digital certificate. The extensions were to become version 3 of the X.509.

Each field in the X.509 version 3 has three parts: the field type, field criticality, and value. The criticality field states whether the field is critical for the operation of the certificate. The certificate is invalid if the field is set to critical and the application does not recognize the information in the field. If the field is non-critical, the values in the field are used for information only and the validity of the certificate does not depend on the field.

The field type is the description of the field, and the certificate uses the associated value. In some cases the X509Extension class is used to retrieve the extensions. Getting the extension is done with the getExtendedValue ( ) method. To retrieve the value through the getExtendedValue ( ) method, the OID of the extension must be passed in as a parameter. The *OID* is an object identifier that maps the field to a specific object. The OID of the matching field is registered as part of the specification. Figure 24-3 maps the certificate extensions for X.509 version 3 with the X509Certificate class.

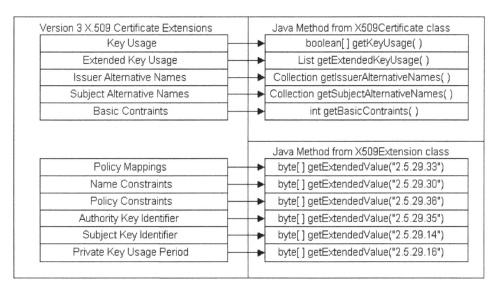

Figure 24-3: Version 3 extensions

The following certificate fields in X.509 version 3 are extended for the key use:

◆ **Key Usage (OID 2.5.29.15):** This field defines restrictions on the operations that can be performed by the public key within the certificate. Some of these operations include digital signature, certificate signing, Certificate Revocation List (CRL) signing, key ciphering, data ciphering, and Diffie-Hellman key agreement.

The certificate issuer may be set to critical or non-critical for KeyUsage. When the KeyUsage is set to critical, the key mechanisms must be enforced by using the public key fields that are set. Otherwise, it is used as a suggestion for operation of the certificate.

The X509Certificate class uses the getKeyUsage ( ) method to get an array of booleans. The boolean array that is returned has a bit set for each true entry. The following list describes what the KeyUsage represents depending on which bit is set:

- **digitalSignature (BitSet 0):** When set to true, this field signifies that the digital signatures must be verified. The digital signature is used to check the integrity of the entity and origin of the data. Other bits that check for different digital signatures are bits 1, 5, and 6.

- **nonRepudiation (BitSet 1):** When set to true, this field signifies that the digital signatures must be verified for non-repudiation services. A *non-repudiation* service is like a third-party notary service that ensures the receiver verified the certificate. Non-repudiation prevents the receiver from denying receiving the certificate. This is discussed in more detail later in the chapter.

- **keyEncipherment (BitSet 2):** When set to true, this field signifies that the subject's key will be used for enciphering keys and other subject information for transport or deciphering information. This flag only encrypts the key for data encryption. See the encipherOnly and decipherOnly flags described later in this list.

- **dataEncipherment (BitSet 3):** When set to true, this field signifies that the user data is encrypted by using the subject's public key when transporting.

- **keyAgreement (BitSet 4):** When set to true, this field signifies that the subject's public key is used for key agreement, such as the Diffie-Hellman key exchange.

- **keyCertSign (BitSet 5):** When set to true, this field signifies that the subject's public key is used for verifying digital signatures for CAs. When the keyCertSign bit is set to true, the associated private key should be used for signing CA certificates only and not for other certificates such as SSL.

- **cRLSign (BitSet 6):** When set to true, this field signifies that the digital signatures must be verified for CRLs.

- **encipherOnly (BitSet 7):** When set to true, this field signifies that the subject's public key can be used only for enciphering data when performing key agreement.

- **decipherOnly (BitSet 8):** When set to true, this field signifies that the subject's public key is used for deciphering data while performing key agreement.

- ◆ **Authority Key Identifier (OID 2.5.29.35):** A CA may have multiple sets of public keys used to verify signatures for certificates and CRLs. This field is used to request the specific set from the CA to verify the digital signature. The Authority Key Identifier is used so that CA's can contain multiple sets of public keys. The Authority Key Identifier field is always marked non-critical. This field must always be included in all version 3 certificates built by a CA. It is used to identify the keys that were used by the CA in certificate chaining. The exception is in self-signed certificates, where it is not necessary. The Authority Key Identifier has three subfields:

- **keyIdentifier:** This field is derived from the public key or a method that generates a unique value. There are two common ways for generating the keyIdentifier. The first is to return 160-bit SHA-1 one-way hash of just the subject's public key. The second is to return a 4-bit type code of 0100 followed by the 60 least significant bits of the SHA-1 one-way hash. The JDK 1.4 returns the first methodology in the form of a byte array.

- **authorityCertIssuer:** This field uses the `GeneralName` format that is described in the "Version 3, Certificate Alternative Names Extensions" section of this chapter. The name defined is the name of the issuing CA.

- **authorityCertSerialNumber:** This field is a unique serial number that is assigned from the CA. This field maps to a `BigInteger` data type class in Java.

♦ **Subject Key Identifier (OID 2.5.29.14):** Certificates may contain multiple keys from the same subject. To identify the specific key to be certified, a field must specify which one to use. The Subject Key Identifier's purpose is to specify the key to certify. This field is always set to non-critical. The field is configured like the `keyIdentifier` field of the Authority Key Identifier.

♦ **Extended Key Usage (OID 2.5.29.37):** This field can be used in addition to or in place of Key Usage to define one or more uses of the public key. This field is intended to extend the `KeyUsage` field for any keys that are not supported in the regular `KeyUsage` field. This extension is used with various protocols such as TLS and smart cards. This field may be critical or non-critical. This field is defined by a list of OIDs. The Java `X509Certificate` class uses the `getExtendedKeyUsage ( )` method, which returns a `List` data type class.

♦ **Private-Key Usage Period (OID 2.5.29.16):** Typically the private key has a different time period than the public key. This field indicates the time period of use of the private key associated with the public key in this certificate. The private key time period must fall between the notBefore and notAfter times that take on the form of a `Date` class in Java.

Some of the fields described in this section do not have a corresponding method to return the extended information in the `X509Certificate` class, such as the Subject Key Identifier field. The `X509Certicate` class is extended by the `X509Extension` class, so that any field may return a byte array by passing the OID of the extension in the `getExtensionValue ( )` method. For instance, the OID for Subject Key Identifier is "2.5.29.14". Passing the OID into the method as `getExtensionValue("2.5.29.14")` will return a byte array for the Subject Key Identifier.

Version 3, Policy Mapping Extensions

Certificates can be issued for many reasons and applications, such as e-mail and an HTTPS server. The certificate policy defines the reason for the issuing of the certificate, such as to facilitate an HTTPS server. The policy contains an OID that the issuer and subject have agreed upon. The OID defines the policy, or reason for the issuing of the certificate. A certificate can contain a list of policies for multiple purposes of the certificate. The OIDs are registered through a Policy Authority that is defined in standard ISO/IEC 9834-1. The Policy Authority issues a set of policies known as a *policy domain*. The issuer and subject access the policy domain to know which OIDs and matching policies are available. The policy domain provides the mapping of OIDs to defined policies. The policy mapping is as follows:

◆ **Policy Mappings (OID 2.5.29.33):** This field is used when the subject of the certificate is a CA. Policy mappings allow an issuing CA to indicate that one or more of the issuer's policies can be considered equivalent to another used policy in the subject's CA's domain. It does this by using Object Identifiers (OIDs) within the issuing CA's domain that are considered to be equivalent to another policy within the subject's CA's domain.

Version 3, Certificate Alternative Names Extensions

You've learned that the subject's and issuer's names are given in the form of a DN to resolve the issuer and subject. This proved to have issues because some applications and protocols required particular name formats that did not match the DN format. Version 3 had to extend the names and add formats to support different protocols that required some other form of naming besides the DN formats. Some of these formats were needed to support a World Wide Web name, IP addresses, e-mail naming conventions, and registered names in an Object Identifier (OID) format, to name a few.

One of the reasons to note why other naming conventions were required is that other applications, such as e-mail, may also use digital certificates. There are two types of Alternative Names, the *Subject Alternative Name* to give different names for the subject of the certificate, and the *Issuer Alternative Name* to give different names to the issuer of the certificate. The Alternative Names are used when the names cannot be defined in the X.500 DN format.

To retrieve the information from an X509Certificate object, the getIssuerAlternative ( ) method is used to retrieve the Issuer Alternative Name and the getSubjectAlternative ( ) method is used to retrieve the Subject Alternative Name. These two methods return a Collection data class type that contains List class entries. Each entry has two fields: an integer for the name type, and the name in the form of a string or byte array. The name type determines if the second field is in the form of a string or byte array. According to RFC 2459, the data type for defining the Alternative Names should be in the form of a *GeneralName*. Internally, the X509Certificate uses a GeneralName class in the sun.security.X509 package. Internally, there are many classes that can construct the GeneralName class through the GeneralNameInterface.

Each name type has a corresponding class to build the name type in an appropriate format. For instance, in the sun.security.X509 package, the URIName class is the corresponding class. The URIName class is responsible for formatting and ensuring the naming convention of the Uniform Resource Identifier name type. Knowing this is important if the Alternative Names are ever created or formatted in a Java application. Following are the names that make up the `GeneralName` and their corresponding integers for the type values:

♦ **otherName (Name Type 0):** This field represents an instance of any other name returned in a byte array format. There is no format currently defined for it except that it returns something. Common uses may be to return an associated OID, such as Kerberos and the KerberosPrincipalName associated with Kerberos. This field makes up for any naming convention not covered in the rest of the name types.

CROSS-REFERENCE: For Kerberos information, review Chapter 16.

♦ **rfc822Name (Name Type 1):** This field represents an Internet electronic mail address defined in accordance with Internet RFC 822. The return type of this name type is in the form of a string and an example is `rhelton@richware.com`.

♦ **dNSName (Name Type 2):** This field represents an Internet domain name defined in accordance with Internet RFC 1035. These are the domain names assigned to an organization registered at the Network Information Center. The return type of this name type is in the form of a `String` and an example is `richware.com`.

♦ **X400Address (Name Type 3):** This field represents an O/R address defined in accordance with ITU-T Rec. X.411 | ISO/IEC 10021-4. An O/R is a originator/recipient that enables a *Message Handling Service* (MHS) to uniquely identify the user to receive the message. The O/R address can take many forms such as the user's name, a terminal name, or a physical address. The return value from the `getSubjectAlternative (` `)` method will return a byte array that will make up one of these O/R addresses.

♦ **directoryName (Name Type 4):** This field represents a directory name defined in accordance with ITU-T Rec. X.501 | ISO/IEC 9594-2. The return value of this field type is Name type from RFC 2253. This field contains a notation for formatting distinguished names.

♦ **ediPartyName (Name Type 5):** This field represents a name of a form agreed upon between communicating Electronic Data Interchange partners. This field is composed of two other fields, the `nameAssigner` and the `partyName`. The `nameAssigner` identifies the authority that assigns a unique value for the names that are assigned in the `partyName`.

♦ **uniformResourceIdentifier (Name Type 6):** This field represents a *Uniform Resource Identifier* (URI) for the World Wide Web defined in accordance with Internet RFC 1630. An example of a URI is `www.richware.com` and the return type is in the form of a `String`.

♦ **iPAddress (Name Type 7):** This field represents an Internet Protocol address defined in accordance with Internet RFC 791, represented as a binary string. An example of an IP Address is `198.198.8.8`. The return type is in a byte array in network byte order.

♦ **registerID (Name Type 8):** This field represents an identifier of any registered object assigned in accordance with CCITT Rec. X.660 | ISO/IEC 9834-1. This field is a *Object Identifier* (OID) that is registered. An example of the OID for the Subject Alternative name field is `2.5.29.17` and the return type is in the form of a string with numbers separated by periods.

Version 3, Certificate Constraints X509Certificate

These version 3 extensions convey additional information when the subject is a CA. These fields can only be used when the subject is a CA.

- **Basic Constraints (OID 2.5.29.19):** This field indicates if a subject can act as a CA. If this field is present, a certification path length may be specified to indicate the number of CA certificates that may follow. For example, if the path length is 0, the subject CA can only issue certificates to the end entity, not to other CAs. If this field is marked as non-critical, the certificate is at the end entity. Otherwise, it must be marked critical. The JDK 1.4 supports this function in the `X509Certificate` class by the `getBasicConstraints ( )` method that will return the integer representing the certification path length. The integer is only meaningful if the CA is set to true, meaning that the subject can act as a CA. If the CA is not set to true, the function will return a "-1".

- **Name Constraints (OID 2.5.29.30):** This field indicates if the subject changes namespace. The namespace change can be an alternative certificate path for the certificate. The format of this field is of the form of two `GeneralSubtrees` (`permittedSubtrees` and `excludedSubtrees`). The `permittedSubtrees` define all the name subtrees that must be included in the defined namespace. The `excludedSubtrees` define all the name subtrees that must not be included in the defined namespace. The form of the `GeneralSubtree` will be a `GeneralName` and optionally two `BaseDistances`. Not all `GeneralName` types are allowed. The `GeneralName` must be a well-defined hierarchical structure such as in the `directoryName GeneralName` type. The `BaseDistances` define the minimum and maximum distance from the top of the subtree to the bottom. The distance basically defines the number of nodes allowed from the top of the tree to the bottom. Having this defined will give applications information on the size the of the directory structure. It is recommended that this field always be marked as critical.

- **Policy Constraints (OID 2.5.29.36):** This field specifies policy path validation by requiring policy identifiers or prohibiting policy mappings. This field may be marked as critical or non-critical.

  - **requireExplicitPolicy:** If this field is set, it requires that all certificates follow the policy identifier that follows the current certificate.

  - **inhibitPolicymapping:** If this field is set, it requires that all certificates do not follow the policy identifier that follows the current certificate.

Certificate Revocation

If a CA is to manage a certificate, the CA must have power to revoke the certificate. If there is any question as to the certificate being compromised, then the certificate is revoked. In these cases, the certificate must be immediately invalidated. The CA is acting as a certificate cop. It will allow valid certificates to pass through and block questionable certificates.

The immediate invalidation occurs when the certificate is added to a CRL. The CRL is a list of certificates that are no longer valid. When a certificate is added to this list, it is no longer authenticated through the CA. CAs are responsible for issuing certificates and adding them to the CRL when revoked. The CA maintains the CRL and the reasons why the certificate is revoked. An organization that receives the certificate should also validate the certificate against the CRL.

This organization acts as a validator of the certificate. If the validator of the certificate is not the issuing CA, the validator is responsible for consulting the CRL to ensure that the certificate is still valid. Some systems are not totally integrated into checking the CRL from the CA and sometimes a revoked certificate may slip through the validation process. The validate ( ) function of the Java Certificate class does not automatically consult the CRL.

> **TIP:** A copy of the CRL needs to be downloaded periodically to validate certificates.

There are several reasons why the certificate gets added to the revocation lists. One example is if the certificate is suspected to be compromised. Another example is if the certificate has expired. Yet another example is if the CA no longer supports the user.

To get the entire lists of reasons, you examine the reason code in the X509CRLEntry. The X509CRLEntry class is a matching entry for each revoked certificate. The X509CRL class is a class that contains the entire CRL and set of the X509CRLEntry classes. These are represented in Figure 24-4.

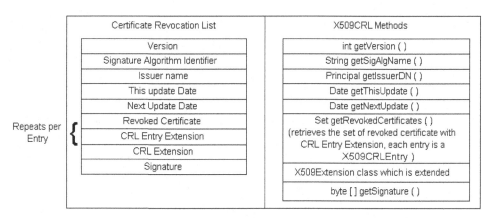

Figure 24-4: The X509CRL and X509CRLEntry classes

There are several means for distributing the CRLs. One way is for an organization to receive an initial CRL from the CA and have the CA only update the CRL. A *Delta CRL* is a CRL that only needs updating; a new CRL is not required every time. A Delta CRL only needs the Delta, or updates, applied to it to become valid. The Delta CRL is useful because a new CRL does not have to be issued every time an update is needed; only the updates are needed.

Another type of CRL update is the Indirect CRL. An *Indirect CRL* is when a CA doesn't update the CRL directly, but another third-party organization does. This third-party organization distributes a single CRL to replace a multitude of CRLs from different CAs. Using a single CRL for an organization that uses multiple CAs is easier than trying to do a lookup on multiple CRLs from different CAs. An organization need only manage a single CRL for many different CAs that it might interface with for digital certificates.

The CRL has fields so that the validator of the X.509 certificate can query the CRL to see if a digital certificate is listed as being revoked. The Java class that is used to support this functionality is the X509CRL class. The fields in the following list do not represent the individual revoked certificates, but the main fields that are needed for the operation of the CRL itself. Several fields are needed for interfacing into the CRL. When checking the individual revoked certificate, the X509CRLEntry class will be used for getting information about the entry. Listing 24-4 demonstrates the ASN.1 notation of the CRL fields and description.

Listing 24-4: The ASN.1 notation of a CRL

```
CertificateList ::= SIGNED { SEQUENCE {
version Version OPTIONAL,
-- if present, version shall be v2
signature AlgorithmIdentifier,
issuer Name,
thisUpdate Time,
nextUpdate Time OPTIONAL, .ISO/IEC 9594-8 : 2001 (E)
revokedCertificates SEQUENCE OF SEQUENCE {
serialNumber CertificateSerialNumber,
revocationDate Time,
crlEntryExtensions Extensions OPTIONAL } OPTIONAL,
crlExtensions [ 0] Extensions OPTIONAL }}
```

♦ **Version number:** This specifies the version number of the X.509 CRL. The version of the CRL is an optional field but if present, it must be v2. Based on the CRL version, the structure of the CRL changes. The method in the X509CRL class to return the version is the getVersion ( ) method that returns an integer of 1 or 2, but should normally be 2.

♦ **Signature Algorithm Identifier:** This field contains the identifier of the algorithm used to sign the CA. The X509CRL class will return a string of the OID with the getSigAlgOID ( ) method. For example, the OID 1.2.84010040.4.3 identifies that the signature algorithm will be SHA-1 with DSA.

♦ **Signature:** This field contains the CA signature bits. The X509CRL class will return a byte array of the signature with the getSignature ( ) method.

♦ **Issuer Name:** This field identifies the DN in X.500 format of the issuer entity.

♦ **This Update:** This field retrieves the date that the CRL was issued. The X509CRL class method to retrieve the Date object of the next update is the getThisUpdate ( ) method.

♦ **Next Update:** This field retrieves the date of the next update of the CRL. The X509CRL class method to retrieve the Date object of the next update is the getNextUpdate ( ) method.

♦ **CRL Entry:** This is the set of revoked certificates. Each revoked certificate is in the form of the Java X509CRLEntry class. The method to return the entire set of revoked entries is the getRevokedCertificates ( ) certificates. To get an individual X509CRLEntry, the BigInteger serial number of the revoked certificate is needed to index into the getRevokedCertificate(BigInteger serialNumber) method.

♦ **CRL Extensions:** These fields were extended in version 2 of the CRL mostly to handle Delta and Indirect CRLs.

♦ **CRL Entry Extensions:** These fields were in the CRL Entry in version 2 to give a reason for revoking the certificate, actions for the certificate, and when it is revoked.

CRL extension

The CRL had to be extended to handle Delta and Indirect CRLs. A CRL was given a CRL Number to keep track of whether the CRL has already been processed. If the CRL has been processed, the next subsequent CRL can be used if the current one has been totally used up for checking certificates. The Delta CRL is needed to keep track of whether the certificate is a Delta CRL or an Indirect CRL. Other modifications were made to differentiate between the key identifiers and issuer when multiple CAs are in an Indirect CRL.

♦ **Authority Key Identifier (OID 2.5.29.35):** This extension can be used to differentiate between multiple CRL signing keys held by a specific CA. This field contains the unique key identifier. The use of this field is mandatory.

♦ **Issuer Alternative Name (OID 2.5.29.18):** This extension associates one or more alternative name forms with the CRL issuer. If there is no DN in the subject field of a certificate, it must have one or more alternative names, and the extension flag must be critical. Otherwise if a DN is specified, the certificate is recommended to be marked non-critical.

♦ **CRL Number (OID 2.5.29.20):** This extension is used to identify a particular CRL. The CRL Number is like a serial number so that if multiple CRLs are listed in an Indirect CRL, the CRL can be kept track of by this unique ID. RFC 2459 recommends its use even though the extension is normally marked non-critical.

♦ **Delta CRL Indicator (OID 2.5.29.27):** This extension identifies the CRL as a delta CRL. If this extension is present, it should be marked critical.

♦ **Issuing Distribution Point (OID 2.5.29.28):** This extension can be used to indicate if a CRL is an Indirect CRL. The extension will identify the CRL distribution point to receive the CRLs. This extension can further define some of the reasons for revocation of certificates and the scope of the CRL. If the extension is present, it should be set to critical.

The CRL can also be generated from the X.509 Certificate Factory as shown in Listing 24-1. The biggest differences are in the type of imported file, which now matches a CRL file, and the use of the `X509CRL` and `X509CRLEntry` classes. Listing 24-5 demonstrates reading a CRL file, the CRL entries, and modifying both (the CRL and the CRL entries) to add extensions.

Listing 24-5: The `RichCRL` class: Importing the CRL and CRL entries and adding extensions

```
package com.richware.chap24;

import java.security.PublicKey;
import java.security.Principal;
import java.security.cert.X509Certificate;
import java.security.cert.CertificateException;
import java.security.cert.CertificateFactory;
import java.security.cert.*;
import java.io.FileInputStream;
import java.io.FileNotFoundException;
import java.util.*;
import javax.security.auth.x500.X500Principal;
import sun.security.x509.*;

/**
 * Class RichCRL
 * Description: A custom demonstration of the Certificate Revocation
List.
 *
 * Copyright:    Copyright (c) 2002 Wiley Publishing, Inc.
 * @author Rich Helton <rhelton@richware.com>
 * @version 1.0
 * DISCLAIMER: Please refer to the disclaimer at the beginning of this
book.
 */
public class RichCRL
{
  /**
   * Method main
   * Description: The main driver to run the methods.
   *
   *
   * @param args (no arguments presently).
   *
   */
  public static void main(String args[])
  {
    try
    {
      System.out.println("Starting RichCRL....");
```

```
    /*
     * Pass in the argument of the keystore file
     * It will be opened in the same directoy as the application
     */
    if (args[ 0] == null)
    {
      System.out.println(
        "This application requires an input file for the location of
the crl");
    }

    String localDirectory = System.getProperty("user.dir");

    System.out.println("Changing directory to Chapter 24");
    System.setProperty("user.dir",
                       localDirectory
                       + "\\com\\richware\\chap24\\");

    localDirectory = System.getProperty("user.dir");

    /*
     * Get the local keystore that contains a trusted certificate
     */
    String localInputFile = localDirectory + args[ 0];

    System.out.println(
      "Opening Chapter 24 plus the input file as an argument: "
      + localInputFile);

    /*
     * Import the certificate revocation list
     */
    RichCRL myCertificate  = new RichCRL();
    X509CRL newcertificate =
      myCertificate.importCertificate(localInputFile);

    System.out.println(
      "***********************CRL *************************");
    System.out.println(newcertificate);
    System.out.println("CRL->Version Number->"
                       + newcertificate.getVersion());
    System.out
      .println("CRL->Signature Algorithm Identifier->"
               + newcertificate.getSigAlgName());
    System.out.println("CRL->Issuer Name->"
                       + newcertificate.getIssuerDN());
    System.out.println("CRL->ThisUpdate->"
                       + newcertificate.getThisUpdate());
    System.out.println("CRL->NextUpdate->"
```

```
                                    + newcertificate.getNextUpdate());

        /*
         * Get the revoked Certificates
         */
        Set             setCRLEntries =
          newcertificate.getRevokedCertificates();
        X509CRLEntry[] newEntries    =
          new X509CRLEntry[ setCRLEntries.size()];
        Iterator        iter          = setCRLEntries.iterator();
        int             current        = 0;

        while (iter.hasNext())
         {
          X509CRLEntry entry = (X509CRLEntry) iter.next();

          System.out.println(
            "***********CRL Entry No Extensions***************");
          System.out.println(entry);
          System.out.println("CRL->Entry->RevocationDate->"
                            + entry.getRevocationDate());
          System.out.println("CRL->Entry->SerialNumber->"
                            + entry.getSerialNumber());
          System.out.println("CRL->Entry->HasExtensions->"
                            + entry.hasExtensions());

          /*
           * Are there any extensions
           */
          if (entry.hasExtensions())
           {
             /*
              * Print the extension OIDs
              */
             Set nonCritSet = entry.getNonCriticalExtensionOIDs();
             if (nonCritSet != null)
              {
                for (Iterator i = nonCritSet.iterator();
                       i.hasNext(); )
                 {
                   String oid = (String) i.next();
                   System.out.println("Extensions in Entry" + oid);
                 }
              }
           }

           /*
            * Else create some extensions
            */
```

```
        else
         {
          /*
           * Create an CRL Extension class to contain individual
extensions
           */
          CRLExtensions extensions = new CRLExtensions();

          /*
           * Create the CRL Reason Code Extension
           */
          CRLReasonCodeExtension reason =
            new CRLReasonCodeExtension(2);
          extensions.set("2.5.29.21", reason);
          //     System.out.println("CRL->Entry->New Reason
Code***********");
          CRLReasonCodeExtension newreason =
            (CRLReasonCodeExtension) extensions
              .get("2.5.29.21");

          //     System.out.println(newreason);
          X509CRLEntryImpl x509crlentryimpl =
            new X509CRLEntryImpl(entry.getSerialNumber(),
                                 entry.getRevocationDate(),
                                 extensions);

          newEntries[ current] =
            (X509CRLEntry) x509crlentryimpl;
         }
       current++;
      }

      /*
       * Create an X500Name from the X500 Principal
       */
      X500Principal currPrincipal =
        newcertificate.getIssuerX500Principal();
      X500Name      name      =
        new X500Name(currPrincipal.getEncoded());

      /*
       * Create a CRL Extension class to contain individual extensions
and set it for the main CRL
       */
      CRLExtensions        crlExtensions = new CRLExtensions();
      CRLNumberExtension crlNumber      =
        new CRLNumberExtension(1);

      crlExtensions.set("2.5.29.20", crlNumber);
```

```
/*
 * Create a new CRL with the extensions in the CRL Entries
 */
X509CRLImpl newCRL =
  new X509CRLImpl(name, newcertificate.getThisUpdate(),
                  newcertificate.getNextUpdate(),
                  newEntries, crlExtensions);

System.out.println(
  "******************CRL with Extensions**************");
System.out.println(newCRL);

/*
 * Iterate through the CRL entries again showing the extensions
 */
setCRLEntries = newCRL.getRevokedCertificates();
iter          = setCRLEntries.iterator();

/*
 * Loop through the entries
 */
while (iter.hasNext())
 {
  X509CRLEntry entry = (X509CRLEntry) iter.next();

  System.out.println(
    "********CRL Entry After Adding Reason Extension**********");
  System.out.println(entry);
  System.out.println("CRL->Entry->RevocationDate->"
                     + entry.getRevocationDate());
  System.out.println(entry.getSerialNumber());
  System.out.println("CRL->Entry->HasExtensions->"
                     + entry.hasExtensions());


  /*
   * the getExtensionValue will return a null because it is not
part of the
   *  supported OIDs mentioned in the JavaDocs
   */
  System.out
    .println("CRL->Entry->Reason Code from method->"
             + entry.getExtensionValue("2.5.29.21"));

  X509CRLEntryImpl x509crlentryimpl =
    new X509CRLEntryImpl(entry.getEncoded());
  Integer          reasonInt         =
    x509crlentryimpl.getReasonCode();
```

```
      /*
       * Print out the Reason Code
       */
      System.out
        .println("CRL->Entry->Reason Code->"
                  + RichCRL
                    .reasonToString(reasonInt.intValue()));

      /*
       * Print out the OIDs found
       */
      Set nonCritSet = entry.getNonCriticalExtensionOIDs();

      if (nonCritSet != null)
        {
        for (Iterator i = nonCritSet.iterator();
                 i.hasNext(); )
          {
          String oid = (String) i.next();

          System.out.println("CRL->Entry->OID->" + oid);
          }
        }
      }

    /*
     *  catches.
     */
  }
  catch (Exception e)
    {
    e.printStackTrace();
    }
}

/**
 * Method importCertificate
 * Description: Import the certificate.
 *
 * @param filename is the file to import.
 *
 * @return the certification.
 *
 */
public X509CRL importCertificate(String filename)
  {
  X509CRL cert = null;
  try
    {
```

```java
    CertificateFactory cf =
      CertificateFactory.getInstance("X.509");

    /*
     * Get the File I/O of the Certificate
     */
    FileInputStream fr = new FileInputStream(filename);

    /*
     *  Construct the certificate based on the import
     */
    cert = (X509CRL) cf.generateCRL(fr);

    fr.close();

    /*
     *  catches.
     */
  }
  catch (java.security.cert.CertificateException e)
   {
    e.printStackTrace();
  }
  catch (java.security.cert.CRLException e)
   {
    e.printStackTrace();
  }
  catch (java.io.IOException e)
   {
    e.printStackTrace();
  }

  return cert;
}

/**
 * Method reasonToString
 *
 *
 * @param i defining the reason for revocation
 *
 * @return the string that maps to the integer
 *
 */
public static String reasonToString(int i)
 {
  switch (i)
   {
  case 0 :  // '\0'
```

```
        return "unspecified";

    case 1 :    // '\001'
        return "key compromise";

    case 2 :    // '\002'
      return "CA compromise";

    case 3 :    // '\003'
        return "affiliation changed";

    case 4 :    // '\004'
      return "superseded";

    case 5 :    // '\005'
        return "cessation of operation";

    case 6 :    // '\006'
      return "certificate hold";

    case 8 :    // '\b'
      return "remove from CRL";

    case 7 :    // '\007'
    default :
        return "unrecognized reason code";
    }
  }
}
```

In the Java code from Listing 24-5, I imported a *VeriSign* CRL. VeriSign is one of the leading CAs, found at www.verisign.com. After importing the CRL, the code is able to add a reason code to each of the three CRL entries for revoked certificates. The application produced the output found in Listing 24-6.

Listing 24-6: The output for Listing 24-5

```
>java com.richware.chap24.RichCRL rich.crl
Starting RichCRL....
Changing directory to Chapter 24
Opening Chapter 24 plus the input file as an argument: C:\
com\richware\chap24\rich.crl
*******************CRL *************************
X.509 CRL v2
Signature Algorithm: MD2withRSA, OID=1.2.840.113549.1.1.2
Issuer: OU=VeriSign Commercial Software Publishers CA, O="VeriSign,
Inc.", L=Int
ernet
```

```
This Update: Fri Mar 23 17:00:00 MST 2001
Next Update: Wed Jan 07 16:59:59 MST 2004

Revoked Certificates: 3
[ 1] SerialNumber: [    1b5190f7 3724399c 9254cd42 4637996a ]   On: Mon
Jan 29 17:
01:24 MST 2001


[ 2] SerialNumber: [    77e65a43 59935d5f 7a75801a cdadc222 ]   On: Wed
Aug 30 18:
00:56 MDT 2000


[ 3] SerialNumber: [    750e40ff 97f047ed f556c708 4eb1abfd ]   On: Tue
Jan 30 17:
00:49 MST 2001

CRL Extensions: 2
[ 1] : ObjectId: 2.5.29.15 Criticality=false
KeyUsage [
  DigitalSignature
  Key_Encipherment
]


[ 2] : ObjectId: 2.5.29.19 Criticality=false
BasicConstraints:[
CA:false
PathLen: undefined
]


Signature:
0000: 18 2C E8 FC 16 6D 91 4A   3D 88 54 48 5D B8 11 BF
.,...m.J=.TH]...
0010: 64 BB F9 DA 59 19 DD 0E   65 AB C0 0C FA 67 7E 21
d...Y...e....g.!
0020: 1E 83 0E CF 9B 89 8A CF   0C 4B C1 39 9D E7 6A AC
.........K.9..j.
0030: 46 74 6A 91 62 22 0D C4   08 BD F5 0A 90 7F 06 21
Ftj.b".........!
0040: 3D 7E A7 AA 5E CD 22 15   E6 0C 75 8E 6E AD F1 84
=~..^."...u.n...
0050: E4 22 B4 30 6F FB 64 8F   D7 80 43 F5 19 18 66 1D
.".0o.d...C...f.
0060: 72 A3 E3 94 82 28 52 A0   06 4E B1 C8 92 0C 97 BE
r....(R..N......
0070: 15 07 AB 7A C9 EA 08 67   43 4D 51 63 3B 9C 9C CD
...z...gCMQc;...
```

```
CRL->Version Number->2
CRL->Signature Algorithm Identifier->MD2withRSA
CRL->Issuer Name->OU=VeriSign Commercial Software Publishers CA,
O="VeriSign, In
c.", L=Internet
CRL->ThisUpdate->Fri Mar 23 17:00:00 MST 2001
CRL->NextUpdate->Wed Jan 07 16:59:59 MST 2004
***********CRL Entry No Extensions****************
SerialNumber: [    750e40ff 97f047ed f556c708 4eb1abfd ]  On: Tue Jan 30
17:00:4
9 MST 2001

CRL->Entry->RevocationDate->Tue Jan 30 17:00:49 MST 2001
CRL->Entry->SerialNumber->155593685987273437918165853798327757821
CRL->Entry->HasExtensions->false
***********CRL Entry No Extensions****************
SerialNumber: [    1b5190f7 3724399c 9254cd42 4637996a ]  On: Mon Jan 29
17:01:2
4 MST 2001

CRL->Entry->RevocationDate->Mon Jan 29 17:01:24 MST 2001
CRL->Entry->SerialNumber->36312672185138585402952177650507422058
CRL->Entry->HasExtensions->false
***********CRL Entry No Extensions****************
SerialNumber: [    77e65a43 59935d5f 7a75801a cdadc222 ]  On: Wed Aug 30
18:00:5
6 MDT 2000

CRL->Entry->RevocationDate->Wed Aug 30 18:00:56 MDT 2000
CRL->Entry->SerialNumber->159374190528741535247094583731252216354
CRL->Entry->HasExtensions->false
*****************CRL with Extensions**************
X.509 CRL v2
Issuer: OU=VeriSign Commercial Software Publishers CA, O="VeriSign,
Inc.", L=Int
ernet

This Update: Fri Mar 23 17:00:00 MST 2001
Next Update: Wed Jan 07 16:59:59 MST 2004

Revoked Certificates: 3
[1] SerialNumber: [    1b5190f7 3724399c 9254cd42 4637996a ]  On: Mon
Jan 29 17:
01:24 MST 2001
    CRL Entry Extensions: 1
    [1]: ObjectId: 2.5.29.21 Criticality=false
    Reason Code: CA Compromise
```

```
[2] SerialNumber: [     77e65a43 59935d5f 7a75801a cdadc222 ]   On: Wed
Aug 30 18:
00:56 MDT 2000
    CRL Entry Extensions: 1
    [1]: ObjectId: 2.5.29.21 Criticality=false
    Reason Code: CA Compromise


[3] SerialNumber: [     750e40ff 97f047ed f556c708 4eb1abfd ]   On: Tue
Jan 30 17:
00:49 MST 2001
    CRL Entry Extensions: 1
    [1]: ObjectId: 2.5.29.21 Criticality=false
    Reason Code: CA Compromise


CRL Extensions: 1
[1]: ObjectId: 2.5.29.20 Criticality=false
CRL Number:     01
NOT signed yet

*******CRL Entry After Adding Reason Extension**********
SerialNumber: [     750e40ff 97f047ed f556c708 4eb1abfd ]   On: Tue Jan 30
17:00:4
9 MST 2001
    CRL Entry Extensions: 1
    [1]: ObjectId: 2.5.29.21 Criticality=false
    Reason Code: CA Compromise


CRL->Entry->RevocationDate->Tue Jan 30 17:00:49 MST 2001
155593685987273437918165853798327757821
CRL->Entry->HasExtensions->true
CRL->Entry->Reason Code from method->null
CRL->Entry->Reason Code->CA compromise
CRL->Entry->OID->2.5.29.21
*******CRL Entry After Adding Reason Extension**********
SerialNumber: [     1b5190f7 3724399c 9254cd42 4637996a ]   On: Mon Jan 29
17:01:2
4 MST 2001
    CRL Entry Extensions: 1
    [1]: ObjectId: 2.5.29.21 Criticality=false
    Reason Code: CA Compromise


CRL->Entry->RevocationDate->Mon Jan 29 17:01:24 MST 2001
363126721851385854029521776505074220 58
CRL->Entry->HasExtensions->true
CRL->Entry->Reason Code from method->null
CRL->Entry->Reason Code->CA compromise
CRL->Entry->OID->2.5.29.21
*******CRL Entry After Adding Reason Extension**********
```

```
SerialNumber: [      77e65a43 59935d5f 7a75801a cdadc222 ]   On: Wed Aug 30
18:00:5
6 MDT 2000
    CRL Entry Extensions: 1
    [1]: ObjectId: 2.5.29.21 Criticality=false
    Reason Code: CA Compromise

CRL->Entry->RevocationDate->Wed Aug 30 18:00:56 MDT 2000
159374190528741535247094583731252216354
CRL->Entry->HasExtensions->true
CRL->Entry->Reason Code from method->null
CRL->Entry->Reason Code->CA compromise
CRL->Entry->OID->2.5.29.21
```

CRL entry

Now that the CRL and the CRL extensions have been discussed, the information in the CRL entry needs to be examined. The CRL entry is the entry for a revoked certificate. The CRL contains a set of all the CRL entries, also known as *revoked certificates*. Each entry represents the individual revoked certificate. The Java class that represents an individual entry in the CRL for a revoked certificate is the X509CRLEntry class. From the X509CRL class, the getRevokedCertificates ( ) method will return the set of X509Entry classes that are found in the X509CRL. Each X509Entry object in the returned set matches an individual revoked certificate.

The object of the X509Entry has methods for reading the information about the revoked certificate. Some of the information that can be read in the X509Entry includes the serial number of the revoked certificate, the date that the certificate was revoked, and any extensions. An example of information in the extension is the reason the certificate was revoked from the CA. The RFC 2549 displays the ASN.1 notation that demonstrates what fields are parts of the CRL entry. The CRL entry is displayed in Listing 24-7.

Listing 24-7: The CRL entry

```
revokedCertificates   SEQUENCE OF SEQUENCE {
   userCertificate   CertificateSerialNumber,
   revocationDate    ChoiceOfTime,
   crlEntryExtensions Extensions OPTIONAL
            -- if present, must be v2
} OPTIONAL

CertificateSerialNumber ::= INTEGER

Extensions ::= SEQUENCE SIZE (1..MAX) OF Extension

Extension ::= SEQUENCE {
   extnId    OBJECT IDENTIFIER,
```

```
critical    BOOLEAN DEFAULT FALSE,
extnValue   OCTET STRING
        -- contains a DER encoding of a value
        -- of the type registered for use with
        -- the extnId object identifier value
}
```

The CRL entry from Listing 24-7 shows that there are only three fields. The revoked certificate contains the serial number of the certificate, the date for being revoked, and the CRL entry extensions:

- ♦ **userCertificate:** This field is the serial number of the certificate that is assigned by the issuer of the CRL. The serial number represents a `BigInteger` data type in Java and is returned in the `X509CRLEntry` class by the `getSerialNumber ( )` method.

- ♦ **revocationDate:** This field contains the beginning date of the revocation for the CRL entry. The revocation date represents a `Date` data type in Java and is returned in the `X509CRLEntry` class by the `getRevocationDate ( )` method.

- ♦ **crlEntryExtension:** This field is the matching CRL Entry Extension.

The purpose of the extensions for each revoked certificate in version 2 of the CRL was simply to extend the reasons for the revocation. It might be that the reason for revocation would be duplicated without knowing the reason for the revocation and information from the CA for holding instructions. If the private key of the issuer was compromised and the certificate was revoked, the issuer might continue to use the private key. The issuer needs to be notified that the key has been compromised. The reason code gives a description of why the certificate was revoked, and it helps inform the parties of issues with the revoked certificate.

The idea is to give enough information to help discover weaknesses with the security and any holes found in the PKI. The organization should be made aware of why some of the digital certificates are no longer in use. The organization should contact the appropriate CA if it feels that further action is needed on the CA's part. If the reason code is that the CA is compromised, the organization should determine with the CA that there are no security breaches.

The hold instructions are actions for the organization to take from the CA to work with any issues of a revoked certificate. The hold instructions are a list of OIDs that the organization looks up for the actions it must take. This OID is information between the CA and the organization using the digital certificates. The OID could be instructions for the organization to call the CA immediately because a security breach has been discovered. It is very important for an organization to understand why some of the certificates were revoked to ensure that the security services are still secure. Here are the fields and their definitions:

- ♦ **Reason Code (OID 2.5.29.21):** This extension specifies the reason for certificate revocation. The reason code is always marked non-critical. Valid entries include the following along with the represented integer for the code.

TIP: A sample for examining the `reason` code is shown in Listing 24-5.

- **unspecified (integer 0):** There was no reason given from the CA for why the certificate was revoked.

- **keyCompromise (integer 1):** The CA believes that the private key of the certificate subject has been compromised. This reason code is applicable to end-entity certificates.

- **cACompromise (integer 2):** The private key of a CA is believed to have been compromised. This reason code is used when revoking CA certificates.

- **affiliationChanged (integer 3):** The name of the subject or other information in the certificate has been changed. This reason code does not imply that the private key has been compromised.

- **superseded (integer 4):** The certificate has been superseded by a newer certificate. This reason code does not imply that the private key has been compromised.

- **cessationOfOperation (integer 5):** The certificate is no longer required for the purpose for which it was issued. This reason code does not imply that the private key has been compromised.

- **certificateHold (integer 6):** The certificate has effectively been suspended or put on hold. If this reason code is used, the `HoldInstructionCode` extension may be specified. Certificates that have been suspended may later be revoked or released and the entry removed from the CRL.

- **removeFromCRL (integer 8):** This reason code is explicitly used for the delta CRLs to indicate that a certificate has expired or has been released from the hold state.

- **privilegeWithdrawn (integer 9):** A privilege that was specified within a certificate has been withdrawn.

- **aACompromised (integer 10):** Indicates that the AA validated in the certificate has been compromised.

- ◆ **Hold Instruction Code (OID 2.5.29.21):** This non-critical extension supports the temporary suspension of a certificate. It contains the OID that describes the action to be taken if the extension exists.

- ◆ **Certificate Issuers (OID 2.5.29.21):** This extension identifies the name of the certificate issuer associated with an Indirect CRL. This should be made critical.

- ◆ **Invalidity Date (OID 2.5.29.21):** This non-critical extension contains a date/time value showing when a suspected or known compromise of the private key occurred.

Summary

This chapter described X.509 in detail along with the associated Java classes. The structure of the digital certificate was discussed in depth as well as the reason for the different fields and their uses. When working with certificates and their associated CRL, it is important to understand the different fields and their uses. An example of a field is the reason code for why a particular certificate was revoked from a trusted source such as the CA. The reason code could point toward an issue regarding the security behind the certificate such as a private key being compromised.

The listings in this chapter give detailed Java examples of manipulating the certificates. The examples are used at the implementer's own risk because they go beyond the information provided in the `JavaDocs`. The Java examples were needed to give detailed information about the digital certificates. To understand how the digital certificate works and its purpose is simply a matter of understanding the individual fields of the certificate and the operations that they perform.

Some elements of the chapter have been left out of the digital signature description, such as a detailed examination of the repository for the certificate and the generation. You can find information regarding the certificate generation in Chapter 7. A detailed examination of PKI, X.500, and LDAP for extending the hierarchy and manipulation of the digital certificate, beyond the individual elements, is contained in the next chapter.

Chapter 25
PKI Management

In This Chapter

- ◆ Understanding the purpose of PKI
- ◆ Working with the operations to perform PKI
- ◆ Learning about the protocols and services used to set up PKI
- ◆ Learning about Java extensions that can be used to extend PKI

Introduction

The previous chapter defined the format of the X.509 digital certificate. The format is a guide to understanding the benefits and limitations of the *Public Key Infrastructure* (PKI). PKI provides the ability to create, store, distribute, manage, and revoke public keys with the use of the X.509 digital certificate format. Very few certificates are actually created by a user, except for testing purposes, because for subjects and issuers that are not inside the same organization, a path of trust must be established to certify that the message was encrypted by the sender's private key.

As a user, you cannot trust everyone who handles a certificate as it is being sent across the Internet, so PKI allows the receiver and sender of the secure message to only be concerned with trust points, commonly known as *Trust Anchors* (TA). The sender and receiver of the message are commonly known as the end entities. The TA is the point that an end entity will trust. A TA is normally a *Certificate Authority* (CA). The CA is a third-party company that is responsible for establishing a TA and a certificate path. The certificate path is the path that a certificate will take to transfer from one end entity to the other. Figure 25-1 gives an example.

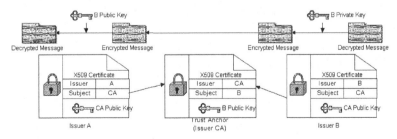

Figure 25-1: Basic certificate path

Here is a description of Figure 25-1:

- The purpose of the public key is to decrypt the message from user B. Because B encrypted the message with her private key, the message can only be decrypted with B's public key.

- If the public key can be guaranteed to come from user B, it follows that the message came from user B.

- If the public key from user B can decrypt the message, only the private key from user B can encrypt the message.

- To decrypt the message, user A needs to get a public key from user B. If user A already has a trusted public key from B, there is no need to get the key.

- If B has sent a message to A, PKI is the means to retrieve the key from user B. When retrieving the key, user A need only trust one entry point in this scenario, the CA. The CA is the Trusted Anchor to both entities in the scenario.

- User A needs to retrieve B's public key but doesn't know how to reach B. User A need only know about their common CA that issues the certificates to user A. User A will get a public key only to their Trusted Anchor (TA). The TA is the public key that the user will receive when registering his organization to the CA.

- User A need only to check its TA's certificate. The path to user B depends on user B's TA. User B also needs to know whom to trust. Because user A trusts the CA and the CA trusts user B, then user A can trust user B.

- User A can then receive user B's certificate and can trust the public key of the certificate. User A can then decrypt the message and know for sure that it came from user B.

> **NOTE:** The path of certificates is also known as the *certificate chain*, which is the chain of certificates needed to get from A to B.

Certificate Chaining

Figure 25-2 demonstrates the concept of certificate chaining. It shows a tree where a Leaf Certificate Authority issues certificates to the end entity, which is the end user or subject. The end entity could be a system, user, or server. The *Intermediate CA* is the CA between the Leaf CA and Root CA. There could be multiple Intermediate CAs between the Root CA and Leaf CA. The number of CAs that are traversed from one end entity to the next is the *path length*.

> **NOTE:** An example of a path length is the number of CAs traversed from the end entity H to I, which would be a path length of 1. If H needs to validate a certificate from the end entity J, the certificate path would be D->B->E. In this case, J has set a Trust Anchor at E.

The Root CA is the Trust Anchor for all CAs and the end entity. It is the most trusted anchor for all CAs. The Root CA is self-signed, meaning that the issuer and subject are the same value. The Root CA is the origin of a certificate tree. From Figure 25-2, the CA issuers will work from the top down to the end entity, each node trusting the higher node. The Root CA is a self-signed certificate because no other CA can issue the certificate to the root. The Root CA will issue the certificate to itself. The Root CA can issue certificates to the next level of Intermediate CAs.

The Intermediate CAs one level above the Leaf CAs will issue certificates to the Leaf CAs. When the Root CA issues a certificate, it will use its private key to encrypt the certificate, and the Intermediate CA will use the Root CA's public key to decrypt it. There is normally only one Trust Anchor per end entity, and it determines the path of the CAs because the certificate path must go through the Trust Anchor of the end entity. The Root CA will issue a certificate to all CAs to establish trust throughout the certificate path. Notice the tree-like structure of the certificate hierarchy. The X.500 protocol produces a directory tree-like structure following a similar hierarchy.

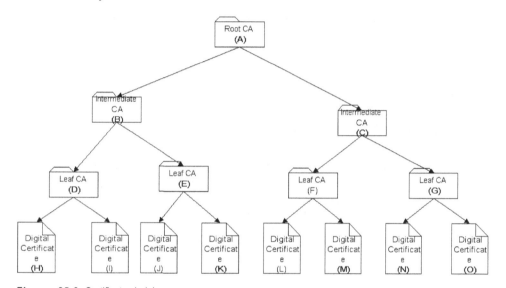

Figure 25-2: Certificate chaining

X.500

The X.500 specification is the first *Lightweight Directory Access Protocol* (LDAP) described in RFC 1487 in 1993 (`http://www.ietf.org/rfc/rfc1487.txt`). The X.500 has even been described as being a mechanism derived from Domain Names in RFC 1279 in 1991 (`http://www.ietf.org/rfc/rfc1279.txt`). I have heard many times that X.500 and LDAP need not be used for security storage, but I wish to qualify that the X.500 protocol is always used for security structures, including X.509.

Although the X.500 is built into protocols and specifications like X.509, an LDAP service may not be required to store the information. The point is that there is a protocol built into the digital certificates, but using servers to manage the X.500 protocol (called LDAP servers) is optional. For those organizations that do not use an LDAP server, the certificates should be stored in a file structure or Relational Database System using the X.500 protocol to define the storage.

A distinguished name

The reason that the X.500 protocol is used is because it defines a *distinguished name* (DN) that is unique to the issuer and subject. The DN is also used to define where to store the certificate because it is unique and can define a path down a tree-like store using the DN fields.

> **CROSS-REFERENCE:** DN fields are described in Chapter 24.

The X.500 directory is made up of entries distributed across a family of servers. Each entry has attributes. An example of an entry is the user `Rich Helton` and attributes are his address, telephone number, and credit card. The attribute value could be `333-333-3333` for the telephone number attribute. In short, an entry can be represented as an object, and the attributes are the fields in the object. An *Access Control List* (ACL) can be used to provide security for the attributes of an entry (`http://www.ietf.org/rfc/rfc1309.txt`). This would prevent others from accessing information such as credit card numbers.

Directory Information Base

The totality of an organization's information in the X.500 protocol is called the *Directory Information Base* (DIB). The entries are organized in a tree structure. Entries higher in the tree describe objects such as countries or organizations, while entries at the bottom of the tree (*leaves*) describe the people, equipment, or processes. An entry below any node is called a *child*. Every entry contains a set of attributes. The attributes depend on the class of the entry, such as country, organization, or organizational person.

The object class determines the types of attribute values that you might expect to find in an entry. There usually will be a small number of mandatory attributes for an entry and a larger number of optional attributes that may be present.

Figure 25-3 represents an example of a DIB. The example demonstrates a tree structure that represents the DNs of certificates, and the attributes at the bottom nodes represent the stored certificates. The distinguished name is made up of components such as country, organization, organizational unit, and personal name. Alias names may also be used to make lookups easier, but searches are normally a path down the tree structure to the end object of the lookup. Sometimes it is necessary to take actions on an entire node. An example of cascading a node is a node that starts with a "development" group. When a product moves to production after the development effort, the access to the servers and databases might have to change. In the X.500 protocol, only the connecting leaf node needs to change.

Figure 25-4 demonstrates a "Development" node that needs to be traversed to reach all of the developers, Developer1, Developer2, Developer3, and Developer4. Instead of changing the attributes of all the developers, the Development node's attribute could be changed to no longer have access to the production machines, thus blocking all developers without changing each developer.

This specific scenario is an example of a group. A *group* applies the same properties to a set of users. To be certain that this is clear, the DIB is the *namespace* to all of the objects that are listed in the tree. The organization of the tree itself is *a Directory Information Tree* (DIT).

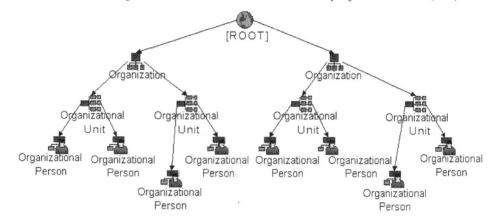

Figure 25-3: An X.500 DIB

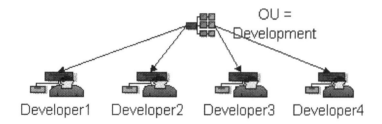

Figure 25-4: OU removal

The DIB is distributed across a community of databases that are controlled by *Directory Service Agents* (DSAs). Users access directory information by means of a *Directory User Agent* (DUA). A DUA provides the user interface for interactive queries and updates and passes user requests to a DSA. The X.500 standard defines a formal protocol that governs the interactions between a DUA and a DSA. There also is a DSA-to-DSA protocol that enables DSAs to relay user queries or download copies of parts of the DIB.

Even if a particular DSA does not have the information a user wants, it will know about other servers that might have the data. A DSA may either pass the address of another server to the DUA, or else may directly contact another server to get the information requested by the user. See Figure 25-5 for a relationship between the user, the DUA, and DSAs.

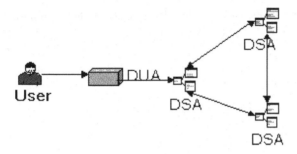

Figure 25-5: DUA

As mentioned before when describing RFC 1279, there are a number of structural similarities between the X.500 directory system and the *Domain Name System* (DNS). Actually, it could be said that DNS evolved into X.500 on the Internet when a tree structure was needed to provide a path and relationships to multiple objects. Both the X.500 and DNS are distributed directory systems. Users of each interact with a local client to reach a designated server, and that server can initiate distributed queries on behalf of the user. X.500 databases are expected to include information that helps users to locate network resources. A user must be able to perform the following operations:

♦ Read information from an entry

♦ Compare a value with the value of an attribute in an entry.

♦ Obtain a list of subordinates of a node.

♦ Search for entries of interest using attribute keys.

♦ Add or remove a directory leaf entry.

♦ Modify an entry.

The X.500 protocol was widely accepted as a format for managing systems, but very few servers were developed explicitly for the X.500 protocol. The reason is that the protocol was defined well, but there was no specification defining the *Software Development Kit* (SDK) for the protocol and many of the details for the communications of the client and server. For these reasons, an RFC was developed in 1995 to extend the X.500 as a version 2, RFC 1777 (http://www.ietf.org/rfc/rfc1777.txt), called *"Lightweight Directory Access Protocol,"* commonly known as LDAP.

LDAP

LDAP is a simplified front end to the X.500 Directory Access Protocol. LDAP reduces the complexity of using X.500 directory services and extends the services from a client and server perspective. Some of the communications that were established between the client and server are defined as an SDK. The LDAP SDK establishes secure transactions between the client and server. In early versions of LDAP, many client-side SDKs were developed to talk to previously defined X.500 servers.

The preliminary LDAP SDK that most LDAP services used as a starting point was the OpenLDAP implementation from the University of Michigan. The LDAP SDK requires that the client authenticate itself before accessing any of the services in the LDAP server. Other noticeable differences were the structure of the internal tables to search not only from top to bottom, but from bottom to top. Other enhancements to the internal tables included global searches, virtual views of a tree, and sorting on a path in the tree. The client differences also included transactional actions, such as rollbacks and commits to be performed on objects.

A lot of these enhancements are very database centric. The X.500 was too OSI network oriented, and it was not optimized for a data store and secure client/server implementation. LDAP decreased the processing time of an X.500 to only 10% of what it was by applying database techniques on top of the network techniques. Searching and sorting the tree was optimized to follow the X.500 schema. LDAP servers are enhanced to follow the X.500 schema, and for that reason they are the mechanism for storing certificates preferred by most certificate vendors.

If a relational database is to be used with the X.500, a lot of the LDAP functionality for managing the certificates will have to be replicated in the database. The X.500 schema is not only recommended for certificates, but it follows most security models in an organization's enterprise. An ACL system, permission system, or any object entry system could easily follow the X.500 schema. The schema also centralizes security information into one central directory for an entire organization. Because it is not directory specific, LDAP has also found its way into various environments, enhancing its interoperability. The LDAP SDK provides a rich API for interfacing into an LDAP server and client.

Many organizations still do not find a need to use LDAP and use relational databases instead to organize security data. This creates a proprietary implementation to an organization that will not communicate with the LDAP SDK. Using a custom implementation inside a *Relational Database Management System* (RDBMS) sometimes limits the applications that organizations can use. Some LDAP servers are becoming more and more tightly coupled to the LDAP SDK. If an organization is ever planning to use protocols or services that are tightly coupled to LDAP, it would be far cheaper to buy an LDAP server than to try to re-invent all of its functionality in an RDBMS. Some developers see building an LDAP server as an intellectual challenge. From an organizational perspective, building an RDBMS to simulate LDAP services could be very costly in maintenance alone.

As mentioned earlier in this section, the LDAP service provides its own authentication mechanisms through its SDK. The authentication types can be anonymous, simple, none, and SASL. SASL is the most secure, and it stands for *Simple Authentication and Security Layer*. RFC 2222 defines SASL (http://www.ietf.org/rfc/rfc2222.txt). LDAP uses this protocol to identify and authenticate a user in the server. The SDK's connection to the LDAP server requires a principal, credentials, and the SASL authentication type.

When the LDAP client tries to authenticate the server, the LDAP server can challenge the authentication. The LDAP client sends responses to the LDAP server, which can challenge as many times as it deems necessary. If the authentication succeeds, it will get a SUCCESS message, otherwise the client will receive an INVALID CREDENTIALS error. SASL is part of the JAAS product and further information can be found in the javax.security.sasl package. If all client and security information is stored in an LDAP server, the LDAP server and SASL protocol can be used as a central choke point for accessing this information. Using LDAP and SASL to handle most of the security namespaces can also limit the information that the development and production teams need to understand and contain the technological scope.

Some of the benefits of the LDAP server are the ability to manage the X.500 schema from an administrative console. The X.500 can manage a group by changing a node on a tree. To accomplish the same task in a RDBMS schema representation would require SQL database calls. The administration console that manages the groups and users is not built in the RDBMS; administration consoles are, however, built-in through an interactive tool like the LDAP administrative console of an LDAP server. Figures 25-6 and 25-7 demonstrate some of the out-of-the-box consoles in the Netscape Directory Server 5.1.

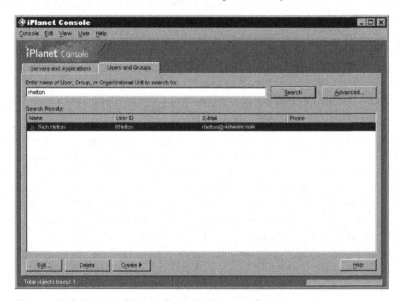

Figure 25-6: Netscape Directory Server 5.1 Users and Groups console

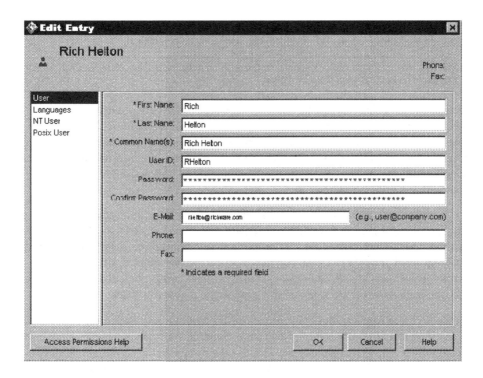

Figure 25-7: User console for the Netscape Directory Server 5.1

Looking at Figures 25-6 and 25-7, you may notice that there is a lot of predefined management information for security that comes out of the box from the Netscape Directory Server 5.1. To replicate the same amount of GUI interaction an X.500 schema requires a lot of work and maintenance. Using the out-of-the-box functionality of a Directory Service provides the out-of-the-box functionality of a Certificate Store. The Certificate Store is used to store certificates in the organization.

Certificate Components

It has been mentioned that a CA will interface to most organizations to issue their certificates and to provide a certificate of the CA as a Trusted Store. Many CAs will transfer certificates across the Internet to the subject's TA. To move from CA to CA, a cross-certification may be required. The X.509 specification (section 8.1.2) defines a cross-certificate in this way:

"A Certification Authority may be the subject of a certificate issued by another Certificate Authority. In this case, the certificate is called a cross-certificate".

CAs are the trusted third party that organizations use to manage their certificates outside of the organization. The CA will use a CRL to check for invalid certificates and send the CRL to the organization to perform any checks that they might require. The CA may also retain copies of private keys in case any are lost and key recoveries have to be performed.

> **TIP:** Some CAs may operate slightly differently, so research on a particular CA such as VeriSign should always be done to understand what services it offers.

When certificates are being transferred, other services besides CAs and users might be processing the certificates. One of these services is the *Registration Authority* (RA). The RA accomplishes the same tasks described for the CA, except that an RA may sit in front of the CA and use human intervention to accomplish some tasks such as getting a revoked certificate, registering a certificate, and reporting key compromises. At no time is the RA part of a certificate trust or certificate path.

An RA is useful to have when human intervention is needed to work with organizations to get set up for certificates. Using an RA will also offload some of the work of the CA just to deal with the trust model. The CA does get a lot of traffic from organizations. After the CA has the certificate registered, it might just deal with the Certificate Server of the CA for most of its functionality. How much human intervention is used with the certificate will depend on which Web and Applications server are being used to process the digital certificate.

Some of the Web and Application servers use a Certificate Repository for storing certificates, usually requiring an LDAP server for the data store. Some of these components may not come standard out of the box, so it might be necessary to extend some of the certificate interfaces through the use of Java. Some of the functionality that Java can provide for certificates has been discussed in the previous chapter. The previous chapter discussed manipulating the X.509 format in certificates. This chapter discusses using Java for extending and validating the certificate path.

Certificate Path Validation

One of the purposes of the JSR-055 (`http://jcp.org/jsr/detail/055.jsp`) that is distributed with the JDK 1.4 is to provide basic path validation. Basic path validation is necessary for many algorithms, such as SSL/TLS and IPSEC. Checking the basic path validation is also important to an organization if it wants to check internally whether the organization's certificate set is valid. The JDK 1.4 distribution provides an API for path validation of certificates.

The PKI documentation (`http://www.ietf.org/internet-drafts/draft-ietf-pkix-new-part1-11.txt`) defines an algorithm that should be used for basic path validation of certificates. The algorithm defines the inputs to be a Trust Anchor, the current date/time, and a certificate to be checked. It also defines indicators for the policy mapping being allowed, the path validation being allowed for at least one of the certificate policies, and an indicator if the `anyPolicy` OID should be used in the validation.

Figure 25-8 demonstrates the basic path validation algorithm where the certificate and values (like the policies) are used to process or validate the certificate, and the algorithm continues till the last certificate in the path.

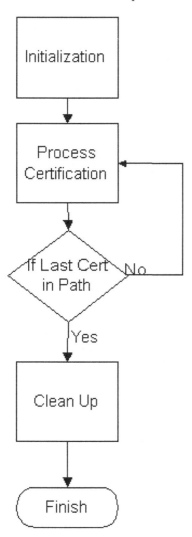

Figure 25-8: Basic path validation algorithm

The initialization begins with, but doesn't end with the creation from the java.security.cert.CertPath class. The CertPath is an engine class that is generated by the CertificateFactory class. Listing 25-1 shows the CertPath initialization example.

Listing 25-1: The `RichPath`: A `CertPath` initialization example

```
package com.richware.chap25;

import java.security.cert.CertPath;
import java.security.cert.CertificateFactory;
import java.security.cert.CertPathParameters;
import java.security.cert.CertPathValidatorResult;
import java.security.cert.CertPathValidator;
import java.security.KeyStore;
import java.security.PublicKey;
import java.security.cert.Certificate;
import java.util.Date;
import java.security.cert.X509CRLSelector;
import java.security.cert.PKIXParameters;
import java.security.cert.PKIXCertPathValidatorResult;
import java.security.cert.PolicyNode;
import java.security.cert.TrustAnchor;
import java.util.Collection;
import java.util.Collections;
import java.security.cert.LDAPCertStoreParameters;
import java.security.cert.CertStore;
import java.security.cert.X509CertSelector;
import java.math.BigInteger;
import java.util.List;
import java.io.FileInputStream;
import java.util.Arrays;
/**
 * Class RichPath
 * Description: A custom demonstration of the path verification
 * for a certificate.
 *
 * Copyright:    Copyright (c) 2002 Wiley Publishing, Inc.
 * @author Rich Helton <rhelton@richware.com>
 * @version 1.0
 * DISCLAIMER: Please refer to the disclaimer at the beginning of this
book.
 */
public class RichPath {
  private static final boolean _DEBUG = true;

  /**
   * Method main
   * Description: The main driver to run the methods.
   *
   *
   * @param args (no arguments presently).
   *
   */
```

```
  public static void main(String args[ ]) {
    try {
      System.out.println("Starting RichPath....");
      /*
       * Pass in the argument of the keystore file
       * It will be opened in the same directory as the application
       */
      if (args[ 0] == null)
      {
        System.out.println(
          "This application requires an input file for the location of
the keystore");
      }

      String localDirectory = System.getProperty("user.dir");
      System.out.println("Changing directory to Chapter 25");
      System.setProperty("user.dir",
                          localDirectory
                          + "\\com\\richware\\chap25\\");
      localDirectory = System.getProperty("user.dir");

      /*
       * Get the local keystore that contains a trusted certificate
       */
      String localInputFile = localDirectory + args[ 0];
      System.out.println(
        "Openining Chapter 25 plus the input file as an argument: "
        + localInputFile);

      /*
       * Import the certificate path keystore
       */
      RichPath myPath  = new RichPath();
      CertPath newpath =
        myPath.importCertPath(localInputFile,"password", "rich2");
      /*
       *   catches.
       */
    } catch (Exception e) {
      e.printStackTrace();
    }
  }

  /**
   * Method importCertPath
   * Description: Import the certificate path from the
   * keystore.
   *
   * @param filename of the keystore to import.
```

```java
 * @param password
 * @param chain
 *
 * @return the certification path.
 *
 */
public CertPath importCertPath(String filename,
                              String password,
                              String chain) {
  CertPath certPath = null;
  try {
    /*
     * instantiate a CertificateFactory for X.509
     */
    CertificateFactory cf =
      CertificateFactory.getInstance("X.509");

    /*
     * instantiate a KeyStore with type JKS
     */
    KeyStore ks = KeyStore.getInstance("JKS");

    /*
     * load the contents of the KeyStore
     */
    ks.load(new FileInputStream(filename),
            password.toCharArray());

    /*
     * fetch certificate chain stored
     */
    Certificate[] certArray = ks.getCertificateChain(chain);

    /*
     * convert chain to a List
     */
    List certList = Arrays.asList(certArray);

    /*
     * extract the certification path from the List of
     * Certificates
     */
    certPath = cf.generateCertPath(certList);
    System.out.println(" CertPath :" + certPath);

    /*
     *    catches.
     */
  } catch (java.security.cert.CertificateException e) {
```

```
        e.printStackTrace();
    } catch (java.security.KeyStoreException e) {
        e.printStackTrace();
    } catch (java.security.NoSuchAlgorithmException e) {
        e.printStackTrace();
    } catch (java.io.IOException e) {
        e.printStackTrace();
    }

    return certPath;
  }
}
```

Listing 25-1 demonstrates the initialization of the `CertPath` class. This `CertPath` object gets the certificate path from the keystore passed in that is called `./keystore`. The certificate chain that will be validated is for the `rich` certificate in the keystore. The password for the certificate in the keystore must be used to retrieve the certificate.

The output of `RichPath` is as follows:

```
>java com.richware.chap25.RichPath .keystore
Starting RichPath....
Changing directory to Chapter 25
Opening Chapter 25 plus the input file as an argument:
C:\com\richware\chap25\.keystore
 CertPath :
X.509 Cert Path: length = 1.
[
==============================================================Certificate 1
start.
[
[
  Version: V1
  Subject: CN=rich helton, OU=development, O=richware, L=denver, ST=co,
C=us
  Signature Algorithm: SHA1withDSA, OID = 1.2.840.10040.4.3

  Key:  Sun DSA Public Key
    Parameters:DSA
        p:       fd7f5381 1d751229 52df4a9c 2eece4e7 f611b752 3cef4400
c31e3f80 b6
512669
    455d4022 51fb593d 8d58fabf c5f5ba30 f6cb9b55 6cd7813b 801d346f
f26660b7
    6b9950a5 a49f9fe8 047b1022 c24fbba9 d7feb7c6 1bf83b57 e7c6a8a6
150f04fb
    83f6d3c5 1ec30235 54135a16 9132f675 f3ae2b61 d72aeff2 2203199d
d14801c7
        q:       9760508f 15230bcc b292b982 a2eb840b f0581cf5
```

```
       g:      f7e1a085 d69b3dde cbbcab5c 36b857b9 7994afbb fa3aea82
f9574c0b 3d
078267
    5159578e bad4594f e6710710 8180b449 167123e8 4c281613 b7cf0932
8cc8a6e1
    3c167a8b 547c8d28 e0a3ae1e 2bb3a675 916ea37f 0bfa2135 62f1fb62
7a01243b
    cca4f1be a8519089 a883dfe1 5ae59f06 928b665e 807b5525 64014c3b
fecf492a

  y:
    9b256cb3 09f61b20 2835df0a 0db97f65 786448dd 2599b6f9 148d1040
79b02014
    df239539 954c69a4 a45d4cb0 7b98ad33 f881e2c4 4481c122 ebf98941
134be3cb
    5077e54a 03774c6d 513f647c 79532772 09c50fea c2f1b5d2 f0d2016c
be4118ce
    f76f757e cfb587c8 376efd44 d961af85 747f4c77 3b03883f 9a5ffb67
6b74ac71

  Validity: [From: Fri Nov 23 22:53:46 MST 2001,
              To: Thu Feb 21 22:53:46 MST 2002]
  Issuer: CN=rich helton, OU=development, O=richware, L=denver, ST=co,
C=us
  SerialNumber: [     3bff35ea ]

]
  Algorithm: [ SHA1withDSA]
  Signature:
0000: 30 2C 02 14 7E 8C 41 2A   2A 3F 9D A8 6C C0 40 58
0,....A**?..l.@X
0010: C8 36 BA 1D EA CC 2B D3   02 14 24 DE E1 54 9E 47
.6....+...$..T.G
0020: AE 33 BF 3D 28 94 9E B6   86 FF 7D 0D E2 DA       .3.=(........

]
==============================================================Certificate 1
end.
]
```

This example does not end the initialization phase of the algorithm. Other values must be initialized such as the current date to ensure that the certificate falls within the current date. A Trust Anchor must also be initialized that will tell the algorithm which path to validate. The certificate path must always go through the Trust Anchor of the end-entity certificate. Any policies that it will be validated against must also be initialized. The class for initializing these parameters to be validated against is the `java.security.cert.PKIXParameters` class. The `PKIXParameters` must be initialized with a Trust Anchor. The Trust Anchor could either be the trusted certificates in the `KeyStore` or a Trusted Anchor created with the `java.security.cert.TrustAnchor` class. Listing 25-2 shows an example of how to build parameters using `PKIXParameters` class.

Listing 25-2: Building parameters with the `PKIXParameters` class

```
/**
 * Method buildParams
 * Purpose: Build the initialization parameters for the
 * certificate validation.
 *
 * @param filename of the KeyStore
 * @param password of the KeyStore
 *
 * @return the parameters built to validate.
 *
 */
public PKIXParameters buildParams(String filename,
                                  String password) {

  /*
   * create CertPathValidator that implements the "PKIX"
   * algorithm
   */
  try {

    /* Pass in a TrustAnchor as a
     * (Collections.singleton(anchor)) or
     * retrieve all trusted certificates
     * from KeyStore as anchor
     * If a TrustAnchor was set here,
     * the caName and publicKey of
     * the CA would have to know
     * or the X509Certificate which is
     * the certificate of the TrustAnchor.
     * Also any nameConstraints.
     */
    if ((filename == null) || (filename.length() < 1)) {
      return null;
    }

    if ((password == null) || (password.length() < 1)) {
      return null;
    }

    /*
     * instantiate a KeyStore with type JKS
     */
    KeyStore ks = KeyStore.getInstance(_keystoreType);
```

```
   /*
    * load the contents of the KeyStore
    */
   ks.load(new FileInputStream(filename),
           password.toCharArray());

   PKIXParameters params = new PKIXParameters(ks);

   /*
    * Parameters used as input for the PKIX
    * CertPathValidator algorithm.
    */
   /*
    *   An example of setting policies would be:
    *   params.setExplicitPolicyRequired(true);
    *   params.setInitialPolicies(policyIds);
    */
   Date currentDate = new Date();
   /*
    * Set the current Date
    */
   params.setDate(currentDate);
   return params;
 } catch (Exception e) {
   e.printStackTrace();
 }
  return null;
}
```

Part of the validation includes checking to see if the digital certificate is revoked. If the digital certificate is not revoked, the certificate is valid to proceed with the certificate path and validation against the parameters. The CRL is returned from a Certificate Store. The Certificate Store is initialized from the `java.security.cert.CertStore` class. A `CertStore` provides access to a collection of untrusted certificates and CRLs that can be used for purposes other than a trusted store. It is different than the `KeyStore` implementation that provides access to a collection of private keys and trusted certificates for an organization. The `CertStore` has two implementations: LDAP and Collection schemas. See Listing 25-3.

Listing 25-3: Retrieving CRLs from the LDAP server

```
/**
 * Method buildLDAPCRLS
 * Purpose: Build a CRL from the LDAP
 * Server satisfying the conditions.
 *
 * @return the Collection of CRL certificates.
 *
 */
public Collection buildLDAPCRLS() {
```

```
try {
/*
 * Access the LDAP Server
 */
  LDAPCertStoreParameters lcsp  =
    new LDAPCertStoreParameters("ldap.sun.com", 389);
  CertStore             cs     =
    CertStore.getInstance("LDAP", lcsp);
  X509CRLSelector           xcrls = new X509CRLSelector();

  /*
   * select CRLs satisfying current date and time
   */
  xcrls.setDateAndTime(new Date());

  /*
   * select CRLs issued by 'O=richwareLLC, C=us'
   */
  xcrls.addIssuerName("O=richwareLLC, C=us");

  /*
   * select only CRLs with a CRL number at least '2'
   */
  xcrls.setMinCRLNumber(new BigInteger("2"));

  Collection crls = cs.getCRLs(xcrls);

  return crls;
} catch (java.io.IOException e) {
  e.printStackTrace();
} catch (java.security
      .InvalidAlgorithmParameterException e) {
  e.printStackTrace();
} catch (java.security.cert.CertStoreException e) {
  e.printStackTrace();
} catch (java.security.NoSuchAlgorithmException e) {
  e.printStackTrace();
}

return null;
}
```

After the certificate is ensured not to belong to the revoked certificate class, the parameters must be validated against the certification path. If the basic path validation is successful, the subject's public key can be returned with other items such as the certificate policy tree. The class that returns the results is the `java.security.cert.PKIXCertPathValidatorResult` class. Listing 25-4 shows the final validation code.

Listing 25-4: Final validation

```
/**
 * Method certPathValidator
 * Purpose: To validate the basic certificate path.
 *
 * @param certPath the certification path.
 * @param params the certificate parameters.
 *
 * @return the results of the validation.
 *
 */
public PKIXCertPathValidatorResult certPathValidator(
        CertPath certPath, PKIXParameters params) {

  /*
   * create CertPathValidator that implements the "PKIX" algorithm
   */
  try {
    CertPathValidator cpv =
      CertPathValidator.getInstance("PKIX");

    /*
     * validate the path and parameters
     */
    PKIXCertPathValidatorResult result            =
      (PKIXCertPathValidatorResult) cpv.validate(certPath,
        params);
    /*
     * retruns the root node of the policy tree
     */
    PolicyNode                   policyTree        =
      result.getPolicyTree();
    /*
     * Get the Subject's Public Key
     */
    PublicKey                    subjectPublicKey =
      result.getPublicKey();

    return result;
  } catch (java.security.NoSuchAlgorithmException e) {
    e.printStackTrace();
  } catch (java.security
          .InvalidAlgorithmParameterException e) {
    e.printStackTrace();
  } catch (java.security.cert.CertPathValidatorException e) {
```

```
        e.printStackTrace();
    }


    return null;
}
```

Non-repudiation

One of the greatest advantages of using digital certificates is non-repudiation. *Non-repudiation* is like receiving a sales receipt when placing an order. Non-repudiation guarantees that when a message is sent to a third-party application, a receipt is returned saying that the message was received.

When working with Business-to-Business (B2B), sometimes it is necessary to get a receipt to ensure that the message was delivered. An example is placing an order through xyzFlowers.com. The company xyzFlowers.com could be a company that doesn't actually deliver flowers, but just handles the ordering process. The company could have a contract with a small flower shop in ABC City, Colorado, a couple of miles from the customer who actually placed an order on the Internet for a flower bouquet to be sent to his wife. xyzFlowers is acting on behalf of the customer by ordering the flowers for the customer without the customer's knowing about the local flower shop. If the customer doesn't receive the flowers in a timely manner, the xyzFlowers organization needs to ensure, without just taking the word of the local flower shop, that the local flower shop truly received the order..

There is no proof that the local flower shop is at fault because there is no proof that it received the order. Non-repudiation is when the client, xyzFlowers, sends a request to the service, the local flower shop, and there is a response and timestamp immediately returned from the service saying that it received the order. The non-repudiation protocol is necessary to find out which organization is currently responsible for the task.

> **NOTE:** The purpose of a non-repudiation service is to establish evidence that a message has had an action performed on it. This evidence is used to ensure that a message was created, sent, submitted, transported, and received.

Non-repudiation services provide an evidence generator that will generate tokens or digital signatures to signify the type of service, the message, and the time that the message provided evidence. The type of service will describe the information that is needed to give evidence of a transaction.

There are four types of non-repudiation services:

- **Non-Repudiation of Origin:** This service covers the case where the sender acknowledges that he created and sent the message.
- **Non-Repudiation of Delivery:** This service covers the case where the recipient acknowledges that she has received the message.

♦ **Non-Repudiation of Submission:** This service incorporates a delivery service that acts as a third party that will receive the message from the sender, acknowledge to the sender that it received the message, and forward it to one or more recipients of the message. It will acknowledge that the message was sent from the sender. It does not guarantee that the recipient received the message, but will make a best effort to forward the message. The sender trusts the delivery service.

♦ **Non-Repudiation of Transport:** This service incorporates a delivery service that acts as a third party that will receive the message from the sender, acknowledge to the sender that the message was received, and place the message in the data store of the recipient. The delivery service acknowledges that the message was placed in the recipient's data store but cannot guarantee that the recipient received the message because it cannot guarantee that the recipient checks the data store.

Summary

To understand the PKI, only two things need to be studied in detail, the X.509 format and how digital certificates are managed in a certificate chain. From those two things you get a lot of information about other protocols such as X.500, LDAP, and asymmetric keying. The purpose of PKI is to transport a secure public key from a sender of a secure message to the receiver of a secure message so that he may decrypt the message. PKI is a means to make the public key secure.

Java has a lot of packages for both formatting the X.509 digital certificate and checking the certificate path. The LDAP SDK also offers a rich API for working with an LDAP server. The LDAP server is important because the X.509 certificate format and certificate path are tightly coupled with the X.500 Directory Service schema for manipulating certificates.

The study of PKI is very extensive and a lot of work could go be required from an organization to support PKI. My suggestion is to take the easiest route. Use LDAP if you can, so that a lot of RDBMS work is not required. Know the services offered by your CA, Web services, and Application services so that you may take advantage of them. I have worked with many companies and types of developers, and many do think that it is cool to write their own LDAP server; however, there is a difference between having to write an LDAP server the night before production and writing one on your own time. Use as much out-of-the-box functionality as possible. Many organizations use PKI, so there are very few things to be discovered in this area for most organizations unless you happen to be an RA or a CA.

Part IX

Enterprise Access

Chapter 26: Java Enterprise Security and Web Services Security

Chapter 27: Securing Client-Side Components

Chapter 28: Securing Server-Side Components

Chapter 29: Application Security with Java

Chapter 26

Java Enterprise Security and Web Services Security

In This Chapter

♦ Understanding how all the different technologies integrate in the Java platform

♦ Learning about the sandbox model

♦ Exploring the security changes included in the J2SDK v 1.4

♦ Understanding Web Services

♦ Exploring Web Services technologies: UDDI, WSDL, and SOAP

By now you should be familiar with the basic tools for security, such as encryption, digital keys, and digital signatures, and you should know about the different security technologies provided by J2EE and the J2SDK v 1.4. This chapter helps you understand how those technologies come together in the overall Java security architecture and their application in Web Services. These technologies form a security framework that allows you to switch among services.

You do not need to implement everything at once, and the framework provides you with a roadmap for your security architecture. The next few chapters explore in more detail how this architecture is used in the client side (Chapter 27), the server side (Chapter 28), and how some applications provide security using these technologies (Chapter 29).

Introduction

Distributed computing has evolved through the years to allow parts of an enterprise system to be located on separate and possibly heterogeneous platforms. These systems may also be located in different geographic areas. For example, there is no reason why a database located in Europe cannot be accessed by a transaction manager in London.

Among the building blocks of distributed computing are distributed objects. *Distributed objects* allow objects that perform a specific task to reside in different machines and to be accessed to provide a complete solution. These distributed objects can be assembled into *components* to encapsulate a behavior or provide a specific solution to part of a problem. The J2EE model can be used to assemble a solution and is one of several enterprise component models in the industry. Other models include those defined by the Microsoft Corporation and the *Object Management Group* (OMG). These distributed solutions typically require security.

When an application (distributed or otherwise) provides security, there is an expectation to safeguard user privacy, to ensure that information (such as transactions and data) is not tampered with either accidentally or maliciously, and to prevent theft. Authorized users should be able to access the information they are authorized to access, and unauthorized users should not. Even so, the level of security needed for the given application depends on the value of the information to be protected and the software and hardware involved. In addition, there are usually compromises that you must make in cost, usability, and security.

Java Security Models

The Java platform has two main goals for security: One is to provide a secure platform on which to run Java-enabled applications, and the other is to provide security tools and services to enable secure applications. The Java platform security at first used the sandbox model, a collection of safe resources that unauthorized code could access, and now it has evolved into a policy-based security model.

The sandbox model

The *sandbox model* refers to the original security model provided by the Java platform. It provided a very restricted environment to run untrusted code. The basic idea was that downloaded code, such as an applet, was not trusted and, therefore, should not access vital resources (such as the file system). Local code, however, was trusted and had full access to system resources. Figure 26-1 shows the original sandbox model.

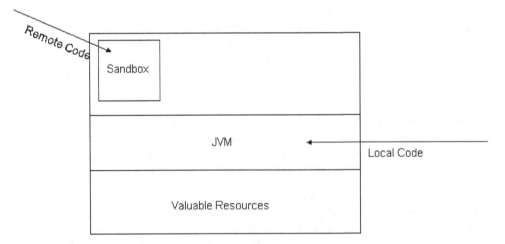

Figure 26-1: The original sandbox model

This model was very restrictive so the JDK 1.1 introduced the concept of *signed applets*. Applets are digitally signed to obtain extra permissions outside of the sandbox. Programs that are not digitally signed continue to be restricted by the original sandbox model. Java 1.1, however, gave unrestricted access to system resources to signed applets. It was an all-or-nothing type of access.

> **TIP:** Recall from Chapter 8 that applets can be signed (as well as configured) using the `policytool`.

The *Extended Java Sandbox* is the default model for digitally signed applets. Under the Extended Java Sandbox, digitally signed Java code is allowed to read and write to a specified directory. In that directory, no executables can run and other Java programs cannot gain access to other network services.

Next, in JDK 1.2, the *Java Protected Domains Security* model gives fine-grain control and selectively grants access to network resources. Under this model, administrators can tailor security policies to match security requirements. For instance, the administrator may grant read access to some files in a directory to all users and write access to managers, all based on the resource being accessed and the identity of the user. The concept of domains is important and is a base for system security.

A *domain* is a group of permissions that are provided to Java code. These permissions are based on the program's origin and its digital signature. The problem with protected domains is that the policy file needs to be modified by the end user, and this requirement is impractical.

Security in J2SDK v 1.4

The J2SDK v 1.4 has enhanced its security; you may want to look at the `http://java.sun.com/security/index.html` site for more information. That site includes documentation, user guides, and articles specific to Java security.

Now the J2SDK provides a security model that is policy-based, which is easily configurable and provides fine-grained access control. The policy guards a resource and specifies which permissions are available. Unless permission is granted to code to access a protected resource, the code cannot access it. This access control can be specified for all Java code such as applications, beans, and applets. There is no longer a built-in concept that all local code is trusted.

Here is a brief summary of the security changes included in the J2SDK v 1.4:

♦ The following packages are now integrated into the SDK instead of being optional packages:

• The *Java Cryptography Extension* (JCE). Recall that, for import control restrictions, the jurisdiction policy files allow strong but limited cryptography.

> **CROSS-REFERENCE:** For more information on JCE, refer to Chapter 15.

- The *Java Secure Socket Extension* (JSSE). Recall that the JSSE implementation, because of import control restrictions, includes strong cipher suites but does not allow the default `SSLSocketFactory` and `SSLServerSocketFactory` to be replaced.

CROSS-REFERENCE: Chapter 23 describes JSSE in more detail.

- *Java Authentication and Authorization Services* (JAAS). The integration of JAAS into the J2SDK makes it possible for the `java.security.Policy` API to handle principal-based queries and for the default implementation policy to support principal-based grant entries. This makes it possible to allow access control, based not only on the code that is running but also on who is running it.

CROSS-REFERENCE: Refer to Chapter 15 and Chapter 19 for more information on JAAS.

- The Java Certification Path API includes new classes and methods to allow building and validating certificate chains.

- The Java GSS-API can be used for exchanging messages between applications using Kerberos v5.

CROSS-REFERENCE: Chapter 17 describes the Java GSS-API in more detail.

- The graphical `policytool` utility now enables you to indicate via the Principal field that a user is granted specified access control permissions.

CROSS-REFERENCE: Chapter 8 and Chapter 18 describe the `policytool`.

- In J2SDK v 1.4, the lifetime of class and permission binding is scoped by the lifetime of the security policy. In previous versions of the SDK, while the class was being loaded, the class was bound with its corresponding permissions and this binding was scoped by the lifetime of the class loader.

J2EE security

The J2EE server enforces security at two levels: authentication and authorization. Authentication is the process by which a user proves his or her identity.

Recall that you define roles and permissions to access resources. In addition, the deployer maps the roles to principals. The details of how the EJB server provides authentication is vendor-specific. Some may use the underlying operating system services and others may use some type of *Public Key Infrastructure* (PKI). Also, the way principal delegation is performed is provider-specific. Recall that the principal of the requestor for a resource is normally propagated. Therefore, the roles and permissions need to be set accordingly. For instance, some beans should be allowed to call other beans that the user may not have access to. This is very similar to the `doPrivileged()` method in `java.security.AccessController`.

NOTE: The `doPrivileged()` method enables a piece of trusted code to temporarily access more resources than are available directly to the application that called it.

JAAS is Java's default security model to grant permissions based on where the code comes from. Authorization is the process to establish whether the requestor to a resource has the proper rights or permissions to access it. Using JAAS, authorization can be accomplished declaratively and programmatically.

> **CROSS-REFERENCE:** J2EE security is discussed in more detail in Chapter 28 in the section "Enterprise Security with EJBs."

Policy file

As mentioned earlier, Java 2 security is *policy-based* and uses the `java.policy` file to specify the security policies that control the resources the application (or applet) can access. In the policy reference implementation, the policy can be specified within one or more policy configuration files. Recall that these files contain a list of entries that map the permissions allowed for code from specific sources.

Also, the policy configuration file may contain a `keystore` entry to look up the public keys of the signers in the grant entries.

> **CROSS-REFERENCE:** Chapter 8 talks about the policy file and the `keystore` entry.

Java Permissions

The permission classes encapsulate the access to system resources. Table 26-1 describes the basic Java built-in permissions. There are many more classes (not only in the security package) that provide specific functionality, such as `java.io.FilePermission` for file permissions.

Table 26-1: Basic Java Built-in Permission Classes

Class	Description
`java.security.Permission`	This abstract class defines the essential functionalities required for all permissions.
`java.security.PermissionCollection`	Each instance of this class holds only permissions of the same type.
`java.security.Permissions`	This class is designed to hold a heterogeneous collection of permissions. Basically, it is a collection of `java.security.PermissionCollection` objects.

> **CROSS-REFERENCE:** See Chapter 19 for more information about Java permissions and the permission set.

Recall that permissions are usually compared against each other. The `implies` method is crucial because it allows for this comparison to happen. For instance, if you have permission to write to a file, it implies that you can read it. That is,

```
java.io.FilePermission("/myfile.txt", "write") implies
java.io.FilePermission("/myfile.txt", "read").
```

> **TIP:** You must be careful how you use the `implies` method because you can give code more permissions than is obvious, such as allowing the setting of system properties. For more information about permissions refer to
> `http://java.sun.com/j2se/sdk/1.2/docs/guide/security/permissions.html`.

Enterprise Component Models

Here is a list of some of the component models used in the enterprise. Most of them are discussed in the next three chapters.

- ◆ *Common Object Request Broker Architecture* (CORBA). CORBA is a standard model for enabling distributed access across components and defines a framework for providing security services to applications via the CORBA *Object Request Broker* (ORB).

- ◆ *Java Remote Method Invocation* (RMI). The RMI framework enables distributed access to components. It enables an object in one JVM to invoke methods in another JVM. It is very popular because it is easy to use, but it lacks interoperability with other languages. That is why it is typically paired with other technologies such as RMI over IIOP, and RMI/IDL.

- ◆ *Applets.* Applets define interfaces between a container and a component that allows Java code to be included in an HTML page. The applet's code is loaded to your system when you access it with a Java-enabled browser and executed by your browser's JVM.

- ◆ *Java Servlets.* Java Servlets are platform-independent server-side application components that are downloaded — on demand — to the part of the system that needs them.

- ◆ *JavaServer Pages* (JSP). The JSP technology is an extension of the Java Servlet technology. It separates the page logic from its design and display, which makes it easy to build Web page applications.

- ◆ *JavaBeans.* A JavaBean is a reusable Java code component that comforms to the JavaBeans specification, which defines the configuration and communication protocol for JavaBeans.

- ◆ *Enterprise JavaBeans* (EJB). The EJB server-side component model simplifies the development of middleware components that are transactional, scalable, and portable.

NOTE: You can find more information on these and other Java products and technologies at the `http://java.sun.com/products/` Web site.

Understanding Web Services

A *Web Service* is any service that uses standard Web protocols, conventions, and namespaces. Web Services are widely used in Business-to-Business (B2B) communications for disparate businesses to communicate with an agreed upon XML document.

TIP: You can find more information at the W3C (World Wide Web Consortium) site (`www.w3.org`), the IETF (Internet Engineering Task Force) site (`www.ietf.org`), and OASIS (`www.oasis-open.org`).

With the invention of *eXtensible Markup Language* (XML), the Web server now no longer need process just GUI messages, but may also take client application requests. XML was designed for document markup and has become the default standard for data transfer. XML documents are now passed between clients and a Web server. The client can format a request in an XML document to get a response from the Web server. The Web server can act as a broker for the requested data to enterprise objects. A typical message broker in a Web server could be a Java Servlet to handle the transactions from the client. The Java Servlet is a server-side component on the Web server.

The transport mechanism for the Web Service is normally HTTP, or HTTPS for secure communication. The client can communicate to the Web server using a synchronous request and reply, or even an asynchronous messaging (sending an XML document to the Web server and asking for a response at a later time). See Figure 26-2 for an overview of a Web Service.

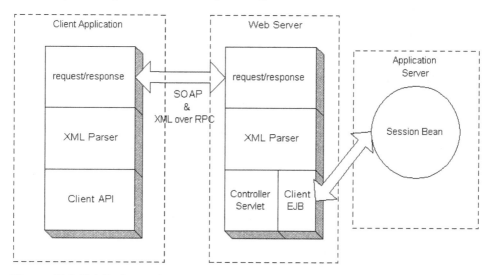

Figure 26-2: Web Service overview

> **NOTE:** To broker an object requires a translation of the XML interface into an API that the enterprise object can communicate with. An example of an enterprise object is an EJB, an ORB, or even a JMS Topic. The XML document needs to identify which object to interface with and the data to pass it; the document does not need to identify the type of object.

The XML document provides a means for different systems to use a decoupled interface from enterprise systems, while still providing a data structure to pass data through in the form of the XML document. Developers have been using architectures very similar to Web Services since XML became available. Web servers provide connectivity out of the box and XML parsers for distilling the XML document. Java provides frameworks for parsing Web Services like JDOM. Much of the work becomes defining the XML structure and defining the associated APIs that are mapped to the XML structure.

> **NOTE:** JDOM is the Java optimized document object model API from jdom.org.

Because of the disparate ways in which developers have chosen to implement their designs, standards have evolved and been defined, and Web Services have become more formalized. The following three technologies have evolved to form Web Services:

- *Universal Description, Discovery, and Integration* (UDDI) was created to be able to register the different Web Services available and provides a discovery mechanism for Web Services that are registered.

- *Web Service Descriptive Language* (WSDL) has become a descriptive language used to define the available interfaces on a single Web Service and its end-to-end connectivity.

- Protocols used to define the structure of the XML stream that the client and server use to communicate to each other. Examples of these protocols include *Simple Object Access Protocol* (SOAP) and XML over RPC. SOAP is the standard for encoding the request and response for the client to the Web Service interface.

These technologies are discussed later in the chapter.

Working with Web Services security

The Web Service is loosely coupled because of the XML stream. A Web Service can be synchronous or asynchronous. Because of the ease of using XML, the data structure of instructions and data can be changed into a human-readable form. Security becomes paramount because of the ease of use and because anyone can tamper with the data as long as it is not secure. The XML stream can be sent through a secure transport, such as HTTPS, PKI or SSL.

Secure transport can secure the connection between the client and the server and the data that passes between the two, but it cannot guarantee the data outside of the transport. For any security outside of the transport, the XML structure must support key exchanges, digital signatures, and encryption. Other protocols like the GSS-API can be used to accomplish some of these features.

> **CROSS-REFERENCE:** Chapters 21 and 22 discuss HTTPS and SSL. Chapter 25 describes PKI, and the GSS-API is discussed in Chapter 17.

XML is simply the mechanism for passing data and identifying the calling objects. Other mechanisms, like key exchanges, may also be needed for encryption and authentication between the client and the server. Some of the predominant key exchanges are X.509 certificates, Diffie-Hellman, and RSA. SOAP and XML structures need these exchanges defined in order to pass keys to different Web Services, and the Web Services that provide security need these mechanisms defined. The XML becomes a defined data container.

> **CROSS-REFERENCE:** X.509 certificates are discussed in Chapter 24. Diffie-Helman and RSA exchanges are addressed in Chapter 4.

Some of the data that it must contain may be secure. If an element in an XML file is encrypted, it must have a mechanism to identify encrypted date from readable data so that a Web Service knows that the data must be decrypted. When a Web Service decrypts data, it has to have a mechanism to get a key to decrypt the data. Key exchanges and encrypted data must be defined in a DTD.

> **NOTE:** Recall — from your XML knowledge — that *Document Type Defenitions* (DTDs) and *XML schemas* are used to describe the syntax of XML documents by declaring a set of allowed elements.

Exploring XML digital signatures

The digital signature in an XML file is used to validate and sign the XML file that is transferred. The digital signature will be extended in the XML structure as an embedded addition to the XML file. To use digital signatures, encryption techniques, and key exchange in Web Services is simply a matter of mapping XML schemas with their appropriate schema standard.

> **NOTE:** For digital signatures, the mapping is to a `http://www.w3.org/2000/09/xmldsig` structure. Likewise, the XML encryption standard is `http://www/w3/org/2001/04/xmlenc`. The SOAP entry into the XML block is done with the `http://schemas.xmlsoap.org/soap/security/2000-12`.

The digital signature can be included to digitally sign an XML document or a Web Service that can ensure data integrity, authentication, and non-repudiation (which have been discussed throughout the book). The XML digital signature specification, `http://www.w3.org/2000/09/xmldsig` and RFC 3275, defines the format of the XML structure. The purpose of the XML digital signature is to provide digital signatures for data objects that can be accessed through a URI through the Web Service.

Visual items that are displayed on a Web server can be digitally signed through the XML signature along with audio files, style sheets, image files, and encoded data. Digital signatures are shown in Listing 26-1.

Listing 26-1: Digital signature

```
<Signature ID?>
        <SignedInfo>
          <CanonicalizationMethod/>
          <SignatureMethod/>
          (<Reference URI? >
            (<Transforms>)?
            <DigestMethod>
            <DigestValue>
          </Reference>)+
        </SignedInfo>
        <SignatureValue>
        (<KeyInfo>)?
        (<Object ID?>)*
        </Signature>
```

Since multiple signature blocks can exist in a given XML structure, the signature ID identifies the signature block. To ensure that the digital signature is not tampered with, a secure hash is applied to the digital signature to ensure that signature has not been changed. A digest block inside the signature is used to specify the hash information. This is achieved with the <DigestMethod> and <DigestValue> elements. The Digest section identifies the properties of the message digest. The algorithm for the message digest, such as the SHA-1 or MD5, must be identified.

CROSS-REFERENCE: MD5, secure hash, and SHA-1 are dicussed in Chapter 9.

The decryption key is stored in the KeyInfo block. The final encrypted signature value is stored in the SignatureValue element. The <Reference> element provides information used to generate the message digest. The information includes any data transformation or normalization used along the way, including canonicalization.

TIP: Canonicalization sets a document into a standard format so that sender and receiver compute the same digest. This is useful because parsers may make insignificant changes such as eliminating whitespace. Canonicalization includes encoding the document in UTF-8, normalizing attribute values, and adding default attributes to the elements. For more information visit the W3C at www.w3.org/TR/2001/REC-xml-c14n-20010315.

The information needs to be carried within the signature using the <Tranforms> element. The <SignatureMethod Algorithm> defines the algorithm to be used for the actual signed value. When the receiver gets the message, the signature is decrypted using the sender's public key, the verified digest, and by verifying the sender's signature.

The reference object has a type, which can be one of many types as long as the type can be referenced in the http://www.w3.org/2000/09/xmldsig specification. An example of a reference is the following:

```
<Reference URI="#TimeStamp"
Type="http://www.w3.org/2000/09/xmldsig#SignatureProperties">
```

The URI reference object in this example is a timestamp. The type of the object can be referenced in `http://www.w3.org/2000/09/xmldsig#SignatureProperties` that defines the type of the object. See `http://www.w3.org/2000/09/xmldsig` for the supported types.

The digital signature can be associated with the XML document in multiple ways, such as:

♦ **Enveloped:** This means that the signature is a child of the data being signed.

♦ **Enveloping:** This means that the signature encloses the data being signed.

♦ **Detached:** This means that the signature is a sibling of the element being signed. The signature is referenced by a local link, or it can be located on the network.

The application has to determine if the key is trustworthy. As with any transportation of data, the XML document can be intercepted and modified if it is not transported through a secure channel. If the `<KeyInfo>` field is omitted, the recipient of the XML document is expected to identify the key to be used. A mechanism supplied by Java that is mentioned is the `KeyStore`. The XML specifications provide mechanisms for key management described in the XKMS specification. The XKMS provides a mechanism to agree on keys through standard key algorithms.

The *XML Key Management Specification* (XKMS) is a specification from the W3C organization to provide the management of keys for supporting other XML specifications like the XML digital signature. XKMS provides a standard set of XML definitions; these definitions allow developers to have a trusted third party locate and provide the appropriate keys and certificates. The trusted third party acts as an intermediary so that the Web Service programmer does not need to track the availability of keys or certificates and ensure their validity.

> **TIP:** VeriSign is one of the primary drivers of XKMS and has a Java toolkit that supports XKMS development (`www.xmltrustcenter.org/xkms/download.htm`).

XKMS provides a simple retrieving method for obtaining a decryption key from a remote source. The retrieval method is defined by XML-SIG and relies on the use of the `<RetrievalMethod>` within the `<KeyInfo>` element. The document assumes that a service exists to provide information about a given key. The following example shows the signer that indicates a Web-resident directory, `www.OurkeyDir.public`, where it has published information about the public key. The following lines show the use of the `RetrievalMethod` element:

```
<ds:KeyInfo>
   <ds:RetrievalMethod URI="http://www.OurkeyDir.public/Key"
      Type="http://www.w3.org/2000/09/xmldsig#X509Certificate"/>
</ds:KeyInfo>
```

For information about a public key, an application client queries a remote service, and the location service defines a set of tags for this purpose. The following code shows the `<Locate>` element. The `<Query>` element has the name of the requested key, and the `<Respond>` element lists the items that the client needs information on.

```
<Locate>
   <Query>
      <ds:KeyInfo>...</ds:KeyInfo>
   </Query>
   <Respond>
      <string>KeyName</string>
      <string>KeyValue</string>
   </Respond>
</Locate>
```

The response to the client looks like the following:

```
<LocateResult>
   <Result>Success</Result>
   <Answer>
      <ds:KeyInfo>
         <ds:KeyName>O=XMLTrustCernter.org OU="Crypto"
                     CN="Rich"</ds:KeyName>
         <ds:KeyValue>...</ds:KeyValue>
      </ds:KeyInfo>
   </Answer>
</LocateResult>
```

The validation service is a trusted third party that validates a binding between a key and an attribute such as a name. The instance is given in the following query:

```
   <Query>
      <Status>Valid</Status>
      <ds:KeyInfo>
         <ds:KeyName>...</ds:KeyName>
         <ds:KeyValue>...</ds:KeyValue>
      </ds:KeyInfo>
   </Query>
   <Respond>
      <string>KeyName</string>
      <string>KeyValue</string>
   </Respond>
```

The validation service should produce the following results:

```
<ValidateResult>
   <Result>Success</Result>
   <Answer>
      <KeyBinding>
         <Status>Valid</Status>
```

```
        <KeyID>http://www.xmltrustcenter.org/assert/20010120-39</KeyID>
        <ds:KeyInfo>
            <ds:KeyName>...</ds:KeyName>
            <ds:KeyValue>...</ds:KeyValue>
        </ds:KeyInfo>
        <ValidityInterval>
            <NotBefore>2000-09-20T12:00:00</NotBefore>
            <NotAfter>2000-10-20T12:00:00</NotAfter>
        </ValidityInterval>
    </KeyBinding>
  </Answer>
</ValidateResult>
```

The `<Result>` and `<Status>` elements have different meanings. The `Success` indicated by the `<Result>` element simply indicates that the request was proposed successfully by the service. The `<Status>` indicates the results of the processing — in this case, the result is `Valid`. The optional `<ValidityInterval>` information shows the `timespan` for which the validate service's results are considered valid.

Because digital certificates and keys are not unconditionally valid, they can be assigned a specific time limit, after which time they are no longer valid. XKMS also defines requests and responses for the following areas:

♦ **Key registration:** Used to register a key with a third-party KMS.

♦ **Key revocation:** Used to send a request to the third-party KMS to tell it that you no longer want it to manage the key on your behalf.

♦ **Key recovery:** Used to recover a key when a user forgets his private key. The XML specification does not not dictate the document structure for recovering a key.

Understanding XML encryption

The XML encryption specification allows data to be encrypted in an XML document. The encrypted part of the document has two new elements: `<EncryptedData>` and `<CipherData>`. The `<EncryptedData>` element defines the encryption scheme to be applied. The `<CipherData>` element is created to contain the encrypted serialization of the `<Items>` element. The result can be contained in a `<CipherValue>` element. As an alternative, you can use the `<CipherReference>` element to point to another location — URI — where the cipher resides. The `<EncryptionMethod>` and `<KeyInfo>` elements are optional. Encryption is done on an as-needed basis.

TIP : The XML encryption specification is defined by `http://www.w3.org/2001/04/xmlenc.`

Registering Web Services with UDDI

UDDI is used to describe the Web Services available for discovering business services that organizations provide. Different types of information can be registered. First, you can register basic company information that allows your Web Service to be discovered by company-identifying information. Secondly, you can register your Web Service based on the categories it satisfies. Finally, you can register your Web Service based on its behavior and functionality.

> **NOTE:** UDDI provides a worldwide registry of Web Services for advertisement, discovery, and integration purposes. For more information visit the UDDI site at www.uddi.org.

The UDDI initiative is a set of standards and specifications. For instance, version 2.0 includes:

♦ **UDDI operators:** UDDI has nodes, and this specification describes the operators and data management requirements. This is not required to be supported by private registries. Most operator nodes implement user name and password for authentication; you can use other types, but they are not defined in the specification.

♦ **UDDI API:** Defines the API that all UDDI registries support. It defines SOAP messages that are supported by by a UDDI registry. You use this specification, UDDI data structure specification, and the UDDI XML API schema to program to a UDDI registry.

♦ **UDDI replication:** A description of the data replication process and interfaces so that replication can occur between sites.

♦ **UDDI data structures:** UDDI has a set of data structures that include:

  • businessEntity: for the business basic information.

  • publisherAssertion: to establish public relationships between two businessEntity structures.

  • businessService: which is a grouping of bindingTemplate structures.

  • bindingTemplate: contains pointers to technical material and reference one or more tModel structures.

  • tModel: contains pointers to the Web Service's specifications.

The Java-based APIs are not defined by the UDDI specification. However, you have a couple of choices:

♦ **JAXR:** This specification defines a way for Java programs to access registries, including UDDI. JAXR is not UDDI-specific but it allows you to access different types of registries. You can find more information about JAXR at http://java.sun.com/xml/jaxr/index.html.

♦ **A custom API:** You can write you own API to access the SOAP API by inserting your XML document in each SOAP message.

♦ **A third-party API:** Systinet is one such solution. Systinet provides an API to UDDI that allows you to program without knowing the details of a UDDI message or SOAP.

Defining Web Service interfaces with WSDL

WSDL describes the Web Service in a standardized fashion and the Web Services endpoints. The Web Service is a server that provides specific data and responses for client requests. WSDL allows disparate clients to automatically interact with a Web Service. A WSDL file is an interface that defines parameters and constraints for runtime communication.

> **TIP:** There are third-party tools that generate the WSDL file based on a Web Service implementation. For example, BEA's Web Logic Server 6.1 provides Ant scripts to generate WSDL based on the implementation of a Web Service (such as an EJB), and SonicXQ (from Sonic Software's) can be used to generate WSDL mapped to services (such as JMS).

A WSDL document contains elements to describe the Web Service and may contain extensions (for example for SOAP). The main elements of a WSDL document include:

- ◆ `<definitions>`: This element is used to describe the service such as the definition of namespaces.

> **NOTE:** Recall that the XML namespace recommendation defines a mechanism to handle name collisions by mapping an element prefix and a URI.

- ◆ `<import>`: This element allows you to include documents into the WSDL document. You can have more than one `<import>` element in your WSDL document.

> **TIP:** You may think of the import element as having similar functionality to the `#include` in C/C++.

- ◆ `<types>`: This element is used to define the data types used in messages. The most common is an XML schema. You can have different types, and you are not constrained to just XML schemas.

> **TIP:** Recall that an XML schema describes the syntax of an XML document; you can use XML schemas to define types and patterns that an XML document must follow.

- ◆ `<message>`: This element allows you to model the communication mechanisms (messages and data) for the Web Service. You can model different messages, and each message may contain different parts (model with a `<part>` subelement). Each part can be a type or a structure. You can reference the types defined in the `<types>` element.

- ◆ `<portType>`: This element defines the endpoints of a Web Service and the set of operations (via the `<operation>` subelement) supported by the Web Service.

> **NOTE:** The operations in the `<portType>` element are just a definition; the actual behavior is described later — an operation may have different behaviors. The WSDL specification defines request-response, solicit-response, one-way, and notification behaviors.

- ◆ `<binding>`: This element is the concrete definition (protocol and data format) of the `<portType>` elements. It is in this element that contains the binding extensions.

- ◆ `<service>`: This element is used to describe the endpoint (described by the `<port>` subelement) of a service. It contains the URL of the Web Service, and it is optional.

Listing 26-2 shows a SWDL document skeleton.

Listing 26-2: A WSDL document skeleton

```
<definition>
        <import>*
        <types> ... </types>
        <message>*
```

```
        <part> ... </part>*
    </message>
    <portType>*
        <operation>*
            <input> ... </input>
            <output> ... <output>
        </operation>
    </portType>
    <binding>*
        <operation>*
            <input> ... </input>
            <output> ... <output>
        </operation>
    </binding>
    <service>*
            <port> ... </port>
    <service>
</definitions>
```

Encoding Web Services with SOAP

The *Simple Object Access Protocol (*SOAP) is an XML-based protocol for representing remote procedure calls and responses. It uses small XML documents to exchange information in a distributed and decentralized manner.

> **NOTE:** All SOAP messages are encoded using XML. SOAP defines two namespaces:
> http://schemas.xmlsoap.org/soap/envelope/ (for the envelope) and
> http://schemas.xmlsoap.org/soap/encoding/ (for the SOAP serialization).

SOAP has four major components:

♦ **A SOAP envelope:** This contains the body of the message. It is addressed to the Web Service that must process the envelope with some instructions on how to process the message. The Header is a generic mechanism for adding features without prior agreement between the sender and receiver. The Body contains the mandatory information (for the ultimate recipient of the message).

♦ **A transport or protocol binding:** SOAP communications (sending SOAP envelopes) use bindings to low-level protocols (such as HTTP and SMTP).

♦ **Encoding rules:** This is a mapping between the application data types and XML tags.

♦ **RPC mechanism:** This is a mechanism to represent remote procedure calls and return values.

Listing 26-3 shows an example of a SOAP request message. This example requests the unit price of an item based on the item's UPC. Listing 26-4 displays the response.

Listing 26-3: A SOAP request message example

```
<SOAP-ENV:Envelope
  xmlns:SOAP-ENV = http://schemas.xmlsoap.org/soap/envelope/
  SOAP-ENV:encodingStyle =
  "http://schemas.xmlsoap.org/soap/encoding/">
  <SOAP-ENV:Body>
      <m:GetUnitPrice xmlns:m="Some-URI">
        <symbol>UPC:2394287410</symbol>
      </m:GetUnitPrice>
  </SOAP-ENV:Body>
</SOAP-ENV:Envelope>
```

Listing 26-4: A SOAP message response example

```
<SOAP-ENV:Envelope
  xmlns:SOAP-ENV= http://schemas.xmlsoap.org/soap/envelope/
  SOAP-ENV:encodingStyle =
    "http://schemas.xmlsoap.org/soap/encoding/"/>
  <SOAP-ENV:Body>
      <m:GetUnitPriceResponse xmlns:m="TheURI">
        <Price>5.75</Price>
      </m:GetUnitPriceResponse>
  </SOAP-ENV:Body>
</SOAP-ENV:Envelope>
```

While the Header and Body are defined as independent elements, they are in fact related. A body entry is semantically equivalent to a header entry intended for the default actor and with a SOAP mustUnderstand attribute with a value of "1". The <SOAP-ENV: mustUnderstand> attribute tells intermediaries that they must know how to understand the header attribute or leave it unprocessed. The value of the mustUnderstand attribute is either "1" or "0". The absence of the SOAP mustUnderstand attribute is semantically equivalent to its presence with the value "0".

As a container for XML-based messages, SOAP 1.1 has responsibilities to support the use of XML-based security technologies. To achieve encryption, authorization, and authentication, an exchange of digital credentials is required. A common form of a credential is the digital certificate X.509.

CROSS-REFERENCE: The X.509 specification is described in Chapter 24.

The XML digital signature has its own namespace contained in the <ds:Signature> element. The wrapper of the signature is <SOAP-SEC:Signature>, which specifies the namespace for the signature and the intended reader of the signature. By extending the SOAP header to use the <SOAP-SEC:Signature> extension, any Web Service can add any type of digital signature to a SOAP message.

The SOAP `encodingStyle` global attribute can be used to indicate the serialization rules used in a SOAP message and may appear on any element. There is no default encoding defined for a SOAP message.

Summary

This chapter has brought together the different security technologies covered throughout the book and discussed how they integrate in the Java platform. In addition, this chapter briefly described Web Services and its associated technologies such as UDDI (Universal, Description, Discovery and Integration), WSDL (Web Service Descriptive Language) and SOAP (Simple Object Access Protocol).

Initially, the sandbox model seemed a good security model, but as time has passed a policy-based security model seemed to satisfy more applications than the restrictive all-or-nothing model that the sandbox presented.

This chapter also described the security changes included in the J2SDK v 1.4. Some of these changes include the integration of previously optional packages, such as JCE and JSSE. It reviewed the basics of authentication and authorization, Java permissions, and the policy file, which are the foundation for the next three chapters. Finally, this chapter briefly described the components that are discussed in more detail in Chapters 27 and 28.

Chapter 27

Securing Client-Side Components

In This Chapter

♦ Learning about Java directory and naming services

♦ Using authetication and authorization from the client-side perspective

♦ Securing Java Applets and applications

♦ Understanding Web configuration via the `web.xml` file

♦ Exploring a hands-on example

♦ Understanding the relationship between JSP and Servlets

Introduction

J2EE applications are deployed in servers, and each J2EE component is installed in different containers. A J2EE server is the runtime portion of a J2EE product and provides EJB and Web containers. The EJB container manages the life cycle of Enterprise Beans, and the Web container manages the execution of JSP pages and Servlets. In addition, there are two more containers: the application client container and the applet container. The application client container runs on the client and manages the execution of application client components. Finally, the applet container manages the execution of applets and consists of the Web browser and a Java plug-in running on the client. Figure 27-1 illustrates these relationships.

This chapter covers security from application, applet, and JSP and Servlets perspectives (EJBs are covered in Chapter 28). In addition, it briefly covers JNDI and presents an example to illustrate these concepts.

Exploring Java Directory Services

A *directory service* adds attributes and extends a naming service. A *naming service* is a set of contexts of the same type, that is, the contexts have the same naming convention. A *context* is a set of name and object bindings and may have *subcontexts,* where each object may be related to another object between the same context. In a system, each object is associated with a name. This association is called a *binding*. Each object can be found by that name via the naming service.

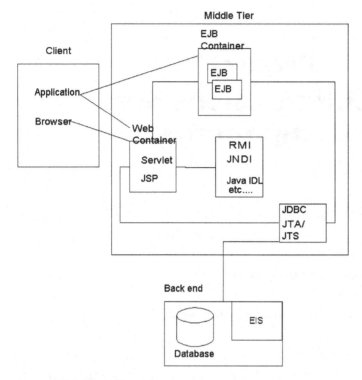

Figure 27-1: The J2EE containers

For instance, the Internet Domain Name Service (DNS) maps machine names to IP addresses, such as `www.sun.com` to 192.9.48.5, and each system has a *naming convention*. An example of a naming convention is the UNIX file system where a file is relative to the root of the file system and uses a forward slash (/), as in `/usr/bin/readmefirst` where `readmefirst` is a file in the `bin` subdirectory of the `usr` directory located at the `root`. In this example, the file system is a context, and the subdirectory is a subcontext.

A directory service provides operations to manage (create, delete, modify, and so on) the attributes associated with the objects within it. You can find the JNDI API at the SUN Web site (`http://java.sun.com/j2se/1.4/docs/guide/jndi/spec/jndi/`).

JNDI architecture overview

The *Java Naming and Directory Interface* (JNDI) is the API that supports the naming and directory functionality to Java applications. The JNDI architecture also provides a *Service Provider Interface* (SPI) to allow different naming and directory services providers to be seamlessly plugged in without affecting the application (which is using the JNDI API). Figure

27-2 illustrates how an application using the JNDI API can use different providers (such as LDAP and CORBA) by the JNDI SPI layer support.

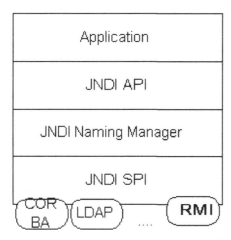

Figure   27-2: The JNDI architecture

The JNDI API provides methods to perform standard directory operations such as associating attributes to named Java objects and searching for those objects based on their attributes.

The packages that form the JNDI API are as follows:

◆ `javax.naming`, which provides the classes and interfaces to access naming services.

The `Context` interface is provided by this package. `Context` is the core interface that defines basic methods such as looking up an object, binding/unbinding objects, renaming objects, and creating and destroying subcontexts.

In JNDI, every name is relative to a context. The `InitialContext` provides a starting point for naming and directory operations. The following code snippet is an example of how to get the initial context and use it to find the Home interface for a Project EJB.

```
Context ctx = new InitialContext();
projectHome = (ProjectHome)ctx.lookup("projinfo.ProjectHome");
```

`Context.lookup()` is the most commonly used operation. You provide the name of the object, and `Context.lookup()` returns the object bound to that name. There are other binding operations such as `Context.listBindings()`, which returns an enumeration of tuples (of the object name, the object's class, and the object itself).

◆ `javax.naming.directory`, which extends the `javax.naming` package to provide access to directories.

Directory objects can have zero or more attributes, and JNDI has the `Attribute` interface and `Attributes` interface (which is a collection of `Attributes`). JNDI also provides implementation of these interfaces in `BasicAttribute` and `BasicAttributes`. The `DirContext` interface represents a directory context and provides methods for examining and updating attributes associated with the directory context. The `DirContext` interface also provides overloaded search methods.

> **TIP:** Use `DirContext.modifyAttributes()` to modify the directory. Modifications to `Attribute` and `Attributes` do not affect the underlying directory.

A *schema* describes the rules that define the structure of the namespace and attributes. Applications can retrieve the schema associated with a directory object when the underlying context implementation provides the necessary support. Using a schema allows for a uniform way to access the directory objects. The schema can be accessed via the `DirContext.getSchema` and `DirContext.getSchemaClassDefinition` methods.

♦ `javax.naming.event`, which provides classes and interfaces for event notification in naming and directory services.

A `NamingEvent` represents an event generated by a naming/directory service. The `NamingEvent` class defines four types of events: `OBJECT_ADDED`, `OBJECT_REMOVED`, `OBJECT_RENAMED`, and `OBJECT_CHANGED`. A `NamingListener` is an object that listens for `NamingEvents`. The `NamespaceChangeListener` interface listens for namespace changes, while the `ObjectChangeListener` listens for changes to an object's contents. For events notifications to be received, the listener must be registered with either an `EventContext` or an `EventDirContext`.

♦ `javax.naming.ldap`, which provides classes and interfaces for using features specific to LDAP v3 not covered by the `javax.naming.directory` package.

This package is primarily for applications that need to use extended operations, controls, or unsolicited notifications. The LDAP v3 (RFC 2251) specifies a way to transmit "yet-to-be defined" operations (these are the *extended operations*). In addition, the LDAP v3 protocol allows any request or reponse to be augmented by "yet-to-be defined" modifiers — these are referred as *controls*.

JNDI classifies the request controls into *connection* (affecting how a connection is created) and *context* (affecting context methods) request controls. The `InitialLdapContext` is the initial LDAP context to perform extended operations and controls.

♦ `javax.naming.spi`, which is the Service Provider Interface that allows different providers to be dynamically plugged in under the JNDI API.

Understanding security with JNDI

JNDI has two main options: with and without security manager. If there is no security manager installed, the code is trusted and the application can access service providers from the local classpath. If a security manager is installed, there is trusted and untrusted code within the same application and access to service providers may be restricted.

JNDI does not define a common security interface for accessing naming and directory servers. The different service providers supply the security operations such as authentication and access control. JNDI, however, provides the means to pass the related security information to the service provider.

> **TIP:** Clients can pass context information of an environment to service providers. You must be careful because the context may contain sensitive information that should not be available to untrusted sources.

Here is a list of some of the environment properties that contain security-sensitive information:

♦ `Context.SECURITY_AUTHENTICATION`: Specifies the authentication mechanism. The following lines of code set the environment to use anonymous authentication via the context.

```
// get initial context
DirContext ctx = new InitialDirContext();
// ...
// set to anonymous authentication
ctx.addToEnvironment(Context.SECURITY_AUTHENTICATION, "none");
```

♦ `Context.SECURITY_CREDENTIALS`: Specifies the credentials of the authenticating entity.

♦ `Context.SECURITY_PRINCIPAL`: Specifies the name of the authenticating entity.

♦ `Context.SECURITY_PROTOCOL`: Specifies the security protocol to use.

The following code example tries to authenticate a user with LDAP, using `simple` authentication, a principal with name Bob, and a password `boby`.

```
// authenticate 'Bob'
env.put(Context.SECURITY_AUTHENTICATION, "simple");
env.put(Context.SECURITY_PRINCIPAL, "cn=Bob, ou=HR, o=XYZ");
env.put(Context.SECURITY_CREDENTIALS, "boby");
```

If the authentication fails because the password is incorrect, a `javax.naming.AuthenticationException` is thrown. Different servers support different authentication mechanisms. If you request one that the server does not support, you get a `javax.naming.AuthenticationNotSupportedException`.

In addition, the service provider is responsible for securing security-sensitive information. For instance, instead of using the context and its properties, the service provider could use JAAS for authorization and authentication purposes. The service provider also could disallow any thread (with execution context or trust level different than the original) from reading the context handle. The service provider could not allow access to sensitive data or allow access to only trusted secure code.

Using Authentication

Application Component Providers determine what application resources should have restricted access. For instance, not all users can access some image files, HTML documents, and so on. At the Web-tier, when a user tries to access a protected Web resource, the Web container prompts the user for a password and username. If the user has an identity that has permission to access the resource, the user can continue. Otherwise, the Web container rejects the request.

Configuring the Web-tier for authentication

The container uses the authentication mechanism defined in the deployment descriptor. The three types of authentication mechanisms that a J2EE Web container must support are as follows:

- *HTTP basic authentication*: The Web browser displays a username and password dialog box. The Web client provides the principal's username and password to the Web server to be authenticated against the realm. This is not a secured authentication because the information (username and password) is not secured during transmission and the server has not been authenticated. The following code fragment shows how to define a basic authentication in the application's `web.xml` file:

```
<web-app>
<login-config>
      <auth-method>BASIC</auth-method>
      <realm-name>myrealm</realm-name>
</login-config>
</web-app>
```

- *Form-based authentication*: This allows the application to use a customized user interface for authentication. This type of authentication is also not secure since the Web server is not authenticated and the username and password are transmitted as plaintext.

The following code fragmet shows how to define a form-based authentication in the application's `web.xml` file:

```
<web-app>
   <login-config>
      <auth-method>FORM</auth-method>
      <form-login-config>
          <form-login-page>/login.jsp</form-login-page>
          <form-error-page>/fail_login.html</form-error-page>
      </form-login-config>
   </login-config>
</web-app>
```

The resource used to generate the HTML form may be an HTML page, a JSP, or a servlet, and is defined in the `<form-login-page>` element. The fields returned from the form elements must be `j_username` and `j_password`, and the action attribute must be `j_security_check`. Here is an example of the HTML code:

```
<form method="POST" action="j_security_check">
  <input type="text" name="j_username">
  <input type="password" name="j_password">
</form>
```

- *HTTPS mutual authentication*: Both the Web client and Web browser use X.509 certificates to establish their identities and the mutual authentication over a an SSL channel. The following code example uses client certificates to authenticate the request:

```
<web-app>
    <login-config>
        <auth-method>CLIENT-CERT</auth-method>
    </login-config>
</web-app>
```

Web containers may also support *HTTP digest authentication*. The Web client sends the Web server a message digest along with the HTTP request message. The HTTP request message and the client's password are combined in a one-way hash to compute the message digest.

In addition, there are hybrid authentication mechanisms in which an SSL channel is used for either HTTP basic, form-based, or HTTP digest authentication. Running these authentication protocols over an SSL session protects the password and all message content for confidentiality. The following example demonstrates how to configure an HTTP basic authentication over SSL using the `transport-guarantee` element:

```
<web-app>
  <security-constraint>
    …
    <user-data-constraint>
        <transport-guarantee>CONFIDENTIAL</transport-guarantee>
    </user-data-constraint>
</web-app>
```

In order for the client authenticator to be fully protected, when using hybrid authentication, the `transport-guarantee` element of each protected resource should be set to `CONFIDENTIAL`.

Exploring Web-tier authentication issues

As discussed earlier, there are several ways to authenticate users in the Web-tier. You, however, must be careful on how applications (multitier and multicomponent) and their resources are protected and used. For instance, the Web-tier does not authenticate a user unless the user is accessing a protected resource (this is known as *lazy authentication*), but an unprotected Web resource may still call protected EJB resources.

In addition, a Web resource usually has a link to another Web resource. For instance, if the link is *relative*, the HTTP container protects the access to the linked resource based on the current resource security properties. When the link is *absolute*, the HTTP client container ignores the context of the current resource and accesses the linked resource based on the URL. For instance, if the URL starts with `http://`, the request is tried over an insecure transport. If the URL starts with `https://`, a secure session is established with the server before the request is sent.

> **TIP:** The application deployer could configure both current and linked resources with a confidential transport guarantee, so the HTTP client container protects the request between them.

Using Access Control

As mentioned in Chapter 26, the J2SDK has integrated JAAS. With this integration the `java.security.Policy` API handles principal-based queries, which allows you to determine who is running the code; so access control now can be based on what code is running and who is running it.

The integration of JAAS also added support for dynamic policies where classes are bound with permissions until a security check is necessary. This binding lasts through the lifetime of the security policy.

> **CROSS-REFERENCE:** Chapter 26 provides a list of the permission classes available in `java.security`, and Chapter 8 provides information on the `java.policy` file.

The `java.security.Permission` class implements the `java.security.Guard` interface. The `Guard` interface provides the `checkGuard` method to perform security checks on an object (which is passed as an argument). The class `AccessControlContext` can be used when access control decisions need to be made in a different context. However, when the resource supplier and consumer are not in the same thread, the access control context may not be available — as when the context is security-sensitive.

The resource supplier can create a `java.security.GuardedObject`. The supplier embeds the resource inside (the guarded object) with security checks that must be satisfied in order for the resource to be accessed. The supplier can then provide the `GuardedObject` to the consumer.

In the following code snippet, the resource to be protected is the `finance.txt` file. The supplier creates a `GuardedObject` that contains the file and its permission information:

```
FileInputStream fFile = new FileInputStream("finance.txt");
FilePermission fPerm = new FilePermission("finance.txt", "read");
GuardedObject myGuardedObj = new GuardedObject(fFile, fPerm);
```

The thread then passes `myGuardedObj` to the consumer, which accesses it via the following line of code:

```
FileInputStream theResource = (FileInputStream) myGardedObj.getObject();
```

The `getObject` method calls the `checkGuard` method of the `Guarded` interface, which in turn calls the `SecurityManager.checkPermission` method. If access is not permitted, an exception is thrown.

Working with Client-Side Security

As you know, J2EE applications are composed of components. The J2EE specification defines three main components, as follows:

♦ Components that run on the client: Application clients and Applets.

- Web components that run on the server: Java Servlets and JSPs.
- Business components that run on the server: EJBs.

In this chapter, I address the first two. EJBs are described in Chapter 28. A J2EE client may be an application client or a Web client.

An application client runs in the client machine. It typically has a GUI (graphical user interface), but a command line is also possible. The application may access server-side components directly (such as EJBs) or may establish a tunnel (such as an HTTP or HTTPS) to the necessary services.

The Web client has dynamic Web pages (HTML, XML and so on). These Web pages are rendered by a Web browser and are generated by the Web components that run in the Web-tier. An Applet may be embedded in a Web page.

> **NOTE:** Recall that an Applet is a small application that is executed by the JVM in the Web browser. They may need the Java plug-in.

The Web components are either Servlets or JSPs, described later in this chapter. The J2EE specification does not consider applets, server-side utility classes, and static HTML pages as part of Web components; but they are usually bundled with Web components during deployment. In addition, EJBs may be included to handle user input and business logic.

Application security

As of this writing, all Java 2 SDK system code invokes the `SecurityManager` method to check the policy in effect and to perform access control checks. There is a security manager for applets implemented by the `AppletSecurity` class, which ensures that classes are loaded only from the applet's host (or code base host).

The security manager is an application-wide object. To perform some operations, classes in the Java packages ask the security manager for permission. An application can set the `java.security.manager` property by invoking the Java virtual machine (JVM) with `—Djava.security.manager` or by installing a security manager by calling the `java.lang.System.setSecurityManager` method.

Applet security

Applets run in a *sandbox* by default. Recall from Chapter 26 that the sandbox is where unsigned code resides and provides a limited use of resources in the machine the code is running on. At the beginning (that is, Java 1.0), the applet was not allowed to go out of the sandbox. That restriction was good for some applications, but it was too restrictive for others. Some of the reasons why an applet may want to access local resources include the need to access a printer (for a word processor applet) or a local inventory database.

Java 1.1 introduced the concept of signed applets. Applets are digitally signed to obtain extra permissions outside of the sandbox. Programs that are not digitally signed continue to be restricted by the original sandbox model. Java 1.1, however, gave unrestricted access to system resources to signed applets. It was an all-or-nothing type of access. The *Extended Java Sandbox* is the default model for digitally signed applets. Under the Extended Java Sandbox, digitally signed Java code is allowed to read and write to a specified directory. In that directory no executables can run, and other Java programs cannot gain access to other network services.

The `java.policy` file (discussed in Chapter 8) provides a way to define specific permissions to the applet. This gives a finer-grained level of security. Administrators can now grant permissions based on the requestor and the resource being accessed. The problem is that the policy file needs to be modified by the end user, and this requirement is impractical.

You use the `jarsigner` to sign a JAR. Java 1.2.1 requires that every class within the same signed JAR package needs to be signed by the same certificate because in previous Java versions, a class loaded from a signed JAR could be altered. Even if the class was altered, it could still be loaded and run but no extra permissions were granted. That provided a way to modify the behavior of the applet. Recall that to sign a JAR file you need a private key and its corresponding certificate, which can be generated by using the `keytool`. After the `jarsigner` has signed the JAR file, the *signature*, *manifest*, and *digital signature* files are created.

> **CROSS-REFERENCE:** Chapter 8 provides a detailed look at the `jarsigner`, `keytool`, and the signature, manifest, and digital signature files.

If the digital signature of the JAR cannot be verified, a security exception is thrown because the JAR has been altered.

Understanding the web.xml file

The `web.xml` file is where you describe how the application is configured. It is the deployment descriptor defined by the Servlet specification and, therefore, all Servlet-compliant containers support this type of file.

For example, suppose that you have an application that requires some of the resources be available to only administrators. The directory structure looks something like the following:

♦ `myApp`: For resources available to anyone.

♦ `myApp/admin`: For resources available to users members of the admin group.

The part of the `web.xml` file that supports this type of structure looks like Listing 27-1. The top element is the `<security-constraint>` element, which has the following subelements:

♦ `<web-resource-collection>`: This element contains the information about the resource you are configuring, such as its name, the subdirectory (`/admin` in this case), and the method that accesses it.

♦ `<auth-constraint>`: This element describes the roles the user must have in order to access the resource (Web pages in this case).

♦ `<user-data-constraint>`: This element describes the authentication configuration (`NONE` in this example; it could be `CONFIDENTIAL` for an HTTPS authentication).

Listing 27-1: Configuring the admin directory structure using the `web.xml` file

```
<security-constraint>
  <web-resource-collection>
    <web-resource-name>AdminPages</web-resource-name>
    <description>
      The pages accessible by authorized administrators
    </description>
    <url-pattern>/admin/*</url-pattern>
    <http-method>GET</http-method>
  </web-resource-collection>
  <auth-constraint>
    <description>
      The roles with access
    </description>
    <role-name>
        admin
    </role-name>
  </auth-constraint>
  <user-data-constraint>
    <description>
       The user data must be transmitted via
    </description>
    <transport-guarantee>NONE</transport-guarantee>
  </user-data-constraint>
</security-constraint>
```

Using Servlets

A Servlet is a module that runs within a request-response server. A request is a call from a client that contains data that the client wants to send to the server. The response is the answer from the server to the client. A Servlet is a Java object that functions the same way as a CGI script but does not need to be restarted for every request.

> **TIP:** If a secure Servlet is requested by a `forward` or an `include`, the security model does not intervene.

The Servlet API provides classes and interfaces to process HTTP requests and keeps the code Web-server independent. When a Servlet is requested, the server checks if the Servlet has been *loaded*. If it has not, the server loads the Servlet. The `init()` method is called so the Servlet can initialize its state (such as reading configuration information). The server gives the request to the Servlet to be processed; at this point the `service()` method is called. When the server needs to shut down the Servlet, the server invokes the `destroy()` method so that the Servlet may prepare for shut down (such as closing database connections).

The Servlet life cycle is managed by a Servlet container that is the connection between the Web server and the Servlets. It is the container that maps incoming requests to the Servlet object registered to process it. In addition, it is the Servlet container's responsibility to convert the response object (created by the Servlet after processing the request) into a response message and send it back to the client.

When a Servlet request is sent to a Web server using a secure protocol, you can use the `ServletRequest.isSecure()` method, which returns a `boolean` stating whether the connection is secure.

If you use HTTPS, a call to `ServletRequest.getAttribute()` returns an array of `javax.security.cert.X509Certificate` objects. In addition, if you use cookies, you can specify whether the cookie needs to be transmitted over a secure protocol. You use the `Cookie.setSecure()` method and pass in a `boolean` value; you can determine the security setting via the `Cookie.getSecure()` method.

Using Java Server Pages

The Java Server Pages (JSPs) are based on the Servlet specification. JSPs allow the development of Web pages that include dynamic content based on, for example, user identity. Once a JSP page is requested by the user, the server translates it into a Servlet, compiles it into a class, and executes it. Finally, the server services the request. The server may pre-compile the JSP code so that the JSP page does not have to go through all these steps every time it is requested. As long as the implementation is not changed, the request is serviced by just invoking the generated class directly. JSPs are just another way to write a Servlet and have the same advantages as a Servlet, such as scalability and security.

A JSP is composed of standard HTML code as well as special JSP elements that allow the server to include dynamic content. When a user requests a JSP, the server executes the JSP elements, merges the results with the HTML code, and then sends the complete content to the browser. Listing 27-2 illustrates how a JSP combines HTML and JSP tags to create a page with a dynamic project name in the header.

Listing 27-2: Simple JSP example

```
<html>
<head>
<title>Project Detail</title>
</head>
<center>
<h2>
<font color=#DB1260>
  <p>
```

```
   <% String projname = request.getParameter("projname");
      String projId = request.getParameter("projid");
   %>
   <strong>
   <%= projname == null ? "": projname %>
   </strong>
   Project Details
 </p>
</font>
</h2>
</center>
<body>
<!-- do something useful ... -->
</body> </html>
```

Listing 27-2 demonstrates a couple of useful things. First, it illustrates combining HTML code with special JSP elements found within the "`<%   %>`". Second, it uses the HTTP request/response model to receive request parameters.

Request parameters can be sent in two ways: as part of the URI or as part of the request message body. In Listing 27-2, the request parameters are expected to be part of the URI. For example:

```
http://localhost:7001/projinfo/projectDetail.jsp?projid=300-
01&projname=Hello
```

When the server executes the `<% String projname = request.getParameter ("projname"); String projId = request.getParameter ("projid"); %>` element, the `projname` string is set to "`Hello`" and the `projId` string is set to "`300-01`".

When you code a URI link in an HTML page using an "`<a>`" element, the request generated uses the `Get` method. The `Get` method always passes parameters as part of the URI and is intended to retrieve a resource. No processing is expected to be done. Here is a way of generating the preceding URI:

```
<a href="/projectDetail.jsp?projid=300-01&projname=Hello>  The Hello
Project Link </a>
```

When it is embedded in a form, the code looks like the following:

```
<form method="Get" action="/projectDetail.jsp">
Project Name: <input name="projname" type="text">
Project Id: <input name="projid" type="text">
<input type="SUBMIT">
</form>
```

Another way to transfer parameters is via the `Post` method. The `Post` method is intended to request a process from the server (such as updating a database). The `Post` method always sends the parameters as part of the body, and you can optionally also add parameters to the

URI. In the code, however, the only thing that changes is the `method` attribute of the `form` element, as follows:

```
<form method="Post" action="/projectDetail.jsp">
```

> **TIP:** The `POST` method is favored over the `GET` method for delivering confidential request data, since data sent via `Get` appears in both client-side and server-side logs.

Different types of JSP elements, such as directives (like the `<%@ include ...%>` element), perform an action based on information obtained at the time the page is requested. Other elements include the action elements: There are standard action elements (like the `<jsp:useBean>` element), which are predefined, and custom action elements, which are defined by the developer. The final type of JSP elements are those used for scripting (such as the expression element `<%! ... %>`, and the expression `<%= ... %>`).

Managing the state

Most applications need a way to keep track of the transaction state. For instance, a shopping cart application needs to remember what the user has selected during the various steps of the transaction. There are two basic solutions: Either the client keeps track of the state or the server does.

Either way, there is a need to let the other side know which state the transaction is in. For instance, if the client keeps the state, it needs to let the server know at each request what the state of the transaction is.

The browser can receive the state information via a cookie. A cookie is a name-value pair the server provides in the response header to the browser. The cookie can be embedded in the URI response where the server sends information to the browser as part of the URI and the browser sends information back as part of the request.

The state information may be embedded as fields in an HTML form. The server may send state information in hidden fields in the HTML form, and the browser may send back information as HTTP parameters.

However, passing information back and forth is inefficient. Therefore, a session is usually established, and a session ID is used to identify parts of the same transaction.

Client-Side Code Example

In this section, I develop an application to access project information of the XYZ Company. The user is required to sign in and is authenticated using a database realm. Based on the permissions granted, the project information is displayed.

The basic project information consists of a unique identifier, a name, and a description. The user has the option to view a project's detail (such as team members and the artifact associated with the project).

In addition:

♦ If the user belongs to the `finance` group, financial information (initial quote, discount, and actual quote) is also displayed along with the project name and description.

♦ If the user belongs to the `admin` group, there is an option to edit the project's information as follows:

- If the user is an `architect`, the artifact information can be modified.

- If the user is a `manager`, the name and description of the project as well as the team member information can be modifed.

- If the user is in the `finance` group, the project quotes can be modifed.

Understanding the design

I decided to call this example the "Project Info App" and illustrate form authentication. I created a `login.jsp`, a `logout.jsp`, a `fail_login.html`, and a `welcome.jsp` to handle the form authentication based on a database realm. First, the user is asked to login via the `login.jsp`. If there is a problem, the `fail_login.html` page is displayed. If the user is authenticated, the `welcome.jsp` page is displayed.

Viewing the project

In the welcome screen the user has the choice to view the project list (other options could also be added). When the user makes the choice to view the projects, she is redirected to the `ProjSelectionServlet`, which retrieves all the project information (via a `Project` EJB) from a project database and displays the project list based on the user's permissions. If the user requests the project details, the `ProjSelectionServlet` redirects to the `ProjectDetail.jsp`.

Editing the project

However, if the user has `admin` rights and chooses to "edit" the project information, there is a redirection to the `admin/editproject.jsp`, where (based on the user rights) different project information may be modified. Once the information is modified, the user may submit it, at which time the `editprojectServlet.java` validates the information and commits it to the project database. At any time the user may select to end the session by the logout option on the pages. Figure 27-3 shows these components and their containers.

Working with user authentication

The first thing the user needs to do is log in to the application, which will be handled by a login JSP. In this example the JSP is called `login.jsp`, as shown in Figure 27-4.

Figure 27-4 shows how the login page looks running in a browser. The code for the page is given in Listing 27-3, the `login.jsp` file.

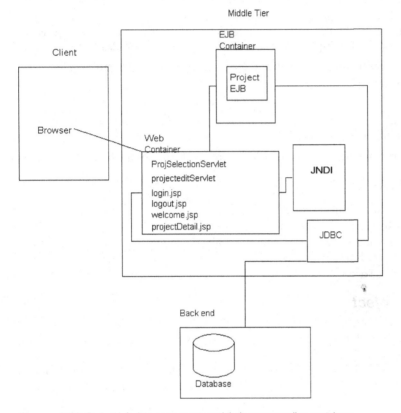

Figure 27-3: Project Info App components and their corresponding containers

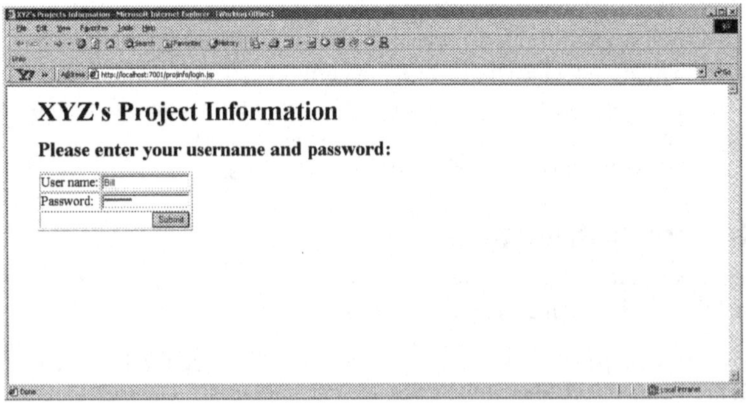

Figure 27-4: The login page for the Project Info App

Listing 27-3: The `login.jsp` file for the Project Info App

```
<html>
  <head> <title>XYZ's Projects Information</title> </head>
 <body>
  <blockquote>
  <h1>XYZ's Project Information </h1>
  <h2>Please enter your username and password:</h2>
  <p>
  <form method="POST" action="j_security_check">
  <table border=1>
    <tr> <td>Username:</td>
     <td><input type="text" name="j username"></td>
    </tr>
    <tr> <td>Password:</td>
     <td><input type="password" name="j_password"></td>
    </tr>
    <tr> <td colspan=2 align=right><input type=submit value="Submit">
</td> </tr>
  </table>  </form>  </blockquote>
</body> </html>
```

If the user authentication fails (for example, if the password is wrong) an error page is displayed. Otherwise, the welcome page (shown in Figure 27-5) is displayed.

> **CROSS-REFERENCE:** Chapter 28 presents a brief discussion on entity beans and contains the `Project` entity bean code.

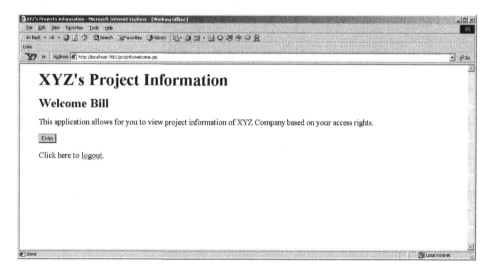

Figure 27- 5: The welcome page for the Project Info App

The welcome page is displayed by the `welcome.jsp`. If the user selects `enter`, the user is redirected to the `ProjSelectionServlet` via the following two lines of code:

```
<form method="Get" action="jasaprjsel">
 <td COLSPAN="2" ALIGN="right"> <input type="SUBMIT" VALUE="Enter">
</td>
```

Working with the web.xml File

Listing 27-3 shows the `web.xml` file that supports this form-based login. It gives access to the `admin` directory to only those users that belong to the `admin` group and defines the `<url-pattern>` for Servlets used by JNDI lookup.

Listing 27-3: The `web.xml` file for the Project Info App

```
<!DOCTYPE web-app PUBLIC "-//Sun Microsystems, Inc.//DTD Web Application
2.2//EN" "http://java.sun.com/j2ee/dtds/web-app_2_2.dtd">
<web-app>
  <display-name>Project Information</display-name>
  <servlet>
    <servlet-name>ProjSelectionServlet</servlet-name>
    <servlet-class>com.richware.projinfo.ProjSelectionServlet</servlet-
class>
  </servlet>
<servlet>
    <servlet-name>editprojectServlet</servlet-name>
    <servlet-
class>com.richware.projinfo.admin.editprojectServlet</servlet-class>
  </servlet>
  <welcome-file-list>
      <welcome-file>welcome.jsp</welcome-file>
  </welcome-file-list>
  <security-constraint>
      <web-resource-collection>
          <web-resource-name>AdminPages</web-resource-name>
          <description>
      The pages only accessible by authorized administrators.
          </description>
          <url-pattern>/admin/*</url-pattern>
          <http-method>GET</http-method>
      </web-resource-collection>
      <auth-constraint>
          <description>
              The roles with access
          </description>
          <role-name>
              admin
          </role-name>
      </auth-constraint>
```

```
            <user-data-constraint>
                <description>
                    This is how the user data must be transmitted
                </description>
                <transport-guarantee>NONE</transport-guarantee>
            </user-data-constraint>
        </security-constraint>
        <login-config>
            <auth-method>FORM</auth-method>
            <form-login-config>
                <form-login-page>/login.jsp</form-login-page>
                <form-error-page>/fail_login.html</form-error-page>
            </form-login-config>
        </login-config>
        <security-role>
            <description>
                An administrator
            </description>
            <role-name>
                admin
            </role-name>
        </security-role>
    <servlet-mapping>
      <servlet-name>ProjSelectionServlet</servlet-name>
      <url-pattern>/jasaprjsel</url-pattern>
    </servlet-mapping>
<servlet-mapping>
    <servlet-name>editprojectServlet</servlet-name>
      <url-pattern>/jasaeditprj</url-pattern>
    </servlet-mapping>
</web-app>
```

Notice that I used form-based authentication but did not define a realm because I wanted to use the default realm. I added my users, defined my groups, added the appropriate users to the groups, and added the appropriate permission to the default realm. In a real application where you need more security, you can use more secure forms of authentication, such as JASA. In addition, throughout this example I use simple text request parameters to pass information among the different resources. As I mentioned earlier in this chapter, you probably do not want to use simple text, because it becomes obvious what technology is being used and may open the application to attacks.

TIP: Using plain URIs may give a hint to a hacker about what technology is being used in your application, such a JSP or Servlet. You may want to map URI patterns using XML elements in the Web application's deployment descriptor and even encrypt them.

To verify whether a user can access a resource, you can also check programmatically if the user belongs to a group by calling the `HttpServletRequest.isUserInRole()` method.

You can call this method from JSPs and Servlets. Listing 27-4 shows how this works in a Servlet.

Listing 27-4: A `isUserInRole` method example

```
if (req.isUserInRole("admin")) {
    System.out.println("\n        user in admin group");
    htmlCode.append("<td>Edit Option</td> \n");
}
```

In essence, you are combining the `<security-role-ref>` and `<security-role>` elements in the `web.xml` file. The way the users and groups are known by the Web container is container dependent. The `<security-role-ref>` element lets you use a role name in the `isUserInRole` method that is not defined by the `<security-role>` element.

Handling a user request

After the user is authenticated the welcome page is displayed and the user can select to `Enter` the application. This action redirects the user to the `ProjSelectionServlet` via a call to the `Get` method. This is handled by the `service` method on the Servlet.

The `ProjSelectionServlet` retrieves the project information from the project database by an EJB (the `Project` EJB) to display a table with the project information. In addition, the Servlet determines what options the user has by using the `isUserInRole` method to determine if the user is in the `finance` group and `admin` group. Listing 27-5 shows the `ProjSelectionServlet` class.

Listing 27-5: The `ProjSelectionServlet` class: The main page for the Project Info App

```
package com.richware.projinfo;

import java.io.*;
import javax.servlet.*;
import javax.servlet.http.*;
import java.util.*;
import javax.naming.Context;
import javax.naming.InitialContext;
import javax.rmi.PortableRemoteObject;

/**
 * Class ProjSelectionServlet
 * Description: The ProjSelectionServlet displays the main page
 *   for this example.
 * If the user has access, it displays the list of all projects
 *   and their rates.
 *
 * Copyright:    Copyright (c) 2002
 * Company:      HungryMinds
```

```
 * @author Johennie Helton <jhelton@richware.com>
 * @version 1.0
 * DISCLAIMER: Please refer to the disclaimer at the beginning of this
book.
 */

public class ProjSelectionServlet extends HttpServlet {
  private ProjectHome projectHome;
  private Vector projects;
 /**
  * Initialize the servlet with all the EJB home objects needed.
  */
 public void init(ServletConfig config) throws ServletException {
    super.init(config);
 try {
       /*
       * Use JNDI for the initialization parameters.
       * Get the initial JNDI context & lookup the user home object
       */
        Context ctx = new InitialContext();
        projectHome = (ProjectHome)ctx.lookup("projinfo.ProjectHome");
       /*
       * get all projects
       */
        Collection col = projectHome.findAll();
        Iterator it = col.iterator();
        this.projects = new Vector();
        while (it.hasNext()) {
         Project prjInfo = (Project)
PortableRemoteObject.narrow(it.next(), Project.class);
          this.projects.addElement(prjInfo);
        }
     } catch (Exception e) {
        getServletConfig().getServletContext().log(e," ");
        throw new ServletException(e.toString());
     }
}
  /**
   * Service a request
   */
   public void service (HttpServletRequest req, HttpServletResponse
resp)
    throws ServletException, IOException {
     String urlStr = resp.encodeURL("jasaprojs");
    /*
     * make sure the user is authenticated. If not redirect to login
     */
     HttpSession session = req.getSession(false);
     if(session == null) {
```

```
        doRedirectToLogin(req,resp,"Please login first.");
      return;
    }
    /**
     * display the project list w/ a logout option at the top
     */
    resp.setContentType("text/html");
    PrintWriter writer = resp.getWriter();
    StringBuffer htmlCode = new StringBuffer();
    htmlCode.append("<!doctype html public \"-//w3c/dtd HTML
4.0//en\">");
    htmlCode.append("<% response.addHeader(\"Pragma\",\"No-cache\");
\n");
    htmlCode.append("   response.addHeader(\"Cache-Control\",\"no-
cache\"); \n ");
    htmlCode.append("   response.addDateHeader(\"Expires\",1); %> \n");
    htmlCode.append("<html> <head><title>Project
List</title></head>\n");
    htmlCode.append("<body bgcolor=\"#FFFFFF\"> <center> <hr><br>  
\n");
    htmlCode.append("<h1> <font size=\"+2\" color=\"red\">Welcome to
XYZ's Projects</font> \n");
    htmlCode.append("</h1> </center> <br>   <hr> <br>   \n");
    htmlCode.append("<a href=logout.jsp>Logout</a>");
    htmlCode.append("<table x:str border=1.0pt solid windowtext;");
    htmlCode.append(" cellpadding=0 cellspacing=0 width=1111> <tr>");
    htmlCode.append(" <td>Project ID</td> \n");
    htmlCode.append(" <td>Project Name</td> \n ");
    htmlCode.append(" <td>Project Description</td> \n");
    // if the user has access to financial information show quotes and
discounts
    if (req.isUserInRole("finance")) {
        htmlCode.append("<td>Initial Quote</td> \n <td>Discount</td> \n");
        htmlCode.append("<td>Actual Rate</td>  \n");
    }
    // if the user is an administrator then show edit choices
    if (req.isUserInRole("admin")) {
        htmlCode.append("<td>Edit Option</td> \n");
    }
    for (int i=0; i < projects.size(); i++){
        Project prjInfo = (Project) projects.elementAt(i);
        htmlCode.append("<tr> <td> <a
href=\"projectDetail.jsp?projid=");
        htmlCode.append(prjInfo.getProjID());
        htmlCode.append("&projname=");
htmlCode.append(prjInfo.getProjName());
        htmlCode.append("\">");
        htmlCode.append(prjInfo.getProjID());
        htmlCode.append("</a>");
```

```
            htmlCode.append("</td> <td> \n");
            htmlCode.append(prjInfo.getProjName());
            htmlCode.append("</td> <td> \n");
            htmlCode.append(prjInfo.getProjDescription());
            htmlCode.append("</td>");
            if (req.isUserInRole("finance")) {
              htmlCode.append("<td> \n");
              htmlCode.append(prjInfo.getInitQuote());
              htmlCode.append("</td> <td> \n");
              htmlCode.append(prjInfo.getDiscount());
              htmlCode.append("</td> <td> \n");
              htmlCode.append(prjInfo.getActualRate());
              htmlCode.append("</td>");
            }
            if (req.isUserInRole("admin")) {
              htmlCode.append("<td> <a href=\"admin\editproj.jsp?projid=");
htmlCode.append(prjInfo.getProjID());
              htmlCode.append("&projname=");
htmlCode.append(prjInfo.getProjName());
              htmlCode.append("\">Edit</a> </td>");
            }
            htmlCode.append("</tr> \n");
        }
    htmlCode.append("</table>");
    htmlCode.append("</form></body></html>");
    writer.println( htmlCode.toString());
    writer.close();
}

    private void doRedirectToLogin(HttpServletRequest request,
            HttpServletResponse response, String msg)
      throws IOException, ServletException {
      String url = "/login.jsp?errorMsg=" + msg;
      response.sendRedirect(response.encodeURL(url));
}
}
```

Figure 27-6 shows the resulting page from Listing 27-5 if the user is not an administrator.

Figure   27-6: The Project List page for the Project Info App

If the user selects the `Project ID` column, the `projectDetail.jsp` page is displayed. Listing 27-6 shows the source code.

Listing 27-6: The `projectDetail.jsp` for the Project Info App

```
<!doctype html public "-//w3c/dtd HTML 4.0//en">
<html>
<!-- The Project Detail Tables -->
<head>
<title>Project Detail</title>
</head>
<center>
<h2>
<font color=#DB1260>
  <p>
    <% String projname = request.getParameter("projname");
       String projId = request.getParameter("projid");
    %>
    <strong>
    <%= projname == null ? "": projname %>
    </strong>
    Project Details
  </p>
</font> </h2> </center> <p/><p/>
<%@ page import="
weblogic.db.jdbc.*,
java.sql.*
" %>
<%!
Connection conn  = null;
String jdbcClass = "COM.cloudscape.core.JDBCDriver";
String jdbcURL   = "jdbc:cloudscape:demo";
public Connection getCon() {
  try {
    Driver myDriver = (Driver) Class.forName(jdbcClass).newInstance();
    conn = myDriver.connect(jdbcURL, null);

  } catch (Exception e) {}
  return conn;
}
%>
<body>
<%
try {
  conn = getCon();
  if (conn != null) {
```

```
    String selectTeam= "select EAUSER.* from PROJ_TEAM, EAUSER WHERE
PROJ_TEAM.projid = '" + projId + "' and EAUSER.userid =
PROJ_TEAM.userid";
    Statement stmtTeam = conn.createStatement();
    stmtTeam.execute(selectTeam);
    ResultSet dsTeam = stmtTeam.getResultSet();
%>
    <center><h2>Project Team </h2></center>
    <table border=1 cellpadding=5>
     <th>Department </th>
     <th>Main contact </th>
<%
    while (dsTeam.next()) {
%>
      <tr>
       <td><%= dsTeam.getString("department") != null ?
dsTeam.getString("department") : " " %> </td>
       <td><%= dsTeam.getString("name") != null ?
dsTeam.getString("name") : " " %></td>
      </tr>
<%
    }
%>
    </table>
<%
    dsTeam.close();
    String selectStm = "select ARTIFACT.* from ARTIFACT,PROJECT_ARTIFACT
WHERE PROJECT_ARTIFACT.projid = '" + projId + "' and
PROJECT_ARTIFACT.ARTIFACT_ID_VERSION = ARTIFACT.ARTIFACT_ID_VERSION";
    Statement stmt = conn.createStatement();
    stmt.execute(selectStm);
    ResultSet ds = stmt.getResultSet();
%>
    <center><h2>Project Artifacts </h2></center>
    <table border=1 cellpadding=5>
     <th>Artifact name </th>
     <th>Artifact description </th>
     <th>Artifact location</th>
<%
    while (ds.next()) {
%>
      <tr>
       <td><%= ds.getString("ARTIFACT NAME") != null ?
ds.getString("ARTIFACT_NAME") : " " %> </td>
       <td><%= ds.getString("ARTIFACT_DESCRIPTION") != null ?
ds.getString("ARTIFACT_DESCRIPTION") : " " %></td>
       <td><%= ds.getString("ARTIFACT LOCATION") != null ?
ds.getString("ARTIFACT_LOCATION") : " " %></td>
      </tr>
```

```
<%
    }
%>
    </table>
<%
    ds.close();
    conn.close();
    out.flush();
    }
    else {
    out.print("Sorry. Database is not available.");
    }
} catch (Exception e) {
  out.print("Exception: " + e);
}
%>
<p> </body> </html>
```

The projectDetail.jsp uses JSP directives to import JDBC (I am using BEA's Weblogic). I also use JSP expressions to help determine what to display if a string is empty and to establish a connection to the database. In addition, I use JSP elements to retrieve the necessary information from the database and parse the result set to determine what needs to be presented to the user. Figure 27-7 shows the resulting HTML page from Listing 27-6.

Figure   27-7: The Project Detail page for the Project Info App

In Figure 27-7 the user selected the `Project Id 300-01`, called `Death-Ray`. These details are determined dynamically when the request is passed to the server and displayed along with the retrieved data from the database based on this selection.

The last detail that needs to be shown here is the `admin/editproject.jsp`, which handles the requests from an `admin` user. This is very similar to the `projectDetail.jsp`. Listing 27-7 shows part of the `admin/editproject.jsp` code.

Listing 27-7: The `admin/projectedit.jsp` for the Project Info App

```
<tr> <td>Project Name: </td>
<%= ds.getString("name") != null ? ds.getString("name") : " " %>
<% if (request.isUserInRole("manager")) { %>
  <td> Change to: <input type="text" name="projname"> </td>
<% } %>
</tr> <tr> <td>Project Description: </td>
<%= ds.getString("DESCRIPTION") != null ? ds.getString("DESCRIPTION") :
" " %>
<% if (request.isUserInRole("manager")) { %>
  <td> Change to: <input type="text" name="projdesc"> </td>
<% } %>
</tr>
<% if (request.isUserInRole("finance")) { %>
  <tr> <td>Inital Quote: </td>
  <%= ds.getString("initquote") != null ? ds.getString("initquote") :
" " %>
  <% if (request.isUserInRole("manager")) { %>
    <td> Change to: <input type="text" name="iquote"> </td>
  <% } %>
</tr>
......
```

Listing 27-7 shows how the `editproject.jsp` uses `isUserInRole` to determine if the information needs to be displayed (in the case of `finance`) and if it needs to be editable (in the case of `manager`). The rest of the code is very similar to Listing 27-6 and is omitted here.

Summary

This chapter covered the essentials of client-side development and security. JNDI provides directory services to Java applications. Not only is JNDI an API, but the JNDI architecture provides a Service Provider Interface (SPI) so that the naming and directory services can be abstracted from the implementation. That allows different providers to be used and interchanged without affecting the application implementation. Security in JNDI is based on the security services given by the underlying implementation and is not specified by the specification.

This chapter also covered client authentication, You have many options to perform authentication, some of which were explored in this chapter. Application deployment via the `web.xml` file, which specifies how the application is configured, was covered as well.

In addition, this chapter discussed Java Server Pages (JSPs) and Servlets, including a brief discussion on how they are affected by security. Finally, you saw an application example (called Project Info App) that was used to illustrate how the different components fit together. With the basic examples explained here and the knowledge that you have gained throughout the previous chapters, you can build an application with robust authentication and authorization.

Chapter 28
Securing Server-Side Components

In This Chapter

♦ Examining options for distributed server-side development

♦ Exploring CORBA security

♦ Understanding RMI

♦ Understanding interoperability

♦ Exploring EJB security

When the term *security* is used, confidentiality, integrity, and accountability come to mind. This chapter explores these characteristics from the server-side development and explores your options for distributed development from the server-side security with emphasis on the J2EE platform. It starts with a brief overview of *Common Object Request Broker Architecture* (CORBA) and CORBA security and then explores RMI, including the `RMISecurityManager` and `RMIClassLoader`. Next, the chapter takes a look at RMI over IIOP and presents how the EJB container can be configured and how it provides security.

Introduction

Enterprise JavaBeans (EJBs) is the default standard for Java server components. It abstracts low-level component service details such as transactions and security, and enables EJBs to be moved to other environments with minimal effort. *Remote Method Invocation* (RMI) is the protocol used in Java for remote communication.

The default industry standard, however, for distributed applications and communication is CORBA. There are two bridges between the two technologies. One bridge is the EJBs that comply with *Inter-ORB Protocol* (IIOP), because it is RMI over IIOP that allows communication between EJB and CORBA components. The other is Java IDL. This gives you the following options for distributed application development (among others):

♦ Java RMI (`http://java.sun.com/j2se/1.4/docs/guide/rmi/index`) allows communication between Java objects on different JVMs and even different physical machines.

♦ RMI over IIOP allows pure Java applications that use RMI to use IIOP as the transport protocol to create a bridge to CORBA components.

♦ Java IDL (`http://java.sun.com/j2se/1.4/docs/guide/idl/index.html`) is the interface to CORBA that allows programmers in Java (just as in other languages like C++ and COBOL) to interface in CORBA Interface Definition Language.

♦ EJBs (`http://java.sun.com/products/ejb/index.html`) use the RMI/IDL CORBA subset for the distributed object model and *Java Transaction Service* (JTS) for the distributed transaction model. With the use of RMI-IIOP, the EJB architecture to CORBA enables interoperability with multivendor ORBs and other EJB servers and non-java platform CORBA clients.

Securing Your Enterprise with CORBA

As you know, CORBA is a product of the *Object Management Group* (OMG) used to create, delete, store, and access distributed objects and to allow them to interact with each other. CORBA provides a set of services that makes it easy for objects to be transactional, lockable, secure, and persistent. CORBA solutions are very flexible because CORBA provides a protocol independent of language and platform implementation.

Review of CORBA

The *Object Request Broker* (ORB) is the CORBA object bus that manages the communication between components in the system and even components on other systems. It provides a set of bus-related services such as the following:

♦ **Transparency:** Your objects are not aware if the services or calls to other components are serviced in the same system or across the network.

♦ **Security and transactions:** The ORB includes context information in its messages to handle security and transactions.

♦ **Static and dynamic method invocations:** You can choose to have static or dynamic method bindings.

The ORB interface is an abstract interface for an ORB to abstract applications from implementation details. This interface provides helper functions such as converting object references to strings. Figure 28-1 shows a generic ORB architecture. The client uses the IDL stub and the implementation (typically known as the servant) uses an IDL skeleton. Both the client and the servant share the ORB interface.

When you write a CORBA application, you define a remote interface that describes the interaction between a server and its clients. You use the *Interface Definition Language* (IDL) to define the object's interfaces to any potential client. This CORBA IDL does not provide implementation details; the methods can be written in any language that provides CORBA bindings such as Java and C++.

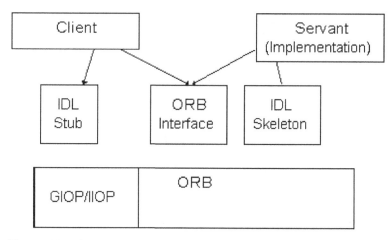

Figure 28-1: Generic ORB architecture

The interface between the client and its ORB is implemented in a *stub,* and the interface between a server object and its ORB is the *skeleton*. This is similar to the concept of stubs and skeletons in RMI. However, in CORBA, the communication is performed by the ORB and not by the stub components themselves.

The *servant* is the implementation of the operations defined in the IDL skeleton. The implementation is built using a language that that provides CORBA bindings such as Java or C++.

For remote invocation requests, CORBA provides a common protocol called *Internet Inter-ORB Protocol* (IIOP). IIOP is the standard *General Inter-ORB Protocol* (GIOP) with TCP/IP specified as the transport protocol. GIOP is the CORBA standard that defines the messages for inter-ORB communication.

CORBA defines a set of services; you may want to take a look at the OMG site (www.omg.org) for more information. Table 28-1 describes some of these services.

Table 28-1: CORBA Services

Service Name	Description
Concurrency Service	Mediates the concurrency control access to an object. If the object is accessed concurrently, its consistency is not compromised.
Licensing Services	Manages the interface to manage software licenses.

Table 28-1 (Continued)

Service Name	Description
Life Cycle Service	Defines operations for the life cycle of objects such as creation, deletion, movement, and copying.
Naming Service	Allows the location of objects that the client intends to use.
Persistence State Service	Provides an interface for persistent storage information.
Query Service	Provides operations for object collections. It is based on the SQL3 specification and Object Query Language (OQL).
Security Service	Provides the overall framework for CORBA security.
Transaction Service	Provides the interfaces for transaction processing essential for distributed applications.

In addition, OMG has defined an IIOP implementation called *Secure Inter-ORB Protocol* (SECIOP). SECIOP provides secure connections between CORBA clients and servers, but it is very complex and many vendors provide SSL implementations as an alternative. In addition, you can tunnel IIOP through an HTTPS connection.

Overview of CORBA security

The CORBA Security Service specification includes authentication, authorization and access control, secure communication, auditing, and non-repudiation. It does not include a specification for cryptography services; however, it does mention that the ORB implementation must be able to use local security policies. OMG has defined an overall security framework with different levels and structured into several feature packages (again you can find more information in the Security Specification at the `www.omg.org` site). Table 28-2 briefly describes these packages, based on the Security Services specification.

Authentication and authorization are not specific to CORBA. You can use different methods with CORBA security for authentication and authorization, and you choose which one to use based on your application needs.

Message integrity, assuring that your message is not tampered, and *message encryption*, for confidentiality, are also supported by CORBA but are not specific to it. CORBA security supports many different types of encryption and addresses all the important ones such as GSS, Kerberos, and SSL. These are explained in Table 28-1.

Non-repudiation, which provides functionality so that neither the sender nor the recipient can deny sending or receiving the message, is provided in an optional package. CORBA security also provides three different levels of privilege delegation. *Privilege delegation* refers to the ability to delegate the initiating principal identity beyond the invoked object. As discussed in Table 28-2, these levels are identity-based policies without delegation, identity-based policies with unrestricted delegation, and identity- and privilege-based policies with controlled delegation.

Table 28-2: CORBA/ORB Security

Functionality	Description
Main Security Functionality Package	*An ORB must provide at least one of these levels before it can be a secure ORB.*
Level 1	Only the identity of the initiating principal is transmitted from the client and can be delegated to other objects. Be careful, because impersonation is possible.
Level 2	Attributes of the initiating principal are transmitted from the client. These attributes can include audit identities, roles, and groups. These attributes can be delegated to other objects, but restrictions may apply.
Optional Security Functionality Package	*Functionality that is expected but not generally required to be part of the main security functionality.*
Non-repudiation	Provides functionality to generate and check evidence so that actions cannot be repudiated.
Security Replaceability Packages	*Specifies if the ORB is structured in a way that allows incorporation of different Security services.*
ORB services replaceability package	The ORB uses interceptor interfaces to call object services.
Security Service replaceability package	The ORB may or may not use interceptors but does use replaceability interfaces. Replaceability interfaces allow the Security services to not be required to understand how the ORB works.
Common Secure Interoperability (CSI) Feature Packages	*These features provide different levels of secure interoperability. All levels support functionality for mutual authentication between client and target, and message protection — for integrity.*
CSI level 0: Identity based policies without delegation	Only the identity of the initiating principal is transmitted from the client to the target. It cannot be delegated to other objects.

Table 28-2 (Continued)

Functionality	Description
CSI level 1: Identity based policies with unrestricted delegation	Only the identity of the initiating principal is transmitted from the client to the target. The identity can be delegated to other objects, and there are no restrictions on its delegation. Be careful, impersonation can happen at this level when an intermediate object can impersonate the user.
CSI level 2: Identity & privilege based policies with controlled delegation	Attributes of the initiating principal are transmitted from the client to the target. These attributes include identities, roles, and groups. The delegation of these attributes to other objects is possible, but subject to restrictions because the initiating principal can control their use.
SECIOP Interoperability Package	*An ORB with the Secure Inter-ORB Protocol can generate and use security information. The ORB can send and receive secure requests to and from other ORBs using GIOP/IIOP.*
Security Mechanism Packages	*The choice of the mechanism and protocol depends on the application mechanism and facilities requirements.*
SPKM Protocol	Supports CSI level 0 using public key technology for keys assigned to both principals and trusted authorities.
GSS Kerberos Protocol	Supports CSI level 1 using secret key technology for keys assigned to both principals and trusted authorities. It may also be used at CSI level 0.
CSI-ECMA Protocol	Supports CSI level 2. It can be used with identity, but not other privileges. Also, if the administrator permits it, it can be used at either CSI level 1 or level 0. It is based on the ECMA GSS-API mechanism.
SSL Protocol	Supports CSI level 0 and does not depend on the SECIOP extensions to IIOP.
SECIOP Plus DCE-CIOP Interoperability	An ORB that supports the SECIOP standard and also provides secure interoperability using the DCE-CIOP protocol.

CORBA principals

A *principal* is an entity that is registered and authenticated to the system. The most common form of authentication is the username and password combination, for humans, or long-term keys associated with the object, for systems. A principal may be associated with different identities for different purposes, such as initiating a message or resource access. In addition, a principal has privilege attributes and the principal may use some or all the attributes at any given session.

Some examples of these attributes include the principal's access identity, roles granted to the principal, and the groups the principal belongs to. The attributes can be obtained by delegation from other principals, may be available through authentication, or may be *public* (that is available to anyone). These attributes are based on access policies.

There are two access policy types. First is the object invocation policy that establishes if the client (based on the current principal) can access the requested operation. The ORB and the security services it uses (for all applications) typically enforce the object invocation policy. The other access policy is the *application object access*, which is enforced within the client and the target object. The ORB is still required to validate the request parameters and ensure delivery.

The object invocations are restricted by security rules, which are based on security policies. These policies include defining whether the client can access the object and perform the operation. Also based on security policies, a client and target object may establish a secure association.

Security mechanisms use cryptography to establish the secure association and to protect the data between client and target. Security mechanisms, however, differ in the type of cryptography used. For instance, there are three types of key distribution: secret, public, and hybrid. Keys are assigned to clients, targets, and trusted authorities. The secret key distribution is used for the distribution of keys for principals and for message protection.

Public key distribution is used for principal key distribution and may use secret key distribution for message protection. Finally, hybrid key distribution uses secret key technology for principal key distribution within an administration domain, and public key distribution for trusted authorities and between domains. The secure association is affected by underlying security mechanisms such as mutual authentication requirements.

> **NOTE:** Recall that a domain is a distinct scope that has common characteristics and rules.

RMI

The Remote Method Invocation protocol was designed to perform simple and powerful networking used by Java for distributed objects to communicate across JVMs and physical systems.

Recall from Chapter 26 that distributed objects are assembled into components to provide a distributed solution. Distributed protocols typically use three components: the *business object,* the *skeleton,* and the *stub.* Each business object class has an associated skeleton and stub classes. For instance, the business object `Order` class is associated with the `Order_Skeleton` and `Order_Stub` classes. The business object and skeleton reside in the server, and the stub resides in the client. Using the RMI protocol, the stub and skeleton classes make the business object appear as if it is running locally in the client's machine. The skeleton and stub are connected via the network.

The business object contains business logic and implements an interface that represents the exposed business methods. The stub implements the same interface. The stub implementation does not contain business logic. Instead, it implements the logic to communicate with the skeleton across the network. At the server side, the skeleton is associated to a port and IP address and listens for requests. When the client calls a method to be serviced by the business object, the stub receives the request. The stub then uses object serialization to marshal (and unmarshal) the method invoked and the parameters passed to the method to send the information to the skeleton.

Because the skeleton is listening, it receives the request, unmarshals it, and identifies which method on the business object to invoke. Any return value is processed similarly: The skeleton receives the value from the business object, streams it, and passes it to the stub. The stub, in turn, passes it to the client as if it were processed locally. Figure 28-2 shows this interaction among the different parts of a distributed object using RMI.

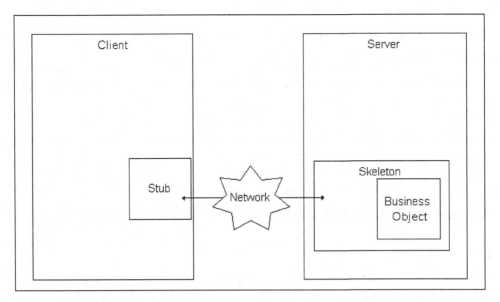

Figure 28-2: Parts of a distributed object using RMI

RMI security overview

To do remote invocation, RMI tries, in turn, the following. Whichever one succeeds first is used for subsequent communications. If none succeeds, the communication fails.

♦ Communicate with the server's ports directly by using sockets. You can create any type of sockets you need, including encrypted sockets, via a socket factory provided by RMI.

♦ Build a URL to the server's host and port and use an HTTP post request on the URL (using the skeleton information as the body). The return information is sent back in the body of the HTTP response.

♦ Build a URL to the server's host using port 80 and a CGI script that forwards the posted RMI request.

The last two techniques allow the communication across a firewall and are significantly slower than the direct socket communication. The `java.rmi.server.disableHttp` property, if set to `true`, disables the use of HTTP for RMI calls; the default value is `false`.

You may want to log information of your RMI application for both client-side and server-side logging. You can use a logging configuration file and the `java.util.logging` API (new in J2SE v1.4) to configure RMI implementation logging. For instance, the `java.rmi.server.logCalls` property corresponds to the `sun.rmi.server.call` logger name and logs server-side remote calls and exceptions; and `java.rmi.client.logCalls` corresponds with the `sun.rmi.client.call` for the client.

RMI security is, not surprisingly, based on the Java security technologies such as automatic bytecode verification and secure class load at runtime. Therefore, the next section explores security managers and class loaders.

The RMISecurityManager

RMI requires that you install a security manager before exporting any server object or invoking a method on a server. You have the option to use the provided `RMISecurityManager` or to write your own. The `RMISecurityManager` restricts downloaded implementations from reading or writing from the computer or connecting to other systems behind your firewall. If you create your own, your classes are loaded using the default `Class.forName`.

> **NOTE:** The *primordial* class loader is used when `java.lang.Class.forName` is directly called. You can think of the primordial class as the root of the class loading tree.

The `RMISecurityManager` class extends the `java.lang.SecurityManager` class and provides the same security features. Chapter 18 describes the `SecurityManager` in more detail. Recall that at this time, the `SecurityManager` class does not provide mechanisms to regulate resources, and so the `RMISecurityManager` does not prevent resource abuse. This means that the RMI system operates within the policies established by the server defined via the security manager and class loader.

The RMIClassLoader

In RMI, the `RMIClassLoader` attempts to load classes from the network and throws an exception if a security manager is not in place. The security manager ensures that loaded classes satisfy Java safety.

> **TIP:** Applications must either define their own security managers or use the restrictive `RMISecurityManager`. If no security manager is in place, an application cannot load classes from network sources.

The property `java.rmi.server.useCodebaseOnly` is used to indicate if it is permitted to download a class from the URL embedded in the stream with a serialized object. This property is applicable to the client and server but not to applets. Classes directly accessed by a class already loaded by the `RMIClassLoader` are subject to the security manager's restrictions because `RMIClassLoader` also loads them. Some static methods of the `java.rmi.server.RMIClassLoader` delegate to an instance of a `java.rmi.server.RMIClassLoaderSpi` (new in J2SE v1.4) Service Provider Interface. This SPI can be configured to augment `RMIClassLoader`.

RMI over IIOP

Remote Method Invocation over Internet Inter-ORB Protocol (RMI-IIOP) simply means that the program uses RMI interfaces and uses IIOP as the transport. It was developed by Sun and IBM and is based on the Java Language Mapping to OMG IDL (`http://cgi.omg.org/cgi-bin/doc?ptc/00-01-06`) specification and the CORBA/IIOP 2.3.1 specification, formal/99-10-07 (`http://cgi.omg.org/cgi-bin/doc?formal/99-10-07`).

RMI-IIOP uses the Java CORBA ORB and IIOP to allow you to write all the code in Java. You do not need to learn a separate IDL or mapping because RMI-IIOP allows developers to pass serializable Java objects between application components. You use the `rmic` compiler to generate the code necessary for connecting your application to any other CORBA-compliant code using IIOP including stubs, skeletons, and OMG IDL. For more information on `rmic` you can visit the `http://java.sun.com/j2se/1.4/docs/tooldocs/solaris/rmic.html` site.

The RMI-IIOP API is supported by the following packages:

♦ `org.omg.CORBA`: Provides the mapping of the OMG CORBA APIs to the Java programming language, including the class `ORB`, which is implemented so that a programmer can use it as a fully functional Object Request Broker (ORB).

♦ `org.omg.PortableServer`: Provides classes and interfaces for making the server side of your applications portable across multivendor ORBs.

In Java, *Portable Object Adaptor* (POA)-based *Dynamic Skeleton Interface* (DSI) servants inherit from the standard `DynamicImplementation` class, which inherits from the `Servant` class. The `PortableServer` module defines the native `Servant` type for the POA. In Java, the `Servant` type is mapped to the Java `org.omg.PortableServer.Servant` class. It serves as the base class for all POA servant implementations and provides a number of methods that may be invoked by the application programmer, as well as methods that are invoked by the POA itself, and may be overridden by the user to control aspects of servant behavior.

♦ `org.omg.CosNaming`: Provides a naming service for Java IDL. The Object Request Broker Daemon (ORBD) also includes both a transient and persistent naming service.

The package and all its classes and interfaces are generated by running the `idlj` tool on the file `nameservice.idl`, which is a module written in OMG IDL.

♦ `javax.rmi.CORBA`: Contains portability APIs for RMI-IIOP. These APIs provide a standard interface between the generated stubs and ties and the RMI-IIOP runtime. They also allow third-party ORBs to be used for RMI over IIOP as an alternative to the ORB supplied by Sun. They are not intended to be called directly from RMI-IIOP applications. See also the `javax.rmi` package.

♦ `javax.rmi`: Contains user APIs for RMI-IIOP. These APIs are provided for use by RMI-IIOP applications, and provide equivalent semantics when running over either IIOP or JRMP. See also the `javax.rmi.CORBA` package.

> **NOTE:** For more information you can visit the RMI-IIOP site at
> `http://java.sun.com/j2se/1.4/docs/guide/rmi-iiop/index.html`.

Enterprise Security with EJBs

As you know, J2EE Enterprise JavaBeans are server-side components that provide a model to simplify the development of transactional, scalable, and portable middleware. EJB servers provide automatic support services such as transactions, security, database connectivity, and more. EJBs encapsulate business logic and provide services to clients. A good resource for EJB information and J2EE in general is Sun's BluePrints site at `http://java.sun.com/blueprints/index.html`.

The EJB architecture defines components, servers, containers, and clients. It is the *EJB container* that provides life-cycle management for the enterprise beans and provides services — by intercepting calls from the client. Examples of these services are security, concurrency control, and transactional services, which are provided to the client, however the client is not aware of the container. The EJB container resides in the *EJB server* that provides services such as directory, naming, and e-mail services.

The home interface provides the methods to create, remove, and get metadata for the EJBs. This interface extends `javax.EJB.EJBHome`.

The remote interface defines the client view set of business methods. It must extend `javax.ejb.EJBObject`, which defines the methods for clients to obtain the home interface, remove an EJB instance, and obtain a handle to the EJB instance, among other things.

The enterprise bean class provides the actual implementation of the business methods of the bean. It must implement the `javax.ejb.EntityBean` or `javax.ejb.SessionBean` interface. It also implements a corresponding `ejbCreate` method for each `create` method in the home interface. In addition, for each finder method in the home interface, the enterprise bean class implements corresponding `ejbFindBy` methods.

The behavior of an EJB is defined partly in the implementation and customized at deployment time via a deployment descriptor.

Understanding EJB components

There are three major types of EJBs: *session, entity,* and *message driven beans.* The specification defines the life cycle for each type of bean. This section describes each EJB type and its life cycle at a high level, skipping many of the details.

Session beans

Session beans model processes, services, and client sessions. They are used as resources only by the client that created them. There are two types of session beans: stateless and stateful. *Stateless* beans do not keep the session data information, also called the *conversational state,* between calls from the client. This type of bean does not survive server crashes since it does not keep its state.

The life cycle of a stateless session bean starts in the does not exist state, which means the instance has not been instantiated. The container creates a new instance via the `newInstance` method and it then calls the `setEntityContext` method. The stateless bean then enters the pooled state where it is ready to provide services (via calls to the exposed business methods). When the container no longer requires the instance, it calls the `ejbRemove` method.

> **NOTE:** A member variable is part of the conversational state if it is a non-transient primitive type or a non-transient Java object.

Stateful session beans keep the state within the bean. That is, the state is kept across multiple methods as well as different invocations of the same method from the client. This works because the client establishes a conversation with the bean. The bean is required to remember the state of the conversation in subsequent calls. Therefore, if the container needs to put the bean in the pool, the bean is *passivated.* A bean is passivated when its conversational state is saved to persistent storage such as the hard disk.

Passivation is required because the state must be available when the client requires a service and a bean instance is required from the pool to service it. The process of retrieving the state from persistent storage is called *activation.* Activation allows the bean instance to have the same conversational state to service the client request, however the bean instance may not be the same as the previous instance before passivation. This process is transparent to the client.

The stateful session bean has four states: the "does not exist," the "non-transaction method-ready," the "transaction method-ready," and the passive state. As with the stateless session bean, the *does not exist state* means that the bean has not been instantiated. The client calls the `create` method on the home interface and the container calls the `newInstance`, the `setSession`, and the `ejbCreate` methods.

At the time of deployment, you specify whether the bean is part of a transaction, and if so, the transaction method-ready state is where the business methods are serviced. In this state the bean cannot be passivated and the bean transitions to the non-transaction method-ready state if there is a commit or a roll back of the transaction. The bean enters the passive state if it has been passivated — from the non-transaction method-ready state and transitions back to it via an `ejbActivate` method call. Non-transactional business methods are serviced in the non-transaction method-ready state. The bean goes back to the does not exist state after an `ejbRemove` method call (from the non-transaction method-ready state) or after a time out (from the passive state).

Entity beans

Entity beans provide a view of persisted data, such as records in a database, and they model real-world objects such as customers and projects. Entity beans instances are created and managed by the *EJB container*. When the client calls `create`, the container creates the instance and calls `setEntityContext` of the entity bean class, which passes the entity context to the bean. The next step in the entity bean's life cycle is the pooled state.

The EJB specification describes an architecture in which the container keeps a free pool of entity bean instances and moves them in and out of this state. In the pooled state, all beans are the same and are not associated to an EJB object. From the pooled state, the entity bean moves to the ready state. In the ready state, the EJB is associated with an object.

There are two ways in which the entity bean is moved to the ready state: Either the container activates it (via the `ejbActivate` method) or the client calls the `create` method. If the `create` method is called, the `ejbCreate` and `ejbPostCreate` methods are invoked by the container; it is in these methods that you perform any necessary logic. When the client calls the `remove` method, the container invokes the `ejbRemove` method and the entity bean is moved to the pooled state. Another way for the entity bean to go to the pooled state is for the container to invoke the `ejbPassivate` method. Finally, the EJB container removes the instance from the pool and invokes the `unsetEntityContext` method.

Message driven beans

Message driven beans (MDBs) allow clients to asynchronously invoke server-side business logic. They are (as of this writing) JMS message consumers, but in the future they may be used to process other types of messages. MDBs work with queues and both durable and non-durable topic subscriptions. To create a new instance, the container instantiates the bean and calls the `setMessageDrivenContext` method.

At this point the instance is in the ready state to process messages. Invocations of the `onMessage` method are serviced in the ready state. These beans are stateless, so any instance may service any message and an instance may service multiple clients as well. The container may pool MDBs and assign any message to any MDB instance. Finally, the `ejbRemove` method is invoked when the bean goes back to the does not exist state.

Using authentication in J2EE components

As described in previous chapters, *authentication* is the mechanism by which an entity (a user or service provider) establishes its identity. That is, it proves that it is acting on the user or system's behalf. So, if the entity establishes the communication without authorization, it is an *unauthenticated* user.

Authentication is required when crossing the boundaries of protection domains. A *protection domain* is a set of entities that trust each other, and so these entities communicate without requiring authentication. You can think of the EJB container as a protection domain because it provides authentication boundaries between its components and their callers. However, container implementations may choose to host components of different protection domains.

There are two main forms of authentication that J2EE components use. The first is called *container-managed resource manager signon*. The other is called *application-managed resource manager signon*. As their names suggest, the main difference is whether the container or the application manages the resource access. For instance, in the *container-managed resource manager signon* case, because components may try to access resources in different protection domains, the calling container is configured to manage the authentication to those resources. In the *application-managed resource manager signon*, it is the application that manages the specification of the caller's identity for resource access.

> **TIP:** If you need to develop your own application-managed resource manager signon, use the connector architecture for portability.

As you probably know, each resource and J2EE component accessed by a component is declared in the deployment descriptor via elements. For instance, the `resource-ref` element declares the resources used by the component, and a `re-auth` element is used to declare the type of authentication required. Components can use can use the `EJBContext.getCallerPrincipal` and `HttpServletRequest.getUserPrincipal` methods to obtain the identity of their caller. The component may map the caller identity to a new identity and/or authentication secret as required by the target enterprise information system.

The authentication context encapsulates the identity. Access to the authentication context can be given in many possible ways through policies and mechanisms such as

♦ to any process the user starts by allowing him access to the authentication context — once the user is authenticated.

♦ once a component is authenticated, access to the authentication context may be made available to trusted components.

♦ by delegation: the caller may delegate the authetication context to the called component.

Using authorization in J2EE components

Recall from previous chapters that an entity may need to be authorized to access a protected resource. For example, a user may be authenticated to use your application but may not be authorized to read certain files that the application may encounter (accounting files, for instance). Authorization is used to restrict access to resources based on constraints. The identity of the caller is available in the authentication context and may be propagated. In addition, it may be an anonymous call where the identity of the caller is not provided.

Similar to the container providing a protection domain for its components, it provides a boundary for authorization as well. The authorization boundary, however, may restrict entities' access to a resource even if they are within the same protection domain.

There are two models for authorization: declarative and programmatic authorization. *Declarative* authorization makes use of the deployment descriptor where security roles and their associations are specified. The EJB container grants access to methods based on these associations. This gives flexibility after the application has been written; all you need to do is modify the deployment descriptor to change the security.

Programmatic authorization provides finer-grain control over privilege and security roles. In the deployment descriptor the element `security-role-ref` is used to link a privilege name to a security role. A component can call the `EJBContext.isCallerInRole` or `isUserInRole` to check whether the caller has been granted the correct privilege to access the requested resource and proceed if the proper rights are encountered.

> **NOTE:** Recall that authorization can be programmatic or declarative. Programmatic authorization is embedded in code and the developer controls (and checks) whether the user is authorized to access the resource or operation. In declarative authorization, the access rules are described in the deployment descriptor and the EJB container is responsible for controlling the access to the operation or resource.

Configuring EJB component security

The deployer is responsible for configuring the container to provide the security and other necessary services. The deployer configures the container for the functionality that it needs to provide services such as message integrity, message encryption, and auditing.

For *message integrity* the container computes and attaches a message signature to the request. The target container verifies the signature of the request and attaches a message signature to the response. The communication fails if the verification fails. Because there is performance overhead, you may want to specify which messages require integrity and specify them through the deployment description.

The deployer configures the container for *message encryption* when the communication between its components and their clients requires confidentiality. Again, there is a performance hit and only those methods that require confidentiality should be identified as such at deployment time. Also, the container needs to be configured to reject any communication that requires confidentiality and is not protected.

Auditing is important, especially when security has been breached, because it allows you to see not only who has been denied access but also who has been given access to the system. The deployer is responsible for the configuration of the EJB container. These constraints should be analyzed and associated with an audit if necessary.

As described, the deployment descriptor, via elements, specifies the access rights (among other things) to resources and components. For example:

♦ The `method-permission` element in the deployment descriptor is used to specify access rights to the methods of the remote and home interfaces for Enterprise JavaBeans. You can give unrestricted access to a resource or method by mapping a role to all the users and giving the role access to the resource. In addition, the `description` subelement (of the `method-permission` element) is used to identify whether the method needs integrity or confidentiality or both.

♦ The element `resource-ref` is used to declare the resources used by a component. If the resources contain sensitive information, they are described in the `description` subelement (of the `resource-ref` element).

♦ The `security-role-ref` element is used to specify the link between a privilege name and a security role.

Server-side code example

Chapter 27 introduced the Project Info App. That application is continued here with the addition of the `ProjectBean` code that the servlets access.

The Project EJB

The Project EJB has the standard home and remote interfaces shown in Listing 28-1 and Listing 28-2.

Listing 28-1: `ProjectHome.java`

```
package com.richware.projinfo;

import java.rmi.*;
import javax.ejb.*;
import java.util.*;
```

```
/**
 * Interface ProjectHome
 * Description: The Project EJB home interface
 *
 * Copyright:    Copyright (c) 2002
 * Company:      HungryMinds
 * @author Johennie Helton <jhelton@richware.com>
 * @version 1.0
 * DISCLAIMER: Please refer to the disclaimer at the beginning of this
book.
*/

public interface ProjectHome extends EJBHome {
    public Project create(String projID, String projName,
          String projDescription,
          double initQuote, double discount,
          double actualRate)
          throws CreateException, RemoteException;

    public Project findByPrimaryKey(String id)
        throws RemoteException, FinderException;
    public Collection findAll ()
        throws RemoteException, FinderException;
}
```

The Project Info application only requires `findByPrimaryKey` and `findAll` methods, which are defined in the home interface and implemented by the container — since this is a container-managed bean.

Listing 28-2: `Project.java`

```
package com.richware.projinfo;

import java.rmi.*;
import javax.ejb.*;

/**
 * Interface Project
 * Description: The Project EJB remote interface
 *
 * Copyright:    Copyright (c) 2002
 * Company:      HungryMinds
 * @author Johennie Helton <jhelton@richware.com>
 * @version 1.0
 * DISCLAIMER: Please refer to the disclaimer at the beginning of this
book.
*/

public interface Project extends EJBObject {
```

```
    public String getProjID() throws RemoteException;
    public String getProjName() throws RemoteException;
    public String getProjDescription() throws RemoteException;
    public double getInitQuote() throws RemoteException;
    public double getDiscount() throws RemoteException;
    public double getActualRate() throws RemoteException;
    public void setProjID(String val) throws RemoteException;
    public void setProjName(String val) throws RemoteException;
    public void setProjDescription(String val)
        throws RemoteException;
    public void setInitQuote(double val)
        throws RemoteException;
    public void setDiscount(double val)
        throws RemoteException;
    public void setActualRate(double val)
        throws RemoteException;
}
```

The remote interface contains all the methods the bean needs to expose to its clients; this includes any business methods required. Listing 28-3 shows the `ProjectBean.java` class.

Listing 28-3: `ProjectBean.java`

```
package com.richware.projinfo;

import java.io.Serializable;
import java.util.Collection;
import java.util.Vector;
import javax.ejb.*;
import javax.naming.InitialContext;
import javax.naming.NamingException;
import javax.sql.DataSource;
import java.rmi.*;
import java.util.*;

/**
 * Class ProjectBean
 * Description: The Project EJB class
 *
 * Copyright:    Copyright (c) 2002
 * Company:      HungryMinds
 * @author Johennie Helton <jhelton@richware.com>
 * @version 1.0
 * DISCLAIMER: Please refer to the disclaimer at the beginning of this
book.
 */

public class ProjectBean implements EntityBean {
    protected EntityContext    context;
```

```java
// flag to determine whether or not the
// bean needs to be written to storage.
private transient boolean isDirty;

// container managed fields
public String projID = null;
public String projName = null;
public String projDescription = null;
public double initQuote = 0.0;
public double discount = 0.0;
public double actualRate = 0.0;

//
// constructor
public ProjectBean() {
  System.out.println(
    "ProjectBean is created by EJB container.");
}

// EJB required methods
// called after activation by the EJB container

public void ejbActivate() throws RemoteException {
    System.out.println("ProjectBean:ejbActivate()");
}

// When the Home Object is called, the Home Object calls
// this method.  Populate the attributes so that the
// container can
// create the database rows needed.

public String ejbCreate(String projID, String projName, String
projDescription,
                        double initQuote, double discount,
                        double actualRate)
            throws RemoteException {

    System.out.println("ProjectBean: ejbCreate ()");

    this.projID = projID;
    this.projName   = projName;
    this.projDescription = projDescription;
    this.initQuote = initQuote;
    this.discount = discount;
    this.actualRate = actualRate;
    return this.projID;
}
```

```java
// updates the object with data from database but
// we are using CMP so we do not need it.
// Just do post-processing needed.
public void ejbLoad() throws RemoteException {
    System.out.println("ProjectBean:ejbLoad()");
}


// called before passivation by the EJB container
public void ejbPassivate() throws RemoteException {
    System.out.println("ProjectBean:ejbPassivate()");
}


// called after ejbCreate.  The instance has been
// associated with an EJB Object and we can get a
// reference via the context if we
// need to.
public void ejbPostCreate(String projID, String projName,
    String projDescription,
    double initQuote, double discount,
    double actualRate)
    throws RemoteException {
  System.out.println("ProjectBean:ejbPostCreate()");
}


// this method is called by the container right before
// removing entity information from the database.

public void ejbRemove() throws RemoteException {
    System.out.println("ProjectBean:ejbRemove()");
}


// updates the database but we are using CMP so we do not
// need it. Just do preprocessing needed.
public void ejbStore() throws RemoteException {
 System.out.println(
      "ProjectBean:ejbStore( " + projID + ")");
 setModified(false);
}

// keep the context so we can access it later if needed
public void setEntityContext(EntityContext ecxt)
   throws RemoteException {
 System.out.println("ProjectBean:setEntityContext()");
 context = ecxt;
}

// disassociate the context
public void unsetEntityContext() throws RemoteException {
    System.out.println("ProjectBean:unsetEntityContext()");
```

```
        context = null;
    }

    //
    // business methods
    public String getProjID() throws RemoteException{
        System.out.println("ProjectBean:getID()");
        return projID;
    }
    public void setProjID(String id) throws RemoteException {
        System.out.println("ProjectBean:setID()");
        this.projID = id;
    }
    public String getProjName() throws RemoteException {
        System.out.println("ProjectBean:getName()");
        return projName;
    }
    public String getProjDescription() throws RemoteException {
        System.out.println("ProjectBean:getDescription()");
        return projDescription;
    }
    public double getDiscount() throws RemoteException {
        System.out.println("ProjectBean:getDiscount()");
        return discount;
    }
    public double getInitQuote() throws RemoteException {
        System.out.println("ProjectBean:getInitQuote()");
        return initQuote;
    }
    public double getActualRate() throws RemoteException {
        System.out.println("ProjectBean:getActual()");
        return actualRate;
    }
    public void setProjName(String name) throws RemoteException {
        System.out.println("ProjectBean:setProjName()");
        setModified(true);
        this.projName = name;
    }

    public void setProjDescription(String name)
        throws RemoteException {
        System.out.println("ProjectBean:setProjDescription()");
        setModified(true);
        this.projDescription = name;
    }
    public void setInitQuote(double initQuote)
        throws RemoteException {
        System.out.println("ProjectBean:setInitQuote()");
        setModified(true);
```

```
            this.initQuote = initQuote;
      }
   public void setDiscount(double discount)
      throws RemoteException {
         System.out.println("ProjectBean:setDisc()");
         setModified(true);
         this.discount = discount;
      }
   public void setActualRate(double actualRate)
      throws RemoteException {
         System.out.println("ProjectBean:setActual()");
         setModified(true);
         this.actualRate = actualRate;
      }
   // Returns whether the EJBean has been modified or not.
   // This method must be public for the container to be
   // able to invoke it.
   public boolean isModified() {
      return isDirty;
   }
   // Sets the EJBean's modified flag.
   public void setModified(boolean flag) {
      isDirty = flag;
      System.out.println("setModified(): " + projID + (String) (flag ?
": requires saving"
                  : ": saving not required"));
   }
}
```

The `ProjectBean` class implements any business methods and any necessary support methods. You identify any security restrictions to these methods at deployment time. The Project Info application does not require these methods to be restricted to different users. In this example, I entrust the Web container to vouch for the identity for users, and the access to the Project EJB is being accessed via secured Web components.

Listing 28-4 provides the `Project-cmp-rdbms-jar.xml` file that is the deployment descriptor for the `User` EJB; I used BEA's Weblogic Server 7.0 (WLS) to deploy this application; therefore, there are some WLS-specific tags.

Listing 28-4: `Project-cmp-rdbms-jar.xml`

```
<!DOCTYPE weblogic-rdbms-bean PUBLIC '-//BEA Systems, Inc.//DTD WebLogic
5.1.0 EJB RDBMS

Persistence//EN'
 'http://www.bea.com/servers/wls510/dtd/weblogic-rdbms-persistence.dtd'>
<weblogic-rdbms-bean>
   <pool-name>demoPool</pool-name>
   <table-name>EAPROJ</table-name>
```

```
<attribute-map>
   <object-link>
      <bean-field>projID</bean-field>
      <dbms-column>projid</dbms-column>
   </object-link>
   <object-link>
      <bean-field>projName</bean-field>
      <dbms-column>name</dbms-column>
   </object-link>
   <object-link>
      <bean-field>projDescription</bean-field>
      <dbms-column>DESCRIPTION</dbms-column>
   </object-link>

   <object-link>
      <bean-field>initQuote</bean-field>
      <dbms-column>initquote</dbms-column>
   </object-link>
   <object-link>
      <bean-field>discount</bean-field>
      <dbms-column>discount</dbms-column>
   </object-link>
   <object-link>
      <bean-field>actualRate</bean-field>
      <dbms-column>actualrate</dbms-column>
   </object-link>
</attribute-map>
<finder-list>
   <finder>
      <method-name>findByPrimaryKey</method-name>
      <method-params>
         <method-param>java.lang.String</method-param>
      </method-params>
      <finder-query><![CDATA[ (= projid)]]></finder-query>
   </finder>
   <finder>
      <method-name>findAll</method-name>
      <finder-query></finder-query>
   </finder>
</finder-list>
<options>
   <use-quoted-names>false</use-quoted-names>
</options>
</weblogic-rdbms-bean>
```

Using RMI to access the Project EJB

Listing 28-5 shows a client using RMI to use the Project EJB. This client is very simple and prints the number of projects found in the database via the `findAll` method. It uses JNDI to look up the home object and JTA to demarcate the transaction. Note that the RMI-IIOP `javax.rmi.PortableRemoteObject.narrow` method is used to cast returned remote objects.

Listing 28-5: `RMIClient.java`

```
package com.richware.projinfo;

import javax.ejb.*;
import javax.naming.*;
import javax.rmi.*;
import javax.util.Properties;
import javax.transaction.UserTransaction;

/**
 * Class RMIClient
 * Description: The RMI client class code that invokes methods on the
Project EJB
 *
 * Copyright:    Copyright (c) 2002
 * Company:      HungryMinds
 * @author Johennie Helton <jhelton@richware.com>
 * @version 1.0
 * DISCLAIMER: Please refer to the disclaimer at the beginning of this
book.
 */

public class RMIClient {
  public static void main(String[] args) {
    try {
      // Get system properties for JNDI
      Properties prop = System.getProperties();
      Context ctx = new InitialContext(prop);
      ProjectHome home = (ProjectHome)
          javax.rmi.PortableRemoteObject.narrow(
          ctx.lookup("ProjectHome"),ProjectHome.class);
      // now use JNDI to find the JTA UserTransaction interface
      // and start the transaction
      UserTransaction utr = (UserTransaction)
          ctx.lookup("javax.transaction.UserTransaction");
      utr.begin();
      // create the Project object and use it
      Project projs = home.create();
      Collection prjcol = projectHome.findAll();
      System.out.println("there are " + prjcol.size()
          + " projects.");
      // now remove the object and commit the transaction
      projs.remove();
      utr.commit();
```

```
    } catch (Exception e) {
       e.printStackTrace();
    }
  }
}
```

Using CORBA to access the Project EJB

Listing 28-6 shows a Java CORBA client that accomplishes the same function as the preceding RMI example. It is somewhat more complex and uses COS Naming to look up the home object, and OTS to demarcate the transaction.

Listing 28-6: CORBAClient.java

```
package com.richware.projinfo;

import java.util.*;
import org.omg.CosNaming.*;
import org.omg.CosTransactions.*;
import org.omg.CORBA.ORB;
import org.omg.CORBA.Object;

/**
 * Class CORBAClient
 * Description: The CORBA client class code that invokes methods on the
Project EJB
 *
 * Copyright:     Copyright (c) 2002
 * Company:       HungryMinds
 * @author Johennie Helton <jhelton@richware.com>
 * @version 1.0
 * DISCLAIMER: Please refer to the disclaimer at the beginning of this
book.
 */

public class CORBAClient {
  public static main(String[] args) throws Exception {
    // init the ORB
    org.omg.CORBA.ORB orb = org.imprise.ejb.Global.orb();
    // obtain naming context
    NamingContext nctx = NamingContextHelper.narrow(
        orb.resolve_initial_reference("NameService"));
    // look up home object
    NameComponent[] components = {
        new NameComponent(ProjectHome","")}
    ProjectHome home = ProjectHomeHelper.narrow(nctx.resolve(
        components));
    // get the OTS Current interface
    Current cTrn = CurrentHelper.narrow (
```

```
    orb.resolve_initial_references("TransactionCurrent"));
cTrn.begin();
// create the Project object and use it
Project projs = home.create();
    Collection prjcol = projectHome.findAll();
System.out.println("there are " + prjcol.size()
    + " projects.");
// now remove the object and commit the transaction
projs.remove();
// commit the transaction
cTrn.commit(true);
}
}
```

Summary

This chapter explored the basics of CORBA and the different services that CORBA provides. Among these services is a security service that provides different levels of security. In addition, the SECIOP package provides interoperability security and the Common Secure Interoperability (CSI) package provides additional levels of security for interoperability. The different CSI levels that different protocols provide for your applications were listed. For instance, the GSS Kerberos protocol provides CSI level 1 but also can be used for level 0. The RMI protocol, its security, and how it can use IIOP for the transport protocol to bridge to CORBA were also discussed.

Finally, Enterprise JavaBeans were explored first by discussing the different types of EJBs that you currently encounter and giving a brief description of their life cycle. The chapter finished with a discussion of authentication and authorization in the J2EE architecture and a description of how the container provides the security mechanisms for EJBs.

Chapter 29
Application Security with Java

In This Chapter

♦ Learning the basics of WebLogic, WebSphere, and Inprise servers

♦ Understanding the security aspects and services available in these servers

As discussed throughout this book, security is more than network security — it affects the entire enterprise solution. I have discussed the security requirements needed for a secure solution. Namely, the following security services are required:

♦ Authentication

♦ Authorization

♦ Data confidentiality

♦ Data integrity

♦ Non-repudiation

This chapter presents a brief description, with emphasis on the preceding security services, of three application servers: BEA's WebLogic, IBM's WebSphere, and Inprise Application Server.

> **TIP:** SUN provides an application server as part of SUN Open Net Environment (SUN ONE), which gives the foundation for enterprise-class application and Web Services. For more information take a look at http://wwws.sun.com/software/.

BEA's WebLogic Basics

WebLogic Server (WLS) contains Java 2 platform technologies. WLS is part of BEA's family of products and, as of this writing, the current version is WLS 7.0 with full support for J2EE 1.3. You can find information at www.bea.com. The BEA WebLogic Server has a three-layered architecture that separates the presentation, business logic, and the data connectivity. The next section presents a brief overview of this popular server.

A brief WLS overview

The WebLogic Server supports Web browsers, other clients that use HTTP, and clients that use *Remote Method Invocation* (RMI) or *Internet Inter-ORB Protocol* (IIOP). WLS supports

J2EE *Connector Architecture* (J2CA), which is a set of contracts for transactions, security, and connection management for EIS connectivity. Connectors are provided by BEA and other third-party companies to allow application integration. Also, WebLogic uses *Simple Object Access Protocol* (SOAP) as the message format and HTTP as the connection protocol.

WLS supports *eXtensible Markup Language* (XML) technology via an XML subsystem that supports standard parsers (and a built-in Apache Xerces), BEA XML editor, XSLT transformers, DTDs, and XML schemas. In addition, WLS implements *Java API for XML Processing* (JAXP) and provides a Web-based administration console for configuring and monitoring WLS services. Configuration is also possible with scripts.

WebLogic provides high availability via EJB components and clustering for dynamic Web pages, backend resource pooling, and connection sharing. It provides tight integration with and support for leading databases, development tools, and other environments. WebLogic provides support for transactions across EJB, JMS, J2CA, and JDBS and an infrastructure for transaction support. It also supports distributed transactions and two-phase commit, and implements *Java Transaction API* (JTA) for the transaction infrastructure. WLS also supports connectivity through CORBA as well as RMI-IIOP.

Understanding the basics of WLS security

WLS enables applications to incorporate security solutions into a pluggable security framework. WLS provides configuration and management via a security policy definition. The policy definition provides a framework and GUI tool for rule-based security criteria; this rule-based security is used to define roles and/or group of users that have access to secured resources. Rules are dynamically calculated and validated at runtime. In addition, WLS provides an administration console for configuring attributes of all applications and services, and captures statistics and audit logs (such as for authentication attempts and for invalid certificates) and manages features of the application server.

External security stores, such as *Lightweight Directory Access Protocol* (LDAP) servers, can be adapted to WebLogic realms, enabling single sign-on for the enterprise. A *security realm* is a logical grouping of users, groups, and *Access Control Lists* (ACLs); a security realm and a single ACL in that security realm protect a WLS resource. Users in a security realm can access resources in that security realm.

> **NOTE:** You use a security realm to define users, groups, and role information. This information can be stored in different types of storage such as an LDAP realm or a third-party realm. WLS v 7.0 provides a set of *Security Service Provider Interfaces* (SSPI) and specialized beans (Security SPI Mbeans) that allow you to write custom security products for WLS. In addition the WebLogic Server Administration Console allows you to modify some of the realm's information but, for more control, it is best if you extend and modify the provided classes.

WLS authenticates and authorizes users by checking the ACL and permissions in that realm and also provides a way to build customized security realms.

WebLogic Server ACLs are instantiated in the WLS at initialization, and realms have dynamic ACLs that can be added or modified without bringing down the server. Also, resources are defined to be protected in the deployment descriptor of the application. These resources include Enterprise JavaBeans, WebLogic Events, HTTP Servlets, and Java Server Pages.

> **TIP:** Using WLS v 7.0 you can use role-based authorization on non-J2EE resources (as well as J2EE ones). In addition, WLS provides a security policy editor.

WebLogic Server supports *Java Authentication and Authorization Service* (JAAS) as discussed in Chapter 19.

WLS has a Security Service Provider Interface that makes it possible to extend WebLogic Security services and to implement WebLogic Security features in applications. In addition, third-party security solutions can be integrated, such as external *Public Key Infrastructure* (PKI).

Data confidentiality is achieved with encryption used for data transfer over a network and communications privacy. WebLogic Server provides *Secure Sockets Layer* (SSL) support for encrypting data transmitted across WebLogic Server, clients, and other servers. WebLogic security realms feature user authentication and authorization for all WebLogic Server services. 128-bit encryption is supported, but restricted by U.S. trade laws.

WLS provides authentication — either with a username and password combination (via HTTP basic authentication, form based) or with a digital certificate (mutual authentication or digest) to permit access to users and deny access to unwanted intruders. WLS supports basic HTTP authentication with Base64 encoding for services protected by firewalls and HTTPS for SSL implementations. It also supports Web Services' end-to-end security model for protection of sensitive data passed from service to service via SOAP. Using WebLogic Server, you can configure one-way and two-way authentication using SSL in servlets and server-to-server SSL.

WLS also provides access control with user and group definitions. It allows the combination of authorized users into groups to set permissions for accessing application functions and services. You can control access to EJB methods as well.

In addition, WLS provides a built-in security data store for role, profile, and entitlement data using LDAP. WLS also supports JAAS for seamless security architecture across J2EE applications.

IBM's WebSphere Basics

IBM's WebSphere Application Server (WAS) (the current version is 4.0) is part of a large family of IBM products designed for e-business solutions. For more information you can visit the `www.ibm.com/software/webservers/appserv/` Web site.

WAS comes in two flavors: Standard and Advanced. Both provide support for Java Servlets, JavaBeans, JSP components, and provide support for *eXtensible Markup Language* (XML), and eXtensible Style Language (XSL).

The Standard edition contains an LDAP client for connection to an LDAP server, and the ACLs can be defined in a granular way at user and group levels. Controls and policies can be established for methods within the application.

The Advanced edition adds — among many other functionalities — "full" support of Web Services (SOAP, UDDI, WSDL, J2EE v 1.2), connectivity through CORBA and ActiveX, Message Beans and JMS Listener support, and internationalization (to accommodate time zones, currencies, and so on). The next section focuses on the Advanced edition.

A brief WAS overview

The *WAS Advanced Edition* (WASAE) architecture is based on the J2EE v 1.2 specification. It provides out-of-the-box support for most of the J2EE containers — the applet container is not included. However, you can configure WASAE by using the IBM Java 1.2.2 Runtime Environment (JRE).

A *WebSphere domain* consists of nodes that can be configured together; this configuration is kept in a single-shared WAS database. Each node may contain multiple application servers. Each server may contain a servlet container and an EJB container. Both of these containers run on a single JVM.

Here are some of the components and tools included in WASAE:

- ♦ The administrator's console, which is used to change the configuration of a WebSphere domain.
- ♦ The Web server, which listens by default on port 80 and supports servers such as IBM's HTTP server.
- ♦ XML Config, which allows the exportation/importation of configuration information to and from nodes. The deployment descriptors are XML files that contain information including security.

Understanding the basics of WAS security

WebSphere security is divided into global security and application security. The application security settings are specific for each application (and may override the global security settings). Global security is common for all applications running in the server and saved in XML configuration files. You can choose among three different user registries for authentication: LDAP, OS, or custom user registry. The user registry is a repository of users and groups. The application security settings (some of which are included in the web.xml file) can be customized using the *Application Assembly Tool* (AAT), the Administrator's Console, and the WebSphere Control Program tool. The configuration and management of application components are supported via these WAS tools as well.

The authentication mechanisms supported by WAS are HTTP basic authentication, HTTPS client authentication, and form-based authentication. You can configure these authentication mechanisms using the Application Assembly Tool.

> **NOTE:** As of this writing, digest authentication is not supported by the WebSphere Server.

WAS provides access controls, which are set using the WAS-provided tools such as the AAT. The Web containers and EJB containers get authentication and authorization services and delegation policies from the security server component of WLS. WebSphere provides method-level security.

WebSphere supports PKI for obtaining a personal certificate and SSL for secure communications. WAS supports SOAP services for Web security. WebSphere administrators may use the IBM `ikeyman` tool to create and manage digital certificates.

> **NOTE:** WAS ships with an `ikeyman` that supports the Java KeyStore (JKS) format.

Security policies (such as role and method permission, login configuration, and data integrity settings) are described in the deployment descriptor of the application. These are XML-based files that can be managed via an administration console. You can associate principals (users and groups) with roles. WLS also has a security collaborator (Web and EJB) that enforces the security constraints and attributes specified in the application deployment descriptors.

WebSphere has the capability to plug in a Reverse Proxy Security Server (RPSS) third-party authentication product. WAS communicates with the RPSS through a plug-in called a "Trust Association Interceptor" and you must implement the `com.ibm.websphere.security.TrustAssociationInterceptor` interface.

Borland's Enterprise Server Basics

Borland Enterprise Server v 5.0 provides an enterprise platform for distributed object technology using CORBA and J2EE components. The server is available in three editions:

- The Web Edition includes the open-source Apache Web Server (v 1.3), the open-source Tomcat Web container (v 4.0), the Smart Agent for object referencing and directory service, and Java Session Service (JSS) for recovery in case of container failure. In addition, it includes IIOP, Dreamweaver, and JDataStore.

- The VisiBroker Edition is primarily used for deploying CORBA components that communicate with non-Java objects. It includes all the features and services of the Web Edition and adds the VisiBroker ORB, the Naming Service (an implementation of JNDI), and the IIOP plug-in for CORBA. It is compliant with CORBA 2.4.

- The AppServer Edition allows Java and CORBA applications that implement the J2EE v 1.3 standard. It includes all features and services of the other two editions and adds an EJB container (for all necessary EJB services), Sonic MQ (a Java Messaging Service), and Borland Security Service. It provides a complete implementation of J2EE v 1.3 and

EJB v 2.0 standards, a support for Web Services, including SOAP and an XML toolkit, and legacy connectivity through CORBA, JCA, and JMS.

For more information you can visit www.inprise.com and www.borland.com/techpubs/.

A brief Borland's Enterprise Server overview

The Borland's Enterprise Server architecture enables you to create not only J2EE applications but also leverage the distributed services of CORBA.

The Borland's Enterprise Server provides a set of three core services:

- ◆ **Web Server:** This includes the Apache Web Server v 1.3 (an implementation of the HTTP protocol), and Borland added an IIOP plug-in to allow the Apache and Tomcat Web Container to communicate via IIOP. In addition, Borland provides Dreamweaver UltraDev plug-in for Web page development (using JSP and servlets).

- ◆ **Sonic MQ:** This is a full implementation of the JMS API and provides support for XML. It is hosted outside EJB containers (for multithread support) and is provided as its own application, which proxies requests to and from EJBs and the message service.

- ◆ **Smart Agent:** This is a distributed directory service provided by the VisiBroker ORB. More than one Smart Agent may be run on the network and if one Smart Agent crashes, all implementation registered with it will automatically register with another Smart Agent.

You can have many partitions. Each partition instance has a Web Container (Tomcat 4.0), an EJB Container (Borland's), a Transaction Service, a Session Service, a Naming Service, and a JDataStore. In addition, the AppServer Edition provides support for JNDI, RMI-IIOP, JDBC, servlets, JSP, JMS, JTA, Java Mail, JCA, JAAS, and JAXP.

Understanding the basics of Borland's Enterprise Server Security

The Management Console allows configuration and management of services and resources. For instance, you can manage servers on the network, and start and stop services and the like from this console. Also, you can access, manage, and set properties of EJB JAR files, *Enterprise Application Resources* (EARs), *Web Application Resources* (WARs), *Resource Adapters* (RARs), and monitor performance.

Deployment information is stored via XML deployment descriptor files. Via the deployment descriptor you can specify the security roles, method permissions, and links between them for an application. This provides access control to the application.

The Enterprise Server, in conjunction with the Borland Security Service, provides multiple levels of security, a console security-based management console, an SSL-based client security, and an implementation of JAAS. In addition, the security service incorporates WJB security with CORBASec security. The administration and configuration of security is provided by the Security Service via properties managed by a Security Services Administrator.

> **CROSS-REFERENCE:** Chapter 28 presents a brief description of CORBA and CORBA security.

The Security Service allows you to establish secure connections between clients and servers. It also integrates with the Web container to allow its own authentication and authorization mechanisms to propagate security information to other EJB containers if necessary. Borland Enterprise Server supports HTTP basic authentication, HTTP digest authentication, HTTPS client authentication, and form-based authentication.

Authentication and authorization is a JAAS implementation, and the authentication policy is determined by properties. The authentication can be achieved by the simple username and password combination or by a certificate. Security realms are defined and correspond to a JAAS `LoginModule`. Authorization is based on the user's identity and the ACLs.

> **NOTE:** Trust is handled like authentication. User-provided JSSE X509TrustManager is supported as well as Java KeyStores.

Authorization domains, which are security contexts used to set authorization permissions, can be established and associated with an EJB in its deployment description. There can be many authorization domains, but all of them need to be registered with the VisiBroker ORB.

Authorization in the CORBA environment allows only identities, in specific roles for a given object, to access that object. The access policy is specified in the protection policy for the *Portable Object Adapter* (POA).

In addition, the Security Service uses JSSE to perform SSL communication. SSL is used for message confidentiality, message integrity, and certificate-based authentication. Public-key encryption is available and digital signatures are supported.

The Borland Enterprise Server supports connectors via the JCA environment, which consists of the implementation of the JCA in the application server and the EIS-specific Resource Adapter. It supports transactions and two-phase commits.

Summary

This chapter presented the basics of BEA's WebLogic Server, IBM's WebSphere Server, and Borland's Enterprise Server, and how they handle security. These three servers are intensive, and it is out of the scope of this book to provide you with a detailed description of what they provide. This chapter gives you a taste of what these servers offer.

Although all three servers are based on the J2EE specification, there are differences among them. When selecting a server for your application you should consider what services the server provides and which one gives the best support for your needs.

Index

A

AAT (Application Assembly Tool), 674

absolute links, 623

acceptor, GSS-API, 354, 374-375
  interaction, implementing, 354-355
  tokens, 355-356

access controller, 384-392, 624
  guarded objects, 387-390
  principal-based, 402-404
  signed objects, 390-392

ACK flag, TCP, 449

ACL (Access Control List), 42, 578

ACLs (Access Control Lists), 426-428

activation, EJBs, 656

active attacks, 17-18
  operating systems, 31

addresses, IP addresses, 444-448

Aggressive mode, key exchange Phase 1, 134-135

AH (Authentication Header), IPSec, 129

AlgorithmParameterGenerator class, 164

AlgorithmParameters class, 164, 293

AlgorithmParameterSpec class, 144

algorithms
  cryptographic algorithms, 140
  differential cryptanalysis, 261
  DSS, 233-237
  ECDSA, 238-239
  hash algorithms, collision resistance, 194
  MD algorithms, 194-204
    implementation, 217-218
    RIPEMD-160, 216-217
    SHA-1 algorithm, 205-216

MD, breakdown, 192-193
MDs and, 191

aliases, 165

APIs (Application Program Interfaces), 39, 114
  Java-based, UDDI and, 612
  UDDI API, 612
  sniffers and, 19

applets, 604
  security, 625-626

Application Component Providers, authentication and, 621-623

application object access, CORBA, 651

application security, 671
  WLS, 671-673

application-level gateway, firewalls, 466-467

application-managed resource manage signon, J2EE, 658

application-managed sign-on, databases, 435-436

AppServer Edition, Borland Enterprise Server, 675

ARP (Address Resolution Protocol), 457

AS (Authentication Server), 338

assurance requirements, CC and, 329-330

asymmetric ciphers, 257

asymmetric encryption, databases, 439

asymmetric keys, 70, 140

attacks
  active, operating systems, 31
  denial of service attacks, 23
  dictionary attacks, 22
  hack attacks
    active, 17-18
    denial of service attacks, 17
    passive, 15-16

sniffers, 16
types, 4-5, 15-18
weapons against, 5
network attacks, 19
monitoring terms, 19
sniffers, 19-21
SSL and, 498-499
viruses, 32-33
auditing, 660
authentication, 6
Application Component Providers, 621-623
components, 47-50
CORBA, 648
credentials, 40
definition, 401
form-based, 622
HMAC, 219
HTTP basic authentication, 622
HTTPS mutual authentication, 622
J2EE components, 658-659
JAAS, 375-418
Kerberos and, 338
Kerberos Server, 47
layers, 41
lazy authentication, 623
MAC, 219-221
mutual, 50
mutual authentication, 338
one-way, 50
PAM, 404-418
principals, 6
principals and, 402
public key, 53
server challenges, 137
server responses, 137
SSL, 497-498
stacked, 407
two-phase process, 414-415
validation and, 6
Web-tier configuration, 622-623
Authenticator, 346
Authenticator class, 481
authenticator, TGS Service tickets, 342
authorization, 7-8
components, 50, 51

CORBA, 648
definition, 401
J2EE components, 659
JAAS, 418-428
layers, 41
permissions, 41-42
principals, 41-42

B

backdoor, 23
viruses, 33-34
Bastion Host
DMZs, 468
dual-homed hosts, 469
packet filtering and, 467
BBS (Bulletin Board Systems), 31
BigInteger class, 80
binding, 617
block algorithms, 259-260
block ciphers, Blowfish, 310-311
Blowfish, 310-311
plaintext files, 313-316
S-boxes and, 311
subkeys and, 311
boot sector viruses, 32
Borland Enterprise Server, 675-677
brute force attacks, DES and, 104
business object, RMI, 652

C

CA (Certificate Authority), 538
components, 583-584
Intermediate CA, 576
path length, 576
PKI and, 575
callbacks, CallbackHandler, 416-417
caller principals, 422
capturing keystrokes, 14
CBC (Cipher Block Chaining), 261
CC (Common Criteria), 327
assurance requirements, 329-330
functional requirements, 328-329
ISO and, 327

origins, 327
CCI (Common Client Interface), 437
certificate alternative names extensions, X.509
      version 3, 554-556
certificate chains, 541
certificate constraints X509Certificate, X.509
      version 3, 556
Certificate message, 492
CertificateFactory class, 164
certificates, 10
    certificate chaining, 576-577
    path validation, 584-594
    revocation, 556-560
      CRL entry, 571-573
      CRL extensions, 559-570
    trusted certificate entries, 165
    validation, 557
CertPath class, 585
challenges, server authentication, 137
channels, 481-484
    transparent, 490
checkPermission( ) method, 385
child entry, DIB, 578
Chinese Remainder Theorem. See CRT, 237
choke points, networks, 463
Cipher Block Chaining. See CBC, 261
cipher engine initialization, 291
ciphers, 257
    asymmetric ciphers, 257
    block ciphers, Blowfish, 310-311
    PKI and, 317-319
    proprietary information, 317
    RC4 stream ciphers, implementation, 299-
      303
    symmetric ciphers, 257-265
    X.509 and, 317-319
CipherSpi class
    implementation, 289-298
    IV and, 290
ciphertext, 53
    confidentiality and, 9
    ECB ciphers, 263
    keys and, 65
circuit-level gateway, firewalls, 465-466
class loader, 382-383

classes
    AlgorithmParameter, 293
    AlgorithmParameterSpec, 144
    Authenticator, 481
    BigInteger, 80
    built-in permission classes, 603-604
    CertPath, 585
    CipherSpi, 289-298
    ClassLoader, 383
    Client_Socket, 475-476
    DHSimpleApp class source code, 72-80
    ECCKeyFactory source code, 119-123
    ECCKeyPairGenerator source code, 123-
      126
    ECCProvider source code, 115
    ECCSimpleApp source code, 116-118
    engine classes, 143
    EngineSpi, 144
    FilePermission, 179-181
    GetProviderInfo source code, 95-96
    InetAddress, 474
    java.math.BigInteger, 70
    KerberosTicket, 350
    KeyGenerator, 141
    KeyPairGenerator, 143
    KeyStore, 164-167
    LoginContext, 406-418
    LoginModule, 406-418
    MessageDigest class, 56-57
    Order_Skeleton, 652
    Order_Stub, 652
    PBEParameterSpec, 306
    Permission class, 385
    PKIXCertPathValidatorResult, 594-595
    PKIXParameters, 591-592
    Provider, 289
    PublicKey, 142
    RichCertificate class, 542-545
    RichMAC, 221-229
    RichProvider, 298
    RMIClassLoader, 654
    RSASimpleApp source code, 96-103
    SecureRandom, 148
    Server_Socket, 477-478
    SocketChannel, 481-484

SocketClient, 454-456
SocketImpl, 479
SocketPermission, 57
SocketServer, 451-454
SSLServer, 516-522
ClassLoader class, 383
ClassLoader interface, 383
CLASSPATH, class loader and, 382
Client tier, J2EE, 433
client/server authentication, TGS, 344
Client_Socket class, 475-476
ClientKeyExchange, pre_master_secret, 493
clients, defined, 444
client-side security, 624-625
    applets, 625-626
    application security, 625
    code example, 630-643
    servlets, 627-628
    web.xml file, 626-627
CN (common name), 539
codeBase property, 180
collision resistance
    hash algorithms, 194
    message digests and, 489
collisions, 190
commands
    DEBUG, 28
    Kerberos, 347-349
commit function, JAAS, 350
component models, enterprise, 604
components, 46-56
    authentication and, 47-50
    authorization and, 50-51
    CAs, 583-584
    confidentiality and, 52-54
    credentials and, 47-49
    EJBs, security configuration, 659-660
    element use components, 46
    GSS-API, 357-374
    integrity and, 54-56
    keys and, 53
        implementation, 52
    KeyStore, 46
    MessageDigest class, 56-57
    permissions

    implementation, 51
    validation, 51
principals, 47-49
    implementation, 51
    validation, 51
security operation components, 46
confidentiality, 8, 487
    components and, 52-54
    keys, 42-43
configuration
    component security, EJBs, 659-660
    Kerberos files, 349-350
connection management, Connector API, 437
connection-oriented Sockets, 479
connections
    socket connections, 504
    sockets, 504
    SSL, 495-498
Connector architecture, databases, 436-439
container-managed resource manager signon,
        J2EE, 658
container-managed sign-on, databases, 435
content type, SSL Record, 494
context tokens, GSS-API, 355
Context.listBindings( ), JNDI, 619
Context.lookup( ), JNDI, 619
contexts, 617
    subcontexts, 617
conversatinal state, EJBs, 656
cookies, JSPs, 27
coordinate system, elliptic curves and, 110
CORBA (Common Object Request Broker
        Architecture), 604-645
    application object access, 651
    delegation, 649
    IDL, 646
    message encryption, 648
    message integrity, 648
    non-repudiation, 649
    ORB, 646-648
    principals, 651
    Project EJB access, 669-670
    remote invokation requests, 647
    security overview, 648-650
    services, 647-648

crackers, password crackers, 22-23
cracks, encryption, 26
cracks in system, 16
CRC (Cyclic Redundancy Code), 191
credentials, 40-41
    authentication and, 6
    components and, 47-49
    JAAS, 422
    validation, 49-50
CRL (Certificate Revocation List), 541
CRL entry certificate revocation, 571-573
CRL extensions, certificate revocation, 559-
        570
CRT (Chinese Remainder Theorem), 237
    RSA and, 93
cryptographic algorithms, 140
crytography, differential cryptanalysis, 261
CSD (Circuit Switched Data), 501
CSMA/CD (Carrier Sense Multiple
        Access/Carrier Detection) protocol,
        450
CTCPEC (Canadian Computer Product
        Evaluation Criteria), 327
Cyclic Redundancy Code. See CRC, 191

D

data integrity, 189
    hash functions, 190
data transfer phase, SSL handshake, 490-493
database security, 433-434
databases
    access types, 433
    application-managed sign-on, 435-436
    connecting, JDBC and, 434-436
    connections, Connector architecture, 436-
        439
    container-managed sign-on, 435
    declarative access, 436
    enterprise data, 439
    resource sign-on, 434
    security context, 434
DatagramSocket, 480
DEBUG command, 28
debugging, 28

declarative access, databases, 436
declarative authorization, 659
decryption, public keys, 164
De-Militarized Zones. See DMZs, 468
denial of service attacks, 17, 23
DES (Data Encryption Standard), 103-104, 305
    brute-force attacks and, 104
    EFF attacks, 104
    modes of operation, 262
    S-boxes
        size, 261
    Triple DES key, 104-106
DH (Diffie-Hellman) algorithm, 54, 488
    man-in-the-middle attacks, 80-92
DH (Diffie-Hellman) key exchange, 70-72
    example, source code, 71
    implementation, 72-80
    DHSimpleApp class, source code, 72-78
        output, 78-80
DIB (Directory Information Base), 578-580
    groups, 579
    namespaces, 579
dictionary attacks, 22
differential cryptanalysis, 261
Diffie-Hellman. See DH
digests, 44-46
digital certificate message, 537
digital certificates, 537
    certificate chains, 541
    DN, 538
    non-repudiation, 595-596
    overview, 537-538
    revoking, 556-560
        CRL entry, 571-573
        CRL extensions, 559-570
    self-signed certificates, 541-550
    signatures, 540
    subject, 537
    transfer management, 537
    validation, 557
    X.500, 538
    X.509 specification, 540
        LDAP service and, 540
digital signature, 54
Digital Signature Algorithm. See DSA

Digital Signature Standards. *See* DSS
digital signatures, 55, 231-232, 488
   direct digital signatures, 489
   DSS and, 232
   legal issues, 56
   NIST and, 232
   PKI and, 231
   XML digital signatures, 607-611
direct digital signatures, 489
directory services, 617-621
discrete logarithmic functions, 66
distributed objects, 599
DIT (Directory Information Tree), 579
DMZs (De-Militarized Zones), 468-470
DN (distinguished name)
   digital certificates, 538
   X.500 and, 539, 578-580
DNS (Domain Name Service), 21, 444, 580
   IP address mapping, 28
   IP addresses and, 446
doAs method, JAAS, 403
doPrivileged( ) method, 385-386
DSA (Digital Signature Algorithm), 140-141
   KeyPairGenerator, methods, 142
   implementation, 239-254
DSAs (Directory Service Agents), 579
DSI (Dynamic Skeleton Interface), 655
DSS (Digital Signature Standard), 232-237,
   488
DUA (Directory User Agent), 579
dual-homed hosts, 469

E

EAI (Enterprise Application Integration)
   systems, 436
EARs (Enterprise Application Resources),
   Borland and, 676
ECB (Electronic CodeBook Mode), 261
ECB ciphers, 263
ECC (Elliptic Curve Cryptography), 109
   mathematics behind, 111-113
ECC key exchange, 113-114
   implementation, as SPI, 114-126

ECCDH (ECC Diffie-Hellman) key exchange,
   113-114
ECCKeyFactory class source code, 119-123
ECCKeyPairGenerator class source code, 123-
   126
ECCProvider class source code, 115
ECCSimpleApp class source code, 116-118
ECDLP (Elliptic Curve Discrete Logarithm
   Problem), 111
ECDSA (Elliptic Curve Digital Signature
   Algorithm), 238-239
EEPROM (Electronically Erasable
   Programmable Read Only Memory),
   320
EFF (Electronic Frontier Foundation), DES
   attacks, 104
EIS (Enterprise Information Systems) tier,
   J2EE, 433
EJB containers, 655
EJB server, 655
EJBHome interface, 655
EJBs (Enterprise Java Beans), 402-418, 645,
   655-660
   component security configuration, 659-660
   entity beans, 657
   session beans, 656-657
Electronic CodeBook Mode. *See* ECB
element use components, 46
Elliptic Curve Cryptography. *See* ECC
Elliptic Curve Digital Signature Algorithm. *See*
   ECDSA
elliptic curves
   coordinate system, 110
   scalar multiplication, 111
encrypted payload, 493
encryption
   ciphertext, 53
   cracks to, 26
   Kerberos, support, 339
   keys, 140
   MD and, 191
   plaintext, 53
   private keys, 164
   public key, RSA, implementation, 266-285
   XML, 611

encryption algorithms, prime numbers, 235
encryption components, GSS-API, 369-374
ENC-TKT-IN-SKEY option, TGS, 341
end-point authentication, 487
engine classes, 143
EngineSpi class, 144
enigma machine, 257
enterprise component models, 604
Enterprise Information Systems. *See* EIS
Enterprise JavaBeans tier, 433
entity beans, 657
ESP (Encapsulating Security Payload), IPSec, 129
Extended Java Sandbox, 601

F

FAT (File Allocation Table), viruses and, 33
Federal Information Processing Standards. *See* FIPS
fields, tickets, TGS, 344-345
file system, 25
    debugging, 28
    sniffing, 25-28
    unsafe memory, 27-28
FileInputStream, security manager, 384
FilePermission class, 179-181
FilePermission type, 42
filters
    port filtering, 473
    protocol filtering, 473
FIN flag, TCP, 449
finishConnect( ) function, 482
FIPS (Federal Information Processing Standards), 205
firewalls, 463-465
    application-level gateway, 466-467
    circuit-level gateway, 465-466
    DMZs, 468-470
    FTP anonymous user, 464
    packet filtering, 467-468
    proxies, 470-473
Fluke LanMeter sniffer, 20
form-based authentication, 622
FORWARDABLE flag, TGS, 343

four pillars of security, 6-10
FQN (Fully Qualified Name), 338
FTP (File Transfer Protocol), 20-21
    anonymous user, firewalls and, 464
Fully Qualified Name. *See* FQN
functional requirements, CC and, 328-329
functions
    finishConnect( ), 482
    getAllByName( ), 474
    getInstance, 166
    getSystemKey( ), 14
    hash functions, MD and, 190-193
    KeyStore, 166
    receive( ), 480
    send( ), 480
    shutdownInput( ), 482
    SocketChannel.open( ), 482
    validate( ), 557
    XOR, 45

G

generating key pairs, 141-157
    implementation, 143-144
    initialization, 152-157
    service providers, 145-146
generating keys, 139-140
    secret keys, 141, 157-160
getAddress function, 481
getAllByName( ) function, 474
getCallerPrincipal, 436
getExtendedValue( ) method, 551
getInstance function, 166
getInstance( ) method, 163
getMIC method, GSS-API, 355
getPort function, 481
GetProviderInfo class source code, 95-96
getSystemKey( ) function, 14
GID (group identification number), 48
GIOP (General Inter-ORB protocol), 647
GIOP (General Inter-ORB Protocol), 471
grant entries, 179-181
    permissions, 385
    policies, 392-398
groups

DIB, 579
JAAS, 423
GSS-API (Generic Security Service-Application Program Interface), 47, 339, 353
   acceptor, 354
      implementation, 354-355
      tokens, 355-356
   acceptors, 374-375
   benefits of, 356-357
   component model, 357-374
   encryption components, 369-374
   getMIC method, 355
   initiator, 354, 374-375
      implementation, 354-355
      tokens, 355-356
   management components, 357-367
   naming components, 367-368
   overview, 354-357
   QOP and, 357
   security context components, 368-369
   unwrap method, 355
   verifyMIC method, 355
GSSCredential interface, 367
GSSManager object, 357-367
GSSName interface, 367
guarded objects, access controller, 387-390

H

hack attacks
   active attacks, 17-18
   cracks in system, 16
   denial of service attacks, 17
   finding hack, 14-15
   IT impersonations, 23-25
   keyboard sniffers, 14-15
   passive attacks, 15-16
   protection from, 35-36
   registery, 26
   replay attacks, 15
   sniffers, 14-16
   social engineering, 15
   types, 4-5, 15-18
   weapons against, 5

hackers, 4
   password crackers, 22-23
   utilities used, 21-25
handshake, SSL, 490-493
   client initiation, 492
hash algorithms, high collision resistance, 194
hash functions, 190
   MD (message digest) and, 190-193
hashed information blocks, 10
hashes, 44-46
   message digests and, 55
   one-way hashes, 192
   secure hashes, 190
HMAC (hash message authentication code), 219
home interface, EJBs, 655
hosts, impersonating, 28
HTTP/SSL comparison, 499
HTTP basic authentication, 622
HTTP digest authentication, 623
HTTP server, DMZs and, 468
HTTP tunneling, 473-474
HTTPS mutual authentication, 622
HttpsUrlConnection, 532-533
HW-AUTHENT flag, TGS, 342

I

ICMP (Internet Control Message Protocol), 458
identities, Kerberos and, 338
IDL (Interface Definition Language), CORBA, 646
IETF (Internet Engineering Task Force), 129, 488
IIOP (Internet Inter-ORB Protocol), 647
   RMI-IIOP, 654-655
   WLS and, 672
IKE (Internet Key Exchange), IPSec and, 130
impersonating hosts, 28
implementation
   CipherSpi class, 289-298
   DH key exchange, 72-80
   DSA, 239-254
   ECC key exchange as SPI, 114-126

key pairs, 143-144
keys, components and, 52
MAC, 221-229
MD algorithms, 217-218
permissions, components and, 51
principals, components and, 51
RC4 stream cipher, 299-303
RSA key exchange, 94-103
RSA public key encryption, 266-285
Indirect CRLs, 558
InetAddress class, 474
init( ) method, 627
InitialContext, JNDI, 619
initialization
cipher engine, 291
keys, 146-157
random numbers, 147
seed, 147-152
specifics, 152-157
initialize( ) method, 146-157
initiating principals, 422
initiators
GSS-API, 354, 374-375
interaction, implementing, 354-355
tokens, 355-356
IKE protocol (SAs), 133
inner header, tunnel mode (IPSec), 131
inner pad, HMAC and, 220
integers, 66
integrity, 9-10
components and, 54-56
digests, 44-46
hashes, 44-46
message digests, 54
interactions, SSLContext, 510
interfaces
ClassLoader, 383
GSSCredential, 367
GSSName, 367
Service Provider interface, 289
Web Services, WSDL and, 612-614
Intermediate CAs, 576-577
Internet Engineering Task Force. *See* IETF
IP (Internet Protocol), 129
IP addresses

DNS and, 446
mapping, 28
networks, 444-448
IP packets, 447
IP spoofing, 29-30
IPSec (IP security protocol), 129-130
AH and, 129
ESP and, 129
IKE and, 130
ISAKMP, 130
transport mode, 131
tunnel mode, 131
irreversibility, message digests and, 489
ISAKMP (Internet Security Association Key
Management Protocol), IPSec and,
130
ISO (International Organization for
Standardization), 327
isolation, 57
isProbablePrime method, 235
IT impersonations, 23-25
ITSEC (Information Technology Security
Evaluation Criteria), 327
IV (initialization vector), XOR function and,
263-265
CipherSpi class and, 290
PBE and, 306

J

J2CA, WLS and, 672
J2EE
authentication and, 658-659
authorization and, 659
security model, 602-603
J2SDK security model, 601-602
JAAS (Java Authentication and Authorization
Service), 47, 350-351, 401-402, 673
authentication, 375-378
authorization, 418-428
commit function, 350
configuration, setup, 417-418
credentials, 422
EJBs and, 402-418
groups, 423

JSPs and, 402-418
LoginModule, 350
permissions, 424-426
principals, 350, 422
subject, 350
subjects, 421-423
JAASAction class, 419-420
JAR (Java Archive), 31
jarsigner tool, 175-178
jarsigner utility, 31
Java
    APIs, UDDI and, 612
    servlets, WAS and, 674
Java API, principals, 47
Java Card Application Programming Interface.
    See JVAPI
Java Card Runtime Environment. *See* JCRE
Java Card Virtual Machine. *See* JCVM
Java Cryptography Extensions. *See* JCE
Java Protected Domain Security model, 601
Java smart cards, 319-323
java.math.BigInteger class, 70
JavaBeans, 604
JavaKeyStore, 165
JavaSockets, 474-484
javax.crypto.KeyGenerator class, 142
javax.crypto.SecretKey object, 142
JAXP (Java API for XML Processing), WSL
    and, 672
JCAPI (Java Card Application Programming
    Interface), 321
JCE (Java Cryptography Extension), 267, 289
JCRE (Java Card Runtime Environment), 321
JCVM (Java Card Virtual Machine), 321
jdb utility, 28
JDBC, database connections, 434-436
JKS (Java KeyStore), 538
JNDI (Java Naming and Directory Interface),
    470, 618-620
    Context.listBindings( ), 619
    Context.lookup( ), 619
    InitialContext, 619
    NamingEvent, 620
    packages, 619
    security manager and, 620-621

JRE (Java RuntimeEnvironment), 382
JSPs (Java Server Pages), 402-418, 604, 628-
    630
    cookies, 27
    state, 630
JSSE (Java Secure Socket Enterprise), 47, 503-
    533
    architecture, 505
    providers, 509
    SSL client sockets, 522-531
    SSLServerSockets, 515-522
JTA (Java Transaction API), 672
JVM, SecurityManager, 382

K

KDC (Key Distribution Center), 338
    primary names and, 338
    principals and, 338-346
kdestroy command, Kerberos, 347
Kerberos, 337
    Authenticator (*see* Authenticator)
    commands, 347-349
    configuration files, 349-350
    JAAS, 350-351
    kdestroy command, 347
    kinit command, 347
    klist command, 347
    kpasswd command, 347
    ksu command, 347
    PD, 346-350
    version 4 vs version 5, 338
Kerberos principal, 48
Kerberos Server, 47
KerberosTicket class, 350
key agreement, 53, 64
key capture, 14
key entries, 165
    keytool, TrustManager, 169
key exchanges, phases, 134-135
key extensions, X.509 version 3, 550-553
key management, 163
    KeyStore class, 164-167
    SPIs and, 164
key material, 139

key pairs, 43, 53, 63-65, 140
    generation, 141-157
        implementation, 143-144
        initialization, 152-157
        service providers, 145-146
    keytool, 53
    logarithms, 66-70
    service providers, 145-146
    SPIs, 143
keyboard sniffers, 14-15
KeyFactory class, 164
KeyGenerator class, 141
KeyManager, 165
KeyPairGenerator, 94-103
    methods, 142-143
KeyPairGenerator class, 143, 164
KeyPairGeneratorSpi, 143
keys, 42-43
    asymmetric, 70
    asymmetric keys, 140
    ciphertext, 65
    components and, 52-53
    cryptographic algorithms, 140
    DES, 103-104
    DH key exchange, 70-80
    ECC key exchange, 113-114
    ECCDH, 113-114
    encryption, 140
    future of key exchanges, 106-107
    generation, 139-140
    initialization, 146-157
        random numbers, 147
        seed, 147-152
        specifics, 152-157
    plaintext, 65
    purpose of, 62-65
    RSA key exchange, 92-103
    secret keys, 140
        generating, 157-160
    symmetric, 70
        RSA key exchange, 103
    symmetric keys, 140
keystore, 53
KeyStore class, 164-167
KeyStore component, 46

KeyStore( ) function, 166
keytool, key pairs and, 53
kinit command, Kerberos, 347
klist command, Kerberos, 347
kpasswd command, Kerberos, 347
KRB_AS_REP message, 340
KRB_ERROR message, 340
ksu command, Kerberos, 347

L

LANs (Local Area Networks), 444
layers, 41
    SSL, 490-495
lazy authentication, 623
LDAP (Lightweight Directory Access
        Protocol), 49, 129, 538, 577
    RDBMS, 581
    X.500, 581-583
    X.509 specification and, 540
LDAP SDK, 581
legal issues, 56
logarithms, 66-70
logic bombs, 33-34
login module, JAAS client, 49
LoginContext class, PAM, 406-418
LoginModule clsss, PAM, 406-418
LoginModule, JAAS, 350

M

MAC (message authentication code), 54-55,
        219-221, 490
    encrypted payload, 493
    implementation, 221-229
macro viruses, 32
Main mode, key exchange Phase 1, 134-135
management components, GSS-API, 357-367
man-in-the-middle attacks, DH and, 80-92
MANs (Metropolitan Area Networks), 444
master_secret, 491
mathematics
    ECC and, 111-113
    key pairs, 65-70
    modular arithmetic, 112

MD (message digest)
  algorithm breakdown, 192-193
  algorithms, 191
  differentiating MDs, 192
  encryption and, 191
  hash functions and, 190-193
  HMAC and, 220
MD algorithms, 194-204
  implementation, 217-218
  RIPEMD-160, 216-217
MDBs (message driven beans), 657
message digests, 54, 489
  digital signatures, 54-55
  hashes and, 55
  MAC (message authentication code), 54-55
message encryption, 660
  CORBA, 648
message integrity, 487, 659
  CORBA, 648
message tokens, GSS-API, 355
MessageDigest class, 56-57, 164
messages, MAC, 219-221
messages digests, MACs, 490
methods
  checkPermission( ), 385
  doAs, 403
  doPrivileged( ), 385-386
  getExtendedValue( ), 551
  getInstance( ), 163
  init( ), 627
  initialize( ), 146-157
  isProbablePrime, 235
  KeyPairGenerator, 142-143
  service( ), 627
  setMessageDrivenContext, 657
  setSeed( ), 148
  verify, 238
MGF (mask generation function), 267
modular arithmetic, 112
modular exponential, 66
mutual authentication, 50
  Kerberos and, 338

N

namespaces, DIB, 579
naming components, GSS-API, 367-368
naming conventions, 618
naming services, 617
NamingEvent, JNDI, 620
needs assessment for security, 330-332
netstat utility, 23
network attacks, 19
  monitoring terms, 19
  sniffers, 19-21
  spoofing, IP spoofing, 29-30
networks
  choke point, 463
  CSMA/CD protocol, 450
  HTTP tunneling, 473-474
  IP addresses, 444-448
  port numbers, 448
  ports, 448
  routing, 457-463
  security
    architecture, 443-444
    overview, 444
  TCP, 448-457
  topology, 447
NICs (Network Interface Cards), 474
NIST (National Institute of Standards and
      Technology), digital signatures and,
      232
nonce, TGS, 342
non-repudiation, 333, 595-596
  CORBA, 649
NSA (National Security Agency), 232

O

OAEP (Optimal Asymmetric Encryption
      Padding), 267
obfuscation, confidentiality and, 8
objects
  distributed objects, 599
  GSSManager, 357-367
  guarded, access controller, 387-390
  SecretKey, 142

signed objects, access controller, 390-392
OFB (Output Feedback), 261
Off-Card Verifier, Java Smart Cards, 321-323
OID (Object Identifier), 47
OMG (Object Management Group), 600, 646
one-way authentication, 50
one-way hashes, 192
operating systems attacks, 31
operations, MD algorithm breakdown, 192
ORB (Object Request Broker), 471, 646-648
Order_Skeleton class, 652
Order_Stub class, 652
OSI (Open Systems Interconnection), 450
OSPF (Open Shortest Path First), 463
OU (organizational unit), 539
outer header, tunnel mode (IPSec), 131
outer pad, HMAC and, 220
Output Feedback. *See* OFB

P

packages, JNDI API, 619
packet filtering, 467-468
packet sniffing, 467
packets
    transport mode, IPSec, 131
    tunnel mode, IPSec, 131
PAM (Pluggable Authentication Module), 404-418
parasitic viruses, 32
passivated, EJBs, 656
passive hack attacks, 15-16
Password Based Encryption. *See* PBE
password crackers, 22-23
path length, CAs, 576
path validation, certificates and, 584-594
PBE (Password Based Encryption), 139, 305-310
PBEParameterSpec class, 306
PCT (Private Communications Technology), 488
PD (Principal Database), 346-350
PEM (Privacy Enhanced Email), digital signatures and, 232
Permission class, 385

permission collection, 397-398
permissions, 41-42, 603
    built-in classes, 603-604
    components and
        implementation and, 51
        validation and, 51
    grant entries, 385
    JAAS, 424-426
    policy files, 179-181
pillars of security, 6-10
ping output, 459
ping utility, 21
PKCS #12 (Public Key Cryptography Standard) KeyStore, 168
PKI (Public Key Infrastructure), 54, 106, 538, 575-576
    ciphers and, 317-319
    digital signatures and, 231
    path validation, certificates, 584
    TA and, 575
PKIXCertPathValidatorResult class, 594-595
PKIXParameters class, 591-592
plaintext, 53
    Blowfish, 313-316
    confidentiality and, 9
    keys and, 65
POA (Portable Object Adapter), 655
POA-based DSI servants, 655
policies, 392-398
policy domains, 554
policy files, 179-181
policy mapping extensions, X.509 version 3, 553-554
policytool utility, 181-185
polymorphic viruses, 32
port filtering, 473
port numbers, 448
port scanners, 23
ports, 448
    netstat utility, 23
    sockets, 449
pre_master_secret, 491
PRE-AUTHENT flag, TGS, 342
PRF (pseudo-random function), 491
primary names, KDC and, 338

prime numbers, 70
  encryption algorithms, 235
principal names, Kerberos and, 339
principal property, 180
principal store, Kerberos, 338
principals
  access control and, 402-404
  authentication and, 6, 402
  authorization, 41-42
  components and, 47-49
    implementation, 51
    validation, 51
  CORBA, 651
  JAAS, 350, 422
  Java API, 47
  KDC and, 338-346
  Kerberos, 48
  user principals, 40
  validation, 49-50
Private Communications Technology. See PCT
private keys
  encryption, 164
  key pairs, 53
private ports, 448
privilege delegation, CORBA, 649
PRNGs (Pseudo-Random Number Generators),
    147, 163
probabilistic primality testing,, 234
processes, ps utility, 23
programmatic access control, 436
programmatic authorization, 659
Project Info App
  client-side security
    design, 631
    user authentication, 631-634
    user requests, 636-643
    web.xml file, 634-636
  ProjectBean code, 660-670
ProjectEJB
  CORBA access, 669-670
  RMI access, 667-669
ProjectHome.java source code, 660-661
properties
  codeBase, 180
  principal, 180

proprietary information, ciphers and, 317
protection, hack attacks, 35-36
protection domains, 658
protocol filtering, 473
protocols
  ARP, 457
  CSMA/CD, 450
  GIOP (General Inter-ORB Protocol), 471
  ICMP, 458
  IPSec, 129-131
  OSI and, 450
  RIP, 457
  SOCKS, 481
  SSL Handshake protocol, 490-493
  TCP, 448-457
  UDP, 448-457
Provider class, 289
PROXIABLE flag, TGS, 343
proxies, 469
  firewalls and, 470-473
proximity cards, 106
ps utility, 23
pseudocode, secret key cipher, 65
pseudo-random function. See PRF
PSH flag, TCP, 449
public key authentication, 53
public key encryption, RSA, 266-285
public keys, decryption, 164
PublicKey class, 142

Q-R

QOP (Quality of Protection), GSS-API and, 357
Quick mode, key exchange Phase 2, 134-136

RA (Registration Authority), 584
random numbers, 70
  key initialization, 147
  PRNGs, 147
  seed, 147-152
RARs (Resource Adapters), Borland and, 676
RC4 stream cipher, implementation, 299-303
RDBMS (Relational Database Management
    Systems), 434, 581
realm, Kerberos, 338

receive( ) function, 480
registered ports, 448
registry, hack attacks and, 26
Relational Database Management Systems. *See*
       RDBMS
relative links, 623
remote invokation requests, CORBA, 647
RENEWABLE-OK option, Kerberos TGS, 341
renew-till field, TGS, 341
replay attacks, 15
replication, UDDI, 612
resource sign-on, databases, 434
responders, IKE protocol (SAs), 133
responses, servers, 137
revoking certificates, 556-560
    CRL entry, 571-573
    CRL extensions, 559-570
RichCertificate class, 542-545
RichMAC class source code, 221-229
    output, 229
RichProvider class source code, 298
RIP (Routing Information Protocol), 457
RIPEMD-160 algorithm, 216-217
RIPEMD-160 protocol, 194
Rivest, Shamir and Adleman key exchange.
    See RSA key exchange
RMI (Remote Method Invocation), 645
    Project EJB access, 667-669
    security overview, 653-654
    skeleton, 652
    stubs, 652
    WLS and, 672
RMI (Remote Method Interface), 604
RMI protocol, 651-652
RMIClassLoader, 654
RMIClient.java source code, 668
RMI-IIOP, 654-655
RMISecurityManager, 653
Root CA, 576
rounds, MD algorithm breakdown, 192
routing, networks, 457-463
RPSS (Reverse Proxy Security Server), 675
RSA public key encryption implementation,
    266-285
RSA digital signature. *See* RSA ds

RSA ds (RSA digital signature) overview, 237-
    238
RSA key exchange, 92-94
    CRT and, 93
    implementation, 94-103
    symmetric keys, 103
RSA Security, 92
RSASimpleApp class source code, 96-102
    output, 102-103
RST flag, TCP, 449

S

SADB (SA Database), 132
salting, 139
sandbox security model, 600-601
SAs (Security Associations), 132-133
SASL (Simple Authentication and Security
    Layer), 129, 136-137, 582
S-boxes
    Blowfish, 311
    size, 261
scalar multiplication, elliptic curves, 111
schemas, JNDI, 620
SDK (Software Development Kit)
    LDAP, 581
    X.500, 580
SECIOP (Secure Inter-ORB Protocol), 648
secret key, 140
    generation, 141, 157-160
    HMAC, 220
    MAC and, 219-221
SecretKey object, 142
secure hashes, 190
secure transport, XML, 606
SecureRandom class, 148, 164
security
    four pillars of, 6-10
    needs assessment, 330-332
    requirements fulfillment, 332-336
Security Associations. *See* SAs
security context components, GSS-API, 368-369
security context, databases, 434
security elements, categories, 40-45
security manager, 383-384

security mangement, Connector API, 437
security models, 600
    J2EE, 602-603
    J2SDK, 601-602
    sandbox model, 600-601
security operation components, 46
security realms, 672
Security Requirements for Cryptographic
    Modules, 163
SecurityException, 382
SecurityManager
    JVM and, 382
    principal-based access control, 402-404
self-signed certificates, 541-550
send( ) function, 480
Server_Socket class, 477-478
servers
    challenges, 137
    EJB server, 655
    responses, 137
ServerSocket, 476
Service Provider Interface, 289
service providers, key pair generation, 145-146
Service tickets (TGS), process modifications,
    342-343
service( ) method, 627
services, 444
servlets, 604
    client-side security, 627-628
    WAS and, 674
SESAME (Secure European System for
    Application in Multi-vendor
    Environment), 353
session beans, EJBs, 656-657
sessions
    socket sessions, 504
    sockets, 504
    SSL, 495-498
setMessageDrivenContext method, 657
setSeed( ) method, 148
SHA-1 algorithm, 205-216
SHA-1 protocol, 194
shutdownInput( ) function, 482
SID, WinNT, 48
Signature class, 164

signatures
    digital certificates, 540
    digital signatures, direct digital signatures,
        489
signed applets, 601
signed objects, access controller, 390-392
Simple Authentication and Security Layer. See
    SASL
skeletons
    ORB, 647
    RMI, 652
SKIP (Simple Key Management for Internet
    Protocols), 106
smart cards, 106, 319-323
sniffer output example source code, 24
sniffers, 14-16
    file system, 25-28
    Fluke LanMeter, 20
    network attacks, 20-21
    networks, 19
SOAP (Simple Object Access Protocol), 472,
    606
    Web Services encoding and, 614-616
    WLS and, 672
social engineering, 15
socket connections, 504
socket sessions, 504
SocketChannel class, 481-484
SocketChannel.open( ) function, 482
SocketClient class, 454-456
SocketImpl class, 479
SocketPermission class, 57
sockets
    connection-oriented, 479
    JavaSockets, 474-484
    ports, 449
        socket pairs, 449
SocketServer class, 451-454
SOCKS protocol, 481
software, virused, 189
source code
    ASN.1 CRL notation, 558
    CertPath initialization example, 586-588
    Client_Socket class, 475-476
    client-side security example, 630-643

CRL retrieval from LDAP server, 592-593

DH key generation, 80

DHAgreement class, man-in-the-middle attack, 83-91

DHSimpleApp class, 72-80

Diffie-Hellman example, 71

doPrivileged action, 385

DSA file example, 177-178

ECCKeyFactory class, 119-123

ECCKeyPairGenerator class, 123-126

ECCProvider class, 115

ECCSimpleApp class, 116-118

FileInputStream, 384

GetProviderInfo class, 95-96

hashes, 45

isUserInRole method, 636

JAASAction class, 419-420

jdk1.4 policy file, 182-183

JSP example, 628

keytool interaction, 171

LoginContext class, 406-407

man-in-the-middle attack output, 81-83

MD5 implementation, 196-203

modular exponential, 66

modulo examples, 112

netstate –rn on Windows 2000 machine, 461-462

ping output, 459

ping with IP record route, 460-461

PKIXCertPathValidatorResult class, 594-595

PKIXParameters class, 591-592

Project.Java, 661-662

ProjectBean.Java, 662-666

project-cmp-rdbms-jar.xml, 666-667

ProjectHome.java, 660-661

RC4 algorithm, 300-303

RichCertificate class, 542-545
    output, 546-547

RichDESKey class, 158-160

RichDSA class, DSA Signature sample, 240-254

RichDSAKey class, 152-154
    output, 154-156

RichGSSService class, creating security context, 358-367

RichGuard class, guarded object example, 388-389

RichMAC class, 221-229

RichPolicy class, policy example, 394-398

RichProvider class, 298

RichRSACipher, RSA cipher implementation, 268-285

RichSeed class, 148-149
    output, 149

RMIClient.java, 668

RSASimpleApp class, 96-103

security context wrap method/unwrap method, 370-374

server socket creation, 507-508

Server_Socket class, 477-478

service providers installed, 94-95

SHA-1 algorithm, 206-216

signing Java2.jar, 176

Sniffer output example, 24

SocketChannel connectin completion, 483

SocketClient class, 454-456

SocketServer class, 451-454

SSLClient class, SSLSocketFactory, 523-528

SSLServer class, 516-522

TestBFCipher class, Blowfish example, 313-316

TestPBECiphers class, PBE cipher testing, 307-310

TestRandomMod class, 67-70

TestRSACiphers class, RSA test for cipher, 294-297

triple-DES three-key implementation, 105

triple-DES two-key implementation, 105

WSDL document skeleton, 613-614

X509-based key manager, 511-512

XOR function, 45

SPD (Security Policy Databases), SAs, 133

SPI (Security Parameter Index), 132

SPI (Service Provider Interface), 39, 114, 618-620
    ECC key exchange as, 114-126
    key management, 164

key pair implementation, 143
overview, 164
SPKM (Simple Public Key GSS-API
Mechanism), 353
SPNEGO (Simple and Protected GSS-API
Negotiation Mechanism), 358
spoofing, IP spoofing, 29-30
SSL (Secure Socket Layer), 487
attacks and, 498-499
authentication and, 497-498
connections, 495-498
handshake, 490
history of, 488
HTTP comparison, 499
layers, 490-495
sessions, 495-498
SSL (Secure Socket Libraries), 47
SSL Handshake Protocol, 490-493
SSL Record, 493-495
SSL/TLS modes, 496-497
SSLContext, 510-512
SSLServer class, 516-522
SSLServerSocket
client authorization, 522
JSSE, 515-522
listener, 522
SSLSession, 514-515
stacked authentication, 407
state, JSPs and, 630
stateful sessions
EJBs, 656
SSL, 495
stateless beans, 656
stealth viruses, 32
stream algorithms, 259-260
stream ciphers, RC4, implementation, 299-303
stub
ORB, 647
RMI, 652
subcontexts, 617
subjects, 40
digital certificates, 537
JAAS, 350, 421-423
subkeys, Blowfish, 311
subnet masks, IP addresses and, 445

symmetric algorithms
block, 259-260
stream, 259-260
symmetric ciphers, 257-265
symmetric encryption, databases, 439
symmetric keys, 70, 140
RSA key exchange, 103
SYN flag, TCP, 449

T

TA (Trust Anchors), PKI and, 575
TCP (Transmission Control Protocol), 131,
446, 448-457
circuit-level gateways, 466
TCP packets, 449
TCP/IP, encryption and, 191
TCSEC (Trusted Computer System Evaluation
Criteria), 327
telnet, 21
TestRandomMod class, source code, 67-70
TGS (Ticketing Granting Server), 338
client/server authentication process,
modifications to, 344
ENC-TKT-IN-SKEY option, 341
modifications to, 339, 344-346
nonce, 342
RENEWABLE-OK option, 341
renew-till field, 341
Service tickets, process modifications, 342-
343
ticket requests
process, 340
version 4, 340-341
version 5, 341-342
tickets, modifications to, 344-346
times section, 341
tiger teams, 34
times section, TGS, 341
TLS (Transport Layer Security), 47, 503
Wireless TLS, 500-501
tokens, GSS-API, 355-356
topology. See network topology
traceroute utility, 21
transaction management, Connector API, 437

transactions
    ORB, 646
    state, 630
Transmission Control Protocol. *See* TCP
transparency, ORB, 646
transparent channel, 490
transport mode, IPSec, 131
Triple DES key, 104-106
Triple-DES, 305
Trojan horses, 34-35
trusted certificate entries, 165
TrustManager, 169
    jarsigner tool, 175-178
    keytool utility, 169-175
truststore, 168
TTL (Time To Live) field, 461
tunnel mode, IPSec, 131
two-phase authentication process, 414-415

U

UDDI (Universal Description, Discovery, and
        Integration), 606
    data structures, 612
    operators, 612
    registering Web Services, 611-612
    replication, 612
UDDI API, 612
UDP (User Datagram Protocol), 446-457
UID (UNIX identification number), 48
    X.509 version 2, 550
unsafe memory, 27-28
unwrap method, GSS-API, 355
upward negotiation, 499
URG flags, TCP, 449
URLs (Uniform Resource Locators), host
        impersonation, 28
user principal, 40-41
utilities
    hackers, 21-25
    jarsigner, 31
    jdb, 28
    keytool, TrustManager, 169-175

V

validate( ) function, 557
validation, 9-10
    authentication and, 6
    certificates, 557
    credentials, 49-50
    paths, certificates and, 584-594
    permissions, components and, 51
    principals, 49-51
variable chain, getInstance method and, 217
verify method, 238
verifyMIC method, GSS-API, 355
viral kits, 33
Virtual Private Network. *See* VPNs
virus attacks, types, 33
viruses, 32, 189
    backdoors, 33-34
    boot sector viruses, 32
    cost of battling, 33
    FAT and, 33
    logic bombs, 33-34
    macro viruses, 32
    parasitic viruses, 32
    polymorphic viruses, 32
    similarity to biological viruses, 32
    stealth viruses, 32
    Trojan horses, 34-35
    types, 32
    worms, 34
VisiBroker Edition, Borland Enterprise Server,
        675
VPNs (Virtual Private Network), 131

W

WANs (Wide Area Networks), 444
WAP (Wireless Application Protocol), 500
WARs (Web Application Resources), Borland
        and, 676
WAS (WebSphere Application Server), 673-
        675
WASAE (WAS Advanced Edition), 674
weapons against hack attacks, 5
Web Services, 605-616

encoding, SOAP and, 614-616
interfaces, WSDL and, 612-614
registering, UDDIs and, 611-612
XML, 605
Web tier, J2EE, 433
web.xml file
client-side security, 626-627
Project Info App, 634-636
WebSphere domains, 674
Web-tier, authentication, configuration, 622-623
well-known ports, 448
whois utility, 21
WLS (WebLogic Server), 671-673
SOAP and, 672
WLS (Wireless TLS), 500-501
worms, 34
WSDL (Web Service Descriptive Language), 606
Web Services interfaces, 612-614
WSP (Wireless Session Protocol), 501
WTLS (Wireless Transport Layer Security), 501
WTP (Wireless Transaction Protocol), 500

X–Y–Z

x,y coordinate system. *See also* coordinate system
X.500 specification, 577-580
LDAP, 581-583
overview, 538
X.509 specification, 540
ciphers and, 317-319
LDAP service and, 540
X.509 specification, version 2
UIDs, 550
X.509 specification, version 3
certificate alternative names extensions, 554-556
certificate constraints X509Certificate, 556
key extensions, 550-553
policy mapping extensions, 553-554
XKMS (XML Key Management Specification), 609

XML (eXtensible Markup Language7), 605
encryption, 611
secure transport, 606
WAS and, 674
WLS and, 672
XML digital signatures, 607-611
XOR function, 45
salting and, 139